MEDIEVAL MANUSCRIPTS IN TRANSITION

Tradition and Creative Recycling

MEDIAEVALIA LOVANIENSIA

SERIES I / STUDIA XXXVI

KATHOLIEKE UNIVERSITEIT LEUVEN
INSTITUUT VOOR MIDDELEEUWSE STUDIES
LEUVEN (BELGIUM)

MEDIEVAL MANUSCRIPTS IN TRANSITION

Tradition and Creative Recycling

Edited by

Geert H.M. CLAASSENS
and
Werner VERBEKE

LEUVEN UNIVERSITY PRESS
2006

ISBN 90 5867 520 3
ISBN 978 905867 520 0
D/2006/1869/2
NUR: 684-635

CONTENTS

PREFACE

Manuscripts constitute the source material par excellence for diverse academic disciplines. Art historians, philologists, historians, theologians, philosophers, book historians and even jurists encounter one another around the codex. The fact that such an encounter can be extremely fertile was demonstrated, once again, during an international congress in Brussels on November 5-9, 2002. Under the title *Manuscripts in transition*, more than 200 scholars from all corners of the world met under the roof of the Royal Library of Brussels. While the theme of the congress, 'recycling manuscripts', provided an ideal occasion for a multidisciplinary and interdisciplinary exchange of ideas, in fact it was the academic diversity of the participants that made such an exchange possible.

A record of these discussions – or at least a part of them – can be found in this volume of the *Mediaevalia Lovaniensia*. The editors selected those lectures that focused on the historical, literary-historical, philosophical and theological aspects of the congress theme as opposed to those with an explicit art-historical perspective. The common thread, however, is always the codicological aspect: what can the study of manuscripts contribute to the literary-historical interpretation or the insight into the functioning of a text in its original context. The various contributions testify to a fearless and unrestrained interdisciplinary approach to the material. The subjects broached cover a broad domain: from the development of classical themes to the transmission of lyrical models, from visual material giving evidence of the reception of literary texts to the artes-literature used as a vehicle for a love story. Just as the gathering in Brussels led to a broadening of horizons for the many participants, so do the editors hope that the reader of this book too will be enriched.

The congress that inspired this publication was organised on the occasion of the exhibition *Medieval Mastery: Book Illumination from Charlemagne to Charles the Bold, 800-1475* (Stedelijk Museum Vander Kelen-Mertens, Leuven 2002) by *Illuminare – Centre for the Study of the Illuminated Manuscript* and the *Instituut voor Middeleeuwse Studies* of the *Katholieke Universiteit Leuven*, in close collaboration with the *Royal Library of Brussels*, the foundation *Bruges 2002 Cultural Capital of Europe* and the *Musée d'Art Religieux et d'Art Mosan* in Liège. The large number of valuable readings and texts submittted to the editorial board has necessitated splitting the proceedings into two separate collections. In addition to this collection in the *Mediaevalia Lovaniensia*, '*Manuscripts in Transition. Recycling Manuscripts, Texts and Images*' – a volume that contains the texts with a pronounced art-historial orientation – has already been published in the meantime in the series *Corpus of Illuminated Manuscripts* (Leuven, Peeters, 2005) by Brigitte Dekeyser and Jan Van der Stock.

We would like to thank the many people who contributed to the organisation and the success of the congress in Brussels, and in particular all authors, especially for their congenial and fruitful cooperation, and their patience on the road to final publication.

Leuven, November 2005
Geert CLAASSENS and Werner VERBEKE

Sharon ARBUTHNOT

MEDIEVAL IRISH COMPILATION: CONSERVATISM AND CREATIVITY

'Compilation' is a largely self-explanatory term. Used of a medieval literary activity, it refers to a recycling process whereby extracts culled from a variety of manuscript sources are cobbled together to create new texts. In a crude, although convenient, analogy, one might suggest that compiling is the textual equivalent of creating a mosaic – the fragments originally belong to very different contexts, a certain amount of compiler-provided 'grout' holds the entirety together, and the end product is a quite distinct artefact in itself. In the twelfth and thirteen centuries, learned Irishmen expended a great deal of energy in this direction, producing, *inter alia*, the compilation in which I am most interested: *Cóir Anmann* ('The Fitness of Names'), a collection of etymological explanations of primarily personal names.[1] Two factors seem indicative of the position this treatise occupied in medieval Irish literary circles: at least three different versions were produced in the space of about a century, and copies of the earliest version have been preserved in some of the most important codices to survive from fourteenth- and fifteenth-century Ireland: the Book of Ballymote, the Book of Lecan and the Book of Uí Maine.[2]

I shall return to *Cóir Anmann* presently. Before focusing on this one work, however, it seems desirable to summarize what has been suggested previously about the circumstances which led to an efflorescence of highly derivative texts in the late Middle Irish period,[3] and about the aims and priorities of the scholars who produced them. In brief, there has been a ten-

1. The latest (?) version of *Cóir Anmann* was edited by Whitley Stokes, '*Cóir Anmann* (Fitness of Names)', *Irische Texte*, 3, Part 2 (1897), 285-444 and 557. Standish H. O'Grady transcribed extracts from the earliest version in *Silva Gadelica – A Collection of Tales in Irish*, 2 vols (London, 1892), where they are scattered throughout II, pp. 455-548. The author is currently preparing editions of all versions for publication by the Irish Texts Society.

2. For approximate compilation dates of the extant versions of *Cóir Anmann* and for the manuscripts in which copies have been preserved, see Sharon Arbuthnot, 'The Manuscript Tradition of *Cóir Anmann*', *Studia Celtica*, 35 (2001), 285-98.

3. The Middle Irish period is generally defined as *c*. 950-*c*. 1250.

dency to regard the compilatory phase in medieval Irish literature as an outcome of certain social, institutional and cultural changes which took place from the eleventh century onwards.[4] Fundamental to these changes was the reform of the church from a monastic system, closely linked to secular power and supporting a network of schools and *scriptoria*, to an episcopal structure similar to that which prevailed in the rest of western Europe. The effect of ecclesiastical reform on the literary life of the country would probably have been considerable in itself in that it impinged on established lines of patronage for the monastic community who cultivated vernacular literature. That this reform was followed by an influx of continental religious orders and, eventually, also by foreign intervention in the form of the Anglo-Normans, is thought to have intensified the threat, actual or perceived, to the traditional custodians of native learning.

It has been suggested then that, unsure of what the future held for themselves and their area of interest, Irish monastic *literati* immersed themselves in the literary yield of previous centuries, collecting, conserving and copying afresh. Perhaps unsurprisingly, exponents of this theory have exhibited little enthusiasm for the vast textual output of these changing times. Proinsias Mac Cana, for example, sensed in compilatory activity 'not so much a creative urge as a conscious effort to regroup and consolidate the resources of native learning'.[5] Edward Gwynn traced an anthology of reclaimed material on placenames, commonly referred to as *Dindshenchas Érenn* (roughly, 'Traditions of Places in Ireland'),[6] to a

4. On social, historical and literary developments in this period, see, for example, Myles Dillon, 'Literary Activity in the Pre-Norman Period', in *Seven Centuries of Irish Learning 1000-1700*, ed. by Brian Ó Cuív (Dublin, 1961), pp. 27-44 (pp. 30-34); Proinsias Mac Cana, 'The Rise of the Later Schools of *filidheacht*', *Ériu*, 25 (1974), 126-46 (pp. 140-42); Kathleen Hughes, *Early Christian Ireland*: *Introduction to the Sources* (1972; repr. Cambridge, 1979), pp. 273-301; Uáitéar Mac Gearailt, 'The Language of Some Late Middle Irish Texts in the Book of Leinster', *Studia Hibernica*, 26 (1991-92), 167-216 (pp. 199-202); Clare Furniss, 'The Historical and Literary Contexts of *Acallam na Senórach*' (unpublished master's thesis, University of Aberdeen, 1997). Bernadette Cunningham, 'Seventeenth-Century Interpretations of the Past: the Case of Geoffrey Keating', *Irish Historical Studies*, 25 (1986-87), 116-28 (p. 122), compared twelfth- with seventeenth-century Ireland (following Reformation and Counter-Reformation, the influx of the 'New English', and a decline in patronage for the learned classes), proposing that at both times there was a feeling that 'things would never be the same' and that 'aspects of society of great antiquity would soon be no more'.

5. 'The Rise' [note 4], p. 141.

6. For editions of this text, see Whitley Stokes, 'The Bodleian *Dinnshenchas*', *Folk-Lore*, 3 (1892), 467-516; idem, 'The Edinburgh *Dinnshenchas*', *Folk-Lore*, 4 (1893), 471-97; idem, 'The Prose Tales in the Rennes *Dindshenchas*', *Revue Celtique*, 15 (1894), 272-336 and 418-84; 16 (1895), 31-83, 135-67 and 269-312; Edward Gwynn, *Poems from the Dindshenchas*: *Text, Translation, and Vocabulary*, Todd Lecture Series, 7 (Dublin, 1900); idem, *The Metrical Dindshenchas*, 5 vols, Todd Lecture Series, 8-12 (Dublin, 1903-35).

time when 'literature from being creative became parasitic'.[7] David Greene threw out the bald remark that in the Middle Irish period 'antiquarianism threatened to choke literature completely'.[8]

Although views such as these have dominated discussion of medieval Irish compilations, they have not been repeated to the exclusion of others. Some time ago, Charles Bowen suggested (apparently intuitively) that genuine borrowings in the *Dindshenchas* were supplemented by mistaken interpretations of sources and onomastic adaptations of traditional material.[9] More recently, Máire Herbert quarried the Middle Irish redaction of a late sixth-century poem, *Amra Coluim Cille* ('The Eulogy of Colum Cille'), to reveal 'scholarship which is dynamic rather than conservative', which does not merely salvage and transmit the poem, but also integrates it into the present.[10] While compilations are not mentioned specifically in Herbert's article, one would assume that her closing argument was intended to embrace these under-studied texts. In it she insisted that characterizing the literary products of post-Viking Ireland as merely antiquarian will no longer suffice: '[W]e must broaden our perspectives on the literature of the Middle-Irish period [...]. We must, in fact, elucidate the source-material before we can begin to estimate the intellectual ethos of the era.'[11]

If we are to follow Herbert's lead and seek to elucidate a compiled text, the initial task is to trace the borrowed extracts to the sources from which they were drawn. Collating the two, we might then hope to establish the extent of agreement between the original and the material based on it, to gain an insight into the methods the compiler employed in appropriating extracts, and possibly even to form some impression of the 'grout' which binds the collection together. Most importantly, of course, an informed assessment of the relationships between a compilation and its sources should prepare the way for a review of the suggestion that such tracts were brought into existence by 'industrious antiquarians'.[12]

7. *The Metrical Dindshenchas* [note 6], v, p. 95.

8. 'Irish as a Vernacular before the Norman Invasion', in *A View of the Irish Language*, ed. by Brian Ó Cuív (Dublin, 1969), pp. 11-21 (p. 21).

9. Charles Bowen, 'A Historical Inventory of the *Dindshenchas*', *Studia Celtica*, 10-11 (1975-76), 113-37 (p. 118).

10. 'The Preface to *Amra Coluim Cille*', in *Sages, Saints and Storytellers: Celtic Studies in Honour of Professor James Carney*, ed. by Donnchadh Ó Corráin, Liam Breatnach and Kim McCone, Maynooth Monographs, 2 (Maynooth, 1989), pp. 67-75 (p. 73).

11. 'The Preface' [note 10], p. 73.

12. This phrase was used by D. A. Binchy, *Scéla Cano meic Gartnáin*, Mediaeval and Modern Irish Series, 18 (Dublin, 1963), p. xxv. Binchy was referring specifically to the compilers of the *Banshenchas*, a twelfth-century Irish learned tract on women.

The remainder of this short contribution is dedicated to the sources of *Cóir Anmann* and to exploring how the scholars responsible for this compilation set about their task; in the process we may learn something about their urges to conserve and to create.

Despite the ravages of eight hundred years or more, a considerable amount of the material contained in *Cóir Anmann* can still be matched to independent prose and verse of demonstrably earlier date. As many extracts could have been drawn from more than one source, it is difficult to tell how many separate works are represented in the extant corpus.[13] It is clear, however, that the *literati* responsible for *Cóir Anmann* were not averse to mixing periods or genres. Indeed, the surviving versions have digested matter which ranges in date from perhaps the eight or ninth centuries to the twelfth, and which originally formed part of genealogies, glossaries, pseudo-historical tracts (mainly *Lebor Gabála Érenn* 'The Book of the Taking(s) of Ireland'), saga literature and hagiography.[14] These were not all used in equal measure in any one of the texts, but in general the evidence suggests that our compilers had an impressive array of literary reference at their disposal.

When we compare a fragment from *Cóir Anmann* with its likely source(s), paying attention, not only to the actual corresponding portion of text, but also to the immediate context, what do we notice? Firstly, as might be expected, some extracts seem to have been simply lifted from the donor-text and dropped bodily into the compilation. Metrical borrowings are almost exclusively of this type.[15] Recycled verse tells us little about the modes by which material was transmitted, however, for medieval Irish verse is largely fixed by rhyme and metre, and arguably relatively easily remembered. When substantial prose passages occur, more or less identically expressed, in two or more sources, there can be scant doubt that the extracts in question passed directly from book to

13. Many literary parallels were noted by Stokes, '*Cóir Anmann*' [note 1], pp. 412-25.

14. On borrowings from glossaries, see, for example, J. Fraser, 'A Note on Cormac's Glossary', in *Féil-Sgríbhinn Eóin Mhic Néill: Essays and Studies Presented to Professor Eóin MacNéill*, ed. by John Ryan (Dublin, 1940), pp. 37-41 (p. 41). On the use of genealogical material, see Donnchadh Ó Corráin, 'Irish Origin Legends and Genealogy: Recurrent Aetiologies', in *History and Heroic Tale: a Symposium*, ed. by Tore Nyberg, Iørn Piø, Preben Meulengracht Sørensen, Aage Trommer (Odense, 1985), pp. 51-96 (p. 86). For editions of *Lebor Gabála Érenn*, see R. A. S. Macalister, *Lebor Gabála Érenn: the Book of the Taking of Ireland*, 5 vols, Irish Texts Society, 34, 35, 39, 41 and 44 (Dublin, 1938-56).

15. Compare, for example, the quatrain on Conaing mac Congail in Stokes, '*Cóir Anmann*' [note 1], §143, with Macalister, *Lebor Gabála Érenn* [note 14], v, p. 508.

book. It is instructive, therefore, to find in the longest version of *Cóir Anmann* episodes which never seriously deviate in wording from, for example, the copies of *Táin Bó Cúalgne* ('The Cattle-Raid of Cooley') and *Tochmarc Ferbe* ('The Wooing of Ferbe'), which are preserved in a major twelfth-century Irish manuscript, the Book of Leinster.[16]

With these instances of borrowing *en bloc* we glimpse compilers at their most passive. Having searched out old material for their new enterprise, they then behave more or less as scribes – and, indeed, contribute to the durability of their sources, in that faithful reproductions have survived (in these cases alongside the original) into the twenty-first century. Where the originals have not come down to us, compilations may be our only means of gauging the content of once-current literary works. The *Cóir Anmann* entry on Conall Cernach,[17] for example, seems to be all that is left to represent the contents of the saga *Compert Conaill Chernaig* ('The Conception of Conall Cernach'), which is mentioned in a tale-list embodied in the tenth- or eleventh-century text, *Airec Menman Uraird meic Coise* ('Stratagem of Urard mac Coise').[18] Thus, it is a simple fact that certain resources of medieval Irish native learning have been preserved by assimilation into compilations – although how close the *Cóir Anmann* material is to the lost (?) tale of Conall's birth, it is impossible to know.

Passages corresponding to *Táin Bó Cúalgne* and *Tochmarc Ferbe* can be found in the longest, and probably also latest, version of *Cóir Anmann*. However, sustained reproduction of a single source is something of an anomaly in the earliest version. More usually in the latter text, quotations are short, and two or more may be brought together in a single entry. In such instances, it is possible to 'explode' the explanation of a name to reveal several distinct elements. The explanation of Connachta ('Connacht' or 'Connachtmen'), a rare example of a population/territorial name tucked amongst a barrage of personal epithets, will serve as a case in point (see Fig. 1). On excavation it would seem that three sources occupy this site. The ninth-century (?) tale *Scéla Mucce Meic Dathó* ('Story of Mac Dathó's Pig') probably supplied the traditions that three hundred Connachtmen were killed in Mac Dathó's hostel and that the servant of

16. See Stokes, '*Cóir Anmann*' [note 1], §§149 and 160. For the corresponding material in *Táin Bó Cúalgne* and *Tochmarc Ferbe*, see Cecile O'Rahilly, *Táin Bó Cúalnge from the Book of Leinster* (Dublin, 1967), p. 57; E. Windisch, '*Tochmarc Ferbe*', *Irische Texte*, 3, Part 2 (1897), 445-556 (p. 516).

17. See Stokes, '*Cóir Anmann*' [note 1], §251.

18. See Proinsias Mac Cana, *The Learned Tales of Medieval Ireland* (Dublin, 1980), pp. 54 and 90, n. 57.

Ailill, king of Connacht, killed Mac Dathó's dog.[19] In the *Cóir Anmann* text, this leads into four lines of verse, for which there is a parallel in *Bruiden Da Choca* ('Da Choca's Hostel').[20] The *Cóir Anmann* entry concludes with an etymological derivation, which is itself also found in *Sanas Cormaic* ('Cormac's Glossary').[21]

Scéla Mucce Meic Dathó

Tri cét do Chonnachtaib romarbtha i mbruidin Maic Dáthó [...] Gilla Ailella romarb in coin i Comor Chinncon. Unde Connachta dicuntur.

Cóir Anmann

Connachta .i. coin-ecta .i. diaro marbsat Ailbi, coin Meic Datho, .i. gilla Oilella ro marb í i Comrair Chind Chon, Connachta dicitur. Trí cét do Connactaib ro marbta i mbruigin Meic Datho.

Bruigen Meic Datho, toirm tend,
gus rangadar fir Erend:
ro caithset a muicc malle
ocus ruccsat uad Ailbe.

Nó Connachta .i. Conn-iucta, [...].i. clanda Cuind. Nam icht .i. clann nó cenel.[22]

Sanas Cormaic

Icht .i. cinél nó cland, ut est Condachta .i. Cond-ichta .i. clanna Cuinn.

Bruiden Da Choca

Bruden Mic da tho, toirm tenn.
gus' tangadar (fir Érenn)
ro caithsit muic immale.
ocus rugsadair Ailbe.

Fig. 1: Probable sources of the entry on Connachta in the earliest version of *Cóir Anmann*.

19. See Kuno Meyer, 'Mitteilungen aus irischen Handschriften', *Zeitschrift für celtische Philologie*, 3 (1901), 17-39, 226-63 and 447-66 (p. 37). The text in Fig. 1 is taken from the editions cited in this and the following two notes.

20. See Whitley Stokes, 'Da Choca's Hostel', *Revue Celtique*, 21 (1900), 149-65, 312-27 and 388-402 (p. 396).

21. See Kuno Meyer, *Sanas Cormaic: an Old-Irish Glossary* (1913; repr. Felinfach, 1994), §787.

22. Dublin, Royal Irish Academy, MS 23 P 12 (536; the Book of Ballymote), p. 250a23-29. Cf. Stokes, '*Cóir Anmann*' [note 1], §76. This entry may be translated as follows: 'Connachta [< *cú* 'hound' + *écht* 'slaughter'], i.e. hound-slaughters, i.e. Connachta is said because they killed Ailbe, Mac Dathó's hound, i.e. Ailill's servant killed it in Comrar Chinn Chon. Three hundred Connachta were killed in Mac Dathó's hostel. Mac Dathó's hostel, secure fame, / to which the men of Ireland came: / they consumed his pig together / and took from him Ailbe. Or Connachta means Conn's peoples. [...]: i.e. Conn's descendants. For *icht* means descendants or kin.' I have translated only the *Cóir Anmann* material, as discrepancies between this text and the sources under discussion tend to be minor.

We are fortunate in having extant texts of three probable sources for the *Cóir Anmann* entry on Connachta. These texts open a window on the working practices of this compiler, for they suggest that he was not only pinpointing and extracting short quotations embedded in manuscript material, but also combining fragments from diverse sources.[23] It is not clear how this would have been achieved. The process could been facilitated in several ways: the passages could have been detached from their original contexts before they reached our compiler,[24] or an entry like that on Connachta could have built up in the course of lost workings of *Cóir Anmann* which predate the earliest extant version. Without textual evidence for either of these scenarios, however, we have to allow that multi-sourced entries were created in a single step. If so, it seems likely that their creation was a demanding task, both in terms of the required knowledge of earlier literature (and, specifically, of written specimens of it) and of the practical organisation of resources.

At this point, I should re-emphasize that the Connachta example discussed above is taken from a version of *Cóir Anmann* which may have appeared before the end of the twelfth century. The longest version of *Cóir Anmann* can hardly be later than the (mid-?)thirteenth century, but includes numerous instances of internal duplication, lengthy quotations from a single source, general biographical matter and formulaic explanation of names.[25] This disparity in content may testify only to the different approaches of different individuals. In the context of the present inquiry, however, it is interesting that, although the early version of *Cóir Anmann* falls well within the period of supposed anxiety and shrinking patronage for the monastic scholar, it was clearly pieced together with precision and patience. The compiler of the emphatically post-Norman version, on the other hand, seems to have been less particular in his selection and combination of material.

Having thus far dealt with (more or less) faithful reproductions of sources from the past, I turn now to some of the more creative uses of

23. Always assuming, of course, that the various elements were not simply called up from the reserves of his learned mind.

24. We know that words and phrases with glosses were initially extracted from texts and collected in ancillary documents (known as *glossae collectae*) before being incorporated into glossaries. See Paul Russell, 'The Sounds of a Silence: the Growth of Cormac's Glossary', *Cambridge Medieval Celtic Studies*, 15 (1988), 1-30 (pp. 27-30); idem, 'Laws, Glossaries and Legal Glossaries in Early Ireland', *Zeitschrift für celtische Philologie*, 51 (1999), 85-115 (pp. 88-90).

25. See, for example, Stokes, '*Cóir Anmann*' [note 1], §§186 and 187 (internal duplication), §92 (biographical matter), and §§277-80 (formulaic explanation of names).

secondary material in Middle Irish compilations. In particular, I am concerned with attempts to convert literary borrowings to purposes they did not originally serve. Apart from Bowen's general remarks regarding the *Dindshenchas*, there has been prior discussion of conversions of this type in *Acallam na Senórach* ('The Colloquy of the Ancients'), a Middle Irish 'frame-tale' in which a miscellany of stories relating to the warrior-bands of Finn mac Cumaill is told to St. Patrick as he journeys around early Christian Ireland.[26] James Carney proposed that two metrical compositions in the *Acallam* are typical of the repertoire of a professional poet.[27] One, he concluded, was a poet's lament for his patron, Cáel mac Crimthainn;[28] the other a metrical notice to a woman with whom the poet intended to lodge.[29] With the assistance of a prose narrative thrown up as a scaffold around these verses, the originator of the *Acallam* presented the former as a woman's lament for her dead husband and put the latter into the mouth of the prospective lover of the woman addressed. Sadly, neither poem is attested independently. Lending support to Carney's suggestion, however, the *Acallam* has also admitted a devotional piece on the eight deadly sins, which is preserved elsewhere as the concluding section of a poem attributed to Máel Ísu Ó Brolcháin, from the monastery of Armagh, who died in 1086.[30] With regard to these specific borrowings, then, the actual material of the poems may have been preserved for posterity in the *Acallam*, but only at the expense of rendering their original function and authorship almost unrecognizable.

Suggesting that extant poems were re-orientated in a new prose environment is less dangerous territory than suggesting that borrowed mate-

26. *Acallam na Senórach* is extant in three versions. For editions of the earliest and best-known version, see O'Grady, *Silva Gadelica* [note 1] I, pp. 94-233; Whitley Stokes, '*Acallam na Senórach*', *Irische Texte*, 4, Part 1 (1900). For a recent translation of this version, see Ann Dooley and Harry Roe, *Tales of the Elders of Ireland* (*Acallam na Senórach*) (Oxford, 1999). There is also a later, longer version, which was edited by Nessa Ní Shéaghdha, *Agallamh na Seanórach*, 3 vols (Dublin, 1942-45). For the shortest version, see Douglas Hyde, '*An Agallamh Bheag*', *Lía Fáil*, 1 (1925), 79-107.

27. James Carney, 'Two Poems from *Acallam na Senórach*', in *Celtic Studies*: *Essays in Memory of Angus Matheson 1912-1962*, ed. by James Carney and David Greene (London, 1968), pp. 22-32.

28. See O'Grady, *Silva Gadelica* [note 1] I, p. 113; Stokes, '*Acallam na Senórach*' [note 26], pp. 24-25; Dooley and Roe, *Tales of the Elders* [note 26], p. 28.

29. See O'Grady, *Silva Gadelica* [note 1] I, pp. 111-12; Stokes, '*Acallam na Senórach*' [note 26], pp. 22-23; Dooley and Roe, *Tales of the Elders* [note 26], pp. 25-27.

30. For the *Acallam* material, see O'Grady, *Silva Gadelica* [note 1] I, p. 160; Stokes, '*Acallam na Senórach*' [note 26], pp. 83-84; Dooley and Roe, *Tales of the Elders* [note 26], p. 90. For Máel Ísu's poem, see Muireann Ní Bhrolcháin, *Maol Íosa Ó Brolcháin* (Maynooth, 1986), pp. 74-76.

rial was internally modified for incorporation into a compiled text. In the latter case, one must bow eventually to the possibility of lost versions more closely related to what is contained in the compilation than those that have been preserved. That said, an investigation of additions to and revisions of sources in *Cóir Anmann* yields intriguing results. In what follows, I consider instances of (i) the creative use of pre-existing lexical material, (ii) general narrative matter exploited for etymological ends and (iii) the same basic material applied to two separate characters.

To begin, then, with a possible adaptation of a lexical source: although there is a small number of entries on proper nouns in early Irish glossaries (such as the *Sanas Cormaic* explanation of Connachta quoted above), common nouns and adjectives predominate amongst the headwords. Inevitably, some of these correspond to the epithets of characters known from other sources, and it would seem that the scholars at work on *Cóir Anmann* were alert to their potential. For example, *Sanas Cormaic* etymologizes the noun *molt*, meaning 'ram', as *mó* [...] *a folt* 'greater its hair',[31] and to explain the name of Ailill Molt, king of Ireland, the longest version of *Cóir Anmann* has *Ailill Molt .i. Ailill mó a fholt* 'Ailill Molt, i.e. Ailill greater his hair'.[32]

'Ailill Molt' is one of a number of entries in *Cóir Anmann* which seem to have been formed when the first names of literary or (pseudo-)historical personages were prefixed to both sides of an explanatory or etymological gloss.[33] Occasionally, probable sources of *Cóir Anmann* do not have an etymological purpose. Let us consider the entry on Áed Sláine.[34] Relating how, following the intervention of religious men, the barren wife of Díarmait Cerball gave birth to a lamb, a salmon and finally a son, this entry is plainly drawing on *Genemain Áeda Sláine* ('The Birth of Áed Sláine').[35] No connection is made between the events preceding the child's birth and his epithet in *Genemain Áeda Sláine*, but interpolated into the borrowing *Cóir Anmann* has a telling line which derives Sláine from the verb *slánaigidir* 'makes whole' and claims that Áed was 'made whole' by the creatures his mother delivered before him. Given that it contains late linguistic forms which are at odds with the conservative

31. Meyer, *Sanas Cormaic* [note 21], §924.

32. Stokes, '*Cóir Anmann*' [note 1], §147. I am not aware of any other source referring to Ailill's hair.

33. Another good example concerns the character Conall Grant. Compare Stokes, '*Cóir Anmann*' [note 1], §129, with Meyer, *Sanas Cormaic* [note 21], §288.

34. See Stokes, '*Cóir Anmann*' [note 1], §133.

35. See O'Grady, *Silva Gadelica* [note 1] I, pp. 82-84.

bulk of the entry,[36] it seems reasonably safe to assume that this line is a postscript to the original episode composed by someone concerned specifically with the origin and meaning of names.

My final category in this section concerns entries in *Cóir Anmann* which echo statements made about other characters in other texts. For an example, I have selected (rather arbitrarily) the entry on Fedlimid Rechtaid ('Fedlimid the Judge'). As can be seen from the passages quoted below, the explanation of this name in *Cóir Anmann* bears a marked resemblance to a reference to Caí Caínbrethach ('Caí of Fair Judgment') in another Middle Irish text, *Scél na Fír Flatha* ('The Story of the *Fír Flatha*'[37]):

> *Cóir Anmann*: Fedlimid Rechtaidh .i. bretha rechta do fhoghnaidís dó [...] Ara mhét dofhoghnaidis bretha rechta dó is aire isberthí Fédhlimid Rechtaid rís.
> ['Fedlimid *Rechtaid*, that is, he used to deliver judgments of the Law (of the Old Testament) [...] From the frequency with which he used to follow the judgments of the Law (*rechta*) he was called Fedlimid *Rechtaid*.'][38]
>
> *Scél na Fír Flatha*: Cai in bretheam [...] Ar at e bretha nobered .i. bretha rechta Maísi [...] Ba siad bretha rechta didiu rofognom do Cormac.[39]
> ['Cai the judge [...] for the judgments which he used to deliver were judgments of the Law of Moses [...] They were judgments of the Law (of Moses), then, that serued for Cormac.']

Of course, it is not certain that the direction of dependency here is from *Scél na Fír Flatha* to *Cóir Anmann*, or even that any direct relationship exists between these two texts. Nevertheless, such correspondences suggest that medieval Irish *literati* did not consider traditions exclusive to particular subjects and that (as one might guess from the explanation shared by *molt* and Ailill Molt) etymological material was likely to be employed wherever it could be made to fit.

Through case-studies of the kind presented above, we gain a sense of the resourceful, playful and even experimental aspects of medieval Irish compilations. Certainly, prose and verse passages were imported, in a rather mechanical manner, from earlier literature. A collation of entries

36. In this line *dob* is used for 3 sg. past tense of the copula and the independent pronoun is found with a passive verbal form (*roslánaigedh é*). These readings are contained in all three extant manuscript copies of this version of *Cóir Anmann*.

37. On the concept of *fír flatha*, literally, 'prince's truth', in medieval Irish literature, see Francis John Byrne, *Irish Kings and High-Kings* (London, 1973), pp. 24-25; Fergus Kelly, *Audacht Morainn* (Dublin, 1976), p. xvii.

38. Stokes, '*Cóir Anmann*' [note 1], §110. His edition and translation.

39. Whitley Stokes, 'The Irish Ordeals, Cormac's Adventure in the Land of Promise, and the Decision as to Cormac's Sword', *Irische Texte*, 3, Part 1 (1891), 183-229 (pp. 193 and 211).

in *Cóir Anmann* with earlier sources suggests, however, that interest in and use of pre-existing material was not incompatible with a creative urge and that compilers were perhaps not overly anxious about whether sources were faithfully copied for posterity, stretched with their own composition or used to fabricate entirely new statements about the principal actors of the Irish literary and (pseudo-)historical traditions. Predictably, there are differences to be observed in the working methods of the various compilers of this period (and, although the matter requires further investigation, also possible changes in compiler activity over time), but, on the whole, it would seem that borrowed extracts were likely to be redirected and revitalized as well as regrouped and consolidated.

How does all of this affect the theory that the production of medieval Irish compilations can be explained in terms of socio-historical factors? Despite the evident non-antiquarian nature of much compiler activity, such a link might be sustained in several ways. Reflections on names played an important part in Irish learning since earliest record,[40] and the flexible and productive approach displayed in *Cóir Anmann*, for example, might be seen as asserting the health of this branch of Irish learning in testing times. It strikes me also that compiling provided a unique opportunity for scholars to demonstrate both their knowledge of earlier material and their ability to take that knowledge forward in fresh realizations. Thus, compiled texts may have had an oblique ideological function relevant to their own day in showing that the monastic scholar was not at the end of his usefulness.[41] In truth, compilations were probably made for a variety of reasons. Based on the findings of this brief study, I would suggest that, alongside a consideration of the world in which compilations were produced, we might wish to take into account their role as vehicles for intellectual play and, especially in the case of *Cóir Anmann*, to acknowledge a continuity from the early Irish glossary tradition whereby glosses on difficult or obscure words were extracted from written texts, combined, ordered and variously adapted.[42] This contribution stands at the

40. See, for example, Bowen, 'A Historical Inventory' [note 9], pp. 114-18; Proinsias Mac Cana, 'Placenames and Mythology in Irish Tradition: Places, Pilgrimages and Things', in *Proceedings of the First North American Congress of Celtic Studies, Ottawa, 1986*, ed. by Gordon W. MacLennan (Ottawa, 1988), pp. 319-41.

41. Huw Pryce, 'The Context and Purpose of the Earliest Welsh Lawbooks', *Cambrian Medieval Celtic Studies*, 39 (2000), 39-63, suggested that a reason for an upsurge in compilations on law in late twelfth- and thirteenth-century Wales was that lawyers 'wished to uphold it, and hence themselves, in the face of potential challenges' (p. 55).

42. See Kuno Meyer, 'The Sources of Some Middle-Irish Glossaries', *Archiv für celtische Lexikographie*, 3 (1907), 138-44; W. J. Mahon, 'Contributions to the Study of Early Irish Lexicography' (unpublished doctoral dissertation, Harvard, 1987), pp. 18-20; Russell, 'The Sounds of a Silence', pp. 27-30; idem, 'Laws, Glossaries and Legal Glossaries', pp. 88-90.

beginning, rather than at the end, of an inquiry into the motivations behind compilation: my intention here has been chiefly to provide an introduction to the mental (and practical) processes involved in recycling manuscript materials in twelfth- and thirteenth-century Ireland.[43]

43. I would like to thank the British Academy for an Overseas Conference Grant which enabled me to travel to Brussels to attend the Manuscripts in Transition International Congress.

Catherine BEL

MÉTAMORPHOSE DES *MÉTAMORPHOSES*: LE CONTE DE *PYRAMUS ET THISBÉ* DANS LES MANUSCRITS DE L'*OVIDE MORALISÉ* EN VERS

Autre fable savoit plus bele,
Plus agreable et plus novele,
Comment la more, qui fu blanche,
Devint puis noire sor la branche,
Ceste li plaist, ceste lor conte.
Or vous raconterai le conte
Et la fable sans ajouster,
Sans muer et sans rien oster,
Si comme uns autres l'a dité
Puis i metrai la verité.[1]

1. INTRODUCTION

En guise d'introduction, l'auteur anonyme de l'*Ovide moralisé* annonce son projet ambitieux: 'traire de latin en romans les favles de l'ancien temps, s'en dirai ce que je entens, selonc ce qu'Ovides les baille'.[2] Il propose en outre de révéler le sens caché des fables.[3] C'est donc là une entre-

1. Ces vers (Livre IV, 219-228) introduisent l'histoire de Pyramus et Thisbé, racontée par une des filles de Mynias, au Livre IV, vv. 219-228, de *l'Ovide moralisé*. Notre édition de référence est celle de Cornélis de Boer, '*Ovide moralisé*', *poème du commencement du quatorzième siècle, publié d'après tous les manuscrits connus*, Verhandelingen der Koninklijke Nederlandsche Akademie van Wetenschappen, Afd. Letterkunde, 4 vol. (Wiesbaden, Martin Sändig, 1920). 'Elle [une des filles de Mynias] connaissait une autre histoire, plus belle, plus agréable et plus nouvelle: comment la mûre, qui fut blanche, devint ensuite noire sur la branche. Elle lui plaît, et elle la leur raconte. A présent je vous raconterai l'histoire et la fable, sans ajouter, sans changer, et sans rien omettre, comme quelqu'un d'autre l'a écrite; ensuite, j'expliquerai le sens' [notre traduction].

2. Ed. De Boer [note 1], Livre I, vv. 16-19. 'Traduire du latin en roman les histoires des temps anciens, et je dirai ce que j'y comprends, comme Ovide les transmet' [notre traduction].

3. 'Mes les mutacions des fables/qui sont bones et profitables/Se dieus le m'otroie, esclorrai/Au plus briement que je porrai/pour plus plaire a ceulz qui l'orront/et maint profiter i porront.' Ed. De Boer [note 1], Livre I, vv. 53-58. 'Mais les métamorphoses des fables, qui sont bonnes et profitables, si Dieu me le permet, je développerai aussi brièvement que je le puis, afin de plaire davantage à ceux qui l'entendront et pourront en tirer maint bénéfice' [notre traduction].

prise qui va au-delà de la pure traduction et qui se veut commentaire. Aussi a-t-il fallu attendre le début du quatorzième siècle pour que quelqu'un s'aventure à recycler ce recueil de polythéisme dans une perspective chrétienne.[4]

Composé entre 1316 et 1328, l'ouvrage aurait été commandé par la reine Jeanne de Bourgogne, épouse de Philippe V.[5] Comme son modèle, le texte s'étend sur quinze livres et suit *grosso modo* le fil des *Métamorphoses* d'Ovide.

L'*Ovide moralisé* nous est parvenu dans vingt-deux manuscrits,[6] dont quelques-uns très richement illustrés. Trois d'entre eux nous serviront ici de corpus; tous sont conservés dans des bibliothèques françaises. La copie gardée sous la cote 1044 à la Bibliothèque municipale de Rouen constitue le témoin le plus ancien; on le situe généralement dans le premier quart du quatorzième siècle (1315-1325).[7] Vient ensuite le manuscrit conservé à Paris à la Bibliothèque de l'Arsenal, sous la cote 5069, qui date des années 1320-1340.[8] Enfin, la copie[9] 742 de la Bibliothèque municipale de Lyon,[10] qui a appartenu au Duc de Berry, est un témoin de la fin du quatorzième siècle.[11]

4. Comme l'exprime si bien Paule Demats: '[...] combien de fils se sont entrecroisés pour former la toile bizarre de l'*Ovide moralisé* [...]!'. Paule Demats, *Fabula. Trois études de mythographie antique et médiévale* (Genève, Droz, 1973), p. 1.

5. En général, la critique est d'accord sur cette datation. Voir éd. De Boer [note 1], pp. 8-11.

6. Marc-René Jung fait état de vingt-deux manuscrits de l'*Ovide moralisé* en vers dont un – Turin, Biblioteca Nazionale Universitaria, anc. Gall. CXVII – est détruit. Certaines copies de sa liste ont des lacunes ou sont fragmentraires, notamment New York, Pierpont Morgan Library, M. 443; Paris, Bibliothèque nationale, fr. 24305 (les sept premiers livres); Londres, British Library, Cotton Julius F. VII. M.-R. Jung, 'Ovide, texte, translateur et gloses dans les manuscrits de l'Ovide moralisé', in Douglas Kelly (ed.), *The Medieval Opus. Imitation, Rewriting, and Transmission in the French Tradition, Proceedings of the Symposium held at the Institute for Research in Humanities, October 5-7 1995, the University of Wisconsin-Madison* (Amsterdam, 1996), pp. 96-97. De Boer mentionnait l'existence de dix-neuf copies.

7. Certaines études réfèrent à ce manuscrit avec la cote « 0.4 ». Il comporte 453 tableautins.

8. Ce témoin est pourvu de 302 images.

9. 57 miniatures embellissent ce manuscrit.

10. Outre le manuscrit de Lyon, Jean de Berry possédait une autre copie de l'*Ovide moralisé*, le manuscrit fr. 373 conservé actuellement à Paris, Bibliothèque nationale. Voir Millard Meiss, *French Painting in the time of Jean de Berry. The late XIV century and the patronage of the Duke*, 2 vol. (New York, 1969; 2e éd.). Quelques tableautins de Lyon ont été reproduits dans l'ouvrage de Jean Seznec, *The Survival of the Pagan Gods. The Mythological Tradition and Its Place in Renaissance Humanism and Art* (Princeton, 1972; 2e éd.), p. 110.

11. Dans ce qui suit, nous désignerons à ces copies respectivement par *Rouen*, *Arsenal*, et *Lyon*.

Rouen et *Arsenal* sont intimement liés par le fait qu'ils proviennent du même atelier – celui du Maître de Fauvel – comme l'ont démontré François Avril,[12] et, plus récemment, les époux Rouse.[13]

Les manuscrits enluminés de l'*Ovide moralisé* ont été classés par Erwin Panofsky, qui les regroupe en quatre catégories.[14] Renate Blumenfeld-Kosinski[15] simplifie cette taxinomie: pour elle, il y a d'un côté les copies dont les miniatures représentent des scènes mythologiques et/ou allégoriques et de l'autre, les copies ornées du portrait des dieux antiques aux frontispices des quinze livres respectifs, sous l'influence de l'*Ovidius moralizatus* de Pierre Bersuire.[16]

Dans la présente étude nous nous laisserons guider par les images qui emmènent le lecteur à travers l'aventure de Pyramus et Thisbé. En français, cette histoire célèbre a mené une vie autonome dans trois manuscrits[17] avant d'être intégrée telle quelle à l'*Ovide moralisé*. C'est dans cette dernière tradition, où l'aventure des jeunes amants infortunés est racontée aux vv. 229-

12. François Avril, in Edward H. Roesner, François Avril, et Nancy Freeman Regalado, *Le Roman de Fauvel in the Edition of Messire Chaillou de Pesstain: A Reproduction in Facsimilé of the Complete Manuscript, Paris, BN fr. 146* (New York, 1990), pp. 46-47 et 'Le parcours d'un enlumineur parisien à la fin du XIVe siècle. La carrière et l'œuvre du Maître du Policratique de Charles V', in Barbara Fleith – Franco Morenzoni, *De la Sainteté à l'Hagiographie. Genèse et Usage de la* Légende dorée (Genève, 2001), pp. 265-282. Carla Lord rappelle cette attribution dans son étude sur le commanditaire du manuscrit de Rouen: C. Lord, 'Marks of ownership in medieval manuscripts: the case of the Rouen *Ovide moralisé*', in *Source,* XVIII/1 (1998), pp. 7-11.

13. Richard H. Rouse and Mary A. Rouse, *Manuscripts and their makers. Commercial Book producers in medieval Paris. 1200-1500*, 2 vol. (Turnhout, Harvey Miller et Brepols, 2000), pp. 209-210.

14. Groupe I: copies à miniatures qui ne sont pas influencées par Pierre Bersuire, groupe auquel appartient Lyon, BM 742; groupe II: les copies qui contiennent la rédaction en prose et dont les enluminures n'ont pas subi l'influence de Bersuire; groupe III: les manuscrits et incunables qui intègrent la traduction française de l'introduction de Pierre Bersuire et qui contiennent les images des dieux antiques et des tableaux narratifs; groupe IV: les témoins qui ne contiennent que les quinze images des dieux antiques décrits par Bersuire. Cette classification a été proposée par Erwin Panofsky, *Renaissance and Renascences in Western Art* (Stockholm, 1965), p. 78, n. 2.

15. Renate Blumenfeld-Kosinski, 'Illustrations et interprétations dans un manuscrit de l'*Ovide moralisé* (Arsenal 5069)', dans *Cahiers de Recherches Médiévales (XIIIe-XVe s.),* 9 (2002), pp. 71-82. Les trois copies que nous étudions appartiennent à la première catégorie proposée par Blumenfeld-Kosinski.

16. Dans le cadre de cette étude, nous ne considérons pas l'influence de Pierre Bersuire sur l'iconographie de l'*Ovide moralisé* qui, certes, est très importante dans certains témoins mais qui est ici hors-propos.

17. Il s'agit de Paris, Bibliothèque nationale, f. fr. 837, f. fr. 19152 et Berlin, Staatsbibliothek, 257. Le texte de *Pyramus et Thisbé* n'est pas illustré dans ces copies. Pour une description, voir F. Branciforti, *Piramus et Thisbé. Introduzione, testo critico, traduzione e note* (Florence, Leo S. Olschki, 1959), pp. 80-88.

1169 du Livre IV, que nous sommes confrontée à l'observation que l'illustration de cet épisode a connu un succès considérable.[18]

Peu de récits ont été si abondamment enluminés dans les manuscrits de notre corpus. Lorsqu'on s'attarde un instant aux histoires de Narcisse ou de Pygmalion, très en vogue à l'époque – pensons au seul *Roman de la Rose* – il est intéressant de constater que celles-ci ont moins retenu l'attention des artistes de l'*Ovide moralisé* que l'histoire de Pyramus et Thisbé.[19]

2. Les images

Les manuscrits de l'*Ovide moralisé* sont des stars célèbres mais n'ont jamais fait l'objet d'une étude d'ensemble, sans doute à cause de l'abondance de leur illustration. Si l'*Ovide moralisé* a été étudié maintes fois sous des angles textuels,[20] son iconographie reste en grande partie inexplorée.[21]

Les deux premiers témoins consacrent chacun dix images à l'histoire de Pyramus et Thisbé, outre une miniature qui évoque l'allégorie chré-

18. Le récit ovidien de Pyramus et Thisbé se lit au Livre IV, vv. 55-167. Notre édition de référence est celle de Georges Lafaye (éd.), *Ovide. Les Métamorphoses*, 3 tomes (Paris, Les Belles Lettres, 1969; 5e éd.).

19. L'iconographie de Pyramus et Thisbé dans l'*Ovide moralisé* a été reprise par l'enluminure de l'*Epître Othéa* de Christine de Pizan. Voir Sandra L. Hindman, *Christine de Pizan's 'Epistre Othéa'. Painting and Politics at the Court of Charles VI* (Toronto, 1986), pp. 93-94.

20. On se reportera, pour le conte de Pyramus et Thisbé, à Edmond Faral, *Recherches sur les sources latines des contes et romans courtois du moyen âge* (Paris, 1913); F. Branciforti, *Piramus e Tisbé. Introduzione. Testo critico, Traduzione e note* (Florence, 1959); Wolfgang van Emden, 'La légende de Pyrame et Thisbé: textes français des XVe, XVIe et XVIIe siècles', in *Mélanges Félix Lecoy* (Paris, 1973), pp. 569-583; William Kibler, 'Piramus et Tisbé: A medieval adapter at work', in *Zeitschrift für romanische Philologie,* XCI (1975), pp. 273-291; Anne-Marie Cadot, 'Du récit mythique au roman: étude sur *Piramus et Tisbé',* in *Romania,* XCVII (1976), pp. 433-461; Robert Glendinning, 'Pyramus and Thisbe in the Medieval Classroom', in *Speculum,* LXI (1986), pp. 51-78; Madeleine Tyssens, 'Les sources du *Pyramus*', in *Mélanges Jean Dufournet* (Paris, 1993), t. III, pp. 1411-1419. Voir aussi notre contribution 'La Rhétorique des mur-mûres dans *Pyrame et Thisbé,* conte du XIIe siècle' à paraître dans *Traduire l'émotion. Actes des Colloques de Cracovie (octobre 2001), Anvers / Louvain (juin 2002)*, études réunies par Jan Herman, Nathalie Kremer, Marcela Swiatkowska, *Les Cahiers de Paralittérature*, 8 (Namur, Editions du Céfal, 2004). Pour une étude du texte de l'*Ovide moralisé*, voir surtout Renate Blumenfeld-Kosinski, *Reading myth. Classical Mythology and Its Interpretations in Medieval French Literature* (Stanford, CA, 1997), Ana Pairet, *Les mutacions des fables: figures de la métamorphose dans la littérature française du Moyen Âge* (Paris, 2002), et Marylène Possamaï-Pérez, *L'*Ovide moralisé. *Essai d'interprétation*, Nouvelle Bibliothèque du Moyen Âge, 78 (Paris, 2006).

21. Sur les trois manuscrits qui retiennent ici notre attention, signalons en particulier le travail fondateur de Carla Lord, 'Three Manuscripts of the *Ovide moralisé*', in *Art Bulletin,* 85 (1975), pp. 161-175. Parmi les études plus récentes, on verra Françoise Clier-Colombani, 'La transposition iconographique du surnaturel dans l'*Ovide moralisé* de Rouen', in *Bien Dire et Bien Aprandre,* 14 (1996), pp. 113-138; Renate Blumenfeld-Kosinski, *op. cit.* [n. 15].

tienne.[22] Cependant, alors que les deux copies proviennent du même atelier, les images d'*Arsenal* ne sont pas identiques à celles de *Rouen*; de plus, elles interviennent dans le texte à des endroits différents.[23] Le manuscrit de *Lyon*, lui, n'offre pour l'aventure des deux jeunes que deux images purement narratives.[24]

La première vignette du cycle de *Rouen* montre au folio 91 deux couples: à droite, les amants s'embrassent; à gauche, une femme et un homme, tous les deux debout. L'homme désigne le couple amoureux de l'index gauche. Plutôt que d'identifier ces deux personnages comme les parents des amants, comme l'a fait Carla Lord, nous pensons que le geste 'accusateur'[25] permet d'identifier l'homme comme le serf qui trahit le couple. Ainsi le précise le texte, particulièrement aux vers 321-322:

> Li douz regars, li simples sens,
> Et li non convenables temps
> Et que nulz biens n'est sans envie
> Et nes uns sers sans felonnie
> Les fist departir et garder
> Qu'ensemble ne porent parler.
> Uns sers nota lor contenance
> Et dist: «Or sai bien sans soutance
> Que mout s'entra'aiment cil enfant,
> Et se il fussent auques grant
> Et il eüssent tel leizir,
> Griez chose fust dou departir;
> Veoir feïssent un tel plait
> Ou il avoit grant mal estrait».
> A la mere a la damoisele
> Porta li sers ceste nouvele [...]. (IV, vv. 307-322)[26]

22. Le programme iconographique de *Lyon* ne comporte à aucun endroit une interprétation allégorique, à travers la copie entière.

23. Lord avance l'hypothèse que les deux copies remontent à un archétype commun qui aurait comporté entre 600 à 650 images. Lord, *op. cit.* [note 21], pp. 166.

24. Voir le tableau en annexe.

25. Pour le geste accusateur de l'index pointé voir François Garnier, *Le Langage de l'image au moyen âge*, vol. 2 (Paris, 1988), p. 109.

26. 'Les doux regards qu'ils échangeaient, l'ingénuité de leurs sentiments, le temps, non encore venu, mais aussi le fait que tout bonheur suscite l'envie et qu'il n'y a pas d'esclave qui ignore la erfidie, eurent comme effet qu'on les sépara et qu'on les surveilla si bien qu'ils ne purent plus se retrouver. Un esclave, qui remarqua leur comportement, déclara: «Je sais bien, il n'y a aucun doute, que ces deux enfants s'aiment beaucoup. S'ils étaient un peu plus grands et qu'ils en eussent la possibilité, ce serait bien difficile de les séparer.» L'esclave vint dire ce qu'il avait vu à la mère de la jeune fille.' Nos traductions sont reprises à *Pyrame et Thisbé. Narcisse. Philomena. Trois contes du XIIe siècle imités d'Ovide*, présentés, édités et traduits par Emmanuèle Baumgartner (Paris, 2000).

Dans *Arsenal* une image analogue se rencontre au folio 40 (fig. 1)[27], à la seule différence près que les couples sont intervertis: à droite, on aperçoit la mère de Thisbé en conversation avec le serf; à gauche, le couple se tient par les bras.[28]

Dans le même manuscrit, une autre vignette précède, au folio 39v, la scène de la délation et ne montre que le couple qui s'embrasse; ce tableautin sert d'introduction à l'aventure.[29] De même, la copie de *Lyon* inaugure l'histoire avec une image charmante: au folio 55v, dans un décor champêtre, un Pyramus de petite taille – l'enlumineur a bien veillé à représenter '*des enfens*' – offre un rameau de fleurs à la jeune Thisbé.[30] L'ambiance est de prime abord assez différente des images de *Rouen* et d'*Arsenal*. Il n'y a pas la moindre allusion à l'issue fatale, pas plus que dans l'image que nous analyserons plus loin.

Les tableaux suivants introduisent la séparation des amants, suite à la trahison du serf; dans les deux plus anciennes copies ils sont quasi identiques. Dans *Rouen*, au folio 92, on aperçoit Pyramus seul dans une chambre voûtée, debout, la tête inclinée à sa gauche. Il porte la main gauche au menton en signe de douleur. Parallèlement, *Arsenal*, au folio 40v[31], montre l'homme, assis sur un banc dans une chambre, à l'intérieur d'une tour crénelée; il porte également la main gauche au menton. Ici encore, il a la tête inclinée à gauche. Cette pose semble voulue par l'imagier. Dans les images suivantes Thisbé se trouve dans sa chambre, dans une position semblable à celle de son ami: la tête inclinée vers sa droite, les jambes croisées, et les mains jointes . *Rouen*, au folio 92v, inclut une image très expressive où la jeune fille est sur le point de tomber du banc où elle est assise, un détail inspiré par le texte: à la fin d'un long monologue, où elle se plaint de la séparation, elle s'évanouit:

27. La rubrique au-dessus de la miniature dit: 'Ci devise comment pyramus et thysbe furent encuse par un serf et du mautalent qui vint entre leur deus peres'.

28. L'interversion est une technique décrite par Carla Lord: on trouve souvent d'une copie à l'autre une transposition 'en miroir' d'une image, technique commune et acceptable si l'on considère que nos deux manuscrits proviennent du même atelier. 'Only about fifty of the Arsenal scenes are very close visually to those of Rouen, although they sometime quote Rouen in reverse [...]. Even then the differences are remarkable, simply because of the enlarged scale of the Arsenal miniatures. Magnified by about one third, many of the Arsenal miniatures have a squared background [...] that suggests not only a decorative foil, but the possible use of a grid system for transfer.' *op. cit.*, [note 21], p. 164; voir aussi notes 27 et 28.

29. La rubrique qui la surmonte dit: 'Ci devise comment pyramus et thysbe commencierent a s'amer li uns lautre des l'aige de sept ans'.

30. La rubrique se trouve en-dessous de l'image: 'comment piramus et tisbe sentramerent des leur enfence'.

31. La rubrique qui accompagne la miniature indique: 'Ci devise comment pyramus se complaignoit pour lamour de thysbe samie a qui il ne pooit parler'.

«Ci fine mes complainz en lermes.
Pasmer mestuet; or est li termes. [...]
La pucele est trois fois pasmee, [...].» (IV, vv. 532-537)[32]

Le fait que les deux amants se trouvent de part et d'autre du mur implique qu'ils se penchent l'un vers l'autre: Pyramus regarde à droite tandis que son amie a la tête inclinée vers la gauche.

Arsenal montre Thisbé à deux reprises au folio 40v. Dans le premier tableau, la jeune fille est assise sur un banc, les mains jointes, la tête inclinée vers le mur qui la sépare de son ami.[33] Elle a les jambes croisées, comme le font deviner les plis de sa longue robe. Une deuxième image[34] ressemble fort à celle dans *Rouen*: Thisbé, assise sur un banc, semble s'évanouir; le buste est penché en avant.

Les images qui enchaînent sur les tableaux de la séparation montrent, dans *Rouen* comme dans *Arsenal*, les jeunes amants debout, de part et d'autre du mur, près de la fente. Ce sont encore une fois, des images spéculaires.

Rouen réserve deux images quasi identiques à cette séquence. La première, au folio 93 (fig. 2), place Pyramus à l'extrême droite; au milieu, on distingue Thisbé, à l'intérieur d'un édicule. Le fente est représentée par l'artiste.

La deuxième miniature, au folio 94, montre les héros au même endroit, mais leurs gestes des bras et des mains sont nettement plus expressifs et font penser à une conversation.

Arsenal ne prévoit pour cette séquence qu'une seule image, spéculaire par rapport à celles de *Rouen*. Au folio 41v (fig. 3), Thisbé se trouve à droite, à moitié à l'intérieur d'une tour crénelée. Elle pose la main gauche sur la fente, mise en évidence par ses dimensions. Il faut rappeler dans ce contexte que c'est bien elle qui a découvert *icel pertus*. Pyramus se tient à gauche, tout près d'elle, l'index droit pointé vers le haut, comme pour prendre la parole. Or, la rubrique[35] et le texte semblent indiquer que c'est plutôt la jeune fille qui parle.

32. 'Ma plainte maintenant s'achève dans les larmes, Je vais m'évanouir, c'en est fait. [...] A trois reprises la jeune fille s'est évanouie [...].' Baumgartner, *op. cit.*, [note 26], p. 41.

33. La rubrique au-dessus de cette image indique: 'Ci devise comment thysbe lamie pyramus se complaignoit pour lamor de ce quele ne pooit parler a lui'.

34. La rubrique en-dessous du tableautin au folio 41 ne réfère pas au contenu de l'image: 'Ci devise comment pyramus et thysbe parloient ensamble par une crevace dune paroi et des complaintes quil faisoient lun a lautre'. Ce sont les vers précédant l'image qui précisent que Thisbé s'évanouit: 'Ci finerai ma plainte en lermes. Pasmer m'estuet or est li termes.' Éd. De Boer [note 1], Livre IV, vv. 532-533.

35. La rubrique précède la miniature: 'Ci devise comment tysbe conforte pyramus son ami par la crevace et comment elle se complaint por lamor de lui'.

Quel chose est ce qu'Amours ne sent?
Li dui amant premierement
Aperçurent icel pertus:
Primes Tisbé, puis Piramus.
Tisbé trouva la creveüre,
Prist le pendant de sa çainture,
S'en fist outre le chief paroir,
Que ses amis le puist veoir. (IV, vv. 555-562)[36]

Bien que l'image ne suive pas le texte à la lettre, puisqu'on ne distingue point la ceinture passant par le trou, l'enlumineur d'*Arsenal* ne semble guère avoir perdu de vue ce détail: tandis que dans les images au folio 40 Thisbé porte une ceinture autour de la taille, elle n'en a plus dans le tableautin illustrant le premier dialogue.

Suite à leur découverte, les jeunes amants décident de partir et de se donner rendez-vous près de la fontaine sous *le morier*. Les épisodes ultérieurs se déroulent donc à l'extérieur.

Au folio 94v (fig. 4), l'imagier de *Rouen* représente Thisbé. Elle grimpe dans un arbre et regarde d'un oeil inquiet le lion près de la fontaine du rendez-vous; la source est peinte comme une simple surface d'eau en forme de larme. L'animal tient dans la gueule le voile de la jeune fille. L'image au folio 42 du manuscrit de l'*Arsenal* présente une scène légèrement différente.[37] Ici, Thisbé, à gauche, prend la fuite, jetant un regard en arrière, en direction du lion. À droite, le fauve, la gueule grand ouverte, menace la belle. Au milieu, on aperçoit la source au pied d'un arbre portant de grands fruits ronds et blancs. Cet arbre dépasse le cadre du tableau, attirant ainsi l'attention du lecteur.

Quand Pyramus croit rejoindre son amie près de la fontaine, il n'aperçoit que le voile taché de sang, ce qui le désespère et le pousse au suicide. C'est ce que représente la miniature au folio 95 de *Rouen*. À gauche, la source au pied du mûrier; à droite, le jeune homme se jette sur son épée et s'écroule. Dans *Arsenal*, au folio 42 (fig. 5), la scène paraît plus pathétique.[38] Debout, face au lecteur, il lève la main droite et se transperce la poitrine d'une épée. L'autre main est levée en signe de douleur. À droite, on voit la source au pied du mûrier. Les fruits de celui-ci ont changé de

36. 'Y a-t-il quelque chose qu'Amour ne puisse percevoir? Les deux amants furent les premiers à remarquer ce trou. D'abord Thisbé, puis Pyrame. Thisbé découvrit la fente, elle prit le pan de sa ceinture et en fit passer la boucle de l'autre côté pour que son ami puisse la voir.' Baumgartner, *op. cit.*, [note 26], p. 43.

37. La rubrique dit: 'Ci devise comment thysbe issi de la meson du pere et vint ala fontaine et comment ele sen foui por la paour du lyon et lessa cheoir sa guimple'.

38. La rubrique précise: 'Ci devise comment pyramus a la fontaine et trouva la guimple thysbe samie toute sanglente et comment il se complaint por ce que il cuidoit quele fust morte et comment il soccist de sespee'.

couleur. La rubrique n'en fait pas mention, mais le texte l'évoque dans un passage ultérieur, notamment en imaginant les dernières paroles du jeune héros:

> 'Mes primes vueil les Diex prier
> Qu'il demonstrent en cest morier
> Signe de mort et destorbier,
> De plour:
> Facent le fruit de tel coulour
> Qui apartiengne a la dolour.' (IV, vv. 1001-1006)[39]

Il faut préciser qu'*Arsenal* est la seule copie qui représente la métamorphose du mûrier; contrairement à sa source ovidienne[40], le texte n'insiste que brièvement sur ce détail.

Dans la même séquence des fatalités irréversibles, *Rouen*, au folio 95v, représente Thisbé revenue sur les lieux. À gauche, la source; au milieu, Pyramus mort par terre. Thisbé le serre dans les bras (fig. 6). À droite se dessine un arbre aux fruits noirs. Une deuxième image, au folio 96v, complète la séquence des retrouvailles nocturnes. La mise en scène est la même, à ceci près que Thisbé, debout devant Pyramus, se jette sur une épée. Dans *Arsenal*, nous n'avons pour ce dernier épisode de l'histoire qu'une seule vignette. Au folio 42v (fig. 7), on trouve la source à droite dans l'image. À gauche, Pyramus gît au bord de l'eau, les yeux fermés, la tête posée sur l'avant-bras gauche. Derrière lui, son amie se transperce; elle adopte exactement la même position que lui au folio 42, accentuant de la sorte le parallélisme de leur trépas. Le mûrier, toujours présent, porte des fruits noirs.

La miniature que *Lyon* réserve, au folio 59v (Fig. 8), à cet épisode – la copie n'en prévoit que deux pour toute l'histoire, nous l'avons signalé –

39. 'Mais avant je veux prier les dieux qu'ils inscrivent sur ce mûrier un signe de mort et de malheur: qu'ils donnent à ce fruit la couleur qui convient à la douleur. [...] Le sang ruisselle sur les branches et noircit le fruit qui était blanc. Jusqu'à ce jour, la mûre avait toujours été blanche mais elle devint depuis de couleur noire, en signe de douleur.' Baumgartner, *op. cit.* [note 27], pp. 71-73.

40. Aux vers IV, 119-127, Ovide décrit minutieusement le processus de la métamorphose comme une conséquence naturelle du suicide de Pyramus: 'Quoque erat accinctus, demisit in ilia ferrum, Nec mora, feruenti moriens e vulnere traxit Et iacuit resupinus humo; cruor emicat alte, Non aliter quam cum vitatio fistula plumbo Scinditur et tenui stridente foramine longas Eiaculatur aquas atque ictibus aera rumpit. Arborei fetus aspergne caedis in atram Vertuntur faciem madefacta sanguine radix Purpureo tingit pendentia mora colore.' À la fin de l'histoire, Ovide réinsiste sur cette métamorphose à travers les dernières paroles de Thisbé: 'At tu, quae ramis arbor miserabile corpus Nunc tegis unius, mox es tectura duorum, Signa tene caedis pullosque et luctibus aptos Semper habe fetus, gemini monumenta cruoris.' IV, vv. 158-161 (Lafaye, *op. cit.*, [note 18], vol. 1, pp. 100-101).

est très particulière.[41] L'enlumineur semble avoir illustré un moment différent de celui qui est retenu dans les deux premières copies.

Dans le tableau, les deux jeunes gens, Pyramus à gauche, Thisbé à droite, – tous deux de petite taille comme dans la première image – se tiennent debout au second plan, surpris par le lion qui flaire le voile de la jeune fille, taché de sang. À l'avant-plan, devant l'animal, on aperçoit une source carrée. Derrière le couple, deux arbres verdoyants. Point de mûrier. Cette scène ne semble pas correspondre au texte où les amants ne sont à aucun moment réunis. Il n'y a aucune allusion à la fin tragique; pas question non plus de la métamorphose de l'arbre.

Peut-être l'artiste s'est-il inspiré directement des vers qui précèdent l'image. Ceux-ci présentent le lion comme protagoniste, justifiant de la sorte la place dominante qu'occupe le fauve dans le tableau:

> Li lions vint a grant effroi.
> A la fontaine esteint sa soi,
> Et quant il est bien assasez,
> Vait s'en deduire par les prez,
> Trueve la guimple en une sente,
> Defoule la et ensanglente; [...]. (IV, vv. 904-909)[42]

En revanche, le contenu de l'image ne correspond guère à la rubrique qui suit. Celle-ci indique *coment piramus et tisbe morurent a la fontaine* et ressemble par ailleurs fort à celle qui accompagne le tableautin au folio 48 pour l'histoire de Narcisse. Le décor en comprend également une fontaine, comme l'annonce la rubrique: *comment narsisus morut a la fontaine*.[43] De fait, au folio 48, dans un paysage fleuri, garni de trois jeunes arbres, le chasseur antique contemple son reflet dans l'eau d'une fontaine carrée située à gauche; à droite, Echo, les mains jointes, est probablement en train de prier Amour de la venger.[44]

41. Nous nous permettons de signaler que le manuscrit Copenhague, Bibliothèque Royale, Thott 399 est la seule autre copie de l'*Ovide moralisé* – vers 1480 – qui enlumine la scène du suicide. Le folio 104v montre à gauche une fontaine hexagonale munie de sculptures, au pied d'un arbre en fleur (qui ne ressemble pas au mûrier); au milieu Pyramus gît mort, l'épée plantée dans la poitrine. Devant lui, Thisbé lève la main gauche et s'enfonce un couteau dans le flanc; elle se jette sur le corps de son ami.

42. 'Le lion approche à grand bruit de la fontaine et il étanche sa soif. Puis, une fois désaltéré, il va folâtrer dans les prés. Il trouve alors le voile dans un sentier, le foule aux pieds et le tache de sang.' Baumgartner, *op. cit.*, [note 26], p. 65.

43. Une seule image sépare la séquence de Pyramus et Thisbé du tableau de Narcisse: au folio 54, on montre les filles de Minyas filant la laine.

44. Ce tableau résume deux actions consécutives: Echo prie Dieu de la venger; ensuite, Narcisse découvre son reflet dans la fontaine. Cette scène qui représente Echo et Narcisse n'est pas racontée dans le texte des *Métamorphoses*, bien que le geste des mains jointes, manifesté par 'quelqu'un' soit décrit: 'Inde manus aliquis despectus ad aethera tollens: Sic amet ipse licet, sic non potiatur amato.' Livre III, vv. 404-405, Lafaye, *op. cit.* [note 18],

La ressemblance des miniatures représentant d'un côté Echo et Narcisse, et de l'autre Pyramus et Thisbé est frappante. L'artiste de *Lyon* a pu être influencé par l'image de Narcisse et Echo qui réunit ces deux personnages dans le même tableau.

Enfin, la dernière image prévue pour l'histoire de Pyramus et Thisbé montre les amants couchés, couverts d'un drap et entourés de personnages portant le deuil. Au folio 96v de *Rouen* les gisants ont la tête tournée vers la droite. Derrière eux se trouvent sept personnages dont, au milieu, un clerc tonsuré. Dans *Arsenal*, au folio 43, Pyramus et Thisbé sont couchés l'un à côté de l'autre (fig. 9). Autour d'eux cinq personnes les pleurent en manifestant des signes de douleur.[45]

Après avoir raconté l'histoire telle que nous la connaissons, l'auteur dévoile le sens caché de la transformation du mûrier en s'appuyant sur la symbolique religieuse: l'arbre représente la croix sur laquelle le Christ est mort pour sauver l'humanité. Les copies de *Rouen* et d'*Arsenal* prévoient chacune une image pour cette allégorie chrétienne. Les deux vignettes se ressemblent très fort. *Rouen* peint au folio 96v une scène violente. Six hommes occupent le tableau. Deux d'entre eux – des martyrs – se trou-

pp. 81-82. L'*Ovide moralisé*, comme son modèle, attribue l'imprécation de vengeance à 'une des victimes': '[...] aucuns ou aucune pria Dieu qu'entre tel fortune li donnast d'amours esprouver, Et qu'il peüst aucun trouver Qu'aussi amast sans joie avoir [...]'. Éd. De Boer [note 1], Livre III, vv. 1533-1537. 'Quelqu'un – homme ou femme – pria Dieu pour que son destin soit celui de tomber amoureux de quelqu'un sans être aimé en retour' [notre traduction]. Le seul texte qui puisse avoir inspiré la position et le geste d'Echo dans la miniature de Lyon est le *Lai de Narcisse*, conte ovidien anonyme du XIIe siècle, où Dané – l'Echo d'Ovide – s'exprime dans un long monologue: 'Vous, diu du ciel et de la terre, Et cil de l'air et de la mer, Vos tuit qui rien savés d'amer Et qui estes en sa baillie, Et tu, Venus, qui m'as traïe Ensamble au die d'amors, ton fil, Giete me hors de cest peril Et de celui prendés vengance Por cui je muir sans esperance! Faites qu'il sace qu'est Amors, Si qu'il ne puist avoir secors!' [Mais vous, dieux du ciel et de la terre, dieux de l'air et de la mer, vous tous qui savez ce qu'est l'amour et qui êtes soumis à son pouvoir, et toi, Vénus, toi qui m'a trahie ainsi que le dieu d'amout, ton fils, sauvez-moi de ce péril et prenez vengeance de celui pour qui, privée de tout espoir, je meurs. Faites qu'il sache qui est Amour et qu'il ne puisse y trouver remède!'. Baumgartner, *op. cit.* [note 26], vv. 616-626. Pour la représentation de Narcisse, thème très fréquemment illustré dans le *Roman de la Rose*, voir l'inventaire établi par Herman Braet, 'Aux Sources du *Roman de la Rose*', dans *Medieval Codicology, Iconography, Literature, and Translation. Studies for Keith Val Sinclair*, ed. by Peter Rolfe Monks et D. D. R. Owen (Leyde – New York – Cologne, 1994), p. 110-120. Le même auteur offre un addendum dans 'L'Illustration de l'illustration: l'exemple et l'image dans le *Roman de la Rose*', dans *Ensi firent li ancessor. Mélanges de philologie médiévale offerts à Marc-René Jung*, ed. Luciano Rossi, Christine Jacob-Hugon et Ursula Bähler, vol. II (Alessandria, Edizioni dell'Orso, 1996), p. 499.

45. La rubrique explique: 'Ci devise comment li parent pyramus et thysbe les trouverent mort dessoz le mourier et les mistrent en un tombiau ensamble'. Une personne au second plan a les paumes levées et dirigées vers l'extérieur; une autre, assise au milieu, juste derrière le tombeau, a les mains en pronation et semble en train de prier. Tous ont la tête inclinée.

vent à genoux, la tête nimbée. Les autres, derrière eux, brandissent chacun une épée pour les frapper.

Arsenal possède au folio 43 une enluminure tout à fait parallèle, bien que la composition soit plus simple.[46] Deux hommes brandissent une épée de la main droite et posent la main gauche sur la nuque de deux hommes à genoux, la tête entourée d'une auréole.[47]

Ces images ferment le cycle; le suivant aborde l'histoire passionnante de Vénus, Mars et Vulcain.

3. Quelques remarques en guise de conclusion

Le thème du recyclage des manuscrits s'applique à merveille à l'*Ovide moralisé* dont le texte et l'iconographie restent un vaste champ de recherche.

Les miniatures qui enrichissent les folios où se lit l'aventure de Pyramus et Thisbé montrent à quel point un cycle d'images peut constituer un univers séparé ayant à sa disposition un langage pictural dans lequel les principaux éléments du texte se trouvent recyclés par le choix et la position des acteurs, par leurs attributs et gestes. La récurrence et la ressemblance de certaines scènes, voire les différences entre leurs éléments – pensons à la métamorphose du mûrier d'une image à l'autre – établissent une histoire parallèle qui peut jeter une autre lumière sur un texte difficile. C'est que l'image, par ses dimensions réduites, a tendance à privilégier l'essentiel d'une histoire, d'en véhiculer le noyau.

Notre analyse a porté sur un corpus fort restreint. Elle permet néanmoins de s'interroger déjà sur le degré d'autonomie du décor accompagnant un texte vernaculaire, – une question qu'il sera difficile de trancher tant qu'on n'aura pas procédé à l'établissement des programmes propres aux manuscrits enluminés des *Métamorphoses* elles-mêmes.[48]

46. La rubrique dit: 'Ci devise lexposicion de la fable du mourier qui estoit blans qui devint noirs pour la mort pyramus'.

47. Cette image a été étudiée récemment par Renate Blumenfeld-Kosinski, qui l'évoque en tant qu'exemple du lien que l'iconographie éclaire ou établit entre le mythe païen et l'allégorie chrétienne. Puisque cette dernière ne mentionne point que les martyrs trouvent la mort par l'épée, l'artiste a dû se laisser guider par l'histoire des jeunes amants qui se suicident de cette manière. R. Blumenfeld-Kosinski, *op. cit.* [n. 15], pp. 71-82.

48. Le catalogue de Franco Munari et ses addenda font état d'une trentaine de manuscrits illustrés des *Métamorphoses*. Lord ne semble pas considérer ces témoins comme une source iconographique de l'*Ovide moralisé;* nous pensons néanmoins qu'une comparaison reste indispensable. F. Munari, *Catalogue of the manuscripts of Ovid's Metamorphoses*, University of London Institute of Classical Studies in Conjunction with the Warburg Institute, Bulletin Supplement, 4 (Londres, 1957); 'Supplemento al catalogo dei manoscritti delle Metamorfosi 'ovidiane', dans *Rivista di filologia e di istruzione classica*, XCIII/3 (1965), pp. 288-297; 'Secondo supplemento al catalogo dei manoscritti delle meta-

Dans le cadre d'une enquête plus large, il reste à examiner pourquoi l'histoire de Pyramus et Thisbé, ainsi que d'autres comme celle de Philomena et d'Arachné, ont été pourvues dans les manuscrits enluminés de l'*Ovide moralisé* de séquences iconographiques fort développées, tandis que des thèmes tels que ceux de Narcisse, de Pygmalion, bien plus répandus, n'ont guère obtenu la faveur des enlumineurs de notre texte. A-t-il existé une tradition antérieure ou parallèle à l'*Ovide moralisé*? Une hypothèse qui tarde à être explorée.

morfosi ovidiane', dans *Studia florentina. Alessandro Ronconi Sexagenario Oblata* (Rome, Edizioni dell' Ateneo, 1970), pp. 275-280. Autres suppléments au catalogue de Munari: F. T. Coulson, 'An update to Munari's catalogue of the manuscripts of Ovid's Metamorphoses', dans *Scriptorium*, XLII (1988), pp. 111-112; F. T. Coulson, 'Newly discovered manuscripts of Ovid's Metamorphoses in the libraries of Florence and Milan', dans *Scriptorium*, XLVI (1992)1, pp. 285-287; F. T. Coulson, 'Addenda to Munari's Catalogue of the manuscripts of Ovid's Metamorphoses', dans *Revue d'histoire des textes*, XXV (1995), pp. 91-127.

Images	Rouen, Bibliothèque municipale, ms. 1044	Paris, Bibliothèque de l'Arsenal, ms. 5069	Lyon, Bibliothèque municipale, ms. 742
Pyramus et Thisbé s'embrassent		f 39v, En babiloine la cite/Furent deus homme renomme (vv. 1-2)	f° 55v En babiloine la cite/Furent deus deus hommes renomme (vv. 1-2)
Pyramus et Thisbé d'un côté, la mère de Thisbé et le serf de l'autre	f° 91 En babiloine la cite/furent dui home renome (vv. 1-2)	f° 40 Et il furent dedens dix ans/ Fu assez leur leece grans (vv. 303-304)	
Pyramus seul	f° 92 Piramus est plains de tristour/ plains de souspir et plains de plour (vv. 375-376)	f° 40 Pyramus est en grant tristeur/ plains de souspirs et plains de pleur (vv. 375-376)	
Thisbé seule	f° 92v Tysbe rest la dedens enclose/ fors dou palais issir n'en ose (vv. 446-447)	f° 40v Thysbe est la dedens enclose/ Hors du palais issir n'en ose (vv. 445-447)	
Thisbé seule		f° 40v Ci finerai ma plainte en lermes/Pasmer m'estuet or est li termes (vv. 532-533)	
Pyramus près de la fente	f° 93 Ensi/fais ie par chascun di/ Tel fief tieng ie de mon ami (vv. 534-536)	f° 41v Amis trop vous desconfortez/ Merveilles est que trop m'amez (vv. 731-732)	
P et T près de la fente	f° 94 Amis trop vous desconfortez/ merveilles est que trop m'amez (vv. 731-732)		
Thisbé et le lion	f° 94 Ensi ferment lor convenant/ Puis departent li dui amant (vv. 820-821)	f° 42 Ainssi ferment leur convenant/ Puis departent le convenant (vv. 820-821)	
Suicide de Pyramus	f° 95 Quant Pyramus ne voit s'amie/ dont cuide il bien qu'el soit fenie (vv. 930-931)	f° 42 Et quant il est des pres issus/et Pyramus y est venus (vv. 910-911)	
Thisbé revient	f° 95v Tysbe repairoit aytant/qu'el ne deceust son amant ((vv. 1023-1024)		
Pyramus mort – suicide de Thisbé	f° 96v Ensi com la fable recorde/ Qui a voire istoire s'acorde (vv. 1158-1159)	f° 42v Thysbe reperoit aitant/ Qu'ele ne decheust son amant (vv. 1023-1024)	
Pyramus et Thisbé près de la fontaine			f° 59v Et quant il est des prez yssus/ Et Piramus y est venus (vv. 910-911)
Pyramus et Thisbé gisants	f°96v Or vous vueil l'exposicion/dire de la mutacion (vv. 1170-1171)	f° 43 Einssi con la fable recorde/Qui a vraie hystoire s'acorde (vv. 1158-1159)	
Les martyrs chrétiens	f° 96v En cest monde plain de vilte/ plain d'ordure et d'iniquité (vv. 1178-1179)	f° 43 Or vous voeil l'exposicion/dire de la mutacion (vv. 1170-1171)	

Figure 1
Paris, Bibliothèque de l'Arsenal, ms. 5069, *Ovide moralisé*, f° 40

Figure 2
Rouen, Bibliothèque municipale, ms. 1044, *Ovide moralisé*, f° 93
«Collections de la Bibliothèque municipale de Rouen.
Photographies Thierry Ascencio-Parvy»

Figure 3
Paris, Bibliothèque de l'Arsenal, ms. 5069, *Ovide moralisé*, f° 41v

Figure 4
Rouen, Bibliothèque municipale, ms. 1044, *Ovide moralisé*, f° 94v
«Collections de la Bibliothèque municipale de Rouen.
Photographies Thierry Ascencio-Parvy»

Figure 5
Paris, Bibliothèque de l'Arsenal, ms. 5069, *Ovide moralisé*, f° 42

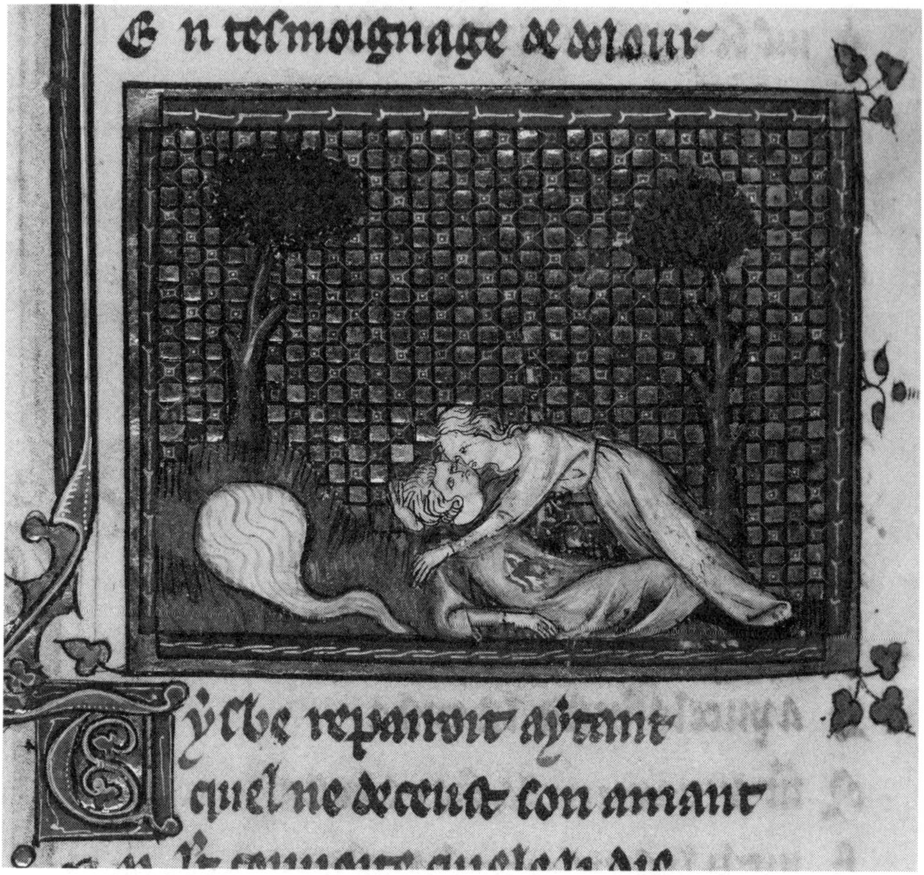

Figure 6
Rouen, Bibliothèque municipale, ms. 1044, *Ovide moralisé*, f° 95v
«Collections de la Bibliothèque municipale de Rouen.
Photographies Thierry Ascencio-Parvy»

Figure 7
Paris, Bibliothèque de l'Arsenal, ms. 5069, *Ovide moralisé*, f° 42v

Figure 8
Lyon, Bibliothèque municipale, ms. 742, *Ovide moralisé*, f° 59v

Figure 9
Paris, Bibliothèque de l'Arsenal, ms. 5069, *Ovide moralisé*, f° 43

Paul Bertrand – Baudouin Van den Abeele

RECYCLAGE DE CONTENUS ET RÉCUPÉRATION DE PIÈCES D'ARCHIVES DANS LE *MACROLOGUS* ENCYCLOPÉDIQUE DE SAINT-LAURENT DE LIÈGE, (*CIRCA* 1470-1480)

L'histoire de l'encyclopédisme médiéval est celle d'une chaîne de textes fortement soudés. Depuis Isidore de Séville au VIIe siècle, en passant par Raban Maur à l'époque carolingienne, puis aux grandes œuvres des XIIe et XIIIe siècles, on y suit le cheminement de contenus transmis par relais successifs, tout en y observant des glissements et des ouvertures multiples. Le genre encyclopédique tout entier – si tant est que l'on puisse parler à juste titre de genre[1] – a pour méthode la compilation, et pour élément de base la citation. Trouver pour chaque réalité à caractériser des passages pertinents dans les œuvres reconnues pour leur *auctoritas*, les reprendre ou les condenser en les juxtaposant avec d'autres extraits, en faire un montage adéquatement structuré, telle semble être la réalité du travail intellectuel des auteurs médiévaux d'encyclopédies. C'est donc à un vaste recyclage de contenus que l'on assiste dans ces textes, et à ce titre le sujet a pleinement sa place dans ce volume *Medieval Manuscripts in Transition*, où l'attention se porte sur la réutilisation de manuscrits, de textes et d'images. Le terme 'recyclage' peut également s'entendre au sens matériel, car de nombreuses pièces d'archives déclassées ont été réutilisées dans le dossier manuscrit qui sera présenté ici.[2]

* P. Bertrand, chargé de recherches au CNRS, responsable de la section de diplomatique de l'Institut de recherche et d'histoire des textes, Orléans; B. Van den Abeele, Chercheur qualifié du FNRS, Université catholique de Louvain.

1. La question est posée explicitement dans deux communications présentées au colloque de Groningue sur l'encyclopédisme: B. Ribémont, 'On the definition of an encyclopedic genre in the Middle Ages', in *Pre-Modern Encyclopedic Texts. Proceedings of the second COMERS Congress, Groningen, 1-4 July 1996*, éd. P. Binkley (Leiden/New York/Köln, 1997), p. 47-62; C. Meier, 'Organisation of knowledge and encyclopaedic «ordo »: Functions and purposes of a universal literary genre', *Ibid.*, p. 103-126.

2. La première partie de l'article, rédigée par B. Van den Abeele, a fait l'objet d'une communication au colloque de Groningue, 'Knowledge, Learning an Cultural Change' (novembre 2002), dont les actes sont en cours d'impression. On y trouvera une version anglaise plus détaillée de ce qui est synthétisé ici, sous le titre 'The *Macrologus* of Liège: an encyclopedic lexicon at the dawn of Humanism'. La deuxième partie de l'article est de la responsabilité de P. Bertrand.

Les études ne manquent pas sur l'encyclopédisme médiéval. La bibliographie sur le père fondateur du genre, Isidore de Séville, occuperait à elle seule un livre, et les titres relatifs aux grands représentants du genre encyclopédique au XIIIe siècle, soit Thomas de Cantimpré, Barthélemy l'Anglais, Vincent de Beauvais et Brunet Latin, se comptent par dizaines pour chacun d'eux. Les XIVe et XVe siècles, en revanche, font figure de parents pauvres, alors qu'ils sont loin de constituer un désert en la matière, mais on a mis longtemps à commencer à s'y intéresser.[3] L'histoire de l'encyclopédisme durant le Moyen Âge tardif reste à écrire et il est assurément trop tôt pour s'y risquer. Toutes les œuvres pertinentes ou presque sont inédites, et les fonds de manuscrits livrent à chaque enquête de nouvelles trouvailles. S'il fallait d'ores et déjà dégager quelques lignes de force de la question, on pourrait formuler quatre éléments de réponse. D'abord, le travail de copie des œuvres du XIIIe s. se poursuit sans interruption, et elles n'ont nullement été considérées comme périmées ou passées de mode, ce qui vaut d'ailleurs aussi bien pour les *Etymologies* d'Isidore, bien plus anciennes. Deuxièmement, on observe une marge d'interventions non négligeable dans l'apport des copistes, en fonction des goûts du commanditaire, de ses moyens peut-être, de la culture du copiste, de son intelligence du texte. La réception d'une œuvre comme celle de Barthélemy l'Anglais montre la variabilité qui affecte ce genre de textes non canoniques.[4] En troisième lieu, parmi les remaniements et les œuvres nouvelles ou semi-originales des XIVe et XVe siècles, on constate le retour en force de la moralisation, de la glose allégorique, du développement édifiant.[5] Ainsi, le *De proprietatibus rerum* de Barthélemy l'Anglais donne lieu au *De proprietatibus rerum moralizate* ou *Liber Septiformis de moralitatibus rerum* de Marc d'Orvieto,[6] au *Liber de exemplis*

3. C'est le mérite de l'équipe de Münster d'avoir organisé, il y a quelques années, un colloque sur les modifications de l'encyclopédisme à la fin du Moyen Age, dont les actes ont enfin paru: *Die Enzyklopädie im Wandel vom Hochmittelalter bis zur frühen Neuzeit*, éd. C. Meier (München, 2002). Voir aussi le volume *Enzyklopädien der frühen Neuzeit. Beiträge zu ihrer Erforschung*, éd. F. Eybl et al. (Tübingen, 1995).

4. Voir l'étude approfondie de H. Meyer, *Die Enzyklopädie des Bartholomaeus Anglicus. Untersuchungen zur Überlieferungs- und Rezeptionsgeschichte von De proprietatibus rerum* (München, 2000).

5. Le versant allégorique n'avait cependant jamais totalement disparu du genre, contrairement à ce que l'on affirme parfois: voir H. Meyer, 'Zum Verhältnis von Enzyklopädik und Allegorese im Mittelalter', *Frühmittelalterliche Studien*, 24 (1990), p. 290-313; B. Van den Abeele, 'L'allégorie animale dans les encyclopédies latines du Moyen Age', in *L'animal exemplaire au Moyen Age (V^{e} – XVe siècles)*, éd. J. Berlioz et M.A. Polo de Beaulieu (Rennes, 1999), p. 123-143.

6. Voir Meyer, *Die Enzyklopädie* [note 4], p. 298-316 et J.B. Friedman, 'Peacocks and Preachers: Analytic Technique in Marcus of Orvieto's *Liber de moralitatibus*, Vatican lat. MS 5933', in *Beasts and Birds in the Middle Ages. The Bestiary and its Legacy*, éd. W.B. Clark et M. McMunn (Philadelphia, 1989), p.179-196.

et similitudinibus rerum de Jean de San Gimignano, au *Multifarium* conservé à Wolfenbüttel.[7] Enfin, une autre tendance nouvelle est la montée du principe d'ordonnance alphabétique. Divers textes encyclopédiques étudiés depuis peu se sont ainsi constitués aux XIVe-XVe s. à travers l'abandon de l'ordre logique ou systématique. Citons le texte nommé *Historia naturalis* de Johannes Egidius (ou Juan Gil) de Zamora dans les dernières décennies du XIIIe s., qui est une compilation alphabétique,[8] le *Omne Bonum* de James le Palmer, écrit à Londres dans les années 1360,[9] le *Repertorium Morale* de Pierre Bersuire, dont l'ampleur semble avoir découragé les chercheurs.[10] Cette tendance occasionne graduellement un rapprochement entre le genre encyclopédique et celui des lexiques et dictionnaires.[11] C'est dans cette dernière veine que s'inscrit le texte étudié ici.

1. Le *Macrologus* : l'œuvre et ses sources

Macrologus, nous dit l'auteur, est le titre choisi, car c'est une œuvre grande et longue, *a macron quod est longum et logos quod est sermo, quia magnum opus est et longum*. Cette explication, à vrai dire assez peu subtile, s'impose à l'esprit quand on considère l'ouvrage. Il s'agit d'un énorme texte en trois gros volumes, conservés à la Bibliothèque Royale de Bruxelles. Le dossier est totalement vierge: le fichier de la Biblio-

7. Pour les deux derniers, voir B. Van den Abeele, 'Moralisierte Enzyklopädien in der Nachfolge von Bartholomäus Anglicus: das *Multifarium* in Wolfenbüttel und der *Liber de exemplis et similitudinibus rerum* des Johannes de Sancto Geminiano', in: *Die Enzyklopädie im Wandel* [note 3], p. 279-304. Pensons aussi au *Liber similitudinum naturalium* de Konrad de Halberstadt, étudié récemment par I. Ventura, 'Der *Liber similitudinum naturalium*' Konrads von Halberstadt und seine Quellen. Ein Fallbeispiel aus der naturwissenschaftlichen Textüberlieferung im Spätmittelalter', *Frühmittelalterliche Studien,* 35 (2001), p. 349-406.

8. L'ouvrage est inachevé, limité dans le ms. de Berlin (SBB-PK, lat. fol. 62) à la lettre A, mais n'en compte pas moins 262 feuillets. Edition par A. Domínguez García et L. García Ballester, *Johannes Egidii Zamorensis, Historia Naturalis* (Salamanca, 1994).

9. Voir L. Freeman Sandler, *Omne Bonum. A fourteenth-century encyclopedia of universal knowledge*, 2 vol. (London, 1996), et Ead., 'The role of illustrations in James le Palmer's *Omne Bonum*', in *Die Enzyklopädie im Wandel* [note 3], p. 305-316.

10. Voir Ch. Samaran et J. Monfrin, 'Pierre Bersuire, prieur de Saint-Eloi de Paris (1290? – 1362)', *Histoire littéraire de la France,* 39 (1962), p. 258-450; M.H. Tesnière, 'Le Reductorium Morale de Pierre Bersuire', in *L'enciclopedismo medievale*, éd. M. Picone (Ravenna, 1933), p. 229-249.

11. Voir O. Weijers, 'Lexicography in the Middle Ages', *Viator,* 20 (1989), p. 139-153; Ead., *Dictionnaires et répertoires du moyen âge. Une étude du vocabulaire* (Turnhout, 1991); K. Grubmüller, *Vocabularius Ex quo. Untersuchungen zu lateinisch-deutschen Vokabularen des Spätmittelalters* (München, 1967), spécialement le chapitre 'Überblick über die lateinische lexikographische Tradition bis zum Ende des 14. Jahrhunderts'; *Les manuscrits des lexiques et glossaires de l'Antiquité tardive à la fin du Moyen Age*, éd. J. Hamesse (Louvain-la-Neuve, 1996).

thèque ne donne aucune référence bibliographique.[12] Il faut donc en présenter le manuscrit, la structure, la genèse et les sources.

Le manuscrit compte trois volumes considérables, qui portent les cotes 9744-45, 9746 et 9747-48.[13] Ils ont chacun une taille in-quarto de 210 sur 300 mm, comptant respectivement 428, 390 et 353 feuillets, écrits à deux colonnes bien serrées. Un simple calcul nous donne un total de 2342 pages ou de 4684 colonnes: c'est dire la masse textuelle. L'écriture, une gothique cursive livresque soignée et nette, semble constante et nous serions tentés d'y voir une seule main (fig.1). On ne connaît pas le nom du copiste ni de l'auteur, et il faut aller à la recherche d'indices dans le texte et dans ses additions. Les filigranes du papier indiquent des dates dans les années 1450 à 1470, et l'écriture concorde avec cette datation tardive.[14] Le prologue fait allusion à un environnement monastique: il est rédigé en l'honneur de 'notre père Benoît', pour l'utilité et l'instruction de 'mes frères', et saint Laurent est nommé comme patron de l'auteur.[15] C'est ce qui a fait supposer aux catalographes de la Bibliothèque Royale qu'il provient de l'abbaye bénédictine de Saint-Laurent de Liège (fichier des manuscrits à la BR), ce qui n'est en soi pas un argument suffisant, et doit être vérifié. En faveur de cette hypothèse, notons d'abord que le manuscrit figure dans le fonds bruxellois parmi une série de cotes qui compte de nombreux manuscrits provenant explicitement de Saint-Laurent.[16] Or, une origine liégeoise du codex n'est pas seulement possible, elle est assurée. En effet, le manuscrit a la particularité d'avoir été très

12. On trouve seulement une fiche descriptive dans le fichier de la Bibliothèque Royale. Il n'existe pas de description publiée de ce manuscrit: il n'est pas dans les catalogues de C. Van den Gheyn, qui ne couvrent de toute manière pas la totalité des manuscrits latins de la BR. La seule notice consacrée à son sujet figure dans le tout récent catalogue des manuscrits en moyen néerlandais de la BR, où le *Macrologus* est brièvement traité pour ses gloses en néerlandais: J. Deschamps et H. Mulder, *Inventaris van de Middelnederlandse handschriften van de Koninklijke Bibliotheek van Brussel*, 3 (Brussels, 2000), p. 5-6. Herman Mulder nous a fort aimablement transmis quelques informations utiles.

13. Dans les références qui suivent, Bruxelles, Bibliothèque Royale sera abrégé en BR.

14. Les filigranes relevés sont proches des types Briquet 1876, 9198 et 15545, attestés dans les années 1462-1479.

15. BR, 9744-45, fol. 6 ra: 'Librum hunc ad omnipotentis Dei, beatissime virginis Marie matris eius, et gloriosissimi martiris Laurentii patroni mei, ac patris nostri Benedicti, et omnium electorum honorem, necnon ad utilitatem et eruditionem meam ac fratrum meorum et omnium intus studere volentium aggressus sum compilare'. On trouvera le texte complet du prologue dans l'article cité à la note 2, annexe 1.

16. De 9706 à 9751, il n'y a guère que des manuscrits de cette provenance. Voir la liste publiée par F. Pirot, 'La bibliothèque de l'abbaye Saint-Laurent de Liège', in *Saint-Laurent de Liège. Eglise, abbaye et hôpital militaire. Mille ans d'histoire*, éd. R. Lejeune (Liège, 1968), p. 125-136. Les trois volumes du *Macrologus* ne sont pas repris dans cette liste.

abondamment complété de notes et d'additions, par la même main à première vue, reportées dans les marges et, au besoin, sur des petits papiers ajoutés et reliés dans le volume: l'étude de ces additions constitue la seconde partie de cet article. En effet, une partie de ces papiers sont recyclés: ils ont été découpés dans des pièces d'archives et comportent au verso des annotations précises. On y relève des noms de personnes et d'institutions, qui sont indiscutablement liégeoises: ainsi, au folio 128bis verso du vol. 3 sont nommés 'Saint Laurent, Vauz Benoît, Beaurepert, Saint Gille, Saint Jacques, les frères Wilhelmins,[17] Saint Paul, Saint Martin'. On ne trahira pas le suspense qui prévaut à tout bon récit en annonçant qu'une étude approfondie de ces extraits, expliquée dans la seconde partie de cet article, confirme la piste de Saint-Laurent de Liège.

L'ouvrage est en essence un vaste lexique encyclopédique en ordre alphabétique, encadré par quelques textes de nature grammaticale. Le prologue, dont il faut commenter quelques éléments, occupe trois colonnes, aux folios 6 recto et verso. Après la dédicace aux patrons de l'auteur et de son institution, il affirme faire œuvre utile, pour soi et pour les frères désireux d'étudier. Il annonce qu'il traitera des huit parties du discours et de certaines règles grammaticales, puis d'une *Exposicio vocabulorum*, et enfin de la production et correction des syllabes. Notons donc que les textes grammaticaux qui encadrent le lexique sont intégrés au projet de l'œuvre. Suit un topos de modestie et une invitation à corriger le texte, mais avec retenue.[18] L'auteur apparaît très soucieux de justifier sa nomenclature et l'ordre alphabétique précis qu'il adopte, en référence à Papias plutôt qu'au *Catholicon* (de Jean Balbi).[19] Il commente ensuite les trois causes qui l'on poussé à la rédaction:

1. Le *Catholicon*, livre utile et nommé ainsi au sens d'universel et comprenant tout, n'est en réalité pas complet et il faut y suppléer.

17. Le couvent des Guillemins.

18. BR, 9744-45, fol. 6 ra: 'In quo parum vel nichil de meo apposui, sed sicut in autoribus comperi, sic ea conscripsi. Unde si quid forte minus bene dictum in eo reperitur, emendet illud corrector si sibi videtur esse corrigendum, non tamen ilico sine deliberacione apponat manum ad corrigendum, nisi omnino certus sit quod male et incorrecte positum sit, quia sepius reperitur quod diversimode aliqua dictio ab autoribus sillabicatur. Nam et Papias aliquas dictiones in libro suo in diversis locis posuit, propter diversitatem sillabicantium. Unde eciam contigit quod liber iste non ponit ordinem vocabulorum secundum positionem Catholicon, sed magis secundum positionem Papie'. Les mots soulignés ici le sont dans le manuscrit.

19. Pour l'*Elementarium* de Papias (circa 1040), il n'existe qu'une édition critique partielle, limitée à la lettre A, par V. De Angelis, *Papiae Elementarium, Littera A*, 3 vol. (Milano, 1977-1980), outre diverses éditions anciennes. Pour le *Catholicon* de Jean Balbi, terminé en 1286, voir Cl. Leonardi, 'La vita e l'opera di Uguccione da Pisa decretista', *Studia Gratiana,* 4 (1956-1957), p. 45-120.

2. Dans d'autres ouvrages, l'auteur a trouvé des sens de mots non attestés dans le *Catholicon*, ainsi que des erreurs.
3. Il voulait disposer en un seul ouvrage de ce qui se trouve chez Isidore, Papias, le *Grecismus* (donc Everard de Béthune), Huguccio, Brito, le *Puericius* et le *Brachilogus*.

Le prologue annonce ensuite que les explications lexicales seront tirées de divers auteurs: Isidore, Papias, le Grecismus, Huguccio, Brito, le *Mammotrectus*, le *Catholicon*, le *Puericius* et le *Braxilogus*. Il y ajoute les œuvres de Jean de Garlande, la *Summa Pisana*, Astaxanus et le *Repertorium magistri Johannis de Hoxhem canonici Leodiensis*. Voici une preuve supplémentaire de l'origine liégeoise du texte: Jean de Hocsem, chanoine de Liège décédé en 1348 après avoir légué ses livres à la collégiale de Saint-Lambert,[20] est un auteur au rayonnement local.[21] L'œuvre en question, un répertoire alphabétique de règles de droit intitulé *Flores utriusque iuris*, est conservée dans un seul manuscrit à Maastricht.[22] L'auteur du *Macrologus* veut donc faire œuvre de compilateur, à partir de sources diverses, avant tout lexicographiques. Le prologue s'attarde ensuite au mode de citation chez Papias et Isidore, et indique les abréviations courantes qui seront utilisées, avant de passer à un point particulier: l'ordre alphabétique sera mis en évidence par un changement de couleur des initiales sur base d'une prise en compte des deux ou trois premières lettres du mot; il insiste sur l'utilité du procédé pour trouver les mots cherchés.[23] Ensuite il est question du titre, expliqué comme il a été dit; peut-être y a-t-il une antithèse voulue au *Braxilogus* cité parmi les sources.[24] L'auteur revient à la question de l'ordonnance des *dictiones* pour signaler qu'elles ne sont pas toutes en vedette mais que certaines sont dans le corps du texte, soulignées au minium, et qu'il y a des entrées qui doivent être déplacées selon des indications ajoutées. Enfin, il fait état de discor-

20. Édition du testament: A. Derolez, éd., *Corpus catalogorum Belgii. The medieval booklists of the Southern Low Countries*, vol. II, *Provinces of Liège, Luxemburg and Namur* (Brussel, 1994), p. 92-94.

21. Voir le *Repertorium fontium historiae medii aevi*, vol. VI (Rome, 1990), p. 334; R. Van Caenegem, 'Johannes de Hocsem', in *Nationaal biografisch woordenboek*, 1 (Brussels, 1964), col. 611-615.

22. Maastricht, Rijksarchief, 215. Voir R. Feenstra, 'Les 'Flores utriusque juris' de Jean de Hocsem et leur édition au XVe siècle', *Tijdschrift voor Rechtsgeschiedenis*, 31 (1963), p. 611-615.

23. Cf. le leitmotiv du *statim invenire* chez les auteurs d'instruments de travail à partir du XIIIe s.: R. et M. Rouse, '*Statim invenire*. Schools, preachers and new attitudes to the page', in *Renaissance and renewal in the twelfth century*, éd. R.L. Benson et G. Constable (Oxford, 1982), p. 201-225.

24. Pour cette œuvre lexicographique, voir ci-dessous, note 29.

dances en matière grammaticale entre les auteurs, et il cite quelques autorités en la matière, qui nous reportent à la région liégeoise: Rolandus de Breda Tongrensis decanus, Godefridus de Kempis, Radulphus de Rivo, Wilhelmus de Werd. Raoul de Rivo, chanoine à Tongres, est bien connu, et on possède de sa main une table alphabétique aux *Etymologies* d'Isidore de Séville conservée à Bruxelles, de provenance liégeoise,[25] mais les autres noms restent à identifier.[26] Le prologue se clôt par une note sur l'usage de Lorenzo Valla dont il sera question plus loin.

Le prologue précède un traité grammatical, qui occupe les cent premier feuillets du vol. I et dont l'incipit est *Vigintitres sunt littere....* Au feuillet 106 débute le lexique alphabétique, qui se poursuit de A à D au vol I, de E à Pal au vol. II, de P à Z au vol. III, f. 324.[27] Suivent enfin, sur une trentaine de feuillets (324v-351v), deux brefs textes grammaticaux, l'un sur l'orthographe, l'autre sur la production des syllabes. Tout cela a été annoncé dans le prologue et nous possédons donc manifestement l'œuvre complète, telle que le compilateur l'a voulue. La conjonction d'une grammaire et d'un lexique, si elle peut étonner un lecteur moderne, n'est pas une singularité complète: le même principe avait été suivi vers 1040 par Papias dans son *Elementarium*, et par Jean Balbi dans son *Catholicon*, terminé en 1286. Le lexique proprement dit du *Macrologus* est organisé sur une base alphabétique stricte.[28] Sa nomenclature inclut toutes sortes de mots courants ou rares, des noms de lieux et de personnes (surtout bibliques), des phénomènes grammaticaux, etc. Les articles donnent en règle générale la forme et sa déclinaison, le genre pour les noms, une définition appuyée d'une ou de plusieurs citations. La longueur des entrées est très variable, et on relève de longues notices: ainsi, 'fenix' ou 'mare' occupent quatre colonnes, 'ethimologia' couvre une page, etc. Quant aux sources citées dans le corps du texte, on constate que ce sont les lexicographes antérieurs qui dominent le tableau. Ainsi, si l'on considère les 500 premiers lemmes, on note une nette priorité pour Papias, cité

25. BR, Ms. II 2548. Le ms. provient de l'abbaye de Saint-Jacques à Liège. Voir, pour l'auteur, C. Mohlberg, *Radulph de Rivo* (Louvain, 1911).

26. L. Reynhout attire notre attention sur un colophon répertorié par les Bénédictins du Bouveret, *Colophons de manuscrits occidentaux des origines au XVIe siècle*, t. II, Fribourg, 1967, n° 5484. Celui-ci renvoie à un Godefridus de Via civitatis Kempensis, qui a signé en 1427 le ms. Wolfenbüttel, HAB, 48. Gud. lat. 2° (cat. 4353) – il y a deux erreurs à corriger dans les *Colophons*, qui donnent la date de 1472 et le n° de catalogue 5353. Il s'agit peut-être de notre Godefridus, mais on n'en sait guère plus.

27. Curieusement, il y a au début du vol. III une reprise des entrées de P à Pal, qui terminent le vol. II.

28. Un échantillon de la nomenclature est donné en appendice 2 de notre article cité n. 2.

257 fois. Il est suivi de Huguccio (68), le *Repertorium,* c'est à dire Jean de Hocsem (36), le *Grecista,* soit Everard de Béthune (32), Isidore de Séville (31), [Guillelmus] Brito (22), le *Catholicon* (14). Avec moins de dix occurrences suivent Priscien, le *Puericius*, Astaxanus, Pierre Comestor, la Bible, le *Mammotrectus*, Jérôme, Bède, Boèce, Cicéron, le *Brachilogus*, le *Doctrinale*, Dioscoride, la Glose, Ovide, le *Physiologus*, Rémi [d'Auxerre] et Servius. Parmi les sources rares, notons le *Puericius* et le *Brachilogus*, tous deux nommés aussi dans le prologue. Le premier est un ouvrage lexicographique rédigé à Anvers vers 1350 par Jean de Mera à l'usage des écoles, *ad puerorum utilitatem*. En 1354 il révisa son ouvrage et il en publia une seconde version, sous le titre *Brachylogus*.[29] Il se fait que la bibliothèque de Saint-Laurent possédait un exemplaire du *Puericius*, conservé actuellement à la Bibliothèque Royale de Bruxelles sous la cote 9638, dans la même série que le *Macrologus*. C'est un manuscrit daté de 1470, dont le papier est de format analogue à celui du *Macrologus*, copié en une écriture différente, mais dont le décor de lettrines bichromes est identique à celui des trois volumes qui nous intéressent. Avec cet argument supplémentaire, la présomption pour Saint-Laurent est très forte et il est temps de rappeler quelques données à propos de cet établissement célèbre.

Saint-Laurent, abbaye bénédictine fondée en 1024 sur les hauteurs dominant la ville de Liège, a participé activement au rayonnement intellectuel de Liège aux XIe et XIIe s.[30] entre autre sous l'abbatiat de Rupert de Deutz.[31] Après une période peu productive aux XIIIe et XIVe s., le XVe s. fut à nouveau très actif au plan intellectuel, sous les abbatiats successifs de Henri Ade (1404-1434) et Henri delle Cheraux (1434-1461). De nombreux manuscrits furent copiés, et certains moines furent également auteurs, tels Jean de Stavelot et Adrien de Oudenbosch. On possède

29. Voir G. Powitz, 'Johannes de Mera, ein Brabanter Lexikograph des 14. Jahrhunderts', *Mittellateinisches Jahrbuch,* 13 (1978), p. 204-226. Ce *Brachylogus* n'est pas à confondre avec l'ouvrage juridique anonyme du même titre, appelé *Brachylogus totius juris civilis* ou *Corpus legum* au XVIe s. Voir A. Gouron, 'L'auteur du Brachylogus: un compagnon de Thomas Becket en exil?', in *A Enrico Cortese*, éd. D. Maffei et L. Birocchi (Roma, 2001), p. 163-173; P. Weimar, P., 'Brachylogus', in *Lexikon des Mittelalters*, 2 (1983), col. 538. Sur le *Puericius*, également J.P. Gumbert, *Die Utrechter Kartaüser und ihre Bücher im frühen 15. Jahrhundert* (Leiden, 1974).

30. Le principal ouvrage sur Saint-Laurent est le volume collectif *Saint-Laurent de Liège. Eglise, abbaye et hôpital militaire. Mille ans d'histoire*, éd. R. Lejeune, (Liège, 1968). Sur le contexte intellectuel, voir C. Renardy, 'Les écoles liégeoises du IXe au XIIe siècle: grandes lignes de leur évolution', in *Revue belge de Philologie et d'histoire*, 57 (1979), p. 309-328.

31. Voir les articles de R. Haacke, H. Silvestre et J. Stiennon dans *Saint-Laurent de Liège* [note 30].

divers inventaires médiévaux de la bibliothèque de l'abbaye, édités récemment par Albert Derolez,[32] et une collection importante de manuscrits provenant de Saint-Laurent est conservée à la Bibliothèque Royale (118 mss).[33] Nous sommes donc assez bien informés sur la bibliothèque et l'activité intellectuelle de l'abbaye,[34] et il s'en dégage, pour la période qui concerne le *Macrologus*, l'image d'un intense vie de copie et de rédaction. Parmi les manuscrits copiés à Saint-Laurent et conservés à Bruxelles, on note le *Puericius*, comme il a été dit, et deux autres volumes comprenant des lexiques, tous écrits au XVe s. Une attention suivie pour les ouvrages lexicologiques caractérise donc le scriptorium de Saint-Laurent, et le *Macrologus* trouvait ici un terreau d'éclosion tout indiqué. Des comparaisons plus larges de manuscrits doivent encore être entreprises pour cerner des influences et des analogies, mais il semble d'ores et déjà acquis que la piste de l'abbaye liégeoise est la bonne, même si l'on s'en tient à une 'simple' étude de critique interne.

Un dernier trait mérite une attention particulière. En bas du prologue a été reportée une note sur des emprunts à Valla: 'Notez que dans ce livre, beaucoup de choses sont ajoutées à partir du livre de Laurent Valla intitulé *De excellentia latine lingue*, qui sont souvent signalées par le nom Valla et parfois par Laurentius Valla'.[35] Effectivement, parmi les innombrables additions marginales ou ajouts sur des bouts de feuilles reliés ensuite dans le volume, la source est récurrente. Dans les trois volumes, pas moins de 243 additions sont mises sous son le nom Valla, très rarement de Laurentius, ou de Laurentius Valla. Le *De elegantiis linguae latinae*, écrit en 1444, a connu sa première édition en 1471, et devint un ouvrage standard pour la stylistique latine.[36] Valla n'est pas le seul humaniste qui apparaît ainsi: diverses additions sont mises sous le nom de Nicholaus Pirotti ou de Nicholaus seul (22 cas). Niccolo Perotti, mort en 1480, a écrit des *Rudimenta grammatices,* édités en 1473, et qui semblent être le texte cité ici.[37] Enfin, on relève une mention de Guarinus

32. Derolez, *Corpus catalogorum* [note 20], II, p. 107-135.

33. Liste dans Pirot, 'La bibliothèque' [note 16], p. 136, n. 59.

34. Voir aussi J. Gessler, 'La bibliothèque de l'abbaye de Saint-Laurent à Liège au XIIe et XIIIe siècle', *Bulletin de la Société des Bibliophiles Liégeois*, 12 (1927), p. 91-135; récemment, R. Dückers, '*Claustrum sine armario castrum sine armamentario.* De bibliotheek van de St.-Laurentabdij te Luik in de 12e eeuw', *Millennium* (1999), p. 105-122.

35. BR, 9744-45, fol. 6 ra: 'Nota quod hic hoc in libro isto multa sunt addita ex libro Laurencii Valla qui intitulatur De excellencia latine lingue, que sepius notantur per illum terminum Valla et aliquando per Laurentium Valla'. Le mot Valla est souligné dans la note marginale.

36. Sur Valla et les autres Humanists cités ici, voir M.M. Cosenza, *Biographical and bibliographical dictionary of Italian Humanists*, 6 vol. (Boston, 1962-1967).

37. C'est un point qui demande encore à être vérifié.

Veronensis (III, f. 20bis). De celui-ci, décédé en 1460, les *Regulae grammaticales* ont été imprimées en 1470. Ces trois utilisations sont dignes d'intérêt, car elles attestent la pénétration bien réelle de l'Humanisme italien dans les milieux liégeois du dernier quart du XVe siècle.[38] Tout porte à croire que l'auteur (ou plus prudemment l'annotateur), a eu accès, après la finition du *Macrologus*, à diverses éditions d'humanistes dans les années 1470, et qu'il a jugé bon de procéder sur ces bases à une campagne d'annotation systématique. On note que les additions de Valla, d'une main identique ou très proche de la main du copiste, sont reportées en une encre noire, tandis que d'autres additions sont notées en une encre brune proche de celle employée pour le texte principal. Le *Macrologus* porte donc la marque de diverses étapes d'additions, et tel que nous l'avons, le triple manuscrit a tout d'un 'work in progress', d'une copie d'auteur soumise à une correction et un enrichissement continus.

On ne peut qu'être impressionné par le travail fourni. Mais ce labeur monumental entrepris à l'abbaye liégeoise est resté isolé. On ne connaît, sous bénéfice d'inventaire, aucune autre copie du *Macrologus*. Sans succès à l'époque, non éditée et pour cause, l'œuvre a également échappé aux érudits. Elle mérite pourtant d'être ouverte et étudiée, d'une part comme témoin tardif d'une longue tradition médiévale de la lexicographie, d'autre part comme point de rencontre entre celle-ci et le genre encyclopédique, auquel elle emprunte le principe de la compilation cumulative, de la citation, de la largeur de sujet. Elle le mérite aussi comme témoin d'une infiltration précoce des écrits grammaticaux des humanistes italiens dans les milieux liégeois. De la sorte, l'abbaye de Saint-Laurent rejoignait le mouvement international, mais tout cela se passait dans le silence derrière les murs monastiques. La prouesse d'écriture est d'autant plus notable que dans ces années 1470, l'heure n'est guère aux loisirs littéraires. C'est un champ de ruines que domine l'abbaye du haut de sa colline, car Liège a été mise à sac et incendiée après sa prise par Charles le Téméraire en 1468.

2. Une enquête sur les notules

Mais, bien avant que la chape d'un silence monastique ne s'abatte sur ce manuscrit, sa première rédaction fit l'objet, très rapidement, d'ajouts

38. Les études sur l'Humanisme à Liège semblent s'être limitées au XVIe siècle: voir A. Gerlo et E. Lauf, *Bibliographie de l'Humanisme belge* (Bruxelles, 1965), p. 93-94; A. Gerlo et H. Vervliet, *Bibliographie de l'Humanisme des Anciens Pays-Bas* (Bruxelles, 1972), p. 114-115.

de la main de l'auteur. Celui-ci a dû, dans les mois ou les années qui ont suivi la rédaction de son ouvrage, au cours de la décennie 1470-1480, prendre connaissance de nombreux ouvrages incunables, de la plume d'humanistes italiens comme Lorenzo Valla, Nicollo Perotti ou Guarino Veronese. L'auteur du *Macrologus* a donc saisi les marges de son dictionnaire puis, quand il s'est avéré que celles-ci étaient trop étroites pour son discours, il a utilisé des fragments de papier, récupérés ici ou là, afin d'y coucher le produit de ses lectures, mais aussi de compléter l'information, d'ajouter de nouvelles entrées (fig. 2). Ce sont ces éléments de papier qui nous intéressent ici, témoins d'une pratique étonnante de récupération et de réutilisation de documents.

Ces fragments de papier, il les a choisis: des grands, 20 cm sur 20 cm voire des feuillets entiers pour de grandes notices, ou au contraire des morceaux larges comme une feuille de papier à cigarettes pour des additions mineures, quelques mots ou quelques lettres. Le rédacteur du dictionnaire a donc démembré et découpé des feuillets de papier afin de constituer ces notules. Certaines, la plupart, sont vierges de toute trace de vie antérieure: découpées dans les marges ou dans des feuillets blancs, elles ne livrent aucun indice de leur origine.[39] Cependant, certaines sont salies ou marquées de plis, comme par l'effet d'une utilisation antérieure bien spécifique.[40] Nous verrons plus loin ce que nous pouvons en tirer. Mais si la plupart de ces fragments sont vierges avant l'intervention de l'auteur de l'encyclopédie, ce n'est pas le cas d'une soixantaine de pièces qui témoignent clairement d'un usage antérieur: il s'agit en réalité de fragments de documents d'archives. Et, dans ce cas, l'auteur du *Macrologus* a pris en compte les quelques lignes ou traces d'écriture qui les jonchent: soit il les a soigneusement grattées, pour se servir du morceau de feuillet de papier comme d'un palimpseste, soit il a laissé ces marques anciennes et a copié son texte au revers, soit encore il a écrit en tenant compte de la présence de ces marques en les contournant (cf. fig. 3), soit enfin il n'a eu cure des quelques mots ou lignes tracées et les a couverts de son texte transcrit à l'encre plus noire, passant à travers tout. Cette dernière solution, la plus radicale, n'est en usage que dans les derniers fragments du dernier volume, des fragments de petite taille et qui avaient été

39. Si ce n'est éventuellement un filigrane, comme par ex. le BR, 9777-45, un feuillet au fol. 49 avec une tête de bœuf.

40. Sur l'importance du pliage comme élément signifiant dans le cadre d'une enquête historique, voir P. Bertrand, 'De l'art de plier les chartes en quatre. Pour une étude des pliages de chartes médiévales à des fins de classement et de conservation', *Gazette du Livre Médiéval,* 40 (2002), p. 25-35.

traversés anciennement de lignes droites, ici consciencieusement surécrites. La solution du 'palimpseste', évidemment difficile à mettre en œuvre (gratter du papier est une opération des plus délicates) ne se retrouve que rarement, si le fragment utilisé par l'auteur ne contenait avant son intervention que quelques mots, une seule ligne dans tous les cas.

Une soixantaine de pièces réutilisées portent donc des traces d'écriture antérieure. Mais le nombre de fragments récupérés et insérés par l'auteur dans son œuvre est considérable! Pour le premier volume, 128 fragments répartis sur 428 feuillets, le second: 108 sur 390 et surtout le troisième: 228 sur 353 feuillets. Soit, en tout, 464 fragments sur 1 171 feuillets! Ces fragments ont-ils été reliés d'office et dès le départ avec le reste de l'œuvre? Probablement: ils semblent tous se trouver au bon endroit dans les volumes, sous la bonne entrée, dans le bon ordre. Vu leur nombre, l'auteur a du s'occuper personnellement de leur reliure au sein de ses volumes.

Mais d'où proviennent ces pièces? Une typologie en est-elle possible, selon leur provenance? Il semble bien que ce soit le cas. On remarque dès le premier abord que bon nombre de ces fragments proviennent de documents d'archives. Mais on peut aller beaucoup plus loin. D'abord, dans tous les volumes, lorsqu'on remploie des pièces d'archives, ce sont surtout des fragments de quinze à vingt centimètres de largeur, sur parfois seulement deux à trois centimètres de hauteur (mais aussi bien plus hauts). Ici, l'auteur a mis à contribution le format de ces pièces d'archives, qui est la plupart du temps comparable aux formats des feuillets de manuscrit en papier. Tandis que les petits morceaux rectangulaires ou carrés, mais de largeur moindre, sont souvent (mais il n'y a pas vraiment de règle, seulement une tendance) tirés d'autres chutes de papier. Lesquelles? D'abord des actes ou copies d'actes en papier, contemporains de l'écriture des documents: brouillons? copies pour procédure? actes à portée locale ou limitée dans le temps?[41] Au-delà des questions, c'est encore une leçon pour l'historien qui voudrait ne pas croire aux destructions documentaires dès le Moyen Âge: ici, c'est une copie d'acte de 1478 qui est mise en lambeaux,[42] et là, une copie d'acte émanant de l'évêque de Liège Louis de Bourbon, en fonction de 1456 à 1482.[43] Soit des documents éminemment récents à l'époque de l'auteur. Ensuite, on trouve

41. Voir notamment BR, 9747-9748, entre les fol. 75-76, 87-88, 131-132, 147-148, 150-151.

42. BR, 9747-9748, entre le fol. 126 et le 127.

nombre de fragments de papiers salis au revers, marqués de pliures diverses et surtout antérieures à leur insertion dans les volumes. Un de ces fragments porte la trace verte, circulaire, d'un sceau. Ces fragments étaient, à coup sûr, des lettres privées, scellées.[44] On en conserve quelques fragments couverts d'écriture, dont deux fragments en écriture cursive étrangement proche de celle de l'auteur, en thiois.[45] L'encyclopédiste aurait-il recyclé son courrier ou ses brouillons?[46]

L'essentiel pour notre propos consiste en ces pièces émanant de registres d'archives. On le sait fort bien, la fin du Moyen Âge voit l'émergence massive d'une culture de l'écrit d'administration, due à la fois au développement de l'écrit en général, à la diffusion du papier et à son coût moindre, à la prise d'importance de la preuve écrite en droit et aussi à la complexification croissante des transactions économiques.[47] Outre les actes des chartriers, certains registres font souvent l'objet d'un grand entretien et peuvent durer: les cartulaires et autres registres consignant des actes de longue durée de vie et d'utilisation, évidemment, mais aussi, quoique plus rarement, les registres consignant les cens et rentes perçus annuellement: en effet, il était habituel que la plupart des rentes et des cens 'chassés' par une institution ne soient pas tous perçus en un an mais soient souvent reportés, cumulés, repoussés aux années suivantes. Il faut donc garder trace des anciennes perceptions, qui sont non seulement des éléments probatoires en cas de litige,[48] mais aussi une base pour la perception des arriérés. Notons cependant que beaucoup de ces documents

43. BR, 9747-9748, entre le fol. 153 et le 154.

44. BR, 9747-9748, entre fol. 209-210, 213-214, 214-215, 224-225, 255-256; une trace de sceau rond en cire verte de env. 25 mm de diamètre sur un frag. de 150X30 mm, avec traces de pliures, entre les fol. 214 et 215.

45. BR, 9747-9748, entre le fol. 271 et 272 et entre le fol. 273 et 274.

46. Un fragment de brouillon – du moins, je l'identifie comme tel – se trouve entre les fol. 75 et 76 du BR, 9747-9748.

47. Pour Liège, on nous permettra de reporter le lecteur à P. Bertrand, *Commerce avec dame Pauvreté. Structures et fonctions des couvents de Mendiants à Liège aux XIIIe et XIVe s.* (Liège, 2004), ainsi qu'à un article du même consacré aux archives des couvents carme et dominicain de Liège du XIIIe au XVe s., à paraître sous peu. Sur l'émergence de cette *Pragmatische Schriftlichkeit*, on renverra le lecteur curieux aux considérations générales et à la bibliographie de *New Approaches to Medieval Communication*, éd. M. Mostert, avec une introduction de M. Clanchy, Utrecht Studies in Medieval Literacy, 1 (Turnhout, Brepols, 1999). Le concept a été au centre des travaux poursuivis par les médiévistes de Münster pendant de nombreuses années (Sonderforschungsbereich 231), ce dont la revue *Frühmittelalterliche Studien* a régulièrement rendu compte durant les années 1990.

48. Par exemple, un tel nous a payé des cens sur tel bien jusque là, puis son successeur ne le fait plus, mais il le devrait, puisque l'usage, coulé dans le registre de perception aux cens et rentes, le prouve.

d'administration ne durent pas au-delà du temps des cerises. Les comptabilités journalières, les copies de baux à terme, les registres à durée d'utilisation limitée ne survivent pas au comptable qui les a transcrits, voire à l'année qui s'est écoulée. Ceux-là, inutiles, ne nous sont pas parvenus ou alors, par hasard. Ainsi, si certaines pièces d'archives peuvent passer l'écueil des ans, ce n'est pas le cas de la plupart d'entre elles, dépendantes de l'intérêt aléatoire du comptable et de l'archiviste, de ses scrupules, de sa conscience professionnelle et de son courage.

C'est ce qui est arrivé aux documents réutilisés par l'auteur du *Macrologus*, ici. On trouve les traces de quelques ensembles documentaires clairement identifiables. D'abord des fragments d'un registre de paiement de cens et de rentes, émanant d'une abbaye, en latin. Ensuite des parties d'un registre de perception de cens et rentes, de la première moitié du XVe s. Enfin et surtout, un 'cahier' issu d'un registre de comptabilité générale des cens et rentes d'un hôpital liégeois, lui aussi de la première moitié du XVe s., a été démembré complètement et réutilisé abondamment par l'encyclopédiste. Nous allons nous attacher plus en profondeur à ces documents.

Le registre de perception de cens et rentes, en latin, n'est pas très présent dans les trois volumes du *Macrologus*: trois fragments seulement (fig. 3).[49] Mais ils sont plus loquaces. Très clairement, c'est un registre qui émane de l'abbaye de Saint-Laurent de Liège: un fragment énumère une série de dîmes, grosses ou petites, perçues par l'institution, et ce sont toutes des dîmes de paroisses dont le collateur n'est autre que l'abbaye de Saint-Laurent: *apud Waseige*,[50] Branchon et Boneffe[51] *pro magna decima*; *ibidem pro minutis decimis de Waseige*; *apud Meffiam pro minutis decimis*,[52] *apud Fexhe Advocati pro minuta decima*,[53] *pro una decima de Avroto*.[54] D'autres revenus, qui sont clairement liés à l'abbaye liégeoise, sont mentionnés dans d'autres documents: un revenu à Leeuw Godefridus,[55] une aime[56] de vin perçue à Noville.[57] Par ailleurs, par deux

49. BR, 9744-45, entre fol. 59 et 60; entre fol. 128 et 129; 9747-48, entre fol. 20 et 21.

50. Voir J. Daris, 'Extraits du cartulaire de Saint-Laurent', in Idem, *Notices historiques sur les églises du diocèse de Liège*, t. 11 (Liège, 1882), p. 217-221.

51. Voir Daris, 'Extraits du cartulaire de Saint-Laurent' [note 50], p. 174.

52. Voir *Ibidem*, p. 205.

53. Voir *Ibidem*, p. 178.

54. Pour Avroy, voir *Ibidem*, p. 137-138.

55. Voir *Ibidem*, p. 201.

56. Mesure de capacité, une aime contient de 113 l. à 153 l., selon les types de mesure, voir Chaineux M.-C., *Culture de la vigne et commerce du vin dans la région de Liège au Moyen Age*, Centre Belge d'Histoire Rurale, 65 (Liège – Louvain, 1981), p. 67-68.

fois les fragments citent l'existence d'un abbé présidant aux destinées de l'institution qui produit le document: *primo domino Stephano abbati huius monasterii ad eius vitam* et *item domino abbati pro sua portione contra conventum.* S'il s'agit bien de l'abbé de Saint-Laurent, alors, le premier cité est Etienne de Marille, abbé de 1388 à 1404, ce qui date le document du tout début du XVe s.[58] L'utilisation du latin dans la confection du registre rend la chose plausible, puisque le latin était en usage dans les premiers registres de comptabilité, comme ceux-ci, avant d'être remplacé par le français.

Mais si ce premier ensemble est clairement lié à l'abbaye bénédictine, ce n'est pas le cas des suivants. Je reste perplexe quant à l'origine de l'ensemble de fragments de registres de perception de cens et de rentes de la première moitié du XVe s., en français: on n'y mentionne aucune institution productrice ni ne trouve d'indice suffisant pour déterminer son origine. Ce qui est certain: il ne provenait pas de l'abbaye de Saint-Laurent, puisque un poste y est consacré à celle-ci par l'institution débitrice, déterminant un revenu à lui fournir: *item alle engliese sans Loren, 3 sous, 6 deniers.*[59]

Le troisième ensemble pose encore davantage de questions. Comme je l'ai dit, c'est un 'cahier'[60] issu d'un registre de comptes généraux qui a été démembré, pillé par l'auteur du *Macrologus*: pas moins de 18 fragments en sont, à l'analyse, décelables. Ce n'est pas l'abbaye de Saint-Laurent qui est à l'origine de ce document, comme de multiples traces l'indiquent: *Chi apres sensiwent ly cens et li capons que la dite maison et hospital at de revenuwe por le dit an 1437 ensi quile appert en registre de dit hospital pour le dit an si est ...*,[61] *chi apres sensiwent les comptez generalx delle mais...*,[62] ou encore cette ligne de titre: *pension a vie que li dis hospital doit.*[63] Il s'agit bien d'un hôpital. On peut tenter d'appro-

57. Voir *Ibidem*, p. 211.

58. Sur Etienne de Marille, voir *Monasticon belge*, t. 2, fasc. 3, *Province de Liège* (Liège, 1962), p. 47 et voir aussi J. Daris, 'Notice sur l'abbaye de Saint-Laurent à Liège' [note 50], p. 103-104.

59. C'est bien de l'abbaye de Saint-Laurent dont il s'agit, puisque elle est citée à sa place dans une liste de cens dus (BR, 9747-9748, fol. 128), entre les cours foncières de la cathédrale et les abbayes du Val-Benoît, de Beaurepart, de Saint-Gilles et de Saint-Jacques. Loin derrière, dans la liste, on trouvera les églises paroissiales: ce ne peut donc en être une ici.

60. Ou, plutôt, un ensemble délimité intellectuellement par l'année 1437.

61. BR, 9747-9748, entre fol. 80 et 81.

62. BR, 9747-9748, entre fol. 305 et 306: jamais on ne parlerait d'une abbaye comme d'une 'maison'.

63. BR, 9747-9748, fol. 183.

cher plus précisément ce qu'était ce registre. En effet, il a été tenu par un comptable du nom de Thonar, dans la première moitié du XVe s.[64] Le cahier pillé a été rédigé en 1437 par le compteur, qui prenait en considération des arriérés de cens depuis 1412 au moins. Mais de quel hôpital s'agit-il? Il devait exister depuis quelques années, au moins depuis 1412, puisque des revenus datant d'alors devaient être perçus pour lui, mais aussi parce que Thonar avait au moins un prédécesseur à la comptabilité en la personne d'un certain Lambert de Cassea.[65]

J'ai tenté une enquête comparative au travers des fonds d'archives existants. Il faut écarter d'emblée l'aumône des Pauvres-en-Île, citée dans les postes du compte comme bénéficiaire d'un revenu dû par l'hôpital. Au fil de l'enquête, deux hôpitaux ont été mis en avant: le premier est l'aumône du béguinage Saint-Christophe (c'est-à-dire l'organe de gestion administrative et caritative du béguinage) et l'hôpital associé au béguinage, dit hôpital Tirebourse, dont le compteur alors est Thonar de Lantremange, officiant à cette période et à l'écriture très semblable.[66] C'est un laïc, probablement un comptable 'professionnel',[67] très certainement à identifier avec 'notre' Thonar. Mais des questions restent en suspens: les sommes finales qui sont en jeu dans notre registre de comptabilité générale n'ont rien à voir avec les sommes importantes manipulées par l'énorme usine à rentes qu'est alors l'aumône de Saint-Christophe et l'hôpital, bien nommé, Tirebourse. L'hôpital qui a émis le registre dont nous nous occupons devrait être plus humble économiquement. Serait-ce alors l'hôpital Saint-Jacques? Cette dernière institution aurait été fondée en 1427 à l'instigation de quelques bourgeois de Liège de retour de Saint-Jacques de Compostelle: un hôpital destiné à héberger les pauvres pèlerins. En 1429, l'abbé de Saint-Laurent, qui possédait le terrain sur lequel se trouvaient les bâtiments de l'hôpital, y autorisa la construction d'une chapelle consacrée à la Vierge et à saint Jacques le Majeur, avec l'approbation de l'évêque, à condition que les comptes de

64. BR, 9746, fol. 134, 147, 159; BR, 9747-9748, entre fol. 15 et 16, 24 et 25, 71, entre 80 et 81, 135.

65. BR, 9747-9748, entre fol. 24 et 25: 'Item rassenat li dis Thonar compteur en debte por lan 1413, 12 et des altez anneez compteit et someit ensemble de temps Lambert de Cassea et dez altrez compteur de devant montent...'. Lambert était toujours vivant en 1437: il percevait une pension de l'hôpital (BR, 9747-48, fol. 183).

66. Par ex., voir Archives de l'État à Liège (désormais abrégé: AEL), Saint-Christophe, 685.

67. Comme c'est souvent le cas à l'époque: P. De Spiegeler, *Les hôpitaux et l'assistance à Liège (Xe-XVe siècles). Aspects institutionnels et sociaux,* Bibliothèque de la Faculté de Philosophie et Lettres de l'Université de Liège, 249 (Paris, 1987), p. 167.

l'hôpital lui soient soumis.[68] Cette institution était donc liée d'assez près à l'abbaye de Saint-Laurent. Ses archives sont conservées, du moins en partie, aux Archives de l'État à Liège. Or, le registre numéroté 293, donnant un aperçu général des recettes et des dépenses, conservé fragmentairement, courant sur la période 1469-1529, présente dès 1469 une structure de comptabilité totalement similaire au registre de comptabilité de 1437. La mise en page des comptes est identique et nous n'en avons pas trouvé de semblable pour les autres institutions hospitalières liégeoises.[69] Restent évidemment deux problèmes: d'abord, ces comptes sont postérieurs de plus de 30 ans aux comptes de Thonar et il n'est peut-être pas prudent de les rapprocher ainsi, d'autant plus qu'aucune autre trace de relation entre la version '1437' et la version '1469' n'est décelable, si ce n'est cette mise en page. Ensuite, et plus fondamentalement, la critique la plus importante est que cet hôpital est censé avoir été fondé en 1427... alors que Thonar, 10 ans plus tard, indique des arriérés de 1412 voire antérieurs. Il n'empêche que la présomption subsiste: les revenus cédés au futur hôpital par les fondateurs étaient peut-être déjà perçus par ceux-ci bien avant 1427 et auraient existé dès avant cela indépendamment. Il est donc possible que Thonar fasse le point en 1437 sur des arriérés de revenus qui n'avaient pas été payés aux fondateurs avant 1427 et continuaient à rester impayés: la chose est tout à fait habituelle et plausible.

On ne peut donc trancher avec exactitude, même si ce dernier hôpital semble bien être à l'origine des pièces comptables étudiées. Ce qui reste certain, c'est que ce 'cahier' démembré (ainsi que, peut-être, le deuxième ensemble de fragments considérés, en français) provient de la comptabilité d'une petite institution hospitalière, récupérée par l'auteur du *Macrologus* après 1437.

Au-delà de l'intérêt proprement diplomatique, au sens large, ainsi que codicologique de ces extraits d'archives, des éléments essentiels à la localisation et la datation du *Macrologus* peuvent en être tirés. Et d'abord la confirmation de la provenance liégeoise de l'œuvre. Plus précisément: il s'agit bien de l'abbaye de Saint-Laurent, comme le prouve le premier ensemble d'extraits.[70] Toute équivoque à ce propos semble bien levée.

68. Voir Daris, 'Extraits du cartulaire de Saint-Laurent' [note 50], p. 161; Fr. Lecomte, *Inventaire des archives de l'hôpital Saint-Jacques à Liège* (Bruxelles, 1982), p. 6-7; P. De Spiegeleer, *Les hôpitaux et l'assistance à Liège* [note 67], p. 85-86; P. De Spiegeleer, 'Les statuts de la confrérie Saint-Jacques de Liège (23 mai 1479)', *Bulletin de la Commission royale d'histoire*, 147 (1981), p. 205-216.

69. Sur la mise en page de la comptabilité, voir les références bibliographiques citées en note 47.

70. Mais aussi comme le laisse penser un extrait de lettre en cursive maniérée, du XVe s., remployé entre les fos. 126 et 127 du BR, 9747-9748: '...nomine voes chier et bien amé... abbé de notre église...et sains Laurens lez moster...'.

Quant à la datation, elle est précisée, elle aussi: la rédaction de l'œuvre elle-même dut avoir lieu avant 1478, date d'une copie d'acte réutilisé comme fragment, ainsi que nous l'avons précisé. Les additions sous forme de notules datent donc des environs de et après 1478.

Il reste à envisager la mise en contexte de ce cas curieux de réutilisation de documents sous forme de fragments par un auteur envahi par ce souci de collection et d'exhaustivité propre au XVe s., souci que l'on retrouve dans les collections de vies de saints, foisonnantes alors.[71] D'abord, c'est un usage habituel dans le monde des registres d'administration, où nombre de recueils sont entrelardés de bouts de papier avec des quittances de paiement, des mises au point concernant l'un ou l'autre tenancier, de petits mémos à l'usage du comptable ou du percepteur des rentes et des cens, qui les réutilisaient pour faire leurs comptes, leurs additions et soustractions et ainsi compléter leurs registres.[72] Certaines constatations font penser que l'auteur du *Macrologus* a dû toucher de près ou de loin à ces activités d'administration au sein de son abbaye: le fait qu'il ait récupéré ici ou là des registres d'archives 'déclassés' tendrait à le confirmer, de même que la constation suivante: au fil des trois volumes de l'encyclopédie, nombre d'entrées montrent l'intérêt de l'auteur pour le droit, notamment le droit de la propriété. Il définit assez précisément (et parfois dans des notules elles-même) des concepts comme le cens (*censa et accensa: se pro eodem, une accense, que datur ad stutum i. ad certum terminum aliquorum annorum*[73]) ou encore l'*allodium*,[74] la *bonorum possessio*,[75] le *feodum*,[76] l'*instrumentum*,[77] l'investiture[78], le

71. Prenons simplement comme exemple les gigantesques compilations de Jean Gielemans, de l'abbaye de Rouge-Cloître, bien connues des chercheurs en hagiographie: voir la prochaine publication de la thèse de V. Souche, '*Terra beata Brabancia*': *l'exaltation de la patrie brabançonne dans l'œuvre hagiographique et historique de Jean Gielemans († 1487)*, thèse de doctorat d'histoire soutenue à l'université de Paris X-Nanterre, le 16 novembre 2002. Voir le résumé dans la *Revue Mabillon*, N.S., 14 (2003), p. 281-282.

72. Ainsi le chassereau des Dominicains de Liège contient-il ce genre de petites notules (AEL, couvent des Dominicains de Liège, 24), voir à propos de ce document P. Bertrand, *Commerce avec Dame pauvreté*, [note 47], p. 384-386.

73. BR, 9744-9745, fol. 286-287: sur un fragment.

74. BR, 9744-9745, fol. 141v-142r.

75. BR, 9744-9745, fol. 237r: 'est ius possessionis certo ordine certoque citulo acquisita': définition confondante de simplicité et de rigoureuse exactitude.

76. BR, 9746, fol. 71v.

77. BR, 9746, fol. 190r.

78. BR, 9746, fol. 197r: 'investire et instituere: idem sonant est autem instituere secundum proprietatem vocabuli, ponere in possessionem quasi intus statuere. Sed in hoc differunt quod institui dicitur quis presencialiter, investiri autem in absencia [...]. Investitura proprie est ipsam possessio'.

redditus ou revenu[79] ainsi qu'un fragment de quarante lignes consacré à l'*ususfructus*.[80] L'auteur du *Macrologus* connaît bien les arcanes du droit des propriétés et s'y intéresse particulièrement, notamment au niveau local. Il a donc dû exercer incidemment des fonctions d'archiviste (ou de compteur), ce qui ne serait pas inhabituel pour ce genre d'intellectuel d'abbaye.[81]

La récupération de documents d'archives dans ce genre de somme encyclopédique n'est pas chose récente: Lambert de Saint-Omer lui-même, au XIIe s., pour son *Liber Floridus*, avait réutilisé en palimpseste des feuillets provenant d'un rouleau de comptabilité des comtes de Flandre, dont on a conservé une languette non grattée, coincée dans la reliure, et qui constitue ainsi un des plus anciens témoins de comptabilité comtale pour le Moyen Âge.[82] La recherche d'exemples similaires, pour comparaison, n'est pas aisée: peu de chercheurs se sont intéressés à ce genre d'enquête, à ce qu'il semble. Un exemple contemporain du *Macrologus*: un manuscrit 'privé' émanant d'un astrologue professionnel, Maître Jorg, de Regensburg, du dernier quart du XVe s. Il s'agit d'un cahier d'annotations en *in-folio*, et d'un dossier de notules de petit format avec des configurations d'horoscope, des configurations de planètes à l'occasion de naissances, des tableaux de localisation de planètes, des tableaux d'ascendance, des prévisions, etc. mais aussi des travaux d'astronomie et d'astrologie pratique, tableaux d'éphémérides, almanachs, géomancies...mêlant donc documents imprimés et manuscrits.[83] L'auteur a aussi annoté son ouvrage dans les marges. Un *opus* similaire donc, même si, ici, c'est plutôt un document à destination privée, un ouvrage de travail à l'usage de Maître Jorg lui-même. Un autre document semblable, bien que plus récent et à usage privé aussi, nommé *De clamatiuncule quedam mei Joh*[ann]*is Grafe prima fetura* : un recueil de sermons et d'extraits de sermons par Johannes Graf, curé à Höchst près de Francfort, entre 1533 et 1548, farci de notules avec des remarques sur les sermons,

79. BR, 9747-9748, fol. 124v: 'redditus, tus, tui, i. reddictio vel id quod redditur vel annualis census'.

80. BR, 9747-9748, entre fol. 316 et 317.

81. Comme l'était Jean de Saint-Victor, par exemple: voir I. Guyot-Bachy, *Le Memoriale historiarum de Jean de Saint-Victor: un historien et sa communauté au début du XIVe siècle*, Bibliotheca Victorina, 12 (Turnhout, 2000).

82. A. Derolez, *The autograph manuscript of the* Liber Floridus. *A key to the Encyclopedia of Lambert of St-Omer* (Turnhout, 1998), p. 16.

83. Berlin SBB-PK Ms. 384 a-i: voir T. Brandis, 'Die Handschrift zwischen Mittelalter und Neuzeit. Versuch einer Typologie', *Gutenberg Jahrbuch* (1997), p. 53-55. Je remercie E. Overgaauw qui m'a fait part de cette information.

des lettres, des extraits de comptabilité, extrait d'acte, calendrier de 1539, testament...[84]

C'est donc, en définitive, un cas très particulier que cette encyclopédie liégeoise. Mais nous restons persuadés que nombre d'autres exemples de ce genre de pratique dorment dans les bibliothèques. L'étude de ces 'récupérations' de documents et de leur réutilisation avec un statut de 'palimpsestes' du bas Moyen Âge offre bien davantage que la possibilité de dater plus précisément un manuscrit ou de le localiser plus exactement, même si ces dernières précisions codicologiques sont essentielles. Ce genre de travail permet aussi de mettre en avant les obsessions des collectionneurs du XVe s., qui ne considèrent jamais leur œuvre close, mais comme en devenir. Les relations avec le milieu des archives en sortent éclairées aussi dans le même temps. Nombre de pièces d'archives jugées obsolètes à l'époque et détruites systématiquement ont dû être réutilisées de la sorte: ces cédules permettront donc de les identifier et donnent l'espoir de bon nombre de découvertes passionnantes. Comme ces comptes généraux d'hôpital, quasi complets dans leurs grandes lignes, entre 1412 et 1437; ou comme ces comptes de l'abbaye de Saint-Laurent, dont bien peu d'archives comptables médiévales nous sont parvenues.[85] Ou encore comme ces extraits de copies d'actes ou de lettres... Les rapprochements effectués ici entre archives et bibliothèques, l'utilisation des ressources conjointes de la diplomatique *largo sensu* et de la codicologie comme levier de l'histoire laissent augurer de nouveaux horizons de recherche.

84. Cod. Pal. lat. 1593 de la Bibliothèque Vaticane: voir le catalogue *Die humanistischen, Triviums- und Reformationshandschriften der Codices Palatini latini in der Vatikanischen Bibliothek (Cod. Pal. lat. 1461-1914)*, W. Metzger, avec la coll. de V. Probst, Kataloge der Universitätsbibliothek Heidelberg, Bd. 4 (Wiesbaden, 2002). Je remercie W. Metzger qui m'a fort aimablement communiqué ce cas et sa notice de manuscrit.

85. Les quelques épaves d'archives provenant de cette abbaye sont conservées aux Archives de l'évêché de Liège (un cartulaire en 7 volumes et un registre de comptes du XVIIIe s., cotés G III 1 à 8) et aux Archives de l'État à Liège.

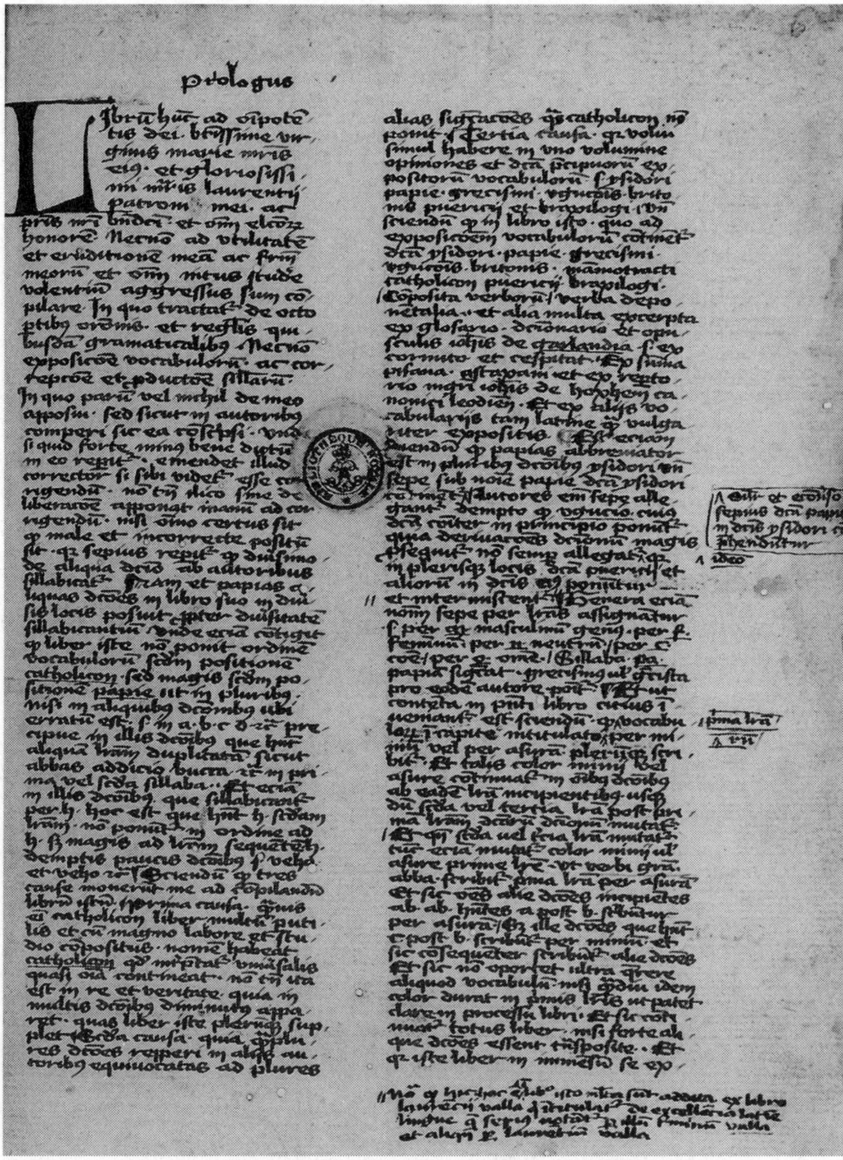

Figure 1
Prologue du *Macrologus*
© Ms. Bruxelles, Bibliothèque royale, 9747-48, f. 6r

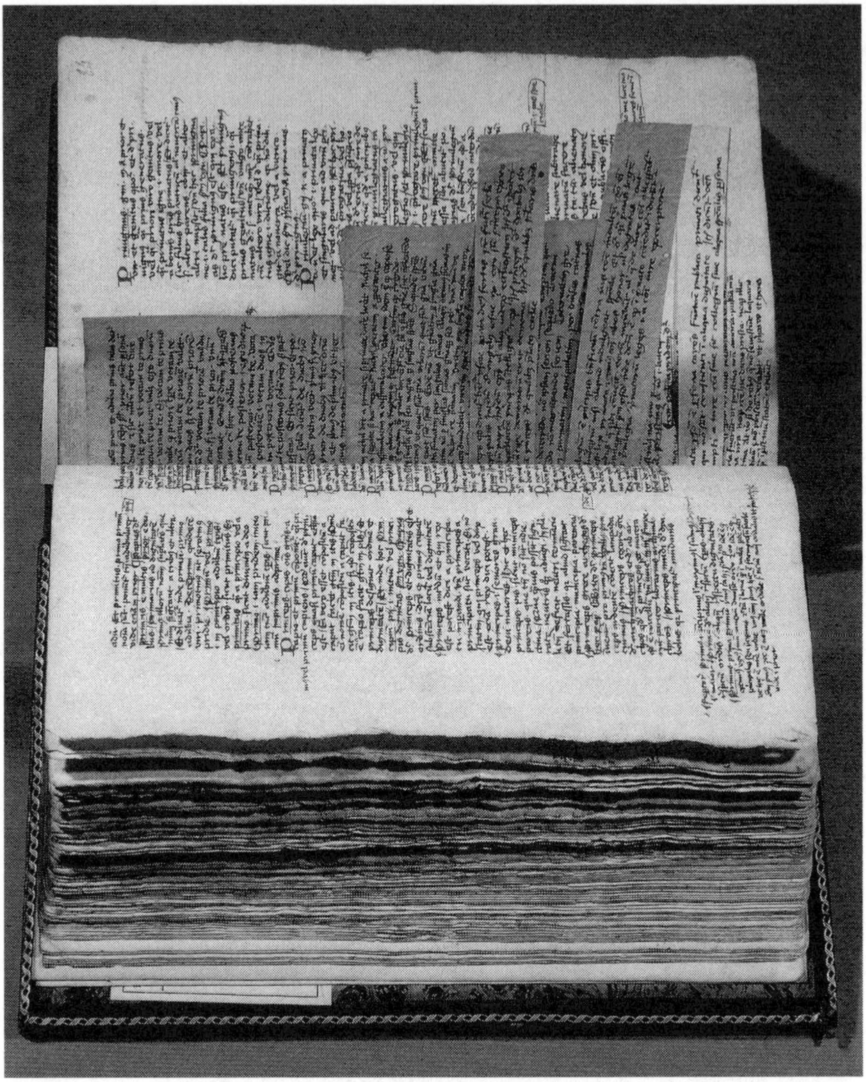

Figure 2
Additions multiples
© Ms. Bruxelles, Bibliothèque royale, 9747-48, f. 83-84

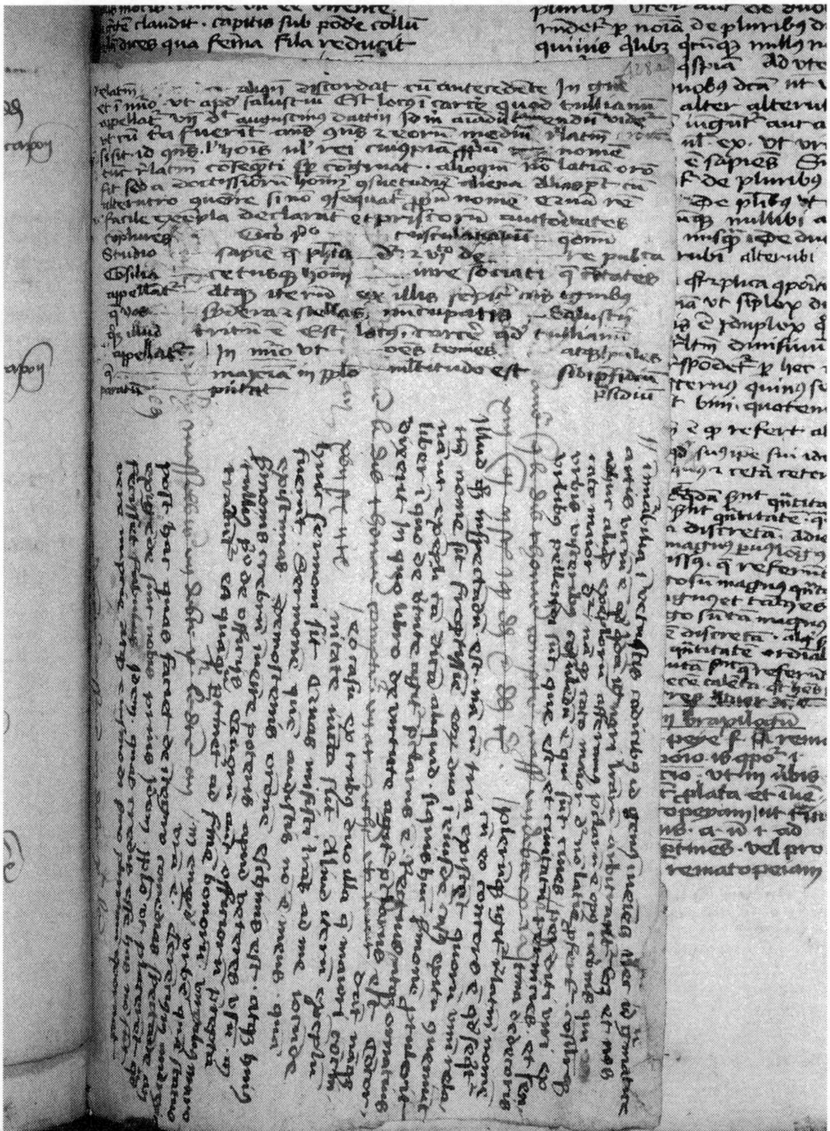

Figure 3
Un document d'archives recyclé
© Ms. Bruxelles, Bibliothèque royale, 9747-48, f. 128a

Pieter BORGHART

THE RECEPTION OF ARISTOTLE'S *ETHICA NICOMACHEA* IN THE *HEIMELIJKHEID DER HEIMELIJKHEDEN* (*SECRET OF SECRETS*) BY JACOB VAN MAERLANT

1. Introduction

The period of the High Middle Ages (twelfth-thirteenth century) is often regarded as a 'renaissance' of the ancient philosophy from a cultural historical point of view. This is especially true for Aristotelism, that was rediscovered from the twelfth century onwards through a real boom in Latin translations of original texts by Aristotle (translated both directly from Greek and indirectly from Arabic), spuria and Arabic commentaries. Although the largest part of the *Corpus Aristotelicum* was already available in Latin at the end of the twelfth century and even a number of so-called 'standard editions' circulated from the thirteenth century onwards, Dod states in his survey of medieval Aristotelism that '[...] Aristotle did not become really important in the academic world until the middle of the thirteenth century'.[1] This was, of course, a consequence of the proscription that was issued in Paris in 1210, which labelled lectures (public or private) on Aristotle's natural philosophy as heresy. Although this ban was effective for merely twenty years, it determined the agenda of the academic society until the middle of the thirteenth century.[2] The decrease of the impact of the proscription from 1250 onwards did not only have positive consequences for the intensity with which Aristotle's writings were studied, but was also accompanied by a thematic shift: while primarily the Stagirite's logics were highly regarded until that moment, after 1250 new standard editions made his writings on natural philosophy accessible for contemporary scholars.[3]

1. Dod (1982: 53).
2. For a brief discussion of this notorious proscription and its consequences for the reception and study of Aristotle's works in thirteenth century Europe, see Dod (1982: 71-73).
3. I refer to the so-called 'corpus vetustius' (middle of the thirteenth century) and the 'corpus recentius' (second half of the thirteenth century and attributed to William of Moerbeke), in which texts were included such as *Physics*, *De caelo*, *De animo*, *De sensu*, etc. See again Dod (1982: 51).

This renewed intellectual climate was, however, not restricted to the major universities as Oxford and the Sorbonne, but expanded also outside the university walls. It goes without saying that certain Aristotelian ideas gradually entered texts in the vernacular, meant for an (courtly) audience that was less qualified in philosophy. In Middle Dutch literature of the thirteenth century Jacob van Maerlant is again the outstanding example.[4] Although little systematic research has been carried out so far on the precise influence of rising Aristotelism in Maerlant's work, *Der naturen bloeme* (ca. 1270), a handbook on nature which runs over 16.000 lines in coupled rhyme, is an often cited example. From the perspective of the evolution in the reception of Aristotelism after 1250, this is not at all illogical, since Maerlant used *De natura rerum* of Thomas van Cantimpré – a follower of the illustrious Albertus Magnus – for this book on biology as his source. As is generally known, both were prominent figures in the reception of Aristotelism, not at least in the field of his natural philosophy.[5]

The intense study of the Stagirite's logics and natural philosophy was, however, not undividedly positive for the reception of other domains of philosophy that Aristotle had explored more than 1500 years before. A case in point is the rather limited attention for the *Nicomachean Ethics* that, in spite of the existence of a sufficient number of translations and the observation that its content had never been on the blacklist of the church, did not gain a firm foothold in the academic world until the second half of the fourteenth century: '[...] it was apparently not until [then] that it was adopted as a regular textbook in the Arts faculties.'[6]

4. Jacob van Maerlant is one of the great figures from the earlier history of Dutch literature: he was the first Middle Dutch author who wrote a vast body of works (containing more than 300.000 verses, among them a biblical history in rhyme (based on Comestor's *Historia Scolastica*) and a world chronicle), and in his day he was considered the 'father of Dutch literature'. For an introduction to all his works see http://www.narrative-sources.be and in particular nr.??? for the *Heimelijkheid der Heimelijkheden*.

5. For a brief survey of Albertus Magnus' commentaries on and explanations of the *Corpus Aristotelicum* known at the time (consisting of both genuinely Aristotelian texts and works erroneously attributed to the Stagirite), I refer to Kübel e.a. (1977-1999), in particular to columns 296-297.

6. Wieland (1982: 657). The available data on the Latin translations of the *Nicomachean Ethics* are the following: 1) twelfth century: an anonymous translation of books II and III ('Ethica Vetus'); 2) early thirteenth century: an anonymous translation of the entire *Ethica*, of which only book I and a number of isolated fragments have been handed down ('Ethica Nova'); 3) 1246-1247: an integral translation by Robert Grosseteste; 4) 1250-1260: a revision of Grosseteste's translation, attributed to William of Moerbeke; see Dod (1982: 77) on this matter.

This rather slow and limited reception of the *Ethica* did not, however, prevent that a number of Aristotle's ethical directives gained acceptance much earlier in medieval thought and behaviour in an indirect way. As mentioned above, the reception of Aristotelism in the Middle Ages was accompanied by an influx of the so-called spuria, texts that were erroneously attributed to Aristotle and of which the pseudo-character was only definitely determined by means of the renewed text critical methods of the renaissance. A representative example is the *Secretum secretorum*, an ethical encyclopaedic treatise that goes back to an Arabic compilation that I will refer to as the *Sirr* for the present time. Although the spurious nature of the *Secretum secretorum* has correctly not been questioned any more since the renaissance, the English scholar Manzalaoui has pointed out that the mirror of princes, which constitutes the core of the Arabic source text, more than likely partially goes back to the *Nicomachean Ethics* of Aristotle through a long text tradition.[7] Because Maerlant's *Heimelijkheid der heimelijkheden* (*Secret of secrets*), a mirror of princes that he wrote on the occasion of the twelve year old Floris V's accession to the throne in 1266,[8] is a Middle Dutch version of the *Secretum secretorum*, it is not improbable that certain guidelines from the *Nicomachean Ethics* already circulated in Middle Dutch ethical literature even before Aristotle's work was – in a Latin translation – widespread and intensively studied in these regions.[9]

Consequently, the aim of this article is twofold. Firstly, I will try to determine to what extent Maerlant's *Heimelijkheid der heimelijkheden* (henceforth *Heimelijkheid*) contains ethical views of Aristotle and in what manner these were assimilated to medieval thought.[10] Secondly, an

7. Manzalaoui's thesis, which constitutes the point of departure of this article, as well as the nature and genesis of the Arabic source of the *Secretum secretorum*, will be extensively elaborated furher on.

8. At the time of the probable composition of the *Heimelijkheid der Heimelijkheden*, Maerlant worked as a sexton in Voorne (Zeeland) for the local house of counts. On the basis of Maerlant's adaptation technique of his Latin source, it has been suggested by Verdenius that the text must have been meant for a youthful listener. An obvious hypothesis, which is still generally accepted, was then that Maerlant would have written this mirror of princes with the accession to the throne of the young Floris V in 1266 in mind, who was then crowned count of Holland and Zeeland.

9. The same applies, *mutatis mutandis*, for 'translations' of the *Secretum secretorum* in other European vernaculars! For a survey for the French and English versions in the vernacular, see Manzalaoui (1977: XXII-L). Please note that Marian Andringa (1994: 38) adopts Manzalaoui's thesis in a recent article on Maerlant's ethics of kings, without, however, further elaboration.

10. The research into Aristotelian influences in Maerlant's *Heimelijkheid der heimelijkheden* is not only interesting from the perspective of the Maerlant studies, but fits in addition into the recent attention in the field of studies in Middle Dutch literature for

attempt will be made to map out – in general terms – the long way that certain ethical concepts of the Stagirite covered from ancient Athens till medieval Flanders and Zeeland.

2. Echoes of Aristotle's ethics in Maerlant

In the following paragraphs, I will compare a number of passages of Maerlant's mirror of princes with the *Nicomachean Ethics* of Aristotle. Few will probably fail to notice that the examples that will be treated, only cover a confined number of passages from the *Heimelijkheid*, which runs to more than 2000 lines in coupled rhyme. I have, however, good reason to do so, as will become clear in the second part of this contribution. Let me, for the time being, just mention the passages in question: ll. 29-287, ll. 288-838 and ll. 1451-1540.

2.1. Lines 29-287

After a general introduction (ll. 1-28), Maerlant starts the *Heimelijkheid* with the statement that there are four kinds of kings, a division based on the binary opposition between the qualities 'liberality' and 'meanness', both with regard to themselves and to the people.[11] Subsequently, this statement is the starting point for an elaborate account on *miltheit* ('liberality') and *vreckeit* ('meanness'), which can, in my opinion, ultimately be traced back to the *Nicomachean Ethics*.[12] For one of the basic theses of Aristotle is the fact that excellence in character is an attitude that has chosen the 'middle', which amounts to 'at the right place, on the right time, towards the right people, etc'. In other words, Aristotle takes for granted the principle that every human virtue must be situated between two poles: the excess and the lack of the characteristic in question. He then applies this thesis on a series of so-called 'good qualities' of man. The first one he deals with is, not accidentally, liberality. The essence of this twofold basic thesis (that is to say: the doctrine of the 'mean' combined with the notion of the 'right place, etc.'), widely elaborated by Aris-

the rise, from the thirteenth century onwards, of ethical texts in the vernacular, and for the image of medieval secularism which can be derived from them. See Reynaert (1994) for a number of representative publications.

11. In this way there are four possible combinations: a king can be generous towards himself and his people, generous towards himself and mean to his people, mean to himself and generous towards his people, and finally mean both to himself and to his people. Subsequently, Maerlant attributes a value judgement to each possibility.

12. For an extensive discussion of Aristotle's view on ethics, I refer to Urmson (1988).

totle in the first six chapters of book IV of the *Nicomachean Ethics*, can also be found in Maerlant's text in lines 97-154.

The first part of this passage (ll.. 97-114) begins with the message that liberality at the right time and towards the right person will bring salvation to the king and his country. A ruler with this attitude should have nothing to fear:

> *Die dan ghevet wel sijn goet,*
> *Alst tijt es ende het noot doet,* [...]
> Sine machte sal menichvouden,
> Ende sine ghebode salmen houden.
> Dese es milde ende ghemate
> Hem ende sinen ondersate;
> (v. 97-98, v. 103-106, p. 119):[13]
> *[He who uses his belongings at the right time and when it is needed,* [...] his power shall grow increasingly and his commands shall be obeyed. Such a person is generous and moderate towards himself and his subjects.]

The other attitude, Maerlant warns, has disastrous consequences:

> [Een koning die...]
> *onwaerden lieden ghevet,*
> Ende sulken dies ghene noot hevet,
> Dien vergaetet te sire scande,
> Die es *verdervere* van sine lande.
> (ll. 109-112, p. 119)
> [[A king who] makes a gift *to people that are not worthy of it*, and to those who are not in need, will be disgraced and will ruin his country.]

Aristotle for his part tells the following about the generous:

> And he will give *rightly*, for he will give to the right people, and the right amount, and *at the right time*, and fulfil all the other conditions of right giving.
> (IV, i, 12-13: 191-193)[14]

And further:

> On the other hand, the liberal man will not give *to the wrong people*, nor at the wrong time, and so forth [...]; and if he spent his money on the wrong objects, he would not have any to spend on the right ones. [...] he that exceeds his means is prodigal.
> (IV, i, 22-23: 195)

13. The used text edition of the *Heimelijkheid* is the one by Verdenius (1917). Italics are mine.

14. The quoted translation is the Loeb-edition (1956), the references refer to the book, the chapter, the paragraphs and the pages of the edition respectively. Italics are mine.

Subsequently (ll. 115-126) Maerlant defends the proposition that a mean king better entrusts his belongings to a confident who is able to deal with wealth and property in a sensible way:

> Vrecheit is oec ene name
> Den landshere sere onbequame; [...]
> So moet die lands here dan
> Kiesen enen goeden man,
> Dien hi ghetrouwe kent ende goed,
> Ende hem bevelen, dat hi hem behoed
> Den orbare van sine lande, [...]
> (ll. 115-116, ll. 119-123, p. 119-120)
> [Meanness is a quality not suited for a sovereign; [...] in that case he would better choose a confident, and order him to administer the profits of his country.]

A similar line of thought can be found in the *Ethica* as well. In the following passage, Aristotle argues that one should strive to entrust wealth and belongings to people who know how to deal with them in an excellent way:

> Now riches are an article of use; but articles of use can be used either well or ill, and he who uses a thing best is he who possesses the virtue related to that thing; therefore that man will use riches best who possesses the virtue related to wealth;
> (IV, i, 6: 191)

In lines 127-138 Maerlant comes to the heart of the matter: the *miltheit* ('liberality') is the middle between *vreckeit* ('meanness') and *dullike verteren* ('prodigality'):

> *Vreckeit ende dullike verteren*
> *Moet hi bede van hem verweren*:
> So mach hi die miltheit bejaghen,
> Ende der mede in sinen daghen
> Sijn lant setten in sulken state,
> Dat langhe blivet in hovescer mate;
> (ll. 133-138, p. 120)
> [The king should *avoid meanness and prodigality*: in this manner he will strive for liberality and he will bring long-lasting prosperity to his country during his reign.]

As this is an approbation of one of the basic principles of Aristotle's view on ethics, the next quote is probably a superfluous illustration:

> *Prodigality and Meanness* on the other hand are both of them modes of excess and of deficiency in relation to wealth. Meanness is applied to those who care more than is proper to wealth [...] we call the unrestrained and those who squander money on debauchery prodigal.
> (IV, i, 2-4: 189)

The last advice that the *Heimelijkheid* gives to the king with regard to 'liberality', is the warning to refrain from the belongings of the people:

Dat hi af trecke sine hande
Vander liede goet vander lande,
[...]
(ll. 141-142, p. 120)
[He should keep his hands off his people's property.]

For the wise Hermogenes claims that the greatest justice lies in the fact

[...] dat hem een lanthere hoede,
Dat hi sine ondersaten
Niene bescatte buter maten.
(ll. 152-154, p. 120)
[[...] that a sovereign should be careful not to impose excessive taxes upon his subjects.]

A similar attitude can be found in the *Ethica*, though in a more general sense:

Consequently the liberal man will not take money from a wrong source [...] But he will acquire wealth from the proper source, that is, from his own possessions [...]
(IV, i, 15-17: 193)

Maerlant concludes the first part of the first book with an example *ex negativo* on the propositions on liberality (ll. 155-168) and with a conclusion (ll. 169-180) in which no new elements are given.

The theme of the second part of the passage in question is another thread in Aristotle's view on ethics. For the Greek philosopher is convinced that all human qualities are based on the 'right reason'. He considers this human quality as a form of common sense (φρόνησις) that all human beings dispose of, contrary to the philosophical contemplation (σοφία), of which only philosophers are capable. An outstanding example, according to Aristotle, of a historical figure that disposed of an excellent φρόνησις but has not in the least become involved in the σοφία, was the statesman Pericles, during whose government Athens reached one of the heights of ancient Greek civilization in the fifth century BC.

A particular type of common sense, which the king should follow when taking important decisions, is also emphasized in Maerlant's treatise:

Die clare verstannesse van sinne,
Die es hovet, entie leret al,
Hoe men lant berechten sal, [...]
Ende waer mesdaet neemt beghin,

Ende wanen verlies coemt ende ghewin;
Ende leert besien wat men sal kiesen,
Ende wat scuwen ende waer an verliesen.
(ll. 182-184, v. 187-190, p. 122)
[*Common sense* is very important and teaches how the country should be ruled [...] when crime begins and when people can expect profit and loss. It also determines which choices will be made, what should be avoided and what will cause loss.]

This *clare verstannesse van sinne* ('clear common sense') is, according to Maerlant, rooted in the pursuit of a good reputation:

Ende van verstannesse es dit tbegin,
Dat een beghert in sinen sin,
Dat hi van goeder name si.
(ll. 191-193, p. 122)
[Common sense begins with the desire for a good name.]

The explanation for this is the following:

Men sal niet willen sekerlike
Coninc sijn om tgrote rike,
Maer men saelt begheren tere
Om die grote name der ere.
(ll. 199-202, p. 122)
[One should not desire kingship for the vast kingdom, but one should want it *for the multiple honours*.]

To put it differently, a good ruler should not aspire after the kingship for its wealth or the position of power that such a function inevitably brings along, but solely for the honour and the good name which a king usually receives. This notion, which is perhaps somewhat more elaborated in the English translation of the Arabic source,[15] matches Aristotle's view on the political meaning of the term 'honour' (τιμή). Honour, he states in book I of the *Nicomachean Ethics*, '[...] may be said to be *the end of the Life of Politics*.' (I, 4: 15). Given the clear indebtedness of the bulk of the initial passages of the *Heimelijkheid* to Aristotle's text, the thesis that the just quoted passage of Maerlant can be traced back to the *Nicomachean Ethics*, seems fairly acceptable. I nevertheless have to nuance this assumption a little: the elaboration of this idea, that is to say: that a king who rules because of his good name, establishes a natural social order and that the opposite leads to resistance and even war, does not find its counterpart at all in the *Ethica*.[16]

15. Cf. Steele (1920: 182-183).

16. Another reason why we may suppose that the emphasis on striving for honour as a purpose of medieval kingship can be traced back to the *Ethica*, is the finding that a sim-

Lines 265-274 of the Middle Dutch text, finally, seem to continue in the same way as the opening passages: Maerlant's ideas again bear strikingly close resemblance to a number of ethical directives that Aristotle had taken down more than 1500 years before. Let me begin by quoting the passage in question:

> Alexander lieve, nu vlie,
> Dat men niet ghevoele an die
> Ghenoechten van den lechame,
> Die *beestelijc* sijn ende sere onbequame
> ende verdervelijc der eren.
> Die hem an svlees wille keren,
> *Sine verstannesse ende sijn sin*
> *Van sire zielen verdervet der in.*
> Weelde hevet in haren sinne
> Verdect vleselike minne;
> (ll. 265-274, p. 124)
>
> [Dear Alexander, beware of carnal pleasures, which are *animal*, highly inappropriate and pernicious for honor. He who turns to the flesh, *spoils his mind, reason and soul*. He who is wise, condemns physical love.]

The basic idea is clear: the king should abstain from carnal desires, because these are more in accordance with animal instinct than with human reason. Aristotle formulates the same message somewhat more prosaic in the chapters on temperance (σωφροσύνη) and intemperance (ακολασία) (*Ethica* III):

> Hence the sense to which [intemperance] is related is the most universal of the senses; and there appears to be good ground for the disrepute in which it is held, because it belongs to us not as human beings but *as animals*. Therefore it is *bestial* to revel in such pleasures, and to like them better than any others.
> (III, x, 1: 179)

The emphasis which both texts lay on the 'animal' character of such desires, is striking. The indebtedness to the *Ethica* becomes even more obvious when one reads Aristotle's chapter on the attitude of a temperate person. In this chapter the philosopher explains that intemperance,

ilar line of reasoning also appears in Maerlant's probable debut *Alexanders geesten* (and is even said by Aristotle himself!). Although *Alexanders geesten* was inspired on the *Alexandreis* of Gautier de Châtillon, Van Oostrom (1996: 241) points out that the passage involved does not appear in Maerlant's source. Elsewhere in his study (1996: 271) this Maerlant specialist explicitly states that the author must have been familiar with the *Secretum secretorum* ever since his debut and has even used it as an additional source (cf. the story of the *poisonous girl*). It is therefore not impossible that this also goes for this passage, so that a link with the *Nicomachean Ethics* is at least plausible.

that is to say the excessive pursuit for physical pleasures, is accompanied by pain, and that it 'apparently is paradoxical to be sad for something that is pleasant.' (III, xi, 6, 181: my translation). He subsequently concludes as follows:

> The man who exceeds these limits cares more for such pleasures than they are worth. Not so the temperate man; he only cares for them as right principle enjoins.
> (III, xi, 8: 183)

On the basis of the above discussed passages, I would like to point out a recurrent intertextual pattern, which in a lesser extent also goes for the examples that will follow. The quoted passages undoubtedly show an indirect (!) dependence of Maerlant's text to the *Nicomachean Ethics*: a number of ethical principles which the Greek philosopher elaborates quite extensively, occur in essence in the *Heimelijkheid* as well. It should be noted, however, that some of Aristotle's ethical directives (and this also holds true for the entire text tradition of the *Secretum secretorum*) were perfectly fitted into the medieval monarchistic order. Time and again the message is: a king who does not keep to the prescriptions, will get into trouble. Moreover, the examples about keeping physical pleasures under control, show how some ethical directives with a presumably Aristotelian origin, are assimilated into the medieval (religiously inspired) world view in general.[17] It thus seems more than likely that the genesis of the passages from the *Heimelijkheid* that possibly go back to Aristotle's work on ethics, can be explained as follows: the theoretical propositions originate in the *Nicomachean Ethics*, while its practical applications on the political and religious medieval world view can be attributed either to the authors of the Arabic mirror of princes, or to the 'translators' of the versions in Latin and several European vernaculars, including Maerlant himself. This hypothesis should, however, be verified into greater detail.

2.2 Lines 288-838

In the second series of lines of Maerlant's *Heimelijkheid* that I would like to compare with guidelines from the *Nicomachean Ethics*, the influence of the Greek philosopher is a lot less explicit than in the previously discussed examples. The nearly systematic indebtedness to Aristotle's

17. See for example lines 275-287 from the *Heimelijkheid* (p.125), in which carnal love is mentioned in one and the same breath with terms such as 'unchastity' (*onscamelheit*), 'unscrupulousness' (*verwaentheit*), 'infamy' (*diefte*), and finally even 'prison' (*karkere ende bande*).

ethics from the beginning of the *Heimelijkheid* has to make way for a number of recurrences, in which only sporadically new ethical guidelines with a possibly Aristotelian core occur. For the whole is mainly made up of passages that often take on the character of philosophical commonplaces of which the precise origin is hard to determine, which are filled up with practical guidelines that have no longer anything in common with the *Ethica*, and which sporadically even are properly monotheistic.[18] I will nevertheless discuss two passages of which the basic idea can also be found in Aristotle and that, in addition, are illustrative for the above sketched intertextual pattern on the level of Maerlants adaptation.

The first passage (ll. 479-501), that can be divided up into three parts, at first sight seems a mere repetition of a number of earlier discussed Aristotelian ethical concepts. The first quote is again a plea not to be led by desire, as wild animals tend to do:

> Scuwe die wreetheit van den diere:
> Dats, dat hi in ghere maniere
> Te haestich si no te fel.
> Horse hovescelike ende wel,
> Ende si hem genadich ende sochte,
> Dien hi met wapinen onderbrochte.
> (ll. 483-488, p.131)
>
> [Shun the cruelty of animals, this means, by no means be too hasty or too fierce. Behave in a courtly and good way, be merciful and gentle towards those whom you have defeated with weapons.]

The king thus primarily has to act mercifully and well thought-out. The next passage, which has the title 'De castitate' in the Latin version, once again gives an explicit warning against the sexual pole of animal lusts:

> Scuwe gulsicheit ende ommate,
> Sijt in dranke, sijt in ate,
> Sijt in slape, sijt in spele,
> *Ende met vrouwen te sine vele,*
> *Want dits swinen sede.*
> (ll. 489-493, p. 131-132)
>
> [Shun greed and excess, whether it is about drink, food, sleep, play or multiple intercourse with women, for these are the habits of pigs.]

In the last part, which is nowhere formulated so explicitly in the entire tradition of the *Secretum secretorum* and hence is a working-out of Maer-

18. Examples of such practical prescriptions, whether or not religiously inspired, are the idea that the king should store corn in view of worse times, the belief that the creator surveys everything, etc.

lant himself, he plays along with that the morality he also propagates elsewhere in his oeuvre:[19]

Ghelovet ghi heren der warede:
Te velen met vrouwen spreken
Doet den lechame tebreken,
Ende cort des menschen leven,
Ende doet doechden begheven,
Wet ende recht scuwen ende laten,
Ende wivelic ene here ghelaten:
Dit maect den dorper doot.
(ll. 494-501, p. 132)
[Believe in the truth, you lords: talking to much to women is damaging to the body, shortens human life and lets the virtues collapse. To shun and omit law and rights, and to behave womanly as a man, is mortal for a citizen.]

Only the last three verses correspond with the content of the Latin and Arabic recension,[20] in the passage in-between Maerlant himself is speaking.

A second passage that is possibly rooted in the *Nicomachean Ethics* (ll. 728-748), is an encitement to the king to give his people the possibility to develop intellectually. Here as well, we can detect an Aristotelian influence, be it to a limited degree. In the last three books of the *Ethica*, which in fact already forms the transitional stage to the *Politica*, the Stagirite postulates that there should be three basic ingredients present to keep man on the rails: natural disposition, habit and education.[21] In the *Heimelijkheid*, there can only be found a few some traces of the idea of education for the people:

Mac scolen, ende doe leren mede
Die kinder van dinen lande.
Sijn si arem, vul hem die hande;
Doe hem hovescheit ende ere,
Dat elc te williker lere.
(ll. 732-736, p. 140)

19. For an elaborate discussion of Maerlant's 'puritan' views on sexuality, see Van Oostrom (1996: 264-279). One of the possible reasons which this scholar puts forward for this, is the fact that there is evidence from medical-historical research that in Maerlant's days venereal diseases, after violence, were the main cause of death amongst aristocratic men.

20. For the passages involved, see Steele (1920: 51, 186).

21. The 'natural disposition' (φύσις) points to the fact that a person who does not possess any potentially good behaviour, will never be able to learn this, with the term 'habit' (ἔθος) Aristotle means that one lives according to the laws of the city-state from childhood on, and 'education' (διδαχή) has the aim to provide insight into those laws and habits.

[Establish schools and educate the children of your country. Fill the hands of the poor; treat them courteously and with honour, so that everyone will be willing to study.]

When comparing, however, the entire passage of the Middle Dutch adaptation to the Arabic and Latin version, one again records that Maerlant uses the text cleverly to perpetuate the prevailing power relations. While the Arabic and Latin text[22] suggest very generally that education will enlarge the reputation of the king, Maerlant applies this proposition to contemporary medieval society by explicitly stating that it is the task of he *clergie* (the clergy, the class of intellectuals) to show off the king to his best advantage through education:

Hier bi soutu clerke wecken,
Dat si diene ere up trecken,
Ende si breden dine name
In worden ende in geesten bequame.
Clergie eerd een conincrike
Ende heren hof sere edellike.
(ll. 737-742, p. 140)
[In particular, you should stimulate the clerks to raise your honor and to proclaim your name adequately in words and stories. The clergy honors a king and its court in a very honourable way.]

2.3. Lines 1451-1540

The third and last passage of Maerlant's *Heimelijkheid* which I will briefly discuss, has the notion 'justice' as its theme. Although Manzalaoui indicates – and not without reason – that the equivalent passages in the Arabic version possibly contain Aristotelian elements, there are no traces of this to be found in the Middle Dutch version.[23] After all, the phrasing of the concrete content of the notion 'justice' is so unclear in the Latin recension, that Maerlant does not seem to have grasped the meaning of it very well and therefore has drawn from contemporary views for the 'translation' of this passage. To conclude this paragraph, I quote the statement in question by Verdenius:

For the translation of the chapter 'de justitia' – a chapter which he probably understood just as little as I do – [Maerlant] proceeds somewhat more independently. His definition of justice, the generally accepted definition in medieval moralizing literature, does not descend from the *Sec.sec*. It reminds

22. For the passages involved, see Steele (1920: 58, 191).
23. An entire chapter (book V) is devoted to this subject in the *Nicomachean Ethics*. For a discussion of Manzalaoui's theses, I again refer to the second part of this article.

us of the well-known Latin legal adage: Justitia est constans et perfecta voluntas Jus suum cuique tribuendi.[24]

3. From Athens to Voorne

Now that it has been stated that there are sufficient arguments for a certain reception of ideas from the *Nicomachean Ethics* in Maerlant's *Heimelijkheid*, we should examine how these 'echoes' from Aristotle got into the work of the Middle Dutch author, and why exactly these passages are involved which have been analysed in the first part of this article. To give a correct answer to these questions, we need to return to the Arabic text tradition that lies at the root of Maerlant's Latin source and which, in English translation, is titled *The Book of the Science of Government, on the Good Ordering of Statecraft*, but is better known under its subtitle *Kitab sirr al-asrar* (henceforth *Sirr*), which literally means *The book of the Secret of Secrets*.[25] In order to make acceptable why we can suppose a certain influence of the *Nicomachean Ethics* on the *Sirr*, I will start with a brief discussion of the hypothesis on the genesis of this work, as it was formulated by Manzalaoui.[26]

In the Arabic tradition, Manzalaoui distinguishes three different recensions, namely the Long Form (henceforth LF), a recension in ten discourses, and a Short Form, which can be divided in a SF7 and a SF8, a shorter version in seven and eight discourses respectively. As philological studies have shown that the LF, which is at the base of the most important Latin branch of the tradition, is in fact an elaboration of the SF, and that '[...] almost certainly, the Short Form, in its eight-book version, is the older form',[27] we can leave the SF7 out of consideration henceforth. De SF8 (henceforth SF), is composed of eight 'discourses', consisting of a mirror of princes (core) and a number of additions, such as a proem and various passages with pseudo-scientific subjects – at least from a mod-

24. 'Iets zelfstandiger gaat hij te werk bij het vertalen van het hoofdstuk *de justitia*, dat hij wellicht evenmin als ik volkomen begrepen zal hebben. Zijn definitie van de gerechtigheid, de gewone in de Middeleeuwse moraliserende geschriften, stamt niet uit het *Sec.sec.* Zij doet denken aan de bekende Latijnsche rechtsspreuk: Justitia est constans et perfecta voluntas Jus suum cuique tribuendi.' (Verdenius, 1917: 103). The translation of the Latin definition of justice is the following: 'Justice is the fixed and complete want to attribute to everyone his part.'

25. The precise Arabic title is *Kitab 'ilm al-siyasa fi tadbir al-riyasa.*

26. The discussion of the *Sirr* is mainly based on Manzalaoui (1974: 147-257 and 1977: IX-XXII).

27. Manzalaoui (1977: X).

ern perspective – that gives the entire text the character of a general encyclopaedic work. LF on the other hand is made up of the eight 'maqualat' of SF and a number of 'abwab', [28] of which the origin can be traced back to the Arabic encyclopaedia *Ikhwan al-safa*. After a process of accretion, these components were finally organised in ten discourses.

The mirror of princes, that forms the core of the eight 'maqualat' of SF, is probably a ninth-century readaptation, compiled during the period of the Abbasid Dynasty (750-1260), from a collection of Greek letters attributed to Aristotle, and translated from a Greek original (or from its Syrian version) into Arabic at the time of the Omayyad Dynasty (660-750), bearing the mark of that period and culture.[29] This collection of Greek letters (or was it a genuine epistolary novel?) was a product of the hellenistic aphoristic tradition, which tended to use gnomologies and summaries.[30] From this point it is only a small step to Aristotle's work on ethics, of which the influence on the *Sirr*, according to Manzalaoui, is '[...] perhaps the most important speculation of all as to its origins, for it indicates the extent to which the *Sirr* may depend ultimately upon a genuinely Aristotelian tradition of studies.'[31]

What reason do renowned *Sirr*-specialists like Manzalaoui and Grignaschi have to attribute a Greek origin to the collection of letters mentioned above? The first argument is the nature of the transcription of Greek names, which deviates in many cases from the traditional transliteration into Arabic. On this matter, Manzalaoui writes: 'Where others might assume these to be due to the ignorance of the scribe, Grignaschi argues that they point to a genuine Greek original, and a transmission into Arabic prior to the scholarly Abbasid movement.'[32] Subsequently, there is a frequent presence of quotes from Homer and other Greek poets in the collection of letters, which would '[...] indicate a familiarity with Greek *imaginative* literature, such as is not found in the philosophical, sci-

28. The Arabic terminology is the following: the term to denote 'discourse' is 'maqualah' (plural: 'maqualat', currently used to denote 'newspaper article'), 'addition' becomes 'bab' (plural: 'abwab'). The eight 'maqualat' of SF hence consist of a mirror of princes and a number of 'abwab'.

29. The Abbasid revision is attributed to a certain Yahya ibn al-Bitriq, as is suggested by the part of the proem that goes back to that period.

30. The hypothesis of the epistolary novel was formulated by Grignaschi and is neither refuted nor accepted to the full by Manzalaoui. With regard to the place of origin of the Greek source text, this scholar suggests Edessa, which was a centre for Aristotelism in the tradition of Syrian hellenism in the period immediately prior to the rise of Islam.

31. Manzalaoui (1974: 201). For a brief survey of the *Sirr's* entire genesis, see Manzalaoui (1974: 193).

32. Manzalaoui (1974: 162).

entific and gnomic tradition of Abbasid and later writers.'[33] Finally, we can detect an unmistakable attention for 'kingcraft' in the philosophy of Plato and Aristotle from which Hellenism has frequently drawn,[34] making their writings extremely suitable to extract elements from for a mirror of princes. This goes, I think, *a fortiori* for the *Nicomachean Ethics*. After all, Aristotle's text was meant for the legislators of the city-state of Athens in the first place, usually middle-aged men who had already gained a lot of experience of life. The Stagirite was convinced that it would not be very meaningful to convey theoretical insights in the ethical conditions that can guarantee citizens a successful life, to youngsters with a very limited empirical knowledge of society. The opposite was, however, true for the future administrators of Athens, so that the *Ethica* can be considered as a kind of manual for future lawgivers and politicians, a function which the medieval mirrors of princes also fulfilled!

As I have already mentioned in the introduction, my research into Aristotelian echoes in Maerlant's *Heimelijkheid* is based on a suggestion by Manzalaoui. On the relation between the *Nicomachean Ethics* and SF, this scholar states the following: 'The first three discourses [...] can be seen to owe a distant but recognizable debt to the *Nicomachean Ethics*.'[35] An attempt to retrieve the corresponding passages of the first three 'maqualat' of SF in Maerlant, however, brings along a number of difficulties. First of all, when we focus our attention on the Latin part of the text tradition, we find two different recensions once more. The first, shorter version, was written by Johannes Hispaniensis (or Hispalensis) and is of no importance for the present discussion, because it is not this recension that is at the root of Maerlant's *Heimelijkheid*. The second Latin translation (first half of the thirteenth century) can be attributed to a certain Philippus Tripolitanus (henceforth PT), about whom there is nothing known with absolute certainty except that he is responsible for this recension of the *Secretum secretorum*.[36] Consequently, the most relevant finding for the present discussion is the fact that Maerlant's text (through the Latin recension of Philippus

33. Manzalaoui (1974: 162).

34. Manzalaoui (1974: 160-161), mentions the dialogues *Euthydemos* and *Politeia* by Plato in this context.

35. Manzalaoui, 1977: X. Please note, however, that Manzalaoui on one occasion speaks about the 'first set of four Discourses' (1974: 191). Further on in the same article, however, he restricts himself to 'Discourses I, II and II' (1974: 201). As he formulates his thesis in the same way in his article from 1977, I have also confined myself to a study of the first three discourses.

36. For more details, see Manzalaoui (1977: XV-XXII), Steele (1920: VIII-XXII) and Verdenius (1917: 55-57).

Tripolitanus) goes back to LF of the Arabic tradition, and not to SF to which the quote of Manzalaoui relates. A second aspect that needs to be taken into account is the observation that the Latin source, although mentioned otherwise in the prologue, omitted the original division into ten discourses.[37] As a consequence, we find a deviant division in twenty-two chapters in Maerlant's *Heimelijkheid* as well.

All this obviously has consequences for the comparison of the table of contents of the respective versions, which should give a decisive answer about the central question which passages of the *Heimelijkheid* go back to the first three 'maqualat' of SF, with LF and PT as intermediate stages? Starting from the perspective of the Arabic branch, I will consequently not refer to the typical division of PT and MA, but to the folios of the Parisian printing from 1520 and to the lines of Verdenius' edition that correspond with the Arabic division in ten discourses respectively. Schematically this can be represented as follows:[38]

Short Form	Long Form		Philippus Tripolitanus	Maerlant's *Heimelijkheid*
I	I		7-9	ll. 29-287
II	IIa		9-17	ll. 288-838
-	IIb	IIb1	17-34	ll.839-1438
		IIb2	34-41	
III	III		41-43	ll. 1451-1540

The survey makes it clear that the text tradition, with regard to discourse I and discourse II of SF (on the types of kings and their behaviour respectively), follows the outlined evolution perfectly: these discourses are identical in both Arabic versions and match the folios 7-9 and 9-17 of Philippus Tripolitanus' translation. In the *Heimelijkheid*, we find the corresponding passages tightly joined in the verses 29-287 (discourse I) and 288-838 (first half of discourse II of LF).

The second part of discourse II of LF, however, is much more problematic. The part IIb of LF, which does not appear in SF and consequently cannot be taken into consideration to echo Aristotle's *Ethics*, can

37. This is an observation by Verdenius, who used the Parisian printing from 1520 for his study. After a thorough examination, he had come to the conclusion that this version is probably closest to the text that Maerlant might have used. For further argumentation, see Verdenius (1917: 103).

38. For this scheme I relied on Manzalaoui (1977: XII-XIV), Steele (1920: 36-126, 176-227) and Verdenius (1917: 2, 103-105, 116-167).

be divided into two parts (IIb1 and IIb2), chapters on hygiene and physiognomy (subjects which are not at all dealt with in the *Nicomachean Ethics*!). The chapter on hygiene (IIb1) appears in PT on the folios 17-34. There is in PT, however, at first sight no trace to be found of physiognomy. Further analysis, however, shows that part IIb2 of LF has been replaced in PT by a chapter that Manzalaoui places under the denominator 'The Occult Sciences'[39] (folios 34-41) and that matches discourse X of LF. In his turn, PT has postponed the part on physiognomy towards the end of the treatise. The second part of discourse II of LF (IIb) corresponds – perhaps not entirely with respect to content, but certainly with regard to length – with the folios 17-41 of PT, which match the lines 839-1438 of Maerlant's text. Finally, the third discourse of SF (on justice), which also appears in LF as such and matches the folios 41-43 in PT, can be found in lines 1451-1540 of Maerlant's 'translation'.[40]

The text tradition of *Secretum secretorum* thus points to the following three passages of Maerlant's text, as going back through a long tradition to the first three discourses of SF, and thus partially originating via an even older tradition in Aristotle's *Nicomachean Ethics*: ll. 29-287, ll. 288-838 and ll. 1451-1540. To what extent this holds true, has been discussed at great length in the first part of this article.

4. Concluding remarks

To conclude: the rather sketchy reconstruction of the text tradition of *Secretum secretorum* shows how complex the subject matter is. To get absolute certainty on the extent of Aristotle's influence on Maerlant's text, one should first dedicate an extensive study to the Greek sources of the *Sirr*, in which every passage should be checked with its supposed source in meticulous detail, to finally determine which passages are of Aristotelian origin, which go back to a younger Greek source and which can be considered as more recent Arabic additions (Manzalaoui has already given the initial impetus to this research in one of his articles on the *Sirr*[41]). Then, a profound analysis should be made of the text tradition that begins with the *Sirr* and ends with (in our case) Maerlant's text, in which one should try to answer questions like: On which source did

39. Manzalaoui (1977: XIV).

40. For the attentive reader: lines 1439-1450 are a personal transitional passage by Maerlant

41. Manzalaoui (1974: 201-202).

Philippus base himself and how faithfully did he deal with it? Which Latin manuscript did Maerlant use and in which way did he adapt it? Moreover, a lot of information has been lost throughout history, so that a sound reconstruction of the entire text tradition is nearly impossible. To give just one example: it is still not clear which manuscript of the *Secretum secretorum* Maerlant used as his source.[42]

To conclude on a positive note, I would like to invoke the impasses to justify the method I have chosen for my discussion. Even Manzalaoui, who has intensively studied the text tradition of *Secretum secretorum*, finally capitulates with the assessment that, even after thorough examination, '[t]he question of the ultimate origin of the *Sirr* remains entirely open.' To resolve this impasse, he only sees one possible solution: 'It seems best, therefore, in studying the *Sirr* [...] to make a study in some depth of the text of the *Sirr* itself.'[43] The same applies, *mutatis mutandis*, to Maerlant's text as well. Consequently, the direct confrontation of the Middle Dutch poet with the famous Greek philosopher which I conducted in the present article, should be viewed against this background.

Bibliography

ANDRINGA 1994: Marian Andringa, 'Vorstenethiek in het werk van Maerlant', in: Reynaert e.a. 1994, 37-53.

ARISTOTLE: *The Nicomachean Ethics* (with an English translation by H. Rackham). [The Loeb Classical Library] (London/Cambridge: William Heinemann LTD/Harvard University Press, 1956).

BRAMS 1999: Jozef Brams, 'Jacob van Maerlants bewerking van het *Secretum secretorum*', in: Rita Beyers (ed.), *Van vader- naar moedertaal: Latijn, Frans en Nederlands in de dertiende-eeuwse Nederlanden*, Handelingen van het colloquium georganiseerd door de Zuid-Nederlandse Maatschappij voor Taal- en Letterkunde en geschiedenis op 23 oktober 1999 (Antwerpen, 1999), 181-194.

DOD 1982: Bernard G. Dod, 'Aristoteles Latinus', in: Kretzmann, Kenny and Pinborg 1982, 45-79.

KRETZMANN, KENNY AND PINBORG 1982: Norman Kretzmann, Anthony Kenny and Jan Pinborg (eds.), *The Cambridge History of Later Medieval Philosophy: from the rediscovery of Aristotle to the disintegration of scholasticism (1100-1600)*. (Cambridge: Cambridge University Press, 1982).

KÜBEL E.A.1977-1999: 'Albertus Magnus', in: *Lexicon des Mittelalters*, 10 vols. (Münich und Zürich, Artemis & Winkler Verlag, 1977-1999), vol. 1, 294-299.

42. Cf. Brams (1999: 184).
43. Manzalaoui (1974: 164).

MANZALAOUI 1974: M.A. Manzalaoui, 'The Pseudo-Aristotelian *Kitab Sirr Al-Asrar*: Facts and Problems', in: *Oriens* 23-24 (1974), 147-257.

MANZALAOUI 1977: M.A. Manzalaoui (ed.), *Secretum secretorum, nine english versions* (Oxford, Oxford University Press, 1977).

MIDDELNEDERLANDS HANDWOORDENBOEK, bewerkt door J. Verdam ('s-Gravenhage, Martinus Nijhoff, 1994; eerste druk: 1932).

REYNAERT 1994: Joris Reynaert, 'Leken, ethiek en moralistisch-didactische literatuur', in: Reynaert 1994: 9-36.

REYNAERT E.A. 1994: Joris Reynaert e.a., *Wat is wijsheid? Lekenethiek in de Middelnederlandse letterkunde* (Amsterdam, Prometheus, 1994).

SCHMITT 1982: Charles B. Schmitt, 'Francesco Storella and the last printed edition of the Latin *Secretum secretorum* (1555)', in: W.F. Ryan and Charles B. Schmitt (eds.), *Pseudo-Aristotle, The secret of secrets, sources and influences* (London, Warburg Institute, 1982), 124-131.

STEELE 1920: Robert Steele, *Secretum secretorum, cum glossis et notulis, tractatus brevis et utilis ad declarandum quedam obscure dicta Fratris Rogeri* (Oxford, E Typographeo Clarendoneano, 1920).

URMSON 1988: J.O. Urmson, *Aristotle's Ethics* (Oxford/New York, Basil Blackwell, 1988).

VAN OOSTROM 1996: Frits Van Oostrom, *Maerlants wereld* (Amsterdam, Prometheus, 1996).

VERDENIUS 1917: A.A. Verdenius, *Jacob van Maerlant's Heimelijkheid der Heimelijkheden* (Amsterdam, A.H. Kruyt, 1917).

WIELAND 1982: George Wieland, 'The reception and interpretation of Aristotle's *Ethics*', in: Kretzmann, Kenny and Pinborg 1982, 657-672.

www.narrative-sources.be : *The Narrative Sources from the Medieval Low Countries*, eds. L. Milis, W. Verbeke, J. Goossens, R. Nip, D. De Boer (Gent, Leuven, Groningen, 2003).

Herman BRAET

DU PORTRAIT D'AUTEUR DANS LE *ROMAN DE LA ROSE*

Je n'i faz riens fors reciter
Si par mon geu (...)
Quelque parole n'i ajoute
Si con font entr'eus li poete
(vv. 15209-15207)[1]

Le *Roman de la Rose*, on le sait, est généralement attribué à deux auteurs: Guillaume de Lorris, qui aurait laissé, vers 1230, une oeuvre inachevée; et Jean de Meun, son continuateur, quarante ans plus tard. On connaît aussi l'importance de ce texte ainsi que l'influence prodigieuse qu'il a exercée sur les lettres et sur la pensée durant trois siècles: c'était l'ouvrage en langue d'oil le plus connu de toute la littérature médiévale, comme l'attestent plus de trois cents manuscrits et fragments conservés.[2] Vu cette popularité, il n'est pas étonnant que bon nombre de ces témoins soient enluminés, ne fût-ce qu'au moyen d'une miniature liminaire.[3] Celle-ci, qui fait office de frontispice, se conforme généralement à un type canonique, auquel nous allons revenir.

Notre point de départ – et point d'arrivée – sera la composition picturale qui précède le texte dans un témoin tardif, le ms. Douce 195 de la

1. Notre édition de référence est celle de Félix Lecoy, *Guillaume de Lorris et Jean de Meun, Le Roman de la Rose,* Classiques français du moyen âge, 92, 95, 98, 3 vol. (Paris, 1965-1970).

2. Au précieux inventaire d'Ernest Langlois, *Les Manuscrits du 'Roman de la Rose'. Description et classement* (Paris, 1910) et à la note additionnelle dans son édition (t. Ier, Paris, 'SATF', 1914, n. 1. aux pp. 49-51), il convient de joindre un certain nombre de copies découvertes depuis lors. On se reportera en particulier au répertoire exhaustif de Heather Arden, *The 'Roman de la rose'. An annotated bibliography* (New York et Londres, 1993), notices 47, 48, 52, 54-57, 63, 67-73, 75 et 77. Consulter encore le catalogue où Mechtild Modersohn décrit quatre-vingt quatre témoins enluminés: M. Modersohn, *Natura als Göttin im Mittelalter. Ikonographische Studien zur Darstellung der personifierten Natur* (Berlin, 1997), pp. 198-244, ainsi que l'inventaire mis à jour aux pp. 193-97.

3. Voir le travail toujours utile d'Alfred Kuhn, 'Die Illustration des Rosenromans', *Jahrbuch der kunsthistorischen Sammlungen des allerhöchsten Kaiserhauses*, XXX 1 (1913-1914), pp. 1-66 et 15 pl. h-t. On trouvera un complément d'information dans notre étude 'Le *Roman de la Rose*, espace du regard', *Studi Francesi,* 35 (1991), pp. 1-11 (Travail traduit d'abord, mais publié sous forme tronquée et mutilée, sous le titre 'Der Roman der Rose, Raum in Blick' dans *Traüme im Mittelalter. Ikonologische Studien*, Stuttgart et Zurich, 1989).

Bodléienne. Daté des années 1487-1495 et probablement copié par Jean Michel, ce volume aurait été enluminé par Robinet Testard et destiné à la cour de Charles d'Orléans et de Louise de Savoie à Cognac.[4]

On distingue au premier folio (fig. 1) les deux volets d'un diptyque.[5] À gauche, un clerc est assis à son pupitre, en train d'écrire dans un livre; à droite, un personnage endormi serre dans la main droite un rouleau de parchemin. Parmi les miniatures liminaires du *Roman*, ce dispositif est exceptionnel et atypique.[6] Quelle est son origine, quelle est sa fonction? Afin de pouvoir répondre à ces questions, il convient tout d'abord de reconduire chacun des deux registres dont il se compose à la tradition des portraits d'auteur, tout en tenant compte du caractère spécifique de l'entreprise romanesque qui se trouve ici inaugurée. Après quoi d'autres solutions peuvent être envisagées.

En fait, Robinet Testard combine deux formules anciennes,[7] toujours en vigueur à la fin du moyen âge, comme en témoigne le relevé des différents types de portraits liminaires dû à Elizabeth Salter et à Derek Pearsall: d'après ces érudits, l'auteur se trouve représenté tour à tour comme enseignant, comme prédicateur, comme lecteur et, bien entendu, dans sa fonction d'écrivain.[8] Ce dernier type remonte comme on sait à l'Antiquité;[9] il a surtout été popularisé par la représentation des évangélistes figurant chacun en tête de sa version,[10] puis par le portrait des prophètes, des pères de l'Église ou encore par celui du roi David.

4. Se reporter à Otto Pächt et Jonathan J. G. Alexander, *Illuminated manuscripts in the Bodleian Library,* I (Oxford, 1966), p. 61 (n° 787) et à *The Douce Legacy. An exhibition to commemorate the 150th anniversary of the bequest of Francis Douce (1757-1834)* (Oxford, 1984), pp. 161-2 (n° 232a). Il est à noter que le ms. est daté vers 1470 par Millard Meiss, *French painting in the time of Jean de Berry. The Limbourgs and their contemporaries* (New York, 1974), n. 118 à la p. 439.

5. Voir au sujet de ce dispositif notre étude, *o.c.* [n.3], pp. 5-6.

6. On se reportera au dépouillement très représentatif de Kuhn, *o.c.* [n. 3].

7. Voir celles que relève Peter Bloch au cours de son étude 'Eine Dialogdarstellung des frühen 12. Jhs.', *Festschrift Dr. h.c. Eduard Trautscholdt* (Hambourg, 1965), pp. 54-62 (56) ainsi que les exemples énumérés dans les n. 7 ss.

8. E. Salter et D. Pearsall, 'Pictorial illustration of late medieval poetic texts: the role of the frontispiece or prefatory picture', in F. Andersen, E. Nyholt, M. Powell et F.T. Stubkjaer (éd.), *Medieval Iconography and Narrative* (Odense, 1980), pp. 100-23 (115-6, avec plusieurs exemples).

9. Au sujet des plus anciens portraits d'auteur conservés, on verra Kurt Weitzmann, *Ancient Book Illumination* (Cambridge Mass., 1959), pp. 116-27 et 154-6, notamment la fig. 130 (*Vergilius Romanus*); les fig. 131-132 et 134 peignent déjà une scène d'enseignement.

10. On trouvera une documentation copieuse – mais regroupant seulement les témoins grecs – chez Albert Mathias Friend, 'The Portraits of the Evangelists in Greek and Latin manuscripts', *Art Studies,* 5 (1927), pp. 115-47; 7 (1929), pp. 3-29. Voir encore Bloch, *loc. cit.* [n. 7]; Robert S. Nelson, *The Iconography of Preface and Miniature in the Byzantine Gospel Book* (New York, 1980), e.a. les figures. 5, 10, 11-12, 26-29, 32; Carl Nordenfalk, 'Der inspirierte Evangelist', *Wiener Jahrbuch für Kunstgeschichte,* 36 (1985), pp. 175-90.

Dès les plus anciennes de ces *Repräsentationsbilder* – qui ne sont évidemment pas à proprement parler des portraits individuels, mais des icônes –, on observe la présence d'un élément qui semble favoriser ou influencer l'acte d'écrire. Une main céleste sortant des nues,[11] l'animal attribut de l'évangéliste[12] ou un ange[13] semblent proposer un modèle ou tendent à inspirer autrement le scripteur. On relèvera en particulier les images montrant la transmission d'un rouleau ou d'un codex, comme si le texte préexistait à sa notation par le sujet.[14] Un peu plus tard, dans un des premiers codices contenant la *Consolation* de Boèce, l'auteur a l'air d'écrire sous la dictée de Philosophie.[15]

11. Par exemple le portrait de s. Matthieu dans York, Minster Libr. 1, f° 22v (fin du Xe, début du XIe s.), reprod. dans Louis Grodecki, Fl. Mütherich, J. Taralon, Fr. Wormald, *Le Siècle de l'An Mil* (Paris, 1973), fig. 234 à la p. 239; ceux de Marc et de Luc aux ff. 60v et 85v du même codex, reprod. dans Elzebieta Temple, *Anglo-Saxon manuscripts 900-1066* (Londres, 1976), fig. 183 et 184; celui de s. Ambroise dans Avranches, B.M. 72, f° 182v (deuxième moitié du XIe s.), dans Gilberte Garrigou, *Naissance et splendeurs du manuscrit monastique du VIIe au XIIe s.* (Paris, 1992), p. 118.

12. Par exemple Londres, Brit. Libr. Cotton Nero D. IV, ff. 93v, 137v, 209v (fin du VIIe, déb. du VIIIe s.), reprod. dans J. J. G. Alexander, *Insular manuscripts 6th to the 9th century* (Londres, 1978), fig. 29 à 31; Paris, B.N. nouv. acq. lat. 1203, f° 2v (Evangéliaire de Charlemagne, dit de Godescal, 781-783), reprod. par Jean Porcher, *Les Manuscrits à peintures en France du VIIe au XIIe s.* (Paris, 1954), fig. 24; Vienne, Ö.N.B. 1224, f° 71v (fin du VIIIe s.), reprod. par Alexander, *ibid.*, fig. 184; Abbeville, B.M. 4 (Evangiles de Saint-Riquier, vers 800), reprod. par Garrigou, *o.c.* [n. 11], p. 98. On verra encore les types de portraits relevés par Wilhelm Köhler, *Die Karolingischen Miniaturen. I. Die Schule von Tours* (Berlin, 1933), Tafelband, pl. 10 à 12 (matériaux du IXe s.), ainsi que Nordenfalk, *o.c.* [n.10], pp. 181-88.

13. Dresde, B.M. A 63, f° 5v (Xe s.), reprod. par Robert Bruck, *Die Malereien in den Handschriften des Königreichs Sachsen* (Dresde, 1906), fig. 8 à la p. 8; Copenhague, Bibl. royale G.K.S. 10, f° 17v (fin du XIe s.), dans Alexander, *o.c.* (1978), fig. 25; Aix-en Provence, Méjanes 7, page 57 (vers 1100), reprod. par Walter Cahn, *Romanesque manuscripts. The twelfth century* (Londres, 1996), fig. 106. Voir encore les exemples dans la note suivante.

14. Par exemple Paris, B.N. lat. 8850, f° 81v (IXe s.), reprod. par Hélène Toubert, *in* Henri-Jean Martin et Jean Vezin (éd.) *Mise en page et mise en texte du livre manuscrit* (Paris, 1990), fig. 342 à la p. 362; Paris, Ste-Geneviève 1190, f° 251v (IXe s.), reprod. par François Garnier, *Le Langage de l'image au moyen âge* II. *Grammaire des gestes* (Paris, 1982), fig. 17 à la p. 319; St-Pétersbourg, lat. Q.v.I 31, f° 20 (IXe s.), reprod. par Tamara Voronova et Andreï Sterligov, *Les Manuscrits enluminés occidentaux du VIIIe au XVIe s. à la Bibliothèque nationale de Russie à Saint-Pétersbourg* (Bournemouth et Saint-Pétersbourg, 1996), fig. 2; Amiens, B.M. 24, f° 108 (deuxième moitié du XIe s.), dans Garrigou, *o.c.* [n. 11], p. 110; Baltimore, Walters Art Mus. W. 17, f° 8v (vers 1100) ainsi que Paris, B.N. lat. 17970, ff. 115v et 181 (début du XIIe s.), dans Cahn, *o.c.* [n. 13], fig. 207, 209 et 210. On lira les observations de Nordenfalk, *o.c.* [n. 10], pp. 187-88.

15. Cracovie, Bibl. Jagellonne Berlin lat. qu. 939 (olim Maihingen, Bibl. Oettingen-Wallerstein 1,2,4° 3) (fin du Xe s.), reprod. par Pierre Courcelle, *Histoire littéraire des grandes invasions germaniques* (3e éd., Paris, 1964), pl. 38 (Philosophie tend un livre ouvert); Madrid, B. N. 10109, f° 2 (XIe-XIIe s.), reprod. par idem, *La 'Consolation de Philosophie' dans la tradition littéraire. Antécédents et postérité de Boèce* (Paris, 1967), frontispice et pl. 28. – La scène fait songer au portrait peut-être très ancien dans l'évan-

Ces éléments adjoints ont leur importance: grâce à eux l'oeuvre apparaît comme émanant d'une instance supérieure. Le scripteur devient dès lors un simple relais, un médiateur entre la source ultime et le lecteur. Bref, l'image frontispice suggère que le texte qu'elle introduit relève d'une autorité extérieure à celui que l'on pourrait considérer comme son auteur.

Il en va de même, nous semble-t-il, d'un autre type de portrait liminaire signalé par les deux érudits anglais[16] – et que l'on retrouve cette fois dans la composition de Robinet Testard. Le poète est couché au lit; il appuie souvent la tête sur l'avant-bras ou sur la main, dans le geste conventionnel du rêveur. Il n'y a rien d'étonnant à ce que la grande majorité des manuscrits enluminés du *Roman de la Rose* s'ouvrent de la sorte:[17] le tableautin y fait écho aux premiers vers, qui donnent effectivement l'entreprise comme étant issue d'un songe que l'auteur aurait reçu lors de sa vingtième année.[18]

À première vue, ce genre de représentation fait signe du côté de l'iconographie visionnaire, à ceci près qu'il n'y apparaît aucun principe surnaturel tel la main de Dieu ou encore, un ange porteur d'une nouvelle. Mais dans sa portée, elle s'avère plus proche des portraits d'évangélistes que nous venons d'évoquer: tout comme ceux-ci, le frontispice habituel du *Roman* vise à éclairer les circonstances de la composition du texte, qui se trouve indexé comme une création au second degré. En somme, cette image cherche à légitimer ce discours en lui assignant une origine extérieure. Jusqu'à la fin du moyen âge, du moins pour les enlumineurs, cette oeuvre éminemment profane n'accède donc pas à l'autonomie,[19] mais se

géliaire de Rossano (Bibliothèque archiépiscopale; Ve-VIe s.?), reproduit dans G. Cavallo, J. Gribomont, W.C. Loerke, *Codex purpureus rossanensis* (Rome et Graz, 1987): saint Marc flanqué d'un personnage (la Sagesse?) qui pose l'index sur la feuille de parchemin où il écrit. D'après Friend, *o.c.* [n. 10], p. 141, cette composition remonterait au schéma hellénistique représentant le Poète visité par sa Muse. On lira par ailleurs sur cette formule les commentaires de Nordenfalk, *o.c.* [n. 10], pp. 175-80 ainsi que O. Kresten et G. Prato, 'Die Miniaturen des Evangelisten Markus im Codex purpureus rossanensis', *Römische historische Mitteilungen,* 27 (1985), pp. 381-99.

16. Salter et Pearsall, *o.c.* [n. 8], p. 116; on verra les illustrations aux pp. 109, 110 et 113.

17. Voir le relevé de Kuhn, *o.c.* [n. 3] et les manuscrits signalés dans notre étude de 1991 [n. 3].

18. Voir les vers 21-33.

19. Michel Zink a montré comment les premiers romanciers français se défendent d'avoir inventé, en se cherchant des cautions. ('Une mutation de la conscience littéraire. Le langage romanesque à travers des exemples français du XIIe siècle', *Cahiers de Civilisation Médiévale* 24, 1981, pp. 3-27, repris dans M. Zink, *La Subjectivité littéraire autour du siècle de saint Louis*, Paris, 1985, pp. 27-46). – Contrairement à Steffen Bogen (*Träumen und erzählen. Selbstreflexion der Bildkunst vor 1300*, Munich, 2001, notamment pp. 305ss.), dont la lecture, en soi fort intéressante, confronte l'iconographie visionnaire et l'une des premières images d'un 'rêve humain', on peut se demander si la présence récurrente de cet incipit visuel dans les manuscrits du *Roman* ne répond pas à un besoin persistant de légitimer la fiction littéraire, en situant sa source dans un ailleurs. On sait que l'alibi du songe sera invo-

donne comme mue par une cause première: elle provient d'une révélation. Le dormeur n'en est que le témoin; l'écrivain, son porte-parole.

Revenons à la composition de Robinet Testard. La mise en écrit y précède la scène onirique. Ce qui répond à l'ordre non pas chronologique mais plutôt logique: Guillaume de Lorris dans son prologue annonce qu'il va consigner le contenu d'un rêve reçu cinq ans plus tôt (vv. 31 et 45-6). La lecture de l'image a l'air de se conformer à l'ordre de présentation des données textuelles. Le poète prend la plume pour évoquer l'expérience du rêveur qu'il a été; l'écrit, à la manière de la métonymie, englobe la source qui l'a fait surgir.

On procède d'ailleurs de cette manière dans un certain nombre de codices contenant le *Pèlerinage de vie humaine* de Guillaume de Digulleville – une oeuvre qui se dit explicitement inspirée par la lecture du *Roman de la Rose*.[20] On y trouve au seuil du texte la même contiguïté des moments de narration et d'action (ou plutôt de réception): la prédication ou l'enseignement (fig. 2) – ou encore, la rédaction[21] – jouxtent et précèdent visuellement le rêve fondateur.[22]

qué dans plusieurs oeuvres tardives, notamment à incidence politique, pour garantir l'impunité à leurs auteurs; Pierre-Yves Badel cite sous ce rapport les *Echecs amoureux* qui soulignent que le procédé permet de 'parler plus seurement' (*Le Roman de la Rose au XIVe siècle. Etude de la réception d'une oeuvre*, Genève, 1980, p. 343).

20. 'En veillant avoie leü (...) Le biaus Romans de la Rose. Bien croi que ce fu la chose Qui plus m'esmut en ce songier' – éd. J.-J. Stürzinger (Londres, 1893), vv. 9-13. – Que l'initiation du rêveur soit amoureuse ou spirituelle, la démarche demeure la même: le cheminement de l'âme pèlerine, chez Guillaume de Deguileville, va doubler la quête de la Rose. On lira par ailleurs avec profit Susan Hagen, *Allegorical remembrance. A study of 'The Pilgrimage of the Life of Man' as a medieval treatise on seeing and remembering* (Athens et Londres, 1990).

21. L'écriture, par exemple dans Paris, B.N. fr. 829, ff. 1 et 1v (daté de 1404) et fr. 828, f° 1 (daté de 1414). Paris, B.N. fr. 377 (vers 1395) combine au f° 1 les deux modes de diffusion; le rêve suit au verso. Contrairement à ce que croient avoir observé Hagen, *ibid.* [n.20], p. 13 et Fabienne Pomel (*Les Voies de l'au-delà et l'essor de l'allégorie au moyen âge*, Paris, 2001, n. 29 aux pp. 256-7), les volets supérieurs du quadriptyque dans Paris, B.N. fr. 823, f° 1 (daté de 1393), ne suggèrent pas, cette fois, comment le songe se trouve enchâssé dans le livre: la première image montre un lecteur et non un scripteur. On pourra se reporter à la pl. 5 chez Hagen [n. 20] ou à la pl. 6, en couleur, dans Michael Camille, *Master of Death. The lifeless art of Pierre Remiet* (New Haven, 1996).

22. Tel est le cas dans plusieurs témoins du milieu ou de la fin du XIVe siècle. Signalons, dans l'ordre chronologique, Paris, B.N. fr. 1818, f° 1; New York, Pierpont Morgan M. 772, f° 1; Munich, Bibl. de Bavière Cod. gall. 30, f°1; Heidelberg, B.U. Cod. pal. lat. 1969, f° 1; Paris, B.N. fr. 1645, f° 1; New York, Pierpont Morgan M. 1038, f° 1; Oxford, Bodléienne Douce 300, ff. 1 et 1v; Arras, B.M. 845, f°76; Douai, B.M. 768, f° 1; Londres, B.L. Add. 38120, ff. 1 et 1v; Bruxelles, B.R. 10176-8, ff. 1 et 1v; Londres, B.L. Harley 4399, f° 1. (Dans Paris, B.N. fr. 377, le f° 1 combine les deux modes, l'écriture et la prédication, ce pendant que le rêve suit au verso). Remarquons toutefois que le dispositif inverse se rencontre lui aussi, quoique plus rarement (à en croire Hagen, *ibid.* [n. 20], p. 16): Paris, B.N. fr. 12462, f° 1; Ste-Geneviève 1130, f° 1; B.N. fr. 829, ff. 1 et 1v; fr. 376, f° 1.

Dans le cas du *Roman de la Rose*, la combinaison choisie par Robinet Testard présente à première vue un intérêt particulier: celui de souligner une innovation romanesque due à Guillaume de Lorris. Non seulement celui-ci est-il dans la littérature médiévale le premier écrivain à raconter son vécu à la première personne, mais il procède d'entrée de jeu à un dédoublement de la personnalité en un narrateur d'un côté, un protagoniste de l'autre (*erzählendes / erlebendes Ich*). Autrement dit, un clivage a été instauré en un moi écrivant d'une part et, de l'autre, un héros agissant, inscrit dans un espace-temps différent.[23] Or beaucoup d'incipit imagés du *Roman* donnent à voir cette stratégie littéraire par le recours à des formules diverses: toutes séparent, au moyen d'une cloison ou à l'intérieur d'un polyptyque composé de deux, trois ou quatre tableautins, la scène originelle des suivantes, qui annoncent les premières péripéties de la *persona* onirique.[24]

Mais le schéma qui inaugure la lecture du poème dans le manuscrit Douce 195 relève-t-il de ce polymorphisme, ou de cette polymodalité? Ce qui est troublant, c'est que parmi les très nombreuses copies enluminées du *Roman de la Rose*, celle-ci apparaisse comme un cas unique: c'est la seule où la miniature liminaire évoque le moment de la composition.

En revanche, un nombre considérable de témoins[25] font intervenir le topos de la mise en écrit non pas en amont mais à la fin du texte de Guillaume de Lorris, aux vv. 4028-9,[26] c'est-à-dire à l'endroit précis où

23. Au sujet de cette stratégie, on lira, parmi d'autres, Paul Strohm, 'Guillaume as narrator and lover in the '*Roman de la Rose*', dans *Romanic Review*, 59 (1968), pp. 1-9; Evelyn Vitz, 'The "I" of the Roman de la Rose', *Genre*, 6 (1973), pp. 49-75 (repris dans E. Vitz, *Medieval narrative and Modern narratology. Subjects and objects of desire*, New York, 1989, pp. 38-63); Rupert Pickens, '*Somnium* and interpretation in Guillaume de Lorris', *Symposium*, 28 (1974), pp. 175-86; Anthony Spearing, *Medieval Dream-poetry*, (Cambridge, 1976), pp. 28-9. – En fait, le scénario institue trois 'je', mais qui ne se trouvent réunis dans aucun frontispice: le narrateur externe, identifié plus loin comme 'Guillaume de Lorris' (v. infra), le narrateur interne, correspondant au rêveur et le personnage d' 'Amant', actant dans le rêve. Quant à la dualité 'historique' de la première instance de production, rappelons déjà qu'elle se trouve résorbée en une seule énonciation, le 'je' de Jean de Meun relayant sans discontinuité celui de Guillaume.

24. Voir encore notre étude de 1991 [n. 3], pp. 6-7.

25. Lori Walters, au terme d'un dépouillement de quatre-vingt onze témoins enluminés avant 1400, a relevé ce signal visuel dans 65% des cas. (L. Walters, 'Reading the *Rose*: literacy and presentation of the *Roman de la Rose* in medieval manuscripts', *Romanic Review*, 85, 1994, pp. 1-26 [4]). On se reportera au précieux inventaire 'Author portraits and textual demarcation in manuscripts of the *Romance of the Rose*', publié par l'érudite en appendice à K. Brownlee et Sylvia Huot (éd.), *Rethinking the 'Romance of the Rose'. Text, image, reception* (Philadelphie, 1992), pp. 359-73. Aj. Le Cap, Grey coll. 4.c.12, f° 24 (2./4 XIVe s.).

26. Correspondant aux vv. 4059-60 dans les éditions de Langlois (t. II, Paris 1920) et de Daniel Poirion (Paris 1974) et aux vv. 4057-8 dans celle d' Alain Strubel (Paris, 1992).

son continuateur aurait (re)pris la plume (fig. 3). Ou encore, quelquefois, cette image intervient vers le milieu de tout le roman (fig. 4), en marge du passage où Jean de Meun nous apprend à brûle-pourpoint qu'il a eu un prédecesseur, que celui-ci s'appelait Guillaume de Lorris, nous informe qu'il est mort et se présente lui, comme ayant pris la relève.[27]

Toutes ces vignettes convoquent un homme, souvent tonsuré, en train d'écrire dans un livre qui manifestement figure le codex que l'on a en main.[28] Il s'agit bien d'un deuxième frontispice ou du moins d'une deuxième miniature liminaire, montrant cette fois le continuateur: la chose est précisée par le grand nombre de rubriques qui à cet endroit signalent 'Cy commence mestre Jehan de Meun'.[29] Dans le ms. Paris, B.N. fr. 12588 (datant de la première moitié du XIVe siècle) nous lisons d'ailleurs, au f° 27, par-dessus l'épaule du scripteur, le mot 'per/du', qui renvoie au premier vers (v. 4029) de la continuation.[30] Dans le ms. Paris, B.N. fr. 380 (daté vers 1400) (fig. 5) on le voit, au f° 28, composer les deux premiers vers de son texte.[31] Et dans Londres, B.L Royal 20 A XVII (datant du XIVe siècle), Jean de Meun est identifié au f° 35v par sa signature: 'ieh*an*'. Apposée au bas de la page, celle-ci fonctionne en quelque sorte comme un titulus intérieur.

Comme c'est parfois déjà le cas dans les évangiles, on est souvent frappé par la pose peu naturelle du scripteur qui, vu de profil, s'applique sur un support présenté au spectateur de face ou de trois quarts: il s'agissait en effet de faire lire les mots qui se trouvent sur la page. Garants de l'authenticité du 'portrait', ces fragments d'écrit enchâssés dans l'image attestent de cette manière l'autorité du texte.

C'est à plus d'un titre que ce deuxième frontispice du *Roman* mobilise la tradition du portrait des évangélistes: il signale l'avènement d'une nouvelle instance écrivante. Mais ce qui est surprenant, c'est que, au seuil de

27. L'épitaphe de Guillaume et la 'prophétie' concernant son successeur sont mises dans la bouche du Dieu d'Amour. Elles se situent plus ou moins – à 500 vers près – au milieu du *Roman* complet (vv. 10531-644 de l'éd. Lecoy; vv. 10561-674 des éditions Langlois, t. III, Paris 1921 et Poirion; vv. 10565-678 chez Strubel).

28. Dans beaucoup de cas, le personnage écrit dans un codex et non sur une feuille: une image non réaliste, qui nous réfère au produit fini. Le texte acquiert de la sorte une épaisseur réelle. La représentation assure encore celle de l'écrivain, qui devient celui qui a produit un codex: l'activité intellectuelle se trouve suggérée par la tâche matérielle qu'elle suppose.

29. Certaines formules mentionnent également Guillaume, mais elles sont rares: voir plus loin, n. 42.

30. 'Et si l'ai je perdue, espoir', v. 4029 de l'éd. Lecoy (v. 4059 chez Langlois et chez Poirion; v. 4057 chez Strubel).

31. On lit: 'Et si lay / ie perd[ue] // despoir'.

l'oeuvre entière, on ne retrouve pas une image qui corresponde à celle-ci. A notre connaissance, le premier poète n'y est jamais montré à l'ouvrage.[32] Il est représenté dans sa fonction d'écriture – et cela dans quelques rares témoins – seulement aux endroits que nous avons indiqués et exclusivement, on le verra, aux côtés de Jean de Meun.

Revenons à ce dernier.[33] Certains frontispices intérieurs mettent en évidence sa secondarité en le peignant dans l'attitude passive d'un lecteur, assis devant un livre ouvert.[34] En revanche, un des plus anciens volumes enluminés (daté de la fin du XIIIe ou du début du XIVe siècle), Paris, B.N. fr. 1569, tend à suggérer par une vignette située au point médian du texte (f° 68) une véritable *translatio* (fig. 6). C'est-à-dire une passation des pouvoirs, ou encore une délégation du rôle auctoriel, car on peut bien supposer que le personnage assis n'est autre que Guillaume, transmettant son oeuvre à son continuateur.[35]

Jean nous apparaît dans un rôle plus actif dans une autre composition binaire – ou bifrons –, qui se retrouve, avec de très légères variantes, dans trois témoins parallèles du XIVe siècle:[36] on y voit travailler les

32. A une exception (très tardive) près: le ms. New York, Pierpont Morgan M. 948 (daté vers 1519) montre au f° 5 un homme assis à côté d'un lit et écrivant dans un livre; devant lui, un miroir comparable à ceux qui figurent la plupart du temps dans les miniatures liminaires du *Pèlerinage de vie humaine* de Guillaume de Digulleville. On pourra utiliser l'édition fac-similé procurée par Margareta Friesen, *Der Rosenroman für François I.* (Graz, 1993, 'Codices selecti phototypice impressi', XCVII). Dans son volume de commentaires, p. 45, cette érudite estime toutefois que la peinture représente plutôt un savant humaniste s'apprêtant à copier le texte figurant sur une feuille posée sur sa table.

33. L'analyse qui suit reprend, mais dans une perspective toute différente – 'Je n'i faz rien fors reciter etc.' – certains des éléments réunis par David Hult, *Self-fulfilling prophecies. Readership and authority in the first 'Roman de la Rose'* (Cambridge, 1986), pp. 77-89.

34. Notons qu'une telle représentation correspond à la démarche de Jean de Meun, dont l'oeuvre se donne comme une relecture du poème de Guillaume. – V. dans l'ordre chronologique, Paris, B.N. fr. 1561, f° 26v; fr. 1564, f° 17; fr. 19157, f° 26v; Arsenal 5209, f° 30; New York, Pierpont Morgan M. 185, f° 30; Oxford, Bodl. E Museo 65, f° 30v. La même subordination est suggérée par l'image dans Paris, B.N. fr. 19153, f° 31 (datant du XVe s.), où Jean remplit l'office d'un copiste, malgré la rubrique qui affirme qu'il 'commence' à cet endroit.

35. Il s'agit d'un modulus ancien, relevé par Bloch, *o.c.* [n. 7], n. 14 à la p. 61, à partir du début du IXe s. Dans deux de ses exemples – le troisième est en fait une *Donationsbild* –, l'ouvrage est remis par l'auteur à un subordonné.

36. Munich, Bibl. de Bavière Cod. gall. 17, f° 28v (deuxième tiers du XIVe siècle), reproduit par Leonardo Olschki, *Manuscrits français à peintures des bibliothèques d'Allemagne* (Genève, 1932), pl. I; Londres, B.L. Stowe 947, f° 30v (daté du milieu du XIVe s.), reprod. chez Hult, *o.c.* [n. 33], fig. 3 à la p. 81; Paris, B.N. fr. 24390, f° 29 (deuxième tiers du XIVe s.). Olschki, *ib.*, p. 7, observe que ce dernier témoin a reproduit fidèlement le codex munichois.

deux écrivains l'un en face de l'autre. Dans le ms Paris, B.N. fr. 24390 les caractères que chacun des auteurs[37] vient de tracer sont parfaitement lisibles (fig. 7). Le premier se trouve rédiger l'incipit du *Roman*: 'Maint[es] gent[s] dient que un songes na se [.] fabl[es]... '. Le second inscrit les premiers mots de la continuation: 'Et si (?) lai ie (?) perd[u]'. On observera que Guillaume de Lorris – montré exceptionnellement comme écrivain – termine la page, ce pendant que Jean en entame une nouvelle pour y faire figurer son propre incipit.[38] La scène expose ainsi à la fois l'antériorité de Guillaume et sa succession.

C'est encore dans un rôle actif que l'on retrouve dans un certain nombre de copies un Jean de Meun enseignant, faisant la lecture publique ou prêchant.[39] Dans le ms. Paris, B.N fr. 1569 (daté de la fin du XIIIe ou du début du XIVe siècle), où le poème s'ouvre sur cette image (fig. 8),[40] le texte que Jean diffuse ainsi est bel et bien le *Roman de la Rose*, comme l'indique l'incipit visible en partie sur le volume ouvert devant lui.[41] Mais ce qui est notable, c'est que cette fois le second registre de la miniature est occupé par la scène canonique du rêve. Exactement comme dans le diptyque de Robinet Testard.

Pour terminer, nous aimerions aligner un certain nombre d'observations permettant d'éclairer ce que l'on vient de voir. Rappelons tout d'abord l'absence de portraits du seul Guillaume de Lorris, confrontée aux nombreux frontispices intérieurs inaugurant le texte de son successeur. Il faut bien en déduire que les enlumineurs (ou les concepteurs des programmes iconographiques) conférent volontiers la dignité auctoriale uniquement au second poète, représenté d'ailleurs la plupart du temps dans l'exercice de ses fonctions: si le propre d'un auteur est d'écrire, alors à

37. Contrairement à ce que suggère Hult, *ibid.* [n. 33], p. 86, il ne s'agit pas de copistes, puisqu'aucun des deux n'a un exemplar sous les yeux.

38. Ce genre de scène nous met en présence du livre en train de se faire: on prend soin de laisser une partie vierge, parfois une ligne entamée mais non encore terminée. Encore une fois, il s'agit de l'activité auctoriale dans sa matérialité.

39. Entre autres dans Rome, Bibl. Ap. Vat. Urbin. lat. 376, f° 26 (peut-être antérieur à 1283; reproduit par Eberhard König, *Der Rosenroman des Berthaud d'Achy. Codex Urbinatus latinus 376. Kommentarband zur Faksimileausgabe*, Zurich et Stuttgart, 1987, 'Codices e vaticanis selecti', LXXI, p. 119 ainsi que dans *idem*, *Die Liebe im Zeichen der Rose. Die Hss. des Rosenromans in der vatikanischen Bibl.*, Stuttgart et Zurich 1992, p. 33); Reg. lat. 1522, f° 68v; Paris, B.N. fr. 1560, f° 27a; Oxford, Bodl. Add. A22, f° 97.

40. Image également reproduite par Hult, *o.c.* [n. 33], fig. 10 à la p. 87 ainsi que par Sylvia Huot, *From Song to Book. The poetics of writing in old french Lyric and lyrical Narrative Poetry* (Ithaca, 1987), fig. 6 à la p. 104. Selon cette érudite, le premier registre montrerait cependant l'Aucteur, *i.c.* Guillaume (p.102).

41. Page de gauche: 'ma/in/te'; page de droite: '(..)/(..)/die'.

leurs yeux, seul Jean de Meun semble avoir droit à ce titre: le livre qu'on est en train de lire aurait été produit par lui.

À cela s'ajoute le sort fait à ce dernier par les rubricateurs. La grande majorité des rubriques à la jonction des deux parties (ou même au point médian) taisent le nom de celui auquel est attribué communément la première.[42] Quelquefois, le libellé tend même à faire passer explicitement Jean pour le seul maître d'oeuvre: le titulus au f° 29v du ms. Paris, Ste-Geneviève 1126 (daté du milieu du XIVe siècle) affirme: 'Ves ci mestre jehan de meun ou il siet en sa chaiere et fet son livre'. Quant au ms. Paris, B.N. fr. 805 (daté du XVe siècle), il inscrit tout de go à son premier folio cette déclaration: 'Cy commence un notable livre appelé le Rommant de la Rose, lequel fist maistre Jehan de Meun'.[43]

Si certains vont jusqu'à offusquer complètement l'existence du premier rédacteur, [44] cela n'a rien de surprenant. A en croire le témoignage de la tradition manuscrite, le poème initial (long de quelque quatre mille vers) n'a été sauvé que grâce à la continuation (qui en compte plus de dix-huit mille);[45] et ce premier effort restait de toutes manières anonyme jusqu'à ce qu'il fût attribué tardivement à un certain Guillaume de Lorris. De plus nous ne disposons à ce sujet que de la parole médiatrice de celui qui se dit son successeur; car Guillaume nous est uniquement connu par

42. Voici les principaux types de libellés relevés dans vingt-huit manuscrits parisiens comportant une rubrique (accompagnée la plupart du temps d'une vignette) à l'un de ces endroits: 'Ci commence mestre Jean de Meun' (quatorze occurrences), 'Ci commence le roman de Jean de Meun et le parfist jusquen la fin' (sept occurrences), 'Ci fine Guillaume de Lorris...et commence J. de M. a parfaire...' et 'Coment J. de M. le parfist a la requeste de G. de L.' (cinq occurrences). Dans au moins trois témoins, comme le rappelle Hult, *o.c.* [n. 33], p. 78, Guillaume est confondu avec le théologien Guillaume de Saint-Amour, qui figure beaucoup plus loin dans le texte de Jean (aux vv. 11548 et 11476-7 chez Langlois). Dans le ms. olim Astor A12 (et olim Stuttgart, Busch), f° 89, le rubricateur l'affuble, cette fois sous l'influence du contexte immédiat, du nom du poète Tibulle (voir figure 4).

43. Dans Londres, B.L. Yates Thompson 21 (daté vers 1380), au point médian du poème, f° 69v, la vignette convoque un Jean de Meun rédigeant les deux premiers vers de l' oeuvre – qu'il a l'air de s'approprier ainsi.

44. On trouve au moins un lecteur averti pour protester. Dans une note en marge du ms. Paris, B.N. fr. 24389, un certain Philibertus signe, au f° 27v, une défense énergique de Guillaume. C'est à celui-ci, 'comme inventeur premier', que revient l'honneur, 'non pas a maistre Jehan de Mehun' – même si celui-ci est également digne d'éloges, ayant su parfaire l'oeuvre au point 'qu'on jugeroit estre tout un'. (Texte d'après Langlois, *o.c.* [n. 2], pp. 58-9). – Que la portée précise de cet hommage soit claire ou non (comp. l'interprétation de John Fleming, *The 'Roman de la rose'. A study in allegory and iconography*, Princeton 1969, pp. 104-5 et celle de Hult, *o.c.* [n. 33], pp. 58-9), on voudra bien noter que même cet ardent défenseur ne nous livre pas le nom du 'premier aucteur'.

45. Comme l'a noté Lecoy, *o.c.* [n. 1], pp. xxxvi-xxxvii. V. aussi Fleming, *ibid.* [n. 44], p. 104, qui renvoie à Alan Gunn, *The Mirror of Love. A reinterpretation of 'The Romance of the Rose'* (Lubbock, 1951); nous n'avons cependant pas identifié ce passage.

la plume de ce dernier. Etant donné que lui-même s'absente de son propre texte, il pourrait parfaitement s'agir d'une fiction.[46]

Jean, en revanche, est un véritable 'aucteur'. Et ceci à plus d'un titre. Selon une confusion très répandue chez les grammairiens du moyen âge, le terme *auctor* est mis en rapport avec les verbes *augere* et *agere*.[47] Or Jean ajoute un supplément de matière et de sens, certes,[48] mais il est encore celui qui préside aux destinées de l'ensemble. Producteur à part entière, c'est comme si aux yeux de beaucoup il avait fini par éclipser ou détrôner un prédécesseur qui n'existait que grâce à lui.[49] Témoin de cette mainmise, Robinet Testard a procédé à une inversion des rôles et a promu le portrait du continuateur à la position initiale. Dans la mise en scène qu'il nous propose, l'attitude active de l'écrivant contraste avec l'état de réception passive du dormeur: le travail de Jean ne semble-t-il pas soustendre toute l'aventure onirique attribuée à son devancier? Celui-ci se trouve enfermé dans la fiction:[50] il apparaît comme le premier actant de

46. On sait que le regretté Roger Dragonetti a été jusqu'à mettre en doute l'existence de Guillaume: comme celui de Jean, son nom ferait partie du montage romanesque conçu par un auteur historique. Ce dernier aurait-il cherché à présenter sous ces 'masques' des approches parfois contradictoires? Voir R. Dragonetti, *Le Mirage des sources. L'art du faux dans le roman médiéval* (Paris, 1987), pp. 211 et 224.

47. Voir Alastair Minnis, *Medieval theory of authorship. Scholastic literary attitudes in the later Middle Ages* (2e éd., Aldershot 1988), p. 10; cf. Cynthia Brown, *Poets, patrons and printers. Crisis of authority in late medieval France* (Ithaca et Londres, 1995), p. 199.

48. On lit encore chez s. Bonaventure (dans son prologue aux *Libri sententiarum* de Pierre Lombard) cette importante *distinctio* entre *auctor, compilator, commentator* et *scriptor*: 'Aliquis enim scribit aliena, nihil addendo vel mutando; et iste mere dicitur scriptor. Aliquis scribit aliena, addendo sed non de suo; et iste compilator dicitur. Aliquis scribit et aliena et sua, sed aliena tanquam principalia, et sua annexa ad evidentiam; et iste dicitur commentator, non auctor. Aliquis scribit et sua et aliena, sed sua tanquam principalia, aliena tanquam annexa ad confirmationem; et talis debet dicitur auctor'. (Proemii qu. 4, conclusio, dans *S. Bonaventurae opera omnia*, 1882-1902, I, pp. 14-5, cité d'après Alastair Minnis, 'Discussions of "authorial role" and "literary form" in late-medieval scriptural exegesis, *Beiträge zur Geschichte der deutschen Sprache und Literatur*, 99 [1977], pp. 37-65 [44]). Cf. Minnis, *o.c.* [n. 47], p. 94. – Notons que Jean réserve le titre d' 'aucteurs' à ceux qui 'les anciens livres firent', lui-même se contentant d'être un 'recitierre' (éd. Lecoy, vv. 15188 ss.; cf. le v. 5688). Mais comme l'observent Minnis, *ibid.* [n. 47], p. 210 et Brown, *ibid.* [n. 47], p. 201, sous cette modestie se cache un écrivain parfaitement conscient de sa valeur.

49. On prolongera cette réflexion en se reportant aux belles pages de Fabienne Pomel, 'La Fonction-auteur dans le *Roman de la Rose* de Jean de Meun: le double jeu et la consécration de l'esquive', dans N. Jacques-Lefèvre et F. Regard (éd.), *Une histoire de la 'fonction-auteur' est-elle possible?* (Saint-Etienne, 2001), pp. 89-106.

50. L'évocation du songe se trouve en quelque sorte englobée dans la scène de la mise en écrit, même s'il y a ici contigüité et non inclusion. Le diptyque ne proposerait-il pas une forme d'*Assistenzporträt*, en intégrant l'auteur à l'action? Signalons dans ce contexte le frontispice intérieur de Paris, B.N. fr. 24392 (XVe s.), qui, au f° 33, montre, dans un premier registre 'maistre Jean' faisant le geste qui parle et, dans le second, le personnage

l'histoire que l'on s'apprête à nous relater. Seul le rouleau que le personnage tient dans la main droite[51] – réminiscence peut-être de celui que l'on tendait quelquefois aux évangélistes – semble rappeller discrètement son statut d'écrivain.

romanesque qui se promène. Le ms. olim Cockerel, Berès, et de Berny – actuellement, Paris, Les Enluminures – (daté de 1360-1365), situe à son premier f° le dormeur et l'écrivant dans le même cadre; au sujet du détail de cette composition, voir notre communication au colloque 'Bribes du moyen âge' (Cracovie, décembre 2002), 'Notes sur l'iconographie de trois mss. du *Roman de la Rose* dans des collections particulières', à paraître dans les *Mélanges Yvan Lepage* (Ottawa, 2006).

51. On songe évidemment à saint Alexis, dont le corps aurait été trouvé, serrant dans la main une "cartre" contenant son histoire (éd. Maurizio Perugi, TLF 529, Genève, 2000, v. 348ss.). Dans l'iconographie chrétienne, selon le *Rationale divinorum officiorum* de Guillaume Durand, les 'rotuli' dans les mains des patriarches et des prophètes marquent des connaissances encore lacunaires; les livres que tiennent les apôtres, le savoir parfait. (D'après Michael Camille, 'Visual signs of the sacred page: books in the "Bible moralisée"', *Word & Image,* 5 [1989], pp. 111-30, notamment p. 111). – On notera que le rouleau, en tant que support ancien, peut emblématiser l'antériorité de celui qui le porte; ou encore, comme c'est apparemment le cas dans le ms. Douce 195, le stade premier du processus créateur.

Figure 1
Le Roman de la Rose
Ms. Douce 195 f. 1ab

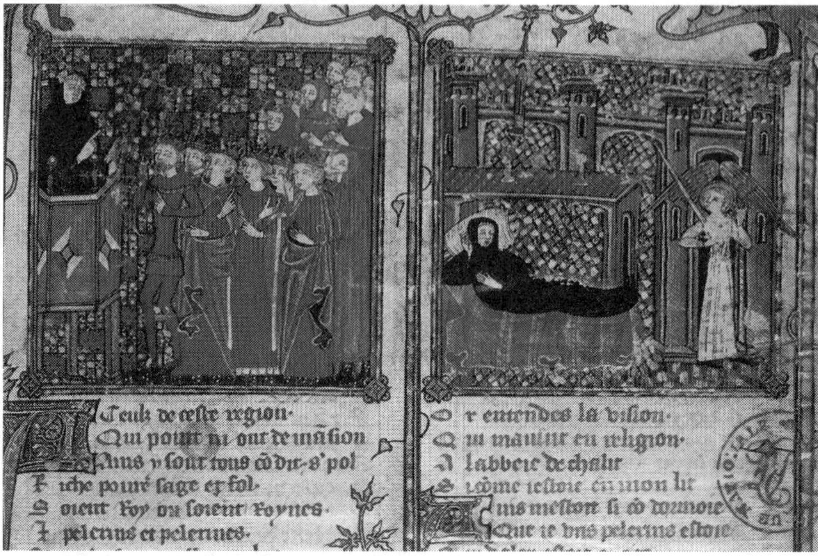

Figure 2
Guillaume de Digulleville, *Pèlerinage de vie humaine*
© Heidelberg, Universitätsbibliothek, Cod. pal. lat. 1969 f° 1

Figure 3
Le Roman de la Rose
© Cambridge, University Library, Gg 4.6 f. 30

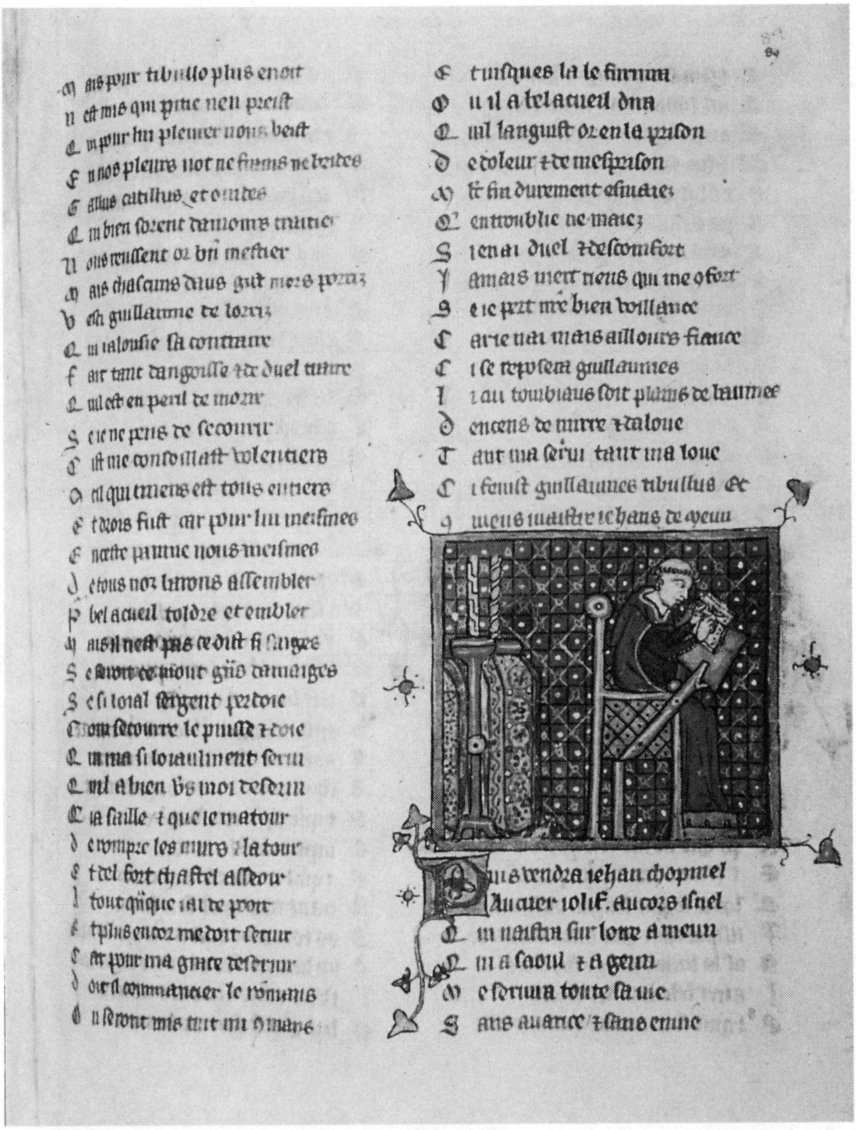

Figure 4
Le Roman de la Rose
olim Busch et Astor f° 89

Figure 5
Le Roman de la Rose
Paris, BnF fr. 380 f. 28v
Cliché Bibliothèque nationale de France, Paris

Figure 6
Le Roman de la Rose
Paris, BnF fr. 1569 f. 68
Cliché Bibliothèque nationale de France, Paris

Figure 7
Le Roman de la Rose
Paris, BnF fr. 24390 f. 29
Cliché Bibliothèque nationale de France, Paris

Figure 8
Le Roman de la Rose
Paris, BnF fr. 1569 f. 1
Cliché Bibliothèque nationale de France, Paris

Geert H.M. CLAASSENS

FROM *ARS* TO *AMOR*: MS. GENT, U.B., 444 AS A LABOUR OF LOVE

1. INTRODUCTION*

Books make great gifts. In fact, a book is always a double gift: an object, and a text. These days such a gift is a relatively straightforward affair, in the sense that there are plenty of books on offer, which is evidently not to say that giving a book is always a cheap option. Beautifully bound volumes printed on high-quality paper can cost an arm and a leg, not to mention the time and brainspace that has to be invested in selecting a book whose worth the recipient will be able to properly appreciate.

In the venerable tradition of the book as a double gift, the value of the gift obviously depends on the availability of books or texts. In the era of the *manuscriptum* a book is a capital present: not only because the material is expensive and the actual production – illuminated or not – may increase the value, but also because of the sheer amount of time invested by the scribe in composing the manuscript. In those cases where the present is offered by the scribe himself (or herself), it could be argued that the gift is even triple: the book as object and as text also represents an amount of congealed time extracted from the life of the giver and introduced into the economy of giving and receiving. The giver hopes the present may establish, improve or consolidate relations, whatever the ulterior motives may be. My contention is that when looking at them from this perspective, we might better understand the idiosyncrasies of a manuscript nowadays kept at the university library of Ghent, under shelfmark 444. I will argue that this manuscript is quite literally 'a labour of love' and as such is an awkward case by medieval standards. With reference to the title of the congress where this case was first presented – *Manuscripts in Transition* –, I would suggest that the aspect of 'transition' in this case is to be found in the intended function of the manuscript. In order to properly back up this hypothesis, I will first briefly sketch

* Geert H.M. Claassens is professor for Middle Dutch literature at the Katholieke Universiteit Leuven. I want to express my sincere gratitude to Katty De Bundel for her careful reading and valuable suggestions and to Ortwin De Graef for his generous and professional help in translating this text into English. If any shortcomings remain, that is certainly not due to their efforts.

some codicological and textual features of the manuscript. Subsequently I will present my arguments for assuming that Ghent 444 is a special codex, made by an otherwise unknown man for his beloved, a lady we very probably know by name.

2 Codicological aspects

Ms. Ghent, U.B., 444 is a paper manuscript containing 59 leaves.[1] It is rather small, the leaves measuring 140 by 105 mm. The watermark in the first four quires allows a safe dating around 1405.[2] This date is corroborated by a statement in the colophon on folium 51recto:

> Dit was ghedae*n* ghemaect met live
> Int jaer ons heere*n* XIIII ^C^ *ende* vive,
> Ten ingane van aprille.[3]
> [This was made with pleasure[4] in the year of Our Lord 1405, at the beginning of April.]

The manuscript contains five quires of six doubleleaves (*senio*), of which the last is incomplete with the eleventh leaf missing. This defect does not cause any loss of text: after folium 52 the manuscript contains only blank leaves.

The manuscript is written by a single hand in a *littera textualis cursiva* that does not strike one as exceptionally beautiful, but it is very legible [**see plate 1 (fol. 1r)**]. The rather frequent use of various types of abbreviations does not diminish the legibility, but justifies the conjecture that it was meant to be read individually, rather than being read aloud.[5]

1. This description is based on J. Reynaert, *Catalogus van de Middelnederlandse handschriften in de bibliotheek van de Rijksuniversiteit te Gent.* Dl. I*: De handschriften verworven vóór 1852* (Ghent, 1984), p. 111-113, with some additions of my own.

2. The watermark in the first four quires is an oxhead, corresponding with nr. IX, 402 in G. Piccard, *Die Ochsenkopfwasserzeichen* (Stuttgart, 1966). This watermark was current in the Low Countries and Germany between 1404 and 1408. In the last quire there is a watermark of a lion, which upto now cannot be identified. Comp. Reynaert, *Catalogus* [see note 1], p. 111.

3. Ghent, U.B., 444, fol. 51r, ll. 3-5. Because the existing editions of the texts (see below notes 10, 13, 15 and 16) are difficult to consult and, moreover, outdated and not without flaws, I quote here and elsewhere in this article from the manuscript. The following conventions were observed: the use of the allographs *v, w, u, i, j* as well as the capitals has been adapted to modern standards; abbreviations have been expanded and marked with italics, Roman numerals are printed in small capitals (skipping possible markers from the manuscript), a punctuation to facilitate reading has been inserted.

4. The words *met live* are ambiguous: they can be understood as 'with pleasure' in a more general sense, but also as the rather more pregnant 'with love'.

5. Some of the abbreviations used are very common: a.o. the superscript stroke for *m* and *n*, an apostrophe for the combination of vowel + *r* (or *r* + vowel), or *en* with super-

The mise-en-page is plain and simple: one column of generally 21 lines. The structure of the text is highlighted with paragraph signs in red, in combination with a red initial on the first folium and 25 lombard letters in red.[6] Four of these lombard letters are decorated with a little flower in red, but there are no traces of further decoration. Because the flowers are perhaps something more than mere decoration, I will return to this aspect later. Another peculiarity might serve as a transition from the codicological description to the survey of the texts. If the opening initial and all of the lombard letters in the first text are read as a string, the following text appears:

MARGARHTAGODEVARTSEWTUDIM

If we put some blanks in this string and are willing to read the W on the twentieth position as a couple of U's and the H on the seventh postion as an E – and this can be justified by assuming a Flemish procope of the H in the word *Hets* – then an acrostichon shows itself: *Margareta Godevartse uut* (from) *Udim*. It seems to me that this otherwise unknown lady from a place called Udim (which as yet remains unidentified[7]) is to be justly considered the addressee of text ánd manuscript. This piece of information, which has been noticed before,[8] lends a personal character to the manuscript, which comes even stronger to the fore when we take a closer look at the texts it contains.

3. Textual aspects

According to modern standards Ghent 444 should be classified as a miscellany: the codex contains more than one text and was from the out-

script stroke for the coordinating conjunction *ende*. In addition to these some less common abbreviations were used to shortcut the endgroup *-en* in – mainly – nouns and verbs.

6. The initial on fol. 1r is only slightly bigger than the 25 following lombard letters, which are two lines high.

7. Perhaps it is the place Udem in the Kleve region, mentioned in the *Klevisches Heberegister* under the year 1318? Comp. Mieke van Doorn en Willem Kuiper, 'Der vrouwen heimlicheid', in: *Spektator,* 6 (1976-1977), p. 539-551, especially p. 545.

8. See K. Deleu, 'Kanttekeningen bij de lectuur van "Der vrouwen heimelijkheid". Dichtwerk der XIVe eeuw", in: *Album Prof. Dr Frank Bauer. Den jubilaris bij zijn zestigsten verjaardag aangeboden door collega's, vakgenoten en oud-leerlingen* (Antwerpen/Brussel/Gent/Leuven, 1948), vol. I, p. 176-181 and Van Doorn en Kuiper, 'Der vrouwen heimlicheid' [see note 7], p. 545. But whereas Van Doorn en Kuiper interpret *Godevartse* as the surname of *Margareta,* Deleu wants to interpret it as the Christian name of the 'sender', the poet-scribe. His argument is not very convincing and involves an intervention in the text, which is unnecessary if *Godevartse* is understood as a surname.

set meant to be a codicological unity.[9] Four separate texts can be distinguished, which I will briefly introduce now.

The first text, the longest of the four, covers folios 1 recto up to and including 44 recto, and is known under the title *Der vrouwen heimelijcheit* [The secrets of women].[10] It is a short gynaecological treatise. In 1.784 rhyming couplets many aspects of pregnancy and procreation are covered, including conception, the evolution of the embryo in the womb, the influence of the planets on the growing child, etcetera. It surely is not an original Middle Dutch treatise, even though it is not yet clear whether an Old French or a Latin text underlies it.[11] Yet it is evident that the text belongs to a widespread European tradition of gynaecological treatises, of which the anonymous – but often attributed to Albertus Magnus – *De secretis mulierum* and Thomas of Cantimpré's *De natura rerum* are the most important Latin representatives.[12]

The second text, covering folios 44 verso up to and including a part of 51 recto, is to be considered as a very short physiognomical treatise in 277 rhyming couplets, completed with a colophon of ten lines, also in rhy-

9. I refer to the definition of 'miscellany' in Thom Mertens, 'Richtlijnen voor de uitgave van Middeleeuwse Verzamelhandschriften uit de Nederlanden', in: M.-J. Govers (eindred.), *Het Geraardbergse handschrift. Hs. Brussel, Koninklijke Bibliotheek Albert I, 837-845* (Hilversum, Verloren, 1994), p. 173-191, especially p. 178. That it is indeed a miscellany can be inferred from the place of the colophon at the end of the second text and from the fact that an initial was used to open the first text, a formal marker that does not appear in the other texts. The presence of a number of blank leaves at the end of the manuscript is another indication that it is a miscellany that was poorly estimated: the colophon indicates that the first two texts were part of the original plan, the last two seem to be mere fillers. But see also below, note 48.

10. Edition in Philippe Blommaert, *Der vrouwen heimelykheid,* Maetschappy der Vlaemsche Bibliophilen, 2e serie, no. 3 (Gent, Annoot-Braeckman, 1848). This edition is outdated and because of the mistakes in the line numbering it is hardly useful as a reference. A new edition is urgently needed. The Middle Dutch texts has been translated in Modern Dutch (L. Elaut, *Der vrouwen heimlicheid. Een middeleeuws gedicht over gynekologie en verloskunde.* Gent etc.: Story-Scientia, 1974), but it is an unreliable translation; see Van Doorn en Kuiper, 'Der vrouwen heimlicheid' [see note 7], p. 540-542.

11. The text itself refers to a Latin source: *Alsoe alst int Lattijn es bescreven, Sal ict in Dietsche voert vertrecken nu* [*as it is written in Latin, so I shall tell you in Dutch*] (fol. 1v, ll. 37-38). Nevertheless it is very doubtful that the Middle Dutch text is an immediate translation of a Latin sourcetext. Comp. M. van Doorn, *Der vrouwen heimelicheid* (Amsterdam, 1981), [unpublished MA thesis], p. 44-59, where strong similarities between the Middle Dutch texts and some Old French counterparts are pointed out.

12. On the *Secretis mulierum* tradition see Brigitte Kusche, 'Zur "Secreta mulierum"-Forschung', in: *Janus,* 62 (1975), p. 103-123. See also Margaret Schleissner, 'Secreta mulierum', in: *Verfasserlexikon*[2], VIII, cols 986-993. Both scholars clearly indicate that the Latin as well as the vernacular *Secretis mulierum* tradition is in need of further research: the authorship has not been satisfactorily established and there is a dire lack of adequate editions, necessary to establish the relationships among the textual representatives.

ming couplets.[13] There might be a relationship between this treatise and a text from 1351, which treats the same matters in prose,[14] but the exact background of the rhymed physiognomy is as yet not sufficiently established.

The third text, on folio 51 recto up to and including a part of 52 recto, is a mini treatise on the sacrament of the eucharist in 40 Middle Dutch verses with crossed rhymes.[15] It opens with a reference to *De civitate Dei* by Saint Augustine, but the exact relationship with this text has as yet not been established.

The last text, a riddle in eight rhyming couplets, can be found on folium 52 recto.[16] Through a circumscription in the form of a protracted question, the riddle asks for the name of a specific person, Caïn. Other known versions of it justify the assumption that it is a commonly known riddle.[17]

At first sight the manuscript seems to be nothing out of the ordinary. A plain and simple appearance, with four texts that might be considered a bit of a strange combination. But if we consider the last two texts – the mini treatise on the sacrament of the eucharist and the riddle – as mere pagefillers,[18] and assume that the first two texts were meant to be the core of the manuscript, then it could be characterized as a rather normal *artes*-manuscript. And as such it is known among scholars in the field of Middle Dutch literature.[19] In themselves, the four texts are indeed not that extraordinary: the first, second and last texts are also known from other manuscripts, but these I will not – for brevity's sake – discuss here.[20] It appears to me that all of the texts are copies made from other

13. Edited in Philippe Blommaert, *Oudvlaemsche gedichten der XIIe, XIIIe en XIVe eeuwen*, Vol. 2 (Gent, Hebbelynck, 1841), p. 60-63.

14. On this prose treatise see Jan Frans Willems, 'Over de Gelaetkunde, een tractaetjen van omtrent het jaer 1351', in: *Belgisch museum*, 3 (1839), p. 231-235.

15. Edition in Blommaert, *Oudvlaemsche gedichten* [see note 13], p. 64.

16. Edition in Blommaert, *Oudvlaemsche gedichten* [see note 13], p. 64.

17. Other copies of this riddle are to be found in mss. Brussels, K.B., 837-845, fol. 104r, and Brussels, K.B., 19.546, fol. 109r.

18. The mini treatise on the sacrament of the eucharist might be linked all the same to the two previous texts on the level of content, see below note 48.

19. Comp. Ria Jansen-Sieben, *Repertorium van Middelnederlandse artes-literatuur* (Utrecht, Hes, 1989), p. 301 (G220).

20. The other manuscripts of the riddle are mentioned above in note 17. *Der vrouwen heimelijcheit* and the physiognomy are preserved together in another complete mansucript: Staatsbibliothek Preussischer Kulturbesitz Berlin, ms. Germ. Oct. 187, possibly a derivative of Ghent 444, written in a dialect of the Lower Rhine area. See on this manuscript Heinrich Hoffmann von Fallersleben, *Horae Belgicae. Studia atque Opera Henrici Hoffmann Fallerslebensis*, 5 vols. (Vratislaviae, 1830-1845), vol. I, p. 120-121. It is to be noted that this manuscript does not contain the peculiarities discussed in this article: the lyrical intermezzi are lacking and the acrostichon is completely garbled (comp. Van Doorn, *Der vrouwen heimlicheid* [see note 11], p. 60 and 67), and the physiognomy is much shorter,

Middle Dutch manuscripts: even though these immediate sources are unknown; this hypothesis is corroborated by the observation that the first and second texts, *Der vrouwen heimelijcheit* and the physiognomical treatise, contain a number of textual anomalies that bear all the marks of typical scribal errors.[21]

4. A LABOUR OF LOVE?

But what arguments and indications might lead us to assume that this manuscript is not that ordinary after all?

The first indication I would like to draw your attention to, is the encoded conclusion of *Der vrouwen heimelijcheit*. On folium 44 recto we find below the column an unusual combination of letters [**see plate 2, fol. 44r**]:

EXPLKCKT SFCRFTXM MXLKFRKS

This rather simple case of encryption can easily be deciphered as *Explicit secretum mulieris*.[22] The use of a code is not in itself remarkable here,[23] what *is* arresting is the use of the singular! In the Latin tradition we usually find a plural, *De secretis mulierum*, and a related Middle Dutch text, belonging to the tradition but not another copy of *Der vrouwen heimelijcheit*, is concluded with *Expliciunt secreta mulierum*.[24] If in the Ghent manuscript *Der vrouwen heimelijcheit* is concluded with 'Here ends the secret of the woman', one is easily tempted to ask: 'which

only 177 verses. A third manuscript is known from a catalogue entry: A. Sanderus, *Bibliotheca Belgica Manuscripta, sive, elenchus universalis codicum mss. In celebrioribus belgii* (Brussels, 1651), vol. I, p. 286, mentions a "Liber, cui Titulus, secreta Mulierum, Versibus Rythmicis Teutonicis, in Membrana, Autoris anonymi, in 8". Of this manuscript, called the Ms. Bultel after its last known possessor, Joannes Gislenus Bultel of Ieper, no trace has been found yet.

21. The texts are plagued with crippled verses and garbled rhymes. An additional argument to assume an earlier circulation of *Der vrouwen heimelijcheit* might be inferred from the fact that Petrus Naghel, previously known as the 'Bibel Translator of 1360', refers to this text in his *historybible*. On this matter see Maria Sherwood-Smith, 'God and Gynaecology: *Women's Secrets* in the Dutch *Historiebijbel van 1360*', in: *German Life and Letters*, 50 (1997), p. 390-402.

22. On the deciphering of the code see Van Doorn en Kuiper, 'Der vrouwen heimlicheid' [see note 7], p. 543.

23. The use of a code might be explained by simple prudence: as the text contains matters that are shrouded in taboos, the scribe might want to conceal the title in this way.

24. See Van Doorn en Kuiper, 'Der vrouwen heimlicheid' [see note 7], p. 543. They refer to *Der mannen ende vrouwen heimelijcheit*.

woman?' Is it the woman in general or Margareta Godevartse from Udim, the lady from the acrostichon, in particular?

The impression that the text is explicitly aimed at a very specific person is strongly enhanced by the way in which the 24 'chapters' of *Der vrouwen heimelijcheit* are concluded. Marked with a paragraph sign and the use of monorhyme, lyrical intermezzi were inserted between all of the chapters. These intermezzi are in no way connected with the contents of the gynaecological treatise, on the contrary. The writer interrupts the course of the treatise to vent his lamentations concerning his beloved and her behaviour towards him, as the following, arbitrarily chosen example can illustrate:

> Die goede es mi worde*n* wreet,
> Dien ic hier desen dienst sende.
> Ic weet wel d*at* ic noeit en kende
> Haers ghelijc van orde tende;
> Sij hout mi altoes in allende.[25]
> [The good one, to whom I offer this service, has become cruel towards me. I am sure that I have never ever met her equal; she keeps me constantly in misery.]

Placed in a single line we could read these lyrical intermezzi as a love story, in which a poet bewails the ups and downs of his 'affair'. These intermezzi do not occur in the Latin tradition, nor in the other Middle Dutch version of the text.[26] We could possibly assume that these intermezzi were meant to cloak a subject matter normally shrouded in taboos,[27] much as the traditional prologue – which, incidentally, does

25. Ghent, U.B. 444, fol. 20v, ll. 4-8. The words *van orde tende* in l. 7 I read as a transposition of *van ende torde* (meaning 'from one side to the other, completely') *causa metri*.

26. An exception must be made for an interesting fragment, Ms. Brussels, K.B., 19.571, consisting of two double leaves in parchment from the second half of the 14th century, forming the remnants of a text known as a *Physiologus*. See on this Jansen-Sieben, *Repertorium* [see note 19], p. 261-262 (B820), who pointed out that in some way or another these fragments are connected with the text of *Der vrouwen heimelijcheit*, even containing the same intermezzi. Indeed, the connection with Ghent 444 has not been sufficiently clarified yet, but I doubt that the presence of a single comparable passage – indeed comparable with one of the intermezzi – in a fragment of limited dimensions is enough to conclude that there is a straightforward, concrete link. But it does support the possibility that lyrical intermezzi were a part of the conventional presentation of this type of *artes*-texts (but, nota bene, the fragment mentioned above does not contain more text that corresponds with *Der vrouwen heimelijcheit*). Jansen-Sieben also mentions the fragments Oudenaarde SA (*idem*, p. 422 (O20)), which I will not bring into account here, because only a 19th-century copy is preserved and the close similarity from these with the above mentioned Brussels fragments opens the possibility that we are dealing here with an unfortunate doublure in the textual history.

27. That possibility is explicitly brought to the fore in the previous note.

occur in other versions – seems to do in rather courtly phrases. But in my view the odds are that these intermezzi indeed should be understood as outpourings of a highly personal nature, because besides these shorter intermezzi – none of them counts more than twelve lines – the text contains one non-lyrical interruption of considerable size.

On the fifth line of folium 17 recto starts a long lamentation of 65 verses in which the poet deplores his vicissitudes: not only is he troubled by the uncertainties vis-à-vis his beloved, he also seems to suffer from serious bodily disorders. Elsewhere I have argued that this lamentation – which is completely out of tune with the gynaecological treatise – in all probability should be interpreted as an aside of an autobiographical nature.[28] This interpolation in the treatise is, as far as I know, unique in Middle Dutch literature. Even if we would consider it to be an intervention of a narrator-in-love, comparable to the one in the Old French chivalric romance *Parthonopeu de Blois* or its Middle Dutch translation, then we should add immediately that in *Der vrouwen heimelijcheit* the gap between the narrator's intervention and the context is much too wide to consider this combination as a meaningful literary game.[29] This personal outpouring is a mixture of hope and despair, partly expressed in the traditional courtly idiom, partly expressed in new, personal, creative phrasing, but always in stark contrast with the discursive context of the treatise.

Now I want to return to the four flowers drawn in margine in the manuscript. Mieke van Doorn and Willem Kuiper investigated the *Der vrouwen heimelijcheit* some years ago and they linked these flowers in a very ingenious way to the female hormonal cycle. The four flowers symbolize the four days of menstruation in the cycle, as the text itself seems to admit on folium 3 recto:

> Die menstrua dat zijn de bloemen
> Die telker maent voert comen.[30]
> [The *menstrua* are the flowers that every month reappear.]

28. Comp Geert H.M. Claassens, 'Een dichter lijdt. De verborgen liefdesgeschiedenis in *Der vrouwen heimelijcheit* (Gent U.B., 444)', in: Karel Porteman, Werner Verbeke, Frank Willaert (eds.), *Tegendraads genot. Opstellen over de kwaliteit van middeleeuwse teksten* (Leuven, Peeters, 1996), p. 93-102.

29. On the narrator-in-love as a literary device see An Faems, *Hiernamaels seldijt bat verstaen. Vertellerscommentaar in de Middelnederlandse ridderepiek* (Leuven, 2002), [unpublished Ph.D. thesis], p. 541-570. On p. 558-561 she presents Ghent, U.B., 444 as another case of a narrator-in-love. It is obvious that I do not agree with her on this point.

30. Ghent, U.B., 444, fol. 3r, ll. 1-2.

Refering to the days of menstruation with the concept 'flowers' is not unique,[31] but the graphic depiction of it [**see plate 3, fol. 10r**] – if it is indeed that[32] – by means of flowers in margine does appear, for the time being, to be unique. This fact seems to point out a rather idiosyncratic processing of an existing tradition, and the same goes for some other, possibly symbolic features of the manuscript which I will not fully discuss here for brevity's sake.[33]

This idiosyncratic processing of traditional materials, which aims at establishing a more personal, intimate communication, appears perhaps even stronger in the ambivalence that *Der vrouwen heimelijcheit* shows concerning the intended audience. Some phrasings can only be understood if a male audience is presupposed,[34] others are clearly meant for a female audience in general,[35] but there are some passages in which an individual women is addressed:

31. Van Doorn en Kuiper, 'Der vrouwen heimlicheid' [see note 7], p. 543, mention a passage in a related treatise, *Der mannen ende vrouwen heimelijcheit*, that gives the same reference, but in a more elaborate form.

32. Perhaps this is nothing but playfulness of the scribe: the position of the flowers [on fol. 10r, l. 4; fol. 28v, l. 11; fol. 36v, l. 9, and fol. 38r, l. 10] shows no meaningful pattern. The flowers do not mark passages with a significant connection to each other, and the lombard letters that are marked in this way – T, T, T, and R – produce no meaningful combination. And, moreover, it is not clear whether the manuscript contains four or five of these 'flowers': on fol. 4r, l. 14 there appears a decorated lombard letter, but is it decorated with a flower comparable to the other flowers?

33. Van Doorn en Kuiper, 'Der vrouwen heimlicheid' [see note 7], p. 543-545, link the four flowers to a numerological interpretation of the *explicit* (see above), in which according to them appear the numbers 9 – reference to 9 months of pregnancy – and 24 which in combination with the flowers should be understood as a reference to the 24 fertile days of the hormonal cycle. At the same place they draw attention to the very simple but remarkable decoration of the opening initial M, the lombard letter E in the middle of the text and the last lombard letter M. They 'read' the E as an overturned M and interprete the three marked M's as a 'hommage aan Maria, de *parel* der vrouwen, aan Margaretha van Antiochië, een bijzonder populaire heilige die als noodhelpster zwangere vrouwen tijdens de bevalling bijstond, en niet in de laatste plaats aan Margareta [Godevartse, GC] zelf' (p. 545). I consider it plausible that these graphic markers once more refer to the name in the acrostichon; Van Doorn and Kuiper give no further arguments as to why these markers *necessarily* refer to the triade 'Mary', 'Margaret of Antioch' and 'Margareta Godevartse'.

34. See as an example Ghent, U.B., 444, fol. 31v, ll. 13-21. In this passage a connection is made between the position of the semen in the womb and the sex of the child, arguing that a man can control that proces and actually choose the sex of the child. In l. 19, *So sal dijn zaet ter rechter ziden varen*, the word *dijn* (your) implies that a male audience is addressed: 'thus your seed will flow into the right side [of the womb, GC]'.

35. See as an example Ghent, U.B., 444, fol. 37v, l. 11-38r, l. 4: in these lines the poet subsequently warns men ánd women for the dangers of having sex during menstruation. Of course the text abounds with places that can be understood as addressing women in general: women is the subject of the treatise.

En docht u, vrouwe, niet mesdaen,
Ic soude u leeren, sonder waen,
Herde wel heefmoeder wesen.[36]
[If you, my lady, do not think it a misdemeanour, then I would surely teach you how to be a very good midwife.]

This indefiniteness concerning the intended audience can to some extent be explained by the evolution of this kind of treatise: in the Latin tradition the dissemination of medical knowledge was predominantly the domain of men; from the moment these texts were translated into the vernacular, women – the party most involved – appear as a target group.[37] The address to an individual woman could be explained from this perspective – the more so because this lady has sometimes been put on the stage in the third person singular! – but could on account of the other indications, especially the acrostichon, equally be interpreted as an address to a concrete female person.

We could discard all these peculiarities as mumbojumbo, as the putting up of a smoke screen around a text that delivers exceedingly intimate details concerning human – and especially female – sexuality. But this can only be maintained if we were to confine our examination to the gynaecological treatise. Which we should not, as I hope to demonstrate. In *Der vrouwen heimelijcheit* the poet interrupts his discourse on the relationship between humoral disposition and different human complexions:

Want ic sal scriven in corter uren
Gemeenlijc alder complexien natuere;
Hoe men an elken mensche mach kinnen
Wat complexien hi hevet binnen,
Oft wat natueren, alsmen hem ansiet.[38]
[Because I will very soon describe in general terms the nature of all complexions; how one can judge from the outward appearance of a person how his inner disposition is and of what nature, just by looking at him.]

These lines are followed by the extensive autobiographical aside mentioned above (see p. 108). But concluding this aside the poet resumes his discourse with the following words:

Om dat complexie ter ander stat
Hier na sal volgen vele bat,
Iet te segghene van haere naturen,

36. Ghent, U.B., 444, fol. 21v, ll. 1-3.

37. On the indefiniteness of the intended audience in *Der vrouwen heimelijcheit* see Dieuwke E. van der Poel, 'Mijn lieve joncfrouwe heeft mi gebeden iet te dichtene', in: *Nederlandse letterkunde*, 1 (1996), p. 249-260.

38. Ghent, U.B., 444, fol. 16v, l. 20-17r, l. 4.

So willic nu te deser uren
Al hier seggen met corten worden
Vandes kindes gheborden.[39]
[Because in another place, further on, there will be ample space to tell something about the nature of different complexions, I will continue now, briefly, about childbirth.]

The first proleptic reference could be interpreted as an announcement of delay within the limits of *Der vrouwen heimelijcheit*, the second on the other hand can only relate to the next text in the manuscript, the physiognomical treatise![40] And if we take a closer look at this latter, we come across an impure couplet which seems to establish a connection with the previous text, the gynaecological treatise:

Bidt voer den ghenen die dit screef
Dat hi verwinnen moet zijn leet.[41]
[Pray for the one who wrote this, that he may overcome his grief.]

Do these words refer to the autobiographical aside in *Der vrouwen heimelijcheit* in which the poet laments his physical suffering as well as his mental distress *mit schönklingender Klage*? This is certainly not improbable, even if only because the alternative assumption that we would be faced here with a fairly conventional scribal request is rendered unlikely by the specificity of the phrasing ('that he may overcome his grief' is not a commonplace in scribal pleas) as well as by its position in the text (as a rule, such pleas appear at the end of a text or a collection of texts).

And this is not the only indication that the physiognomy was adapted by the same person who adapted *Der vrouwen heimelijcheit*. In the physiognomy too we find interventions in which a specific person is addressed. The prologue of this text, for example, addresses the beloved immediately, in the second person singular. Compared to the prologue of *Der vrouwen heimelijcheit*, which evokes the addressee in the third person singular, this is an intensification of the directness. The intrusion of the personal in the physiognomy appears even more clearly at the end of the treatise, where the poet in a digression of 55 verses – on a total of 277 verses – discusses his own character, informing the reader that he has subdued his inclination to lasciviousness by studying the philosophers.[42]

39. Ghent, U.B., 444, fol. 18v, ll. 9-14.

40. That a proleptic reference to the physiognomy is meant here can with certainty be inferred from the fact that in *Der vrouwen heimelijcheit* no more attention is given to the matter of complexions at all.

41. Ghent, U.B., 444, fol. 50v, ll. 18-19.

42. The opening of this digression is revealing: *Lieve kint, dats waerheit (...)* [Dear child, it is the truth (...)] (Ghent, U.B., 444, fol. 49v, l. 18) evokes the addressee in a very personal way.

But he also 'implicates' the lady he adores in a subtle way: he announces that he will reveal her complexion, but for discretion's sake he will not go into details. In this game of 'I will tell you, but I wont tell you' he reveals her name:

> Nu hoert welc haer name zij:
> Si es gheheeten Sangwinna,
> Na dat ic mi best versta.[43]
> [Now listen to what her name is: she is called Sangwinna to the best of my understanding.]

Sangwinna is, of course, not the same as Margareta, but the immediate context of this revelation – a treatise on the connections between humoral disposition, outward appearance and character – justifies a metaphorical reading of this name.[44] His beloved one is of a sanguine nature, passionate, warm-blooded, but:

> Wat van h*aer* ghescreven es,
> D*at* willic haer alleene sc*ri*ven.[45]
> [What is written about her, I want to write for her alone]

5. Conclusion

Some of my arguments have been only briefly presented, some of my observations are not entirely new. Especially Van Doorn and Kuiper drew attention to the enciphered conclusion of *Der vrouwen heimelijcheit*, to the flowers in margine and the possible use of numerological symbolism. But their conclusion was that *Der vrouwen heimelijcheit* circulated in two distinct versions: a didactic version and a lyrical version.[46] The Ghent manuscript, in their view, is a representative of the lyrical version *in optima forma*, the other manuscript represents the didactic version.[47] The possibility that the Ghent manuscript contains a unique, personal, individualised version of *Der vrouwen heimelijcheit*, turning this treatise touching on labour into a touching labour of love for a single, specific person – Margareta Godevartse –, that possibility was not contemplated by

43. Ghent, U.B., 444, fol. 50v, ll. 9-11.

44. Faems, *Hier namaels seldijt bat verstaen* [see note 29], p. 560-561 already pointed out that this naming is ambiguous: the poet presents the complexion of his beloved as if it were her Christian name.

45. Ghent, U.B., 444, fol. 50v, ll. 13-14.

46. See Van Doorn en Kuiper, 'Der vrouwen heimlicheid' [see note 7], p. 549.

47. The other manuscript Van Doorn and Kuiper are referring to is Berlin, SPK, Ms. Germ. Oct 187, discussed above in note 20.

them. As will no doubt have become clear from the above, I am strongly in favor of this possibility. The more so because the physiognomy is adapted in the same way as *Der vrouwen heimelijcheit*.[48] Or should we assume a lyrical and a didactic version for this text too?

If my argument is at all sound and we may indeed assume that the anonymus crafted the Ghent manuscript as a gift with which he hoped to win the favour of Margareta Godevarste from Udim, the question remains whether Margareta was susceptible to this kind of gift and whether our scribe's strategy was successful. In the absence of external evidence, we can obviously never be sure, yet for our poet – if he deserves that name – it may just have worked. In the lyrical intermezzi we can follow the course of his wooing, and if we may take his word at face value, than he finally reached his goal. Here are the last words of his final digression:

> (…) van miere liever vrouwen
> Die mi ghetroest heeft met trouwen:
> Sij seide, sij en mochte niet anscouwen
> Dat ic bevaen ben met rouwen.[49]
> [(…) of my beloved lady, who consoled me faithfully. She said, she could not bear seeing me caught up in grief.]

48. Here I want to suggest, with cautious reservation, that the mini treatise on the sacrament of the eucharist too was added to the texts in the manuscript for 'personal reasons'. The treatise very explicitly states that the sacrament of the eucharist brings forgiveness for all sins that ensue from *lichte spraken* [frivolous talk]. And because our poet on several occasions in the previous texts showed his fear of being judged on his utterances and outpourings, we might, perhaps, consider this aspect of the mini treatise to be a significant link with the previous texts.

49. Ghent, U.B., 444, fol. 43v, ll. 3-6.

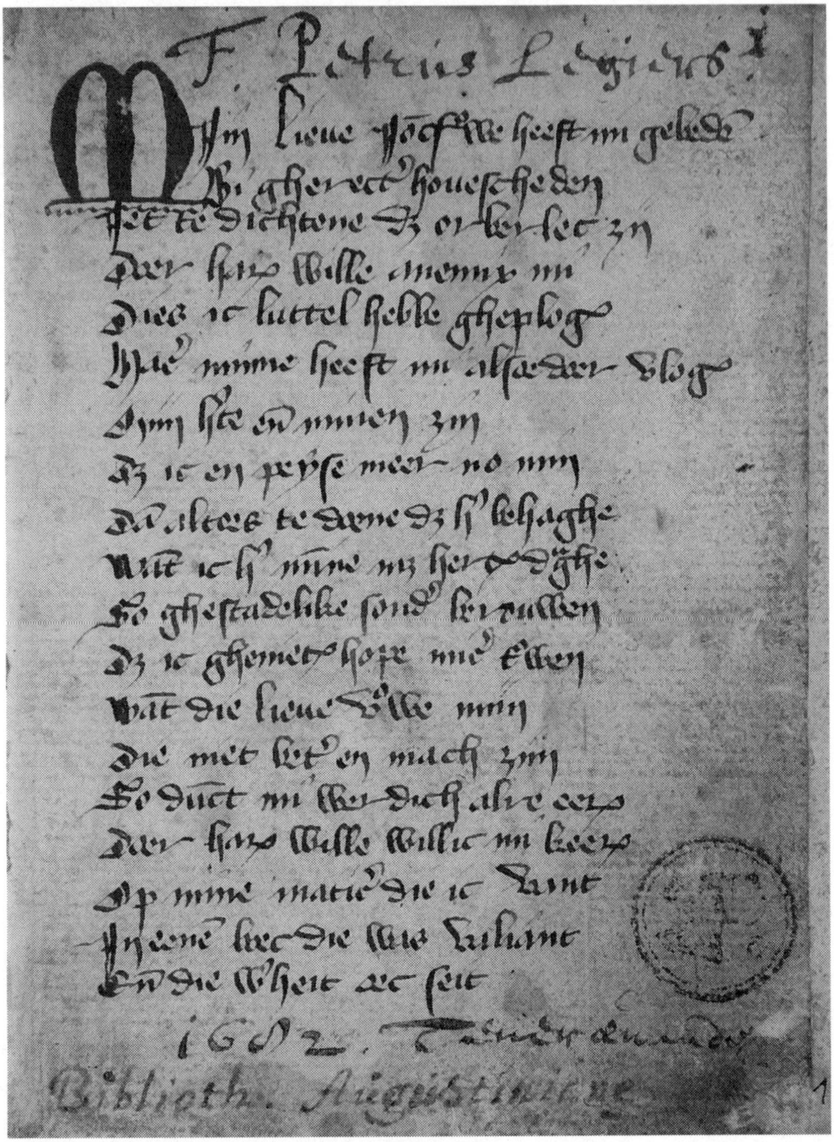

Plate 1
Ghent, Universiteitsbibliotheek, Ms. 444, fol. 1r

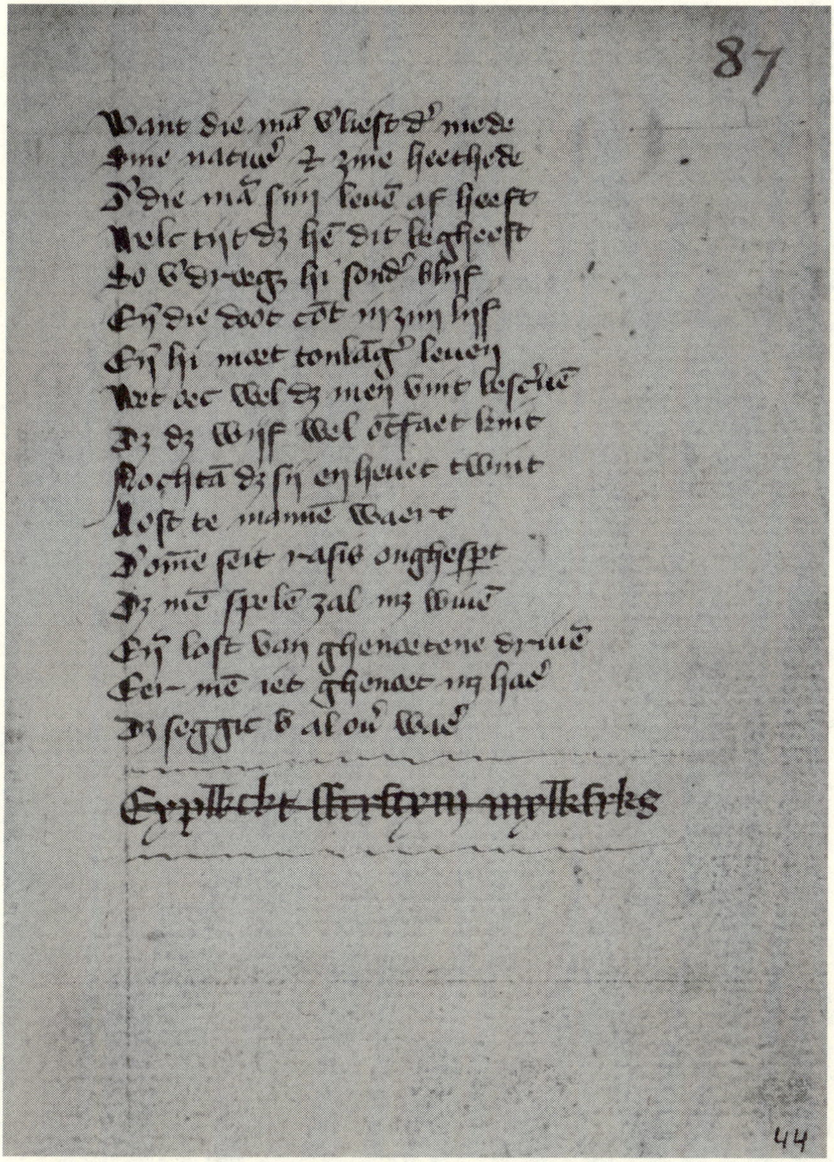

Plate 2
Ghent, Universiteitsbibliotheek, Ms. 444, fol. 44[r]

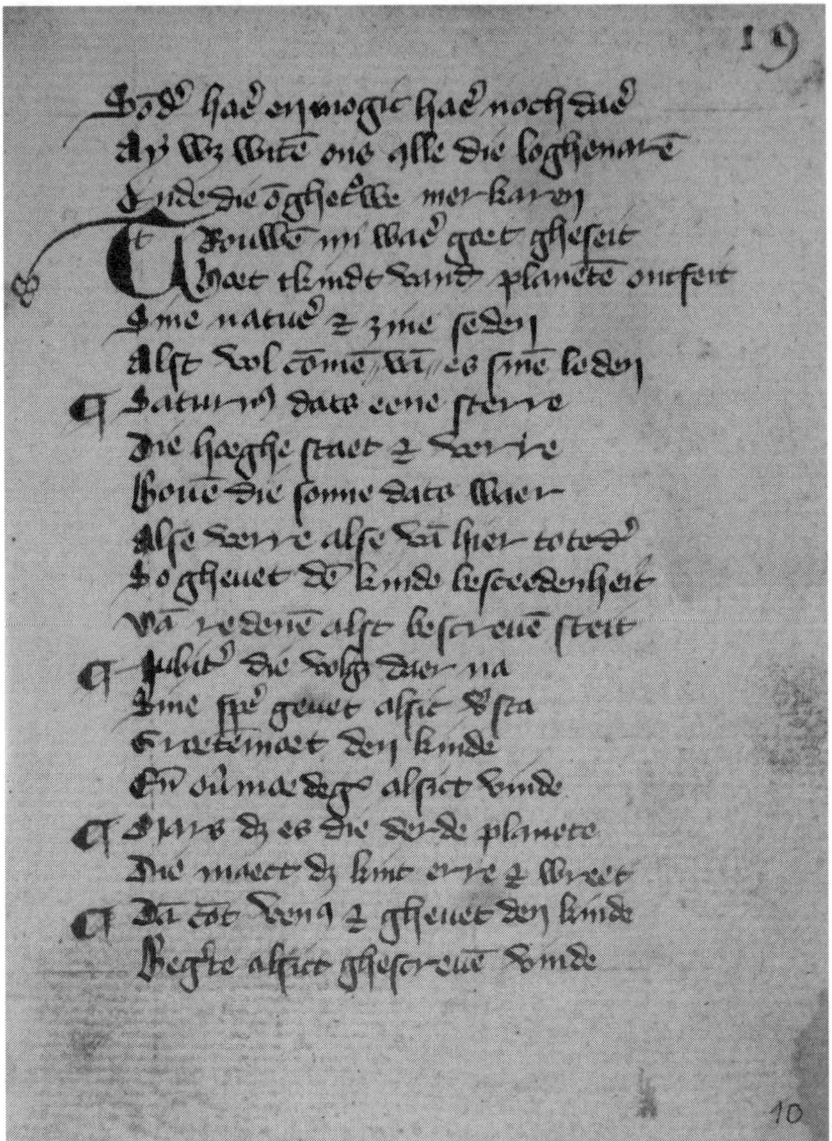

Plate 3
Ghent, Universiteitsbibliotheek, Ms. 444, fol. 10r

Katty DE BUNDEL

A FEMALE SCRIBE REVEALS HERSELF: THE MAKING OF MS. LEUVEN, THEOL. 842S

1. Introduction*

Although research on the position of women in the literary cultural landscape of the Middle Ages has increased considerably in recent years, a specific aspect of this position is still underexposed. Female patronage and reception have received a great deal of attention, but when we speak of the direct involvement of women in the total production of a book – writing/translating, scribal work and commissioning – a great deal of work remains to be done, especially for the Dutch speaking regions. This task is hampered by a lack of direct data, which forces us to weigh and interpret as much as possible all available information from manuscripts and archival material.

I would like to make a contribution to this research by presenting a case based on a manuscript kept in the library of the Faculty of Theology at Leuven University under signature 842S.[1] As is evident from the colophon, this manuscript was commissioned by Sister Margriete Swilden and Sister Clare Baerts and was completed in 1437:

> Dezen bouc was ghescreve*n* en*de* vulhent met der gracie Gods int jaer Ons Heren MCCCC en*de* XXXVII den XIsten dach in october, ende heeft ghedaen scriven ende hoort toe zuster Margriete Swilden en*de* zuster Clare Baerts, ten laetsten live va*n* he*m* beden.[2]
> [This book was written and completed by the grace of God in the year 1437 on the eleventh day of October by order of Sister Magriete Swilden and Sister Clare Baerts, and belongs to them until they both should die.]

* I would like to thank Geert Claassens for his suggestions and critical remarks when writing this article, and Miltiades Papatheophanes and David Johnson for their generous help with the English translation.

1. This manuscript has been known for some time, but there has been no in-depth research yet into the codicological and content-related aspects of it. See De Bruin 1977-1978, p. 150, De Bruin 1980, p. VII, and De Vreese 1931, p. XXVI-XXVII. In Appendix II A of the latter work, p. 111-123, De Vreese has published a critical edition of some fragments from the text (fol. 3ra-3va and 5ra-12va).

2. Leuven, Theol. 842S, fol. 2v. I refer here and elsewhere in this article to the manuscript itself; quotations from the text adhere to the following conventions: the allographs *v, w, u, i, j* have been standardised; capitalisation has been adapted to modern use; abbreviations have been expanded and put in italics; Roman numerals are reproduced in small capitals (without any markers); grammatically reliable punctuation has been used. Furthermore, I refer to the modern numbering in pencil in the manuscript. Unfortunately, folio 73 has been numbered twice, so, if necessary, the second folio 73 will be referred to as 73bis.

In what follows, I will present the Leuven manuscript as a codicological object and subsequently discuss its contents and provenance. The core of this article concentrates on the – in all likelihood – female figure behind this manuscript, whose contours are dimly perceived through some features of the codex and of the translation and adaptation technique used.

2. Description of the manuscript

What kind of book did Sisters Clare Baerts and Margriete Swilden commission? The codex numbers 150 parchment leaves of varying quality.[3] The leaves measure on average 150-152 x 208-211 millimetres, but it is obvious that the pages were trimmed during a subsequent rebinding.[4] The text is laid out in two columns of 31 lines each, and was written and corrected by one hand in a *littera textualis*.[5] There is a contemporary opening numbering in Roman numerals on the verso of the leaves, to which the table of contents on folio 1r-2r refers. The manuscript is decorated in a modest, functional way: embellished initials and rubric work are intended first and foremost to make the hierarchically arranged articulation of the text graphically more explicit. The decorated initials are set at the highest level of the text articulation. The first text opens on folio 3r with a beautifully embellished initial over five lines [see plate 1]. The individual chapters of the text are marked with initials over two or three lines. At a lower level (paragraphs and sentences), the text is articulated by means of paragraph signs (alternatingly in red and blue) and with capitals highlighted with rubric. Chapter headings are underlined in red and marked by a preceding paragraph sign, alternatingly in red and blue [see plate 2]. This hierarchical text articulation system was departed from

3. Two paper end leaves were added to the front and back of this original book-block when it was rebound.

4. This can be seen from the fact that on fol. 3r, a cut-off caption is still partly legible in the top margin. It cannot be ascertained whether this occured in the most recent rebinding. At present, the book-block is bound in a late 18th – early 19th century calfskin binding. The dating is based on the ex-libris affixed on the interior side of the front plate, which is attributable to Joseph Antoine Aybert Idesbalde van Huerne (1752-1844). The bookbinder himself is unknown, but it is plausible that Van Huerne commissioned the rebinding of the manuscript. For the identification of the ex-libris, see Linnig 1910, p. 215-216. It is there indicated that the year in which Van Huerne died is unknown, but on the frontispiece of Dullaert and Vandervin 1844, 31 May 1844 is given as the date of death.

5. Quite a number of corrections have been made in the text, which is not to say that the text was carefully checked and corrected. The corrections appear to be by the same hand, with the script being smaller and the ink of a lighter colour.

in several cases to stress passages of important contents.[6] Miniatures are lacking in the manuscript, but there is a remarkable illustration with an obvious devotional function on folio 107v [see plate 3]. The text here speaks of the wound in the side of the crucified Christ, and this wound is imitated in the text column in the form of a *mandorla* surrounded by a crown of thorns and filled with a Latin inscription.[7]

3. Contents

According to the title shield on the spine of the new, modern binding, the codex contains the *Leven ons Heeren Jesus Christus* [Life of Our Lord Jesus Christ], but this title gives a false impression of the contents. The codex is actually a miscellany containing a number of religious Latin prose texts in Middle Dutch translation, sprinkled with Latin quotations.

Folios 3ra-140rb provide an incomplete translation/adaptation of the *Meditationes Vitae Christi*, formerly ascribed to the Franciscan Saint Bonaventure (1221-1273) but currently assumed, with some reservations, to be the work of his younger fellow monk Johannes de Caulibus.[8] The work can be characterised as an accessible meditation book that looks back on the most important moments of Christ's life and passion in a particularly evocative and affective style, and encourages the reader to empathise and suffer with Jesus.

On folios 140rb-141va follows an excerpt from a hitherto unidentified devotional text. The contents can be distinguished into two parts: initially, Christ is urging people to reconsider His passion, while the subsequent part presents a dialogue between God and Saint John the Evangelist on the effect of Jesus's intercession for God's forgiveness.

6. The chapters dedicated to the birth of Christ (fol. 15va), the passion of Christ (fol. 91rb), the first revelation of His resurrection (fol. 118va) and His Ascenscion (fol. 133ra) are marked with an initial executed in the same format and decoration level as the large opening initial on fol. 3ra. A possible explanation for this deviation is given in paragraph 5 of this article.

7. The following text is entered in the wound: *Hec* est *longitudo* et *latitudo* et *magnitudo vulneris lateris* Cristi, *monstrata relogiose* persone *a Deo*. Quicumque *devoto corde in die aspexerit, per die*m *securus manebit a mortali* peccato *et* omnium *venaliu*m *peccatoru*m *indulgencia*m pro*merebit*ur. This illustration, which pretends to represent the wound of Christ in life size, functions as an amulet: whoever looks on it, will be safeguarded from cardinal sin and will receive forgiveness for his pecadillos. The representation of the wound of Christ in this form, as well as the inscription, are highly conventional. Cf. Gougaud 1924, p. 223-227.

8. Published in Stallings-Taney 1997. On the authorship of the *Meditationes Vitae Christi* see Stallings-Taney 1997, p. IX-X, and De Bruin 1977-1978, p. 144. A brief introduction to this work is provided by De Bruin 1977-1978, p. 144-150.

The last folios, 141vb-149vb, contain a number of excerpts from the *Stimulus amoris maior* of pseudo-Bonaventure,[9] a work that may be qualified with the term 'passion mysticism'.[10]

Given the prevailing religious climate at the time, the choice of the texts is not remarkable in itself,[11] but their position in the late medieval vernacular literature of the Low Countries deserves a brief explanation. Both the *Meditationes Vitae Christi* and the *Stimulus amoris maior* enjoyed a rather limited transmission in Middle Dutch. It is remarkable that both texts in the Leuven manuscript are independent from the other known translations.[12] This independent status of the Leuven texts at once raises questions about the manuscript: is it an autograph or an apograph of an independent translation, or only a copy thereof? The manuscript itself offers no clear clues for resolving these questions. I do not exclude the possibility that this codex is the autograph of a translation made for the sisters, perhaps an apograph (the first clean copy of the translation), and I wish expressly to keep open the possibility that the translation and

9. The *Stimulus amoris maior* is an adaptation of the *Stimulus amoris minor*, written in the second half of the thirteenth century by Jacob of Milan (cf. Piana 1986). Although the *Stimulus amoris maior* is included in the *opera omnia* of St. Bonaventure (Peltier edition, 1864-1871, XII, p. 631-703) on account of the high content of Bonaventurian and pseudo-Bernardian passion mysticism, it is generally agreed today that this great Franciscan theologian was probably not the one who adapted and expanded the text of Jacob of Milan. See a propos Eisermann 1995.

10. I will deal with these excerpts in greater detail in paragraph 5, below.

11. For more on this, see Van Herwaarden 1981, p. 185-191.

12. In addition to this text in the Leuven manuscript, some other Middle Dutch translations of the *Meditationes Vitae Christi* have been transmitted. With one exception, more specifically the manuscript Bruges, Municipal Library, 408 (written in 1487), these are only very partial translations. The most complete survey of the surviving Middle Dutch (partial) translations of the *Meditationes Vitae Christi* is to be found in Stooker and Verbeij 1997, I, p. 204, n. 44, where the Leuven manuscript is not included. Furthermore, De Bruin 1977-1978, p. 50, n. 32, refers to two other Northern Netherlandish translations of this Latin text. The Leuven manuscript was not used for the translation in the Bruges manuscript, see De Vreese 1931, p. XXXVI-XXVII and De Bruin 1980, p. VII. Some excerpts from the Bruges manuscript have been published in De Vooys 1902, p. 137-139 and De Vreese 1931, p. 124-132 [Bijlage II B].

There is another Middle Dutch translation of the *Stimulus amoris maior* as well. Cf. Ruh 1956, p. 274 and 276-277 (the partial translation of the *Stimulus amoris maior* in the Leuven manuscript is not mentioned here). This translation was produced in 1387 – under the title *Den gaert der minnen* – by a very productive translator known as the 'Bible translator of 1360' (for more on the Bible translator of 1360, see De Bruin 1967-1971, Coun 1980, Kors 2000 and Kors 2003. A very brief introduction is provided by Claassens 2001). A comparison with his translation clearly shows that the same Latin source text was used, but that this existing translation was not used in the Leuven manuscript. For this comparison, I have used Peeters 2000 and Leyts 2000, who have printed the corresponding passages diplomatically after manuscript Brussels, Royal Library, 15.087-90.

writing work was carried out by one and the same person – even if I henceforth refer to this person by the term 'scribe'.

4. Dating and localisation

The aforementioned colophon ultimately provides little information about the origin of the manuscript: aside from the dating of the codex and the names of the otherwise unknown commissioners, we do not know very much. That the names of the commissioners are preceded by the predicate 'sister' justifies the conclusion that they were nuns. We can also suppose, with Stooker and Verbeij, that they – as was the case in many convents – had only elementary if any training in Latin.[13] The following was subsequently added to the abovementioned colophon by another hand [see plate 4]:

> Nu behoorse zuster Jaco*m*ine Magriete Lijsabette van Themse. Na ons zal[s]e hebben die Sinte Barbele verware*n* zal altos vorgande. A*n*no LXXXI.[14] [It now belongs to Sister Jacomine Margriete Lijsabette van Themse. After us, it will become the possession of those who Saint Barbara will always protect in a consummate manner. Anno [14]81.]

On the premise that the manuscript went from the private possession of Sisters Margriete Swilden and Clare Baerts via Sister Jacomine Margriete Lijsabette van Themse to the collective possession of a Saint Barbara's convent, we can possibly assume that all these sisters belonged to the same convent.[15] But which convent of Saint Barbara was it?[16] In other words: where should we localise the Leuven manuscript?

13. Cf. Stooker and Verbeij 1997, p. 142.

14. Leuven, Theol. 842S, fol. 2v. The addition to the colophon is written by a very inexperienced hand: the name '*Jacomine*' is difficult to read and a 'c' instead of the expected 's' appears to have been mistakenly written in the word '*zal[s]e*'.

15. Private owners of manuscripts in monasteries parted with their books only after their death, whereby these were usually left to a fellow monk or nun, or to the monastery. Cf. Stooker and Verbeij 1997, p. 137.

16. Given this explicit mention of the name of the convent, it is strange that De Vreese, in a note to the famous *Bibliotheca Neerlandica Manuscripta* (http://www.leidenuniv.nl/ub/bnm), localises the codex in the convent of Saint Andries near Bruges and the Bruges Carthusian convent of Sint Anna ter Woestijne [Saint Anne of the Desert]. The latter localisation is, however, accompanied by a question mark. Ydewalle 1945, p. 183-187 provides a list of the Carthusian sisters who stayed at Saint Andries from 1350 to 1580. The commissioners of the Leuven manuscript do not appear on this list, so in my view this location can be dismissed. De Vreese does not provide arguments for this localisation in the Bruges area in this BNM note. Elsewhere, he gives another localisation – South-Eastern Flanders – but once again, without any arguments in support, cf. De Vreese 1931, p. XXVI. The remark should perhaps be understood as a localisation on the basis of dialectological characteristics, but as already said, there is no support for this position whatsoever.

An analysis of the regional language features, one of the standard tools for a localisation, identifies the language of the Leuven manuscript as West Flemish.[17] Although western Flanders is a relatively small area, this means that we are still looking for a needle in a haystack. In the text itself, however, we find a firm lead for a more precise localisation of the manuscript. The chapter entitled *De meditacie te tiertsen* (fol. 100rb-102ra) recalls Jesus's road to Calvary. Following the Latin text, the Leuven manuscript wants to give the audience a very graphic idea of the distance that Jesus covered with His heavy cross. In the *Meditationes Vitae Christi*, this distance is described as follows:

> (...) mons Caluarie, ubi fuit crucifixus, distabat a porta ciuitatis quantum locus noster a porta Sancti Geminiani.[18]
> [The Calvary Mount, where He was crucified, was as far from the city gate as our place is from Saint Geminianus's Gate.]

In the Middle Dutch text the same strategy is used, but the 'coordinates' have been adapted to fit another audience:

> De berch va*n* Calvarie*n*, d*aer* Du ghecruust w*aer*s, staet wel also verre van der porte van der stat alst es va*n* der Smedeporte tote *Sinte* Baefs.[19]
> [The Calvary Mount, where You died on the cross, is just as far from the city gate as the Smiths' Gate is from Saint Bavo.]

This connection of the *Smedeporte* [Smiths' Gate] and Saint Bavo undoubtedly refers to the Bruges region,[20] which means that the text in the Leuven manuscript was written by someone who not only spoke a West Flemish language, but also was familiar with Bruges. For this description to deliver a maximal effect, the audience had to recognise these places. We can therefore situate the sisters mentioned in the colophon in a Saint Barbara's convent in the Bruges region.[21] It is not

The fact that the localisation is not argued further by De Vreese is perhaps the reason why the Leuven manuscript was not included in the repertory of Stooker and Verbeij 1997.

17. This means that I cannot subscribe to De Vreese's characterisation of the language (see above). See further appendix 1, where a detailed analysis of the regional language features in ms. 842S is provided.

18. Stallings-Taney 1997, p. 269, l. 63. Here and elsewhere, the spelling of this edition is rendered literally.

19. Leuven, Theol. 842S, fol. 101vb.

20. The Smith's Gate looks out onto the parish of Saint Bavo, a rural parish which originated shortly before 1216 and is situated south-west of the Bruges city walls. See e.g. the map in the historical atlas of Bruges by Ryckaert 1991, p. 100-101. On p. 88 of the same work, a brief introduction to the history of this parish is provided. The 'Saint Bavo' mentioned in the quotation supposedly refers to a chapel.

21. It goes without saying that if the Leuven manuscript should turn out to be a copy after all, this localisation is no longer unconditionally usable. In that case the question, whether the Bruges place names were already present in the scribe's exemplar or not, becomes very urgent. Only if the scribe deviated from the exemplar by using the Bruges place names, this localisation remains valid.

unlikely that Sisters Margriete, Clare and Jacomine belonged to the convent of Saint Barbara, also known as '*Magerzo*', a convent of the Third order of Saint Francis situated in the *Ganzenstraat* [Goose Street] in the city centre of Bruges.[22]

Now we know approximately where, but still not by whom the manuscript was produced. Perhaps Margriete Swilden and Clare Baerts had entrusted this task, as was often done at the time, to a clergyman in charge of the pastoral care of the nuns at the convent. It is not to be excluded, however, that another sister carried out this task. The codicological data and characteristics of the translation and adaptation technique yielded by the manuscript, seem to indicate that a woman was involved in the production of this codex. In my presentation of these indications, I will necessarily touch only briefly on some of them, so that others can be discussed at greater length.

5. Codicological indications

An initial hypothesis that I will put forward here, is that the manuscript was produced by an inexperienced scribe. The quire structure gives the first indication. The first quire – a double leaf – contains only the table of contents, and was added to the codex after it was completed.[23] Then follow 18 regular quires of four double leaves (*quaternia),* after which the book-block was closed with four single leaves which are not bound, but glued,[24] which can point to a poor estimate of the scribal work. We may assume that this codex was initially intended to include only the adaptation of the *Meditationes Vitae Christi*. The colophon on folio 140rb

22. The convent of Saint Barbara is included in the repertory of West-Flemish monasteries and abbeys, where it is dated in the period from 1311 to 1535 (Nuyttens 1997, p. 23). However, in Simons 1987, p. 161-162, 1342 is suggested as the year of foundation. The convent's alternative name, '*Magerzo*' [lean food], allegedly refers to the poor living conditions of its inhabitants. See also Ryckaert 1991, p. 198 and Goyens 1922, p. 181-185. The location of the convent of Saint Barbara can be seen on the map in Ryckaert 1991, p. 179 or De Smet 1944.

23. This is evident from the fact that in the table of contents (fol. 1r-2r) the individual chapters are referred to by the opening numbering (from I up to CXLVIIJ) in the manuscript. An evident mistake in this same table of contents provides an additional argument. On fol. 2r we read: *Tiene scone artikelen ¶ zouc* CXL. For the sequence to be correct, this lemma should change places with the preceding one (*Item van den zelven* CXLIJ). It appears that, while drawing up the table of contents, the scribe had initially forgotten the reference to the *tiene scone artikelen* and added it later, albeit that the reference to the chapter on opening 142 had already been included at that moment.

24. It is just possible that these four leaves are the remains of a disintegrated *binio*, which were glued together in the rebinding.

and the irregular use of the opening initials indicate that the inclusion of the excerpts was not originally planned.[25] After the first text, a great deal was left blank in the last quire, and it was probably decided only then to fill it up with excerpts. This led to a shortage of writing space, and single leaves were then added to the planned quires in the hope of being able to close the codex at a natural cesura in the texts which were included as excerpts. It appears that this was tried, but that, once four single leaves were added, it was in the end nonetheless decided to put an abrupt end to the codex. The nature and sequence of the excerpts and the striking conclusion of the text on the last leaf support this supposition. The excerpts – which were presumably chosen for their content-related affinity with the subject of the first text[26] – are not entered in the sequence of the Latin text. Furthermore, the last excerpt breaks off abruptly in the middle of the text, albeit after a full sentence, on the last line of the last folio [see plate 5].[27] It would appear that the last words on the last line of folio 149vb were painted over in red ink, to force a text ending. A larger *Amen* written in red is centred in the lower margin, above a triangular ornament in red. In a certain sense, we could suppose that the codex was nonetheless concluded in a traditional manner, but that clashes with the observation that the owner's note, unlike what the formulation would

25. The translation of the *Meditationes Vitae Christi* expressly ends with the following closing formula on fol. 140rb: *Ende ald*us *so es hier ghehent die ghuldine bouc va*n *de*n *levene Ons Heren* Jhesu Cristi, *de welke met goudene letteren sculdich ware ghescreven te zine* [In this way ends here the golden book on the life of Our Lord Jesus Christ, which ought to be written in gilded letters]. The opening of the first text with a decorated initial over five lines, might lead one to expect the beginning of the other texts to be decorated in a similar manner. However, further in the manuscript it becomes clear that those other texts open with initials over two or three lines, comparable to the initials used in the first text to mark the individual chapters (see fol. 140rb and 141vb).

26. The chapter *Qualiter ho*mo *potest ampli*us *etcetera. Hoe dat die mensche voor dan in duechden* profiteren *mach ende Gode temeer ghelieven* (fol. 141vb-144ra) contains a translation of the *Stimulus amoris maior*, book II, chapter 1 (cf. Peltier 1864-1871, XII, p. 662a-663a) and the (untranslated) prayer that follows the second chapter of the first book of the *Stimulus amoris maior* (Peltier 1864-1871, XII, p. 638a). The last chapter but one, *O Broeders zouct alo*mme *en*de *ve*rw*ondert tons* w*aert die caritate Gods (…)* (fol. 144rb-148rb), offers a translation of the *Stimulus amoris maior*, book I, chapter 1 and the (again untranslated) subsequent prayer (cf. Peltier 1864-1871, XII, p. 633a-635b). In the last chapter (fol. 148rb-149vb), *Stabat iuxta cruce*m Jhesu *mater eius. Bi de*n *cruce van* Jhesu *stont zij*n *zoete moeder (..)*, a translation of the *Stimulus amoris*, book I, chapter 3 (cf. Peltier 1864-1871, XII, p. 638a-639a) is given.

27. The *explicit* of this chapter in the *Stimulus amoris maior* is as follows: *Si autem nec quidquam dixeris, tunc cor meum vulnerabitur tristitia et dolore, et sic sine dolore non recedam* (Peltier 1864-1871, XII, p. 639a). When we compare the excerpt, as it is included in the Leuven manuscript, to the corresponding passage of the *Stimulus amoris maior*, it is clear that the text of the Leuven excerpt is incomplete.

lead one to suppose, is not given as a concluding colophon on the last folium, but on the blank verso of folio 2 of the subsequently added table of contents.

Not only the way in which the size of the book was estimated shows a lack of skilfulness, unprofessionalism seems to be a feature of the translation technique as well.

6. Translation technique

'Incompetence' is a word that inevitably springs to mind when assessing the translation technique used. As mentioned above, the Leuven manuscript is bilingual. The larger part of the text is however written in Middle Dutch, and the Latin passages present are – generally – subordinate thereto. There are many Latin quotations in the text, which are in general clearly marked as such and followed by a Middle Dutch translation.[28] Often, they are Latin citations in direct speech, such as:

> En*de* als dat die Coni*nc* horde, so seide Hi: "Penitet Me fecisse homine*m*." Het beraut Mi dat Ic de*n* mensche ghemaect hebbe.[29]
> [When the Lord heard this, He said: "Penitet Me fecisse hominem." I am sorry that I created man.]

Here and there, (a part of) a Latin phrase is embedded, and then – but not always – translated, in a Middle Dutch sentence:

> Warachtelike, sine*n* lof staet wel i*n* dit ewa*n*gelie, d*aer* me*n* va*n* he*m* seit dat hi es vir iustus, een gherechtich man.[30]
> [In truth, his praise is written in this gospel, where it is said of him that he is a vir iustus, a righteous man.]

This secondary status of the Latin compared to the vernacular can be explained by the fact that this text was intended for a female audience.[31] It is commonly accepted that women in general had only a limited knowledge of Latin.[32] Offering both the Latin text and a Middle Dutch trans-

28. The marking of the Latin quotations is graphically identical to that of the chapter headings.

29. Leuven, Theol. 842S, fol. 6va. Numerous other examples can be found, e.g. on fol. 6ra, 6va, 14vb, 17va, 22vb, 30va-b, 35vb, 36vb, 40vb, 42ra, 44vb, 46va, 60rb, 63ra, 65vb-66ra, 70va, 76ra, 76va-b, 78ra, 78vb, 79ra, 80ra, 83vb, 88va, 89rb, 89vb, 90ra, 90rb, 90vb, (...).

30. Leuven, Theol. 842S, fol. 14rb. See for other examples fol. 3ra, 5rb, 5va, 9va, 12rb, 16ra, 16rb, 18ra-b, 31va, 43ra, 43vb, 75rb, 83va-b, 92vb, 94ra, 112rb, 119va, 124vb, 143rb, 148ra, (...).

31. Cf. Wackers 1996, p. 33 and Stooker and Verbeij 1997, p. 271.

32. On the knowledge of Latin of women in the Middle Ages, see e.g. Stooker and Verbeij, p. 117, Scheepsma 1996, Scheepsma 1997, p. 26.

lation allowed the audience various possibilities of use, depending to the degree that he or she knew Latin and had access to the Latin sources. The Latin phrases make the connection with the original Latin text (if this was available) and confer a certain authority on the translation. Thanks to the Middle Dutch translation, those who did not know Latin could easily skip the Latin text.[33] Such a translation method may also have had an instructive function, for instance learning important Latin phrases, from which a great spiritual power could be drawn.[34] As mentioned above, not all Latin quotations are translated. In certain cases, the audience is assumed to be thoroughly familiar with them, such as the untranslated lines from the *Ave Maria* in the following passage:[35]

> En*de* rechte voort so staet Elisabeth up ... en*de* neemtse blidelike in hare aerme*n* en*de* roupt en*de* seit: "Benedicta tu i*n* mulierib*us* et b*enedictus* f*ructus* v*entris* t*ui*."[36]
> [And Elisabeth stood up at once... and embraced her [Maria] full of joy and called out: "Blessed art thou among women and blessed is the fruit of thy womb."]

It goes without saying that this supposition does not apply to all untranslated Latin sentences, and certainly not to the longer embedded excerpts in Latin which do not fit directly in the vernacular context. I am thinking here of the text in the illustration of the wound of Christ and certain prayers in the excerpts from the *Stimulus amoris maior*.[37] For a good

33. Cf. Wackers 1996, p. 33.

34. I am thinking here of the biography of Trude van Beveren in the *sister book* [zusterboek] of Diepenveen. In her *vita* we read that she often carried a book with her, containing the texts for that day, so as to ask a sister with a better command of Latin for explanation whenever she had the opportunity. Her biography recounts how one day she was drawing water when an applicable Latin phrase that she had read in the matins sprang to her mind (*Haurietas aquas in gaudio de fontibus salvatoris* ...). These words gave her so much strength that she forgot the heavy labour and hardly knew anymore what she was doing. Cf. Scheepsma 1997, p. 54. According to Scheepsma, this passage shows how the daily life of the nuns of Windesheim got interwoven with liturgical texts. I would like to add that these *vitae* serve as an example and the fact that such an event was recorded seems in this respect highly significant to me, for it indicates that a lot of interest was taken in (acquiring) knowledge of Latin – a language considered, after all, to be superior to Middle Dutch – even if only in the form of a single applicable phrase.

35. Fixed prayers such as the *Pater Noster* and *Ave Maria* were undoubtedly known in Latin by the monials, cf. Scheepsma 1997, p. 91.

36. Leuven, Theol. 842, fol. 13ra. On fol. 10ra another untranslated quotation of the *Ave Maria* can be found.

37. For the location of these Latin passages in the Leuven manuscript, see above. It is remarkable in this respect that on fol. 143vb a number of Middle Dutch lines in between two longer Latin passages are underlined in red. Must we deduce from this marking that the Latin passages were simply to be skipped?

understanding of the text, the audience will consequently have been obliged to use all its available knowledge of Latin.

Like many Middle Dutch translations of Latin texts, the translations in the Leuven manuscript also show a strong word-for-word tendency. Often, the imitation of the Latin syntax yields an ungrammatical Middle Dutch sentence.[38] This is still no reason to accuse the translator of incompetence.[39] The way in which the translator solved lexical problems posed by the Latin text, does, however, justify such an accusation. Paul Wackers has provided a summary of the common strategies used at that time to solve such problems:[40] the term from the source can be used – accompanied by an explanation (e.g. gloss) or new words can be formed that refer to the meaning or the form of already existing words. Another possibility is using French or words borrowed from French, if the public can be presumed to know French. If necessary, the term in question can be described, and finally it can be translated by means of doublets.

These strategies are rarely used in the Leuven translations. Here and there we encounter an original translation,[41] but in general the text contains, in addition to a large number of Latinisms,[42] also quite a number

38. Compare e.g. the following Middle Dutch passage: *Nu es ghezien dit niet wel te vullen connen te zegghene; want niet allene die pijnlike* ende *die stervelike crusijnghe Ons Heren* Jhesu Cristi, *maer ooc die* daer *voren gaen*, *die dijnghen zijn van* <+*der*> *aldermeester* compassie ende *bitterheden zere te verwonderne* (fol. 91va), to its source in Stallings-Taney 1997, p. 253, l. 27-30: *Videtur autem michi posse non incongrue dici quod non solum illa penalis et mortalis crucifixio Domini, sed ea que precesserunt eandem sunt uehementissime compassionis, amaritudinis et stuporis.*

39. Cf. Wackers 1996, p. 25.

40. Cf. Wackers 1996, p. 20-31.

41. Innovative translations seem to be (at least they are not attested in the MNW): *handemaels* (fol. 67rb) for *manualiter* [manual], *vulstandelike* (fol. 61vb, 77rb, 90ra) for *constanter* [persevering], *verfinekene* (fol. 107va) for *flectere* [to mollify], *hantvichters* (fol. 134va) for *pugiles* [boxers], *si namen een verper* (fol. 77vb) for *sumentes occasionem* [seize the opportunity]. Furthermore, the verb '*luusscht*' is used on several occasions (fol. 71ra, 124rb, 132va) as a translation for the word '*relucet*' [flickers, shines], which can be derived from the original meaning of *luuschen* as 'to hide'. Compare e.g. *Dus moghes du merken ooc hier die ghecostumeerde goedertierheit, minne* ende *omoedicheit Ons Heren* Jhesu Cristi, *de welke luusschen in al zine ghewerken* (fol. 132va) to *Potes eciam hic considerare benignitatem, caritatem et humilitatem Domini ... in omnibus factis eius relucent* (Stallings-Taney 1997, p. 334-5, l. 25-27). However, the use of '*curieus rover*' [strange robber] on fol. 41va and 70ra as a translation of *curiosus explorator* [prying investigator] strongly deviates from the original meaning, as does the meaning of '*vetselinghe*' (fol. 53rb), usually denoting a jewel or brooch, as *dat nederste deel van den clede* [the lower part of the cloth].

42. I give here some examples of occuring Latinisms, in each case with just one location; *abhominabile* (fol. 10va) < *abominabile*; *abstineerne* (fol. 59va) < *abstinendum*; *vele afflictien* (fol. 8rb) < *multa affliccione*; *aldercuriaelste* (fol. 54rb) < *curialissimus*; *ampulose woorden* (58va) < *ampullosa verba*; *circonstancien* (fol. 80rb) < *circumstanciis*; *cir-*

of untranslated Latin words. Some of these words, such as '*prohemium*' (fol. 1ra, 3ra) and '*cenaculum*' (fol. 86rb, 86vb) may have been known to the public, while in the case of others, such as '*parulimphus*' (fol. 10ra, sic), this is highly questionable.[43] And here is the rub: glosses are lacking in the manuscript, and added explanations are the exception to the rule.[44]

Should we conclude, therefore, that the audience, for which this translation was intended, had a very thorough knowledge of Latin? Or rather that the translator had only a moderate command of that language? Some striking examples can illustrate this.

On folio 51ra-b is related the healing of the centurion's servant (Mat. 8, 5-13; Luc. 7, 1-10). Whereas in the Latin text, the centurion refers to his servant with the words '*puer meus*',[45] the Leuven text has '*mijn kij*n*t*' [my child].[46] Given the context, it is very strange that the translator opted for the – admittedly most current – meaning of the word '*puer*'. Should we deduce that this was the only meaning known to the translator? Another striking error is the translation of Joseph's occupation, *magister lignarius* [carpenter], as the incomprehensible *meest*er *van bindene*.[47] Per-

culacie (fol. 3ra) < *circulacione*; *composicie* (fol. 86rb) < *composicio*; *conquestrerende* (fol. 73va) < *conqueritur*; *curialike* (fol. 44ra) < *curialiter*; *delibereerden* (fol. 81rb) < *deliberauerunt*; *detractien* (fol. 117vb) < *detractionis*; *diffijtselste* (fol. 45vb) < *difficilius*; *dissimulacie* (fol. 70rb) < *dissimulationem*; *generen van contemplacie*n (fol. 72rb) < *genera contemplacionis*; *forme* (fol. 130vb) < *formam*; *ghedefraudeert* (fol. 65vb) < *defraudasti*; *ghedeputeert* (fol. 65vb) < *deputatus*; *ghenoteert* (fol. 80vb) < *notaretur*; *ghesustineert* (fol. 71ra) <*sustentari*; *impedimenten* (fol. 73vb) < *impedimentis*; *perplex* (fol. 80vb) < *perplexitatem*; *specie* (fol. 68vb) < *specie*; *legacie* (fol. 11va) < *legacionem*; *numerende* (fol. 125vb) < *numerando*.

43. Other untranslated words are e.g.: all declined forms of Christ, *bauila* (fol. 13vb), *cubitus* (fol. 16va), *magnalia* (fol. 22va), *ydeota* (fol. 35va), *architriclino* (fol. 49va), *raboni* (fol. 121ra), *proprie* and *approprietate* (in the sentence *Dit sulstu niet proprie verstaen maer approprietate* on fol. 6vb), *regulus* (fol. 51rb) and *puerilia* (fol. 29va).

44. In the case of *puerilia* and *regulus* (see above), the Latin word is followed by an explication in Middle Dutch as e.g. in: *(...) dinghen die puerilia sij*n *dats kijnderachtich* (fol. 29va). However, the explanation of regulus is also present in the Latin text (cf. Stallings-Taney 1997, p. 104, l. 11). Once, more specifically on fol. 54vb, a content related explanation is added. The translation (...) *multiplicaui peccata super numerum arene maris* (...) (Stallings-Taney 1997, p. 111, l. 26) goes as follows: *Ende mine zonden zijn vermenicht boven den zande van der zee. Maer dat es dus te verstane: nichte me dan men zoude connen ghetellen dat zant van der zee of de sterren van den hemele, so en zoude men connen ghetellen die menichte van minen zonden* [My sins have outnumbered the sand of the sea. But this is thus to be understood as: no more than one could not number the sand of the sea or the stars in heaven, one could count the mass of my sins].

45. Stallings-Taney 1997, p. 104, l. 8.

46. Leuven, Theol. 842S, fol. 51ra.

47. Leuven, Theol. 842S, fol. 15vb.

haps the translator did not know the word '*lignare*' and therefore translated for convenience's sake the closest known word, '*ligare*' as '*binden*' [to bind].[48] That Joseph's occupation was apparently not self-evident to the translator suggests a very superficial knowledge of this rather well known gospel story.[49]

With this succinct summary of the translation technique, we have arrived at some of the most characteristic features of the knowledge profile – poor knowledge of Latin and the Bible[50] – of the average medieval woman/nun. Should we then accept, on these grounds, that this translation was produced by a woman?[51]

7. Adaptation technique

Fortunately, the sex of the translator need not be determined exclusively on negative grounds, but may also be gauged from certain creative adaptations of the Latin text. As the title clearly indicates, the *Meditationes Vitae Christi* contain the important moments from the life of Jesus, presented as graphically as possible and accompanied by detailed indications for meditation, which urge the reader to empathise with the story. Yet, the insistent character of the Latin text was not enough for the translator, as can be seen from certain interventions in the text, which were intended to make that text even more personal and even more suitable for the practice of meditation.

For instance, we frequently encounter a reversal of the narrator's perspective in the Middle Dutch text. Where the Latin text tells of the vicissitudes of the characters in the third person, such as when Mary regains consciousness after she has seen how Longinus pierced Jesus's side with

48. Possibly, a nasal line was lacking in the Latin exemplar, causing the word '*lignarius*' to be read as '*ligarius*', which was consequently translated as '*binden*'. But then the fact remains that the translator's knowledge of the Gospel was insufficient so as to correct this mistake in the exemplar. That this is not a single, unnoticed error in the Leuven translation becomes evident from another, even darker translation of *magister lignarius* as *meester van scotele*n *te bij*n*dene* on fol. 28vb.

49. A similar mistranslation, also pointing to a poor command of Latin and of the Gospel is the rendering of *Capharnaum erat quidam centurio, id est centum militum dominus (…)* (Stallings-Taney 1997, p. 104, l. 3) as *In Capharnau*m *was een man die hiet Centurio, de welke hadde* c *ridders onder he*m *(…)* [In Capharnaum lived a man, called Centurio, who had 100 knights under his command …] (fol. 51ra).

50. On the labourious access of women to the Bible, see Stooker and Verbeij 1997, p. 198.

51. In the conclusion of this article, I will return to the validity of this argument in relation to the status of the manuscript.

his lance: *Excitatur autem Domina, surgit quasi euigilans, querens quid sit de dilecto filio suo (...)*,[52] we see that the Middle Dutch text sometimes uses the second person singular, which creates a different narrator's perspective, strongly suggesting a dialogue: *En*de *Maria, zoete moeder, als du becomen zijs so vraechs du hoe dat es met dinen ghemin*den *zone*.[53] [And sweet mother Mary, when you regained consciousness, you asked how your beloved son was.]

In the following example, the narrative perspective is also changed, but in a somewhat different way: in the Latin phrase *(...) auerte autem parumper oculos a diuinitate et eum purum hominem considera. Et uidebis iuuenem elegantem (...)*,[54] the attention of the audience is focused on the humiliated and suffering Christ, which is intensified in the Middle Dutch text in

> O mijn alderliefste Here en*de* mij*n* zoete mi*n*lic Heer, so willic Di nu bezien recht als een puer mensche, sonder die godheit, en*de* dan so mach ic zien enen vrome*n* scone*n* jonghelinc.[55]
> [Oh my dearest Lord and my sweet, precious Lord, I now wish to look on you purely as a man, without divinity, and then I see a pious, beautiful youth.]

In addition to this type of change, we also encounter additions to the Latin text, chiefly situated in the meditatively tinted passages of the *Meditationes Vitae Christi*. For instance, in the five chapters devoted to the meditation on the passion for matins, primes, midday and noon (together in one chapter), vespers and complines, no fewer than eight prayers appear.[56] Except in one case, these are always closed with the words

52. Stallings-Taney 1997, p. 278, l. 53.

53. Leuven, Theol. 842S, fol. 108ra. Another example can be found on fol. 14va (compare to Stallings-Taney 1997, p. 28, l. 22-29). It is not surprising that these reversals of the narrator's perspective frequently occur in the more meditatively tinted passages. Especially in the chapters dedicated to the meditation on the passion of Christ (see also further) these reversals become extremely frequent. Compare e.g. in the chapter on the meditation of the passion for the matins fol. 93ra-b, 93vb, 94va-b, 95ra and 95rb to the Latin source (Stallings-Taney 1997, respectively p. 256, l. 5-11; p. 256, l. 26-27 and p. 257, l. 32; p. 258, l. 68-73 and l. 75-76; p. 259, l. 81-83 and 88-89; p. 259, l. 97-98).

54. Stallings-Taney 1997, p. 268, l. 13 a.f.

55. Leuven, Theol. 842S, fol.100va. Other examples are on fol. 100vb, 107rb-va and 108 ra (compare to Stallings-Taney 1997, respectively p. 268, l. 23 a.f.; p. 277, l. 39-40; p. 278, l. 56-57).

56. The chapter on the meditation for the matins takes up fol. 93ra-98ra, the meditation for the *priemen* fol. 98ra-100rb, the meditation for midday and noon fol. 102ra-106va, the meditation for the vespers fol. 106va-109vb and the meditation on the complines fol. 109vb-114ra. The prayers are on fol. 97vb-98ra, 100rb, 105vb-106ra, 106ra-b, 106va, 107va, 109vb and 113vb-114ra.

'*Pater noster*', a clear indication that the audience has to pray here. The meditation *Te middaghe en*de *te noenen*, for instance, ends with the remark:

> Waer bi dat ic da*n* wel zegghe*n* mach dat in hem noch zin noch vroescepe en es, die Dine pine passie ende ziecheit niet en beleft noch en bevoelt.
> [Where I can say that he, who does not experience or feel Your passion and suffering, has no understanding or wisdom.]

Here, the following prayer was added:

> O goede zoete *Jhesus*, dat ic dit niet en doe, dat wille mi v*er*gheve*n*, biddic di vrie*n*delike, en*de* gracie v*er*lene*n* dat ic betere*n* moet. Amen. Pater *noster*.[57]
> [Oh good, sweet Jesus, please forgive me that I do not do this, and I beseech you to give me grace to improve myself. Amen. Pater noster.]

Another addition at the end of the meditation of complines refers explicitly to the practice of meditating (I quote only a part of the addition):

En*de* ooc so biddic di, zoete moeder, dat du mi met dine*n* zoete*n* ghezelscepe dine helighe benedictie nu gheve*n* wils also, als dat ic te deser oufeni*n*ghe mi altoos en*de* i*n* allen duechden also devotelike bekeren moet, als dat ic dine*n* gheminde*n* zone *Jhesum* en*de* di hier in en*de* i*n* allen duechde*n* altoos ghelieve*n* moet. Ame*n*. Pater *noster*.[58]

[And I also beseech you, sweet mother, to grant me your holy blessing with your sweet presence, so that I can always strive, through this meditation, towards all virtues in such a devoted manner as to please your beloved son Jesus and yourself in all virtues at all times. Amen. Pater noster.]

However, not only prayers are added, as can be seen from the following example. In a meditation on Jesus returning from Egypt, the audience is urged to seek out the child Jesus:

> En*de* dan so zal Hi di leden tote sij*n*re zoeter vriendeliker moeder en*de* curialike di vor haer eere*n* en*de* segghen: "Zie, zoete w*aer*de moeder, dits onse speciale vrie*n*deghe die ons aldus ghetrauwelike comt visiteren." En*de* dan so kniele vor he*m* lieden en*de* doe he*m* lieden eere en*de* w*aer*dicheit.[59]
> [And then He [Jesus] will lead you to his sweet, friendly mother and will honour you courteously before her and say: "See here, sweet, dear mother, this is our special friend who comes to visit us in faith." And then kneel before them and show them honour and dignity.]

The added sentence, *Ende segghen zie zoete waerde moeder dits onse speciale vriendeghe die ons aldus ghetrauwelike comt visiteren*, which is

57. Leuven, Theol. 842S, fol. 106va.
58. Leuven, Theol. 842S, fol. 113vb-114ra.
59. Leuven, Theol. 842S, fol. 29vb.

included seemlessly in the original text, speaks directly to the female audience and uses the strikingly female form '*vriendeghe*', which must be understood as 'female friend'.[60]

The changes mentioned above can be understood from the intended purpose, namely to produce a practical book of meditation – with an admittedly enhanced prayer dimension – customised for a female audience. This in itself does not suffice however to explain some other changes, where both a 1st person singular and a feminine form are pressed on the Latin text. The example of the feminine form '*zondarighe*' in the following passage, which is added to the meditation for midday and noon, may illustrate this:

> O Maria, mine zoete lieve moeder, nu biddic di vriendelike, in de ghedinkenesse van der utenemender zericheit die du nu hebs als du dine*n* lieve*n* zone dus zies sterven, dat du nu met dese*n* zoete*n* en*de* ooc nu zerighe*n* ghezelscepe wils impetreren die gracie an dine*n* ghemi*n*den zone *Jhesum Cristum* dat hi mi v*er*lene*n* wille dat ic he*m*, aerme zondarighe, nu ghebede*n* hebbe en*de* ooc al dat mij*n*re aerme ziele zalich es. Ame*n*. *Pater noster*.[61]
> [Oh Mary, my sweat, dear mother, I implore you, in remembrance of the inordinate pain that you now suffer when you see your son die, that you may use this sweet and now also suffering companionship to obtain grace from your beloved son Jesus Christ, so that he may grant to me, poor sinner, what I have beseeched him, as well as everything that can bless my poor soul Amen. Pater Noster.]

On folio 39va we find a striking change in the translation of the Latin sentence *Factus estis sicut unus ex nobis, peregrinus et aduena sicut omnes patres nostri, factus estis seruus, ut nos reges fiamus*.[62] The Middle Dutch text here reads:

> Du sijs ghemaect ghelijc een van ons lieden; peelgrijn ende vreemde. Du sijs worden een knecht om dat ic wesen soude ene coneghinne.[63]
> [You are made as one of us, namely a pilgrim and a stranger. You have become a servant so that I could be queen.]

The unspecified plural form '*reges*' (kings and queens) from the Latin text is here converted into the exclusive feminine form in the singular

60. An adaptation with a similar effect occurs in the translation of *(…) et quantum potes sta familiaris Domine et puero Iesu* (Stallings-Taney 1997, p. 35, l. 147-8). On fol. 18ra the Middle Dutch text here reads: *(..) ende in al dat du vermoghes, so si dienighe* v*an Onser Zoet*er *Vrauwen en*de *van haren zoeten kindekine* Jhesum [and be a servant to the best of your ability to our sweet Lady and to her sweet little child Jesus]. Again, the exclusively feminine form '*dienighe*' specifically appeals to a female audience.

61. Leuven, Theol. 842S, fol. 106ra-b.

62. Stallings-Taney 1997, p. 74, l. 33 a.f.

63. Leuven, Theol. 842S, fol. 39va.

'*coneghinne*' [queen]. Such feminisations also occur in the Latin citations from the *Stimulus amoris maior* that have been left untranslated. In the *Stimulus amoris maior* we read the following lines:

> Domine sancte, Pater omnipotens, aeterne Deus, propter tuam largitatem, et Filii tui, qui pro me sustinuit passionem et mortem, et Matris ejus excellentissimam sanctitatem, atque beati Francisci, et omnium Sanctorum merita: concede mihi peccatori, et omni tuo beneficio indigno, ut te solum diligam (...).[64]
> [Holy Lord, almighty Father, eternal God, owing to your clemency and that of your son, who suffered and died for me, and of his all-holy mother, and Saint Francis, and the merits of all the saints, grant me, a sinner not worthy of your benefaction, so that I can honour you alone (...).]

The corresponding passage has been shortened somewhat in the Leuven manuscript, but also shows some striking changes:

> *Domine, Sancte Pater,* rogo Te, p*ro*pter Tua*m* largitatem, et Filii Tui, q*ui* p*ro* me sustinuit mortem, *et* Matris Tui excellente*m* *sancti*tate*m* et *omnium Sanctorum* tuo*rum* merita, ut co*n*cedas michi peccatrici, et *omni* beneficio tuo i*n*digna, ut te solu*m* diligam.[65]

In place of the masculine '*peccatori*' (dat. m. sing.) we find here the exclusively feminine '*peccatrici*' (dat. f. sing.). The rest of the sentence construction fits in: also *indigno* has been feminised to *indigna.*[66]

Such changes seem to presuppose a female scribe, since such a high degree of identification with the intended female audience can scarcely be expected from a male author.[67] Furthermore, the additions and changes to the source text can be read as the report of her meditation on the text, while she translated it.

8. Concluding remarks

In the preceding paragraphs the argumentation has been built up departing from the (assumed) premise that the Leuven codex is an autograph,

64. Peltier 1864-1871, XII, p. 635.
65. Leuven, Theol. 842S, fol. 148rb.
66. Another example appears on fol. 144ra, where the Latin phrase *Et tu, clementissima Domina, impetra mihi ut suae et tuae semper deditus sim servituti (...)* (Peltier 1864-1871, XII, p. 663a) has been feminised in *Et tu, clementissima* Domina, *Virgo semp*er, *Maria, michi indignissima impetra ut perfecte sim dedita tue servituti* [And you, most merciful Lady, eternal Virgin, Mary, grant me, unworthy, my wish to be rendered entirely in your service.]
67. I will deal with the validity of this assumption in relation to the status of the Leuven manuscript in the concluding paragraph of this article.

perhaps an apograph, for reasons of simplicity and plausability. For if manuscript 842S is assumed to be merely a copy, matters become highly complicated. In that case, it becomes not so much a question of whether a woman was responsible for the production of this manuscript, but rather how many women were involved in the production process. As far as the translation technique is concerned, the outcome of the discussion still holds. For, as we have seen above, the translator delivered a text that must have been hard to swallow for an audience ignorant of Latin. It follows from the fact that in the copy the most obvious mistranslations have not been corrected – something a professional scribe would not have failed to do –, that the scribe's knowledge profile was not necessarily worse, but certainly not better than that of the translator. Thus, the female profile discerned in the limited command of Latin and the Bible not only applies to the person responsible for the translation, but also to the scribe of that translation. When we subsequently return to the third, and admittedly strongest argument, i.e. the presence of a female first person narrator in the text, the possibilities – and their accompanying uncertainties – are significantly multiplied. Who is responsible for the feminisations in the Leuven text? The answer could be 'the scribe,' but can we reasonably assume that the scribe had a sufficient command of Latin so as to toy with the Latin quotations of the *Stimulus amoris maior*? However, 'the translator' is just as valid an answer to the question just posed. Do we have to assume then, since the Leuven manuscript contains two (identified) texts, that these feminisations were already present in the copied translation of the *Meditationes Vitae Christi* and of the *Stimulus amoris maior*? How great are the chances that the Bruges scribe disposed of two texts, written by and for women? Furthermore, if the scribe departed from existing translations, how do we account for the *ad hoc* interventions pointing to a poor estimate of the space in the codex required to accommodate the text?

To avoid getting lost in a dense fog of doubts and improbabilities, let us look again at the data (not all of which is hard evidence) yielded by the Leuven manuscript. To start with, there is nothing that contests the assumption of the Leuven codex to be an autograph. On the contrary, this assumption is corroborated by the homogeneity of the language in the Leuven codex,[68] and by the circumstances of its origin. Although this is not explicitly stated as such in the colophon, we can assume that the commissioners of the Leuven manuscript, two sisters belonging to

68. See appendix 1 on the regional language features in ms. 842S.

a poor convent after all, joined hands to finance the production of this rather expensive manuscript. An outlay that hardly seems justified were it not for the fact that it provides a previously non-existent translation of the texts mentioned. Furthermore, the complete absence of transmission of the Leuven texts enhances the character of the translations as incidental and intended for private use only. Combined with the established features of the codex, translation and adaptation technique used, which each in itself carries insufficient proof but gain probative value in their internal coherence, a feminine authorschip of the Leuven manuscript becomes reasonably plausible. If my arguments have any validity, manuscript Leuven, Theol. 842S must be considered to have been produced by women, for women.[69]

Further research into comparable manuscripts should help clarify whether the Leuven manuscript is an incidental case,[70] or that we are here on the trail of a significant development in late medieval manuscript and text production, possibly limited to the – broad – genre of 'devotional books', where an important role was charted for women.

Appendix 1: Regional language features in ms. 842S[71]

When looking at regional language features in ms. 842S, the limits of research have to be taken into account. The current state of affairs in the historical linguistics of the Dutch language still shows a remarkable hiatus for the period 1450-1550 (*grosso modo*), the transitional period between Middle Dutch and Early Modern Dutch. Ms. 842S dates from the

69. By way of a short comparison, I would like to draw attention to a fifteenth century manuscript, dedicated by an unknown woman to the English queen Elizabeth Woodville, wife of Edward IV. This English text translated from Latin, which is given the contemporary title *Hours of the Guardian Angel*, is wellnigh unique: it has come down in only two, independent translations. The translation itself is awkward and contains obvious mistakes as well as strikingly feminine forms – reasons to suppose that the donour of the manuscript was presumably the author as well. On this manuscript, Liverpool University Library, Liverpool Cathedral, ms. Radcliffe 6, see Sutton and Visser-Fuchs 1996, especially p. 239-240.

70. I am thinking here e.g. of the following manuscripts, kept in Brussels in the Royal Library: IV 1265, IV 105, IV 165, 21371 and IV 1228. These are all fifteenth-century books of hours and prayer books, featuring strikingly feminine forms, of which nothing else is known unfortunately. Deschamps and Mulder 1998-2001.

71. I would like to thank sincerely prof. dr. A. Berteloot (Münster) for his critical remarks on an earlier version of this appendix. His comments have removed to some extent the chronological limitations of the research literature and prevented me from overinterpreting the material.

year 1437, whereas the tools available for investigating the regional features of the language used are all based on older materials, up to the year 1400.[72] Consequently, the analysis of the regional language features of the Middle Dutch text given below does not pretend to be exhaustive or definitive: I wish merely to sketch in broad outlines how the regional language is to be classified.[73]

Departing from the regional language features listed by Van Loey in his *Middelnederlandse spraakkunst*,[74] I have looked in Berteloot's *Klankatlas* to those maps yielding the most exclusive features.[75] It soon became clear that particularly the Flemish language features offered the most useful leg up to this analysis.

As common Flemish features are to be named:

- ☐ '*(be)kennen*' for Modern Dutch (further Mod.Du) 'inzien, erkennen' [realize, recognize]. There are 29 hits, once we find the eastern form '*kinnen*' [Berteloot 1984, II, map 28].
- ☐ Palatalisation of '*o*' to '*u*': '*vul*' for Mod.Du 'vol' [full], (the form '*vul*' has been used exclusively in words such as *vul, vulmaecste, aldervulmaecste, vulmaectelike, onvulmaect(er), vulmaecheit, vulcomen(e), vulhent, te vullen, vuldaen, vulweghen, vulheit, vulstandich(eden), vulstandelike, vulcomelike, onvulmaecten*) [Berteloot 1984, II, map 63]; '*up*' for Mod.Du 'op' [up], (used exclusively in the following words: *up, (alder)upperste, upvaert, upgheblasenen*) [Berteloot 1984, II, map 64]; '*bus*' for Mod.Du 'bos' [wood] (used exclusively in the words *busachtighen* and *busschen*) [Berteloot 1984,

72. I refer here to the material that has been brought under what is known as the 'corpus Gysseling', and especially to the collection of official records which can relatively easily be dated and lokalised (see Gysseling 1977). This corpus contains material up to and including the year 1300, which has been used for linguistic research in e.g. Berteloot 1984 and Mooijaart 1992. Very recent is Rem 2003, in which the year 1400 is used as chronological upper limit. However, this work could not be taken fully into the investigation anymore.

73. This leads us to yet another problem: if we are able to name the regional language in the manuscript (perhaps even accurately), do we know then where the manuscript has been produced? For the result of an investigation of regional language features initially concerns the origin of the scribe's regional language (and possibly the exemplars used), and cannot simply be 'translated' in terms of the environment or milieu of origin of the manuscript. See a propos e.g. Van den Berg 1986, p. 305-306. A scribe may very well have been active outside the immediate environment where he learnt his regional language variant.

74. See Van Loey 1968, p. 123-129.

75. Cf. Berteloot 1984. The complete text of manuscript 842S has been incorporated into this investigation of regional language features. Unless only one specific form occurs in the manuscript, I have given the number of hits and deviating forms. For exceptional cases I have also mentioned the location.

II, map 62]; '*wulf*' for Mod.Du 'wolf' [woolf] (we only find the word *wuluen* on fol. 78ra) [Van Loey 1968, §25b]; '*nuchtens*' voor Mod.Du "s ochtends' [in the morning] (only *nuchtens*) [Van Loey 1968, §25b]; '*mul*' for Mod.Du 'zand' [sand] (only *mul*) [Van Loey 1968, §25b].

- ☐ the *u* in '*sulc*' and '*rudder*': '*sulc*' for Mod.Du 'zulk(e)' [such] (used exclusively in words such as *sulc, sulctenighe(r), zulc, zulctenighe, zulke(n), zulker*) [Berteloot 1984, II, map 53]; '*rudder*' for Mod.Du 'ridder' [knight] (5 hits for *ridder*, *rudders* has been used once on fol. 104ra) [Berteloot 1984, II, map 48].
- ☐ the exclusively used form '*gaet*' for Mod.Du 'gaat' [goes] [Berteloot 1984, II, map 79].
- ☐ '*broeder*' for Mod.Du 'broeder' [brother] (only *broeder(s)*) [Berteloot 1984, II, map 112].
- ☐ '*bede*' for Mod.Du 'beide(n)' [both] (exclusively used in words such as *bede(n), hem beden, si beden, in bede*) [Berteloot 1984, II, map 116].
- ☐ '*helig(he)*' for Mod.Du 'heilig' [holy] is to be considered a common Flemish form, attested till Mechelen. Ms. 842S contains only *helighe(n/r)* [Berteloot 1984, II, map 118].
- ☐ the exlusively used form '*s/zu*' for Mod.Du 'zij' [she] (pronomen 3 sing. fem.) [Berteloot 1984, II, map 121].

In addition to these common Flemish features, the Leuven manuscript also contains forms which can be located more specifically in a certain region. This material admittedly shows some variety, which does not differ significantly however from the average variety found in Middle Dutch texts. Significant are the following, rather West Flemish features:

- ☐ the exclusively used form '*of*' for Mod.Du 'af' [of] [Berteloot 1984, II, map 10].
- ☐ the exclusively used form '*brocht*' for Mod.Du 'bracht' [brought] [Berteloot 1984, II, map 12].
- ☐ the exclusively used form '*socht*' for Mod.Du 'zacht' [soft] (in words such as *aldersochtmoedig*, *sochtmoedig*, *zochtmoedig*) [Van Loey 1968, §3 rem.1].
- ☐ once we find the West Flemish form '*darst*' (fol. 140va) for Mod.Du 'dorst' [thirst], next to 10 hits on words with the form '*dorst*' such as *dorst, dorstede, mi dorst, dorstich, dorstende* [Van Loey 1968, §10].
- ☐ depalatalisation in *er*+consonant: '*varre*' for Mod.Du 'ver' [far] (one hit for *varren* (fol. 41rb), next to 21 hits for *verre(n)*). In addition, the four times that this word was expanded, the form '*wa(e)rue(n)*' for Mod.Du 'maal' [time] has been used [Berteloot 1984, II, map 16].

Other examples of the same feature are the exclusively used forms '*bardere*' on fol. 86vb for Mod.Du 'plank' [plank], '*caerker*' for Mod.Du 'kerker' [prison] and '*scaerp*' for Mod.Du 'scherp' [sharp] (in words such as *scaerp(en)* and *scaerpede*).

- the '*e*' in stead of '*o*' before *r*+consonant. Once we find the form '*herkelen*' (derived from '*horken*' for Mod.Du 'luisteren' [listen], fol. 50 va), next to the forms '*aerclende*' (fol. 49vb) and '*haerkelde*' (fol. 115ra) [Van Loey 1968, §10a].
- the form '*omme*' for Mod.Du 'om' is used exlusively in ms. 842S [Berteloot 1984, II, kaart 130].
- the form '*cam*' for Mod.Du 'kwam' [came] is typical of the Flemish language, even the more western Flemish [Berteloot 1984, II, map 147].
- the frequent occurrence of the aphaeresis of the '*h*' (e.g. *ondertvout* instead of *hondertvout* (fol. 67va); *olflinghe* (fol. 4rb) instead of *halflinghe*; *eerlijcste* (fol. 49va) instead of *heerlijcste*) and, above all, the prosthesis of the '*h*' (e.g. *huutnemende* (fol. 88ra) instead of *uutnemende*, the exclusively used form '*heescht*' instead of '*eescht*', *hachtede* (fol. 35rb) instead of *achtede*, *hende* (fol. 35va, 88rb, 89ra) instead of *ende*, *gheheert* (fol. 50va) for Mod.Du 'geëerd', *here* (fol. 61rb, 84va, 86ra) for Mod.Du 'eer', *hore(n)* (fol. 76vb, 93vb) for Mod.Du 'oor(en)' is an important Flemish feature, attested more specifically in north-western Flanders [Berteloot 1984, II, map 140 and 141]. Aphaeresis and prosthesis of '*h*' sporadically also occurs in the northern part of the Low Countries, among others in material from Bergen op Zoom, Breda, Amsterdam and Dordrecht.
- the form '*sonderlanghe*' [strange, odd], which occurs six times (*z/sonderlanghe(ste)*), in addition however to a majority of words with the form '*(s/z)onderlinghe*' (29 hits), is West Flemish [Van Loey 1968, §2 rem. 3].
- in general we find the form 'mensche' for Mod.Du 'mens' [human (being)] in words such as *mensche(n), menschelijcheit, menscheliker, euenmensche*. Four times however the form '*meinsche*' occurs, a very rare spelling that is only attested for Gent and Bruges [Berteloot 1984, II, map 36].
- the '*e*' instead of '*ie*': e.g. the exclusively used form '*speghel*' for Mod.Du 'spiegel' [mirror] and the only once occurring form '*heldedes*' (fol. 126rb) for Mod.Du 'hield' [held] [Van Loey 1968, §53].
- the word '*striewelen*' for Mod.Du 'strooien' [scatter] is typical of the West Flemish language. Manuscript 842S contains words such as

striewelen, gestriewelt and *striewelinghe*) [Van Loey 1968, §84, rem. 2].

- the expression '*nichte me*' (fol. 54vb) for Mod.Du 'niets meer' [nothing more], which occurs once in the manuscript, is typical of West Flemish [MNW, vol. 4, col. 2380-2381].
- a feature typical of West Flemish is also the occurrence of feminine forms on *–e/ighe*: *dienighe* (fol. 7ra, 8ra, 18ra, 47va, 47vb), *dieneghe* (fol. 48ra), *vriendeghe* (fol. 29vb), *personeghe* (fol. 110ra), *verbiddighe* (fol. 113vb), *zondarighe* (fol. 106rb), *apostelighe* (fol. 125rb), *minneghe* (fol. 20vb), *viandeghe* (fol. 77va) [Van Loey 1964, p. 178-179].

On the basis of the analysis given above, it is acceptable for the language in manuscript 842S to be characterized as West Flemish. A further specification would presumably have to be considered too speculative, but we can safely state that the language used can very well be reconciled with the hypothesis of a Bruges scribe (at least, the result of the investigation is not contradictory thereto). To some extent this analysis also sheds some light on the (assumed) premise mentioned above, that the Leuven codex is an autograph c.q. apograph. The search for a linguistic upper and lower layer in a prose text (in contrast to a rhimed text) is far from easy, but the linguistic material seems homogeneous enough so as to corroborate the assumption that there is no exemplar in another regional language at the basis of this manuscript.

Bibliography

BERTELOOT 1984: A. Berteloot, *Bijdrage tot een klankatlas van het dertiende-eeuwse Middelnederlands,* 2 vols. (Gent, 1984).

CLAASSENS 2001: Geert H.M. Claassens, 'Bible Translator of 1360', in: John Jeep (ed.), *Medieval Germany. An Encyclopedia* (New York/London, 2001), p. 61-64.

COUN 1980: Th. Coun, *De oudste Middelnederlandse vertaling van de Regula S. Benedicti,* Regula Benedicti Studia, Supplementa, 8 (Hildesheim, 1980).

COUN 1985: Th. Coun, 'De Middelnederlandse vertalingen van Ekbert von Schönau's *Sermo de vita et passione Jesu Christi*', in: *Ons Geestelijk Erf,* 59 (1985), p. 515-532.

DE BRUIN 1967-1971: C.C. de Bruin, 'Bespiegelingen over de "Bijbelvertaler van 1360": Zijn milieu, werk en persoon', in: *Nederlands Archief voor*

Kerkgeschiedenis, Nieuwe serie, 48 (1967-1968), p. 39-59; 49 (1968-1969), p. 135-154; 50 (1969-1970), p. 11-27; 51 (1970-1971), p. 16-41.

DE BRUIN 1977-1978: C.C. de Bruin, 'Middeleeuwse Levens van Jesus als leidraad bij meditatie en contemplatie', in: *Nederlands Archief voor Kerkgeschiedenis,* Nieuwe serie, 58 (1977-1978), p. 129-155.

DE BRUIN 1980: C.C. de Bruin, *Tleven ons Heren Ihesu Cristi. Het pseudo-Bonaventura-Ludolfiaanse Leven van Jezus,* Corpus Sacrae Scripturae Neerlandicae Medii Aevi, Miscellanea, 2 (Leiden, 1980).

DE SMET 1944: J. De Smet, 'De Brugsche straatnamen in 1399, in het cijnsboek van den disch der Brugsche O.L.Vrouwkerk', in: H. Draye (ed.), *Feestbundel H.J. Van de Wijer,* Vol. I (Leuven, 1944), p. 331-363.

DE VOOYS 1902: C.G.N. de Vooys, 'Middelnederlandsche proza-verhalen over de geboorte van Jezus', in: *Nederlandsch Archief voor Kerkgeschiedenis,* Nieuwe serie, 1 (1902), p. 125-162.

DE VREESE 1931: W. de Vreese, *Die eerste bliscap van Maria* ('s-Gravenhage, 1931).

DESCHAMPS 1972: J. Deschamps, *Middelnederlandse handschriften uit Europese en Amerikaanse bibliotheken* (Leiden, 1972 [tweede, herziene druk]).

DESCHAMPS and MULDER 1998-2001: J. Deschamps and H. Mulder, *Inventaris van de Middelnederlandse handschriften van de Koninklijke Bibliotheek van België. Eerste [-vierde aflevering]* (Brussel, 1998-2001).

DULLAERT AND VANDERVIN 1844: A. Dullaert and H. Vandervin, *Catalogue des collections de tableaux, dessins, gravures, antiquités, curiosités, et objets d'histoire naturelle, formant le cabinet Van Huerne (...)* (Gent, 1844).

EISERMANN 1995: F. Eisermann, 'Stimulus amoris', in: B. Wachinger *et al.* (eds.), *Die deutsche Literatur des Mittelalters. Verfasserlexikon* (Berlin/New York, 1970-2000 [second, revised edition]), Vol. 9 (1995), col. 335-341.

GOUGAUD 1924: L. Gougaud, 'La prière dite de Charlemagne et les pièces apocryphes apparentées', in: *Revue d'histoire ecclésiastique,* 20 (1924), p. 211-238.

GOYENS 1922: J. Goyens, 'Soeurs du Tiers Ordre à Bruges. Textes inédits', in: *Franciscana,* 5 (1922), p. 181-193.

GYSSELING 1977: M. Gysseling, *Corpus van Middelnederlandse teksten (tot en met het jaar 1300).* M.m.v. en van woordindices voorzien door W. Pijnenburg, Reeks I, *Ambtelijke bescheiden* ('s-Gravenhage, 1977).

KORS 2000: M.M. Kors, 'Bijbelvertaler van 1360', in: B. Wachinger *et al.* (eds.), *Die deutsche Literatur des Mittelalters. Verfasserlexikon* (Berlin/New York, 1970-2000 [second, revised edition]), Vol. 11 (2000), col. 249-256.

KORS 2003: M.M. Kors, 'Die Schenkung einer *Legenda aurea*-Handschrift aus dem 14. Jahrhundert und die Identität des Bijbelvertalers', in: A. Berteloot, H. van Dijk en J. Hlatky (red.), *"Een boec dat men te Latine heet Aurea Legenda" Beiträge zur niederländischen Übersetzung der Legenda aurea,* Niederlande-Studien, 31 (Münster, 2003), p. 19-34.

LEYTS 2000: S. Leyts, *Den gaert der minnen I. Een diplomatische editie van Brussel, K.B., hs. 15.087-15.090, fol. 3r-49va met een onderzoek naar de passiemystiek in Den gaert der minnen I* (Leuven, 2000 [onuitgegeven licentiaatsverhandeling]).

LINNIG 1910: B. Linnig, *Nouvelle série de Bibliothèques et d'Ex-libris d'amateurs belges aux XVIIe, XVIIIe et XIXe siècle* (Buxelles, 1910).

MNW: E. Verwijs – J. Verdam, *Middelnederlandsch Woordenboek*, 11 vols. ('s-Gravenhage; 1885-1041).

MOOIJAART 1992: M.A. Mooijaart, *Atlas van Vroegmiddelnederlandse Taalvarianten* (Utrecht, 1992).

NUYTTENS 1997: M. Nuyttens, *Repertorium van kloosters en abdijen in West-Vlaanderen* ..., Bibliografische inleiding tot de Belgische kloostergeschiedenis vóór 1796, 11 (Brussel, 1977).

PEETERS 2000: J. Peeters, *Den gaert der minnen II. Een diplomatische editie van Brussel, K.B., hs. 15.087-15.090, fol. 49va-81ra met een onderzoek naar de vertaal- en bewerkingstechniek* (Leuven, 2000 [onuitgegeven licentiaatsverhandeling]).

PELTIER 1864-1871: A.C. Peltier, *S.R.E. Cardinalis S. Bonaventura, ex ordine minorum episcopi albanensis, doctoris ecclesiae seraphici. Opera omnia,* 15 vols. (Parijs, 1864-1871).

PIANA 1986: C. Piana, 'Il "Fr. Iacobus de Mediolano Lector". Autore dello pseudo-Bonaventuriano *Stimulus Amoris* ed un convento del suo insegnamento', in: *Antonianum,* 61 (1986), p. 329-339.

REM 2003: M. Rem, *De taal van de klerken uit de Hollandse grafelijke kanselarij (1300-1340): naar een lokaliseringsprocedure voor het veertiendeeeuwse Middelnederlands*, Uitgaven Stiching Neerlandistiek VU, 39 (Münster, 2003).

RUH 1956: K. Ruh, *Bonaventura deutsch. Ein Beitrag zur deutschen Franziskaner-Mystik und -Scholastik* (Bern, 1956).

RYCKAERT 1991: M. Ryckaert, o.l.v. A. Verhulst en J.-M. Duvosquel, *Brugge*, Historische stedenatlas van België, 2 (Brussel, 1991).

SCHEEPSMA 1996: W. Scheepsma, '"Verzamelt de overgebleven brokken, opdat niets verloren ga": Over Latijnse en Middelnederlandse levensbeschrijvingen uit de sfeer van de Moderne Devotie', in: P. Wackers e.a., *Verraders en bruggenbouwers. Verkenningen naar de relatie tussen Latinitas en de Middelnederlandse letterkunde*, Nederlandse literatuur en cultuur in de Middeleeuwen, 15 (Amsterdam, 1996), p. 211-238 en 334-346.

SCHEEPSMA 1997: W. Scheepsma, *Deemoed en devotie. De koorvrouwen van Windesheim en hun geschriften,* Nederlandse literatuur en cultuur in de Middeleeuwen, 17 (Amsterdam, 1997).

SIMONS 1987: W. Simons, *Bedelordekloosters in het graafschap Vlaanderen. Chronologie en topografie van de bedelordenverspreiding vóór 1350* (Brugge, 1987).

STALLINGS-TANEY 1997: M. Stallings-Taney, *Iohannis de Cavlibus. Meditaciones vite Christi olim S. Bonauenturo attributae,* Corpvs Christianorum, Continuatio Mediaeualis, 153 (Turnholti, 1997).

STOOKER and VERBEIJ 1997: K. Stooker and Th. Verbeij, *Collecties op orde. Middelnederlandse handschriften uit kloosters en semi-religieuze gemeenschappen in de Nederlanden*, 2 vols., Miscellanea Neerlandica, 15-16 (Leuven, 1997).

SUTTON and VISSER-FUCHS 1996: A.F. Sutton and L. Visser-Fuchs, 'The cult of angels in late fifteenth-century England: An hours of the guardian angel presented to queen Elizabeth Woodville', in: J.H.M. Taylor and L. Smith (eds.), *Women and the book. Assessing the Visual Evidence* (London, Toronto,1996), p. 230-265.

VAN DEN BERG: E. Van den Berg, 'Over het lokaliseren van Middelnederlandse rijmteksten', in: *Verslagen en Mededelingen van de Koninklijke Academie voor Nederlandse Taal- en Letterkunde* (1986), p. 305-322.

VAN HERWAARDEN 1981: J. Van Herwaarden, 'Geloof en geloofsuitingen in de veertiende en vijftiende eeuw. Eucharistie en Lijden van Jezus', in: J.D. Janssens (ed.), *Hoofsheid en devotie in de middeleeuwse maatschappij. De Nederlanden van de 12^{e} tot de 15^{e} eeuw,* Handelingen van het wetenschappelijk colloquium te Brussel 21-24 oktober 1981 (Brussel, 1981), p. 174-207.

VAN LOEY 1968: A. Van Loey, *Middelnederlandse spraakkunst. II. Klankleer* (Groningen, 1968 [vijfde herziene uitgave]).

VAN LOEY 1964: A. Van Loey, *Schönfelds historische grammatica van het Nederlands: klankleer, vormleer, woordvorming* (Zutphen, 1964 [zevende druk]).

WACKERS 1996: P. Wackers, 'Latinitas en Middelnederlandse letterkunde: ter inleiding', in: P. Wackers e.a., *Verraders en bruggenbouwers. Verkenningen naar de relatie tussen Latinitas en de Middelnederlandse letterkunde,* Nederlandse literatuur en cultuur in de Middeleeuwen, 15 (Amsterdam, 1996), p. 9-42.

YDEWALLE 1945: S. d'Ydewalle, *De Kartuize Sint-Anna ter-Woestijne te Sint-Andries en te Brugge, 1350-1792,* Andreana-reeks, 1 (Brussel/Brugge, 1945).

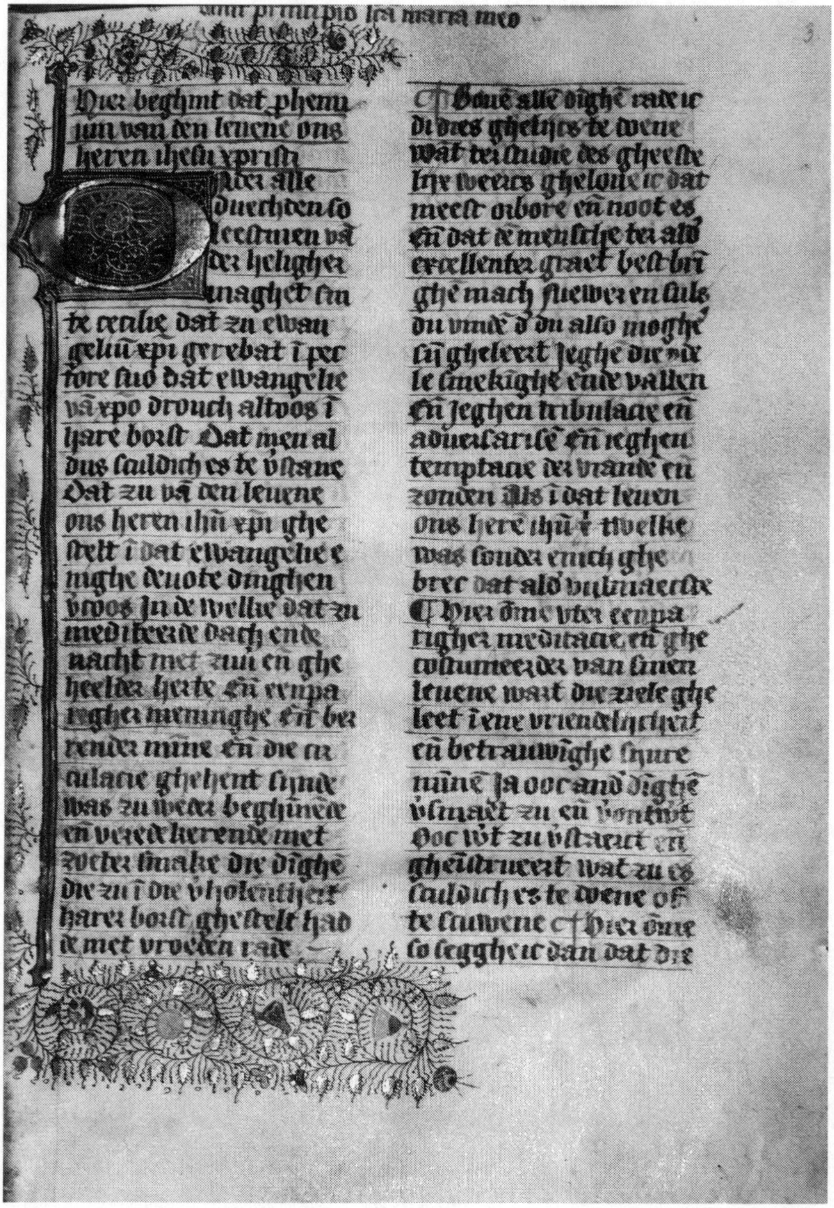

PLATE 1
Leuven, Bibliotheek van de Faculteit Godgeleerdheid, Ms. 842S, fol. 3r
Decorated opening initial of the first text

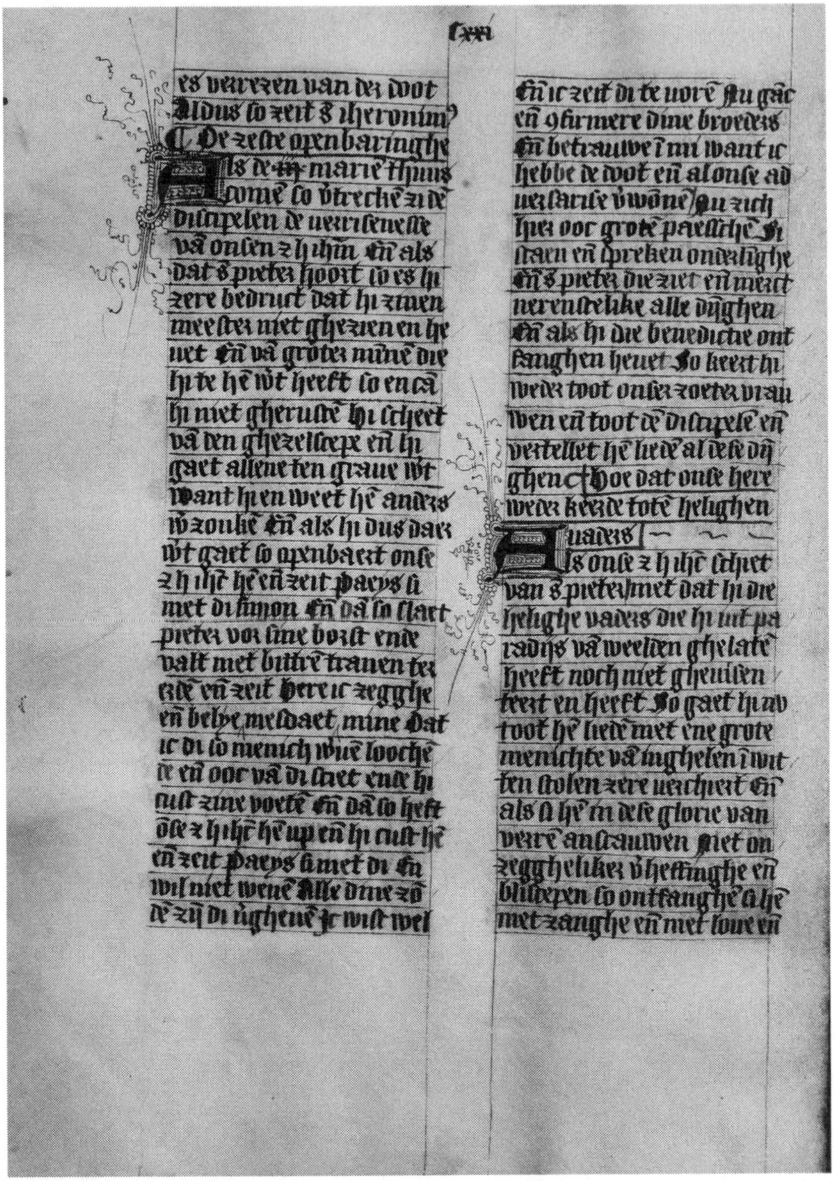

PLATE 2
Leuven, Bibliotheek van de Faculteit Godgeleerdheid, Ms. 842S, fol.122v
Decoration of individual chapters and chapter headings

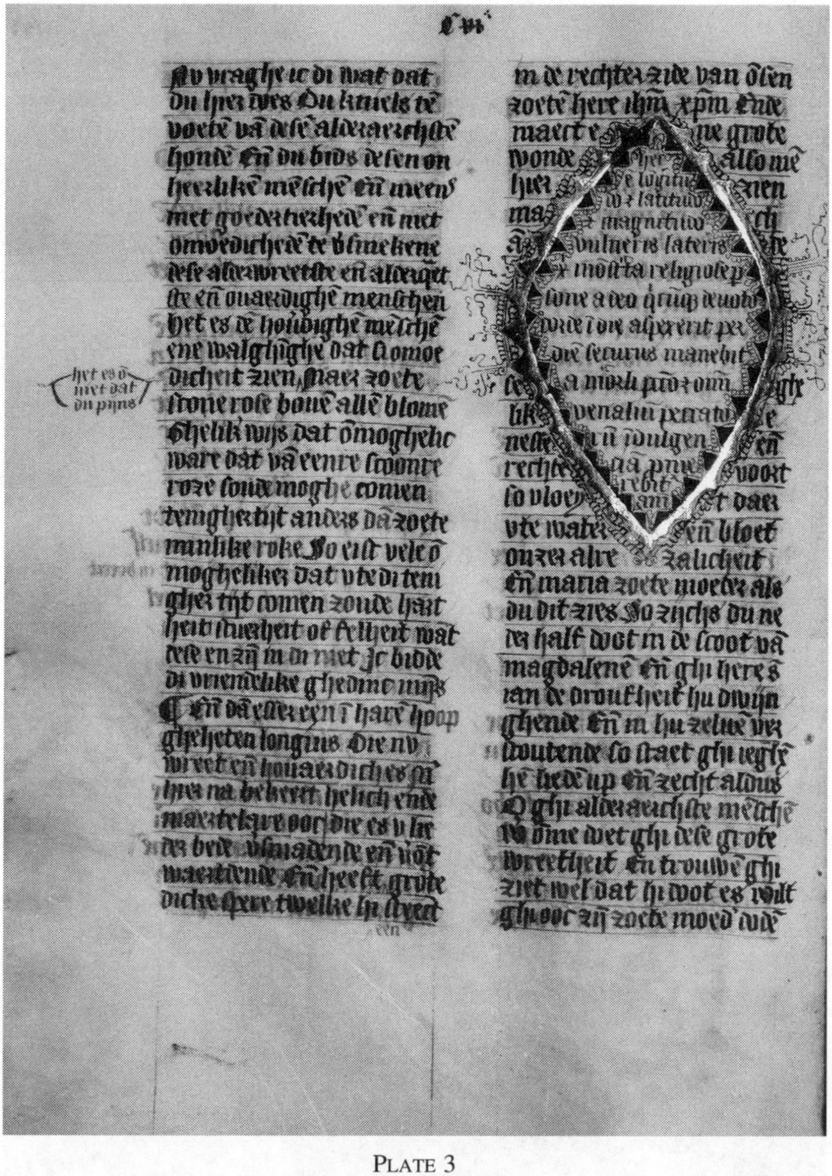

PLATE 3
Leuven, Bibliotheek van de Faculteit Godgeleerdheid, Ms. 842S, fol. 107v
Wound of crucified Christ

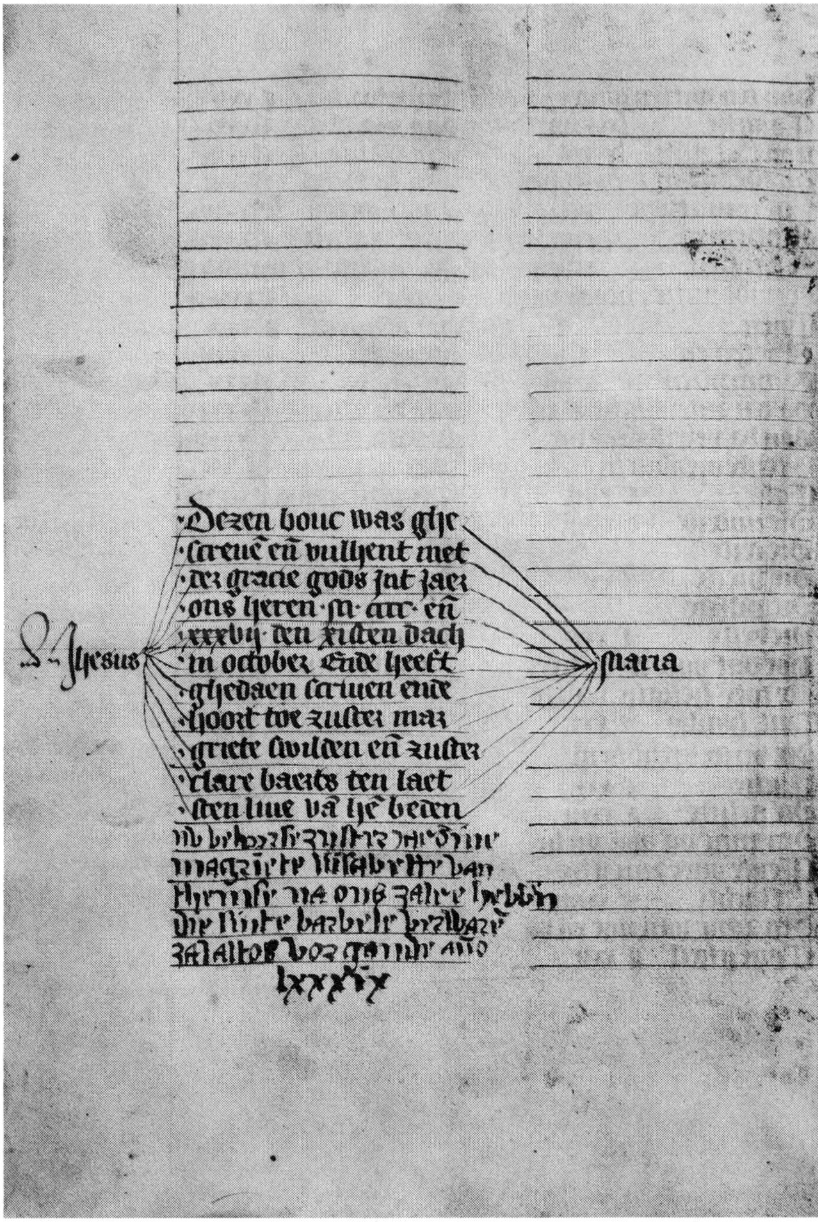

PLATE 4
Leuven, Bibliotheek van de Faculteit Godgeleerdheid, Ms. 842S, fol. 2v
Colophon

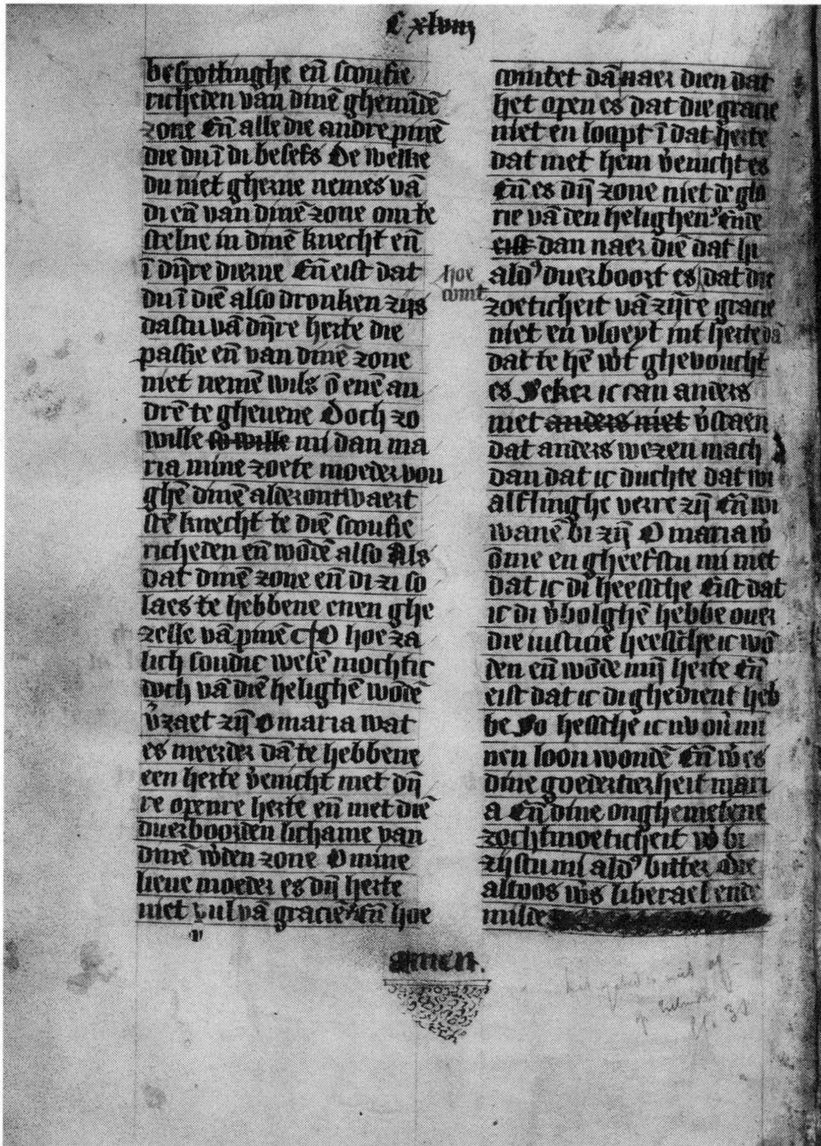

PLATE 5
Leuven, Bibliotheek van de Faculteit Godgeleerdheid, Ms. 842S, fol. 149v
Abrupt ending of the last excerpt

Yitzhak HEN

THE RECYCLING OF LITURGY UNDER PIPPIN III AND CHARLEMAGNE

The age of Pippin III (d. 768) and Charlemagne (d. 814) was a significant period of liturgical formation in the early medieval West. For the first time in the history of western Christendom a concerted interest in liturgy was demonstrated by rulers who obviously recognised the political and social advantages that lay within the patronage of liturgy.[1] Several unrelated sources clearly associate Pippin III with the introduction of the *cantus Romanus* into Francia, and consequently credit him with replacing the *cantus Gallicanus* with what were understood to be Roman musical traditions.[2] Walahfrid Strabo (d. 849) even recounts that it was Pippin himself who asked Pope Stephen (d. 757) to bring with him on his visit to Francia some material to enable this reform.[3] Pippin's modest beginnings were shortly overshadowed by his successor's grandiose reform programme.

Under Charlemagne the Carolingian reformatory zeal received a more official expression. Already in his first capitulary, dated to around 769, Charlemagne showed some interest in liturgy and in the way it was celebrated, and thus ordered that each priest '(...) should always in Lent report and explain to the bishop the method and procedure [in which he performs] his ministry, concerning baptism, the Catholic faith, the prayers, and the *ordo* of the mass'.[4] Furthermore, in the same capitulary he decrees that

1. On the patronage of liturgy in the early Middle Ages, see Y. Hen, *The Royal Patronage of Liturgy in Frankish Gaul to the Death of Charles the Bald (877)*, Henry Bradshaw Society, subsidia 3 (London, 2001).

2. *Epistola Karoli Calvi Imp. ad clerum Ravennatem*, in A. Jacob, 'Une lettre de Charles le Chauve au clergé de Ravenne?', *Revue d'histoire ecclésiastique*, 67 (1972), 409-22 (at 417); *Admonitio generalis*, c. 80, ed. A. Boretius, Monumenta Germaniae Historica [hereafter cited as MGH] Capitularia regum Francorum I (Hannover, 1883), no. 22, p. 61; *Karoli epistola generalis*, ed. Boretius, ibid., no. 30, p. 80; *Libri Carolini*, I.6, ed. A. Freeman, MGH Concilia, supplementum 1 (Hannover, 1998), 135-6; Walahfrid Strabo, *Libellus de exordiis et incrementis quarundam in observationibus ecclesiasticis rerum*, c. 26, ed. and trans. A.L. Harting-Corrêa, Mittellateinische Studien und Texte, 19 (Leiden, New York and Cologne, 1996), 168-9.

3. Walahfrid Strabo, *Libellus de exordiis* (cf. note 2), c. 26, p. 168-9. On the fact that Walahfrid Strabo did not know the *Libri Carolini*, see ibid., 230-1.

4. *Karoli Magni capitulare primum (c. 769)*, c. 8, ed. Boretius (1883), no. 19 (cf. note 2), p. 45: '(...) et semper in quadragesima rationem et ordinem ministerii sui, sive de baptismo sive de fide catholica sive de precibus et ordine missarum, episcopo reddat et osten-

> priests, who do not know properly [how] to perform their ministry and are not too busy to learn with all their energy according to the order of their bishops, or [those who] seem to disregard the canons, must be removed from the office itself, until they should know these completely without any mistakes.[5]

Charlemagne, it appears, took more than a supervisory interest in the details of liturgical worship and ceremonies. Liturgy, as noted by Gregory Dix, was a subject upon which his views were decided and obstinate.[6] With the assistance of his advisers, most notably Alcuin of York (d. 804) and Theodulf of Orléans (d. 820),[7] Charlemagne published a whole series of legislation in which he took straightforward measures to reform the liturgical practices of the Frankish Church. In the *Admonitio generalis*, which contains the clearest statement of his programme for the reform of the Frankish Church, Charlemagne reiterated his father's instructions that the clergy should learn the Roman chant and employ it throughout the office.[8] In the same capitulary he also introduced the Roman practices regarding the kiss of peace and the recitation of the names of the dead during mass,[9] and subsequent legislation as well as conciliar decrees repeated these demands, either in general or in particular terms.[10] What is noteworthy about Charlemagne's legislation is not so much that it was original, but that it was clearly stated and consistently applied.

dat'. This canon repeats *Karlomanni principis capitulare (742)*, c. 3, ed. Boretius (1883), no. 10 (cf. note 2), p. 25. The authenticity of this capitulary is disputed by scholars; see T.M. Buck, *Admonitio und Praedicatio. Zur religiös-pastoralen Dimentionen von Kapitularien und kapitulariennahen Texten (507-814)*, Freiburger Beiträge zur mittelalterlichen Geschichte, 9 (Frankfurt, 1996), 292-5, and see the further references listed there.

5. *Karoli Magni capitulare primum (c. 769)*, c. 15, ed. Boretius (1883), (cf. note 2), p. 46: 'Sacerdotes, qui rite non sapiunt adimplere ministerium suum nec discere iuxta praeceptum episcoporum suorum pro viribus satagunt vel contemptores canonum existunt, ab officio proprio sunt submovendi, quousque haec pleniter emendata habeant'.

6. G. Dix, *The Shape of Liturgy*, 2nd ed. (London, 1945), 575.

7. The amount of literature on Alcuin and Theodulf is vast, and cannot be listed here. A useful summary on both is provided by J.M. Wallace-Hadrill, *The Frankish Church* (Oxford, 1983), 205-25, and see there pp. 430-2 for a fuller bibliography. On Alcuin, see also the seminal studies by D.A. Bullough, 'Alcuin and the kingdom of heaven: liturgy, theology and the Carolingian age', in idem, *Carolingian Renewal: Sources and Heritage* (Manchester, 1991), 161-240 [originally published in *Carolingian Essays. Andrew Mellon Lectures in Early Christian Studies*, ed. U.-R. Blumenthal, Washington DC, 1983, 1-69]. See also *Alcuin of York*, eds. L.A.J.R. Houwen and A.A. MacDonald, Germania Latina, 3 (Groningen, 1998); M. Garrison, *Alcuin's World through his Letters and Verse* (Cambridge, forthcoming).

8. *Admonitio generalis (789)*, c. 80, ed. Boretius (1883), no. 22 (cf.note 2), p. 61.

9. Ibid., cc. 53-54, 57.

10. See, for example, *Karoli epistola generalis*, ed. Boretius (1883) (cf. note 2), 80; *Capitulare Francofurtense (794)*, cc. 50-1, ed. A. Werminghoff, MGH Concilia, I (Hannover, 1906), no. 19(G), 171.

The rather unusual royal interest in liturgical practices under Pippin III and Charlemagne also had its effect on the production of liturgical texts. First, a new type of sacramentary – the so-called eighth-century Gelasian Sacramentary – emerged during the reign of Pippin III; and subsequently, a Roman sacramentary was imported by Charlemagne and disseminated throughout the Frankish kingdom. The circulation of these two new types of sacramentaries punctuated the history of the Frankish rite in the second half of the eighth century, and in both cases recycling had an important role in shaping the liturgical scene of Carolingian Europe.

Let us begin with Pippin III. The so-called eighth-century Gelasian Sacramentary, also known as the Frankish Gelasian, the Mixed Gelasian, the Young Gelasian (*Junggelasiana*), the Sacramentary of King Pippin III, or the Sacramentary of St Boniface, is known to us only from a series of a dozen or so manuscripts which transmit what are thought to be derivative versions of the original copy.[11] These versions have several peculiar features in common. First, all these sacramentaries 'have a certain Benedictine flavour about them', for they provide a set of masses for the feast of St Benedict and his name appears in the *communicantes* of the Canon.[12] Second, all these sacramentaries commemorate the feast of the Frankish St Praiectus (d. 676), and they all have a mass in honour of St Chrysogonus (d. *c.* 304), thought to be rewritten when his basilica was restored in Rome under Pope Gregory III (d. 741).[13] Finally, and more

11. The most important manuscripts of this type of sacramentary are listed by M. Metzger, *Les sacramentaires*, Typologie des sources du Moyen Age occidental, 70 (Turnhout, 1994), 107-8; C. Vogel, *Medieval Liturgy: An Introduction*, trans. W. Storey and N.K. Rasmussen (Washington DC, 1986), 71-3. See also *Codices liturgici latini antiquiores*, ed. K. Gamber, 2nd ed., 2 vols., Spicilegii Friburgensis subsidia, 1 (Freiburg, 1968), with a supplement by B. Baroffio et al. eds., Spicilegii Friburgensis subsidia, 1A (Freiburg, 1988), nos. 801-898 [hereafter cited as *CLLA*]. The following discussion on the eighth-century Gelasian Sacramentaries is based on A. Chavasse, 'Les sacramentaire gélasien du VIIIe siècle. Ses deux principales formes', *Ephemerides liturgicae,* 73 (1959), 249-98; idem, *Les sacramentaires dans le groupe dit gélasiens du VIIIe siècle*, 2 vols., Instrumenta Patristica, 14 (Steenbrugge, 1984); B. Moreton, *The Eighth-Century Gelasian Sacramentary: A Study of Tradition* (Oxford, 1976); Vogel, *Medieval Liturgy,* 70-78; E. Palazzo, *A History of Liturgical Books from the Beginning to the Thirteenth Century*, trans. M. Beaumont (Collegeville, 1998), 46-8; Metzger, *Les sacramentaires,* 107-13. See also M. Klöckener, 'Sakramentarstudien zwischen Fortschritt und Sackgass', *Archiv für Liturgiewissenschaft,* 32 (1990), 207-30.

12. Moreton 1976 (cf. note 11), 15-16; Vogel 1986 (cf. note 11), 73.

13. See L.C. Mohlberg, 'Elementi per precisare l'origine del sacramentario Gelasiano del secolo VIII', *Atti della Pontificia Accademia Romana di Archeologia*, 7 (1932), 19-32; Vogel 1986 (cf. note 11), 73-4; and compare B. Moreton, 'Mohlberg, Chrysogonus, and the eighth-century Gelasians', in *Studia Patristica*, 10, ed. F.L. Cross, Texte und Untersuchungen, 107 (Berlin, 1970), 391-5. See also B. Moreton, 'A pastoral festival? Saint Praiectus and the eighth-century Gelasian Sacramentary', *Journal of Theological Studies,* 27 (1976), 370-80.

importantly, all these sacramentaries show a great similarity to one another in terms of content, arrangement and use of prayers. Hence, a single archetype was postulated, and scholars have reached the conclusion that it was assembled by a team of Benedictine monks, most probably at the Burgundian monastery of Flavigny, late in the reign of Pippin III.[14]

The content of this new sacramentary is very revealing. It is commonly accepted nowadays that the eighth-century Gelasian sacramentaries are basically Gallican modifications of Roman usage (similar to the one represented by the ninth-century Sacramentary of Padua),[15] based on earlier Frankish exemplars of the Old Gelasian Sacramentary and with ample use of prayers from the later Merovingian period.[16] The recycling of Gallican elements, it appears, was crucial in the gathering of the eighth-century Gelasians. In some cases, like, for example, in the feast for the Invention of the Cross, the entire Old Gelasian mass set was copied by the compilers of the eighth-century Gelasian, with minor changes or variations.[17] In other cases, the compilers of the eighth-century Gelasian picked and mixed various bits and pieces from the Frankish liturgy (mainly from the so-called Old Gelasian tradition) and re-arranged them in new masses for various occasions. In most cases, the choice of prayers to be recycled was not random, and a thematic association connected the older prayers with their new function. For example, the similarity and close affinity between the story of the Seven Brothers (local Roman martyrs of the second century) and that of the Maccabees, may explain why the compilers

14. *Liber sacramentorum Gellonense*, ed. A. Dumas and J. Deshusses, 2 vols., Corpus Christianorum, series latina [hereafter cited as CCSL] 159-159A (Turnhout, 1981), II, xxiii-xxvi; Vogel 1986 (cf. note 11), 74-6. Moreton argues that the archetype was produced by a Benedictine community in the Rhaetian Alps, on account of the fact that the derivative versions from that area are the least affected by outside traditions. See, Moreton 1976 (note 11), 173.

15. Padua, Biblioteca Capitolare D 47 (S. Germany; s. ix^{med}); *CLLA*, no. 880. For an edition, see *Le sacramentaire grégorien. Ses principales formes d'après les plus anciens manuscrits*, ed. J. Deshusses, 3 vols., Spicilegium Friburgense 16, 24 and 18 (Freibourg, 1979-82), I, 609-84. On the Sacramentary of Padua, see Vogel 1986 (cf. note 11), 92-7, and see the further bibliography listed there.

16. See Vogel 1986 (cf. note 11), 74-5; Moreton 1976 (cf. note 11), passim.

17. See, for example, *Liber sacramentorum Gellonense*, cc. 944-8, ed. Dumas and Deshusses 1981 (note 14), 127-8; *Liber sacramentorum Engolismensis*, cc. 939-43, ed. P. Saint-Roch, CCSL 159C (Turnhout, 1987), 139-40; *Liber sacramentorum Augustodunensis*, cc. 747-51, ed. O. Heiming, CCSL 159B (Turnhout, 1987), 90-91. For the Old Gelasian mass for the Invention of the Cross, see *Liber sacramentorum Romanae aecclesiae ordinis anni circuli (Sacramentarium Gelasianum)*, cc. 869-72, ed. L.C. Mohlberg, L. Eizenhöfer and P. Siffrin, Rerum ecclesiasticarum documenta. series maior 4 (Rome, 1960), 138. See also Moreton 1976 (cf.note 11), 111 and 134-5.

of the eighth-century Gelasian chose various elements from an Old Gelasian mass *in natale plurimorum sanctorum* and incorporated them into a mass for the Maccabees.[18] Apparently, this particular Old Gelasian mass for unspecified saints was used in Rome, as attested by the so-called Leonine Sacramentary, for the feast of the Seven Brothers.[19] In other examples, the connection is even more straightforward, such as the recycling of the Old Gelasian mass for the feast of St Peter (29 June) as part of the eighth-century Gelasian mass for the *Cathedra Petri*,[20] or the recycling of the mass for St Marcellus (d. 309) in the mass for St Leo (d. 461).[21] While in the former St Peter himself inspired the recycling, in the latter it was the fact that both saints were popes. On top of all that, these newly formed prayer books recycled and preserved many Frankish practices, such as Rogation days,[22] consecration of churches,[23] and more significantly, the Frankish episcopal blessings.[24]

As far as liturgical uniformity is concerned, there is no doubt that the eighth-century Gelasian sacramentaries demonstrate a high degree of

18. See, for example, *Liber sacramentorum Gellonense*, cc. 1277-81, ed. Dumas and Deshusses 1981 (cf. note 14), 168-9; *Liber sacramentorum Engolismensis*, cc. 1156-8, ed. Saint-Roch 1987 (cf. note 17), 171-2. For the Old Gelasian mass, see *Sacramentarium Gelasianum*, cc. 1113-1114, ed. Mohlberg et al. 1960 (cf. note 17), 169. See also Moreton 1976 (cf. note 11) 112-16.

19. See *Sacramentarium Veronense*, cc. 398-9, ed. L.C. Mohlberg, L. Eizenhöfer and P. Siffrin, Rerum ecclesiasticarum documenta, series maior 1 (Rome, 1956), 54. On this sacramentary, see D.M. Hope, *The Leonine Sacramentary. A Reassessment of its Nature and Purpose* (Oxford, 1971); Vogel 1986 (cf. note 11), 38-46; Palazzo 1998 (cf. note 11), 38-42.

20. See, for example, *Liber sacramentorum Gellonense*, cc. 234-7, ed. Dumas and Deshusses 1981 (cf. note 14), 29-30; *Liber sacramentorum Engolismensis*, cc. 238-41, ed. Saint-Roch 1987 (cf. note 17), 33; *Liber sacramentorum Augustodunensis*, cc. 244-8, ed. Heiming 1987 (cf. note 17), 29-30. For the Old Gelasian mass for the feast of St Peter, see *Sacramentarium Gelasianum*, cc. 918-20, ed. Mohlberg et al. 1960 (cf. note 17), 144. See also Moreton 1976 (cf. note 11), 145.

21. See, for example, *Liber sacramentorum Gellonense*, cc. 866-9, ed. Dumas and Deshusses 1981 (cf. note 14), 118; *Liber sacramentorum Engolismensis*, cc. 897-900, ed. Saint-Roch 1987 (cf. note 17), 133-4; *Liber sacramentorum Augustodunensis*, cc. 675-8, ed. Heiming 1987 (cf. note 17), 82-3. For the Old Gelasian mass for St Marcellus, see *Sacramentarium Gelasianum*, cc. 810-14, ed. Mohlberg et al. 1960 (cf. note 17), 130-131. See also Moreton 1976 (cf. note 11), 145.

22. See, for example, *Liber sacramentorum Gellonense*, cc. 890-4, ed. Dumas and Deshusses 1981 (cf. note 14), 121-4; *Liber sacramentorum Engolismensis*, cc. 959-63, ed. Saint-Roch 1987 (cf. note 17), 142-4; *Liber sacramentorum Augustodunensis*, cc. 697-707, ed. Heiming 1987 (cf. note 17), 85-6.

23. See, for example, *Liber sacramentorum Gellonense*, cc. 2415-24, ed. Dumas and Deshusses 1981 (cf. note 14), 360-62.

24. On these episcopal blessings, see E. Dekkers, '"Benedictiones quas faciunt Galli". Qu'a voulu demander saint Boniface?', in *Lateinische Kultur im VIII. Jahrhundert. Traube-Gedenkschrift*, ed. A. Lehner and W. Berschin (Saint-Ottilien, 1989), 41-6.

structural unity, which undoubtedly derives from the fact that all surviving manuscripts can be traced back to a single archetype. However, even within this unity, a striking degree of diversity was created by various alterations, additions and omissions.[25] An excellent case in point is the mass for the feast of the above-mentioned Pope Marcellus. While the Gellone Sacramentary recycles the Old Gelasian mass for St Marcellus the centurion (d. 298) and adds to it two prayers, one from the Gothic Missal's *missa unius confessoris* and one from the Leonine Sacramentary's mass for St Laurentius (d. 258);[26] the Sacramentary of Angoulême combines the Gellone mass for Pope Marcellus with that for St Marcellus the centurion;[27] the Rheinau Sacramentary recycles only the Gellone mass for St Marcellus the centurion;[28] and the Sacramentary of Autun, like the Rheinau Sacramentary, recycles the Gellone mass for St Marcellus the centurion, to which it adds one prayer from the Old Gelasian and one new prayer, which is found nowhere else.[29]

Shortly after its production, the eighth-century Gelasian enjoyed a vast circulation, as the various manuscripts of its derivative versions suggest. Yet, the reasons for its popularity could only be postulated. It could be that the eighth-century Gelasian was perceived as a sacramentary with some kind of royal approval, since its archetype was put together at the monastery of Flavigny, which enjoyed the king's patronage and commemorated the king's patron saint.[30] Yet, it is more likely that this new type of sacramentary was appreciated by many contemporary ecclesias-

25. See Moreton 1976 (cf. note 11), 170-72; idem, 'The *liber secundus* of the eighth-century Gelasian sacramentaries: a reassessment', in *Studia Patristica* 13, ed. E.A. Livingstone, Texte und Untersuchungen 116 (Berlin, 1975), 382-6.

26. *Liber sacramentorum Gellonense*, cc. 140-145, ed. Dumas and Deshusses 1981 (cf. note 14), 17-18. For the Old Gelasian mass for St Marcellus, see *Sacramentarium Gelasianum*, cc. 810-14, ed. Mohlberg et al. 1960 (cf. note 17), 130-131. For the prayer from the Gothic Missal, see *Missale Gothicum*, c. 466, ed. L.C. Mohlberg, Rerum ecclesiasticarum documenta, series maior 5 (Rome, 1961), 111; also E. Rose, *Communitas in commemoratione. Liturgisch Latijn en liturgische gedachtenis in het Missale Gothicum (Vat. reg. lat. 317)*, PhD thesis, University of Utrecht, 2001, 162. For the Leonine prayer for St Laurentius, see *Sacramentarium Veronense*, c. 746, ed. Mohlberg et al. 1956 (cf. note 19), 94.

27. *Liber sacramentorum Engolismensis*, cc. 135-43, ed. Saint-Roch 1987 (cf. note 17), 18-19. For the Gellone mass for St Marcellus the centurion, see *Liber sacramentorum Gellonense*, cc. 146-8, ed. Dumas and Deshusses 1981 (cf. note 14), 18-19.

28. See *Sacramentarium Rhenaugiense*, cc. 119-21, ed. A. Hänggi and A. Schönherr, Spicilegium Friburgense, 15 (Freiburg, 1970).

29. See *Liber sacramentorum Augustodunensis*, cc. 144-9, ed. Heiming 1987 (cf. note 17), 17-18. On the eighth century Gelasian mass for St Marcellus, see also Moreton 1976 (cf. note 11), 136-9.

30. See Hen 2001 (cf. note 1), 59-60, and see the bibliography cited there.

tics as a more complete, more up-to-date and more handy composition, properly adapted for the Frankish rite. They could certainly recognise its familiar Gallican tone, which was the result of a unique process of recycling and grafting older prayers from the prevailing repertoire of the Merovingian liturgy.

Things, it seems, were about to change dramatically during the reign of Charlemagne. Sometime in the early 780s, taking advantage of Paul the Deacon's visit to Rome on his way back to Montecassino, Charlemagne bid him to ask Pope Hadrian for a copy of the authentic sacramentary put together by Pope Gregory the Great. This request must have embarrassed the pope, for no sacramentary used in Rome at that time went back to Pope Gregory's pontificate. Nevertheless, after some delay, a copy of the so-called Gregorian Sacramentary reached the court at Aachen between 786/7 and 791. On account of this gift, the particular type of the Gregorian Sacramentary sent by Pope Hadrian to Charlemagne is commonly known as the *Hadrianum*.[31] But this sacramentary was neither a copy of the sacramentary arranged by Pope Gregory the Great, nor was it the current sacramentary used in Pope Hadrian's time. What Charlemagne received was a copy of a sacramentary that was redacted, most probably, under Pope Honorius I (d. 638) and augmented in the course of the seventh and the eighth centuries.[32]

Given the fact that the Gregorian Sacramentary which served as the basis for the *Hadrianum* was originally designed for papal use and, consequently, contained mainly stational masses to be celebrated in the basilicas of Rome,[33] the *Hadrianum* was ill-suited for the needs of any Frankish episcopal church, let alone a parochial one. No wonder then, that on its arrival at Charlemagne's court, the *Hadrianum* was given the cold shoulder by Alcuin of York, the mind behind Charlemagne's reforms.[34]

31. On the *Hadrianum*, see *Le sacramentaire grégorien*, ed. Deshusses 1979-82 (cf. note 15), I, 60-3; Vogel 1986 (cf. note 11), 80-85; Palazzo 1998 (cf. note 11), 48-54; Metzger 1994 (cf. note 11), 78-80.

32. See *Le sacramentaire grégorien*, ed. Deshusses 1979-82 (cf. note 15), I, 50-61; Vogel 1986 (cf. note 11), 79-80; Metzger 1994 (cf. note 11), 57-80.

33. On the stational liturgy of Rome, see A.A. Willis, *A History of Early Roman Liturgy to the Death of Gregory the Great*, Henry Bradshaw Society subsidia series 1 (London, 1994), 68-77.

34. On Alcuin and the Carolingian reforms, see F.C. Scheibe, 'Alcuin und die *Admonitio generalis*', *Deutsches Archiv*, 14 (1958), 211-19; idem, 'Alcuin und die Briefe Karls des Großen', *Deutsches Archiv*, 15 (1959), 181-93; L. Wallach, *Alcuin and Charlemagne: Studies in Carolingian History and Literature*, rev. ed. (Ithaca NY, 1968), 198-226; Bullough 1991 (note 7); T.F.X. Noble, 'From brigandage to justice: Charlemagne, 785-794', in *Literacy, Politics and Artistic Innovation in the Early Middle Ages*, ed. C.M. Chazalle (Lanham, New York and London, 1992), 49-75, at 59-61.

'What need is there for new when the old are adequate?',[35] he wrote to Eanbald of York, and continued to use older sacramentaries.[36]

Not so long after its arrival and subsequent diffusion throughout the Frankish kingdom, the shortcomings of the papal sacramentary sent to Charlemagne were noted, and therefore it was reorganised, corrected and supplemented. Benedict of Aniane (d. 821), held by Cyrille Vogel as the 'reformer *par excellence* of the Carolingian period',[37] took upon himself to revise and adapt the *Hadrianum* for use in Francia.[38] In the course of his revisions, Benedict supplemented the *Hadrianum* mainly with Sunday and votive masses, to which a series of *praefationes*, episcopal blessings and texts for the ordination of the minor orders, were appended.[39] As he clearly states in the preface to his supplement, throughout his revision Benedict extracted from older versions of Frankish sacramentaries available to him, mainly from copies of the Old Gelasian and the eighth-century Gelasians. For example, being a sacramentary for the papal stationary liturgy, the *Hadrianum* had no mass for the king, not the least because it is hard to imagine the pope praying for the success and welfare of the Lombard kings, his closest neighbours and most terrifying nemesis. Thus, Benedict incorporated into his supplement the Old Gelasian mass *pro regibus*, which was earlier recycled by the compilers of the eighth-century Gelasian as well.[40] But still, Benedict was not satisfied, and he com-

35. Alcuin, *Epistolae* 226, ed. E. Dümmler, MGH Epistuale 4 (Berlin, 1895), 370: 'Quod opus est nova condere, dum vetera sufficiunt?'

36. J. Deshusses, 'Les anciens sacramentaires de Tours', *Revue bénédictine*, 89 (1979), 281-302.

37. See Vogel 1986 (cf. note 11), 86.

38. Although in the past scholars attributed the *Hadrianum*'s supplement to Alcuin of York, it is nowadays almost unanimously attributed to Benedict of Aniane, following the argument put forward by Jean Deshusses. See J. Deshusses, 'Le supplément au sacramentaire grégorien: Alcuin ou Saint Benoît d'Aniane?', *Archiv für Liturgiewissenschaft*, 9 (1965), 48-71; idem, 'Le sacramentaire grégorien pré-hadrianique', *Revue bénédictine*, 80 (1970), 213-37; *Le sacramentaire grégorien*, ed. Deshusses 1979-82 (cf. note 15), I, 62-70 and III, 66-75; Vogel 1986 (cf. note 11), 85-92; Palazzo 1998 (cf. note 11), 53-4; Metzger 1994 (cf. note 11), 114-19; R. McKitterick, *The Frankish Church and the Carolingian Reforms, 789-895* (London, 1977), 130-8. More recently Philippe Bernard argued that it was not Benedict of Aniane who composed the *Supplementum* and its preface, but a councillor at the royal court of Charlemagne, most probably Alcuin. Furthermore, Bernard attributes the impetus for the composition to Charlemagne himself, and dates the composition to an earlier stage of Charlemagne's reign. See Philippe Bernard, 'Benoît d'Aniane est-t-il l'auteur de l'avertissement "Hucusque" et du Supplément au sacramentaire "Hadrianum"?', *Studi Medievali* 39 (1998), 1-120. However, Bernard's learned and interesting analysis is untenable.

39. For an edition of Benedict's *supplementum*, see *Le sacramentaire grégorien*, ed. Deshusses 1979-82 (cf. note 15), I, 351-605 [hereafter cited as *Supplementum*].

40. *Supplementum*, cc. 1266-9, ed. Deshusses 1979-82 (cf. note 15), I, 424-5. For the Old Gelasian mass *pro regibus*, see *Sacramentarium Gelasianum*, cc. 1505-9, ed. Mohlberg

posed a new mass *pro rege*, which he added right after the mass he copied from the Old Gelasian.[41] In his *Missa specialis sacerdotis*, to give just one more example, Benedict recycled a prayer from the Bobbio Missal,[42] to which he added some newly composed prayers to complete the mass.[43] Moreover, most of the *praefationes* which he added were taken from various versions of the eighth-century Gelasian Sacramentary.[44] The result was a unique compendium of old Frankish prayers carefully chosen by Benedict of Aniane, with some newly composed additions. This was appended to the *Hadrianum*, and from then onwards was circulated with it in various forms.[45]

Apart from posing an intellectual exercise for scholars who wish to trace the sources and evolvement of the eighth-century Gelasians and the *Supplementum* to the *Hadrianum*, the recycling of liturgy at the time of Pippin III and Charlemagne is of crucial importance to our understanding of the nature and scope of the liturgical development and reforms under the early Carolingians. The Merovingian age was a prolific period of liturgical activity. New prayers were composed, sacramentaries and lectionaries were shaped, and new celebrations were instituted.[46] It was the formative period of the so-called Gallican liturgy, in the course of which a rather defined corpus of Gallican prayers was formed. Although bishops and priests were free to institute feasts, fasts and vigils, or to compose prayers and prayer-books of their own, a general reluctance to do so emerged during the early Carolingian period, and it is clearly reflected in the recycling of Gallican prayers under Pippin III and Charlemagne.

The recycling Merovingian prayers in the Carolingian period rightly puts into question the traditional understanding of the liturgical reforms promulgated by the Frankish kings. It seems that the neat textbook description of early Carolingian attempts to impose a form of liturgical

et al. 1960 (cf. note 17), 217-18. For the eighth century masses, see, for example, *Liber sacramentorum Gellonense*, cc. 2624-8, ed. Dumas and Deshusses 1981 (cf. note 14), 410-11; *Liber sacramentorum Engolismensis*, cc. 2311-16, ed. Saint-Roch 1987 (cf. note 17), 359-60; *Liber sacramentorum Augustodunensis*, cc. 1637-41, ed. Heiming 1987 (cf. note 17), 201-2.

41. *Supplementum*, cc. 1270-72, ed. Deshusses 1979-82 (cf. note 15), 425-6.

42. Ibid., c. 1280, 428. For the prayer from the Bobbio Missal, see *The Bobbio Missal: A Gallican Mass Book*, c. 414, ed. E.A. Lowe, Henry Bradshaw Society, 58 (London, 1920), 123.

43. *Supplementum*, cc. 1281-4, ed. Deshusses 1979-82 (cf. note 15), 428-9.

44. See ibid., cc. 1516-1737, 495-575.

45. See ibid., I, 62-74.

46. On the liturgical activity in Merovingian Gaul, see Y. Hen, *Culture and Religion in Merovingian Gaul, A.D. 481-751* (Leiden, New York and Cologne, 1995), 43-153; Hen 2001 (cf. note 1), 25-41.

unity through the imposition of Roman liturgical practices and books, can no longer be accepted at face value. Although there were indeed successful attempts at reform through the introduction of Roman books, this was not the case as far as the Frankish liturgy is concerned. Whether one looks at the compilation of the eighth-century Gelasians or the grafting of the *Hadrianum*'s supplement, it is obvious that no Romanisation was at stake, and that local and indigenous traditions were abundantly preserved.[47] Hence, the recycling of old Gallican prayers in the eighth-century Gelasians and in the *Supplementum* of the *Hadrianum* are, I would submit, the most eloquent witness to the force and vitality of the Gallican rite, even at the second half of the eighth century.

Despite the prevailing image of unity and Romanisation which our sources generate, the Carolingian period was an age of considerable liturgical experimentation and diversity. The concern and preoccupation with authority, orthodoxy and correctness, which characterised the late Merovingian and, more particularly, the early Carolingian period, gave rise to what I would call 'rhetoric of reform' that emphasised, among other things, the reformatory qualities of Pippin III and Charlemagne, and subsequently stressed correctness, uniformity and compliance with Rome.[48] This 'rhetoric of reform' crops up in a variety of sources all of which originated in the royal court of Charlemagne and his successors. Subsequently, words such as *corrigere*, *emendare*, *renovare*, *reformare* and their synonyms, readily became the instruments for achieving unity, and unity gave the Christian empire of Charlemagne *pax*, *caritas* and *concordia*.[49] No doubt this rhetoric was conditioned by the Carolingian political ideology and the perception of kingship that evolved in the late eighth and early ninth century. It was echoed in each and every description of the king, his duties and the reforms he promulgated.[50] As a result,

47. On this issue, see Hen 2001 (cf. note 1), 42-95, and see the bibliography cited there. See also Y. Hen, 'Liturgische hervormingen onder Pepijn de Korte en Karel de Grote: de illusie van romanisering', *Millennium,* 15 (2001), 97-113.

48. On this 'rhetoric of reform', see Hen 2001 (cf. note 1), 86-9.

49. These ideas come up time and again in a great variety of sources from the Carolingian period. See, for example, Alcuin, *Epistolae* 41, 121, 129, 136, 219, 257, ed. Dümmler 1895 (cf. note 35), 84, 176, 192, 209, 363, 415 respectively; idem, *Disputatio de rhetorica et de virtutibus,* ed. W.S. Howell, Princeton Studies in English 23, Princeton, 1941; Theodulf of Orléans, *Carmina* 28-29, ed. E. Dümmler, MGH Poetae 1, Berlin, 1881, 493-520. For further references, see H.H. Anton, *Fürstenspiegel und Herrscherethos in der Karolingerzeit,* Bonner Historische Forschungen, 32 (Bonn, 1968).

50. See N. Staubach, '"Cultus divinus" und karolingische Reform', *Frühmittelalterliche Studien* 18 (1984), 546-81, especially 563-73. See also Y. Hen, 'The uses of the Bible and the perception of kingship', *Early Medieval Europe,* 7 (1998), 277-89; idem, 'The christianisation of kingship', in *Der Dynastiewechsel von 751*, ed. M. Becher and J. Jarnut (Munich, 2004), 163-177.

the royal patronage of liturgy in this reforming context, whether it was merely implementing changes that were already set in motion by the king's predecessors (as in the case of Pippin and the Roman chant), commissioning a new liturgical book from Rome (as in the case of Charlemagne and the *Hadrianum*), or introducing a few Roman practices to the Frankish rite and calendar, became an integral part of this rhetorical discourse. The colossal recycling of old Gallican prayers by the compilers of the eighth-century Gelasian and by Benedict of Aniane proves that such 'rhetorical' objectives were not implemented in actuality.

Notwithstanding the importance of Merovingian prayers in the formation of the Carolingian liturgy, a different kind of recycling endangered the very existence of the older Gallican liturgical corpus. The diffusion of the eighth-century Gelasians and the subsequent rise of the *Hadrianum* in its supplemented form – two phenomena which dominated the liturgical scene of the late eighth and the early ninth century – had some devastating effects on the copying and preservation of older Gallican liturgical texts. Francia was flooded with new copies of sacramentaries and lectionaries, and many older liturgical compositions were simply swept away and doomed to oblivion. By the end of the eighth century, the Merovingian liturgical books were old-fashioned, inadequate, and in many cases were already replaced by new, revised and well-adapted compositions. Once the old sacramentaries and lectionaries were no longer suitable for use, they were discarded, and this process is clearly reflected in the liturgical palimpsests from the late eighth and early ninth century.[51] Most of the liturgical palimpsests known to us from that period are palimpsests of older Gallican texts, some of which found their way to the newly composed eighth-century Gelasian or Benedict of Aniane's *Supplementum*, other survive only in a mutilated form,[52] and many were lost forever. Thus, paradoxically, while one process of recycling helped to preserve the Gallican liturgical tradition and carry it on to the Carolingian period, another process of recycling threatened to eradicate it.

51. On the liturgical palimpsest from Francia, see Y. Hen, 'Liturgical palimpsests from the early Middle Ages', in *Early Medieval Palimpsests*, ed. G. Declercq (in press). See also E.A. Lowe, '*Codices rescripti*. A list of the oldest Latin palimpsests with stray observations on their origins', in *Mélanges Eugène Tisserant* (Vatican City, 1964), V, 67-112 [reprinted in idem, *Palaeographical Papers, 1907-1965*, ed. L. Bieler, Oxford, 1972, II, 480-519].

52. See, for example, Munich, Bayerische Staatsbibliothek, Clm 14429; *CLLA* 211. For an edition, see *Das irische Palimpsestsakramentar im Clm 14429 der Staatsbibliothek München*, eds. A. Dold and L. Eizenhöfer, Texte und Arbeiten, 53-54 (Beuron, 1964). On the importance of this sacramentary, see Y. Hen, 'Rome, Anglo-Saxon England, and the formation of the Frankish liturgy', *Revue bénédictine,* 112 (2002), 301-22.

To sum up, the age of Pippin III and Charlemagne has often been regarded as a formative stage in the evolution of western liturgical rites and practices. In many cases this is true, yet one should be extremely careful not to read too much into the sources and not to overemphasise the significance of the liturgical reforms promulgated by the Frankish kings and their advisers. Roman books and liturgical practices were undoubtedly introduced to the Frankish kingdoms, both voluntarily and by legislation, but the traditional non-Roman rites were neither deliberately suppressed nor lost. Many of the old Gallican prayers and feasts were recycled in the new liturgical compositions of the late eighth century, and the continuity in liturgical celebration is apparent. No general Romanisation of the entire Frankish practice was ever desired by the Frankish kings or their bishops, and no outright exchange of an existing liturgical corpus for a wholly different one was aimed at. As far as liturgy is concerned, the time of Pippin III and Charlemagne appears to have been a great age of recycling.

Donna MAYER-MARTIN

RESPUN MELODIES FOR THE VIRGIN: *TROUVÈRE* MODELS FOR THE SONGS OF GAUTIER DE COINCI

1. Introduction

Les Miracles de Nostre Dame, adapted by Gautier de Coinci in the early thirteenth century from now lost Latin sources, witnessed such immense popularity during the late Middle Ages that they are preserved today in almost eighty manuscripts. Carefully interpolated amongst the Marian narratives in several of these manuscripts are Gautier's songs in praise of the Virgin – songs for which Gautier wrote the words but borrowed the melodies. The musical genres chosen by Gautier as models for his Marian chansons are extremely diverse, and they reveal an intimate knowledge of all of the major musical practices of the late twelfth and early thirteenth centuries in northern France. At the Abbey of Saint-Médard, the study of plainchant would have been an important part of the young Gautier's instruction, and his *Miracles* are full of musical allusions. Gautier's musical models for his chansons include *trouvère* chansons, a sequence, and Latin organa and conductus from Notre Dame. For the purposes of the present study, I will consider only those Marian songs that are based upon melodies preserved in *trouvère chansonniers.* As we shall see, Gautier used as models for his *chansons pieuses* melodies by some of the most renowned creators of the northern courtly lyric and, by composing new texts for these borrowed courtly melodies, he sang the praises of his own *belle dame,* Mary, the mother of Christ. In the course of considering each of the eight chansons in this group, I have examined all extant manuscript appearances of Gautier's melodies and those of his musical models. These examinations shed light on manuscript transmission practices in the *trouvère chansonniers* at the same time that they illuminate transmission patterns in the manuscripts containing Gautier's songs. Just as important, they suggest which *specific* versions of *trouvère* melodies were familiar enough to Gautier for him to choose them as models for his songs.

2. The manuscripts

In her seminal study of the manuscript tradition of Gautier's *Miracles de Nostre Dame,* Arlette Ducrot-Grunderye divided the seventy-nine extant manuscripts into three groups.[1] Mme Ducrot based her manuscript groups on the relative completeness of the two Marian cycles that make up the basic structure of Gautier's work, and she assigned sigla of capital letters to those manuscripts she found to be most comprehensive. It is within this broad sub-group that the twelve manuscripts that preserve Gautier's melodies are found.

Gautier's *Miracles de Nostre Dame* are organized as follows in the majority of manuscripts considered most comprehensive by Ducrot:

Book One: Prologue to Book One
Prologue to the chansons
Seven Marian chansons
Thirty-five Marian miracles
Three chansons in honor of Sainte-Léocade

Book Two: Prologue to Book Two
Seven Marian chansons
One Marian miracle
De la chasteé as nonains (moralist poem)
Twenty-three Marian miracles
An Epilogue and three related writings
Chanson, *Entendez tuit ensemble et li clerc et li lai*
Four prayers
Three additional Marian chansons (preserved in only a few manuscripts)

The number of Gautier's musical works, then, is twenty-two, if one includes the final three chansons and one chanson not included as part of a cycle, *La fontenele i sourt clere.*

The manuscripts that preserve Gautier's chansons with their melodies are listed in Table I. Ducrot's sigla (DG) are included here and, to their right, are the sigla used earlier by Friedrich Gennrich (GENN).[2] We will use Gennrich's numerical sigla in this discussion in order not to confuse

1. Arlette Ducrot-Granderye, *Études sur les 'Miracles Nostre Dame' de Gautier de Coinci. Description et classement sommaire des manuscrits.* Annales Scientiarum Fennicae, B, XXV, 2 (Helsinki, 1932).

2. Friedrich Gennrich, 'Die beiden neusten Bibliographien altfranzösischer und altprovenzalischer Lieder', *Zeitschrift für Philologie,* XLI (1921), 294-346.

Ducrot's sigla with those (also capital letters) used by scholars to identify the *chansonniers*. The manuscripts listed in Table I date from the thirteenth and fourteenth centuries, with the earliest being Manuscript XVI, dated by its scribe, Guillaume, monk of the Abbey of Morigny, in 1266, just thirty years after Gautier's death.[3]

The musical contents in these manuscripts are remarkably complete. The only two exceptions are two thirteenth-century sources, Paris, BN, 986 (Gennrich's XIII), which contains music only for the first cycle of miracles, and Brussels, BR, 10.474 (MS V), which has staves but no music for the last three songs in the first cycle.

The best-known of Gautier's manuscripts was originally kept at the Grand Séminaire at Soissons. Although we know that Gautier wrote his *Miracles* while he was prior of the chapel at Vic-sur-Aisne, which was closely affiliated with the neighboring Abbey of Saint-Médard, Soissons was the home of Saint-Médard where Gautier later would serve as abbot from 1233 until his death in 1236. The Soissons Manuscript (MS I), which had disappeared for much of the twentieth century and is now in the Bibliothèque nationale de France as Paris, BN, n. acq. 24.541, is justly famous for the beauty of its visual images. The melodies in the Soissons manuscript are preserved in mensural notation; this is the only occurrence of rhythmic indications for Gautier's melodies with the exception of a few half-hearted attempts at metric notation in Paris, BN, 22.928 (MS II) and the St. Petersburg Manuscript, Hermitage, fr. F.v.XIV 9 (MS XIX).

Table Two lists the titles of Gautier's Marian chansons as they appear in the Soissons manuscript (MS I), which also is the most typical order of their appearance in the other manuscripts that contain music. The first cycle of seven songs, in this manuscript preserved in folios 4v to 6v, is preceded by Gautier's Prologue to Book One and the brief Prologue to the chansons themselves. The seven chansons are followed by thirty-five narrative miracles. Following these, on folios 110r to 111v, is preserved a cycle of songs (with music) in honor of Sainte-Léocade, the Spanish saint whose relics were carefully guarded at the chapel in Vic-sur-Aisne under Gautier's stewardship. The second cycle of seven Marian chansons appears on folios 115r to 118r. Three additional Marian songs, which are not a part of the two cycles, do not appear in the Soissons manuscript and are listed in Table II as numbers 20, 21, and 22. Musicologist Jacques Chailley and literary scholar Frederick Koenig both believe Gautier may

3. The signature reads: "Explicit liber domni Galteri, prioris de Vi, scriptus per manus Guillelmi monachi Maurigniacensis, anno Domini MCCLX secto." See L. Delisle, *Le cabinet des manuscrits de la Bibliothèque nationale*, t. II (Paris, 1874), 385.

have written these last three songs during the three years following the completion of his *Miracles* in 1233 and his death in 1236.[4] The remaining song in Table II, *Entendez tuit ensemble et li clerc et li lai,* is preserved on folio 240r in the Soissons source.

As mentioned earlier, Gautier borrowed melodies from *trouvère chansonniers* for eight of his Marian chansons. These particular chansons, which include works from both Marian cycles and from the last three songs, are listed below:[5]

Qui que face rotruenge novele (RS 603, 748)
Efforcier m'estuet ma vois (RS 1836)
Quant ces flouretes florir (RS 1677)
Pour la pucele en chantant me deport (RS 1930, 1600)
D'une amour coie et serie (RS 1212)
Ja our yver, pour noif ne pour gelee (RS 520)
Pour mon chief reconforter (RS 885)
Puisque voi la fleur novele (RS 600)

Because discussions of these eight chansons entail consideration of their multiple manuscript sources and of the multiple sources that contain their models, it would be helpful at this time to provide information on the relevant *trouvère chansonniers*. Table III presents those *trouvère* manuscripts that contain models for Gautier's chansons, with corresponding identifying sigla and the approximate dates of each manuscript.[6]

3. Analyses of Gautier's Chansons and Their Models

3.1. *Qui que face rotruenge novele* (RS 603, 748)

Gautier's chanson *Qui que face rotruenge novele* borrows its melody from a chanson by the famous *trouvère,* Blondel de Nesle. The poems of both poets consist of stanzas of nine decasyllabic lines with the rhyme scheme a'ba'b/bbba'b. Gautier's chanson is preserved in ten manuscripts: I (twice),

4. Jacques Chailley, *Les Chansons a la Vierge de Gautier de Coinci* (Paris: Heugel, 1959), 35-41. *Les Miracles de Nostre Dame par Gautier de Coinci,* 1. ed. V. Frederic Koenig (Geneva: Librairie Droz, 1966), xxx.

5. RS numbers are from Hans Spanke, G. *Raynauds Bibliographie des Altfranzösischen Liedes,* Erster Teil (Leiden: E.J. Brill, 1980).

6. The alphabetical sigla of *trouvère chansonniers* in Table III have no relationship to Ducrof's alphabetical sigla for Gautier's manuscripts. For an in-depth discussion of the musical contents of all of the *trouvère chansonniers* as well as the music manuscripts of Gautier de Coinci, see Donna Mayer-Martin, *Thematic Catalogue of Troubadour and Trouvère Melodies, with a study of the manuscripts* (Stuyvesant, NY: Pendragon, 2006).

II, III, IV, V, VIII, X, XI, XIII, and XIX. Blondel's poem, *Bien doit chanter qui fine amor adrece* (RS 482), also survives with its music in no fewer than ten *chansonniers:* MSS K, M, N, P, R, T, U, V (twice), X, and a.[7]

There are three different melodic readings that appear in the ten manuscripts preserving Gautier's chanson. The first two phrases of all three readings are presented as Examples la, 1b, and lc. The first two melodies, found in MSS II and VIII, are closely related to one another in melodic contour, although the melody in MS II (which is similar to melodies found in MSS I, III, IV, and XIX) explores a melodic range a fourth below that in MS VIII (which shares its melody with that in MS X). The third melody, in MS V (Example lc), differs in almost every way from the previous two. This is the only reading of this melody preserved in any of Gautier's manuscripts.

Upon examining Blondel's chanson, one finds there are three readings for his melody as well. The first, preserved in MS K, is presented as Example 1d, and the second, in MS T, as Example le. A closer look shows these two readings to be similar to one another, with their opening descending sweep through the interval of a seventh in the first phrase, followed by a second phrase that hovers around the middle range of the first phrase. The third reading of this chanson, preserved in MSS R and V, is loosely related to the above two readings. The next step, of course, would be to explore relationships between Blondel's melodies, preserved in the *chansonniers,* and Gautier's melodies. However, since such a comparison involves qualitative as well as quantitative considerations of the sources involved, it would be well to consider briefly stemmatic interrelationships relevant to each of the two sets of manuscripts.

The *chansonniers* of the *trouvèeres* may be loosely divided into three families, or collections, based upon their contents and upon similarities in orthography, ordering of stanzas, and their accompanying melodies. The most cohesive of the three families is that made up of MSS K, N, P, and X (these four MSS are so similar they may well have been copied at the same atelier) and MSS O, B, and part of R. A second family, also very reliable in its readings, includes MSS M, T, A, Z, and a. The third family, which includes MSS F and U, contains much less music than the other two collections and therefore is more difficult to evaluate.[8]

7. Blondel's *Bien doit chanter qui fine amor adrece* is also the probable model for Minnesinger Ulrich von Gutenberg's song, *Ich hôrte wol ein merlikîn singen.* See James McMahon, *The Music of the Early Minnesang* (Columbia, South Carolina: Camden House, 1990), 137-139.

8. This is not to dismiss the importance of MS U (Paris, BN, 20.050) in particular, which is considered the earliest collection of troubadour and *trouvère* song extant.

In addition to assigning sigla of capital letters to the most comprehensive of Gautier's manuscripts, Ducrot further classified them according to what she termed "particularités externes", in which category she included omissions, interpolations, ordering of materials, rubrics, and glosses. Following this, she added a further classification based upon textual variants.[9] According to these criteria, Ducrot discerned the following groupings: CG, BHv, DIf, FL, bx, and adgr. In his exemplary edition of Gautier's *Miracles,* Frederic Koenig reviewed more recent manuscript scholarship and he found Ducrot's initial classifications to be essentially sound.[10] Koenig based his own edition of the *Miracles* on MS L (Gennrich's II) because, at the time he began his work, the other two manuscripts he considered to be most carefully executed and reliable, MSS R (XIX) and S (I), were unavailable to him. Jacques Chailley based his edition of Gautier's melodies on MS S (I). The reasons for choosing a manuscript dated so late (early fourteenth century), appears to have been because it is the only manuscript that preserves Gautier's songs with rhythmic notation throughout. Although this solved the problem of how to deal with the rhythmic question for the edition, it did not present a reading that would have been contemporary with Gautier. For our musical purposes, then, we will refer primarily to Ducrot's and Koenig's studies of the manuscripts.

As we return to the chanson *Qui que face rotruenge novele* and its model *Bien doit chanter qui fine amour adrece*, I notice that, while variants of Gautier's melodies found in Manuscripts II and VIII (Examples 1a and 1b) survive in fully ten of the eleven preserved sources, it is only the melody preserved in Brussels, BR, 10.747 (MS V) that is closely related to Blondel's melody (compare particularly Examples 1c and 1e). Although Gautier's melody lacks the dramatic opening downward sweep of Blondel's melody, it nevertheless is strikingly similar in both pitch and melodic contour. Blondel's melody, beginning either on F (Example 1d) or on C (Example 1e), is preserved with few variations in nine of the manuscript sources for this melody and, in the other two (MSS R and V), there are obvious similarities. It would appear, then, that only one of Gautier's manuscripts preserves what was evidently a very popular reading of Blondel's melody, and that is MS V. See the plate (at the end of this contribution) for a facsimile of this chanson.

9. Ducrot, *Études* [see note 1], 124-139.
10. Koenig, *Gautier de Coinci* [see note 4], xxxix-xlv.

3.2. *Efforcier m'estuet ma vois* (RS 1836)

The melody for Gautier's chanson, *Efforcier m'estuet ma vois,* is singularly static in relation to Gautier's other borrowed melodies. It appears in all nine of its surviving musical sources (MSS I, II, III, IV, VIII, X, XI, XIII, XIX) as a simple, syllabic melody based on a D mode, and devoted primarily to repetition on its dominant, the A located a fifth higher. While Chailley suggests a relationship with Moniot de Paris's famous chanson, *Lonc tans ai mon tans usé* (RS 475),[11] the sequential pattern of the movable reciting tone of the latter chanson appears to disqualify this possibility. In this case, matching metric schemes in the texts (9-line stanzas with 7- and 6-syllable lines and refrains) has not yet produced a viable candidate for a melodic source for this chanson.

3.3. *Quant ces flouretes florir* (RS 1677)

The source for this chanson is readily apparent. Gautier's poem and its model, Vielart de Corbie's *De chanter me semont armours* (RS 2030), both consist of stanzas of eight octosyllabic lines with a rhyme scheme, abab/abab. Gautier's melody is preserved in nine sources: MSS I, II, III, IV (twice), VIII, X, XI, XIII, and XIX. With the exception of the final phrase, which is presented in a variant reading in manuscripts II, III XIII, and XIX, all appearances of Gautier's melody are remarkably similar.

Vielart de Corbie's chanson survives in only four sources, MSS K, N, P, and X. As stated earlier, these four manuscripts not only belong to the same *chansonnier* family, but are so similar in their contents that they may well have been copied at the same atelier. It is interesting to note that the only divergence among these four readings is in the final phrase, where MSS K and N offer melodies more closely related to the predominant readings in Gautier's manuscripts (particularly MSS I, IV, VIII, and X), while MSS P and X present a related, but somewhat different, opening melodic gesture. Example 2 presents both chansons in their entirety. The reading of Gautier's chanson is that in MS XIX (fol. 44v), the Hermitage Manuscript, and Vielart de Corbie's chanson is from MS K (fol. 227r). One notices that Gautier's melody is somewhat more florid than that of its model (see particularly phrases 1 and 6). The single critical difference between the two chansons lies in the final phrase: because MS XIX presents what has been referred to above as a variant reading of Gautier's melody, the chanson here ends on F rather than the pitch above,

11. Chailley, *Les Chansons* [see note 4], 51.

G, which is the norm for all of Vielart's readings and for the majority of Gautier's as well. The final cadence on F results in a strong pull away from the remainder of the chanson which has been centered around a G mode.

3.4. Pour la pucele en chantant me deport (RS 1930,1600)

Gautier's music for *Pour la pucele en chantant me deport* is preserved in ten sources: MSS I (twice), II, III, IV, V, VIII, X, XI, XVI, and XIX. The work on which it is modeled, *Chanter me fet ce don't je crien morir* (RS 1429), most likely written by Pierre de Molins, although also attributed to Gace Brulé, was equally popular – as shown in its preservation in ten *chansonniers* which cross all three *trouvère* manuscript families. This text and melody are in sequence rather than chanson structure, with the text following the pattern ab ab ab ba with the music in open and closed versicles of aa aa bb cc. The readings of Pierre's, or Gace's, melody in all *chansonniers* are very similar to one another. Surprising, though, is the fact that among Gautier's readings, only MS XVI (the earliest source), and MS III (also an early source), provide matches with Gautier's model.

Example 3a presents the first two phrases of Gautier's *Pour la pucele en chantant me deport* as it appears in MS V (fol. 107r). This reading is very similar to those found in MSS I (both appearances), II, IV, VIII, X, XI, and XIX and, as can easily be seen from the example, has nothing in common with Pierre's melody (Example 3c) related to melodic shape, range, or cadences. On the other hand, the melody in Gautier's MS III, presented here as Example 3b, is in every important instance virtually identical to its model.

3.5. D'une amour coie et serie (RS 1212)

Although Gautier's chanson *D'une amour coie et serie* has two metric correspondances (Thibaut de Champagne's *Contre le tens qui debrise* (RS 1620), and the anonymous *Ferus sui d'un dart d'amour* (RS 1945), one can find both a metric and a musical match in a chanson by Gilles de Vies-Maisons, *Je chant c'est mout mauvés signes* (RS 200, 1356). Gilles's poem consists of eight heptasyllabic lines with the rhyme a'ba'b/bba'b. Gautier added to Gilles's structure a refrain of three lines: 4B 6A' 6B. Eight manuscripts preserve Gautier's melody: MSS I, II, IV, V, VIII, X, XI, and XIX, and all eight readings are distinctly similar to one another. *Je chant c'est mout mauvés signes* is preserved only in the one closely-related manuscript family K, N, P, and X – where the melodic readings are almost identical.

Example 4 presents the opening four lines of both chansons where one can note subtle but significant musical alterations by Gautier from his model. For instance, while Gilles's melody consists of four phrases all cadencing on G, Gautier has changed his to an open-closed cadential pattern with the first and third phrases serving as musical antecedents to their following phrases. Gautier also returns by a leap of a fifth immediately upon the openings of phrases one and three to the higher melodic register and then develops that register with more florid motion than his model. These small changes suggest a skillful musician with a better ear for mode and musical expansion than that displayed in the model.

3.6. *Ja our yver, pour noif ne pour gelee* (RS 520)

Gautier chose another chanson by Blondel as his model for *Ja our yver, pour noif ne pour gelee*. Blondel's song, *Li plus se plaint d'amors mes je n'os dire* (RS 1495), survives in nine manuscripts that demonstrate an unusually wide spread of *trouvère* sources. These include readings from MSS K, N, P, M, T, R, V, Z, and a. Only the third *chansonnier* family is missing. The music for Gautier's chanson, however, is preserved only in MSS I, II, III, and XIX. The stanzaic form of the poem is eight decasyllabic lines with the rhyme scheme a'ba'b/ba'ba'. To Blondel's structure, Gautier has added three refrains, one for the first two verses, the second for verses three and four, and a third refrain follows the fifth verse. The four sources that preserve Gautier's music present melodies very similar to one another for both the body of the chanson and for Gautier's added refrains; the principal variants are related to cadential patterns in lines one and three of the chanson. In contrast, Blondel's chanson appears in three different variations across its nine manuscript appearances. The majority of the readings, however, are related more or less closely to that found in manuscript family K, N, and P. As one can see from Example 5, Gautier's melody, taken from MS XIX, fol. 142v, is once again similar to the music preserved in this *chansonnier* family. One notices, however, that Gautier has altered his opening two phrases from the model; this proves to be the case in all four manuscript appearances of Gautier's version.

3.7. *Pour man chief reconforter* (RS 885)

Gautier's chanson *Pour mon chief reconforter* presents a most interesting study in musical borrowing. The melody first appeared as the lower voice in a conductus from Notre Dame with words by Walter of Châtillon, *Sol sub nube latuit*. The *trouvère* Thibaut de Blaison, who was connected with the court at Poitiers until his death in 1229, borrowed that melody and fashioned from it his chanson, *Chanter et renvoisier seuil* (RS 1001). Thibaut's chanson is preserved in six *chansonniers*. Its poetic structure consists of pairs of seven-syllable lines using a repeated ab rhyme pattern, and the melody reflects this structure. Five of the six manuscripts that preserve Thibaut's music, MSS K, N, P, X, and O, present remarkably similar melodies; the sixth manuscript, MS V, contains an unrelated variant reading. Gautier's adaptation survives in only one source, the early manuscript XVI. His melody is obviously related to that of Thibaut de Blaison's but, in several instances, appears more closely related to the original conductus source. In addition, Gautier's chanson extends another four phrases beyond that of Thibaut's adaptation, matching the structure of the conductus, and Gautier includes as well, in his last phrase, a lengthy penultimate melisma that reflects the conductus's ending cauda. This suggests that Gautier was familiar with both sources and that his own chanson is not merely an adaptation of the single model by Thibaut de Blaison.[12]

3.8. *Puisque voi la fleur novele* (RS 600)

The final chanson by Gautier that we are considering, *Puisque voi la fleur novele,* also survives in only one source and, again, the source is Manuscript XVI. Its model, Gautier de D'Argies's *Au tens gent que reverdoie* (RS 1753), is in typical chanson structure, with six heptasyllabic lines followed by three lines of three, seven, and three syllables respectively. The rhyme pattern is a'ba'b/a'a'ba'b. Gautier de D'Argies's chanson is preserved in three sources, MSS K, N, and P with virtually identical readings; Gautier's adaptation is almost identical to these with, again, some creative variations at points of cadence.

4. Concluding remarks

There are a number of conclusions one may draw from a close consideration of these eight chansons. The first is a purely musical one. As

12. The source for *Sol sub nube latuit* considered is Wolfenbüttel, Herzog August Bibl. 677 (Wl), fol. 110v.

Gautier adapted his new poems for the Virgin Mary, he did not blindly use borrowed melodies as contrafacta. Rather, after selecting some of the best songs available from the current *trouvère* repertoire, Gautier adapted these melodies to his needs with alterations of modal patterns and melodic gestures – the latter almost always moving towards a more florid style than his models, a musical style associated in plainchant with praise. Gautier in some instances further elaborated his models with the additions of refrains, as is evident in *D'une amour coie et serie* and *Ja our yver, pour noif ne pour gelee.*

When considering manuscript transmission, it becomes obvious from the close relationships of Gautier's melodies with specific models that the chansons as they would be preserved in *trouvère* manuscripts K, N, P, and X were well known in the region of Picardie during Gautier's lifetime. Gautier's music manuscript tradition appears to be more cohesive in its contents than that of the *trouvère* tradition at large; this is not surprising given the smaller number of works and focused years of composition. Nevertheless, one does recognize individual strengths and differences among Gautier's sources. The Brussels Manuscript (MS V) appears to be a central source for Gautier's chansons; in fact, it is the sole manuscript preserving the melody for *Qui que face rotruenge novele.* This makes it even more dismaying that the manuscript is missing notation for the staves provided for the following three chansons.

However, the manuscript source of most interest musically may be the earliest surviving source for the melodies, MS XVI (Paris, BN, fr. 2163), dated thirty years after Gautier's death. While MS XVI preserves only three of the eight chansons considered in this study, two of these, *Pour mon chief reconforter* and *Puisque voi la fleur novele,* are unica. The first of these is particularly compelling because of its association with musical repertoire from Notre Dame, and suggests further possibilities in the quest for information about Gautier's advanced musical studies following his early years at Saint-Médard. Based upon the quality of Gautier's musical models, and also upon his adaptations of these models, it appears he may well have been an active participant – at the least as student and listener – in the extraordinarily vibrant musical culture of early-thirteenth-century Paris. What better place or better time for the young monk to begin gathering the many-colored musical and spiritual images that he would later weave into the rich tapestry of his songs for the Virgin.

TABLE I: MANUSCRIPTS CONTAINING THE MUSIC OF GAUTIER DE COINCI

DG: sigla of Arlette Ducrot-Granderye (1932)
Genn: sigla of Friedrich Gennrich (1921)

	Approximate Date	**DG**	**Genn**
Paris, BN, n. acq. fr. 24541 (anc. Soissons, Grand Séminaire)	Early 14thC	S	I
Paris, BN, fr. 22.928	14thC	L	II
Paris, BN, fr. 25.532	13thC	N	III
Paris, Arsenal, 3517	13thC	D	IV
Paris, Arsenal, 3518	13thC	D'	IV
Brussel, BR, 10.747	13thC	B	V
Paris, BN, fr. 1530	13thC	G	VIII
Paris, BN, fr. 1536	13thC	I	X
London, BL, Harl. 4401	13thC	C	XI
Paris, BN, fr. 986	13thC	F	XIII
Paris, BN, fr. 2163	1266	M	XVI
St. Petersburg, Herm., fr. F v. XIV 9	14thC	R	XIX
London, BL, Egerton 274	13thC	10bis.	–

TABLE II: GAUTIER'S CHANSONS WITH MUSIC

Order of Chansons in Paris, BN, n. acq. fr. 24.541 (anc. Soissons, Grand Séminaire), MS I

First Cycle (fol. 4v-6v)
1. *Amours qui bien set enchanter*
2. *Qui que face rotruenge novele*
3. *Roïne celestre*
4. *Talens m'est pris orendroit*
5. *Efforcier m'estuet ma vois*
6. *Quant ces flouretes florir*
7. *Pour conforter mon cuer et mon corage*

Cycle of Sainte Léocade (fol. 110r-111v)
8. *Las las las las, par grant delit*
9. *Seur cest rivage, a ceste crois*
10. *De la sainte Leochade*

Second Cycle (fol. 115r-118r)
11. *Pour la pucele en chantant me deport*

12. *Mere Dieu, Virge senée*
13. *S'amours dont sui espris*
14. *D'une amour coie et serie*
15. *Hui matin a la journee*
16. *Ja our yver, pour noif ne pour gelee*
17. *Ma viele*

Chanson not in a Cycle (fol. 149v)

18. *La fontenele i sourt clere*

Third Cycle (fol. 240r)

19. *Entendez tuit ensemble et li clerc et li lai*

[Chansons not in MS I]

20. *Hui enfantez fu li filz Dieu*
21. *Pour mon chief reconforter*
22. *Puisque voi la fleur novele*

TABLE III: *TROUVERE CHANSONNIERS* CONTAINING MODELS FOR THE CHANSONS OF GAUTIER DE COINCI

	Approximate Date	**Siglum**
Arras, Bib. Mun., 657	13thC	A
Paris, Arsenal, 5198	13thC	K
Paris, BN, fr. 844	13thC	M
Paris, BN, fr. 845	13thC	N
Paris, BN, fr. 846	13thC	O
Paris, BN, fr. 847	13thC	P
Paris, BN, fr. 1591	14thC	R
Paris, BN, fr. 12.615	13thC	T
Paris, BN, fr. 20.050	13thC	U
Paris, BN, fr. 24.406	13thC/14thC	V
Paris, BN, n.a. fr. 1050	13thC	X
Siena, Bib. Com., H.X.36	13thC/14thC	Z
Rome, Vatican, Reg. 1490	14thC	a

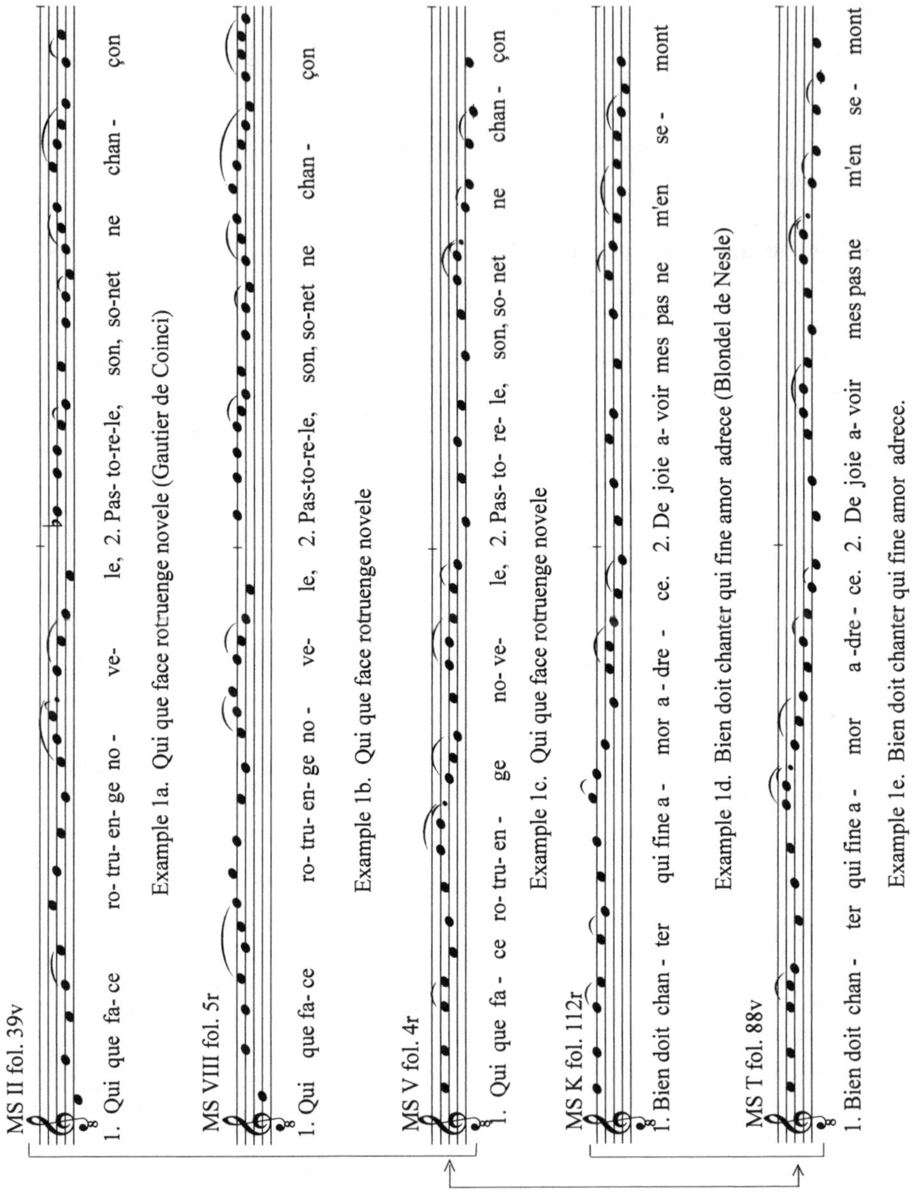

Example 1a. Qui que face rotruenge novele (Gautier de Coinci)

Example 1b. Qui que face rotruenge novele

Example 1c. Qui que face rotruenge novele

Example 1d. Bien doit chanter qui fine amor adrece (Blondel de Nesle)

Example 1e. Bien doit chanter qui fine amor adrece.

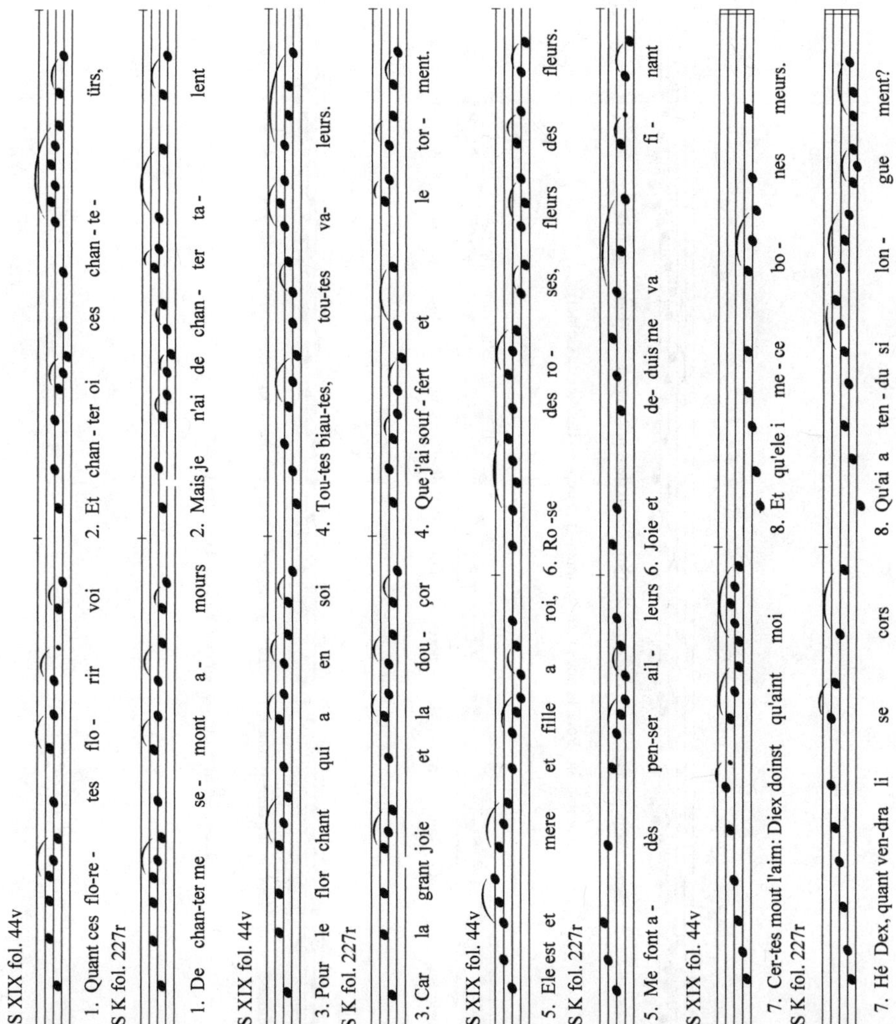

Example 2. Quant ces floretes florir voi (Gautier de Coinci) and De chanter me semont amours (Vielart de Corbie)

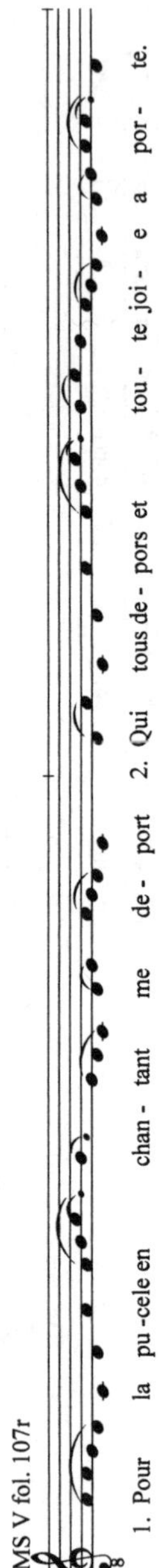

Example 3a. Pour la pucele en chantant me deport (Gautier de Coinci)

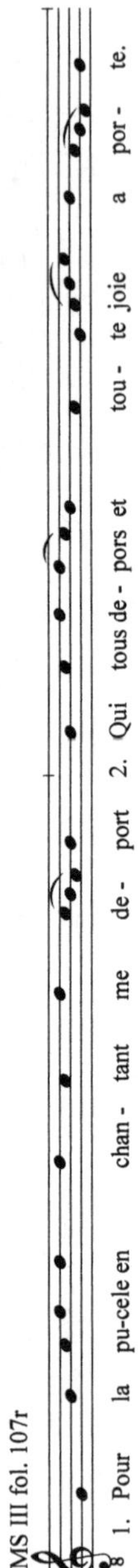

Example 3b. Pour la pucele en chantant me deport

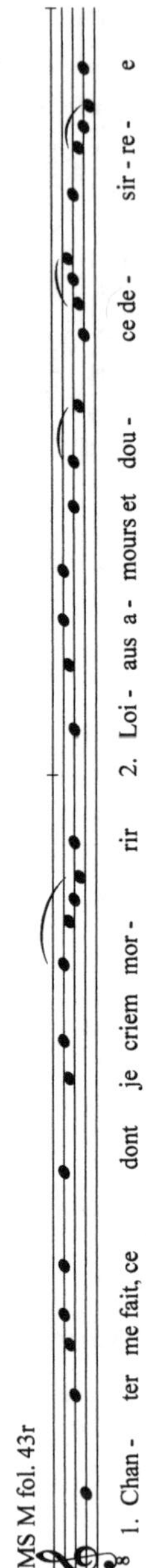

Example 3c. Loiaus amours et douce desirree (Pierre de Molins)

Example 4. D'une amor coie e serie (Gautier de Coinci)
and Je chant mès c'est mauvès signes (Gilles de Viès-Maisons)

Example 5. Je pour yver, par noif ne pour gelee (Gautier de Coinci)
and Li plus se plaint d'amors mes je n'os dire (Blondel de Nesle)

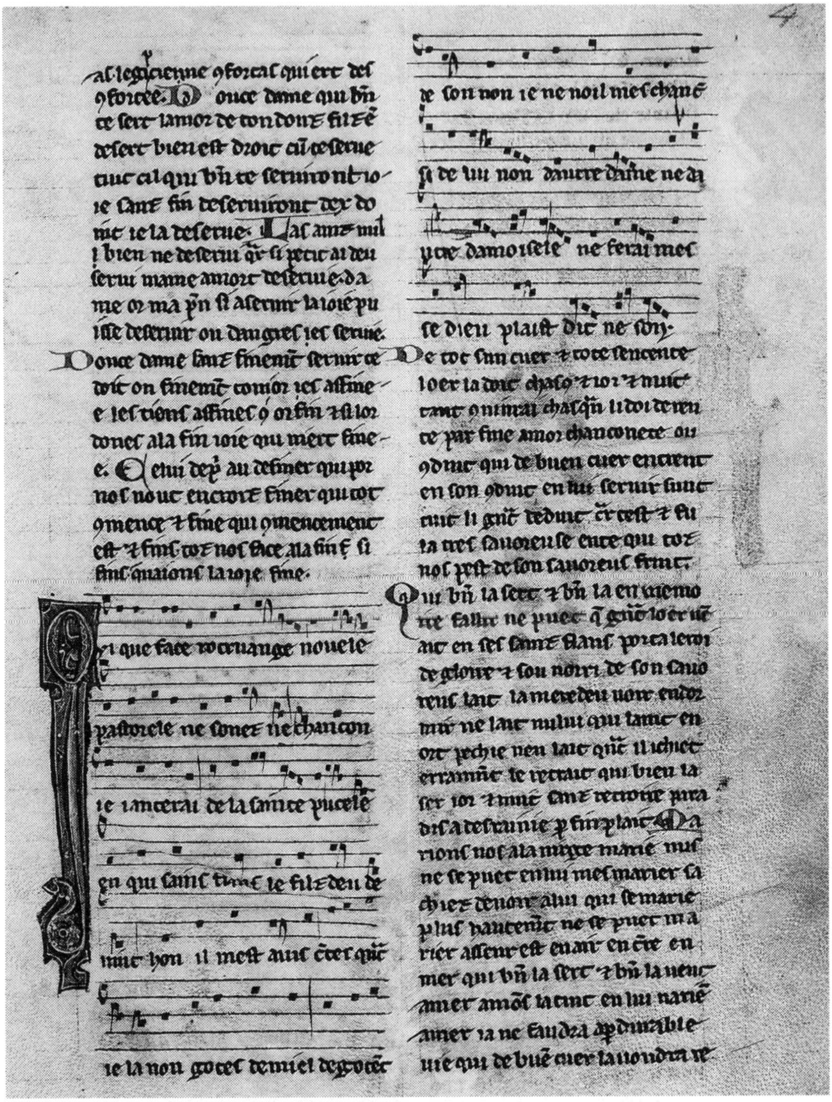

Gautier de Coinci, *Qui que face rotruenge novele*
Brussels, Bibliothèque royale, Ms. 10.747, fol. 4r
© Brussels, Bibliothèque Royale

Martine MEUWESE

THE SECRET HISTORY OF THE FOX AND THE HARE IN TRINITY B.11.22

1. INTRODUCTION*

Whereas miniatures or historiated initials generally attempt to illustrate the relevant text, marginal images need not do so. The abundant marginal decorations in psalters and prayer books are often text-independent, for they usually do not illustrate the accompanying religious text. In the margins artists could indulge their imagination, reverse roles, and even mock the authority of Christian doctrine. Marginal themes may refer to the accompanying text, to works of 'literature' such as sermons, romances, fables and bestiaries, but also to the activities of daily life such as hunting or children's play, or to a whole range of oral discourse, whether sayings, proverbs, riddles, or tales not written down originally.[1]

The Flemish Book of Hours Cambridge, Trinity College B.11.22 is dated around 1300 and is supposed to have been made for secular patrons, perhaps for a lady. The calendar contains Franciscan elements and refers to the region of Bruges and Ghent.[2] This splendid little Book of Hours has abundant marginal decoration on every page, covering a wide range of themes and sources.[3] Apart from general themes such as saints, games, obscenae, parody, humour (a man with bagpipes blown by a mouse on his shoulder), or images where the world is turned upside-down (a hare catching a man, a cow milking a woman), several images seem to refer

* I should like to thank Lilian Randall, Beatrix Zumbült, André Bouwman, Paul Wackers, Bart Besamusca and Sophie Oosterwijk for stimulating discussion and useful comments.

1. L.F. Sandler, 'The Study of Marginal Imagery: Past, Present, and Future', in: *Studies in Iconography*, 18 (1997), 1-49, esp. 27.

2. K.B.E Carlvant, 'Collaboration in a Fourteenth-century Psalter. The Franciscan Iconographer and the two Flemish Illuminators of MS 3384,8 in the Copenhagen Royal Library', in: *Sacris Erudiri. Jaarboek voor Godsdienstwetenschappen,* 25 (1982), 135-166, esp. 147. M. Meuwese, 'Jacob van Maerlant's *Spiegel Historiael*: Iconography and Workshop', in: M. Smeyers and B. Cardon (eds.), *Flanders in a European Perspective. Manuscript Illumination around 1400 in Flanders and Abroad. Proceedings of the International Colloquium Leuven, 7-10 September 1993* (Leuven, Peeters, 1995), 445-456.

3. The marginal decoration of Trinity B.11.22 has been described in M.R. James, *The Western Manuscripts in the Library of Trinity College, Cambridge. A Descriptive Catalogue* (Cambridge, Cambridge University Press, 1900), no. 261, but his iconographical list is by no means complete.

to a specific context. A motif that probably derives from an oral source, perhaps a proverb, is the man hatching on a nest of eggs. This marginal motif, which only occurs in a few stylistically related Flemish manuscripts dating from the late thirteenth century, can be considered as an allusion to human folly.[4]

One of the many bestiary themes illustrated in the margins of Trinity B.11.22 is the panther, beautifully spotted in all colours, followed by animals that are attracted to his irresistable scent. Other animals that refer to the bestiary tradition are a beaver castrating himself, a man playing the harp to a swan, the capture of an ape when he puts on shoes, an ostrich with a horseshoe in its beak, a magpie pecking the eyes of a corpse in the water, a sea-knight, a pelican, a mole, and a spider in a web. The artist is so familiar with bestiary iconography that it would be surprising if he had not illustrated some kind of bestiary before. He also seems familiar with fables, as he illustrates the fable of the grasshopper and the ant.

A different and remarkable motif is a knight who visits a hermit living in a tree. The theme of a knight confessing to a hermit is not surprising for a Book of Hours made for wealthy secular patrons, but the motif of a dendrite, a hermit who lives in tree-tops, is definitely striking. Alison Stones first noticed the similarity of this scene with a miniature in a *Lancelot en prose* manuscript that is supposed to have been produced in the same workshop.[5] In this French Arthurian romance the motif has a more specific meaning. The surrounding text and the knight's arms (containing two red hearts) identify this knight as Lancelot, the famous lover of Queen Guinevere. According to the text, Lancelot confesses to a hermit, but it was the illuminator's choice to make the latter live in a tree. Specific motifs could apparently be used in quite different contexts.

4. L.M.C. Randall, 'A Mediaeval Slander', in: *The Art Bulletin*, 42 (1960), 25-38 connects this motif with an anti-English sentiment. According to Randall the motif of a man hatching on a nest of eggs also occurs in Baltimore, WA, 82, Psalter-Hours; Brussels, KB, 10607, Psalter of Gui de Dampierre; Cambrai, BM, 102, Breviary; New Haven, Beinecke Library, Yale 229, *Lancelot en prose*; Oxford, Bodl., Douce 5-6, psalter; Paris, BNF, lat.10435, psalter.

5. Oxford, Bodleian Library, Douce 215, fol. 14r. See A. Stones, 'Indications écrites et modèles pictureaux, guides aux peintres de manuscrits enluminés aux environs de 1300', in: *Artistes, artisans et production artistique au Moyen Age,* III *Fabrication et consommation de l'oeuvre* (Paris, Picard, 1990), 321-349, esp. pl. 6-7. In the Trinity manuscript it is placed at the hours of the Holy Ghost, and does not seem to be related to this prayer.

2. Reinaert and Cuwaert

A motif with ramifications for another literary genre is a marginal illustration of a lion king enthroned, legs crossed, holding a sceptre, and giving a sealed letter to an animal, probably a fox (Fig. 1). An enthroned lion king and a fox will no doubt have reminded spectators of King Noble and Renart the Fox. King Noble presiding over his court is a common motif in the *Roman de Renart* (Fig. 2). The animals are gathered in front of the lion king, who is sitting on a throne, legs crossed, holding a sceptre in his left paw and stretching out his right paw.[6] All these elements (throne, scepter, crown, crossed legs, outstretched arm, and the presence of subjects) indicate that the lion is acting as a judge, as this configuration is also common in a human setting.[7]

Much depends on the messenger's identity for the interpretation of the scene. If it is a lion cub, for example, the image should be considered as a parody on human activities, with lions in the role of humans. Compare for instance the marginal decoration 'aping' human conduct in a stylistically related psalter, where an ape king gives a sealed letter to an ape messenger.[8] Comparison with the animals in the other marginal decoration of the Trinity Book of Hours suggests that the animal before the lion king is most likely meant to be a fox. In the upper margin of fol. 22r., for example, a fox carries off a bird, and in the lower margin of the same page a sledge on which lies a fox with tied paws is drawn by an ape riding a white sledge-dog (Fig. 3).[9] The fox before King Noble is somewhat

6. Six miniatures in a group of three *Roman de Renart* manuscripts (Paris, BNF, fr. 1580, fol. 55r., 114v.; Oxford, Bodl. 360, fol. 1r., 36v.; London, BL, Add. 15229, fol. 6r., 92v.) show this court scene. See B. Zumbült, 'Approaching the Medieval Illustration Cycles of the Fox-Epic as an Art Historian: Problems and Perspectives', in: *Reinardus, Yearbook of the International Reynard Society*, 15 (2002), 191-204, pl. 16-27.

7. Zumbült 2002 [note 6], 193 n. 7 assumes that Noble crossing his left foot above the right in the miniatures might be a visual sign of turning the world upside down, but this rendering is a common representation of crossed legs in miniatures. Hence Noble does not deviate from the iconographic tradition of rulers as judges. For examples see H. Martin, 'Les enseignements des miniatures. Attitude royale', in: *Gazette des Beaux-Arts*, 55 (1913), 173-188.

8. Oxford, Bodl., Douce 6, fol. 157v., reproduced in M. Camille, *Image on the Edge. The Margins of Medieval Art* (London, Reaktion, 1992), fig. 77.

9. A fox carrying off a cock, chicken, or bird is a common motif in marginal decoration. See L.M.C. Randall, *Images in the Margins of Gothic Manuscripts* (Berkeley-Los Angeles, University of California Press, 1966). S. Huot, *The Romance of the Rose and its medieval readers: interpretation, reception, manuscript transmission* (Cambridge, Cambridge University Press, 1993), 287 mentions a fox bearing off a rooster in the margins of *Roman de la Rose* manuscript Paris, BNF, fr. 25526, illustrating Faux Samblant's final boasts of hypocrisy in the accompanying text, and a fox carrying off a chicken elsewhere

atypical, as it lacks the pointed snout and has a brown instead of a reddish pelt, but it will not represent a cat, as cats look even more different from the animal receiving the letter.[10]

Perhaps the allusion to the Renart stories in a general sense is all that is intended here. This marginal decoration could be considered as a metaphor for King Noble summoning Renart to court, or the document with a seal might be interpreted as the 'pax', a symbol of peace in the animal kingdom.[11] In that case, it might be ironical that Renart receives the 'pax', as he usually is the one to break the peace.

Three late thirteenth-century Flemish manuscripts contain a marginal motif that refers to a specific scene in the Renart stories. A hare, seated between the legs of a fox, reads in a book while the fox seems ready to bite off the hare's head. This motif only occurs in the Psalter of Gui de Dampierre, a stylistically related *Lancelot en prose* manuscript in Yale, and in another psalter that is currently in Dublin (Fig. 4).[12] As two of these manuscripts are written in Latin and one in French, it is all the more surprising that the marginal motif refers to an episode that only occurs in the Middle Dutch *Van den vos Reynaerde*. This so-called Cuwaert episode is supposed to be an elaboration by the Dutch author. It does not occur in the French *Roman de Renart,* and as far as we know it is not part of

in the margins. See for other foxes and birds K. Varty, *Reynard, Renart, Reinaert and Other Foxes in Medieval England. The Iconographic Evidence* (Amsterdam, Amsterdam University Press, 1999). The sledge-scene, however, is uncommon. Marginal decorations sometimes depict Renart's funeral procession, but that is not the case here. For the funeral motif see F. McCulloch, 'The funeral of Renart the Fox in a Walters Book of Hours', in: *The Journal of the Walters Art Gallery*, 25-26 (1962-1963), 8-27, and S.K. Davenport, 'Illustrations Direct and Oblique in the Margins of an Alexander Romance at Oxford', in: *Journal of the Warburg and Courtauld Institutes*, 34 (1971), 83-95.

10. On fol. 56r., for example, a cat and a bird beat a fur blanket with sticks.

11. Compare for instance the fox summoned to court by a hare-messenger holding a sealed letter in the margins of the Smithfield Decretals, illustrated in England ca. 1335 (London, BL, Royal 10 E IV, fol. 53v.; reproduced in Varty 1999, fig. 167). On the 'pax' motif in *Van den vos Reynaerde* see J. de Putter, 'Vrede ende pays in *Van den vos Reynaerde*', in: *Millennium. Tijdschrift voor middeleeuwse studies*, 14 (2000), 86-103.

12. Brussels, KB, 10607, fol. 86r.; Yale, Beinecke Library, Yale 229, fol. 133v.; Dublin, Chester Beatty Library, 61, fol. 61r., reproduced in Randall 1966 [note 9], figs. 193-5 (figs. 193 and 194 should be interchanged). Randall's index describes the motif as: 'fox reading over hare's shoulder'. In a letter of September 2002 Lilian Randall kindly informed me that she has not found any further examples of the motif since. Note the striking overlap with the group of manuscripts in which the marginal motif of the man sitting on a nest of eggs occurs. The assistant painter of Yale 229 also worked on Brussels 10607. See A. Stones, 'The Illustrations of BN, fr. 95 and Yale 229: Prolegomena to a Comparative Analysis', in: K. Busby (ed.), *Word and Image in Arthurian Literature* (New York-London, Garland, 1996), 203-283.

an animal-fable tradition either.[13] In this episode in the Middle Dutch romance, the fox Reinaert promises Cuwaert the hare to teach him the *credo* and make him a chaplain. The fox positions the hare firmly between his legs and both begin to spell and read, and to sing the *credo* out loud.[14] Reinaert meanwhile intends to bite off Cuwaert's throat. The hare narrowly escapes this fate.

To 'teach someone the *credo*' is an ambiguous expression. In the literal sense it means teaching the confession of faith, but there is also the indecent meaning of having sexual intercourse with someone.[15] The Dutch Reinaert-expert André Bouwman suggested that it is this sexual connotation, which the Middle-Dutch author hints at between the lines, that has suggestively been visualised in the marginal decorations. The phrase 'firmly between his legs' seems to be an extra argument for a sexual interpretation, and such a topic would not interfere with the often obscene nature of marginal decoration.[16]

13. See A.Th. Bouwman, *Reinaert en Renart. Het dierenepos Van den vos Reynaerde vergeleken met de Oudfranse Roman de Renart*, Nederlandse literatuur en cultuur in de Middeleeuwen, 3, 2 dln (Amsterdam, Prometheus, 1991), vol. 1, 65; J.D. Janssens, 'Wereldse literatuur in het dertiende-eeuwse Vlaanderen', in: R. Beyers (ed.), *Van vadernaar moedertaal. Latijn, Frans en Nederlands in de dertiende-eeuwse Nederlanden. (Handelingen LIII, van het colloquium georganiseerd door de Koninklijke Zuid-Nederlandse Maatschappij voor Taal- en Letterkunde en Geschiedenis op 23 oktober 1999)*, (Brussels, 2000), 119-135, esp. 123-125; J. Janssens en R. van Daele, *Reinaerts streken. Van 2000 voor tot 2000 na Christus* (Leuven, Davidsfonds, 2001), 56-62.

14. *Van den vos Reynaerde* has been edited by F. Lulofs, *Van den vos Reynaerde. De tekst kritisch uitgegeven, met woordverklaring, commentaar en tekstkritische aantekeningen* (Groningen, Wolters Noordhoff, 1985), and by A. Bouwman and B. Besamusca, *Reynaert in tweevoud. vol. 1: Van den vos Reynaerde* (Amsterdam, Bert Bakker, 2002). It concerns the verses 142-148: '[Hi hem] ghelovede te leerne sinen crede / Ende soudene maken capelaen. / Doe dedine sitten gaen / Vaste tusschen sine beene. / Doe begonsten si over eene / spellen ende lesen beede / Ende lude te zinghene crede.' ['The fox promised to teach him his *credo* and to make him a chaplain. Then he made him sit down firmly between his legs. Then they began to spell together and read and sing the *credo* aloud.']

15. See Lulofs (1985), 207 no. 143, and W.Gs Hellinga, 'Het laatste woord is aan Firapeel', in: *Maatstaf. Maandblad voor letteren*, 6 (1958-1959), 353-373 (reprinted in: H. van Dijk and P. Wackers (eds.), *Pade crom ende menichfoude: het Reynaert-onderzoek in de tweede helft van de twintigste eeuw*. Hilversum, Verloren, 1999, 37-50).

16. It has been repeatedly suggested that the text implies homosexual activities here, but according to the bestiary tradition hares change gender every year, so caution should be exercised. Furthermore, as will be explained later on in this essay, sexual interpretations of phrases such as 'het *credo* leren' always refer to a heterosexual context. M. Camille, 'Manuscript Illumination and the Art of Copulation', in: K. Lochrie, P. McCracken, J.A. Schultz (eds.), *Constructing Medieval Sexuality* (Minneapolis-London, University of Minnesota Press, 1997), 58-90 writes on 74-75: 'Committing sodomy with one's wife, however, was deemed as sinful as committing the act with a whore or a man. It was not so much the gender of the partner as what parts were put where that was labeled "against nature" (...) Sexual relations between members of the same sex were never represented in thirteenth-century manuscript illumination, to the best of my knowledge'.

The Trinity Book of Hours not only refers to the Renart stories by means of the motif of King Noble and Renart with the charter. Later on in the manuscript the marginal decoration seems to continue the Cuwaert story mentioned just now by showing a scared hare that obviously has been reading from a book (Fig. 5).[17] Hares reading books are rare, even in marginal decoration, but the bloodied bottom of the hare is extremely unusual. The paint of this big red blot is of exactly the same colour as the vermilion used elsewhere in the decoration, and hence must be original. A hare can be covered with blood because he has been bitten by a dog or hit with a stick, but then the wounds would be elsewhere on the body and the offender would probably also be around. The combination of the hare disturbed in his reading and the bloodied bottom suggest a continuation of the Cuwaert episode as represented in the three examples just mentioned. Here the victim is the focus of the illustration.[18] The book and the blood serve as a visualisation of Reinaert's penetration of the hare. Furthermore, the Middle Dutch text mentions Cuwaert's wounds afterwards.[19] In the literal sense, these injuries refer to Reinaert's attempted murder by biting the throat of the hare, but in the sexual variant represented in the marginal decorations, these wounds would be the result of Reinaert's penetration.[20]

17. Both 'Renardian images' have been placed next to the Hours of the Holy Ghost in the Trinity Book of Hours.

18. It remains unclear whether there originally was also a fox around on the facing page, as the next folium has been cut out. The Trinty artist sometimes devoted a folium or opening to a particular motif. See for example the two foxes on fol. 22r., or the opening fol. 55v. - 56r. On the verso a man dies in a bed covered with a fur blanket (indicating that he is rich), there is a doctor in the margins and a priest next to his bed, two angels take up his soul in a cloth, and in the lower margin two men clothe a corpse in a cowl while a third man hold his nose because of the stench; on the recto a cat and a bird beat a fur blanket with sticks. S. Huot (1993) [note 9], 290 comments on the marginal decoration in the *Roman de la Rose* manuscript Paris, BNF, fr. 25526: 'the artist devoted one or even both sides of a bifolium to a single motif. One finds entire bifolia with scenes of children's games, or with hybrids, or with knights riding to battle'. This Cuwaert motif could very well function on its own, hence a fox in the surroundings is by no means necessary.

19. *Reinaert* v. 162-164: 'Siet hier noch die verssche wonden / Ende die teekine, heere coninc / Die Coewaert van hem ontfinc' ['Behold, lord king, the fresh wounds and scars that Coewaert received from him'.]

20. D. Wolfthal, 'A Hue and a Cry: Medieval Rape Imagery and its Transformation', in: *The Art Bulletin*, 75 (1993), 39-64 describes how rape images are sympathetic to the victim and make clear that rape is a savage act. To convict a rapist, court demanded evidence. The victim's cries for help during the rape were of critical importance, but also evidence relating to the victim's appearance was required. Courts demanded that the victim show torn clothes and disheveled hair. It remains unclear whether the bloodied bottom of Cuwaert the hare in the Trinity manuscript indicates rape, or that it mainly functions as a visual sign to draw attention to the act of sexual intercourse. Compare M. Camille, 'Play, Piety and Perversity in Medieval Marginal Manuscript Illumination', in: K. Kröll and

The sexual connotation of this seemingly innocent visual motif could only be understood by viewers who knew the relevant story, and perhaps that was part of the fun for the illuminator inserting it in the pictorial program of the Latin religious text. Illustrated psalters and books of hours not only served as devotional literature, such books were also used to learn to read, thus enabling persons to recite the psalms and prayers. The insertion of the ambiguous theme of the reading hare in psalters and books of hours might therefore also be a nodding reference to the use of these books.

3. Monks and nuns

Apart from such expressions as teaching or reading the *credo*, literary texts also mention phrases such as 'learn the paternoster', 'read the psalter' or 'read the hours together' as metaphors for sexual intercourse, especially when it concerns caricatures of the clergy. Monks and nuns, who should be outstanding examples of celibacy, are the favourite targets for these allusions.[21] But there seems to be visual evidence for a sexual interpretation of such phrases as well. The marginal decoration on the opening page of a new text branch in a stylistically related *Lancelot en prose* manuscript in London is very interesting in this respect. The abundant marginal decoration on this folium emphasises the beginning of a new text. One of the marginal scenes at the opening of the *Lancelot*, on the lower right of the page, shows a nun sitting on a hillside (Fig. 6). The nun caresses the chin of a hermit, who is sitting between her legs with an open book in his hands, while he touches the nun under her garment and sucks at her breast. All elements are there: sitting between someone's legs, a visual reference to reading, and the allusions to sexual occupations.[22]

H. Steger (eds.), *Mein ganzer Körper ist Gesicht. Groteske Darstellungen in der europäischen Kunst und Literatur des Mittelalters* (Freiburg im Breisgau, Rombach, 1994), 171-192. On 176 Camille writes with reference to the marginal decoration in the set London, BL, Add. 36684 – New York, PM, 750: 'On nearly every page there is an anal image, in either human or ape form. The anatomical puckered point is stressed with a touch of red around the black hole (…).'

21. See the examples mentioned in R. van Daele, 'Die burse al sonder naet. Scabreuze elementen in *Van den vos Reynaerde*', in: R. van Daele et al. (eds.), *Literatuur en erotiek* (Leuven, Peeters, 1993), 9-64 and G. Herchert, *Acker mir mein bestes Feld. Untersuchungen zu erotischen Liederbuchliedern des späten Mittelalters. Mit Wörterbuch und Textsammlung* (Münster, Waxmann, 1996), esp. 165-172, 300-304.

22. M. Müller, *Minnebilder. Französische Minnedarstellungen des 13. und 14. Jahrhunderts* (Köln etc., Böhlau, 1996), fig. 81 reproduces a marginal decoration in a northern French Breviary dated 1288 (Heidelberg, Universitätsbibliothek, Cod. Sal. 9.51, fol. 272v.), depicting a priest and nun gambling; the monk tries to touch the nun's breast, while she kicks him with her foot.

The explicit erotic continuation of this hilarious scene is shown at about the same place on the opening page of the next text branch in this set of manuscripts (Fig. 7). This text, the *Queste del Saint Graal*, focusses on the theme of chastity, which is an essential virtue for the knights who want to succeed in achieving the Holy Grail, but the margins on the opening page represent a less chaste story. The nun now lies on her back on the hill with her dress tucked up, and the hermit lies between her legs and kisses her. Two nuns on the left are looking at this lovemaking scene: one points at the couple and the other covers her eyes.[23] The example of this 'to be continued' episode not only shows that the miniaturist of these *Lancelot en prose* manuscripts was subtle and had a sense of humour, but it also proves that the motif of reading in a book while seated between someone's legs does have sexual connotations.

In this respect it is interesting that on both sides of poor Cuwaert in the Trinity Book of Hours, a hybrid bishop and a nun reading a book, both sprouting from a leaf-tendril, look meaningfully at each other.

4. Middle Dutch texts and oral transmission

The Middle Dutch *Van den vos Reynaerde* is supposed to have been written in Flanders, possibly in Ghent, in the second or third quarter of the thirteenth century. Thus it is not surprising that the Cuwaert motif occurs in manuscripts that were produced in Flanders at the end of the thirteenth century. Two manuscripts can even be connected to the Dampierre court in Ghent. Yet it is also a remarkable phenomenon: one

23. This continuation of the marginal decoration in the preceding text branch has more ramifications. There appears to be a variation of the scene of the hermit sucking at the nun's breast in the Additional *Lancelot* (London, BL, Add. 10393, f. 1r; see fig. 6), again at the same place on the page, in the border of the opening page of the *Mort Artu* in the Rylands manuscript, which was illustrated by the same illuminator (Manchester, John Rylands University Library, Rylands fr. 1 vol. 2 fol. 212r.; reproduced in M. Camille, 1992, fig. 12). Here a monkey sucks at the breast of a nun. See M. Meuwese, 'To be Continued. Shared Iconographical Themes in the *Lancelot-Grail Cycle*' (forthcoming). For a marginal decoration of a nun and a monk copulating on a hillside next to a pack mule loaded with a basket of phalluses in the margins of a *Roman de la Rose* manuscript illustrated by the Montbaston workshop (Paris, BNF, fr. 25526, fol. 111v.), see A.M. Koldeweij, 'A Barefaced *Roman de la Rose* (Paris, B.N., ms. fr. 25526) and some Late Medieval Mass-Produced Badges of a Sexual Nature', in: M. Smeyers and B. Cardon (eds.), *Flanders in a European Perspective. Manuscript Illumination around 1400 in Flanders and Abroad. Proceedings of the International Colloquium Leuven, 7-10 September 1993* (Leuven, Peeters, 1995), 499-516, esp. fig. 6, and Huot 1993 [note 9], 292-3. Randall 1966 [note 9] mentions a monk and a nun having intercourse in the Gorleston Psalter, England, ca. 1310-1325 (London, BL, Add. 49622, fol. 98v., partly erased).

literary text in French, two Psalters in Latin, and a Book of Hours written in Latin with rubrics in French, containing marginal decorations based on a Middle Dutch text![24] That would suggest that the miniaturists had at least some knowledge of Middle Dutch.

In the Trinity Book of Hours there is indeed evidence that the illuminator was familiar with Middle Dutch. On two pages, a short Dutch text turns up in the hands of marginal creatures. In the first instance, a hybrid man sprouting from a line filler holds a wax tablet with the words: 'ic bidde ghenaden soeteh lief ic sen desen brief min [art]' (I pray for mercy, my sweet, I send this writing...).[25] On another folium, a hybrid creature holds a scroll in its hands saying: 'ic bidde wor alledeghene die miere die i(n) sonden sin' (I pray for all my beloved who are in sin).[26] It can be assumed that the illuminator and not the scribe wrote these words in the marginal decorations. Short and terse as these sentences are, they nevertheless contain sufficient information to pin down the dialect to a specific region: Ghent.[27] Other manuscripts illustrated in the same atelier also point to this city, and therefore it can be assumed that this workshop probably was based in Ghent.[28]

There remains the question of the source of inspiration for the marginal decorations depicting the Cuwaert episode. The Middle Dutch *Van den vos Reynaerde* itself has never been illustrated, as far as we know. Would

24. W.P. Gerritsen, 'Vertalingen van Oudfranse litteraire werken in het Middelnederlands', in: R.E.V. Stuip (ed.), *Franse literatuur van de Middeleeuwen* (Muiderberg, Coutinho, 1988), 184-207 mentions on 191 that the Yale *Prose Lancelot* manuscripts is one of the six codices that contain the version on which the Middle Dutch *Lancelotcompilatie* has been based. J.D. Janssens, 'De "Vlaamse" achtergronden van de Lancelotcompilatie. Wat onzekerheden op een rijtje: Vlaams, Brabants of Hollands?', in: B. Besamusca and F. Brandsma (eds.), *De ongevalliche Lanceloet. Studies over de Lancelotcompilatie* (Hilversum, Verloren, 1992), 21-43, suggests that manuscript Yale 229 might have been one of the source-texts at the *Lancelotcompilatie* author's disposal. B. Besamusca and A. Postma, *Lanceloet. De Middelnederlandse vertaling van de Lancelot en prose overgeleverd in de Lancelotcompilatie.* Pars I (Hilversum, Verloren, 1997), 25 raise some objections to this view.

25. The inscription on the scroll is in garbled Middle Dutch; the transcription is correct.

26. Reproduced in Meuwese (1995), fig. 4. The word 'wor' is a corruption of the Middle Dutch 'vor' or 'voor' [see note 25].

27. Evert van den Berg told me in a personal communication that the word 'deghene' does not occur in western Flanders: in Brughes 'deghone' would be used. The word 'soeteh', which will be a corruption of either 'soeten' or 'soete', in Brabant would be written as 'sute'. In Ghent both 'deghene' as 'soete(n)' can be used.

28. See Meuwese 1995 and E.B. Moore, 'The urban fabric and framework of Ghent in the margins of Oxford, Bodleian Library, MSS Douce 5-6', in: *"Als Ich Can". Liber Amicorum in memory of Professor Dr. Maurits Smeyers*, vol. 2 (Leuven, Peeters, 2002), 983-1006.

this marginal imagery, for lack of visual models, then have been inspired by oral material or by a reading of the written text by the miniaturist?[29] The complete lack of illustration for the Middle Dutch *Van den vos Reynaerde* might be an indication for a mainly oral circulation of the story.[30] Hence I consider it most likely that the extremely popular Reinaert story was transmitted to the illuminator by means of oral storytelling.

5. Conclusion

A book containing marginalia is likely to include visual references to more than one textual or oral tradition, but also in illustration programs of miniature cycles specific motifs from different contexts were inserted.[31] Through their illustration work, miniaturists were familar with a wide range of texts, and thus had a wealth of visual motifs at their disposal. They could easily adapt or adopt iconographic motives, sometimes reusing the connotations of their model or, on the contrary, intentionally playing with the expectations of a spectator. Unfortunately it is almost impossible to tell whether such nodding references were always understood by a medieval reader, and what the response will have been.

Should we, for example, conclude that the primarily French speaking court in Ghent was familiar with the Middle Dutch *Van den vos Reynaerde*, and that the patrons must have understood the visual reference

29. See Sandler 1997 [note 1], 28: 'It should first be considered whether the text source was generally illustrated. If so, it is only reasonable that for the artist a known pictorial image would be a more likely inspiration than the text it accompanied. More perplexing, though, is the question of the sources of marginal illusrations that are related to texts not usually illustrated... Are such illustrations to be understood as derived from a reading of the relevant text in its written form, by the artist or by some hypothetical "scholarly adviser", or rather should such marginal imagery be supposed to share the same fund of oral material drawn upon by written texts?'

30. Norbert H. Ott, 'Texte und Bilder. Beziehungen zwischen den Medien Kunst und Literatur in Mittelalter und Früher Neuzeit', in: H. Wenzel, W. Seipel, G. Wunberg (eds.), *Die Verschriftlichung der Welt. Bild, Text und Zahl in der Kultur des Mittelalters und der frühen Neuzeit* (Wien, Kunsthistorisches Museum, 2000), 105-143, writes on 110: 'Während Texte, die länger als andere mündlich überliefert sind – wie etwa die der germanischen Heldenepik –, nie oder erst sehr spät und dann noch immer höchst zurückgenommen illustriert werden, gehören solche die von Beginn an anspruch auf literarizität vertreten, zu den am frühesten bebilderten überhaupt, und ihre Handschriften zeichnen sich zudem durch ein ausgesprochen hohes Ausstattungsniveau aus'. See Meuwese (1995) [note 2] for something similar in the miniature illustrating the battle of Ronceval in the *Spiegel Historiael*. For oral delivery and the Reinaert tradition see J. Janssens, 'De middeleeuwse vos in beeld. Van Avignon over Murano naar Brugge', in: *Tiecelijn*, 11 (1998), 2-8.

painted in their books, or was it more likely a secret amusement of the illuminators to include a subtle reference to this Middle Dutch text in manuscripts, written in different languages, that were made for the court? It is obvious that miniaturists were inventive and had a good sense of humour. Especially in the margins they could indulge their imagination and display malicious pleasure at the misfortunes of others, be it Cuwaert the hare or just an anonymous poor hare, suspended by its ears from a tendril by a mischievous ape (Fig. 8).

Images isolated from a fuller thematical context, such as the Reinaert episodes in the margins of the Trinity Book of Hours, are not the easiest to recognise or explain. A better understanding of the significance of literary themes in medieval society can best be achieved by the study of the visual as well as the written manifestations of those themes. Only by means of this interaction shall we be able to unravel the reception of literary and visual motifs.

31. See M. Meuwese, 'Die Illumination der Detmolder *Der Naturen Bloeme*-Handschrift', in: A. Berteloot and D. Hellfaier (eds.), *Jacob van Maerlants Der naturen bloeme und das Umfeld. Vorlaüfer, Redaktionen, Rezeption*, Niederlande Studien, 23 (Münster, Waxmann, 2001), 135-152, fig. 14-28; and 'Recycling Sacred Iconography. The Adaptation of Biblical Scenes in Arthurian Illustration' (forthcoming).

Ill. 1. © Cambridge, Trinity College Library, Trinity B.11.22, *Book of Hours*, Ghent, ca. 1300, fol. 205r. King Noble and Reinaert.

Ill. 2. © Paris, Bibliothèque nationale de France, fr. 1580,
Roman de Renart, ca. 1340, fol. 114v. King Noble presides over his court.

Ill. 3. © Cambridge, Trinity College Library, Trinity B.11.22,
Book of Hours, Ghent, ca. 1300, fol. 22r. Foxes.

Ill. 4. © Dublin, Chester Beatty 61,
Psalter, Flanders, end of 13th cent., fol. 61r. Reinaert and Cuwaert.

Ill. 5. © Cambridge, Trinity College Library, Trinity B.11.22,
Book of Hours, Ghent, ca. 1300, fol. 214v. Cuwaert.

Ill. 6. © London, British Library, Add. 10293, *Lancelot*, Flanders or northern France, ca. 1316, fol. 1r. Monk and nun.

Ill. 7. © London, British Library, Add. 10294, *Queste del Saint Graal*, Flanders or northern France, ca. 1316, fol. 1r. Copulating monk and nun.

Ill. 8. © Cambridge, Trinity College Library, Trinity B.11.22, *Book of Hours*, Ghent, ca. 1300, fol. 42v.
Monkey suspends a hare by its ears from a tendril.

Virginie MINET-MAHY

LE RECYCLAGE DES MÉTAPHORES DANS LA LITTÉRATURE ALLÉGORIQUE: DE L'HISTOIRE DU SENS À LA CRÉATION POÉTIQUE

L'image de la harpe et de l'harmonie universelle

La contribution de la philologie à une réflexion générale sur le thème du recyclage et de la translation des images dans les manuscrits et dans les textes présente divers intérêts. Elle permet de situer le débat à un niveau conceptuel: l'image verbale est un matériau abstrait qui incite à porter son attention sur les mécanismes généraux de la récupération des métaphores et à tenter de résoudre des questions qui touchent aux raisons idéologiques, psychologiques, sociologiques, culturelles, politiques qui président à la transmission des imaginaires. Si la période médiévale est longue et qu'il faut éviter tout effet d'écrasement des strates chronologiques et des domaines d'application, il n'en reste pas moins que de la période patristique à l'aube de la Renaissance, l'image affiche dans le texte profane comme dans le texte chrétien des qualités mnémoniques et un pouvoir heuristique qui en font un objet de méditation spirituelle, un lieu de souvenir et d'invention rhétorique autour duquel se construit la pensée.[1] Élément central de la *préstructure*, de la programmation de la lecture, la métaphore implique le destinataire de la communication et suscite chez lui la réaction.[2] Elle a un pouvoir d'agir sur l'interprète. Cette

1. Mary Carruthers, *The Book of Memory. A Study of Memory in Medieval Culture*, Cambridge Studies in Medieval Literature, 10 (Cambridge, Cambridge University Press, 1993²). Idem, *The Craft of Thought. Meditation, Rhetoric, and the Making of Images 400-1200*, Cambridge Studies in Medieval Literature, 34 (Cambridge, Cambridge University Press, 1998).

2. Nous reprenons la théorie de l'esthétique de la lecture de Wolfgang Iser (*L'acte de lecture. Théorie de l'effet esthétique*, trad. de l'allemand par Evelyn Sznycer, Bruxelles, Mardaga, 1985) comme un des cadres théoriques de cette recherche (un des autres théoriciens de référence est Paul Ricoeur, *La Métaphore vive*, Paris, Seuil, 1975) qui prend part à une thèse de doctorat soutenue à l'Université Catholique de Louvain en mai 2003, sous la direction de Claude Thiry et dont le titre est 'La *refiguration* du sujet et du monde dans l'œuvre allégorique aux XIVᵉ et XVᵉ siècles. Les tensions du sens: Écriture/Lecture, Histoire/Fiction'. À travers un corpus de textes situé à la charnière des XIVᵉ et XVᵉ siècles (Eustache Deschamps, Jean Gerson et Alain Chartier), sous le règne de Charles VI, la thèse étudie comment la figure du lecteur est impliquée dans les mécanismes d'écriture allégorique, les relations entre les images et les discours de personnifications et les systèmes de représentations socioculturelles et littéraires afin de déterminer l'implication de la fiction dans un programme de réformation d'une société en crise. La rhétorique du texte allégorique tend à des effets esthétiques sur le lecteur intégré dans la structure textuelle.

force heuristique et pragmatique provient de la sélection qu'elle opère au sein d'un *répertoire* (terminologie de Iser) de normes socioculturelles et de bagage littéraire, en s'intégrant dans une structure textuelle nouvelle dans laquelle elle reçoit une nouvelle fonction esthétique.

Le mode de fonctionnement de l'image remonte à la Bible, ce grand réservoir de résonance imagée où le sens allégorique se construit inlassablement à travers les diverses combinaisons que chaque génération de lecteur parvient à tisser dans une chaîne de reprises. La métaphore ne peut se lire qu'en contexte; dans le contexte de représentation d'une société dans laquelle émerge l'œuvre, dans le contexte historique de ses *pré-textes*, de ses modèles littéraires, dans le contexte de la nouvelle structure, de la forme d'accueil qui organise les tensions entre les signes intégrés et orientés vers le même effet esthétique. Par une sorte de sédimentation du sens, la métaphore est une mémoire et une projection vers des reprises futures.[3]

La présente étude a pour objectif de décortiquer les mécanismes qui sous-tendent le travail de l'intertextualité et de la continuité des imaginaires à travers un corpus de texte restreint à trois auteurs du moyen français: Evrart de Conty, Jean Gerson et Jean Molinet, autour d'une même image, la harpe et l'harmonie universelle. Les trois personnages offrent l'intérêt d'opérer leur activité d'écrivain dans une sphère proche du pouvoir princier et d'organiser à l'adresse du souverain un message de perfection politique par le biais d'un réseau d'images cosmiques et musicales. Ils tirent parti du passé textuel de métaphores pour actualiser leur potentiel heuristique et pragmatique en direction d'un certain effet esthétique.[4]

3. 'Cette circulation entre la démarche abstractive et la démarche de concrétisation fait que la signifiance est un travail inachevé, un "incessante Odyssée". C'est le dynamisme sémantique, propre au langage naturel, qui donne à la signifiance une "historicité": de nouvelles possibilités de signifiance sont ouvertes, qui trouvent un appui dans les significations déjà acquises. Cette "historicité" est portée par un locuteur qui, voulant dire une expérience neuve, cherche dans le réseau déjà fixé des significations un porteur adéquat de ses intentions.' Paul Ricœur, 'Huitième étude. Métaphore et discours philosophique', in *La Métaphore vive* [note 2], pp. 377-378.

4. Signalons l'étude intéressante de David Cowling au sujet des metaphores chez les rhétoriqueurs. La métaphore du bâtiment pour signifier la pensée et l'acte d'écriture transite dans les textes allégoriques en français, en particulier dans le milieu des rhétoriqueurs bourguignons qui trouvent dans le comparant architectural un système de représentation polysémique propre à désigner également l'édification de l'État. Selon Cowling, le succès de l'image de l'édifice dans la littérature bourguignonne dérive d'une appropriation culturelle imaginaire tendant à dépeindre la maison de Bourgogne, puis l'arche d'Autriche comme le pendant au 'jardin de France'. Les revendications 'nationales' passent aussi par la construction d'univers symboliques. L'étude investigue sur le double champ des représentations socioculturelles liées à un milieu et des réminiscences littéraires et parvient ainsi à mettre en évidence en quoi l'efficacité esthétique du texte découle de l'implication du

La harpe et l'harmonie musicale témoignent de manière particulièrement exemplaire de la translation diachronique d'une mémoire signifiante de la métaphore verbale.[5] L'image remonte à l'Antiquité, aux spéculations pythagoriciennes et platoniciennes sur le nombre comme entité à la base de la création et sur la musique universelle. Les divers ordres du cosmos consonnent dans une harmonie globale issue des rapports de proportions numériques. Rapidement la métaphore féconde trouve des applications multiples qui enrichissent sa signification et qui transitent jusqu'à la fin du Moyen Âge. Virgile en fait une image de la création poétique, tandis que Cicéron y voit le modèle de la concorde politique de la République. L'exégèse et les poètes latins tardifs récupèrent le bagage antique et transfèrent la métaphore au Christ, poète de la Rédemption, de l'harmonie retrouvée;[6] à l'Église, corps organique composé de parties diverses; à l'Écriture sainte; à l'âme au diapason avec le divin. Lorsque Jean de Salisbury écrit son *Policraticus* en guise d'enseignement au prince, il vante les vertus de la musique, rappelant les théories platoniciennes du *Timée* sur le nombre et l'harmonie universelle.

La harpe, symbole du pouvoir sur l'univers puisqu'elle touche aux principes numériques de la création du cosmos est vouée à une réelle fécondité de lecture. Au vu de cette richesse symbolique, ce n'est que dans une archéologie et dans une restauration de la chaîne des transmissions que l'on saisit le sens plein de chaque actualisation. Dans le domaine français, les occurrences sont nombreuses, du *Tristan* à Eustache Deschamps en passant par l'*Ovide moralisé* en vers et Guillaume de Machaut.

En 1424, Jean Gerson adresse au médecin et conseiller de Charles VII une lettre par laquelle il fait don au roi de Bourges d'un opuscule organisé autour de la métaphore du psaltérion décacorde.[7] L'association déjà ancienne de l'instrument de musique avec les dix commandements de

lecteur dans le texte. David Cowling, *Building the Text. Architecture as Metaphor in Late Medieval and Early Modern France*, Oxford Modern Languages and Literature Monographs (Oxford, Clarendon Press, 1998).

5. Entre autres études, signalons: Helmut Giesel, *Studien zur Symbolik der Musikinstrumente im Schrifttum der alten und mittelalterlichen Kirche*, Kölner Beiträge zur Musikforschung, 94 (Regensburg, Gustav Bosse Verlag, 1978). Martin Van Schaick, *The Harp in the Middle Ages. The Symbolism of a Musical Instrument* (Amsterdam-Atlanta, Rodopi, 1992; 1988[1]).

6. Et dans la volonté de forger un art poétique chrétien s'attribue la métaphore christique: l'écrivain est lui-même la harpe. Jacques Fontaine, 'Les symbolismes de la cithare dans la poésie de Paulin de Nole', in *Études sur la poésie latine tardive d'Ausone à Prudence. Recueil de travaux de Jacques Fontaine* (Paris, Belles Lettres, 1980), pp. 393-413.

7. Jean Gerson, *Œuvres complètes*, 13 vol. intr. texte et notes par Mgr Glorieux (Paris, Desclée de Brouwer, 1960-1974).

Moïse fait date. Mais le décalogue fonde aussi, dans les traités d'enseignement aux princes, et particulièrement dans le *Policraticus* de Jean de Salisbury, traduit pour Charles V par Denis Foulechat en 1378, la base de la loi dont le roi doit se porter le défenseur et le garant. Gerson établit donc un raccord entre le bagage signifiant de l'image biblique et le discours politique pour construire son propre modèle de réformation du royaume. Le chancelier se présente comme 'prophète' chargé par Dieu de la mission de composer un 'psaltérion' pour inscrire le souvenir de la loi dans la mémoire du souverain.

> At vero potissimum in praefato versiculo voluit meditatio mea recipere compositionem cantici novi psalteriique decacordi moralis et mystici, hoc adjecto jussisse Deum per Moysen regi noviter instituto sub hiis verbis *alto corde* ponendis. (vol. 2, lettre 52, p. 250)
> [Mais c'est surtout sur le verset ci-dessus que ma méditation s'est attardée: se mettre à la composition d'un cantique nouveau et d'un psaltérion décacorde au sens moral et mystique, ajoutant à ceci que Dieu donna cet ordre, par Moïse...]

Plusieurs manuscrits conservent la séquence du psaltérion décacorde. Deux d'entre eux offrent un noyau plus complet: Paris, BNF, lat. 17487 et Tours B.M. 379, manuscrits jumeaux issus, semble-t-il, de l'atelier de Thomas de Gerson (vers 1440).[8] On y retrouve un ensemble de pièces latines et françaises dont la cohésion est assurée par le thème de la musique et l'image du psaltérion (Fig. 2). L'*isotopie*[9] figurative témoigne de l'intégration que le poète entrevoit entre les ordres cosmiques et leur modèle divin: l'âme et le corps social tendent vers la même réalisation de la métaphore christique de la harpe de la passion. L'édition des textes par Glorieux qui dissémine la séquence à travers les neuf tomes, a empêché de saisir pleinement l'engagement des traités dans le dessein de refiguration du lecteur idéal, le prince. Il est donc important de retourner à la composition globale du manuscrit pour saisir l'intention du programme scripturaire sous-tendu par une implication des images riches de leur passé littéraire et de leur ancrage socioculturel.[10] Le *Collectorium super Magni-*

8. Gilbert Ouy, 'Manuscrits jumeaux et copies en facsimilé: deux couples de manuscrits gersoniens', in *Codices Manuscripti*, 11 (1985), pp.124-136.

9. Nous empruntons le concept à Alguirdas Julien Greimas, *Sémantique structurale. Recherche de méthode*, Langue et langage (Paris, Larousse, 1966), p. 93. Dupriez en donne une définition claire: 'Le type de réalité évoqué par l'ensemble des éléments du texte constitue l'univers du discours ou isotopie.' Bernard Dupriez, *Gradus. Les procédés littéraires (Dictionnaire)*, 10/18 (Paris, Union Générale d'Éditions, 1984), p. 268.

10. Nous ne donnons pas ici la description complète du manuscrit qui nécessiterait une contextualisation trop longue. Voir: Virginie Minet-Mahy, *Esthétique et allégorique à l'époque de Charles VI*, Bibliothèque du XVe siècle, 68 (Paris, Champion, 2005), pp. 377-379.

ficat (f. 1-167, éd. t. 8, 418) et le *Super Cantica canticorum* (f. 234-272, éd. t. 8, 422) ouvre et ferme le manuscrit Paris, BNF, lat. 17487. Entre ces deux grands textes de théologie mystique que traverse la métaphore de la musique spirituelle de l'âme scandée par les cinq lettres/notes mystiques, on trouve des dessins à la plume de main musicale[11] (f. 231), de psaltérions décacordes (f. 229 et f. 230 [Fig. 2]), d'échiquiers [Fig. 1], le *Tractatus de Canticis*, des pièces françaises (*Canticordum du pelerin*, f. 167v-180v, t. 7, 305), etc. Des indices épars dans le manuscrit attestent du programme de réformation spirituelle et politique adressé au dauphin. Citons, outre la lettre de dédicace au médecin du roi,[12] le poème *Dictamen de sancto Ludovico* qui fait l'éloge de la royauté très chrétienne (f. 180 v), le *Canon pro psalterio mystico* où le lys emblématique de la maison de France côtoie la croix, figure du sacrifice christique qui réalise l'harmonie du psaltérion mystique, et les figures des échiquiers où les membres de la société sont placés sur l'instrument de musique et invités à réaliser des harmonies imitant la perfection divine.

Gerson exploite la mémoire du motif musical pour construire dans son propre système de représentation un message spirituel d'élévation mystique, adressé en particulier au roi, rédempteur de la Nation. Le chancelier accentue la symbolique des chiffres quatre et cinq en vue de marquer les relations proportionnelles qui s'établissent entre les ordres de l'univers et leur modèle divin. Gerson arrange les cinq notes associées à cinq affections de l'âme *Joye, Espoir, Pitie, Paour, Doleur* correspondant res-

11. Sur la main musicale comme figure de méditation dans des manuscrits de dévotion antérieurs, voir: Geneviève Hasenhor, 'Méditation méthodique et mnémonique: un témoignage figuré ancien (XIIIe-XIVe s.)', in *Mélanges d'histoire, d'histoire de l'art et d'archéologie offerts à J. Stiennon*, éd. par Rita Lejeune et J. Desckers (Liège, Mardaga, 1982), pp. 365-381.

12. La métaphore musicale et la métaphore thérapeutique sont elles-mêmes liées étroitement par le même idéal d'harmonie et de consonance cosmique. Plusieurs pièces de l'ensemble des opuscules portent sur la figure de l'échiquier et renvoient à un autre texte de la fin du XIVe siècle où l'on retrouve le croisement entre l'évocation du cosmos et la métaphore du corps social associé à la concorde musicale et l'image de la harpe, Le *Livre des Eschez amoureux moralisés* [Evrart de Conty, *Le Livre des Eschez amoureux moralisés*, éd. par Françoise Guichard-Tesson et Bruno Roy, Bibliothèque du Moyen Français, 2, Montréal, CERES, 1993]. Curieusement, l'auteur, Evrart de Conty est, comme Jean Cadart, destinataire de la lettre de Gerson, médecin du roi, ici en l'occurrence Charles V. *Le Livre des Echez amoureux moralisés* est une glose d'une œuvre en vers, *Les Echecs amoureux*, elle-même commentaire du *Roman de la Rose*. Dans le prologue du *Livre des Echez amoureux moralisés*, l'auteur glose l'échiquier. Il le compare au mouvement des étoiles qui produit une musique. Le soleil, au centre du système correspond au roi qui influence tous les membres de son royaume, et au cœur dans le corps de l'homme qui règle la vie (pp. 9-51). Les *Echez amoureux moralisés* offrent une image idéale du prince éclairé, 'cosmocrator' assimilé au cœur de l'univers.

pectivement aux lettres vocales A, E, I, O, V et les organise en figure de croix dont le centre est le I. Le psaltérion décacorde, symbole de la loi mosaïque et modèle du gouvernement juste s'associe avec l'image du cœur [Fig. 3] (symboliquement rattaché au roi, centre cosmique de la société) et de la croix, figure du sacrifice rédempteur du Christ (le roi étant lui-même rédempteur de sa nation et coordinateur de la concorde poltique).[13] La quadrature de la figure est particulièrement signifiante. La *Pitié* ou la *Paix*, vertu politique aussi, au centre donne le ton comme le soleil au centre des planètes et dans la musique des sphères. Le chiffre cinq mis en avant par les cinq notes rappellent les cinq blessures du corps du Christ,[14] les cinq sens, les cinq doigts,[15] les cinq livres du psautier de David. Les deux figures du psaltérion à dix cordes glosées par les dix commandements et du cœur couplé aux notes mystiques encadrent le poème 'un cuer seulet mis en esmay' (Un cœur seul, ébranlé) dans lequel revient la figure du roi David, exemple de sagesse royale dans l'idéologie très chrétienne française (f. 230r-v [Fig. 2-3]). La croix inscrite dans une sphère représente la perfection et place le schéma de la figure dans une dimension cosmique.[16]

Dans ses discours et sermons adressés au roi et à la cour, Gerson construit une image de l'Église et de l'État comme corps mystique et cosmique. La harpe et l'image de la perfection harmonique parachèvent la représentation de la concorde des ordres du cosmos. Au même titre que l'âme, le corps mystique de l'État doit chanter la louange de Dieu, prendre en soi la forme du psaltérion pour le salut du peuple. Gerson identifie

13. La harpe et la croix se confondent dans l'image de Gerson, comme dans le frontispice du commentaire sur les psaumes de Pierre Lombard daté du XIIe siècle, Londres, Beatty collection, 32, f. 1r (Illustration dans Van Schaik, *The Harp* [note 5], 23, p. 226).

14. Dans le poème *Pratique du psaltérion mystique* (338, vol. 7, 'Ung cuer seulet',) Gerson fait clairement référence aux cinq plaies du Christ: 'O cuer devot, ie te pry, voy / En lumiere de vraie foy / Comme en Jhesus pendant en croix / Ces cinq poins sont et cinq voix. / En cinq lieux est playe tout nu / Comme ung tympaine est estendu; / En Jhesus mis en passion / Que vois tu fors compassion?' (pp. 422-423) [Oh, cœur dévot, je te prie, regarde, comme vers Jésus sur la croix, il y a cinq points et cinq voix. Il y a une plaie en cinq lieux du corps nu, il est étendu comme un tambour; en Jésus Christ conduit à la passion, que vois-tu, excepté la compassion?]

15. 'Scimus in manu quinque digitos esse… Hae sunt quinque lampades mysticae, lucentes in manibus virginum prudentum ad illuminationem sensuum quinque suorum.' [Nous savons qu'il y a cinq doigts sur la main… Il y a cinq lampes mystiques, brûlant dans les mains des vierges sages pour illuminer les cinq sens.) *De canticordo*, in *Tractatus de Canticis*, 460, vol. 9, p. 584.
Dans le manuscrit Paris, B.N.F., lat. 17487, f. 231, la main est dessinée et associée à la gamme.

16. Anna Esmeijer, *Divina Quaternitas: A Preliminary Study in the Method and Application of Visual Exegesis (*Van Gorgum Assen, 1979).

l'image de l'Époux parmi les lys du Cantique et la croix au milieu des fleurs, attribut héraldique de la royauté française dans le *Canon pro psalterio mystico*.[17]

> Lilia trina fidem, spem designant et amorem;
> Cor cruce signatum pascitur inter ea.
> Nostra Jhesus lex est crucifixus, quam medio cor
> Justi fert et eam nocte dieque canit.
> Psalterium reparas,... (vv. 19-23)
> [Les trois lys désignent la foi, l'espérance et l'amour, paissant au milieu d'eux est le cœur marqué d'une croix. Jésus notre loi est crucifié, que le cœur du juste porte en son milieu et qu'il chante nuit et jour. Tu reprends le psaltérion]

L'union mystique du roi avec le divin consiste en l'imprégnation de la loi résonnant dans le cœur du souverain comme un chant céleste garant de l'harmonie du royaume. Il faut appréhender à la fois la composition globale du manuscrit et l'histoire des images pour reconstituer la cohérence du système figuratif. La lecture des pièces isolées de leur contexte, tant historique, qu'intertextuel et matériel (composition du manuscrit) prive la métaphore de son sens pragmatique et de sa force d'intégration dans un monde imaginaire cohérent et engagé. Le *Canticordum du pelerin* (f.167v-180v) trouve une lecture d'autant plus pertinente lorsque l'on resitue le dialogue entre *Cœur seulet* et *Cœur mondain* dans le cadre d'un enseignement de la sagesse et de l'imitation du Christ qui sied par excellence au cœur de la société, le prince. Le jeu des citations bibliques peut être analysé à l'aune de cet horizon particulier. Il fait intervenir des discours sur la question de la paix, dans un contexte historique troublé par le Schisme et la crise de la royauté. La réévaluation de la métaphore: de la sélection qu'elle opère dans le répertoire des antécédents littéraires et des représentations socioculturelles par l'inscription dans un nouveau projet, permet de relire le texte globalement, de redéfinir le rapport entre les signes linguistiques.

Gerson s'approprie la métaphore de la harpe en mettant l'accent sur ses connotations corporelles et cosmiques afin de poser le modèle christique comme idéal de concorde, non seulement de l'âme, mais également de l'Église et de l'État. La même circulation signifiante entre harmonie musicale, perfection du macrocosme et du microcosme, paix politique et modèle divin s'effectue à travers l'image de l'échiquier, autre instrument à cordes posées sur un caisson de bois.

17. Texte n° 106, vol. 9, p. 1.

Dans les figures d'échiquier français, Gerson rappelle l'association traditionnelle entre le cœur et le roi déjà présente dans le *Livre des Echecs amoureux moralisés* d'Evrart de Conty (487-488-489, vol. 9 éd. Glorieux, voir également figure 1 en annexe). *Humble de cuer* se situe au centre des sept clefs de l'échiquier, clefs qui mettent en mouvement les cordes de l'instrument, comme le soleil au centre du système planétaire et la mèse dans les tons musicaux. Il y a donc une continuité figurative qui se profile entre les deux auteurs. La communauté des systèmes de représentation traduit en même temps une parenté idéologique relative au pouvoir. Evrart de Conty amorce l'édification symbolique du corps cosmique de l'État et l'image de l'harmonie musicale, signe de perfection du gouvernement, par le biais de la métaphore de l'échiquier et de la harpe. Celle-ci est un des trois attributs d'Apollon dont les correspondances symboliques avec le roi sont subtiles. Elle représente la perfection cosmique dont Apollon est le modérateur, comme le soleil parmi les planètes et le souverain dans la société.

La harpe chez Evrart est un des attributs d'Apollon, assimilé symboliquement au roi, centre de la société. Elle est aussi celui de l'art de versifier et de composer la prose qui est pris dans l'isotopie cosmique de la musique et mis en rapport étroit avec la représentation du pouvoir et de l'univers céleste. Confirmant l'attraction d'une nouvelle réalité de l'ordre cosmique dans le système de la musique universelle, l'image de la harpe reparaît dans la description des pièces de l'acteur comme figure gravée sur l'écu de *Doulx Parler*, un des deux cavaliers. Avec Orphée, elle représente la perfection de la parole et son pouvoir d'action sur le monde est rattaché à son rôle dans le gouvernement de la cité. L'accord de sagesse et d'éloquence (d'Orphée et d'Eurydice dans l'explication de la fable) convient au bon gouvernement (p. 723). La parole poétique figurée par la harpe est un élément du cosmos et outil d'action sur le pouvoir dont elle partage le système de représentation.

La musique, métaphore de la perfection du macrocosme, du microcosme et du corps social, se métamorphose complètement chez Molinet en l'expression du talent d'écrivain. Le transfert s'articule autour de l'image de la harpe. Dans *le Naufrage de la Pucelle*,[18] prosimètre daté de 1477, les connotations véhiculées par l'imaginaire musical jouent un rôle de premier plan. Marie, fille de Charles le Téméraire, est laissée seule sur le trône de la Bourgogne suite à la mort tragique de son père. Elle doit

18. Jean Molinet, *Les Faictz et Dicts*, éd. par Noël Dupire, t. 1, SATF (Paris, Didot, 1936), pp. 77-99.

choisir un parti pour conclure une alliance matrimoniale. Molinet représente la nef de l'État bourguignon chavirant et menacée par les ambitions de la France. *Noblesse Debilitee* sur le navire est séduit et trompé par le chant des sirènes, qui s'associe à la baleine et au dauphin, alias la France pour séduire Marie de Bourgogne. *Coeur leal*, le compagnon positif de la duchesse de Bourgogne, porte un nom symboliquement marqué au regard de la tradition de la métaphore musicale et cosmique. Du cœur-roi, on passe au cœur bon conseiller du pouvoir. Molinet l'appelle le 'mignon cler' qui apporte consolation à Marie après sa déploration initiale. Il entre dans le registre positif de la musique.[19] L'éloquence du clerc qui guide et épaule la régente des États bourguignons résonne comme la harpe d'Orphée.[20] Dans la bouche de *Noblesse Debilitee* se profile un éloge à la musique trompeuse du dauphin. Celui-ci est un jeune enfant qui ne sait pas encore parler, ni chanter et qui a besoin de l'artifice de *Circés, la fine magicienne*.[21] Le chant des sirènes est d'emblée entaché de connotation de tromperie face à la véridicité du dire du *clerc* qui sait *obvier leurs deceptions sophistiques* (p. 92, l. 4). L'immaturité linguistique du 'jeune prétendant' le disqualifie symboliquement. La parole vraie et sage du clerc l'emporte sur le défaut langagier. Alors que l'acteur et *Coeur leal* parle du son de la musette ou de la busine[22] pour définir le

19. 'A pou se la tres noble jouvencelle avoit donné fin a sa doloreuse complaincte, quant Cœur leal, son mignon cler, astut et de bonne indole, la regarda d'ung oeul de pité et voiant qu'elle estoit a demy chutte en pamoison, sans avoir une onche de joie, par la suavité de sa melliflue eloquence, plus armonieuse que la harpe orpheyne, se prins a consoler en telle maniere.' [A peine la très noble jeune fille eut-elle terminé sa triste complainte, quand, Cœur Loyal, son mignon clerc, rusé et de grand talent, la regarda avec pitié et voyant qu'elle était presque sans connaissance, sans avoir une pointe de joie, par la douceur de son éloquence ruisselant de miel, plus harmonieuse que la harpe d'Orphée, se mit à la consoler.] (p. 83).

20. Les trois compagnons de Marie sur la nef, figure de l'État, rappellent les trois ordres traditionnels de la société: *Noblesse debilitee*, *Coeur leal* et *Communauté (femenine)*. *Coeur leal* reçoit aussi la caractérisation de *tres prudent bacheller*, p. 92, l. 3, renvoyant à un titre universitaire.

21. 'Mais pour ce qu'il estoit jeune et ne sçavoit aincores ne parler ne chanter et que, de sa nature proprietaire, avoit chant humain et instrumens musicaux, Circés, la fine magicienne, qui jadis avoit charmé les compaignons Ulixés, luy envoia deux seraines de l'autre monde qui faisoient merveilles d'enchanter gens.'

22. La busine est l'instrument associé à la guerre. Jean Molinet dans la *Chronique* présente le duc Charles le Téméraire comme un personnage guerrier, 'inspiré de Mars, le dieu des batailles, le restor d'Ulixes, ung second Scipion, (...) qui les provinces voisines a merveilleusement resveilliét au son de ses buisines et a fait plus que le possible du très chevalereux art d'armes, (...)' [Inspiré de Mars, le dieu de la guerre, le nouvel Ulysse, le second Scipion... qui a éveillé les provinces voisines au son des trompettes et a réalisé plus qu'il n'est possible, des exploits d'armes.]

chant émis par les sirènes et la baleine,[23] *Noblesse debilitee* prouvant son incapacité à soutenir Marie y déchiffre le son de la harpe.[24]

Le *Naufrage de la pucelle* oppose la musique et la harpe de *Coeur leal*, conseiller-clerc du pouvoir et la tromperie du parti français appuyant la tentative de séduction de Marie de Bourgogne par le chant des sirènes et la *busine*. Les connotations politiques de la musique remontent à l'Antiquité et transitent dans la pensée médiévale par le biais des poètes latins tardifs qui transfèrent dans la symbolique chrétienne un bagage classique important.[25]

Molinet invoque l'autorité d'Augustin dans un emploi précis de l'image de la harpe au sein du poème *Petit Traité de la harpe*, sans que l'on puisse cibler où le rhétoriqueur à puiser chez l'évêque d'Hippone, comme nous allons le voir. Le parallèle très net entre le passage de la *Cité de Dieu* et le *Naufrage de la pucelle* ne témoigne-t-il pas d'une inspiration 'décalée' par rapport aux allégations de Molinet?

Le *Petit Traité de la harpe* renoue avec les connotations christiques de l'instrument pour exprimer la création poétique.[26] La harpe 'orpheÿne' qui

Jean Molinet, *Chroniques*, publiés par Georges Doutrepont et Omer Jodogne, t. 1 (1474-1488), Académie Royale de Belgique, n° 51 (Bruxelles, Palais des Académies, 1935), p. 27.

23. 'La ballaine aspirant après sa proie, a demy rompue de sa pretente, voeulle elucider son occulte conception, se mist en paine de ravoir par force ce qu'elle promettoit a garantir par amour et fist venir Triton, ung buzineur, qui a sa tube adulatoire congrega hideux marsuins, fluvieux ypotames, serpens aquaticques, coeullevres marines, (...)' [La baleine, désirant sa proie, à moitié acquise par ses agissements – je veux élucider son occulte manière – se mit en désir de gagner par la force, ce qu'elle promettait d'obtenir par amour, et fit venir Triton, un trompettiste, qui avec sa trompe doucereuse rassemblait les affreux marsouins, les hippopotames fluviaux, les serpents aquatiques, les couleuvres marines.] (p. 96).

24. 'Quel nom, quel cry, quelz armes vous sont plus precieuses que les sacrés fleurons du real liligere? Vostre grand bruit, triumphe et glore resone, repose et resplend en la catholicque auriflambe: vecy la souefve balleine qui aspire après vous pour vous sauver, comme elle sauva jadis le grand prophete; vecy le petit dauphin qui vollette auprés de vous et vous festoie pour vous mener a port de salut, comme jadis il mena Arion, le bon instrumentaire, pour la suavité musicalle que il trouva au son de la harpe (...)' [Quel nom, quel cri, quelles armes vous sont plus précieux que les fleurons sacrés du lis royal? Votre grande renommée, triomphe et gloire reposent et resplendissent dans l'oriflamme catholique: voici la douce baleine qui vous désire pour vous sauver, comme elle sauva jadis le grand prophète, voici le petit dauphin qui s'agite près de vous et vous fait la fête pour vous mener au port du Salut, comme jadis il mena Arion, le bon musicien, à cause de la douceur de la musique qu'il trouva dans sa harpe.] (pp. 93-94).

25. Cicéron utilise la comparaison de l'accord musical pour signifier l'unité de l'État dans le *De Republica* II, 42-43. L'image est récupérée par Augustin dans les Livre II, 21 et XVII, 13 de la *Cité de Dieu*. La pensée politique de l'évêque d'Hippone a profondément marqué le Moyen Âge.

26. Jean Molinet, éd. Dupire, t. 2, 1937, pp. 439-442.

sert de terme de comparaison à l'éloquence de *Coeur leal* dans la *Naufrage de la Pucelle*, revient dans le *Petit Traictiet de la harpe*, où Molinet s'attarde plus longuement sur le pouvoir d'action du 'prudent cithariste' (v. 1) qui agit sur les éléments du cosmos. La figure de David présentée dans la deuxième strophe prolonge l'image du pouvoir du musicien sur l'univers. 'David, qui sceut ses accords accorder, / Chascune corde au parfaict accorda, / Sans nul discord qui sceusit discorder (...)' [11-13: David, qui sut accorder ses accords, accorda chaque corde au parfait, sans aucune discordance qui eût provoquer une discorde]). Le motif de David accordant sa harpe est très fécond dans les représentations iconographiques, en particulier dans l'illustration de la lettre B du Psaume 1 ou dans le frontispice des manuscrits de psautiers. Le roi psalmiste se trouve représenté portant en main une clef pour régler l'instrument. Van Schaick y lit une préfiguration du Christ-Logos qui vient rétablir l'ordre dans la création.[27]

Molinet s'adresse, dans la troisième strophe, a 'vostre reverence' pour lui offrir l'instrument métamorphosé en image verbale glosée, instrument élu pour son pouvoir d'action.

> Puisque David, menant ses aigneaux paistre,
> Sceut accorder sus la harpe musicque,
> Et luy estant cithariste campestre
> Fut tant plaisant a nature angelicque,
> Puisque Orpheüs le turbo plutonicque
> Sceut endormir au reson de sa lire,
> J'ay bien vollut cest instrument eslire
> Pour ung present digne de preference,
> Comme porrés en après oïr lire,
> Sy ne desplait a vostre reverence.
> [Puisque David, conduisant ses agneaux paître sut accorder la musique sur la harpe et étant un cithariste champêtre, il fut tellement agréable à la nature angélique, puisque Orphée sut endormir Cerbère au son de sa lyre, j'ai voulu choisir cet instrument pour un don digne de préférence, comme vous pourrez l'entendre lire, s'il plaît à votre majesté.]

Molinet renchérit sur le rôle de la harpe évoquant la pacification des éléments par le biais d'une autre lecture du motif: l'apaisement de la rage de Saül, roi d'Israël. L'Ancien Testament enseigne aussi sur la manière de gouverner.[28] Molinet se priverait-il d'offrir à son destinataire un miroir

27. Van Schaick, *The Harp* [note 5], p. 50: 'A similar symbolic meaning is attached to David tuning the harp: David is the reflection of the Christ-Logos who maintains the order of the macrocosmos.'

28. Jacques Verger, 'L'exégèse de l'Université', in *Le Moyen Âge et la Bible* (Paris, 1984), pp. 199-232. Philippe Buc, 'Pouvoir royal et commentaires de la Bible (1150-1350)', in *Annales E.S.C.*, 43/3 (1989), pp. 691-713.

du rapport prince/clerc dans le couple David/Saül, glorifiant par cette occasion la dignité de sa fonction? La harpe (choisie comme métaphore du poème offert) restaure 'meilleur sens et raison'. Le rhétoriqueur opte ensuite pour l'exploitation de l'identification traditionnelle du psaltérion de forme triangulaire[29] et de la Trinité.[30] Honorius d'Autun notamment dit que 'Le psaltérion est un instrument de musique, avec dix cordes, triangle, à la manière de la forme de la lettre *delta* (...). Le psaltérion est construit en triangle, comme en reconnaissance de la Trinité, et par les dix cordes, il s'agit des Dix Lois.'[31] On retrouve l'association de la harpe et de la Trinité dans certaines représentations iconographiques, notamment dans l'*Hortus deliciarum* dans la représentation de la parabole du festin céleste où le siège sur lequel est installé le Père a une forme de harpe.[32]

L'appropriation du schéma trinitaire dans le chef œuvre de Molinet semble aller dans le sens de l'ouverture de la métaphore à l'expression de la création poétique. Le Père correspond à l'art, l'Esprit à la main et le Fils à la corde. La dernière attribution entre dans le registre traditionnel de l'image. La corde tendue symbolise la passion, notamment chez saint Bernard et dans les *Passions*.

Mais les couples art/Père; main/Esprit[33] ressortissent de l'imagination propre à Molinet et offrent des éléments de raccords avec l'expression de l'activité scripturaire.

> En la harpe trois choses il convient,
> Ains qu'il y ayt souffissance au parfaict:

29. Si Molinet allègue une source augustinienne ('La glorieuse et saincte Trinité / Lassus regnant sans principe et sans fin / Puis figurer sans incongruité / Sus la harpe, selon sainct Augustin, / Docteur devot, secretaire divin;...' [La glorieuse Trinité, régnant dans les cieux sans commencement ni fin, je puis la figurer sans incongruité par la harpe, selon saint Augustin, docteur dévot et secrétaire de Dieu.] vv. 51-55) nous n'avons pas pu situer chez l'évêque d'Hippone d'assimilation claire entre l'instrument et la Trinité. Ses commentaires nombreux sur le motif portent plus sur la distinction entre cithare (incarnation et passion du corps du Christ) et le psaltérion (esprit glorieux de la mort).

30. Martin Van Schaick, *The Harp* [note 5], chap. 3: 'The delta Harp', pp. 62-90.

31. Honorius d'Autun, *Expositio in Psalmos selectos*, *PL* 172, col. 269 et 272. (Nous traduisons). Raban Maur parle également de la lettre delta et de l'assimilation à la Trinité: 'La cithare, à propos de laquelle on parle, a la forme spirituelle de l'Église. Elle qui a une forme à trois côtés, avec les vingt-quatre dogmes anciens, à la manière de la lettre delta, signifie la foi en la sainte Trinité (...)': Raban Maur, *Commentarium in Paralipomena*, lib. I, *PL* 109/3, col. 346. (Nous traduisons).

32. Gérard Cames, *Allégories et symboles dans l'Hortus deliciarum* (Leiden, E.J. Brill, 1971), pl. LXXI.

33. Dans l'iconographie, l'inspiration divine issue du Saint-Esprit médiateur entre le monde céleste et le monde terrestre est figurée par une main sortie du ciel.

L'art l'accorde, puis la main qui le tient,
Sans laquelle tout demeure imparfaict
L'art voeult dicter tout ce qui y est faict,
La main après donne mesure et touche,
Et la corde donne armonie doulce,
Et toutefois l'art par qui tout consonne
N'est point oÿ, ne la main qui la touche:
C'est seullement la corde qui resonne.
[Il convient qu'il y ait trois choses dans la harpe, afin que ce soit suffisant pour la perfection: l'art accorde, ensuite la main qui tient, sans laquelle tout reste imparfait. L'art veut dicter tout ce qui y est fait, la main ensuite donne mesure et touche et la corde donne la douce harmonie. Et néanmoins, l'art qui donne la consonance n'est pas entendu, ni la main qui touche: il n'y a que la corde qui résonne.]

L'art qui descend du Père veut 'dicter'. Le vocable 'dicter' renvoie à l'acte d'écrire ou d'enseigner et sa proximité avec le terme 'art' pointe vers le syntagme 'art de dictier'. Molinet entend-il placer sa conception de l'écriture sous l'autorité divine et emprunter une image christique du pouvoir harmonique sur l'univers pour signifier sa propre activité? La main de l'Esprit qui 'donne mesure et touche' recouvre une valeur ambivalente et peut exprimer tant l'action sur l'instrument que la matérialité de la main qui tient la plume et versifie. Le vocabulaire propre à la rhétorique semble affleurer à nouveau dans la septième strophe. La résonance de la corde, l'incarnation a lieu par la 'disposition du Père' et 'l'operation' de l'Esprit. Si la 'disposition' désigne la volonté du Père, elle fait également penser à la 'dispositio' une des cinq parties des arts de rhétorique, qui indique l'art de débuter ou d'agencer les arguments.[34]

Mais a esté par disposition
De Dieu le pere et operation
Du Sainct Esprit, c'est chose souveraine (...).
[Mais il a été par la disposition de Dieu le Père et par l'opération du Saint-Esprit, c'est une chose souveraine.]

D'Orphée au Christ en passant par David, Molinet exprime à travers son poème le pouvoir du verbe sur le monde, et par excellence de ce Verbe divin incarné dans la grande Poésie biblique. Le Logos-Christ rétablit par la vérité de son dire l'harmonie du cosmos. Après avoir été chez Gerson miroir du prince, la harpe qui l'exprime est-elle ce même instrument que le poète veut 'eslire' comme modèle de son activité d'écrivain? C'est bien à 'lire' (v. 29) qu'est destinée la harpe du poète. L'image glisse

34. L'opération (l'œuvre du Saint-Esprit) ferait penser à l'*actio*, la récitation, la performance.

et transite, d'Orphée à David, au Christ, puis à l'âme et au souverain idéal pour signifier enfin la vocation de l'écrivain à agir comme le Verbe sacré, garant de l'harmonie du cosmos, chantre de la paix des nations.

En 1470, Molinet présente un chant royal à la confrérie du puy Notre-Dame à Amiens.[35] Le refrain proposé par le maître de la confrérie, Jean Barbier 'Harpe rendant souveraine armonie' donne lieu chez le rhétoriqueur à un poème de louange à la Vierge figurée par l'instrument. Les sept planètes sont mises en relation avec les sept accords musicaux et avec les sept vertus (trois théologales et quatre cardinales). L'allusion à l'arbre de Jessé rappelle la filiation de Marie, descendante de David. Dans certaines représentations iconographiques, notamment sur la lettrine du psaume 1 du manuscrit conservé à New-York, Pierpont Morgan Library, 43, f. 27v. (XIIe siècle), David est représenté portant la harpe, et la Vierge dans le médaillon sous le Christ. Molinet fait également allusion à l'Assomption (['Devant son filz, qui endura mort sure, / Est assumpté, et en gloire infinie / Resonne, et est, par compas et mesure, / Harpe rendant souveraine armonie.' [A côté du Fils qui a enduré une mort amère, elle est montée et en gloire infinie, elle résonne, par ordre et mesure. Harpe rendant harmonie souveraine.]), motif figuré au sommet du cadre entourant la lettre historiée: Jésus couronne la Vierge. Le texte de Molinet manifeste donc une grande proximité par rapport aux représentations des psautiers. À l'initiale encore du psaume 1 du psautier d'Oxford, Bodleian Library 284, f. 1r (début XIIIe siècle), on retrouve les figures de David à la harpe et de la Vierge portant l'enfant Jésus.[36] La maternité qui permet l'incarnation divine se trouve fortement associée au psalmiste. Mais la Vierge de Molinet est l'occasion aussi de glorifier la parole poétique dont Marie se fait porteuse et qui est l'occasion même de son élection divine, de la rédemption.[37] C'est à entendre les chansonnettes de Marie dans le

35. Édition Noël Dupire, t. 2, pp. 447-449. Jean Molinet, 'Art de seconde rhétorique', *Recueil d'Arts de Seconde Rhétorique*, publié par Ernest Langlois, Collection de Documents inédits sur l'histoire de France, 12 (Paris, Imprimerie nationale, 1902), pp. 242-244.

36. Voir Van Schaik, *The Harp* [note 5], illustration 32, p. 231.

37. Chez Gerson, l'âme/la Vierge sont *verbigènes* et elles engendrent le Christ dans un élan d'amour qui provoque le chant (le *Magnificat*, commenté par Gerson, t. 8, 418, *Collectorium super Magnificat*; et le *canticordum*.) Notons que la dévotion à la Vierge et la communauté imaginaire qui unit la louange de Marie et du pouvoir ne sont sans doute pas innocents, dans le chef de Gerson et dans celui de Molinet qui s'approprie les représentations du prince 'français' pour la gloire du duc de Bourgogne. Les rois de France ont voué une dévotion particulière à la Vierge, et selon Colette Beaune, le choix du lys dans l'héraldique royale au XIIe siècle n'est pas étranger à l'attribution du motif à la Vierge à la même époque (notamment dans la lecture du Cantique). Voir: Colette Beaune, *Naissance de la nation France*, Bibliothèque des Histoires (Paris, Gallimard, 1985), pp. 237-263.

temple que Dieu l'a choisie et envoie l'ange Gabriel ('Au temple fut presentée et sonna / Si hault que Dieu oy ses chansonnettes; / Riche Salut Gabriel lui donná [Au temple, elle a été présentée et résonna, tellement haut que Dieu entendit sa chansonnette. Gabriel lui fit une salutation riche]). L'immaculée conception s'exprime par la métaphore du don de l'art de musique. La naissance du Verbe en son sein lui donne les traits d'une musicienne qui sait aussi manier les mots pour sauver le genre humain:

> Car a ce mot deïté s'accorda
> Au genre humain marchant sus espinettes;
> Si doulx accort sa corde recorda
> Quelle endormi serpenteaux et raynettes;
> Si trés doulx mos sont de sa bouche issus
> Que les haulz cieulx de Dieu fais et tissus,
> Jadis fermez, lui ont fait ouverture
> Et ont brisié infernale closture.[38]
>
> [Car à ces mots, la divinité s'accorda au genre humain en marchant sur des épinettes; sa corde rendit un accord si doux qu'elle endormit les serpents et les grenouilles, des mots tellement doux sont sortis de sa bouche que les hauts cieux créés et façonnés par Dieu, autrefois fermés lui ont été ouverts et ont brisés la prison de l'enfer.]

Le poète présente l'incarnation comme la conséquence de la séduction du Très-Haut par les paroles et les chants de la Vierge. Le pouvoir de la parole c'est le Verbe incarné, mais aussi la mère, protectrice et promotrice de la poésie. La Vierge du puy inspire la création et donne au poète ses gloires:

> Prince du puy, qui chantez d'aventure,
> Donnez accort, plain chant et floriture
> A l'humble fleur des vierges espanie,
> Et vous orrez en la glore future
> Harpe sonnant souveraine armonie.[39]
>
> [Prince du puy, qui chantez quelquefois, donnez accord, plain-chant, et fioritures à l'humble fleur des vierges épanouie, et vous entendrez dans la gloire future, la harpe résonnant d'harmonie souveraine.]

C'est en composant en l'honneur de Marie que le créateur peut espérer sortir victorieux du concours et recevoir, comme récompense céleste, d'entendre résonner la harpe qui l'inspire. L'attribut de la concorde universelle est offert au poète comme matière à sa composition. La harpe insuffle au poète harmonie et pouvoir.

38. Édition Noël Dupire, t. 2, pp. 447-449.
39. Idem.

Si l'intention du livre des psaumes écrit par David est 'de nous inciter à l'imitation du Christ, de sorte que par lui-même, nous sommes rachetés pour la gloire éternelle, que nous avons perdue par Adam dans la plus grande misère',[40] la figure du psaltérion qui accompagne l'illustration de nombreuses initiales, comme attribut du roi David et signe de l'Incarnation du Verbe, sert à méditer ce message. Image riche de sens, alimentée par des générations de commentaires bibliques et de reprises iconographiques, elle connaît une série d'actualisations qui permettent de saisir la dimension diachronique du sens. Fort de la lecture et de l'imprégnation d'une tradition figurative, le créateur adapte les possibilités offertes par l'univers imaginaire déployé devant lui et l'inscrit dans la perspective d'une interprétation de son propre monde et de ses propres représentations socioculturelles, de la place même qu'il doit tenir dans la société.

Dans le bréviaire de Charles V, le manuscrit de Paris, B.N.F., lat. 1052, réalisé dans un atelier parisien, peut-être celui de Jean Lenoir, on peut observer au folio 261r Dieu assis sur un trône et portant le globe, signe de puissance, et Charles V agenouillé devant lui.[41] La miniature illustre le psaume 109 dans lequel Yahvé proclame le sacerdoce et la royauté universelle du Christ.[42] L'image ne veut-elle pas signifier le transfert au roi Charles V de la puissance accordée par le Père à son Fils, renforçant par la même occasion la fonction de roi-prêtre revendiquée par les propagandistes de la royauté très chrétienne et la typologie Christ rédempteur/roi? Le psautier, livre de prière, trouve par la même occasion une nouvelle fonction: il s'adresse au souverain pour lui enseigner la dignité de sa fonction. Même jeu que la figure du psaltérion dans l'œuvre de Gerson, d'abord métaphore du Christ, elle devient modèle pour l'âme humaine, et en particulier pour le corps mystique de l'État.

Dans l'illustration du Psautier de Charles V, l'image permet de 'recycler' le message biblique au sein de l'idéologie et de la mystique royale.

40. Honorius d'Autun, *Selectorum Psalmorum expositio*, *PL* 172, col. 271 A. (Nous traduisons).

41. La miniature souvent reproduite figure dans le livre de Jeannine Quillet, *Charles V. Le Roi lettré* (Paris, Perrin, 2002; 1984[1]).

42. Psaume 109: 'Oracle de Yahvé à mon Seigneur: «Siège à ma droite tant que j'aie fait de tes ennemis l'escabeau de tes pieds.» Ton sceptre de puissance, Yahvé l'étendra: depuis Sion, domine jusqu'au cœur de l'ennemi. À toi le principat au jour de ta naissance, les honneurs sacrés dès le sein, dès l'aurore de ta jeunesse. Yahvé l'a juré, il ne s'en dédira point: «tu es prêtre à jamais selon l'ordre de Melchisédech.» À ta droite Seigneur, il abat les rois au jour de sa colère; il fait justice des nations, entassant des cadavres, il abat les têtes sur l'immensité de la terre. Au torrent il abreuve en chemin. C'est pourquoi il redresse la tête.'

Le manuscrit se fait lieu de transition de la pensée, de récupération historique. De même l'image au sens purement conceptuel, l'icône verbale transite de manuscrit en manuscrit, d'auteur en lecteur. Elle véhicule l'histoire d'une signification qui se sédimente et sans laquelle elle reste vide et accessoire, pur ornement. La relation texte/image tellement riche au sein du manuscrit peut aussi être intériorisée. L'image est alors perçue comme un des éléments internes qui fait circuler le rapport entre création et interprétation. Elle fonctionne comme un lieu d'interrogation où le sens ouvert tend vers la reprise et la continuation. L'illustration témoigne de la réception du texte et témoigne du pouvoir de l'écrit d'agir sur son monde d'accueil. De la même manière, l'image s'entend comme une réponse à l'appel du/des texte(s) qui la véhicule(nt) en amont et qui tracent en aval des perspectives de lecture et d'interprétation ouverte du monde.

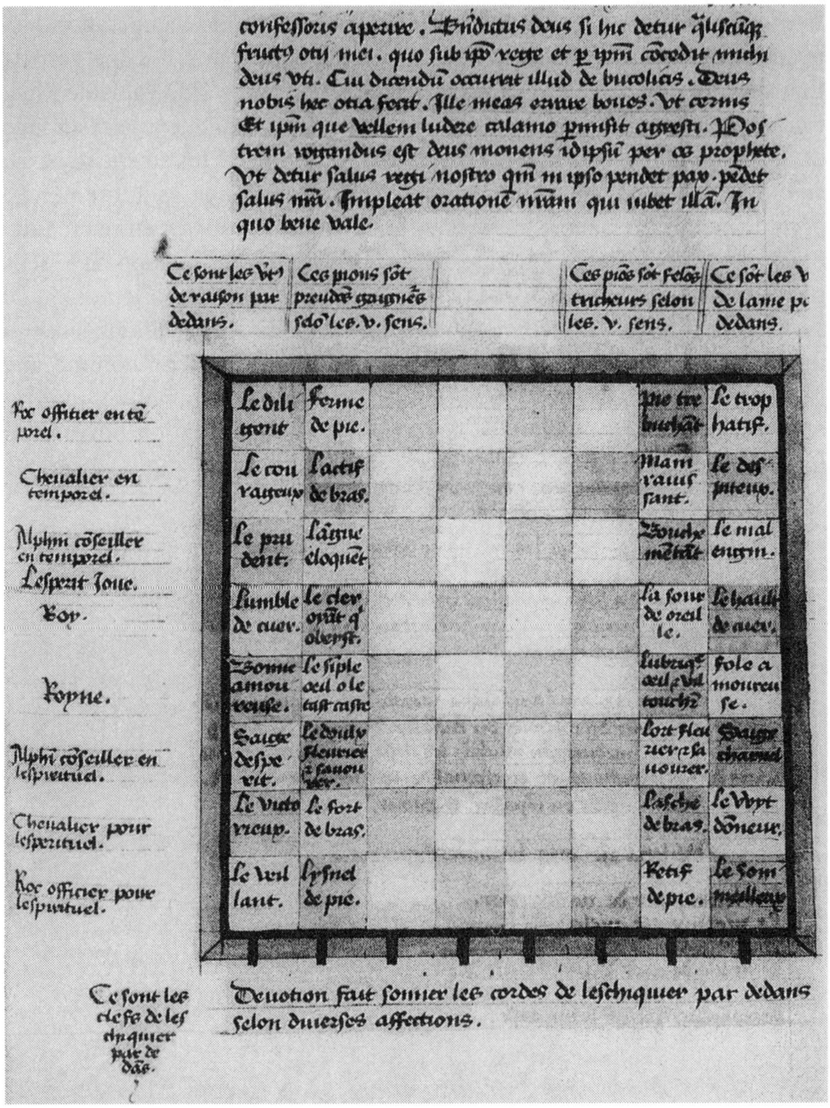

Figure 1

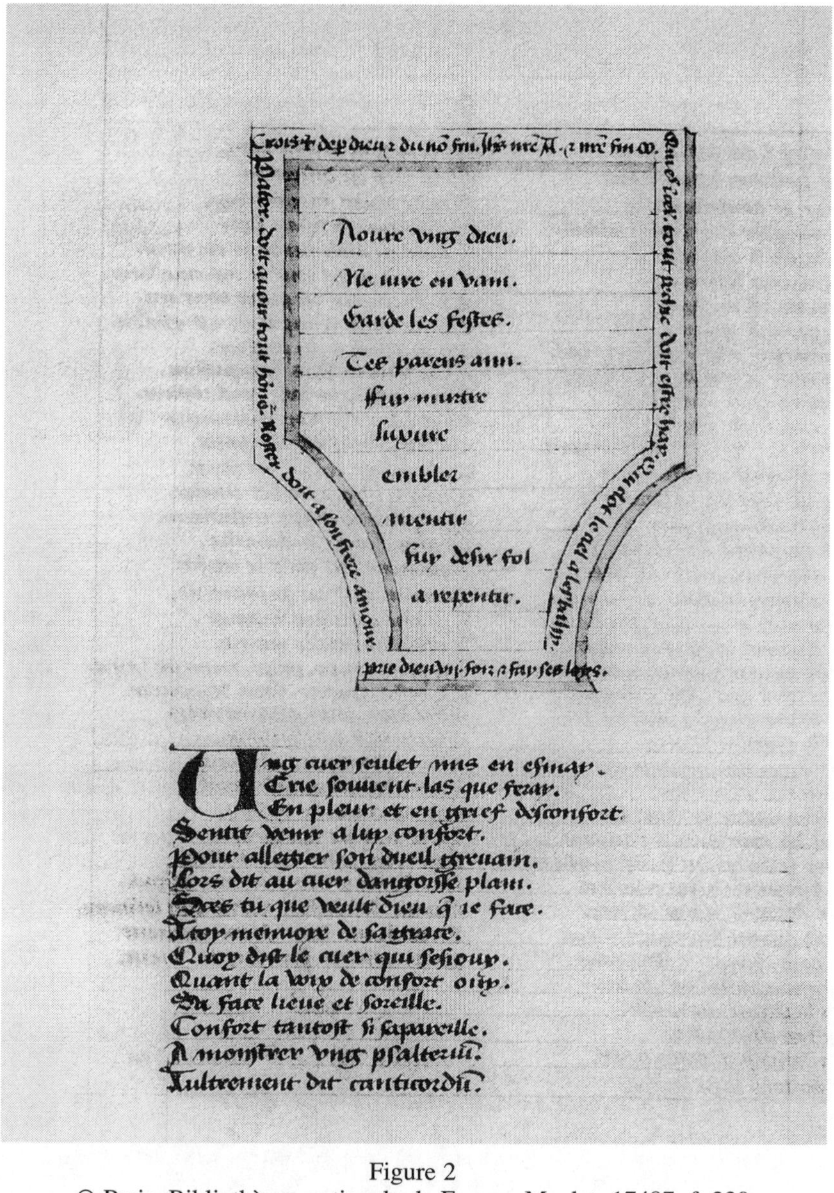
Aoure ung dieu.
Ne iure en vain.
Garde les festes.
Tes parens aim.
Fuy murtre
luxure
embler
mentir
fuy desir fol
a repentir.
Ung cuer seulet mis en esmay.
Crie souvent las que feray.
En pleur et en grief desconfort.
Sentit venir a luy confort.
Pour alleger son dueil grevain.
Lors dit au cuer dangoisse plain.
Confort tantost si sapareille.
A monstrer ung psalterium.
Autrement dit canticordium.

Figure 2

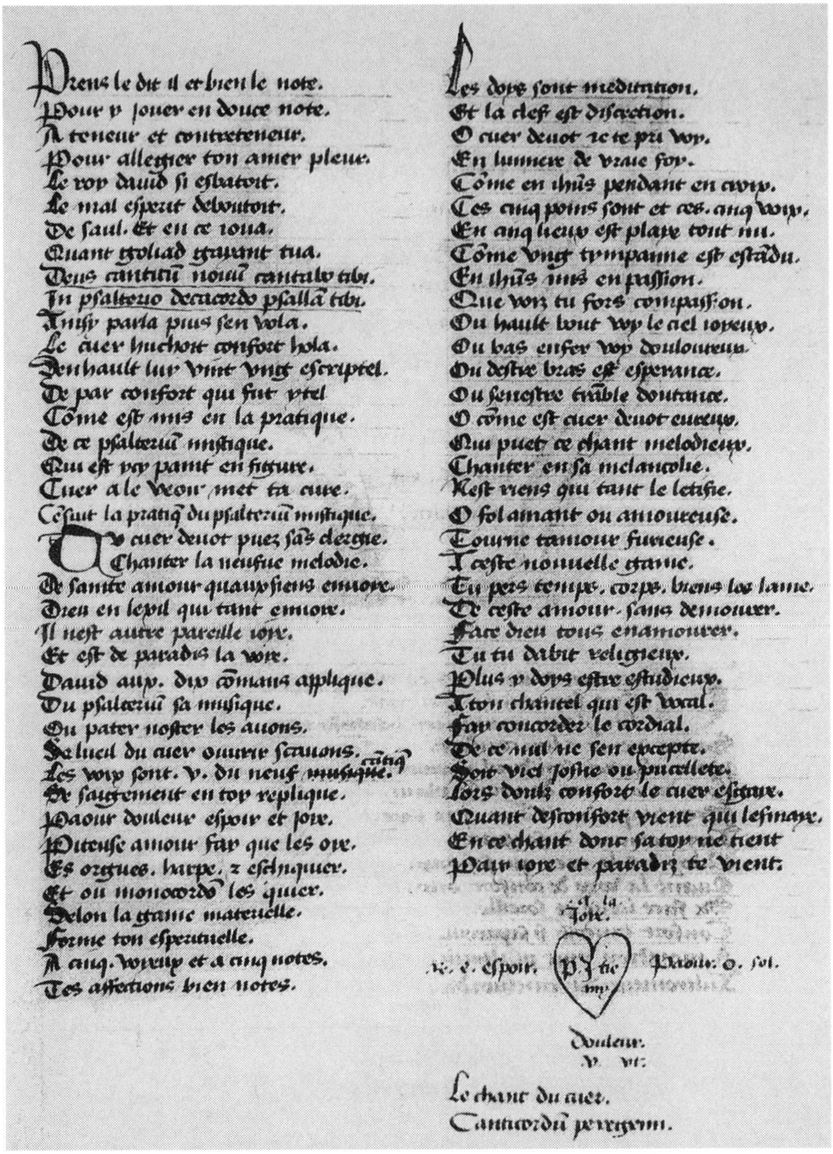
Prens le dit il et bien le note.
Pour y jouer en douce note.
A teneur et contreteneur.
Pour allegier ton amer pleur.
Le roy david si esbatoit.
Le mal esperit deboutoit.
De saul. Et en ce iona.
Quant goliad geauant tua.
Deus canticu̅ nouu̅ cantabo tibi.
In psalterio decacordo psalla̅ tibi.
Ainsy parla puis sen vola.
Le cuer huchoit confort hola.
Den hault lui vint vng escriptel.
De par confort qui fut ytel
Co̅me est mis en la pratique.
De ce psalteriu̅ mistique.
Qui est cy paint en figure.
Cuer a le veoir met ta cure.
Cesuit la pratiq̅ du psalteriu̅ mistique.
Ov cuer deuot puez sa̅s clergie.
Chanter la neufue melodie.
De sainte amour quauxsiens enuoie.
Dieu en lexil qui tant ennoie.
Il nest autre pareille ioie.
Et est de paradis la voie.
David aux. dix co̅mans applique.
Du psalteriu̅ sa musique.
Ou pater noster les auons.
Seluel du cuer ouurir scauons.
Les voix sont. v. du neuf ~~musique~~. ca̅tiq̅
Se saigement en toy replique.
Paour douleur espoir et joie.
Piteuse amour fay que les oie.
Es orgues. harpe. z eschiquier.
Et ou monocordo les quier.
Selon la grame materielle.
Forme ton espirituelle.
A cinq. voieux et a cinq notes.
Tes affections bien notes.

Les doys sont meditation.
Et la clef est discretion.
O cuer deuot ie te pri voy.
En lumiere de vraie foy.
Co̅me en ihu̅s pendant en croix.
Ces cinq poins sont et ces. cinq voix.
En cinq lieux est playe tout nu.
Co̅me vng tympanne est esta̅du.
En ihu̅s mis en passion.
Que voiz tu fors compassion.
Ou hault voit voy le ciel ioyeux.
Ou bas enfer voy douloureux.
Ou destre bras est esperance.
Ou senestre trouble doutance.
O co̅me est cuer deuot eureux.
Qui puet ce chant melodieux.
Chanter en sa melancolie.
Nest riens qui tant le letifie.
O fol amant ou amoureuse.
Tourne tamour furieuse.
A ceste nouuelle grame.
Tu pers temps. corps. biens los lame.
De ceste amour. sans demourer.
Fait dieu tous enamourer.
Tu tu debit religieux.
Plus y doys estre estudieux.
A ton chantel qui est vocal.
Fay concorder le cordial.
De ce nul ne sen excepte.
Soit viel josne ou pucellete.
Lors doulz confort le cuer esiouxe.
Quant desconfort vient qui lesinaxe.
En ce chant dont sa toy ne tient
Paix ioye et paradiz te vient.

la
Joie.
. e. espoir. P z tie Paour. o. sol.
doleur.
. v. vi.
Le chant du cuer.
Canticordu̅ peregrinu.

Figure 3

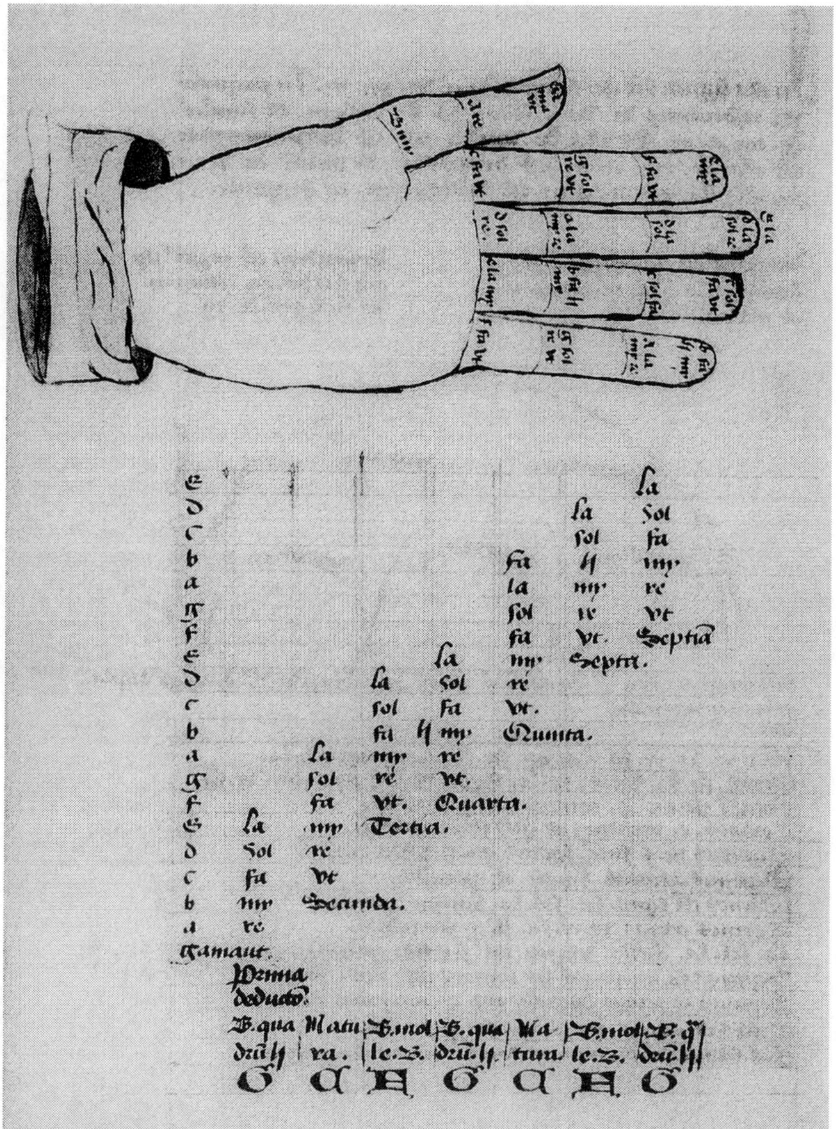

Figure 4

© Paris, Bibliothèque nationale de France, Ms. lat. 17487, f. 231

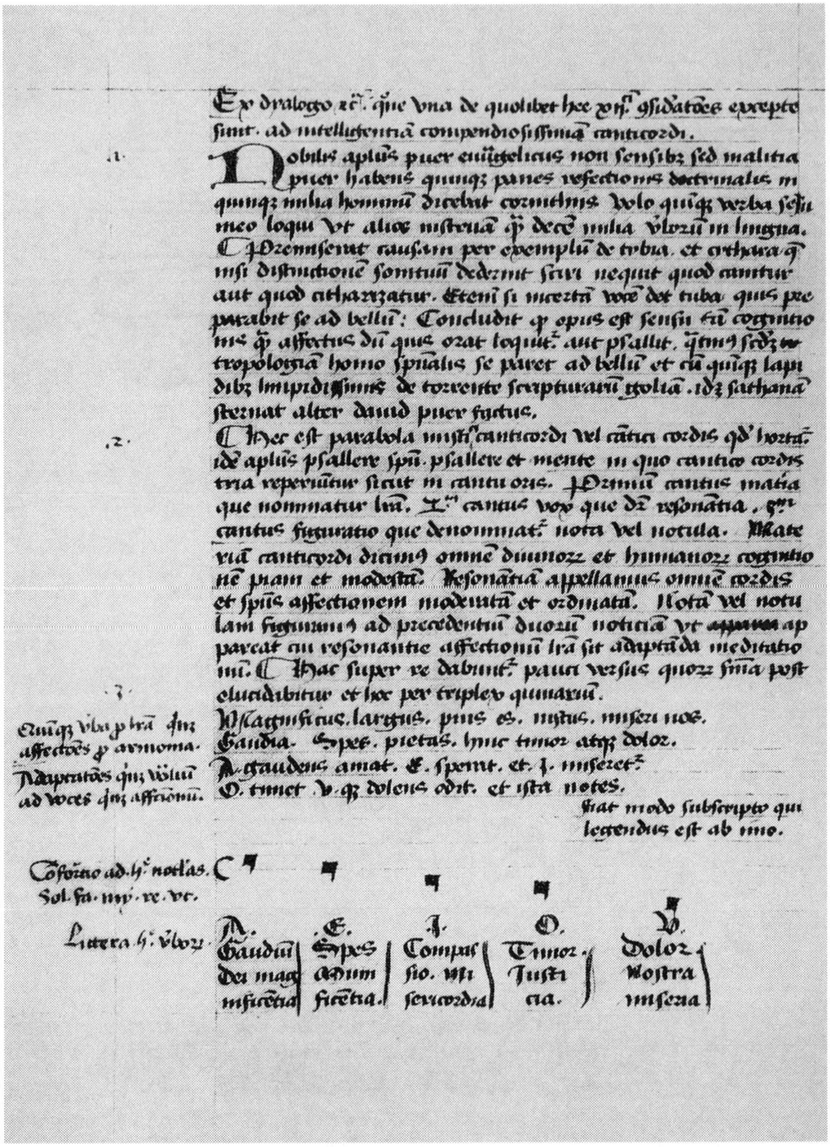

Figure 5

Esther M. MULDERS

MEDIEVAL MANIFESTATIONS OF EROS:
The Ancient God of Love in a Christian Setting

1. INTRODUCTION

Although early authors such as Vasari and Ghiberti have attempted to make us believe otherwise, nowadays it is generally agreed upon that the antique inheritance did not die during the Middle Ages. Consequently, the ancient tradition was never revived during the Renaissance. Renaissance scholars inherited their antique treasure from their medieval ancestors. Medieval thought, writings and imagery, for their part, borrowed significantly from the antique tradition.[1]

This contribution traces the ways in which Eros, the ancient god of love, was reused – or more appropriately maybe: continued to exist – during the Christian Middle Ages.

The story of Eros' medieval fortunes can be told in several ways: broadly speaking, the deity's medieval adventures link up nicely with the abandoned ideas as described before. On a superficial view the pagan god of love appears to have nearly died during the Middle Ages. By the end of this era the god seems to have made his most impressive comeback, like a phoenix who rises from his ashes.

One can reach another, very fascinating, reading of Eros' medieval vicissitudes by studying the network of the transmission of ideas and texts concerning the god's character. Evidently the medieval doctors struggled to saveguard the antique inheritance and they took a fair amount of effort to harmonize the antique god of love with medieval Christian thought. In order unveil Eros' medieval significance, the doctors' hidden agenda must be brought to the surface, the particular nature of this mythological fig-

1. See for example: J. Elsner, *Art and the Roman viewer. The Transformation of Art from the Pagan World to Christianity* (Cambridge, 1995), p. 1-14; A. Grabar, *Christian Iconography. A Study of its Origins* (Princeton, 1968), p. xli-l; E. Male, *The Gothic Image. Religious Art in France of the Thirteenth Century* (New York, 1972), p. 332-354 (*L'Art Religieux du XIIIe siecle en France*, Paris, 1898); E. Panofsky, *Renaissance and Renascences in Western Art* (Stockholm, 1960), p. 42-52; H. Rahner, *Griechischen Mythen in Christlicher Deutung. Gesammelte Aufsatze* (Zurich, 1945); J. Seznec, *The Survival of the Pagan Gods. The Mythological Tradition and Its Place in Renaissance Humanism and Art* (New York, 1953), p. 3-7 (*'La Survivance der Dieux Antiques', Studies of the Warburg Institute*, vol XI, London, 1940).

ure must be unraveled and coordinated to its contemporary context. An image of Eros in *De Universo* by Hrabanus Maurus serves the purpose in this article (ill. 5).

The methodology used in this survey can be characterised as 'synthetic'. Neither the visual sources, nor the literary sources can be considered as independent categories. Instead, the various sources are closely related to each other. In addition, the source material stands in relation to its contemporary context. This article focusses not only on the relations between images and texts and their interactions with their historical, ideological and functional backgrounds. It proposes that Eros' presence and significance in medieval Christian context was also influenced by the ideosyncrasy of both the phenomenon of mythology and that of the innate character of the god of love.

The god Eros is probably the most ambiguous deity in the pagan Pantheon. First, the god is both the personification and the cause of the idea of love. Secondly, there are as many aspects to love as there are to the god Eros. As is evidenced by the variety of myths about Eros that have come down to us from Antiquity onwards, the complexity of love was an issue no less intriguing than it is today. His participation in the world of mythology, provides the god of love with even more dynamics. A myth or a mythological figure aims to create an image, either visually or literarily, of an abstract reality. The particular position of the mythological figure, in the realm between the immaterial idea and the physical world, supplies it with its own level of abstraction. This quality furnishes the mythological figure with an immense flexibility: both the mythological figure, and any of its interpretations, are ever capable of changing readings, depending of their contexts. In addition, since the concept of love is more complex and variable than any other abstraction, the mythological image that is drawn to embody the concept is more real than the realities referred to: Eros' features are fixed. His significance on the other hand is exceptionally flexible.

This pagan idol of many faces found its way into the Christian Middle Ages. The notions of the medieval doctors concerning physical reality as an image of metaphysical truth, interplaying with the peculiarities of mythology in general and the deity's character in particular, have turned the god into a true medieval symbol.

2. The story of the phoenix

The history of Eros' perception, from its early beginnings in Antiquity onwards, seems to corroborate the, theoretically abandoned but in practice still quite persistant, aforementioned notion of history to unfold in undulations.[2]

At the beginning of his career, the god of love was a great expert. Hesiod (ca. 700 BC) was the first author to describe Eros as a person. This Greek author staged Eros in his *Theogonia* as a god of great beauty and as the basic impulse that brought about the union between Chaos and Gaia. Hesiod saw the god as the deep and creative love behind the genesis of life.[3] Following this great act of creation Eros remains, according to Hesiod, in function as the driving force behind the continuation of all life.[4] The lyrical poets, in the seventh and sixth centuries BC, described Eros as cunning, cruel, handsome and unpredictable. Plato, just like Hesiod, assigned Eros an important and constructive place in the supernatural world. He considered the god Eros to be the regulating and uplifting principle at the basis of all good.[5]

The veneration of the deity's power and domination in both the natural and the supernatural worlds appears to decline in the course of history. In the early third century Eros is presented, for the last time in centuries, as one of the greatest powers of nature: in 212 AD Pseudo-Oppianus dedicated a poem about the art of hunting using dogs, the *Cynegetica*, to the emperor Antonius (Caracalla). The text of the *Cynegetica* survives in eighteen manuscripts, of which three are illustrated. The oldest illustrated specimen dates from the tenth century and is kept in Venice (ill. 1 – 2).[6] The manuscript contains 150 illustrations. The major part of these illustrations is directly related to the text, showing the appropriate tools and dogs to be used by the hunter. A small portion of the illustrations is of a mythological character. Two of these mythological images show the god Eros. The poet praises the immense power of the god of love. Eros not only dominates earthly life, but also his fellow gods on top of the Olympus. Quite rightly, the inhabitants of both worlds tremble in fear in confrontation with this deity: if Eros' authority would ever be challenged, life would cease to exist.[7] The first image shows Eros who

2. Due to the division of history in distinguished ages, one is inclined to define differences or antithesises between periods.

3. Hesiod, *Theogonia*, 120-123, tr. S. Lombardo (Cambridge, 1993), p. 64.

4. Hesiod, 201, tr. Lombardo [note 3], p. 67.

5. Plato, *Symposion*, 178 B, 199 C-212 C, tr. T. Griffith, intr. R. B. Rutherford (New York, 2000), p. 15, 47-86.

6. Venice, Biblioteca Marciana, Cod. Gr. 479: Pseudo-Oppianus, *Cynegetica*, tenth century, fol. 20,33.

7. Pseudo-Oppianus, *Cynegetica*, II 410-425, Gr. text & tr. in Latin J.G. Schneider (Strassbourg, 1913).

is aiming his arrow at the animals (ill. 1). In the second image he is aiming at the Olympic gods (ill. 2). Athena is depicted next to Eros. On her left hand side Hermes is attempting to escape. Pan, with his goat's feet, is running towards Aphrodite, who is wearing a nimbus. The scene is placed in front of a cella above which Zeus is depicted. On the right a second scene is added. Two men are fighting over a lady, who is watching them from her window.[8]

The original notion of the power of Eros was strayed as time went on and a more earthly view on the deity came into being. As early as in Hellenism Eros was merely considered to be a beautiful young man who had been responsible for many cases of unhappy infatuation. Eros gradually turned into a troublesome todler, playing silly and childish games. The Roman poets, who were to become an important source of mythological information in the Middle Ages, finally furnished the god with a moral significance and turned love into a dangerous, painful and retarded state of mind.[9]

The Churchfathers, in their turn, did not reject the Platonic principle of love. Instead, they adopted the concept and transformed it into a theory of Divine Love, that they named *Agape, Caritas* or *Amor Spiritualis.* Contrary to Plato, they dissociated the ancient god of love from this concept. More remarkably even: Eros was made to present an antithesis to the idea of Divine Love. Hesiod had described the love represented by Eros as life, and as present before time and space; the Eros of Plato was the ordering principle at the basis of all good. Both of these interpretations are reminiscent of the creative love of the Christian God. This connection between divine, creative love and earthly reproduction, however, was denied by medieval scholars. The Church Fathers had decided to seize upon the duality of love, emphasizing the existance of a divine love and an earthly love. Eros was dissociated from divine love and was turned into a symbol of earthly love. Having lost his esteemed reputation as an omnipotent and creative force Eros lived on to embody *Cupiditas* or *Amor Carnalis*, the various forms of earthly love.[10]

8. A. W. Byvanck, 'De Geillustreerde handschriften van Oppianus' Cynegetica', *Mededelingen van het Nederlands Historisch Instituut te Rome,* V (1925), p. 34-64, K. Weitzmann, *Greek Mythology in Byzantine Art* (Princeton, 1951), p. 123-130.

9. E. Panofsky, *Studies in Iconology, Humanistic Themes in the Art of the Renaissance* (New York, 1962), p. 104-105.

10. R. Berliner, 'God is Love', *Gazette des Beaux Arts*, 56 (1953), p. 9-26; A. Nygren, *Eros and Agape*, (London, 1953), p. 41-48; Panofsky [note 9], p. 99-100. J.C.M. van Winden, 'Wat heet liefde? Over eros en agape in het vroeg-christelijke denken', *Mededelingen van de afdeling Letterkunde / Koninklijke Nederlandse Akademie van Wetenschappen*, nieuwe reeks dl. 56, 3, (1993), p. 5-27.

As early as the fourth century, in Prudentius' very influential *Psychomachia,* Eros was presented as the personification of the vice of earthly love.[11] In this poem Prudentius reworked the antique notion of a perpetual battle of the mind within a Christian setting. After Tertullianus' *De Spectaculis* female personifications of the virtues and the vices are presented as warriors in an arena, fighting a bloody battle.[12] Eros appears on the scene as a follower of the vice *Luxuria* (Voluptuousness) which has taken on the form of the goddess Venus. Contrary to the other vices, who are shooting arrows, *Luxuria* strews rose petals and violets. These unexpected tactics confuse the virtues and they are about to surrender to *Luxuria* when, just in time, the virtue *Sobrietas* (Modesty) leaps in front of *Luxuria*'s chariot, carrying a cross in her hand. The horses are frightened and jump; the chariot topples over and *Sobrietas* kills *Luxuria* with a single blow of a stone. *Luxuria*'s host is terrified and is forced to flee. Eros, pale with fear, throws off his bow and arrow. [13] An eleventh-century copy of the *Psychomachia*, which is kept in Leiden, shows the winged and naked idol running away, while he looks round and drops his quiver (ill. 3).[14] The illuminator of a tenth-century copy, also in Leiden, chose to dress the fleeing Eros in a short tunic (ill. 4).[15] At the end of the battle the virtues are triumphant.[16]

This reading of Eros, as the inferior and defeated vice of earthly love, must have been what Hrabanus Maurus, abbot of Fulda and later archbishop of Mainz, had in mind when he introduced the deity into his encyclopaedia, *De Universo*, also known as *De Rerum Naturis* (ill. 5). The Carolingian original of this encyclopaedia has been lost; this copy, now kept in the monastery of Montecassino, is the oldest specimen of only three existing illustrated copies of *De Universo* and was manufactured in 1023.[17]

11. R. Newhauser, *The Treatises on Virtues and Vices in Latin and the Vernacular* (Turnhout, 1993).

12. Tertullianus, *De Spectaculis,* XXIX.

13. Prudentius, *Psychomachia*, 436-438: (Fr. tr. M. Lavarenne, Paris, 1933, p. 168).
Dat tergum fugituus Amor, lita tela ueneno
Et lapsum ex umeris arcum faretramque cadentem
Pallidus ipse metu sua post uestigia linquit.

14. Leiden, Universiteitsbibliotheek, ms. Voss. Lat. O. 15 VIII, Prudentius, *Psychomachia,* eleventh century, fol. 40 v.

15. Leiden, Universiteitsbibliotheek, ms. Burm. Q 3, Prudentius, *Psychomachia,* tenth century, fol. 135 v.

16. Prudentius, *Psychomachia*, 310-438, Fr. tr. Lavarenne [note 13], p. 158-168.

17. The Montecassino manuscript (Montecassino, Biblioteca dell'Abbazia, Hrabanus Maurus, *De Universo* or *de Rerum Naturis,* Cod.132, book 15, chapter 6, 1023, fol 389) was, in turn, copied in the fiteenth-century (Vatican, pal. Lat. 291). Another image of the god of love, copied after the montecassino manuscript, suvives in a fragment made in Catalonia at the end of the fourteenth century (Berlin, Staatsbibliothek Preussischer Kulturbesitz, Ms Lat. fol. 930).

The three gods, depicted in the image, look rather stiff and motionless. They are lined up orderly in frontal postions, while showing their attributes to the observer. They wear broadly the same hairstyles and their gowns are draped in simple folds. Not much is left of Eros, the powerful spirit that once stood at the basis of creation. The Eros in the image is powerless and motionless. He is no longer flying about, shooting his arrows. Although the Olympic gods could not resist him, he could not lord over medieval Christianity. The perpetual battle of the mind seems to be settled now. Eros was beaten and had been encapsulated into a new moral system, one of the symbols of which was the Christian encyclopaedia.

The monumental translations of the encyclopaedia too, for example the cycles of the virtues and the vices, show the same immobile and caged idol, leaning on his torch with his eyes closed.[18] Master Wilighelmus even chose to add an ibis to Eros' image (ill 6). According to the bestiaries the ibis fears clean water and eats contaminated food. The ibis doesn't know how to dive and prefers to stay in the shallow water. As an antipole to the true Christian, the *homo universalis,* who is reborn through the water of the Holy Spirit, the ibis, the *homo carnalis,* is used to emphasize Eros' ill character.[19]

At times the complete story of the *Psychomachia* is repeated in the encyclopaedias. For example in one of the most famous encyclopaedias of the twelfth century, the *Hortus Deliciarum* by Herrad of Landsberg, abbess of the abbey in Hohenburg. Unfortunately the original manuscript was destroyed during the bombing of Strassbourg in 1870 and its texts and illustrations only survive in a nineteenth century reconstruction (ills. 7-8).[20] Herrad constructed her encyclopaedia from the 'juices of the Holy Scripture' and many philosophical writings.[21] Herrad's encyclopaedia opens with the creation of the angels and the fall of Lucifer. She describes the heavenly spheres and the creation of the universe and the world. She gives a detailed account on the Old Gospel and reconciles it with the New Gospel. The Church is presented to Christ and is crowned.

18. Modena Cathedral, west facade, Master Wiligelmus, ca. 1170.
E. Panofsky, [note 1], p. 94.

19. *Physiologus,* ger. tr. O. Seel (Zurich, 1960), p. 59-60.

20. Strassbourg, Bibliothèque de la Ville, Herrad of Landsberg, *Hortus Deliciarum,* nineteenth century reconstruction: fol. 201 v, 202 v.
As early as the nineteenth century A. Straub and G. Keller had started reconstructing the *Hortus.* Their contributions are included in A. D. Caratzas, *Hortus Deliciarum* (New York, 1977). Another reconstruction was made under the guidance of R. Green, *Hortus Deliciarum* (London, 1979).

21. Herrad of Landsberg in the edition by Green [note 20], II, p. 3.

This event is followed by the battle of the virtues and the vices, after Prudentius *Psychomachia*. The context of Herrad's encyclopaedia in its entirety, the great effort Herrad took to comprise and to explain the whole of creation and its history in it, clearly indicates the position of the *Psychomachia*. Contrary to Prudentius, who referred to a perpetual battle of the mind, Herrad referred to the victory of Christianity. Being part of the *Hortus Deliciarum,* the *Psychomachia* relates how the glory of the Christian virtues came about at some point in history. The perpetual battle was over and Eros and all the other vices had been defeated by the Christian virtues. The virtues and the vices are depicted as knights when they enter the battle field. They wear coats of mail, shields and nose protection (ill. 7). The virtues are under the command of Humility. They carry swords, symbolizing the word of God. The vices are under the command of Pride. They carry long spears, symbolizing the sting of seduction. After their defeat the vices wear long gowns. Their hair is ruffled. They are desperate and bewildered (ill. 8).

In the thirteenth century the tide turned for the ancient god of love: the concept of courtly love came into being. This concept established a reconciliation between *Caritas* and *Cupiditas*. This conciliation came to exist alongside the old antithesis which the churchfathers had initiated. The ecclesiastical principle, in which Eros functioned as the beaten personification of the dark side of love, survived as a very useful construction to edify and instruct the common herd. The 'nouveau riches' at the courts of the feudal kings designed their own exclusive system of virtue.[22]

Courtly culture arose in an atmosphere of aristocracy, knighthood and codes of honour, and sublimated love between men and women into a sacred art. The love of a noble man for an unapproachable woman will expand courtly virtues inside the lover's heart. Unconsumated love will make the man chaste, disciplined, persistent and mild. For the first time in many centuries earthly love stood at the basis of true virtue; a new synthesis was found between the earthly and divine aspects of love.

The allegorical tale, the *Roman de la Rose* can be considered as the most famous product of the courtly culture. The rhymed text was written in the vernacular by Guillaume the Lorris and Jean le Meung. Nearly three hundred copies of the *Roman de la Rose* still exist today. Guillaume de Lorris describes the fortunes of a young man who arrives in a garden which is crowded with personifications. The young man meets the god

22. G. Duby, *De Middeleeuwse liefde en andere Essays (*Amsterdam, 1990), p. 79-112 (Male Moyen Age. De l'Amour et autres essays, Paris, 1988), Panofsky, [note 9], p. 82.

of love; he is caught by one of the god's arrows and falls madly in love with a rosebud. From that moment on the young man lives to pick and kiss the rosebud. He swears loyalty to the god of love who locks his heart and gives him his blessing. The young man is the vassal and the god of love is the feudal prince.[23]

The text, and also the images in the illustrated copies of the *Roman*, show, considering what went before, a rather unexpected blend of Christianity and worldliness. A thirteenth-century specimen, which is one of the oldest illustrated copies of the *Roman* and which is kept in the Vatican, contains an initial showing the god of love who is kneeling and praying to Jupiter who appears from a cloud in the sky, wearing an cross-nimbus. [24] Another image shows the god blessing one of the courtly lovers, who is kneeling in front of him, as if the god were a Christian bishop.[25] One of the images in an early fourteenth-century specimen of the *Roman*, also in the Vatican, disseminates an almost unthinkable mixture of sacred and secular worlds: the god of love is depicted as a crowned angel, sitting on top of a tree. Worshippers are kneeling at the foot of the tree. With his spread-eagled arms the god seems to bless the lovers.[26] The image strongly reminds one of the crucified Christ or the tree of Jesse with the Virgin on top.[27]

In short, the original significance – or the appreciation of the original significance – of Eros as formulated by Hesiodos, as one of the greatest supernatural powers, seems, at first glance, to have been lost in the course of the centuries. This process was initiated in Antiquity and adopted and elaborated by the learned men of the Middle Ages. After many centuries of being imprisoned and humiliated, the god of love managed, in the thirteenth century, to rise from his ashes. As the great causal entity at the basis of courtly virtue he regained his esteemed place in the world of divinity.

Contrary evidence proves, however, that the god had never died and was, consequently, not really resurrected into his antique glory. The god of love had developed into a medieval symbol, due to his particular nature and as a natural an logical result of the foregoing historical and ideolog-

23. G. de Lorris and J. le Meung, *Roman de la Rose,* Dutch tr. and intr. E. van Altena (Baarn, 1991).

24. Vatican, Urb. Lat. 276, G. de Lorris and J. le Meung, *Roman de la Rose*, thirteenth century: fol. 65.

25. Idem note 24, fol. 63.

26. Vatican Reg. Lat. 1522, G. de Lorris and J. le Meung, *Roman de la Rose,* fourteenth century: fol. 12.

27. E. König, *Die Liebe im Zeichen der Rose* (Zürich, 1994), p. 54.

ical processes.The above-mentioned image of Eros in the encyclopaedia by Hrabanus Maurus, which is kept in the Montecassino monastery, may serve to illustrate which processes of historical transmission have helped the ancient god Eros to transform into a medieval phenomenon (ill. 5).

3. The survivor's genealogy

Hrabanus Maurus (780-856), was abbot of Fulda. Later in life he was appointed archbisshop of Mainz and he was one of the most important theological and didactical authors of his age. Under Hrabanus' direction, de monastic school of Fulda developed into a leading European centre of learning. Hrabanus considered the arts and sciences important means to convey the message of Christianity.[28] *De Universo* is his most extensive work, consisting of twenty-two books, which synthesize and Christianize the entire body of science that had been developed up until the ninth century. It was meant for the students in the monastic school who were to teach the laity after finishing their studies.

The text accompanying the image of the god Eros harks back to the beginning of the great medieval encyclopaedic tradition. Hrabanus based his encyclopaedia – including his description of the god Eros – largely on the *Etymologiae* written by Isidore of Sevilla, the first of the medieval encyclopedists, not long before his death in 639. Isidore gathered and systematized all knowledge available to him, for the glory of God and his creation and hoping to educate the newly converted Visigoths. In doing so, in praise and for the sake of preservation and education, he reconciled paganism with Christianity. Of his *Etymologiae,* however, no illustrated copies survive.

The eighth book of Isidore's *Etymologiae* is devoted to the cults and lists many pagan gods. Isidore describes the appearance of most of them, together with a short account of their significance. Hrabanus, in the fifteenth book of his *De Universo*, faithfully copied his predecessor.[29] Both authors mention Eros.

28. F. Saxl, *Lectures* (London, 1957), I, p. 233-234.

29. It has been argued that a large number of the images of the *Universo*, including the image of Eros, were based on a now lost specimen of the *Etymologiae*. Be this as it may, it is generally accepted that the miniatures in the Montecassino manuscript were copied after an illustrated Carolingian specimen which in turn reached back to a model (or models) conceived in the Mediterranean area. See: N. Himmelmann, *Antike Götter im Mittelalter* (Mainz, 1986), p. 8-11; M. Reuter, *Text und bild im Codex 132 der Bibliothek von Montecassino "Liber Rabani de originibus rerum"* (München, 1984), p. 22-23, F. Saxl, *Lectures* (London, 1957), I, p. 224-241.

In the Montecassino copy of *De Universo* Eros is depicted between Aphrodite and Pan. From Antiquity onwards Eros had usually been associated with Aphrodite.[30] The appearance of the goddess, however, is not described in the accompanying texts. Pan, the amorous pastoral god, is depicted – as he is also described – with goat's feet and pan pipes. The beams of the sun and the moon shine from his temples. The staff in his left hand, possibly a sheperd's crook is not mentioned in the text.[31] In both encyclopaedias the god Eros is described as a lascivious demon. He is winged, because he is a flighty and whimsical demon. He is depicted as a child, because he is unwise and irrational. He is shown carrying an arrow and a torch. With his arrow he stabs the hart. With his torch he sets the heart on fire.[32]

In writing his passage about the god of love, Isidore was inspired by the Roman poet Propertius (ca 50-15 BC).[33] In the second book of his *Elegies*, in which Propertius mainly sang of his beloved Cynthia (also known as Hostia), he gives a description of the outward features of the god Eros, possibly based upon a depiction of the god in a painting. In addition, the poet furnishes the appearance and the attributes of the deity with a meaning:

> "Quicumque ille fuit, puerum qui pinxit Amorem,
> nonne putas miras hunc habuisse manus?
> is primum vidit sine sensu vivere amantis,
> et levibus curis magna perire bona.
> idem non frustra ventosas addidit alas,
> fecit et humano corde volare deum:
> scilicet alterna quoniam iactamur in unda,
> nostraque non ullis permanet aura locis.
> et merito hamatis manus et armata sagittis,
> et pharetra ex umero Cnosia utroque iacet:
> ante ferit quoniam tuti quam cernimus hostem,
> nec quisquam ex illo vulnere sanis abit."

> [Whoever he was who painted love as a boy,
> Think you not he had wondrous skills?

30. In Hesiod's *Theogonia*, 201 [note 2], Eros was a witness to her birth and became her companion. Later mythological traditions describe him as her son.

31. Reuter [note 29], p. 175-176.

32. 'Cupidinem vocatum ferunt propter amorem. Est enim daemon fornicationis. Qui ideo alatus pingitur, quia nihil amantibus levius, nihil mutabilius invenitur. Puer pingitur, quia stultus est et irrationabilis amor. Saggitam et facem tenere fingitur. Saggitam, quia amor cor vulnerat; facem quia inflammat.': Hrabanus Maurus, *De Universo*, XV, 6, in: *Patriologiae cursus completus...Series Latina*, ed. J. P. Migne, dl. 111, col. 435; Isidori Hispalensis Episcopi, *Etymologiarum Sive Originum, libri XX*, ed. W.M. Lindsay, 2 vols. (Oxford, 1911), 1, VIII, 80.

33. Panofsky [note 9], p. 104-105.

He was the first to see that lovers behave childishly
And that great blessings are lost through their petty passions.
He too with good reason added fluttering wings,
And made the god to fly in the human heart,
Since in truth we are tossed by the waves,
This way and that,
And with us the wind never sits in the same quarter.
And justly his hand is armed with barbed arrows,
And a cretan quiver is suspended from his shoulder,
Since he strikes while we feel safe and do not see the foe,
And from that wound no one departs unscatched.[34]]

Propertius compares the childlike nature of the god to the thoughtlessness of the lovers. His wings, flying in the wind, show how fancifully the god flits about in the heart; and lovers too, lack all direction. His arrows suggest the pain wich the god inflicts in the heart.

Indirectly, therefore, the text about the god of love in Hrabanus' encyclopaedia, copied from Isidore, harks back to an image, possibly a tangible painting, of the god.

Propertius, in his efforts to illustrate his feelings, provided the visual image of the god of love with a moralizing significance. In doing so, he unwittingly made his work into a fascinating source of information for writers such as Isidore, whose self-appointed task it was to adjust antique learning to the medieval Christian mind by explaining its underlying moral meaning. Propertius does not mention the torch depicted in the Montecassino image; it was, however, one of Eros' usual attributes in Antiquity.[35] Apparently Isidore, with his exeptional kowledge of the Greek and Latin writings, must have come across the torch in the work of another author. He explains the torch in a familiar moralizing fashion: it is used by Eros to set the heart on fire.[36]

Clearly, the text about Eros accompanying the Hrabanus image reaches back to an antique personification of love as described by the love-sick Propertius; a fluttering toddler who attacks people at random, hurting them with his arrows, and who manages to transmit his infantility to his victims, in whose hearts he will flit around capriciously.

When one looks at the image, not much is left of the foolish amorousness the god personified in Propertius' text – the ultimate source of Hrabanus text as copied in the Montecassino manuscript. This Eros is hardly

34. Propertius, *Elegiae*, II, p. 12; Eng. Tr. G.P. Gould (Cambridge, 1990).

35. The torch can be found e.g. in Ovidius, *Metamorphoses* I, 461 ff. or in the *Ars Amatoria*, I, 22, by the same author.

36. Panofsky, [note 9], p. 104-105.

about to shoot one of his arrows, nor can we imagine him flying about lightheartedly. In the Montecassino image, Eros is hardly a reckless toddler. He is a static entity, an icon of his own self.

Although the image reaches back to Propertius, the medieval predicament of the earthly Eros clearly differed from the Roman one. Though Propertius, Isidore, and his follower Hrabanus refer to Eros' worldly aspect in their descriptions of the god of love, as opposed to his divine qualities, the deity changed status as time went on. The defeat of the vices in the *Psychomachia* caused an important shift in the position of the power of eartly love. Prudentius' *Psychomachia* showed the god for the first time as the vice *Cupiditas* and for the last time in centuries in action. The motionless Eros of the Montecassino image is the personification of earthly love as a medieval vice, which had been beaten by Christianity and imprisoned in a Christian encyclopaedia. The defeated vice was no longer connected to either the esteemed deity from early Classical mythology or to the personification of Propertius' fanciful emotions.

4. A MEDIEVAL 'IMAGE'

Although the literary sources give important information on the historical processes of transmission, they cannot be used as reference works. To shed light upon the medieval Eros, not just the ways in which ideas and interpretations were 'recycled' and pressed into medieval Christian morality's service, but also the accumulations and transformations of ideas should be taken into consideration. Evidently, any 'borrowed' interpretation of a concept holds a new meaning which is closely related to its contemporary ideological context. In addition, the general nature of mythology and of Eros' particular character stand in relation to medieval ideology.

A myth forms the 'image' of a universal concept. It mirrors a particular interpretation of the concept, as it has been developed in a specific place and in a specific stage in history. Consequently, a different context involves different interpretations of the same abstractions, so that new myths arise. Moreover, in being a mirror to the world of universal ideas, a myth or a mythological figure finds itself in the realm between the abstract concept and the natural world. This furnishes a myth and any new interpretation of a myth with a universality of its own and it can, in its turn, be interpreted in many ways, depending on its context. From this point of view a myth or mythological figure is a symbol rather than the original human construction that was designed to mirror a fixed abstraction.

Eros is possibly the most dynamic figure in the mythological world. On the one hand, the idea of love has had a most malleable content within the memory of men. On the other hand, the image of love, Eros is very constant. Eros is consistently depicted – either in words or in a tangible image – winged, carrying his bow and arrows and possibly his torch. His apparent meaning as the cause of love is equally unchanging. The kind of love he causes and personifies however, is subject to change to such a degree that one might even say that the mythological 'image' of love is more real than the realities it refers to. From this point of view the god Eros can be seen as a natural phenomenon, which can be furnished with a great variety of meanings. This view manoeuvres the god into a special position; it provides Eros with an even higher symbolic quality than any other mythological figure.

Once more, the Montecassino image may serve as a point of departure (ill. 5). The Roman Propertius and medieval Isidore alike, were free to choose or to create any interpretation of Eros to answer their needs. To Propertius the god of love had been a suitable symbol to communicate his emotions. Propertius had been seeking a proper 'image' to reflect his personal emotional state. The poet did not create a personification. Instead, he found an existing figure, whose content could be modified to such an extent that it could be used as a symbol of his own feelings. In doing so, he imbued an existing image with a new meaning. Similarly, Isidore and his follower Hrabanus treated the ancient god of love as a symbol, rather than as a personification, and supplied him with an appropriate content. Yet, it must be noted that the interest taken by Propertius and Isidore and his follower Hrabanus in the deity, stemmed from different motives.

Although both Proportius and Isidore provided the 'image' of love with a symbolic significance, Isidore looked at the ancient god from a totally different perspective. Isidore did not try to personify an abstract idea – quite the contrary. Isidore experienced Eros as a common reality of the visible world. To him Eros existed in the natural world God had created, a world imbued with meaning. Every detail of this reality needed to be recorded and systematized in the encyclopaedia, which, in turn, aimed to reflect the universe and to unveil its harmony. Eros was as much part of God's sacred scheme as any other aspect of creation, and similarly reflected a deeper cause. No less than any other creature he was an 'image' of metaphysical truth that needed explanation and preservation.

By looking at Eros from this perspective, Isidore turned the god into a true medieval symbol and admitted him into the first veritable Christian encyclopaedia, a symbol of God's creation.

The inactive Eros in the Montecassino encyclopaedia, by Isidore's follower Hrabanus, hardly reminds one of either a myth or a human emotion. The accompanying text is a bare catalogue of his distinguishing marks, supplied with a unadorned explanation of their meaning. The image shows an Eros consisting of the sum of his traits as represented by his outward features. He is placed between other motionless pagan gods who also show their personal appearance to the viewer, with the purpose of calling to mind their moral meaning. The image of Eros in the Montecassino encyclopaedia cannot be seen as an illustration of the accompanying text. The image hardly adds anything to the understanding of the text. Nor can it be said that the image inspired the accompanying text. Yet the image was not meant to be understood in isolation from the text: its sole audience was that of the literate monks. Text and the image in the Montecassino manuscript have a similar meaning. Both 'describe' Eros. In addition, the text provides an explanation of the symbolic content of Eros' outward features and thus explains the image. Considering the medieval perception of creation as existing of interconnected visible 'images' of a deeper cause needing explanation, it is clear that images are fundamental to the medieval mind. Although an image of Eros such as the one in the Montecassino encyclopaedia was probably not the inspiration for the accompanying text, the passage *does* explain the 'image' of Eros as a true existing figure, part of the visible world. From this point of view his depiction in the encyclopaedia – as the depiction of any other aspect of the physical world – seems very appropriate to medieval thought.

Paradoxical as it may seem, the synthesis between the earthly and divine aspects of love, that had been established in the concept of courtly love does not contrast with the underlying ideals of the enclopaedists. The renewed reputation of the god of love is no dramatic 'comeback'. Instead, it should be considered as a logical consequence of the foregoing developments. The courtly system, like the encyclopaedia, is a medieval construct aiming to harmonize all aspects of creation within one ideology. Both systems managed to incorporate the image of earthly love and to explain its role in the whole of creation. Courtly love crowned the work of the encyclopaedists; it succeeded to harmonize the natural world with the religious by placing earthly love at the basis of Christian virtue.

5. Conclusion

Today, the mythological god Eros is still famous and often expressed in both images and texts. The deity fulfilled a similar function adequately during the Christian Middle Ages. Superficially, the god of love seems to have been merely tolerated in the medieval Christian context, as a precious memory of a remote past that has been made harmless. A closer look, however, has brought some more complex underlying mechanisms to the fore.

Myths, mythological figures and interpretations of both are alive and ever open to new readings. Its existence in the realm between the world of metaphysical ideas and the visible world provides mythology, much like a fairy tale, with a particular level of abstraction and consequently with flexibility. Moreover, the god Eros shows a particular pliability of his own. First, the god is both the cause and the personification of love. Secondly, the views on the character of love are widely divergent. Although Eros' meaning is highly paradoxical, his features are fixed. In other words: the image that is designed to embody the abstract reality of love seems more real than the concept it refers to.

It may not have been easy to adapt the pagan personification of love to medieval Christian dogma. Yet, the medieval doctors had no alternative. God's creation included the wealth of the past, the present and the future and was, in itself, an 'image' of supernatural truth. In praise of their Creator and for the purposes of education, the medieval authors were expected to record creation and to unveil its underlying harmony. Fortunately Eros' character is quite symbolic and can function as an 'image' of a variety of contents. The medieval learned men had great freedom to explore the possiblities to incorporate Eros into medieval principles.

Evidently, there are several options to harmonize earthly love with medieval Christian theories. Although the explanations of the 'image of love' seem, from the thirteenth century onwards, contrary to each other, in truth they stem from the same motives. The highly systematic character of medieval thought is evident in both the encyclopaedias and the concept of courtly love. Both show a great effort to gather up and to explain what is experienced in the visible world, and to reconcile it with the virtuous will of God. Within these medieval views on creation any interpretation of the image of love must have been appropriate.

Ill. 1. – *Eros dominating nature*, miniature from Pseudo-Oppianus, *Cynegetica*, tenth century. – Venice, Biblioteca Marciana, cod. Gr. 479, fol. 20 (copyright: Venice, Biblioteca Marciana).

Ill. 2. – *Eros dominating the Olympic gods*, miniature from Pseudo-Oppianus, *Cynegetica*, tenth century. – Venice, Biblioteca Marciana, cod. Gr. 479, fol. 33 (copyright: Venice, Biblioteca Marciana).

Ill. 3. – *Eros fleeing*, miniature from Prudentius, *Psychomachia,* eleventh century – Leiden, Universiteitsbibliotheek, ms. Voss. Lat. O. 15 VIII, fol. 40 (copyright: Leiden, Universiteitsbibliotheek).

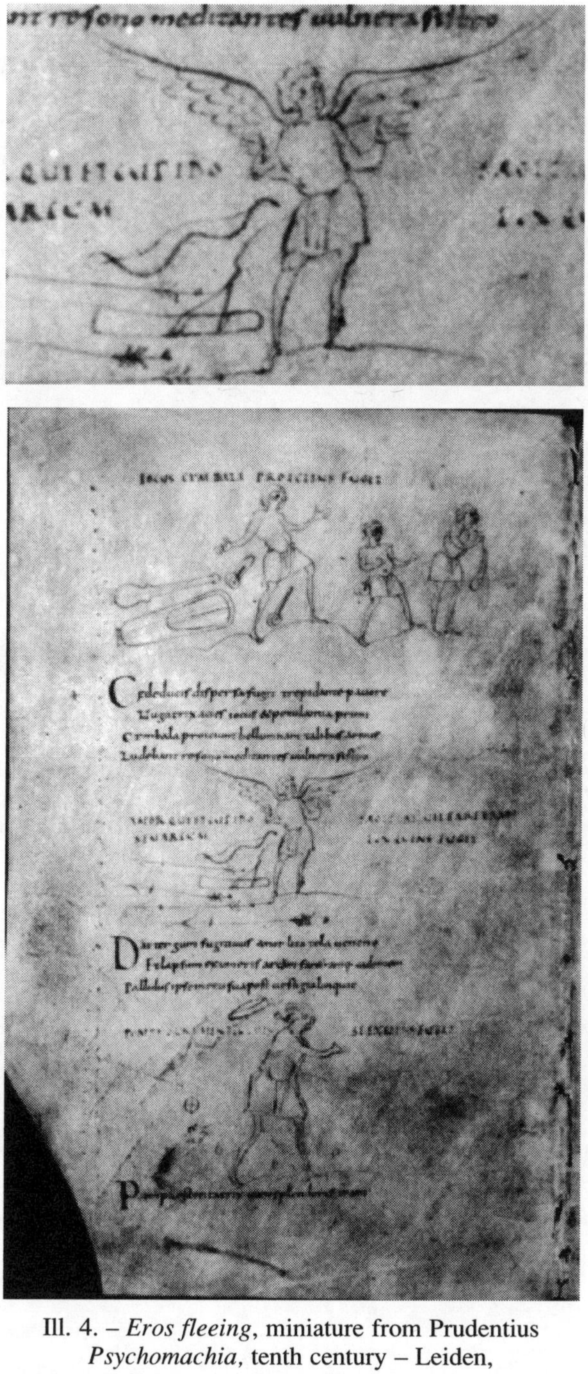

Ill. 4. – *Eros fleeing*, miniature from Prudentius *Psychomachia*, tenth century – Leiden, Universiteitsbibliotheek, ms. Burm. Q 3, fol. 135 v. (copyright: Leiden, Universiteitsbibliotheek).

Ill. 5. – *Aphrodite, Eros and Pan*, miniature from Hrabanus Maurus, *De Universo,* or *De Rerum Naturis*, 1023 – Montecassino, Biblioteca dell'Abbazia, cod. 132, Lib. 15, c. 6, fol. 398 (copyright: Montecassino, Bibliotheca dell'Abbazia).

Ill. 6. – Master Wilighelmus, *Eros with an Ibis*, sculpture, ca. 1170 – Modena Cathedral, west – façade (Copyright: City of Modena).

Ill. 7. – *Luxuria and her followers in the chariot*, miniature from Herrad of Landsberg, *Hortus Deliciarum*, nineteenth century reconstruction – Strassbourg, Bibliothèque de la Ville, fol. 201v. (copyright: Strassbourg, Bibliothèque de la Ville)

Ill. 8. – *The defeated vices*, miniature from Herrad of Landsberg, *Hortus Deliciarum*, nineteenth century reconstruction – Strassbourg, Bibliothèque de la Ville, fol. 202v.
(copyright: Strassbourg, Bibliothèque de la Ville)

Susie SPEAKMAN SUTCH

LA PRODUCTION D'UN MANUSCRIT DU POÈME INTITULÉ *LE CHEVALIER DÉLIBÉRÉ* D'OLIVIER DE LA MARCHE

1. INTRODUCTION

Le manuscrit 80-11 de la Collection de la Société des Manuscrits des Assureurs Français (S.M.A.F.) en dépôt à la Salle des Manuscrits de la Bibliothèque nationale de France comporte deux ouvrages de nature très différente. Le premier, un traité moral en prose que Ghillebert de Lannoy a écrit à l'intention du futur duc de Bourgogne, Charles le Téméraire, s'intitule l'*Instruction d'un jeune prince pour se bien gouverner envers Dieu et le monde* (fol. 1r – 39r). Le second, *Le Chevalier délibéré* (fol. 39v – 100v) d'Olivier de La Marche, est une allégorie didactique en vers qui, sous la forme d'un pèlerinage de la vie chevaleresque, enseigne aussi des leçons édifiantes. Selon la description la plus récente de ce manuscrit, le premier texte aurait été transcrit et enluminé à Tours ou à Bourges, 1479-1483, et on reconnaît dans ses miniatures la main du Maître du *Mamerot* de Vienne, connu aussi sous le nom du Maître du *Missel de Yale*.[1] Le second texte reste problématique, et pour sa datation, et pour sa localisation. Tandis que les notices qui décrivent le manuscrit s'accordent sur la France comme le lieu de sa production,[2] il a été impossible

1. J.B. Lebigue, *Manuscrits du Moyen-Âge et manuscrits littéraires modernes. La collection de la Société des Manuscrits des Assureurs Français* (Paris: Bibliothèque nationale de France, 2001), pp. 80-86; N. Reynaud dans F. Avril et N. Reynaud, *Les Manuscrits à peintures en France 1440-1520* (Paris: Flammarion / Bibliothèque Nationale, 1993), p. 152.

2. Lebigue, *op. cit.* [note 1], p. 81 dit seulement, France, après 1483. D'autres descriptions de ce manuscrit se trouvent dans C.W. Carroll (ed.) et C.W. Carroll et L.W. Wilson (trs.), *Olivier de La Marche, Le Chevalier deliberé (The Resolute Knight)* (Tempe, Arizona: Arizona Center for Medieval and Renaissance Studies, 1999), p. 19; Avril et Reynaud, *op.cit.* [note 1], p. 155; Londres, vente Sotheby, 10 décembre 1980, lot 88, pp. 55-59 et 10 juillet 1972, lot 30, pp. 23-25; E. Picot et H. Stein, *Recueil de pièces historiques imprimées sous le règne de Louis XI reproduites en fac-similé avec des commentaires historiques et bibliographiques* (Paris: Pour la Société des Bibliophiles françois [Francisque Lefrançois, Libraire], 1923, Texte, p. 321; *Mitteilungen aus der Königlichen Bibliothek. Herausgegeben von der Generalverwaltung*. IV Kurzes verzeichnis der Romanische Handschriften (Berlin: Weidemannsche Buchhandlung, 1918), p. 11; M. Huisman, 'Inventaire des nouveaux manuscrits concernant l'histoire de la Belgique par la Bibliothèque royale de Berlin' (Bruxelles, 1899 [extr. des *Bulletins de la Commission royale d'histoire de Belgique*, 5e série, t. ix], pp. 367-369); I. Bekker dans *Bericht über die zur Bekanntmachung geeigneten Verhandlungen der Königlichen Preussische Akademie der Wissenschaften zu Berlin* (Berlin: Druckerei der Königlichen Akademie der Wissenschaften, 1853), pp. 3-13. Pour l'identification du manuscrit de la S.M.A.F., voir

jusqu'ici de proposer une localisation plus précise. Malheureusement, je ne peux pas non plus apporter plus de précisions à ce sujet. En revanche, dans l'article qui suit je voudrais émettre l'hypothèse selon laquelle l'exemplaire du *Chevalier délibéré* que renferme ce manuscrit serait en fait une copie presque exacte – une sorte de fac-similé[3] – du manuscrit de Cambridge University, Fitzwilliam Museum, ms 166.[4] Une étude comparative de ces deux manuscrits servira à établir leur filiation.

2. La Filiation des deux manuscrits: Cambridge, Fitzwilliam Museum ms. 166 et Paris, S.M.A.F., ms. 80-11

Tout d'abord les deux manuscrits ont à peu près le même format: le manuscrit de Cambridge mesure 239 x 160 mm, celui de la S.M.A.F. 252 x 175 mm.[5] Plus significatif est le fait que la mise en page des deux

S.S. Sutch, 'Notice sur l'identification d'un manuscrit 'inconnu' du *Chevalier délibéré* d'Olivier de la Marche,' dans *Romania*, 114 (1996), pp. 246-253.

3. J.J.G. Alexander fait une distinction entre 'replica' et 'facsimile' et emploierait peut-être 'replica' pour décrire ce manuscrit étant donné que pour lui le mot 'replica' définit une copie 'produced at the same time or after only a short interval.' ('Facsimiles, Copies and Variations: The Relationship to the Model in Medieval and Renaissance European Illuminated Manuscripts,' dans *Retaining the Original: Multiple Originals, Copies, and Reproductions* (Washington, D.C.: National Gallery of Art, 1989), p. 64.) Mais je préfère fac-similé qui 'suggests a copy as accurate as possible' dans le cas du manuscrit de la S.M.A.F.

4. La datation de ce dernier manuscrit est 1490 selon M.R. James, *A Descriptive Catalogue of the Manuscripts in the Fitzwilliam Museum* (Cambridge: Cambridge University Press, 1895), p. 366. Nous pouvons considérer cette date approximative, 1490 étant à mi-point entre la date à laquelle La Marche a achevé d'écrire son poème et la date de sa mort en 1502. Étant donné que ce manuscrit reste aussi silencieux en ce qui concerne le lieu de sa production, un examen des miniatures et de la décoration aiderait à le préciser. Les costumes sont bien de l'époque de Charles VIII (1483-1498), mais la décoration marginale est frappante par son style archaïsant. À l'exception du premier folio (Figure 10), la décoration de bordure imite un style de décor français des années de la génération antérieure et pourrait donc indiquer que ce manuscrit a été produit dans un atelier provincial peu au courant des nouvelles modes de décor marginal. Le style des miniatures paraît très provincial. Grâce aux recherches de Mme Anne-Marie Legaré, nous pouvons suggérer que les miniatures du manuscrit de Cambridge ont été peintes par un artiste provincial dans un style parisien où se révèle l'influence prononcée de Maître François. Ce manuscrit comporte dans le bas de page du premier feuillet les armoiries de la famille d'Albret. Je tiens à exprimer mes très vifs remerciements à M. F. Avril, à Mme N. Reynaud et à Mme A.-M. Legaré qui m'ont fourni des renseignements précieux sur l'enluminure et sur la décoration de ce manuscrit.

5. La différence de dimensions des deux manuscrits provient en partie des effets de reliure. Cependant, l'examen de la réglure et de la justification du texte démontre que le format du manuscrit de la S.M.A.F. était toujours plus haut et plus large que celui du Fitzwilliam Museum, la justification de ce dernier (148 x 72 mm) étant bien plus étroite que celle du manuscrit de Paris (148 x 90 mm). Nous verrons plus loin les conséquences de ce changement de réglure surtout dans la reproduction des miniatures.

manuscrits est identique en tous points: chaque feuillet contient les mêmes strophes, le placement des rubriques et des miniatures dans le manuscrit de la S.M.A.F. suit exactement leur placement dans le manuscrit de Cambridge, ce qui veut dire que la foliotation est donc identique.[6] Le texte du *Chevalier délibéré* comprend précisement 62.5 feuillets (c'est-à-dire 123 pages) dans les deux cas.

Non seulement le scribe qui a transcrit le manuscrit aujourd'hui en dépôt à Paris respecte la mise en page et la foliotation du manuscrit de Cambridge, mais il préserve aussi un petit espace après la lettre initiale de chaque vers. Cet espace est accentué par une deuxième réglure de 5 à 6 mm – qui manque dans l'exemplaire de Cambridge – servant à encadrer la lettre initiale de chaque vers (Figure 1). Mis à part ce trait distinctif et à l'exception de quelques variations d'orthographe ou d'abbréviation sans importance, il copie fidèlement le manuscrit de Cambridge. Il y a un moment en particulier où il révèle sa dette au manuscrit du Fitzwilliam Museum par une particularité assez intéressante. Au vers 2700 le scribe de Cambridge avait écrit 'Que liuer est en son exiL' (Figure 2); son collègue reproduit le mot 'exil' en écrivant un 'l' qui a plus de traits en commun avec sa formation de 'l' majuscules que de 'l' minuscules (Figure 1).

Les rubriques du manuscrit de la S.M.A.F. témoignent aussi d'une sorte de contrainte qui laisse supposer que ses rubriques sont copiées sur celles du manuscrit de Cambridge. Sur plusieurs exemples que nous pourrions citer, nous en relevons trois seulement. Au folio 79r du manuscrit de la S.M.A.F., qui correspond au folio 40v du manuscrit de Cambridge, nous voyons que le scribe respecte strictement l'espace qui lui est accordé pour sa rubrique (Figure 3) alors que le scribe du manuscrit de Cambridge déborde la marge de droite (Figure 4) et envahit l'espace réservé à la décoration de la bordure de droite.[7] Ce même phénomène se reproduit au

6. Il faut tenir compte du fait que le texte du *Chevalier délibéré* qui se trouve dans le manuscrit Paris, S.M.A.F., ms. 80-11, suit le traité de *L'Instruction d'un jeune prince* de Ghillebert de Lannoy et commence donc au verso du folio 39 tandis que celui du manuscrit Cambridge, Fitzwilliam Museum, ms. 166, constituant le seul texte du manuscrit, commence au recto du premier folio.

7. Normalement les deux scribes du texte du poème respectent scrupuleusement l'espace laissé pour la transcription des strophes démarqué par la réglure de justification. Nous pouvons voir pourtant au folio 1r du manuscrit de Cambridge que le texte de deux vers déborde la réglure de la justification du texte et donc envahit l'espace envisagé pour la bordure (Figure 10); étant donné que la largeur de la justification du manuscrit de la S.M.A.F. est de 90 mm, le scribe du manuscrit de Paris évite de déborder la marge (Figure 9). Ce débordement se reproduit au folio 44r du manuscrit du Fitzwilliam Museum tant pour la rubrique de la miniature que pour le deuxième vers de la strophe suivante; en se servant d'une abbréviation dans la rubrique et en serrant les mots du vers, le scribe du manuscrit de la S.M.A.F. a réussi à respecter la réglure de justification (f. 82v). En revanche, comme

folio 49v (Figure 5) – à comparer au folio 11r du manuscrit du Fitzwilliam Museum (Figure 6) – mais bien que la deuxième ligne de la rubrique déborde la réglure de marge de droite, il semble ne pas envahir autant l'espace pour la décoration que ne le font la première et la troisième lignes de la même rubrique du manuscrit de Cambridge pour la simple raison que l'artiste de la bordure a repoussé la bordure de droite. Un troisième exemple, où il s'agit de la coupure d'une rubrique en cinq lignes différentes, démontre aussi que le scribe du manuscrit de la S.M.A.F. copiait sur le manuscrit du Fitzwilliam Museum. Au folio 91r de ce dernier (Figure 7) le scribe laisse un espace blanc à la fin de la troisième ligne où il aurait très bien pu écrire le 'Et' de la phrase suivante. Or le scribe de la rubrique du manuscrit de Cambridge remplit totalement l'espace alloué au folio 52v (Figure 8).[8] Tous ces détails d'ordre graphique m'apportent la certitude que le scribe du manuscrit de la S.M.A.F. avait sous les yeux celui de Cambridge et qu'il l'a transcrit consciencieusement.

Cependant, ce qui prouve définitivement mon hypothèse selon laquelle le manuscrit de la S.M.A.F. est une copie exacte de celui de Cambridge est une mauvaise transcription due à une faute de reliure dans ce dernier manuscrit où le quatrième cahier, le cahier 'd', atteste l'inversion du troisième et du quatrième bifolia (ff. 27-30). Cette inversion rompt l'ordre normal des strophes que tous les autres manuscrits que j'ai consultés attestent et rend illogique la lecture de cette partie du poème.[9] Le manuscrit, Paris, S.M.A.F., ms. 80-11 reproduit cette

Mme N. Reynaud me l'a signalé dans une communication privée, dans le cas du manuscrit de la S.M.A.F. c'est l'artiste de la bordure qui repousse sa bordure de droite pour accommoder le texte qui déborde la marge de droite, voir par exemple la Figure 5, tandis que l'artiste de la bordure du manuscript de Cambridge maintient sa règle rigoureusement (Figures 4, 6 et 8). Je voudrais exprimer ma profonde gratitude à Mme N. Reynaud d'avoir discuté ce manuscrit avec moi. Dans la présente discussion la dette que je lui dois est manifeste.

8. Un autre exemple est à noter: la rubrique pour l'image représentant l'Acteur et Fresche Memoire dans son cimetière, qui se trouve au-dessous de la miniature, comprend cinq lignes. Le scribe du manuscrit de Cambridge arrive à la fin de la cinquième ligne et il lui reste le mot 'livre' à écrire. Il n'a d'autre choix que de déborder la réglure de droite et ainsi d'envahir l'espace de la bordure (f. 29r). Le scribe du manuscrit de Paris arrive tout juste à accommoder tous les mots de la rubrique dans l'espace qui lui est alloué en les serrant un peu (f. 67v).

9. Cette inversion donne l'ordre suivant aux strophes: 136-138 (f. 26v), 145-147 (f. 27r), 148-150 (f. 27v), 139-141 (f. 28r), 142-144 (f. 28v), 157 plus l'illustration et la rubrique (f. 29r), 158-160 (f. 29v), 151-153 (f. 30r), 154-156 (f. 30v), 161-163 (f. 31r). Je tiens à exprimer mes remerciements chaleureux à Mme P. Stirnemann d'avoir eu la gentillesse de vérifier cette leçon pour moi.

leçon illogique (ff. 65v – 69r).[10] Et puisque le texte du poème commence au verso du folio 39, l'inversion des strophes dans ce manuscrit ne peut aucunement être le résultat d'une faute de reliure, mais renvoie directement au manuscrit original sur lequel il a été copié.[11]

Non seulement le texte verbal du manuscrit, Paris, S.M.A.F., ms. 80-11 représente une transcription du texte du manuscrit du Fitzwilliam Museum, mais l'artiste qui a peint les miniatures, lui aussi, a copié celles du manuscrit de Cambridge. La mise en page, le contenu, et la disposition des figures dans ses miniatures leur sont identiques en presque tous

10. Selon K. Heitmann ('Die spanischen Übersetzer von Olivier de la Marches 'Chevalier délibéré': Hernando de Acuña und Jerónimo de Urrea', *Studia Iberica. Festschrift für Hans Flasche* [Bern et München: Francke Verlag, 1973], p. 234) il y a deux autres manuscrits qui font partie de la même famille de manuscrits copiés sur un exemplaire aujourd'hui inexistant; ce sont Paris, B.N., Fr. 15099 et B.N., Fr. 2361 tous les deux des manuscrits in-quarto. Paris, B.N., Fr. 15099, qui mesure 198 x 142 mm et reste inachevé en ce qui concerne la décoration (il contient en effet seulement la première miniature), suit la même mise en page que celle des deux autres manuscrits dont il est ici question: c'est-à-dire trois strophes par page avec les rubriques et les blancs laissés pour les enluminures prévues aux mêmes endroits. Les rubriques sont presque complètes; la rubrique manque seulement aux folios 5v et 16v. Dans ce dernier cas, le scribe transcrit la strophe qui suit la séquence image-rubrique et néglige donc de laisser assez de place pour la rubrique qui suit l'image dans les deux exemplaires que j'étudie ici. Ce lapsus signifie que jusqu'au folio 23r il y a un décalage d'une strophe, mais qu'en écrivant la rubrique pour la miniature représentant l'Acteur devant le Palais d'Amour au folio 23r et en laissant un blanc équivalant à deux strophes pour la miniature au folio 23v le scribe a pu éliminer ce décalage et reprendre une mise en page identique à celle des manuscrits du Fitzwilliam Museum et de la S.M.A.F. Normalement, le placement des rubriques dans ce manuscrit est identique à celui des deux autres, à l'exception de la rubrique du folio 44v qui précède l'image au lieu de la suivre comme elle le fait dans les deux manuscrits que je compare dans cette étude. Enfin la foliotation de ce manuscrit est elle aussi identique. La feuille de garde étant fol. 1, par conséquent le texte du *Chevalier délibéré* va de f. 2r à f. 63r et comprend précisément 62.5 feuillets (c'est-à-dire 123 pages). Cependant contrairement au manuscrit Paris, S.M.A.F., ms. 80-11, Paris, B.N., Fr. 15099 préserve l'ordre correct des strophes 139-160. Quant au manuscrit Paris, B.N., Fr. 2361, qui mesure 212 x 142 mm et qui lui aussi reste inachevé du point de vue de la décoration, il lui manque les deux mêmes rubriques que dans le manuscrit décrit ci-dessus aux folia 5v et 18v. Pour les 22 premiers folios ce manuscrit ne suit pas la mise en page des trois autres manuscrits de cette famille; puis, entre folio 23r et 25v, sa mise en page suit celle du manuscrit Paris, B.N., ms Fr. 15099 (c'est-à-dire, ff. 20v-23r) mais, bien qu'il reproduise trois strophes par page à partir du folio 26r, ce ne sont pas les mêmes que dans les trois autres. Ainsi, là où le manuscrit Fr. 15099 reprend la mise en page des manuscrits du Fitzwilliam Museum et de la S.M.A.F., le manuscrit Fr. 2361 diverge. Et enfin, comme le fait le manuscrit Fr. 15099, le manuscrit Fr. 2361 préserve l'ordre correct des strophes 139-160.

11. Cf. les catalogues de vente Sotheby: 'The text of the present manuscript is good – at several points where it differs from the Gouda edition it is clearly correct – but seems to be derived from a manuscript in which the two innermost bifolia of a gathering had been inverted (25 stanzas on ff. 65b to 69b are out of order)' (1972, p. 24; 1980, p. 58).

les détails, y compris les couleurs.[12] Il reproduit la forme des miniatures du manuscrit de Cambridge: carrée ou arrondie selon leur emplacement identique sur la surface de la page. La seule exception quant à la forme est la première miniature: celle du manuscrit de la S.M.A.F. au folio 39v a une forme arrondie (Figure 9) tandis que celle du manuscrit de Cambridge au folio 1r a une forme plutôt rectangulaire (Figure 10).[13]

Nous pouvons constater que l'artiste de l'exemplaire de la S.M.A.F. a copié les enluminures du manuscrit de Cambridge et non pas vice versa grâce à plusieurs petits traits de composition ou de détails qui se subdivisent en trois catégories: le remplissement de l'espace, l'emploi de l'ombre et les détails qui manquent. Tous ces traits peuvent se voir aisément si nous comparons les deux miniatures qui représentent la joute à pied de Philippe de Bourgogne contre Débile, un des deux lieutenants de la déesse de la Mort, Atropos, qu'on voit dans la tribune des juges (Figures 3 et 4).

Mis à part le fait que les deux combattants dans l'image du manuscrit de Cambridge (Figure 4) semblent plus dynamiques et plus actifs que dans la miniature du manuscrit de Paris (Figure 3) – ce qui sera d'ailleurs vrai pour toutes les miniatures –, nous sommes frappés tout d'abord par le fait que toute la scène de la Figure 4 semble légèrement en recul et plutôt rectangulaire dans le sens de la hauteur: ainsi toutes les figures nous semblent plus à l'aise à l'intérieur de l'espace qui leur est consacré. Cette miniature mesure 85 x 72 mm. Cependant, les dimensions de la Figure 3 paraissent plutôt carrées, et en fait l'image qui mesure 85 x 90 mm est plus large que long de 5 mm, ce qui impose des contraintes à l'artiste. Il est à noter que les dix personnes qui partagent la tribune avec Atropos dans la Figure 4 se tiennent droit et ont des attitudes plus ou moins normales. Leurs treize confrères dans la tribune de la Figure 3, en revanche, sont entassés les uns sur les autres et doivent se pencher parce qu'il n'y a pas assez de place pour eux. Ce même effet s'observe dans la Figure 5 où le plafond est tellement bas qu'Entendement doit se courber pour mon-

12. De même, l'artiste qui a peint les bordures du manuscrit de la S.M.A.F. a imité le style archaïsant des bordures du manuscrit du Fitzwilliam Museum. Ce qui distingue ces bordures de celles du manuscrit de Cambridge est la présence de paons et de grotesques dans les bordures, un trait qui provient, à mon avis, du fait que les bordures du premier texte du manuscrit sont ornées de paons. Or dans le manuscrit de Cambridge il n'y a qu'un paon, dans la bordure de gauche du folio 1r (Figure 10).

13. Un des deux autres manuscrits de cette même famille, Paris, B.N., ms Fr. 15099, n'a qu'une miniature au premier folio du texte (f. 2r) représentant le même sujet que celles de Cambridge, Fitzwilliam Museum, ms 166 et Paris, S.M.A.F., ms. 80-11. Quant à sa forme elle reproduit la forme rectangulaire de la miniature de Cambridge.

trer ses reliques à l'Acteur. Dans la Figure 6, par contre, les deux figures se tiennent normalement.

Etant donné que la lumière vient du côté du lecteur dans la Figure 4 et porte sur la palissade de la lice, l'écu et l'épée que tient Philippe de Bourgogne jettent une ombre par terre derrière lui. Ce même effet est produit aussi par l'arme que porte Débile. Cet effet d'ombre se reproduit dans toutes les enluminures du manuscrit du Fitzwilliam Museum, que ce soit une scène d'extérieur ou d'intérieur, sauf la dernière (Figure 8). La lumière venant toujours du devant, l'artiste a peint consciencieusement l'ombre quelle que soit sa source: les pattes de cheval, les corps humains ou même les cailloux parsemés sur les chemins. Cet effet est complètement absent dans la miniature provenant de l'exemplaire de la S.M.A.F. (Figure 3) et par ailleurs dans toute l'enluminure de ce manuscrit.[14]

Enfin nous remarquons dans la Figure 4 que le fourreau de l'épee de Philippe de Bourgogne se voit très nettement entre ses jambes. Bien que nous voyions la poignée de son épée dans la Figure 3, son fourreau manque complètement. Ce dépouillement se remarque aussi si l'on compare les Figures 9 et 10: dans la seconde nous voyons le coin du livre au-dessous du bras armé du chevalier. Or, dans la première ce petit coin de livre reste invisible.[15] De plus, quand nous comparons les Figures 7 et 8, nous remarquons que la petite image qui orne le chevet du lit à dais dans la Figure 8 manque entièrement dans la Figure 7.

Si ces trois catégories de différences ne suffisent pas tout à fait à prouver que le miniaturiste du manuscrit de la S.M.A.F. a copié les images du manuscrit du Fitzwilliam Museum, ajoutons la déformation de certains détails d'ordre ornemental ou architectural qui démontre que cet artiste copie, mais d'une façon moins compétente, les miniatures de son confrère. Un seul exemple de cette déformation d'ordre ornemental suffit à soutenir notre hypothèse: les armoiries de Philippe de Bourgogne sont parfaitement reproduites dans l'image provenant du manuscrit de Cambridge et sur son armure et sur le drapeau qui flotte au-dessus de son pavillon (Figure 4). Ce n'est plus le cas dans la miniature du manuscrit de Paris où ses armoiries sont représentées vaguement par des taches d'or

14. Voir les Figures 6 et 10 à contraster avec les miniatures du manuscrit de la S.M.A.F., les Figures 5 et 9.

15. Un autre lapsus révélateur se trouve dans l'enluminure qui représente la lutte de Charles de Bourgogne contre Accident. Cette image montre deux joutes: au premier plan une joute à cheval, puis à l'arrière plan une joute à pied dans un champ clos entouré d'une palissade. Dans la miniature du manuscrit de Cambridge les quatre côtés de la lice sont visibles (f. 44r) tandis que dans l'image de Paris, S.M.A.F., ms. 80-11, le quatrième manque (f. 82v).

et d'azur parsemées de fleurs de lys ou de raies d'or mais dépourvues d'une définition nette de ses charges; et ses armoiries disparaissent entièrement du drapeau de son pavillon pour être remplacées par trois fleurs de lys (Figure 3).[16]

Nous observons cette même sorte de déformation quand nous étudions la reproduction de détails d'ordre architectural. Dans deux miniatures qui représentent une scène intérieure aux folios 3r et 7v du manuscrit de Cambridge, le plancher est composé en damier de carreaux foncés et clairs. Cette alternance disparaît dans le manuscrit de Paris, où les carreaux sont d'un gris foncé uniforme (ff. 41v et 46r). La reproduction des fenêtres dans les images du manuscrit de la S.M.A.F. est aussi assez maladroite comparée à l'execution des fenêtres dans le manuscrit du Fitzwilliam Museum.[17] Plus révélatrice est l'ornementation architecturale qui décore les portes et les fenêtres, dont nous voyons un exemple dans la Figure 6. Ce détail décoratif reste un des traits distinctifs de l'artiste du manuscrit de Cambridge; en revanche quand l'artiste du manuscrit de Paris rend ce détail dans les miniatures qu'il peint, soit il emploie un gris clair comme dans les Figures 5 et 7,[18] soit sa peinture en blanc ne fait que suggérer ce détail ornemental[19], soit encore il néglige complètement de peindre ce détail.[20] Cependant, ce peintre prête beaucoup plus d'attention aux détails de ligne et de décoration de tissu (Figure 7) que son confrère (Figure 8). Nous observons cette attention dans la représentation des plis de la couverture et dans la décoration du lit à dais.[21] En fait, c'est probablement à cause de son enthousiasme pour l'élaboration de la décoration du tissu que

16. Le même phénomène se reproduit dans les deux miniatures représentant les joutes de Charles de Bourgogne contre Accident. Dans l'image au folio 44r du manuscrit de Cambridge ses armoiries sont lisibles; elles ne sont que vaguement suggérées par des taches d'or et d'azur rayé d'or ou parsemé de fleurs de lys dans l'exemplaire de Paris (f. 82v).

17. Voir ff. 6r, 7v et 15v du manuscrit du Fitzwilliam Museum, à comparer aux ff. 44v, 46r et 54r du manuscrit de la S.M.A.F. Le folio 46r est reproduit dans Londres, vente Sotheby, 1972, Illustration, Lot 30.

18. De même pour la miniature au folio 67v à comparer au folio 29r du manuscrit de Cambridge.

19. Voir ff. 7v et 15v du manuscrit du Fitzwilliam Museum à comparer aux ff. 46r et 54r de la S.M.A.F. Le folio 46r est reproduit dans Londres, vente Sotheby, 1972, Illustration, Lot 30.

20. Voir folio 6r du manuscrit de Cambridge à comparer au folio 44v du manuscrit de Paris.

21. Cette même extravagance de lignes décoratrices peintes en or s'observe aussi bien dans la reproduction de la couverture du cheval d'Accident au folio 82v que dans la représentation de la robe et de la tente de Marie de Bourgogne, archiduchesse d'Autriche au folio 86r. Les deux miniatures du manuscrit de Cambridge sont plus simples à cet égard (ff. 44r et 47v).

l'artiste néglige de reproduire l'image au-dessus de la tête de l'Acteur couché dans cette dernière miniature du manuscrit.

On peut donc conclure, grâce à cette comparaison de détails graphiques et iconographiques, non seulement que l'exemplaire du *Chevalier délibéré* se trouvant dans le manuscrit, Paris, S.M.A.F., ms. 80-11 est identique au manuscrit Cambridge University, Fitzwilliam Museum, ms. 166, mais encore qu'il constitue une copie aussi exacte que possible de ce dernier.

3. L'ENIGME DU MANUSCRIT DE LA S.M.A.F.

Comment comprendre l'action de compilation que représente le manuscrit de la S.M.A.F., qui semble inattendu pour le premier texte aussi bien que pour le second?[22] Comme le note Mme N. Reynaud, le texte de Lannoy 'est généralement couplé avec d'autres ouvrages d'enseignements moraux'.[23] Le poème allégorique de La Marche, pour sa part, se trouve à trois reprises dans une compilation avec *Le Pas de la Mort*, poème didactique d'Amé de Montgesoie auquel le texte du *Chevalier délibéré* fait référence dans la cinquième strophe (v. 34-35).[24] Pourrait-il s'agir d'une action intentionnelle destinée à récupérer, voire recycler, un manuscrit, qui n'a peut-être pas atteint son destinataire déclaré,[25] ou bien encore à le transformer pour un autre destinataire toujours inconnu, grâce à l'ajout d'un texte de genre et de style littéraire différents mais non moins essentiel pour une éducation princière qu'est le *Chevalier délibéré*? Car ce qui est sûr, c'est que la juxtaposition de ces deux textes, malgré leurs différences visuelles et textuelles,[26] crée un ensemble qui met en relief la thématique du 'miroir des princes' bien présente, mais peu commentée,

22. Lebigue, *op. cit.* [note 1], p. 81, suit Reynaud, dans Avril et Reynaud, *op. cit.* [note 1], p. 155, lorsqu'il dit 'Ce volume est le produit d'un montage factice, juxtaposant deux textes sans rapport ni pour le contenu ni pour la présentation. La variation entre les types de réglures et d'écritures met en valeur la division du manuscrit en deux sections'.

23. Reynaud, dans Avril et Reynaud, *op. cit.* [note 1], p. 155.

24. Paris, B.N., ms Rothschild 2797 (Hainaut, Valenciennes?, 1487/8-1490); Vienne, ÖNB ms 2654 (Flandre?, vers 1520); Oxford, Bodleian Library, Douce 168 (Flandre, fin XVIe ou début XVIIe siècle). On le retrouve transcrit aussi dans des recueils qui regroupent plusieurs manuscrits de types différents datant du XVIe siècle.

25. Le premier ouvrage du manuscrit commence par une lettre, en guise de prologue, écrite par Bernard de Béarn, Bâtard de Comminges, à l'intention de 'Monseigneur le Prince de Navarre' à qui il dédie son manuscrit. Ce prince était très probablement le jeune roi de Navarre, François Phoebus, qui est mort prématuré en 1483.

26. Le style des bordures démontre cependant une tentative d'harmoniser la présentation de ces deux textes. Voir note 12.

dans le récit du poème de La Marche. La lecture traditionnelle de ce poème a tendance à le considérer comme une simple allégorie sur la vieillesse et la mort. Or, dans la partie centrale du récit (la quatrième partie du livre, strophes 219-281), l'Acteur décrit les joutes fatales auxquelles il assiste avec son guide Fresche memoire dans la lice de 'la deesse de la mort', Atropos. Ces joutes opposent d'abord Philippe le Bon, duc de Bourgogne, à Débile et ensuite duc Charles le Téméraire et Marie de Bourgogne, archiduchesse d'Autriche, à Accident, le second des lieutenants d'Atropos. La description de ces combats et l'éloge qui suit la mort de chacun de ces grands personnages les présentent comme des parangons des vertus princières. Alors la conclusion s'impose selon laquelle ces deux textes seraient en effet complémentaires: le traité de Lannoy présentant la partie théorique du miroir des princes; le poème de La Marche les *exempla* à suivre. Mais tout ceci n'est qu'hypothétique. Nous devons attendre à ce que de nouveaux éclaircissements sur le manuscrit de la S.M.A.F. voient le jour.[27]

27. Je voudrais remercier très chaleureusement Mme Laura Truffaut et Mme Elodie Lecuppre-Desjardin d'avoir corrigé et amélioré sensiblement le français de cet article.

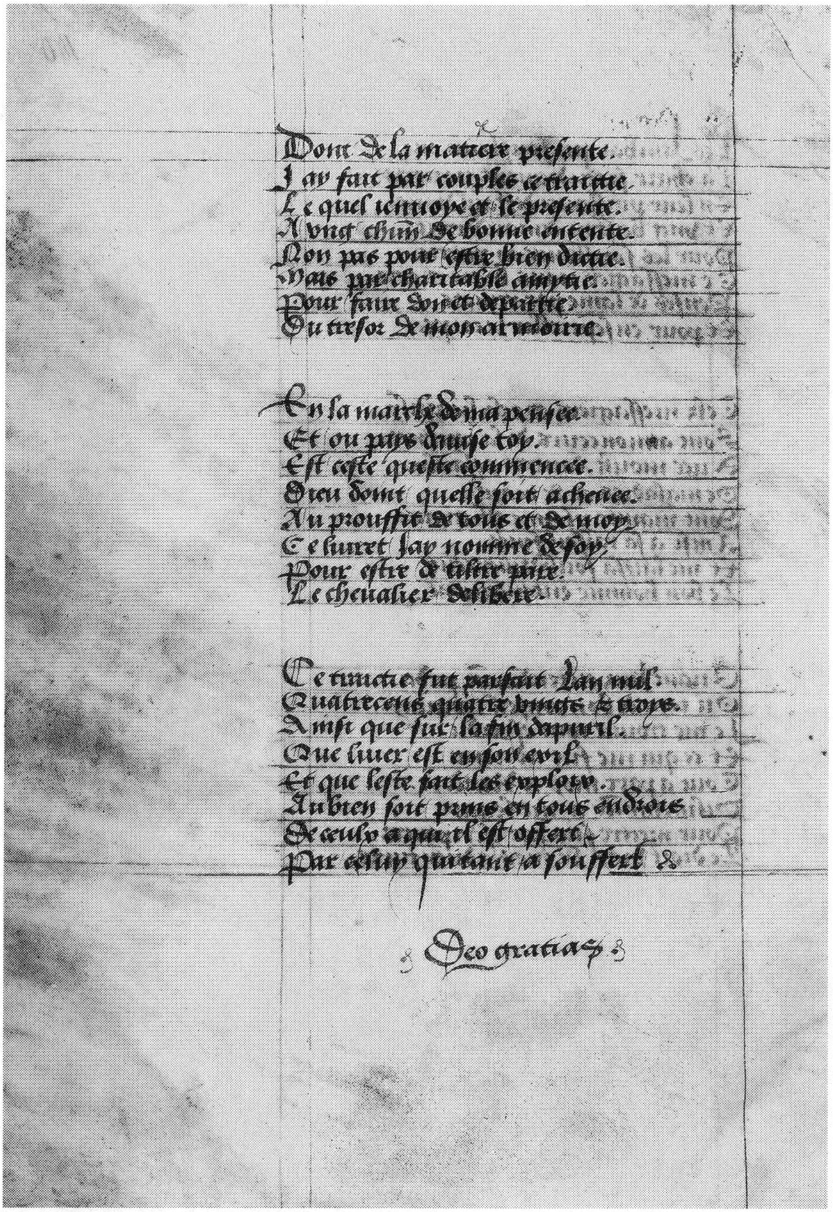

Figure 1
Les trois dernières strophes du *Chevalier délibère* (v. 2681-2704)
Paris, S.M.A.F., ms. 80-11, f. 100v

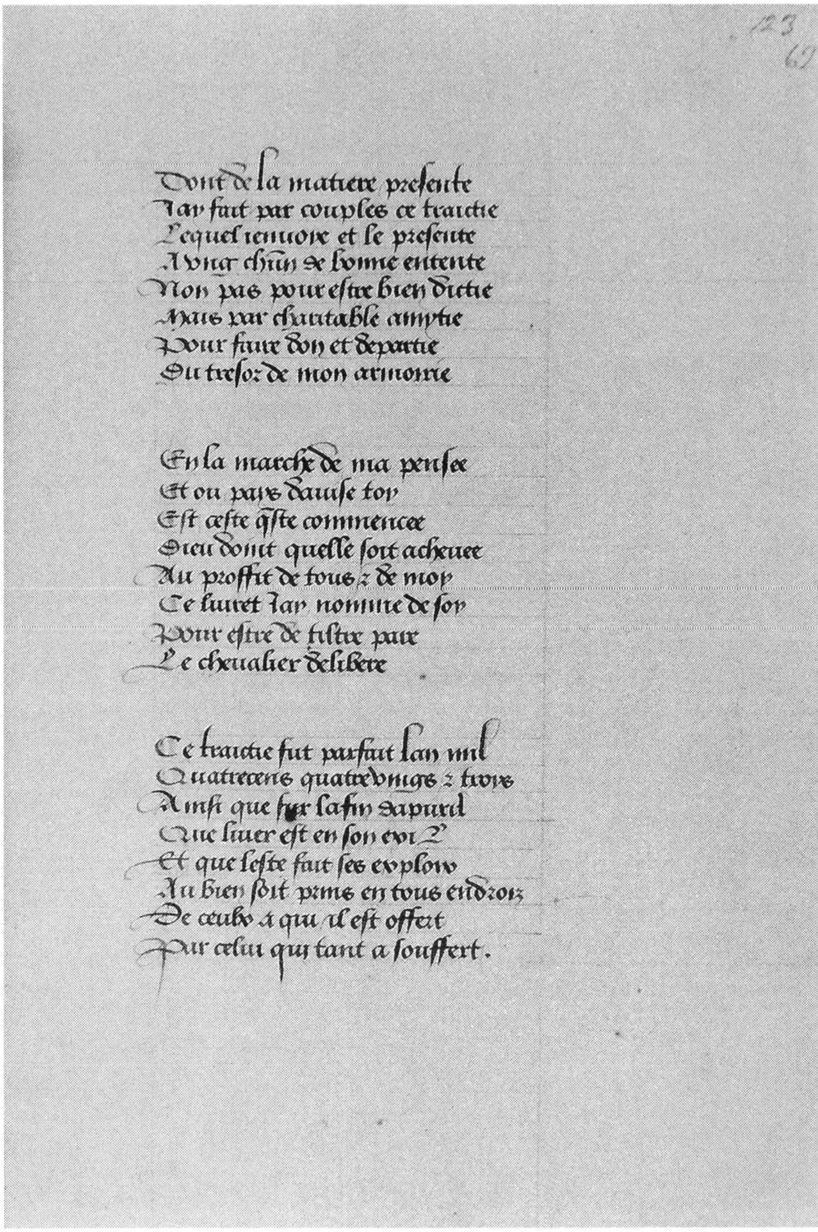

Dont de la matiere presente
Jay fait par couples ce traictie
Lequel jenvoye et le presente
A ung chascun de bonne entente
Non pas pour estre bien dictie
Mais par charitable amytie
Pour faire don et departie
Du tresor de mon armoire

En la marche de ma pensee
Et ou pays dausse toy
Est ceste queste commencee
Dieu doint quelle soit achevee
Au proffit de tous z de moy
Ce livret jay nomme de soy
Pour estre de tiltre pare
Le chevalier delibere

Ce traictie fut parfait lan mil
Quatrecens quatrevings z trois
Ainsi que hyer la fin dapvril
Que liver est en son exil
Et que leste fait ses exploix
Au bien soit prins en tous endroiz
De ceulx a qui il est offert
Par celui qui tant a souffert.

Figure 2
Les trois dernières strophes du *Chevalier délibére* (v. 2681-2704)
Cambridge, Fitzwilliam Museum, ms. 166, f. 62r

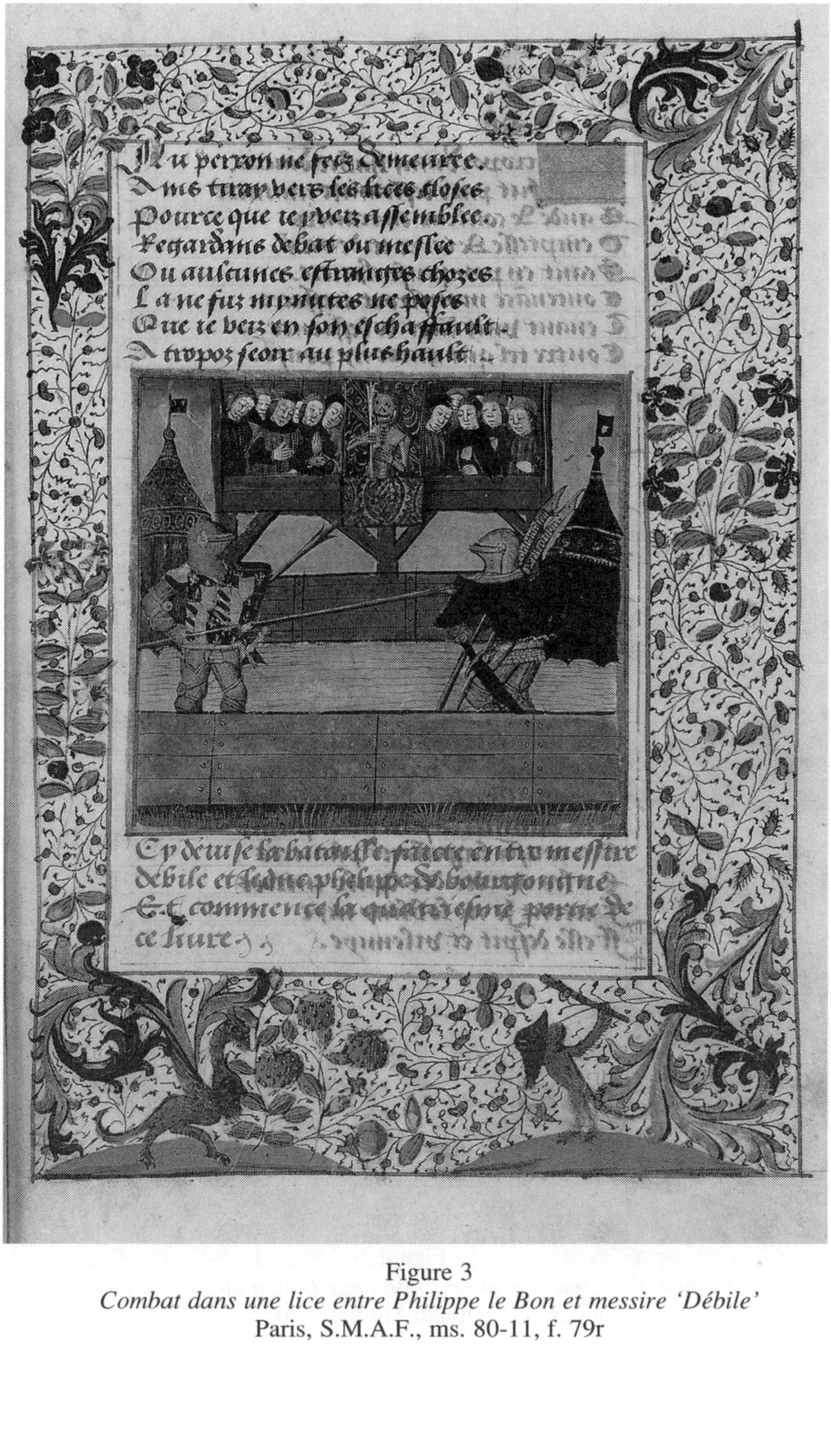

Figure 3
Combat dans une lice entre Philippe le Bon et messire 'Débile'
Paris, S.M.A.F., ms. 80-11, f. 79r

Figure 4
Combat dans une lice entre Philippe le Bon et messire 'Débile'
Cambridge, Fitzwilliam Museum, ms. 166, f. 40v

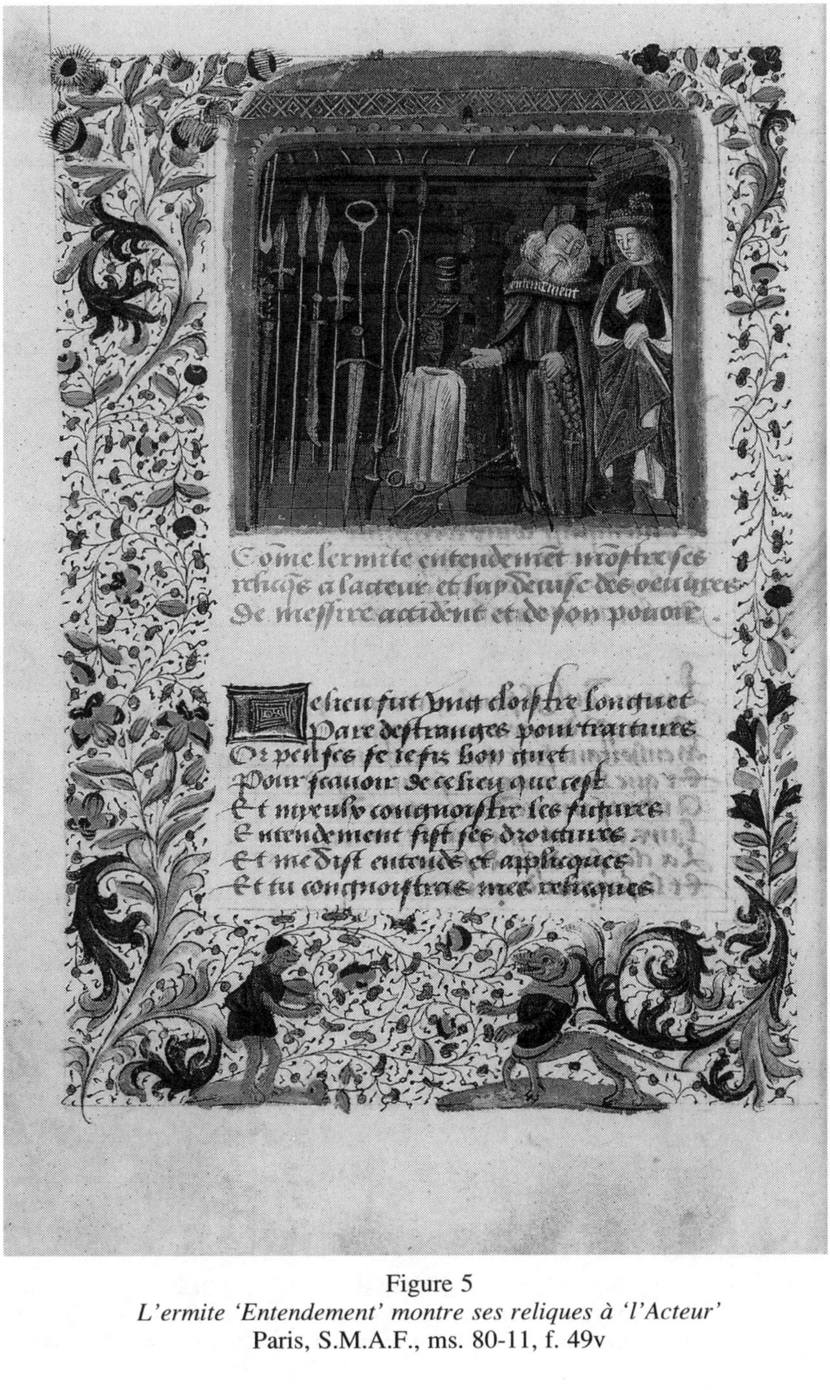

Figure 5
L'ermite 'Entendement' montre ses reliques à 'l'Acteur'
Paris, S.M.A.F., ms. 80-11, f. 49v

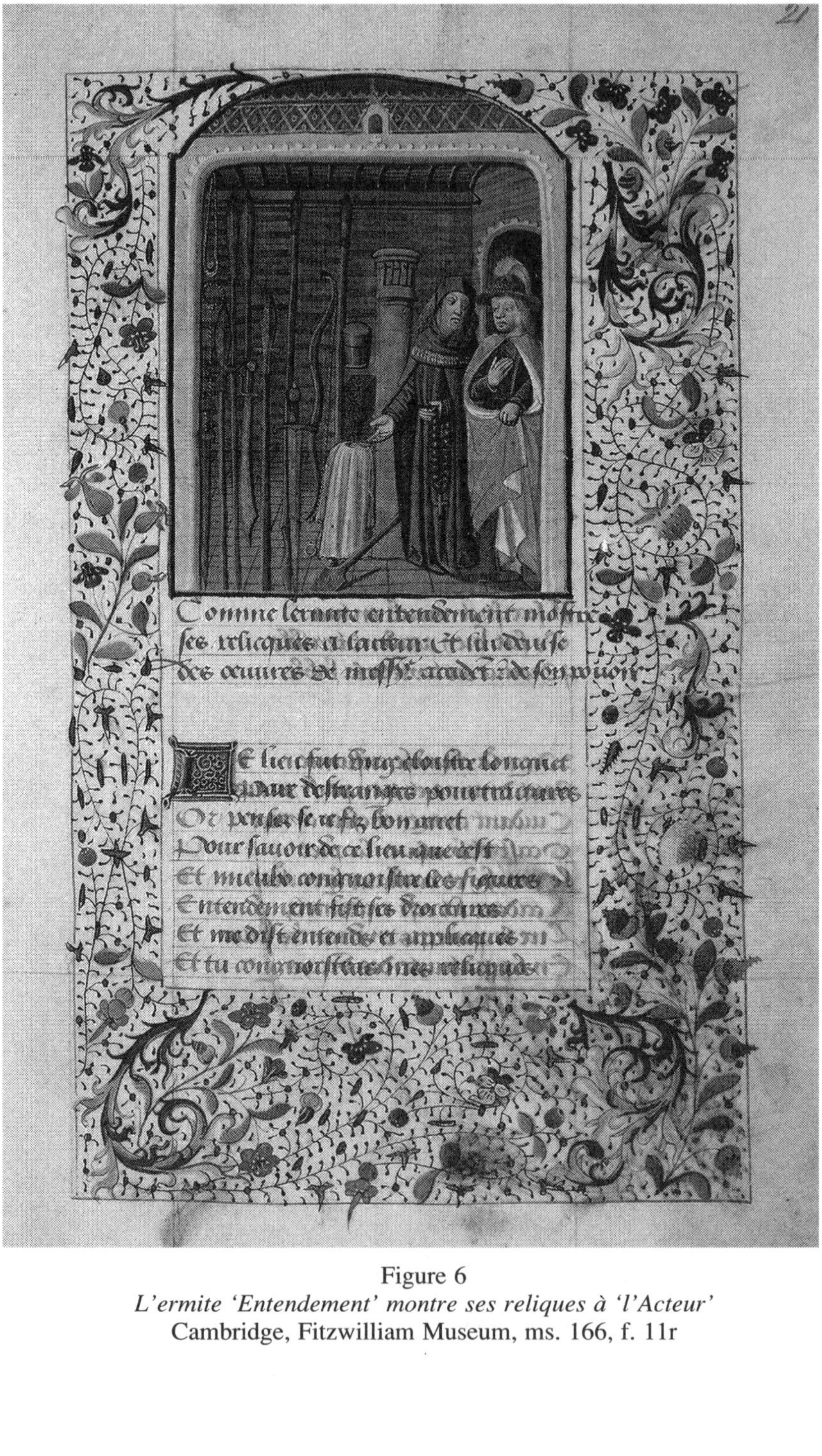

Figure 6
L'ermite 'Entendement' montre ses reliques à 'l'Acteur'
Cambridge, Fitzwilliam Museum, ms. 166, f. 11r

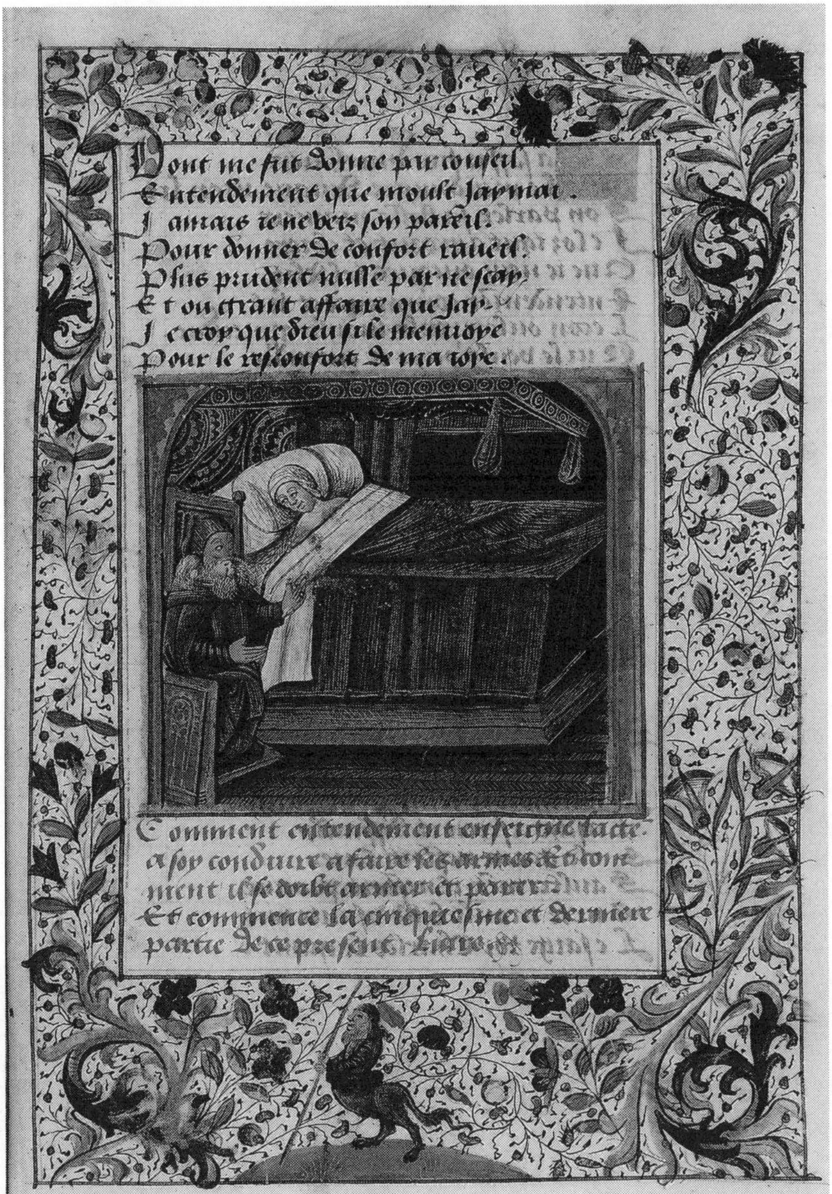

Figure 7
'L'Acteur' écoute l'enseignement de l'ermite 'Entendement'
Paris, S.M.A.F., ms. 80-11, f. 91r

Figure 8
'L'Acteur' écoute l'enseignement de l'ermite 'Entendement'
Cambridge, Fitzwilliam Museum, ms. 166, f. 52v

Figure 9
Le Chevalier délibéré
Paris, S.M.A.F., ms. 80-11, f. 39v

Figure 10
Le Chevalier délibéré
Cambridge, Fitzwilliam Museum, ms 166, f. 1r

Gilbert TOURNOY

AN ITALIAN SCRIBE AT BRUGES IN THE SECOND HALF OF THE FIFTEENTH CENTURY: FRANCESCO FLORIO

This contribution deals with a topic which, like a medal, has two sides, an Italian one and a Bruges one. Both parts started to be studied some forty years ago, in the sixties of the last century.[1] They each had a quite independent development, not unlike two tracks of a railway, which have the same starting point, but may or may not ever meet again.

The first track started when I was studying the Neo-Latin *novella* in the Italian Quattrocento. A certain Franciscus Florius happened to be the author of one of these short stories, which I had to examine in that context. It was published several times at Paris and elsewhere,[2] between 1470 and 1500, with the title:

Francisci Florii Florentini de amore Camilli et Emilie Aretinorum.

For biographical details concerning that author I had to rely on the scanty information provided by old reference works such as the *Nouvelle Biographie Générale,* which published the entry on Florio in 1858, or the *Biographie Universelle,* which had an entry on him in 1856. In volume 17 of the *Nouvelle Biographie Générale,* one even could read that (col. 957): 'on est même allé jusqu' à nier son existence'. But the redactors of the *Nouvelle Biographie Générale,* as well as their colleagues of the *Biographie Universelle* two years earlier, were unaware of the fact that in 1855 the French scholar André Salmon had published another work composed by Francesco Florio, his *De probatione Turonica,* a description of the city of Tours.[3]

1. This is in essence the text read at the Conference on 'Manscripts in Transition' (Brussels, November 2002). I have added only a few footnotes and a first edition of Florio's *Visio mirabilis.* I am grateful to my friend and colleague Ron Truman for the correction of my English.

2. See *Gesamtkatalog der Wiegendrucke*, VIII (Berlin -Stuttgart, 1978), coll. 524-527. Because of the dedication of the novella to Guillaume Tardif, the compiler(s) of the lemma erroneously wrote that the *novella* had been composed in the house of Guillaume Tardif, confusing in this way the dedicatee, who was indeed Guillaume Tardif, and the 'Guillermus Archiepiscopus Turonensis = Guillaume Larchevesque', in whose house the *novella* had been finished, according to the colophon.

3. A. Salmon, 'Description de la ville de Tours sous le règne de Louis XI, par F. Florio', *Mémoires de la Société Archéologique de Touraine*, 7 (1855), 82-108.

One had to wait for more than a century until somebody else re-opened the Florio file. In 1963 the Scottish scholar Charles Finlayson dealt with three Latin manuscripts copied by Francesco Florio (Paris, Arsenal, MS 1183; Edinburgh, University Library, MS 195; Oxford, Merton, MS A.3. 1.). In a second contribution he drew attention, justly I believe, to the autobiographical character of the *novella*.[4] Nevertheless, still in 1971, our colleague Lionello Sozzi from the University of Torino stated: 'La figura del Florio è anch'essa del tutto oscura e meriterebbe, senza dubbio, accurate indagini.'[5]

My own research yielded in the first place the autograph manuscript of Florio's *novella,* which had been in private hands for centuries, until it was acquired by the Cambridge University Library. It was the late Professor Albinia de la Mare, whom I met at an Oxford Conference back in 1984 – at that time she was still attached to the Bodleian Library – who put me on the right track leading to that manuscript.[6]

In addition to the *novella* and several other manuscripts transcribed by Florio, a few other original and unpublished works written by Florio also emerged: a tract *De laudibus rethorice,* composed at Paris in April 1466, and the autograph manuscript of his *Visio mirabilis supra arcana Galliae* ('a marvellous vision of the secrets of France').[7]

It is the combination of the various autobiographical elements present in the original works as well as in the manuscripts transcribed by Florio, and especially in their extensive colophons, which have enabled us to outline the life and whereabouts of Francesco Florio.

Let us start with the *novella,* which marks the début of Florio on the literary scene. In it he tells the love story of two youngsters from Arezzo, Camillo and Emilia. In doing so, he followed in the footsteps of Enea Silvio Piccolomini, the future Pope Pius II, who had composed his *novella*, his *Historia de duobus amantibus Eurialo et Lucretia,* some twenty years earlier, in 1444. This latter short story immediately met with an enormous success and was, for instance, one of the first three dated tracts that were printed in the Low Countries, viz. by Dirk Martens at Aalst in 1473.

4. Charles P. Finlayson, 'Florius Infortunatus', *Scriptorium*, 16 (1962), 378-380, and Id., ''Florius Infortunatus', Scribe and Author', *Scriptorium*, 19 (1965), 108-109.

5. L. Sozzi, 'Petrarca, Tardif e Denys de Harsy (con una nota su Francesco Florio)', *Studi francesi*, 43 (1971), 78-82 (81, n. 2).

6. Now kept at Cambridge, University Library, Ms. Add. 8446. See G. Tournoy, 'Francesco Florio's *novella* Revisited', *Humanistica Lovaniensia*, 50 (1991), 30-42.

7. The first of these has been published, but in a most unsatisfactory way, by E. Beltran, 'Un discours inconnu de Francesco Florio sur la Rhétorique', *Bibliothèque d'Humanisme et Renaissance*, 50 (1988), 101-109; the text of the second, kept at Rome, Biblioteca Nazionale, MS V.E. 428, can now be read in the appendix to this contribution.

Now for the contents of Florio's *novella De amore Camilli et Emilie Aretinorum.*

> Camillo is the son of an extremely poor craftsman from Arezzo, a knife-maker, who is not able to feed his numerous family. At the age of three he is adopted by the wealthy family of Emilia, whose father decides that both children should be brought up together. The two grow up, become inseparable – almost like Piramus and Thisbe – and gradually their friendship turns into a tender sentiment of burgeoning love. At the age of fourteen they are separated, but this separation only increases their mutual affection. Three years later Emilia is given in marriage to a young man of her own social class, and Camillo is left alone, broken-hearted. But soon the two lovers find a way to exchange love letters and, still better, to spend many nights in each other's embraces. This continues until another young man, attracted by Emilia's irresistible beauty, stands guard before her house day and night. And when he sees, one night, Camillo secretly enter the house, he sounds the alarm, convinced that Camillo is a burglar. Camillo's subsequent imprisonment does not decrease his passion for Emilia but only increases the lovers' caution. The two are again separated when Emilia is sent by her husband to his castle outside Arezzo, Camillo at first not being able to find out where Emilia has been taken. But then Lady Fortune comes to his aid. Camillo finds a job as organ player in a church half-way between Arezzo and the castle, and quite by chance the two lovers meet one day on the doorstep of that church. Their first new rendez-vous, however, is interrupted by the unexpected arrival of the suspicious husband. But while he is searching for witnesses, Camillo escapes, thanks to a hazardous jump out of the window, and Emilia has to suffer all by herself the wrath of her husband. So she decides to walk out on him. After having roamed through the woods for several days, she is found and brought back, not to her husband though, but to her parents. The poor husband does everything possible to regain his spouse's confidence, but in vain: her door opens only for Camillo. He, however, cannot stay forever. And while he is studying in Florence, the plague is raging in Arezzo. Emilia is infected and dies piously. Camillo has some masses celebrated for the salvation of her soul and then, not yet twenty-five years old, he goes wandering all over the world.

In his introduction Florio guarantees the veracity and the authenticity of the whole story. The only things he has changed, so he claims, are the names of the *dramatis personae*.

If indeed one can take one's departure from the autobiographical character of this *novella*, and especially from the identification between the author (Florio) and the protagonist (Camillo), a number of elements could be helpful in reconstructing the life of our author.

From the very beginning though, one meets with a difficulty. The very title of the *novella* reads: 'Francisci Florii *Florentini* de amore Camilli et Emilie Aretinorum'.

Camillo thus is a native of Arezzo, while Florio presents himself as Florentine, and so Paolo Viti, for instance, simply writes in his entry in the *Dizionario biografico degli Italiani*: 'Si sa che nacque a Firenze'[8]

In order to solve this problem, one has to bear in mind that, at that time, the city of Arezzo, for more than a century already, had been politically dependent on the republic of Florence. Furthermore, there are other similar cases. One example only: when our colleague Michele Feo, now at the University of Florence, some years ago read a Latin poem in an old manuscript kept at the library of Gotha in Germany – a poem that was attributed to a 'Franciscus Florentinus' – he immediately felt that this was a major discovery.[9] And indeed, this poem was a completely forgotten one and the 'Franciscus Florentinus' turned out to be no one other than Petrarch himself, who in fact was born at... Arezzo!

Similarly in the case of Florio there are several other indications that support the thesis that Arezzo, and not Florence, was his native city:

- first of all, in his *novella* Florio presents Camillo and Emilia as his compatriots;
- secondly, Florio starts his short story with a eulogy of the city of Arezzo, where a whole series of prominent figures have been born: Francesco Petrarca, Leonardo Bruni, Carlo Marsuppini and the brothers Accolti;
- thirdly, in his *Visio mirabilis,* the Muse addresses him in this way: 'Atqui gignasiis Caroli Aretini compatriotae tui nutritus, ore eius ac Venusini sententia eruditus' ('you who were brought up in the school of Carolus Aretinus, and were educated by his words and the thoughts of Horace'). Now, this Carolus Aretinus is no one else than the well-known Florentine humanist Carlo Marsuppini, who after the death of Leonardo Bruni in 1444 became Chancellor of the Florentine Republic until his own death in 1453.

Accepting the autobiographical character of the *novella* is also essential to establish the precise date of Florio's birth. In the prefatory letter Camillo is presented as not yet having reached his fortieth year. Since Florio finished his *novella* at the end of 1467, he must have been born in 1428. This date is now confirmed by the discovery of a juridical manuscript kept at the Vatican library (MS Vat. Lat. 6054, containing

8. Paolo Viti, 'Florio, Francesco', in *Dizionario biografico degli Italiani*, 48 (Roma, 1997), pp. 363-366.

9. Michele Feo, 'Primo dossier sul Petrarca di Gotha', *Quaderni Petrarcheschi*, 4 (1987), 9-120.

the *Decretalium libri quinque*). At the end of this manuscript (fol. 306r) the extensive colophon informs us that Tristan de Salazar (†1519), archbishop of Sens since 1475, had the various parts of the entire *Corpus iuris canonici* transcribed by Francesco Florio, a major undertaking that would occupy the copyist for more than five years. Indeed, Florio started this work on 9 July 1478, transcribing the *Decretum Gratiani* (Paris, Arsenal, MS 1183). At the end of this first part, finished 12 March 1480, Florio still presented himself – as he was accustomed to do in the other manuscripts he previously had copied – as 'Florius ille infortunatus' (see ill. 15):

> Summe sit Trinitati laus et gloria, ad cuius utriusque ecclesie decus et utilitatem hoc presens Gratiani decretum sumptu notabili ac impensa Reverendissimi patris et domini domini Tristandi de Salazar divina clementia Senonensis archiepiscopi, manu autem ac maximo labore mei Francisci Florii Florentini inceptum Senonis nona iulii, et agente peste mediatum apud Sanctum Iulianum XX augusti post anni cumulum; sed tandem divino aspirante favore spatio viginti mensium et trium dierum ab operis inceptione hac Gregorio dicata die XII Martii M°CCCC°LXXX° a nativitate Domini in domo domini decani Riparie apud Villam Novam archiepiscopi feliciter consummatum est. Deo Gratias. Florius Ille Infortunatus.

In the colophon of the Vatican MS (see ill. 16)[10] he states that he is now happy in the service of Tristan de Salazar, but he has been unfortunate ('infortunatus') until the age of fifty. Since he entered the service of Tristan de Salazar in 1478, his year of birth must indeed be 1428.

Back to the *novella* once more. Following its chronology, we find that Camillo studied together with his adoptive sister till the age of fourteen, the two last years being reserved for their musical education. This brings us to 1442/43. The musical qualities of Camillo, which are repeatedly stressed in the *novella,* appear to constitute another match between Camillo and Florio. Our author indeed, in his description of Tours, dwells at great length and enthusiastically on the Flemish musician Jan

10. MS Vat. Lat. 6054, fol. 306r: Iam virginis ora phebus aureus illustrarat, cum benigniori quodam fato astra coeli Florium aspicere satagebant. Arridebat iam Tonantis soror et querulas Infortunati voces verterat in cantum, quando largifluo sumptu domini Tristandi Senonum archipresulis presens decretalium opus manus Francisci Florii die prima Septembris M°CCCC°LXXXIII feliciter explevit. Summe igitur Trinitati gloria lausque perennis, quae sua ineffabili bonitate dies Florio tribuit incolumes, ut post transcriptum Gratiani aureum opus etiam has Decretales perficere concessit. Non deneget tandem, rogo item, vitae spatium ad presentiam, ut simul hac et Sextum et Clementinas Florius ille, ad L.^{mum} usque annum Infortunatus, iam fortuna ac sospitate per omnia felix valeat explere. Amen.

Quinta luce post fata Iciuodul Siger Murocnarf. (= Ludouici Regis Francorum)

Ockeghem, who from 1465 onwards was appointed by the French king to be master of the music of the royal chapel[11].

In the *novella* Camillo and Emilia are then separated for a period of three years, after which the young lady is given in marriage. But their relationship continues without difficulties for another two years. This brings us from 1442/43 to 1447/48. When Camillo is caught in Emilia's house, he is sentenced by an ecclesiastical court, because he is a 'clericus'. Here we have another possible match with Florio, who in his prefatory letter to Guillaume Tardif counters in advance the man's possible objections, stating: 'Quod si non multum mee professioni dixeris convenire, scias profecto tecum mihi furere dulce esse.' The expression 'non multum mee professioni (...) convenire' already suggests a clerical status.[12] This possibility became a certainty after the discovery of yet another MS in the Municipal Library of Toulouse (MS. 214), the colophon of which reads:

> Millesimo quadringentesimo sexagesimo quinto, ad honorem individue Trinitatis et virginis Marie gloriam, explicit prima pars Summe Theologice viri sanctissimi preclarissimique doctoris fratris Thome de Aquino, ordinis sacri Predicatorum, scripta per Franciscum Florium, de provincia Romana, eiusdem almi ordinis Dominici fratrem, spacio dierum centum; nam XXIIa mensis Mai anno supra notato, in vigilia scilicet Ascensionis Parisius incepta, eiusdem anni Augusti mensis XXVIIIa die, videlicet Augustino dicata, feliciter fuit ad finem redacta pariterque expleta. Deo gratias. Amen.

The formula 'Franciscum Florium, de provincia Romana, eiusdem almi ordinis Dominici fratrem', proves that Florio was a member of the Dominican order.

In this context it also becomes clear why Florio, in his description of Tours, calls the church of Santa Maria sopra Minerva at Rome 'sacrarium nostrum'. This church indeed was built in the thirteenth century by two Dominican friars, fra Sisto (†1290) and fra Ristoro (†1284). It is also in this church that another prominent Florentine, fra Angelico, found his final resting-place.

11. See J.M. Vaccaro, 'Jean de Ockeghem, trésorier del'église Saint Martin de Tours de 1459 (?) à 1497', in *Johannes Ockeghem en zijn tijd. Tentoonstelling gehouden in het Stadhuis te Dendermonde 14 november – 6 december 1970*, Oudheidkundige Kring van het Land van Dendermonde, Buitengewone uitgaven, 24 (Dendermonde, 1970), pp. 60-76 (62: 'maistre de la chapelle de chant du roy nostre sire').

12. As had been noted already by Salmon, 'Description' [note 3], p. 86, who finds further confirmation in the fact that Florio lived at Tours in the house of a canon of the cathedral, and that in his description of Tours, he takes especial delight in focusing on churches and ceremonies.

Back to the *novella*: Three years after Camillo's arrest, a rumour is spread that the soldiers of the King of Naples, Alfonso of Aragon, are about to invade the territory of the Florentine Republic. This is a historical event that can be pinpointed without the shadow of a doubt. The treaty between Naples and Venice, concluded in June 1451, aimed at a joint attack against Florence. But, precisely as our author indicates: 'adventus eius usque in alium annum protenderetur', this attack was postponed until the summer of the following year.

Camillo and Emilia do not see each other until September 1451. And at their first rendez-vous, they are surprised by her husband. Camillo flies, Emilia flies and returns to her father's house; after a while Camillo goes to study at Florence. Florio also studied at Florence, with Carlo Marsuppini, as we have seen before: 'Atqui gignasiis Caroli Aretini compatriotae tui nutritus' ('you who were brought up in the school of Carolus Aretinus').

This Carlo Marsuppini (1398-1453) not only taught Latin in Florence but, from 1451 onwards, also Greek. Traces of his teaching can be found in the works and manuscripts copied by Florio, who indeed adds at the end of his *Visio mirabilis* his name and surname in Greek characters, though not without some orthographical errors (see ill. 6):

Φρανκισκωσ Φλωρηοσ Φλορεντινοσ.

Shortly afterwards, Emilia dies and Camillo, broken-hearted, decides to roam through the world. And again this corresponds with Florio's statement in his description of Tours: 'Florius tuus, postquam actus satis Etruriam deseruit' ('Impelled to do it, your Florio left Etruria').[13]

And further on: 'cum tamen omnem fere Europae Asiaeque partem lustraverim' ('since I have wandered through almost the whole of Europe and a part of Asia'), and again: 'Nec mihi quis Tyburtina loca aut Tarentina praedicet, nemo laudet Thessala Tempe, cum et ego illa viderim et ista probaverim' ('Nobody has to extol for me the beauty of Tivoly or Taranto, nobody has to praise the valley of Tempe (in Thessaly), since I have seen Tivoli and Taranto and I have admired the Tempe valley').[14] Thus, just like Camillo, Florio had been roaming through the world.

13. I quote here the text of MS. Paris, B.N., 12879, pièce 308, ff. 282r-292v. The text published by A. Salmon 'Description', p. 91, reads: 'postquam actu stultitiae Etruriam deseruit.'

14. With an allusion to the famous seventh ode of Horace's first book of odes, beginning with 'Laudant alii claram Rhodon', the fourth line of which has the combination 'Thessala Tempe', while in the following lines Horace also mentions Tivoli, its sacred wood and its waterfall.

A first conclusion perhaps is in order here: our knowledge of the first part of Florio's life is essentially based on the autobiographical nature of his *novella*. This hypothesis is by no means without foundation: the *novella* indeed is composed partly with literary themes, but partly also it is interwoven with a wealth of details, which do not further the development of the action but are so precise in their correspondence to historical events and to the figure of Florio that sheer coincidence has to be excluded.

For the second part of Florio's life it is mainly his other literary works that are instructive, and no less so the manuscripts he copied and adorned with highly elaborate colophons. In his description of Tours, to begin with, Florio states that he has left Italy, or at least the Republic of Florence, more than fifteen years since: 'iam extra patriam sextum decimum annum agens'. After his wandering through the world he came to France, entering the service of John V, count of Armagnac. This count had come to Rome in 1461, hoping to be absolved by Pope Pius II from his sins. He indeed had for many years lived together with his sister Isabelle, who bore him three children. Although the Pope interceded on his behalf with Charles VII, it was not until the autumn of that year 1461, when Louis XI had become the new King, that a decree was issued which enabled the count to return to his country. And it may have taken a few months before Florio became aware of the changed situation of the count and decided to try his luck with him. But soon our Italian humanist was deceived in his expectations. He left the count and started wandering through France before he settled at Paris for three years, as Florio himself states in his description of Tours: 'a quo ut comperit se delusum, totum prius Francorum regnum lustravit, atque Parisium incoluit per triennium.'[15] This Paris stay, from 1464 to 1467, is documented by his tract *De laudibus rethorice*, given as a speech in April 1466, and by the colophon of several manuscripts:

- the MS 214 of the Municipal Library of Toulouse written at Paris between 22 May and 28 August 1465;
- the MS Med. Pal. 109 of the Biblioteca Laurenziana in Florence transcribed at Paris in August 1467;
- it is highly probable that two other MSS were copied during that same period, viz. the tragedies of Seneca (kept at Oxford, Merton, MS A.3. 1.) and a Vergil MS (kept at Edinburgh, University Library, MS 195).

15. Salmon, 'Description' [note 3], p. 91.

The Florentine MS doubtless marks the end – or at least the provisional end – of Florio's stay at Paris. Shortly afterwards, he left Paris for Tours. There he finished his *novella* in December 1467, writing to Guillaume Tardif in his dedicatory letter that four months had passed since their last contact.

We now pass over – for the moment – a short period of Florio's life to find him in the second half of the 1470s and in the 1480s in the service of the Archbishop of Sens, Tristan de Salazar. For him Florio transcribed the juridical manuscripts of the entire *Corpus iuris canonici*, starting with the *Decretum Gratiani* (Paris, Arsenal, MS 1183) and completing the *Decretalium libri quinque* (MSS Vat. Lat. 6054 and 6055) on 1 September 1483. After the transcription of these manuscripts, Florio vanishes into thin air, without leaving a trace. He was by then fifty-five years of age.

This was the first track we have followed until now. The second track starts at Bruges, when the late Dom Nicolas Huyghebaert (1922-1981) of the Benedictine abbey of Zevenkerken at Sint-Andries (Bruges), published in 1966 a first list of manuscripts ordered or possessed by Jan Crabbe, abbot of the Dunes abbey at Koksijde from 1457 until his death in 1488.[16] A few years later, in 1969, he dealt more particularly with three manuscripts of Jan Crabbe: one at the Seminar library at Bruges (MS 112/111), a second one now at the Royal Library at Brussels (MS II.7842), and a third one in the Cathedral Archives of Tournai (MS 4). These manuscripts were closely connected to one another: they were bound by the same Bruges bookbinder, viz. Antoon van Gavere (1459-1505); they were written by the same anonymous scribe, and decorated by the same anonymous artist. Dom Huyghebaert stated that there was no colophon which could help to identify the copyist, but he was convinced that it was highly unlikely that these manuscripts, bound and decorated in a Bruges style, could have been copied by an Italian scribe, even if the handwriting clearly showed some Italian influence. He moreover drew attention to a particularity present in all three manuscripts which served as a signature, viz. the special use of the word 'Finis' or 'telos' (in Greek characters) at the very end of each work.[17]

Taking up Huyghebaert's suggestion that Crabbe's manuscript collection until then had not received the attention it rightfully deserved, a

16. N. Huyghebaert, 'Abbaye des Dunes à Koksijde et à Bruges', in *Monasticon belge*, III, 2 (Liège, 1966), pp. 353-445 (404, n. 8).

17. Id., 'Trois manuscrits de Jean Crabbe, abbé des Dunes', *Scriptorium*, 23 (1969), 232-241.

young historian Noël Geirnaert started a thorough study of the entire collection. The opportunity to publish the first results of his investigation presented itself in 1981 on the occasion of the Bruges exhibition *Vlaamse kunst op perkament*. In the catalogue accompanying this exhibition Geirnaert was able to identify a few more manuscripts copied by the same scribe.[18] On the basis of some common characteristics, such as the catchwords written vertically and the aforementioned characteristic writing of the word 'Finis' betweeen two dots in the middle of the line, he rather boldly jumped to the conclusion that these manuscripts were copied by the Greek expatriate Georgius Hermonymus of Sparta, who around 1473 dedicated a MS of the *Sententiae gnomicae* to abbot Jan Crabbe (Paris, Arsenal MS 1139). In so doing he was simply following the authority of the French scholar Henri Omont, who in 1885 had listed this particular MS. amongst the manuscripts copied by Hermonymus.[19] But this hypothesis did not meet with much approval, and Geirnaert himself took a more cautious position later on.[20]

Until now, we have seen two quite different tracks, an Italo-French one and a Bruges one. The connection between those two was established by the the discovery of yet another MS, kept at the Escorial (S.III.4). The transcription of this MS, containing the *Dicta et Facta memorabilia* of Valerius Maximus, was finished, according to the first colophon on fol. 215^{v}, at Bruges on 8 December 1469. On the very last leaf the copyist put his name, in Greek characters: Φρανκησκοσ Φλωρηοσ ανηρ (see ill. 8). Looking at the small changes Florio introduced in his first name in comparison with the subscript at the end of the *Visio mirabilis* (Φρανκισκωσ Φλωρηοσ Φλορεντινοσ), it is obvious that the first one

18. Paris, Bibliothèque de l'Arsenal, MS 1139 and Holkham Hall, Library of the Earl of Leicester, MS 311.

19. Henri Omont, 'Georges Hermonyme de Sparte, maître de grec à Paris et copiste de manuscrits, suivi d'une notice sur les collections de manuscrits de Jean et Guillaume Budé et de notes sur leur famille', *Mémoires de la Société de l'Histoire de Paris et de l'Ile-de-France*, 12 (1885), 65-98; *Bulletin de la Société de l'Histoire de Paris et de l'Ile-de-France,* 12 (1885), 45-50 and 13 (1886), 110-113. I quote from the offprint once present in Omont's own library, pp. 7 and 35. In vol. 47 (1920) of the same *Bulletin*, H. Omont published 'Nouveaux manuscrits grecs copiés à Paris par Georges Hermonyme'.

20. Noël Geirnaert, 'De bibliotheek van de Duinenabt Jan Crabbe (1457/58-1488)', in *Vlaamse Kunst op perkament. Handschriften en miniaturen te Brugge van de 12de tot de 16de eeuw* (Brugge, 1981), pp. 176-206. Id., 'Classical Texts in Bruges around 1473: Cooperation of Italian Scribes, Bruges Parchment Rulers, Illuminators and Bookbinders for Johannes Crabbe, Abbot of Les Dunes Abbey (C.U.L., MS Nr. III.5)', *Transactions of the Cambridge Bibliographical Society*, 10 (1992), 173-181 (= *Fifteenth-Century Flemish Manuscripts in Cambridge Collections*).

is due to iotacism, while the shortening of the last vowel may point to the progress in Greek he had made probably thanks to his collaboration with Georgius Hermonymus.

Much more important, however, was the fact that the discovery of this MS thus signed by Florio proved that he had been active at Bruges as a copyist. When one looked for more evidence in that direction, it soon became clear that a considerable number of MSS which had been transcribed at Bruges were unmistakably in Florio's upright, slightly gothicizing humanistic handwriting, and also presented the same codicological features that were present in the autograph MSS of his own works and in the other MSS he transcribed. A few examples:

- in the autograph MS of his *novella* and in that of the *Visio mirabilis,* one finds at the very end the word 'finis' written in capitals between two dots in the midle of the line; the same features are present in MS Arsenal 1183 and Vat. lat. 6054 (fol. 306^r).
- Perpendicular catchwords at the extreme lower right of the previous pages are present in the autograph MS of the *novella* on fol. 12^v, 24^v, 36^v and 47^v; in that of the *Visio mirabilis* on fol. 8^v, 16^v, 24^v and 32^v; and also, in the Escorial MS, on fol. 10^v, etc.

These same codicological features are present in several manuscripts transcribed for Jan Crabbe, viz.

- the two volumes of the Vergil MS in the Library of the Earl of Leicester at Holkham Hall (MS 311), copied in February – March 1473; if other evidence is required, it might be noted that the copyist still follows the 'calculus florentinus', 'Annunciation Style', when he writes (vol. II, fol. 31^r): '... feliciter explicit. 24 martii die mercurii in vigilia annunciationis dominice anno 1473 *incoante*' (my italics);
- the Sallust MS in the Royal Library at Brussels (II.7842), copied in 1473;
- the Caesar MS in the Cambridge University Library (Nn.3.5, ff. 121-244), copied in 1474;
- the MS kept at the Bruges Seminary, containing Cicero's *De officiis* and Boethius's *De consolatione philosophiae,* copied in or shortly before 1474 (MS 112/111);
- The letters of St. Paul, kept at the Chapter Library of the Cathedral of Toumai, MS A.18, copied in or about the same period;

- the *Sententiae gnomicae* by Georgius Hermonymus, kept at Paris, Arsenal MS 1139, copied in or about the same period.

This last MS faces us with several questions, such as:

- was there a relationship between Florio and Hermonymus, and what kind of relationship was it?
- when and where did they meet, and how and where did they enter into contact with Jan Crabbe? Was it already at Rome perhaps, where Hermonymus was living during the 1450s in the circle of Cardinal Bessarion?[21]
- did they enter together the service of Tristan de Salazar, to whom Hermonymus also dedicated, after 1475, a work of his, viz. a Latin translation of Aristotle, *De virtutibus* and the letters of Themistocles and Plato (Paris, Arsenal, MS 814)?

These problems cannot be tackled here and now, but it might be evident already that Florio during the years he spent in Flanders – from 1469 until 1474 at least – might have copied a lot more manuscripts than the few discovered so far, and it can be hoped that they will emerge sooner or later.

To conclude: what would seem especially worthwhile to me is a thorough investigation of the MSS which hitherto have been ascribed to Hermonymus. A plausible hypothesis might be that, if both expatriates indeed collaborated for some time, Hermonymus mainly took care of the transcription of the Greek texts, and Florio of the Latin ones.

P.S.

Em. Prof. Dr. Elizabeth A.R. Brown (The City University of New York) is currently working on yet another manuscript which most probably is copied by Francesco Florio around 1485 and now is kept at the New York Public Library, MA 45. It is a lavishly illustrated *Book of Hours*, which was owned by Galeas de Salazar (d. 1523), a younger brother of Archbishop Tristan de Salazar, and by Galeas's wife Claude d'Anglure, who may have predeceased her husband. It has recently been described by James H. Marrow in the catalogue *The Splendor of the Word: Medieval and Renaissance Illuminated Manuscripts at the New York Public Library*, ed. by J.G. Alexander, J. Marrow and L. Freeman-Sandler, Studies in Medieval and Early Renaissance Art History, 44 (Turnhout: Brepols, 2005), pp. 250-254, no. 53.

21. Cf. John Monfasani, 'Testi inediti di Bessarione e Teodoro Gaza', in *Dotti bizantini e libri greci nell'Italia del secolo XV. Atti del Convegno internazionale Trento 22-23 ottobre 1990*, a cura di Mariarosa Cortesi e Enrico V. Maltese (Napoli, 1992), 231-255 (240).

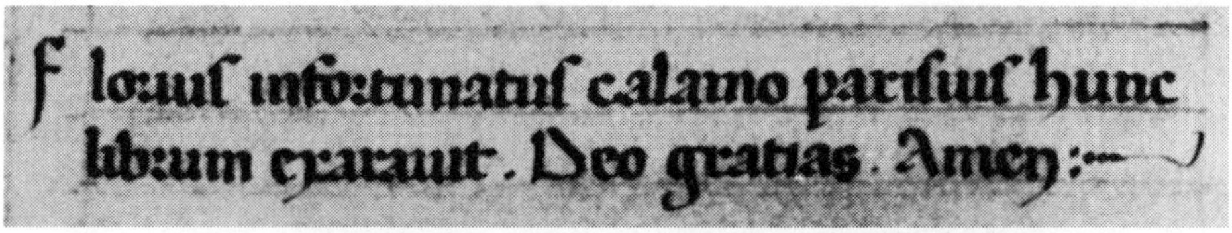
Florius infortunatus calamo parisius hunc
librum exarauit. Deo gratias. Amen:—

Ill. 1 Edinburgh, University Library, MS 195, fol. 208r

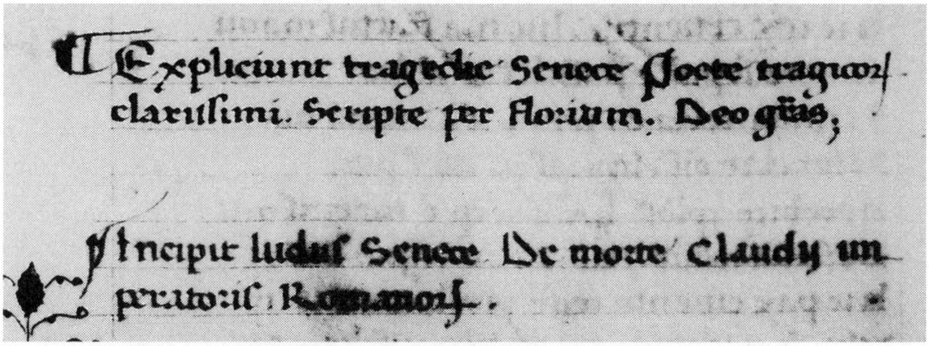
Expliciunt tragedie Senece Poete tragicorum
clarissimi. Scripte per Florium. Deo gratias;

Incipit ludus Senece De morte Claudij im
peratoris Romanorum.

Ill. 2 Oxford, Merton College, MS A.3.1

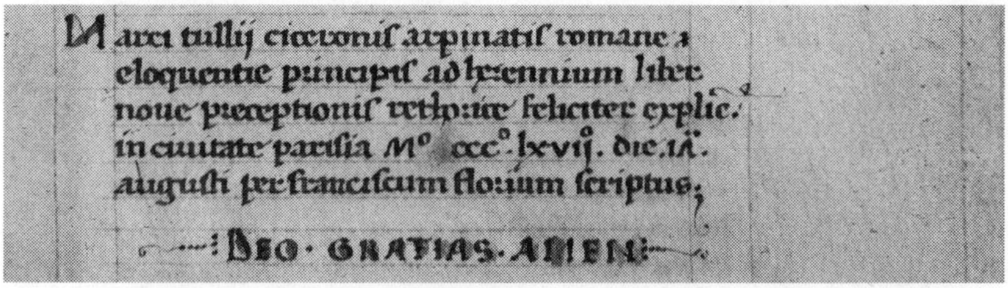
Marci tullij ciceronis arpinatis romane
eloquentie principis ad herennium liber
noue preceptionis rethorice feliciter explic.
in ciuitate parisia M° ccc° lxvij. die ix.
augusti per franciscum florium scriptus;
DEO · GRATIAS · AMEN:

Ill. 3 Firenze, Biblioteca Laurenziana, MS Med. Pal. 109, fol. 55r

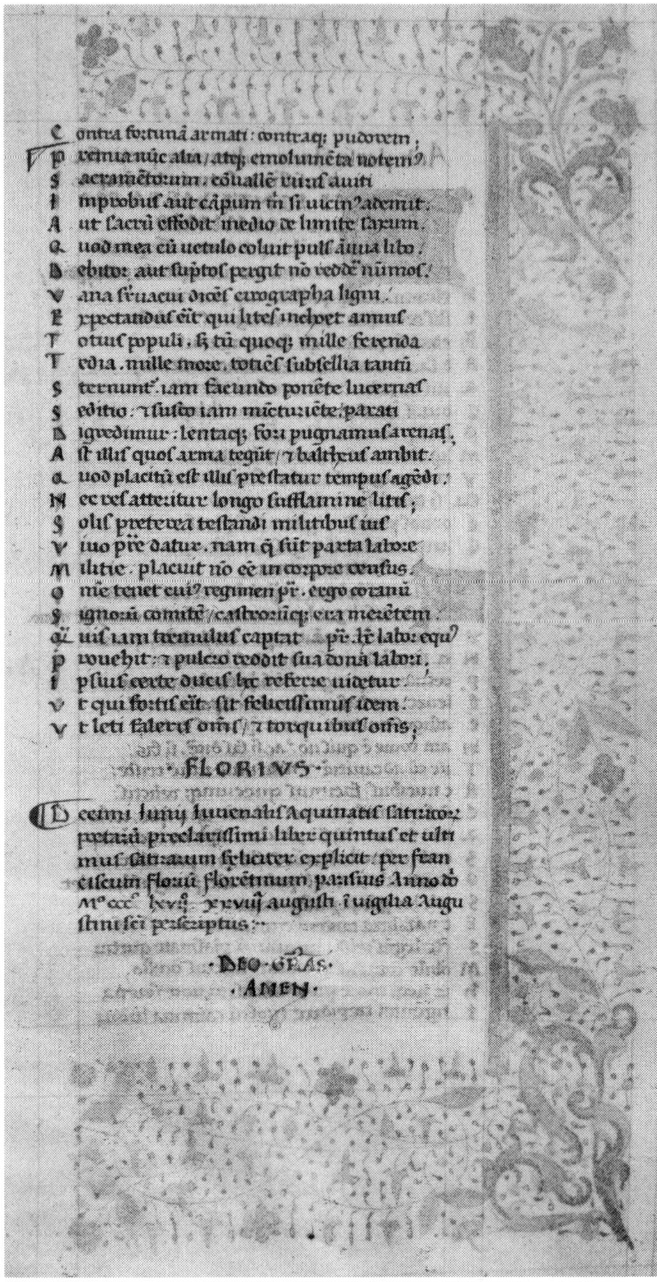

Ill. 4 Firenze, Biblioteca Laurenziana, MS Med. Pal. 109, fol. 104r

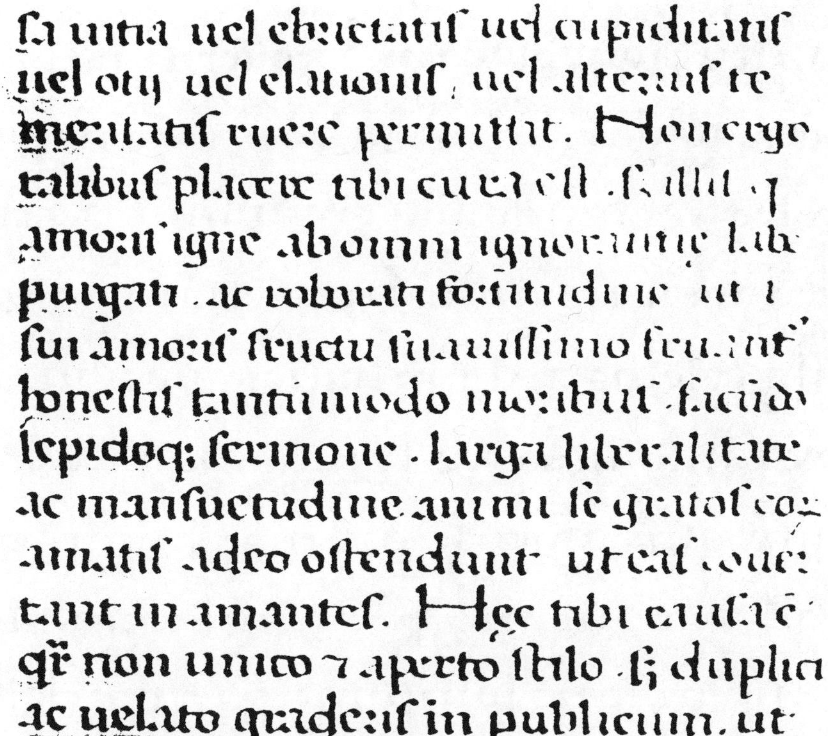

sa uitia uel ebrietatis uel cupiditatis
uel otii uel elationis, uel alterius te
meritatis ruere permittit. Non ergo
talibus placere tibi cura est. sed illis q
amoris igne ab omni ignorantie labe
purgati ac uoluntati fortitudine ut i
sui amoris fructu suauissimo fruantur
honestis tantummodo moribus. facundo
lepidoque sermone. larga liberalitate
ac mansuetudine animi se gratos co
amatis adeo ostendunt ut eas conuer
tant in amantes. Hec tibi causa e
qr non unico et aperto stilo. s duplici
ac uelato gradieris in publicum. ut
sic solus ipse guilhelmus te noscat nec
claudicare. uel si qui sint i aliquo
illi sileat. s recto pede procedere. et
si ignorantia audaces te in oibus e
incultum et deformem uoluerint af
firmare. Te igitur corrigat ut lube
bit; humiles preces porrigere ne uere
re guilhelmo. cui milies et florium
suum recomissum face;
FINIS.

Ill. 5 Cambridge, University Library, MS Add. 8446, fol. 53r

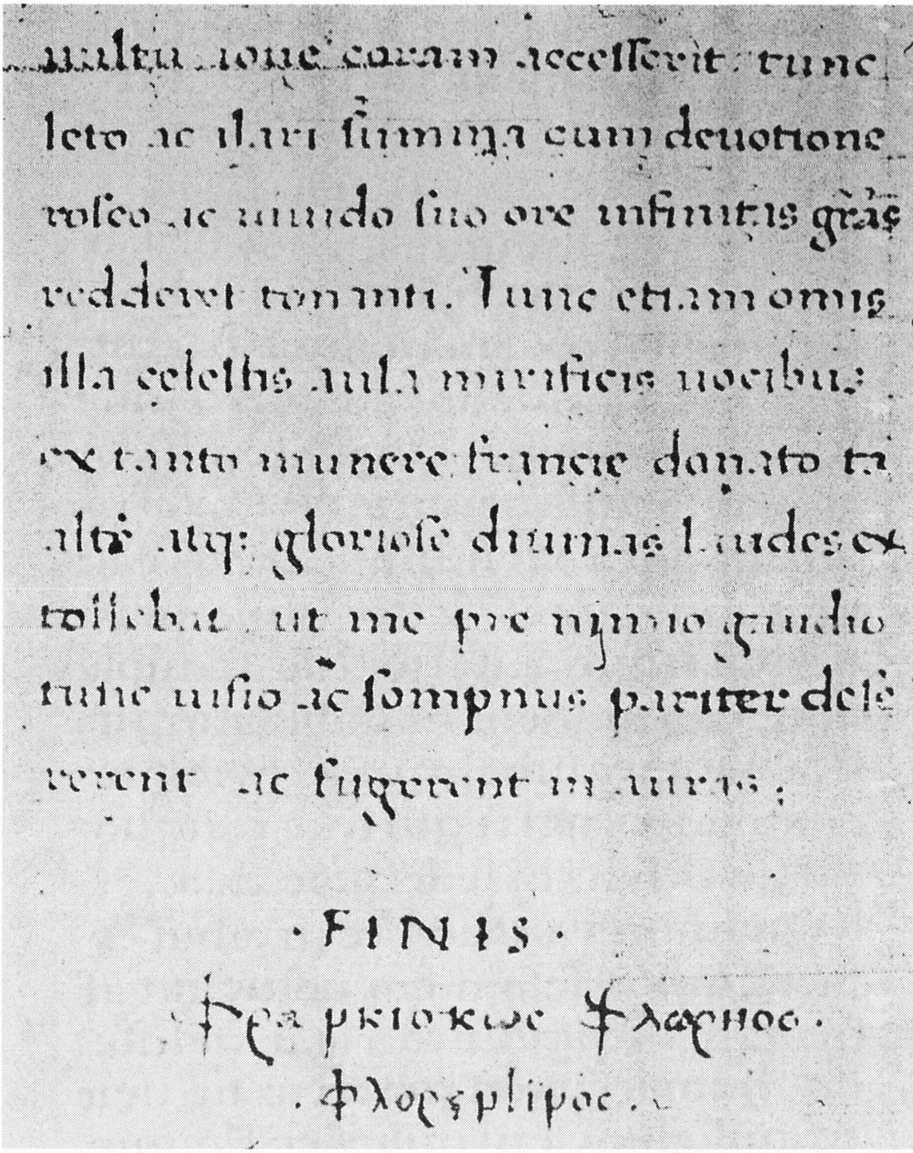

Ill. 6 Roma, Biblioteca Nazionale Centrale, MS V.E. 428, fol. 33r

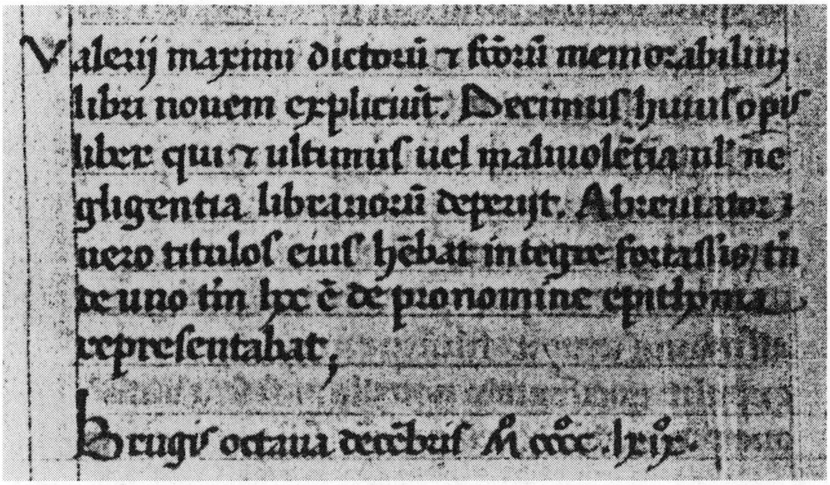

Ill. 7 Escorial, MS S.III.4, fol. 215v

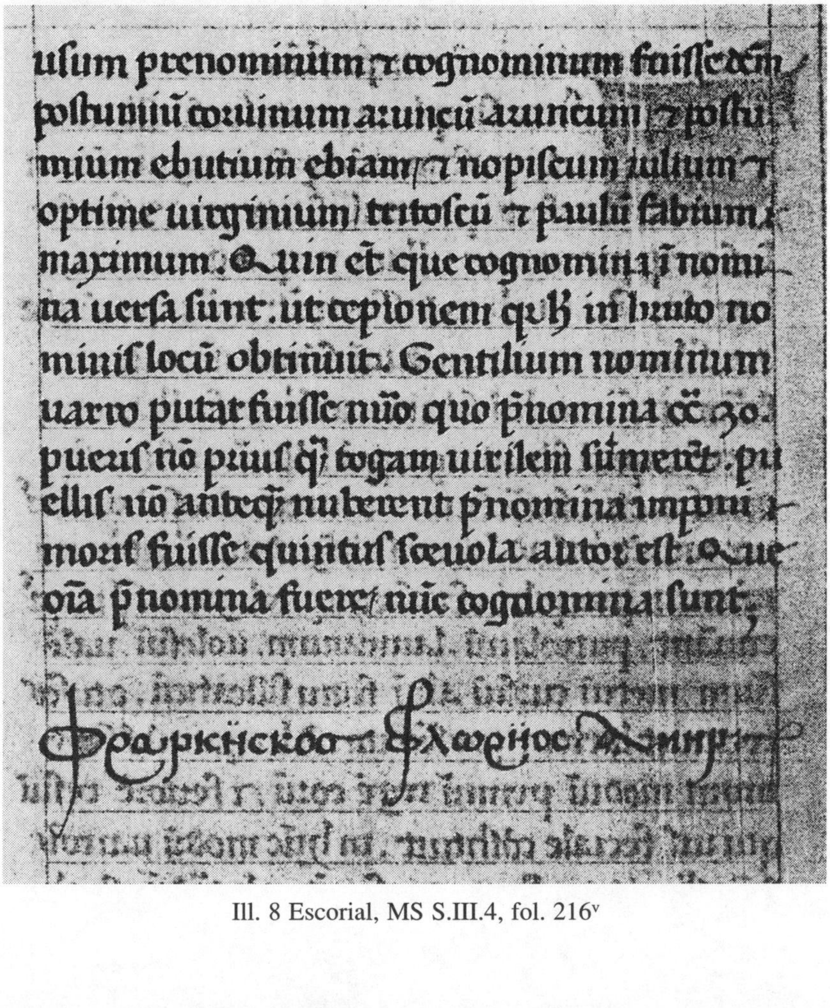

Ill. 8 Escorial, MS S.III.4, fol. 216v

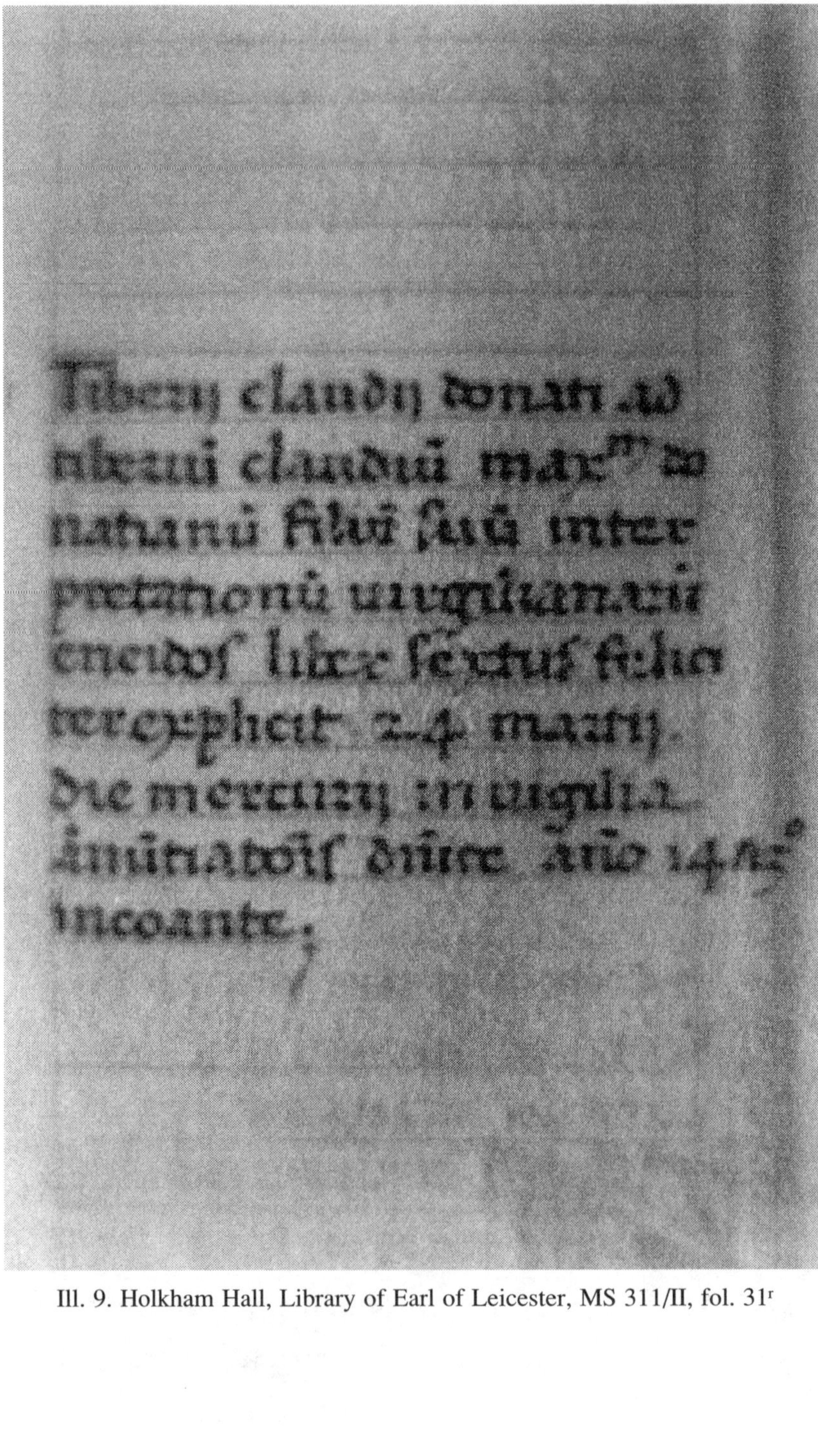
Tiberij claudij donati ad
tiberiũ claudiũ max.m do
natianũ filiũ suũ inter
pretationũ uirgilianarũ
eneidos liber sextus felici
ter explicit 24 martij
die mercurij in uigilia
ãnũtiatois dñice ãno 1465
incoante.

Ill. 9. Holkham Hall, Library of Earl of Leicester, MS 311/II, fol. 31r

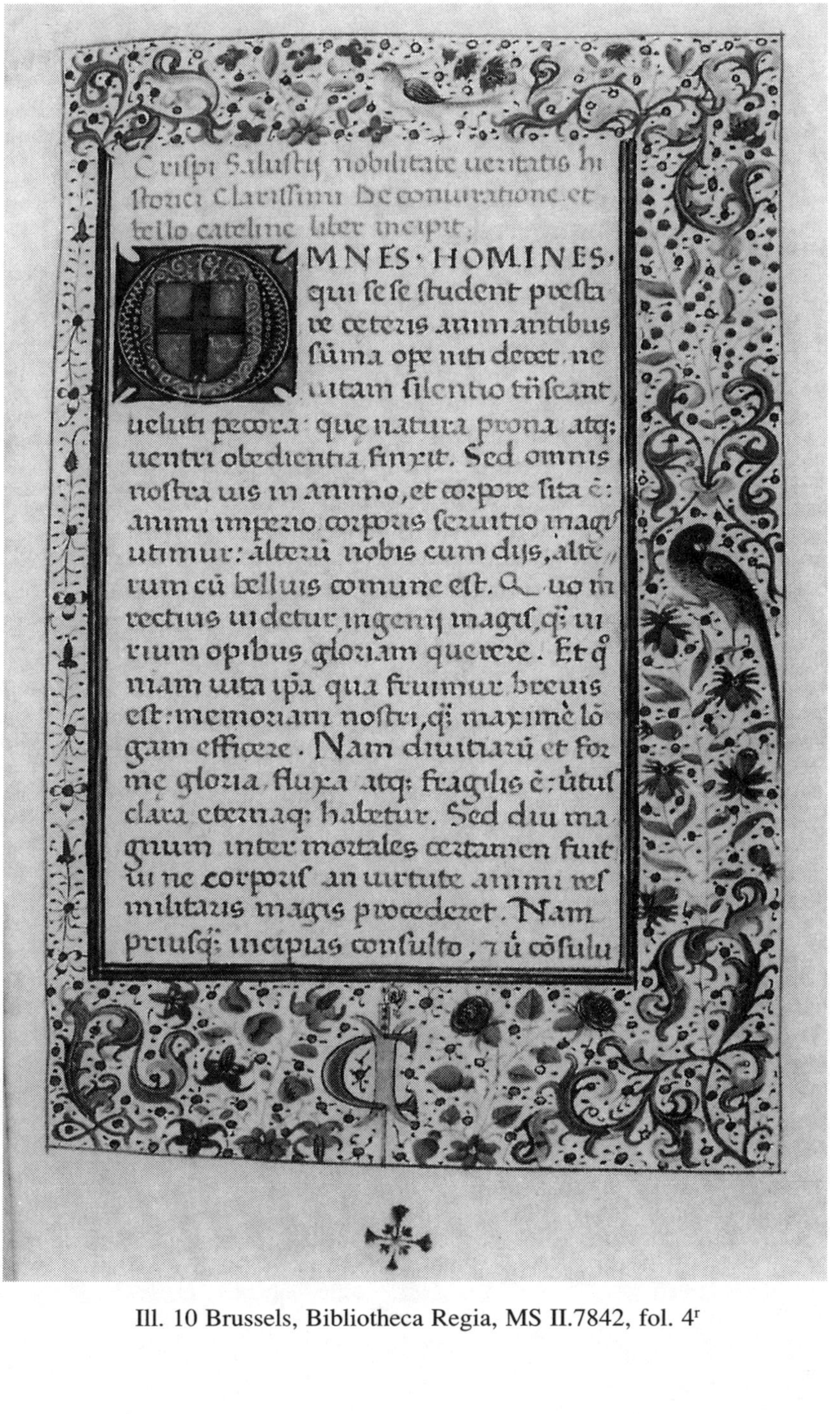

Ill. 10 Brussels, Bibliotheca Regia, MS II.7842, fol. 4r

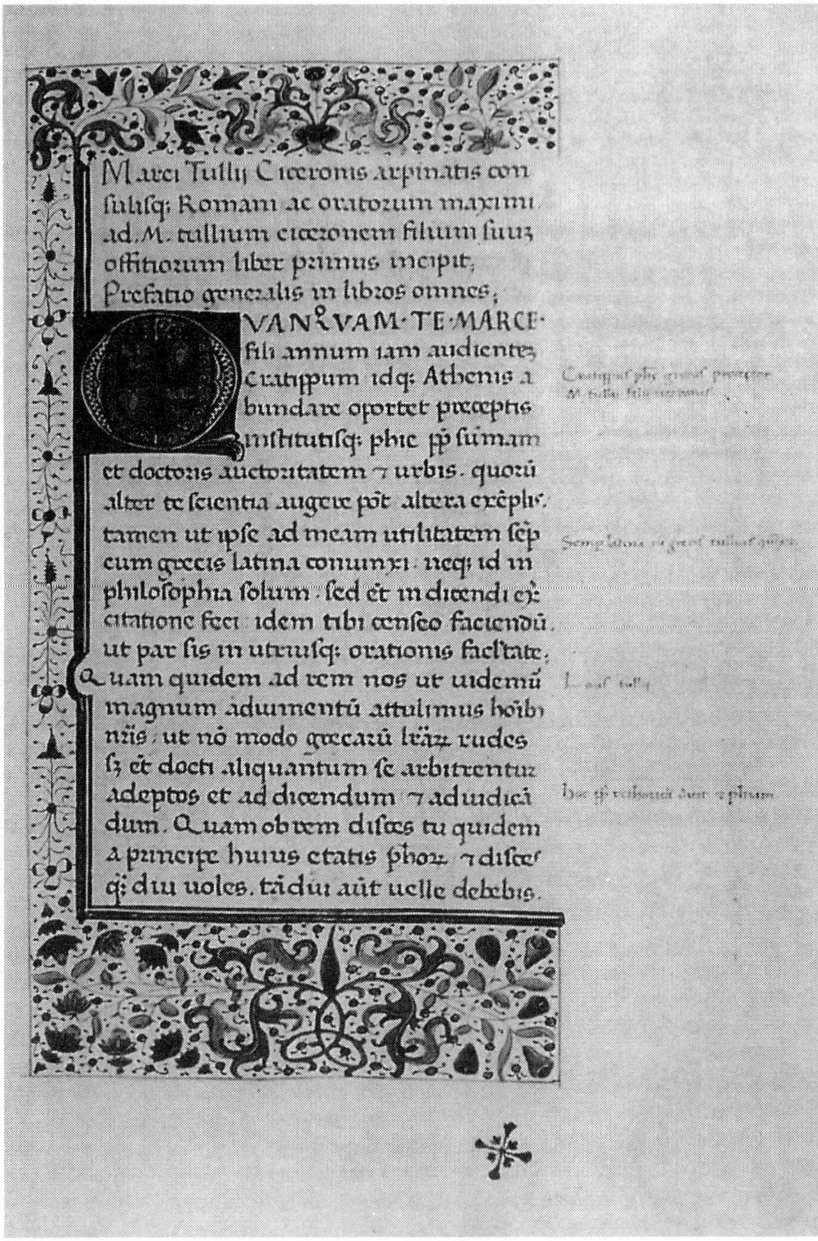
Marci Tullij Ciceronis arpinatis con
sulisq; Romani ac oratorum maximi
ad M. tullium ciceronem filium suu[z]
offitiorum liber primus incipit;
Prefatio generalis in libros omnes;
QVANQVAM TE MARCE
fili annum iam audientem
Cratippum idq; Athenis a
bundare oportet preceptis
institutisq; phie pp summam
et doctoris auctoritatem 7 urbis. quorū
alter te scientia augere pōt altera exēplis.
tamen ut ipse ad meam utilitatem sēp
cum grecis latina coniunxi. neq; id in
philosophia solum. sed et in dicendi ex
ercitatione feci idem tibi censeo faciendū.
ut par sis in utriusq; orationis facultate.
Quam quidem ad rem nos ut videmū
magnum adiumentū attulimus hoībi
nr̄is. ut nō modo grecarū lr̄az rudes
sz et docti aliquantum se arbitrentur
adeptos et ad dicendum 7 ad iudicā
dum. Quam ob rem disces tu quidem
a principe huius etatis phoz 7 disces
q; diu uoles. tādiu aūt uelle debebis.

Ill. 11 Brugge, Grootseminarie, MS 112/111, fol. 119r

Ill. 12 Cambridge, University Library, MS Nn.3.5, fol.121r

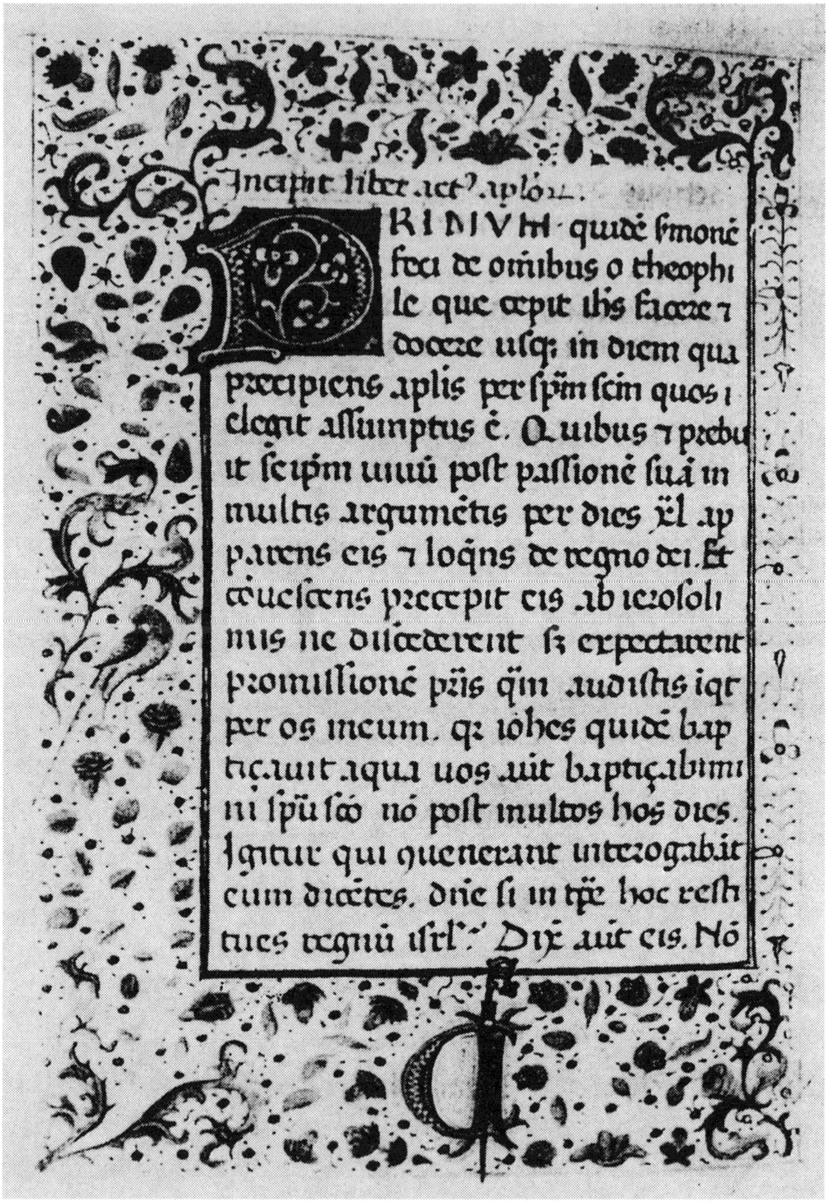

Ill. 13 Tournai, Cathédrale, Archives Capitulaires, MS 4, fol. 179v

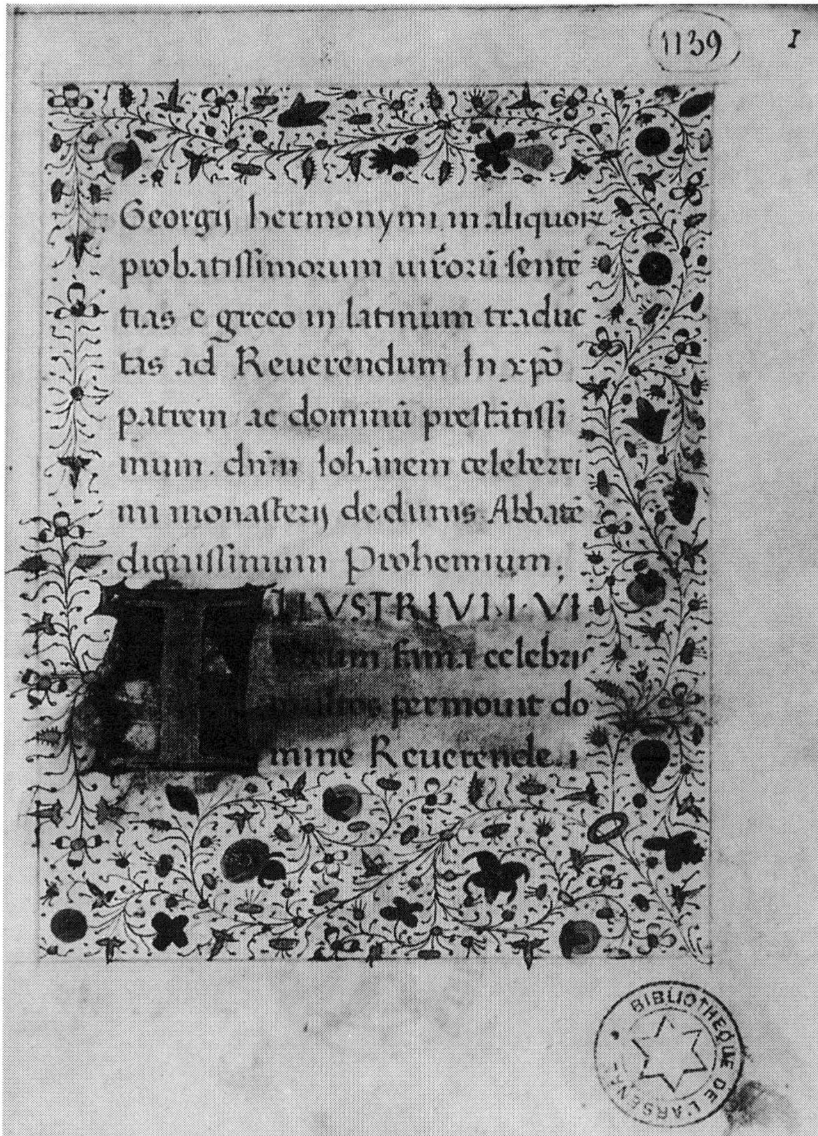
1139

Georgij hermonymi in aliquor
probatissimorum virorū sente
tias e greco in latinum traduc
tas ad Reuerendum in xpō
patrem ac dominū prestantissi
mum. dnm Iohanem celeberri
mi monasterij de dunis Abbatē
dignissimum Prohemium.
ILLVSTRIVM VI
rorum fama celebris
permount do
mine Reuerende

Ill. 14 Paris, Bibliothèque de l'Arsenal, MS 1139

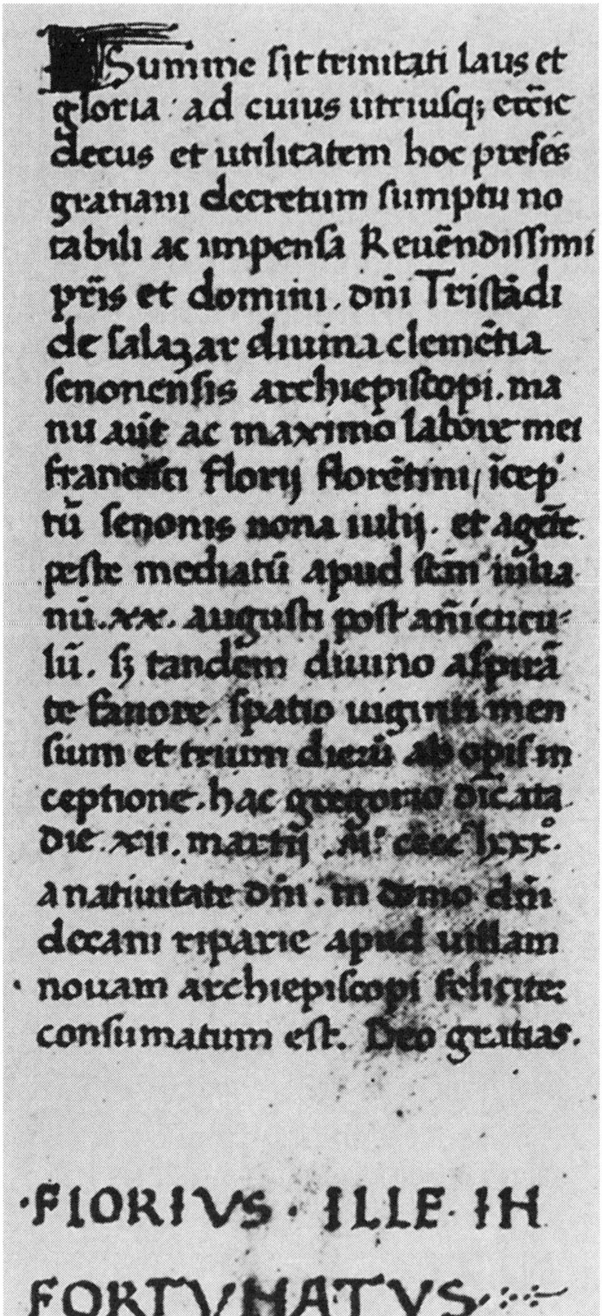

Summe sit trinitati laus et
gloria ad cuius utriusq; ecc̄ie
decus et utilitatem hoc presēs
gratiani decretum sumptu no
tabili ac impensa Reuēndissimi
p̄ris et domini. dñi Tristādi
de salazar diuina clemētia
senonensis archiepiscopi. ma
nu autem ac maximo labore mei
francisci flory florētini, icep
tū senonis nona iulij. et agēte
peste mediatū apud sctm iulia
nū .xx. augusti post añicircu
lū. s; tandem diuino aspirā
te fauore. spatio uiginti men
sium et trium dierū ab opis in
ceptione. hac gregorio dicata
die .xii. martij .M°. cccc lxx°.
a natiuitate dñi. in domo dñi
decani riparie apud uillam
nouam archiepiscopi feliciter
consumatum est. Deo gratias.

FLORIVS · ILLE · IN
FORTVNATVS

Ill. 15 Paris, Bibliothèque de l'Arsenal, MS 1183

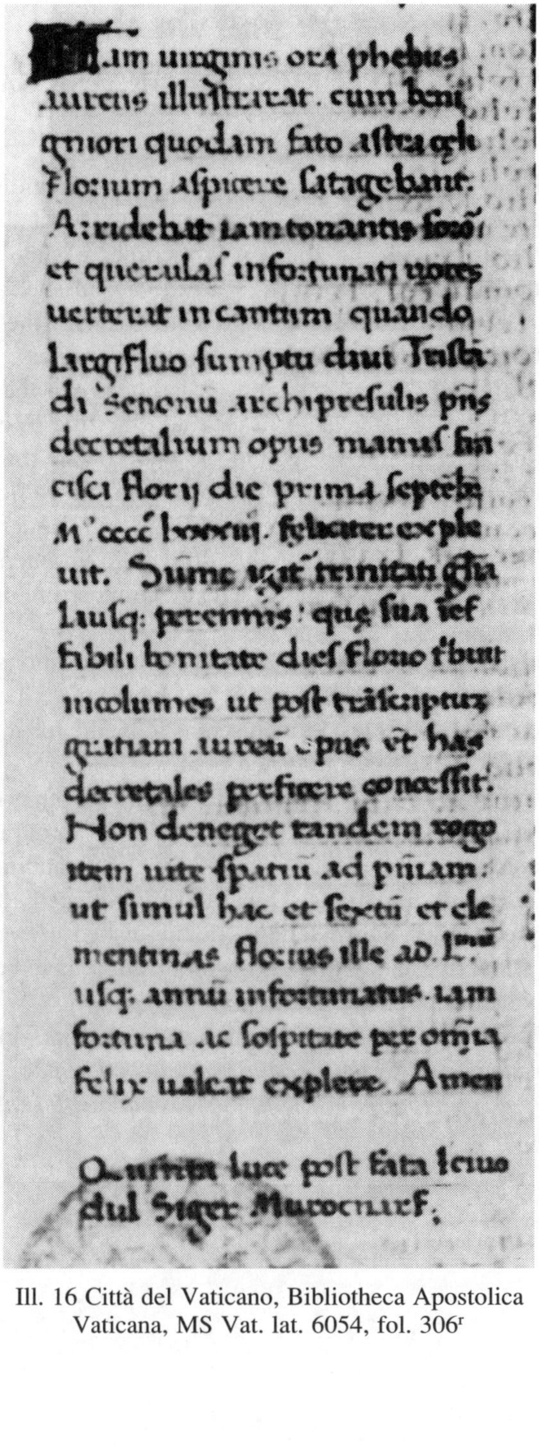

Iam uirginis ora phebus
aureus illustrarat. cum beni
gniori quodam fato astra celi
florum aspicere satagebant.
Arridebat iam tonantis fauor
et querulas infortunati uoces
uerterat in cantum quando
largifluo sumptu domini Tristi
di Senonum archipresulis pns
decretalium opus manus Fran
cisci Florij die prima septebris
M°cccc°lxxviij. feliciter exple
uit. Summe igitur trinitati gloria
lausque perennis: que sua ines
fabili bonitate dies Florio fbunt
incolumes ut post transcriptum
gratiani aureum opus et has
decretales perficere concessit.
Non deneget tandem rogo
item uite spatium ad primam:
ut simul hac et sextum et cle
mentinas Florius ille ad L^mum
usque annum infortunatus iam
fortuna ac sospitate per omnia
felix ualeat explere. Amen

Q̃uarta luce post fata lenio
dul Siger Mucocnarf;

Ill. 16 Città del Vaticano, Bibliotheca Apostolica Vaticana, MS Vat. lat. 6054, fol. 306r

APPENDIX

VISIO MIRABILIS FLORII SUPRA ARCANA GALLIAE

The only known MS is kept at Rome, Biblioteca Nazionale Centrale Vittorio Emanuele, MS V.E. 428. On the verso side of the cover two owners' marks are found: in the top left corner a small rectangular vignette of the Biblioteca Nazionale, with the actual shelf-mark 'MSS. Vitt. Eman. 428'; in the centre a large vignette with the arms of the Borghese family, encircled by the following text in capitals: 'Ex libris M. A. Principis Burghesii'. The first folio (I) is blank. On the recto of the second one (II) a much later hand has written the title 'Visio Mirabilis Florii supra arcana Galliae / 1544'. On the recto of the third folio (III), the same hand has written '1544. Die 8 xbris hora xxii in florentia tonuit et glandinavit', followed by some scribblings and, underneath these, 'Anno 1544'. On the verso side of this third folio an attempt has been made to restore the first lines of Florio's text: 'Gravi errore oppressus animus in arcem.'

The rest of the volume presents three different foliations: one in the top right corner, another in the bottom right-hand corner beneath, and a third at centre-bottom; this last, which seems to be the most recent, is the one indicated within the text published here.

In publishing this tract, I have generally respected the orthography of the manuscript, since we clearly have to do with an autograph. In order, however, to enhance the readability and ready understanding of the text, I have made a few modifications. Thus I have introduced a few emendations, silently expanded abbreviations, distinguished u/v and written ii instead of ij. Modern punctuation and capitalization have been provided and also a division into chapters and paragraphs.

As for references to classical authors and their works in the notes, I adopted the system used by the *Thesaurus Linguae Latinae... Index librorum scriptorum inscriptionum ex quibus exempla afferuntur*, 2nd edn (Leipzig: Teubner, 1990).

1.1. Gravi merore oppressus animus in arcem † mentis vires subductus [f. 1r] lilio † [1] qui postea quam nec voluntate nec ratione meo dolori potuerit prestare medelam, solis vitalibus naturalibusque virtutibus me valde turbatus dimisit. 2. Tum, cum maior tristitiae aditus pateret, ut oculi se in fontem converterent, lachrimarum copia data est, et nubila suspiria fractique singultus pectore procederent ex imo, ac si solum contra Fortunae acerbitatem impiasque fatorum dispositiones hoc mor/talibus favor esset [f. 1v] atque tutamen. 3. Angebat me profecto preteritorum eventuum memoria presentique mei vulneris dolori vim ministrabat, dum me solum Fortunae ludis expositum intendebam. Numquam enim mihi videbatur Fors aspera nimis vultu placido arrisisse, ni forte ut in eius fallaci confisum volubilitate me acrius in precipitium deiceret.

2.1. Verum post longas mei infortunii quaerelas, post uberrimum lachrimarum profluvium, ut victus ac lassus coelum unquam hausisse indignatus, secretum mei incolatus cubiculum solum mearum cogitationum conscium / fidissimum intravi, in quo non post multum temporis spatium [f. 2r] pressi oculi sompnum capere sunt coacti. 2. Hoc namque miseris unicum solamen est, hoc singulare ac precipuum refrigerium, quo mens turbata in lucem redit rationis, ad equalitatem humor incensus reducitur, refoventur spiritus, visque omnis naturalis lassa quietatur. 3. Sed dum sola fantasiae virtus otio potiri minime vellet, nec in quiete secura consistere, nescio quo tramite per devia vallium ac montium anfractus me in magnam ac tenebrosam cuiusdam silvae opacitatem perduxit.

3.1. Tunc novus pavor / exortus est, gelidusque tremor per ossa cucurrit[2]; [f. 2v] tunc mihi arrectae stetere comae et vox faucis hesit[3], dum non tantum varias beluarum formam inmaniumque ferarum ymagines prospicere visus sum, sed et tetra horrendaque monstra, quae non solum mihi natura timido, verum Alcidae orbis domitori[4] et talium visioni assueto, non parum timoris potuissent incutere. 2. Siquidem hinc inde centauri stabulabant, satyri atque silvani fauni ac Panes, hinc geminae Scillae, atque triformis Gerionis umbra, hinc centimanus Gigas[5] Lerneusque serpens una cum tristi Gorgone omnem mihi viam evadendi preclude-

1. The first lines have been rewritten. In an attempt to restore the original text the copyist corrupted a few words into '... subdursutilo'.
2. Cf. Verg. *Aen.* 8, 390: 'per ossa cucurrit.'
3. Cf. Verg. *Aen.* 2, 774: 'Obstipui steteruntque comae et vox faucibus haesit.'
4. Hercules; cf. Sen., *Herc. f.*, 619: 'ille domitor orbis.'
5. Cf. Hor. *carm.* 2, 17, 14 and 3, 4, 69: 'centimanus Gyges' ('gigas' in the mss.).

bant.[6] 3. Sicque omnis mihi spes / salutis septa atque occlusa erat, [f. 3r] ut sola mors, quam omni conamine appetebam, mihi solatio posset adesse. 4. Sed heu! Quam surda tunc aures a miseris avertit, cum totis vocibus eam invocant infoelices! 5. Tanta nempe angustia cor meum undique circumsepsit, ut illo in statu mihi et vita et mors pariter odio existerent.

4.1. Ceterum divinum illico mihi adfuit solamen, novique splendoris michi radius effulxit. 2. Nam cum nec rectus nec prostratus omnino iacerem, sed in ipso precipitio laborantem, mulier pulcerrima cadenti astitit, meeque cervici[7] iam deflexae supposuit levam, ac sua dextra meae superimposita dextrae[8] me pronum / ac in baratro ruentem supra pedes [f. 3v] rectum voluit consistere. 3. At ego infoelix acrius in eam visum figens faciem non mihi omnino ignotam prospexi, quae me tanto suae frontis claritate gaudio respersit, ut qui prius mortem desiderarem, tunc maxime vitam appetere videbar.

5.1. Haec paulo fixius in me oculorum suorum radios dirigens, 'Agnoscisne', inquit, 'nutricem, cuius lacte a pueritia alitus ac propriis in laribus educatus, postquam in magnum virum poteras evadere, eius doctrinam ac salutaria precepta despicere ac vilipendere non erubuisti? 2. Sed non tali omine te mihi sororibusque me/is educandum Apollo [f. 4r] tradidit atque Minerva, ut etsi coros nostros amenaque vireta contempneres, ego te tamen deserere aut tui oblivisci unquam possem.[9] 3. Sed quid nunc te in hoc baratro detrusit, nisi inconcessa Venus, insatiabilis Iuno, honoris ac reverentiae libido? Quae te nunc super vario bellorum eventu cogunt fluctuare? 4. Non quod ad te spectet quis fratrum victoria potiatur, sed quia ne longius tibi Cupido faveat pertimescis.

6. Cf. Verg. *Aen.* 6, 285-289:
Multaque praeterea variarum monstra ferarum,
Centauri in foribus stabulabant Scyllaeque biformes
et centumgeminus Briareus ac belua Lernae
horrendum stridens, flamisque aramata Chimaera,
Gorgones Harpyiaeque et forma tricorporis umbrae.

7. cervici *corr. ex* pernici *cod.*

8. Cf. Vulg. *cant.* 2, 6 and 8, 3:'Laeva eius sub capite meo, et dextera illius amplexabitur me.'

9. Cf. Boeth. *cons.* 1, 2, 1-4: 'Tum vero totis in me intenta luminibus: Tune ille es, ait, qui nostro quondam lacte alitus, nostris educatus alimentis in virilis animi robur evaseras? Atqui talia contuleramus arma quae nisi prior abiecisses invicta te firmitate tuerentur. Agnoscisne me? Quid taces? Pudore an stupore siluisti?'

6.1. Sed heu! quam facile per temetipsum ab hoc curarum sollicitudinumque onere poteras animum alleviare, si nostri alumpni Flacci documenta, quae ex Castalio nostro fonte potavit, sectasses: /

'Musis amicus tristitiam et metus [f. 4v]
Tradam protervis in mare Creticum
  Portare ventis, quis sub Artho
  Rex gelidae metuatur orae,

Quid Tiridaten terreat, unice
Securus'.[10]

3. An forte opinabaris philosophiae precepta sequi te minime posse, ni velut insanum ac magis fluctu mobile vulgus nos tanquam scenicas meretriculas[11] prius abiecisses? 4. Hic, arbitror, error fuit tuus, qui etiam complures amentes persaepe detinere solet. 5. Atqui gignasiis Caroli Aretini compatriotae tui nutritus, ore eius ac Venusini sententia eruditus, poteras hoc te solvere vinculo hereseos, cum non minus philosopho quocum/que gravi poetam vita pollere deceat ac moribus. [f. 5r]

7.1. Unde

'   quantas
Virtutes habeat sic collige: vatis avarus
Non temere est animus; versus amat, hoc studet unum;
Detrimenta, fugas servorum, incendia ridet.
Non fraudem sotio puerove incogitat ullam
Pupillo. Vivit siliquis et pane secundo.
Militiae quanquam piger et malus, utilis urbi,
Si das hoc, parvis quoque rebus magna iuvari.
Os tenerum pueri / balbumque poeta figurat, [f. 5v]
Torquet ab oscenis iam nunc sermonibus aurem,
Mox etiam pectus preceptis format amicis,
Asperitatis et invidiae corrector et irae.
Recte facta refert, orientia tempora notis.
Instruit exemplis, inopem solatur et egrum.
Castis cum pueris ignara puella mariti
Disceret unde preces, vatem ni Musa dedisset?

10. Cf. Hor. *carm.* 1, 26, 1-6. The text quoted by Florio is the one given in most manuscripts.

11. Boeth. *cons.* 1, 8: 'Quis, inquit, has scenicas meretriculas ad hunc aegrum permisit accedere.'

Poscit opem chorus, presentia numina sentit, /
Caelestes inplorat aquas, docta prece blandus, [f. 6r]
Avertit morbos, metuenda pericula pellit,
Impetrat et pacem et locupletem frugibus annum.
Carmine di superi placantur, carmine Manes.[12]

2. An haec tibi philosophiae preceptis adversari videntur, quae etiam nos colit ac veneratur? Sed auxilio nunc opus est, non tui nunc erroris correctione'. Et simul his dictis nescio quo tramite me in desideratam lucem restituit.

8.1. Non multis autem meam ductricem sum passibus assequtus, quod iuxta castellum quoddam / Pario lapide constructum[13] limpidissimoque [f. 6v] fluvio circumdatum perveni. 2. Huius profecto arx summa caelum tangere visa est, quae miris ac variis pretiosis lapidibus contexta iocundum subtilissimis intuitibus aspectum comprestabat. 3. O quam foelices tunc illius loci incolas fore ymaginabar. Intra tunc me ipsum tanto ardore accensus sum, ut arroganter aliquid mihi incondecens petivissem, ni meam salvatricem sua candida manu me semper tenentem erga portam tendere prospexissem. 4. Variis figuris in summo culmine portae velut quidam elementorum apices insigniti erant, qui etsi primo aspectu non multum aspi/cientes delectare viderentur, maximam tamen postea iocunditatem [f. 7r] comprestabant. 5. Hanc autem portam mulier quaedam perpulcra vestibus quatricoloribus ornata claudere sola atque aperire poterat, quae honesta tum virorum tumque puellarum caterva circumsepta meae ductrici aditum reverenter exhibuit.

9.1 Postquam ergo primam portam introgressi sumus, meorum oculorum visui quidam oblati sunt, qui lento gravique incessu eos qui mulieri illi proximiores erant sectabantur, inter quos reverendo aspectu quidam suo libello Latinam linguam clarius illustrans eminebat.[14] 2. Hunc prope ille erat qui fructus ac flores / Maronis impartiebatur;[15] cuius dextrum latus [f. 7v] tenebat qui barbari comici librum decoravit;[16] quem iuxta Acron,

12. Hor. *epist.* 2, 1, 118-138.

13. Paros was famous for its white marble. Cf., e.g. Hor. *Carm.* I, 19, 5, and Verg. *Aen.* I, 592: 'Pariusve lapis'.

14. Obviously Marcus Terentius Varro (116-27 BC), author of *De lingua Latina*.

15. Servius (4th cent. AD), who left an extensive commentary on Vergil.

16. Aelius Donatus, the 4th-century author of the celebrated commentary on Terence (*Commentum Terenti*).

Augelius[17], Nonius, Festusque pluresque alii assidebant. 3. At velut in partem quidam togatus quirinali solus sedebat, qui aliorum vestigia despiciens acribus morsibus antiquorum famam carpere nitebatur.[18] 4. Huic ex adverso Raudensis[19] etsi non tam veloci, gravi tamen gressu atrocique vultu restistebat, cui multum favoris Tortellus[20] comprestabat.

10.1. Horum ego visione letus cum ductrice fida ad secundam portam perveni, cui due mulieres ut custodes astabant, diversae forma ha/bituque non parum, quarum manu duas aspides gestabat una, visu terribilis [f. 8r] aspectuque severa, etsi comis impessis vesteque inculta appareret et maxime. 2. Huic multa profecto plebeia caterva famulabatur, quae in duas distincta partes equales: una verba solum fumumque terminorum; alia res cum verbis considerabat. 3. Hi quippe leves atque velut satiri dicaces subsannatoresque videbantur. Illi vero incessu graves et verbo aequa trutina verum discernebant a falso. 4. Verum altera quae cum hac muliere custos preerat portae non sic inhumano aut barbarico ritu / oculis se presentabat intuentium, sed veste quinque coloribus distincta [f. 8v] flores suavissimi odoris ambabus manibus gerebat. 5. Qui vero eius dexteram tenebant, quid fit, quidve in urbe fiendum subtili acie contemplabantur oculorum; qui vero sinistram, solum quod factum est iure vel iniuria ornato gratiosoque respectu curare videbantur. Hi profecto in tanta numerositate fulgebant, ut vix primiores (*sic*) etiam ex parte poteram agnoscere, inter quos nostri habitus Livius Patavinus, Veronensis Plinius, Trogus, Salustius, Curtius[21], atque Hebraicae sectae quidam[22] splendida clamide redimitus altius capita extollebant. / 6. Sed non minori gloria hi [f. 9r] qui illius mulieris dexterae adherebant, nitere videbantur, quorum primus

17. From the Middle Ages onwards quite common orthographic rendering of Aulus Gellius.

18. The Roman humanist Lorenzo Valla (*c.* 1405-1457), author of the *Elegantiarum Linguae Latinae libri sex.*

19. The adversary of Valla was Antonius Raudensis (*corr. ex* Randensis *cod.*), the Franciscan friar Antonio da Rho (°*c.* 1398). At first Valla was on good terms with the friar, and introduced him as an interlocutor in his dialogue *De vero falsoque bono* (Milan 1433). Later on their relationship deteriorated, and Valla dedicated to his good friend Tortelli his *In errores Antonii Raudensis adnotationes* (1443). Cf. Mariangela Regoliosi, 'Nuove ricerche intorno a Giovanni Tortelli. III. La vita di Giovanni Tortelli', *Italia Medioevale e Umanistica*, 12 (1969), 129-196 (pp. 137-138).

20. Giovanni Tortelli (Arezzo, *c.* 1400-1466). His favourable disposition towards Antonio da Rho is obviously most probably to be dated before the enmity between the Minorite and Valla arose.

21. Titus Livius (59 BC – 17 AD), author of the *Ab urbe condita libri* in 142 books; Gaius Plinius Secundus, born not at Verona, but at Como 23 AD, author of the encyclopaedic *Naturalis historia*; Pompeius Trogus, 1st cent. AD, author of the first universal history in Latin literature; and finally the historians Gaius Sallustius Crispus (86-23 BC) and Quintus Curtius Rufus (1st – 2nd cent. AD).

22. The Jewish historian Flavius Josephus (*c.* 37-110 AD).

ac velut in acie princeps Arpinas[23] rutilabat, quem Hyspanus quidam[24], quia eum precellere non potuit, non parum emulabatur. 7. Pari Arpinatis gradu ille incedebat Graecus[25], qui sua lingua diserta a furibundo Orientis domitore suam civitatem servavit; cui Eschines[26] velut invitus deferebat. 8. Transeo Gorgiam[27], taceo Vectorinum[28], atque complures innumerabiles quos obscura fama recondit. 9. Augebatur in horas gaudium atque per temporum momenta interna letitia gestire videbar, quando fida comes iterum se / accingebat ad iter. [f. 9v]

11.1. At postquam virenti prato variis ornato floribus tertiam portam attigimus smaragdis, topatiis ac omni pretioso lapide roboratam, coepi egomet stupidus tacite contemplari, si unquam Crassi[29] vel Attali[30] opes, Augusti an Macedonis[31] potentia, Dedali[32] ingenium vel Phidiae[33] aut Praxitellis[34] industria tale possent opificium proferre in lucem. 2. Atque dum concludebam mecum, virtute humana tale quid fieri impossibile fore, subito meis oculis mulier spetiosissima apparuit, quam tum pompa sublimi, tum superbo comitatu miratus sum illam meae ductrici exhibuisse honorem, / ac si ancilla potius quam domina extitisset. 3. Mirabar utique [f. 10r] ipsius oculis varios ac unum ex illis mobilem et summe, eiusque vestes aureas albo viridique colore flosculis contextas, quas miro quodam splendore divinus radius perlustrabat. 4. Eos inter qui illius stabilitatem contemplabantur summus cum suis Perypatheticis apparebat Aristoteles, quem duo propinquius sequebantur, et qui servus erat, precedere eius dominum conabatur. Hos turba innumera comitabatur Latio Achivoque

23. Marcus Tullius Cicero, born at Arpinum 106 BC.

24. Marcus Fabius Quintilianus, born *c.* 35 AD. at Calagurris in Spain.

25. Demosthenes, 384-322 BC, who delivered four *Philippics* against King Philip of Macedon.

26. Aeschines (first half of 4th cent. BC), pupil of Socrates, author of the *Dialogi*.

27. The famous sophist Gorgias (480-380 BC).

28. Fabius Marius Victorinus, celebrated professor of Roman rhetoric (4th cent. AD).

29. The cognomen 'Crassus' was bequeathed to a branch of the gens Licinia; several members of this family were so famous for their riches that they were explicitly called 'Dives', an attribute which is attested from the time of P. Licinius Crassus Dives (*c.* 240-183 BC); some other prominent members of the family were P. Licinius Crassus Dives Mucianus (*c.* 180-130 BC) who supported the Gracchi, and M. Licinius Crassus Dives, the triumvir (†53 BC); cf. Cic. *off.* 1, 25 and Plin. *nat.* 33, 134.

30. Attalus I (269-197 BC), the first king of Pergamum, whose wealth was proverbial.

31. Alexander the Great (356-323 BC).

32. Daedalus was an Athenian craftsman and inventor, who built in Crete the labyrinth to house the Minotaur for King Minos who imprisoned him there later on; but Daedalus escaped together with his son Icarus on waxed feather wings.

33. Phidias (active at Athens *c.* 465-425 BC) was considered by the ancients to be the greatest of Greek sculptors; cf. Quint. *inst.* 12, 10, 9 and Plin. *nat.* 36, 15-19.

34. Praxiteles was another famous Athenian sculptor, active *c.* 357-330 BC; cf. Plin. *nat.* 36, 20-21.

ritu decorata, quae clara vestigia posteris leta relinquebat. 5. Plato vero cum suis Achademicis / pari gressu discipulum assotiabat Aristotelem, cui [f. 10v] non parum honoris ac famae Plotinus[35] reddere videbantur. 6. Sed mulieris[36] levam Socrates tenebat atque Crisippus[37] cum Stoicis, quibus ex adverso Aristippus[38] cum fratre magna cum societate resistebat eundo. 7. Hi omnes variis habitu cultuque ornati dominam sequebantur quocumque ibat. Quae suo aspectu uno eodemque intuitu primam omnium causam simul cum creaturis ac moribus prospiciebat.

12.1. Modo simili cum mea ductrice lento gradu per quatuor alias portas intravi, in quarum qualibet mulier formosa presidens extabat magna comitante caterva: quae omnes reveren/do suo aspectu animos intuentium alliciebant. [f. 11r] 2. Et harum alia varias figuras, alia numeros, alia modulationum proportiones, et quarta ipsa sidera et solem et lunam cum firmamento acuta subtilique indagine considerare videbantur.

13.1. At postquam portarum ultimam cum fida comite ingressus sum, in amenissimum pratum amplum spatiosumque deveni, arboribus variis consitum[39], quod clarus pulcerque rivus nunquam irrigare cessabat. 2. Tum ibi propriis suis manibus me totum in fluvio lavit perdocta nutrix, ter me in illo submergens, adeo ut pene multum ex aqua illa ore hauserim invitus. 3. Cum vero de me / fecit ut voluit, nescio quo modo aut via fluvium post [f. 11v] terga reliqui indutus. Tum ibi suavissimus ut mihi videbatur avium concentus[40] aures demulcebat, tum clarissimo intuitu Proserpinam atque Phebum[41] sidereaque omnia lumina prospiciebam. 4. Non ibi turbida Iuno[42] regnabat aut Eolus[43], non Vulcanus vorax aut frigidus Boreas, sed aura quaedam levis non profundis emissa cavernis, nec humores corrumpens, sed eorum conservans equalitatem totum illud hemisperium perflabat. 5. Tales quidem opinor finxisse poetas Insulas existere Fortunatas vel campos illos Elisios, quos Grae-/cia quandoque mirari solebat.[44] [f. 12r]

35. Neoplatonist philosopher AD 205-269/70.
36. mulieris *corr. ex* mulieres: *cod.*
37. Chrysippus of Soli (*c.* 280-207 BC) succeeded Cleanthes as head of the Stoa in 232.
38. Aristippus of Cyrene (*c.* 435 – *c.* 366 BC), an associate of Socrates, was, according to Xenophon, the champion of sybaritic hedonism. He often gets confused with his grandson of the same name, who founded the Cyrenaic school.
39. Cf., *e.g.*, Ov. *met.* 1, 598: 'consitaque arboribus.'
40. Cf., e.g., Verg. *georg.* 1, 422.
41. The moon and the sun.
42. Cf. Stat. *silv.* 3, 4, 14-15: 'quem turbida semper / Iuno videt.'
43. Aeolus, the mythic king of the Aeolian Islands, who was given control over the winds by Jupiter.
44. Cf. Verg. *georg.* 1, 38: 'quamvis Elysios miretur Graecia campos.'

14.1. At dum taciti voluptuosum illud viridarium perambulabamus, in partem venimus ubi secreta atque mirabilia videre nescio quo fato mihi concessum est, quae vix mens unquam potuit concipere humana aut lingua explicare mortalis; atque dum magis in lucem quod vidi atque audivi nunc aedere conor, tanto profundius confundor in me ipso. 2. Saepe namque humanus intellectus apprehendere videtur, quod tamen ob rei excellentiam lingua nequit verbis explicare. Mihi quidem tunc supra me ipsum rapto videbar divinae spetiei / aliquam similitudinem degustare, quae adeo animum [f. 12v] meum interno gaudio ac letitia perfundebat, ut absque omni sensuum operatione beatum esse me censerem. 3. At dum locum locique amoenitatem contemplabar, Apollinem sua lyra personare prospexi, qui cum suis puellis ad sonum illum dulcissimum suavissime cantantibus coelestem illam militiam summa iocunditate delectabat. 4. Ibi Diana cum suis sacratis nimphis choros ducebat, modo atque arte imperceptibili, quae non solum astantes, sed antiquum illum etiam dierum <dominum>[45] ad gaudium videbatur allicere, qui cum sua Minerva beatus / in se existens et solus suo [f. 13r] divino sceptro et summas et infimas causas regens atque in suos disponens fines minima etiam quaeque gubernabat.

15.1. Ego vero dum mecum tacitus in tantam maiestatem, omnipotentiam summamque illius sophiam ac bonitatem infinitam mentis meae oculos defigebam atque caetera despiciens solum in tantae gloriae contemplatione distractus permanebam, tanto coram Deo ac maiestatis splendore mulierem quippe formosam per Cyllenes filium[46] presentari conspexi. 2. Haec profecto etsi substantia mortalis[47] erat, forma tamen et dignitate una videbatur multum dilecta Tonanti, cuius ve-/stes zaphiri colorem aureaque [f. 13v] lilia effingebant. 3. Hanc quidem venerandam aspectu atque habitu mulierem complures nimphae sectabantur, quae omnes etsi gravi incessu, moesto tamen vultu atque demisso procedebant; inter quas una caeteris formosior illius dominae dexteram humero sustentabat.

16. 1. Postquam vero devota ac supplex propius accessit, sic obortis lacrimis[48] roseo suo ore[49] in haec verba suaviter prorupit. 2. 'Gemens ac

45. The reading of the MS 'dierum' needs correction. Obviously Jupiter is meant here; instead of adding a word such as 'dominum' or 'patrem', one could perhaps read 'Diovem' instead of 'dierum'.

46. Cyllene is a mountain in Arcadia, where Mercury was born; cf. Verg. *Aen.* 4, 258: 'Cyllenia proles'.

47. Cf. Mart. Cap. 2, 141: 'quippe caducae mortalisque substantiae istaec esse munimina memorabat.'

48. Classical iunctura; cf., *e.g.*, Verg. *Aen.* 3, 492; 4, 30; 6, 867; 11, 41; Ov. *met.* 4, 684; 6, 495; 7, 689; 10, 419, etc.

49. Classical iunctura; cf., *e.g.*, Verg. *Aen.* 2, 593 and 9, 5.

supra modum pavida tremendum tuae hodie maiestatis tribunal adii, o, qui
solus res hominum deorumque / regis, universi arbiter ac rector, summe [f. 14r]
Iuppiter, supplici prece expostulans ut meis quaerelis aures benignus
parumper accomodes, atque si dignae sint eterna tua infallibilique pro-
videntia, qua totum legibus orbem gubernas, tandem meis erumpnis atque
calamitatibus miseratus finem imponas et modum. 3. Neque enim in me
ipsa diffidere possum te solum pium atque clementem, cuius proprietas
summa est misereri semper et parcere, meis votis acquiescere debere,
cum non nisi apud te potestas mihi succurrendi sit, apud neminem sapi-
entia nisi in te consistat, nulla mea nisi in te / spes firma atqua confiden- [f. 14v]
tia quiescit. 4. Nec de tua in me voluntate benigna male opinari phas est,
quae sola vult omnes salvos fieri atque in suum tandem finem ultimum
devenire. 5. Bella fremunt,[50] fratres bella minantur[51], o summi Olimpi
rector[52], iam lituus ac tuba praelia cient, iam sonipes ungula terram fodit[53],
et gladio accinctus eques alterno milite currens mortem adversario
machinatur. 6. Mars sanguineus, quem solus cruor delectat[54], acies in bel-
lum movet et armata Pallas[55] torvis oculis[56] hastam quatit indesinenter.
7. Iterum Tenari[57] claustra panduntur, et dirae Stigii[58] lacus aves[59] per
viridia prata Gal-/liarum benignos animos in furorem accendentes vagan- [f. 15r]
tur. 8. O quot animae Acherontia[60] littora videre festinant! Quo parva

50. Cf. Stat. *Theb.* 3, 568-569: 'iam bella tubaeque / comminus absentesque fremunt sub pectore Thebae.'

51. Florius alludes here to the revolt of the French high nobility against Louis XI (the War of the Public Weal), which lasted from March to October 1465. This rebellion was supported by the Duke of Burgundy, Philip the Good, and his son Charles, Count of Charolais, by the Duke of Brittany, François II, by the Count of Armagnac Jean V, by the Duke of Bourbon and even by Louis' own younger brother Charles, Duke of Berry (1446-24/25 May 1472). A very detailed account of these events is to be found in Philippe de Commynes, *Mémoires*, édités par Joseph Calmette. Vol. I (1464-1474), 2nd ed. (Paris, 1964). See also Henri Stein, *Charles de France, frère de Louis XI* (Paris, 1921), passim.

52. Cf. Verg. *Aen.* 7, 558: 'summi regnator Olympi.'

53. Cf. Verg. *Aen.* 8, 595-596: 'it clamor, et agmine facto / quadripedante putrem sonitu quatit ungula campum.'

54. Sen. *Herc.f.* 403 'bella delectat cruor.'

55. Sen. *Ag.* 529: 'armata Pallas quidquid aut hasta minax.'

56. Ov. *met.* 5, 92: 'ille tuens oculis inmitem Phinea torvis.'

57. The Taenarum was a promontory in Laconia, the south-eastern district of the Peloponnese, where an entrance to Hades was situated.

58. The Styx: a river in the Underworld, and hence the Underworld itself.

59. The Harpies, mythological monsters, half bird and half woman; cf. Verg. *Aen.* 3, 262:'Dirae obscenaeque volucres', and 3, 214-215:

Tristius haud illis monstrum, nec saevior ulla
pestis et ira deum Stygiis sese extulit undis.

60. This adjective does not occur in classical or later Latin, where one finds the forms 'Acheronteus' or 'Acheronticus'. The Acheron is the river in the Underworld, that had to be crossed by Charon transporting the souls of the dead in his boat ('cymba').

cimba iam premitur pondere Gallorum! Quis unquam inter tuae omnipotentiae cultores audivit talia vel similia contigisse? 9. An, o summi regnator coeli, in me miseram Thebana fata[61] conversa sunt, ut nunc velut alter Pollinices Ethioclem ferro petat regnantem frater atque collecto undique milite non Thebas sed et Thebis et Argis nobiliorem potentioremque tui cultus gloriam atque decus urbem Parisiam, mei regni caput ac meae fortitudinis fundamentum gravissima obsidione premat? 10. Hinc siquidem / agros Burgundi vastant, hinc Britanni effreni pauperum tecta [f. 15v] solo diripiunt, hinc Armaniacus eques omnia intercipit, ac Borbonius armiger omnia vastat in vindictam.[62] 11. Et quae michi spes tot angustiis oppressae relinquitur? Quod mihi auxilium aut unde nisi ex te potest adesse? Heu mihi parum liceat mea infortunia deflere, ut sic saltem solatio miserae mihi lachrimae existant.

17.1. Ego quae quondam sola tua dispensatione mari videbar imperare ac terris, nunc meis viribus premor atque confundor. 2. Laudes ac ingentia facta Caroli transeo Martelli maiora / adhuc taceo Pipini. Ad magnum meum Ca- [f. 16r] rolum[63] devenio, qui ob eius mirifica gesta id Magni cognomen adeptus est, quod Macedo ille Alexander orbe subacto, et Gneus Pompeius, et Constantinus primus clarissimis rebus meruere.[64] 3. Hic enim Normanis, Aquitanis, Saxonibus totiens religioni tui Unigeniti rebellantibus Christi iugum imposuit suave.[65] Hic Ungaros coercuit, Lombardos contrivit, Graecos ex Apulia expulit, ex Trinacria Saracenos deturbavit, citeriorem Hispaniam ex Maurorum manibus eripuit. Hic Anthiochiam, Tholomaidam, Alexandriam atque nostrae / salutis officinam Ierosolimam ex barbarorum dentibus extraxit. 4. [f. 16v] Hic usque ad Eufraten et Tigrin crucis vexillum portavit, ac ipsam Mesopotamiae urbem Christiano nomini gloriose restituit.[66] Hic vexatam atque omnibus modis a tyrannis oppressam apostolicam sedem in pristinam

61. Eteocles and Polynices were the two sons of Oedipus who had agreed to reign in alternative years over Thebes. When Eteocles refused to give up the throne at the end of his first year, a fierce battle was fought in which the two brothers killed each other.

62. The allies in the revolt against Louis XI marched from all sides towards Paris. The Count of Charolais, who came from the north, pitched camp on 3 July 1465 between Saint-Denis and Paris. His army defeated that of Louis XI on 15 July at Monthléry. The King retired to Paris, which for several weeks remained besieged. See Commynes, *Mémoires*, pp. 15-51 and Stein, *Charles de France*, pp. 89-99.

63. Charles Martel (*c.* 676-741), his son Pepin III (the Short, 714-768) and his grandson Charlemagne (*c.* 742-814).

64. That is, Charlemagne deserved the same surname as Alexander the Great (356-323 BC), Gnaeus Pompeius Magnus (106-48 BC) and Constantine I the Great (*c.* AD 273-337). A similar idea in F. Petrarch, *fam.* 1, 4, 7 'Carolum regem quem Magni cognomine equare Pompeio et Alexandro audent.'

65. Vulg. Matth. 11, 30: 'Iugum enim meum suave est, et onus meum leve.'

66. Charlemagne indeed christanized the Saxons in the north, defeated the powerful tribe of the Avars on the Danube, and conquered the kingdom of the Lombard king

libertatem atque gloriam reduxit.[67] 5. Non ignota tibi loquor, cuius oculus non tantum mortalium facta, sed et renes et corda atque cogitationes rimatur.[68] Quid ultra mei sponsi preconia commemoro, qui etiam tuae tantum placuit maiestati ut Romanorum rex esset semper Augustus et mihi / imponeret coronam? [f. 17r]

18.1. At nunc misera, quae tantis totque quondam preclaris titulis fui illustrata, ad quid devenerim considera. Me mei lacerant, et qui me hactenus soliti sunt defendere, nunc illi acrius me pro libito dilaniant. 2. Sed parva quidem adhuc sunt ista, si inter duos germanos Mars nunc seviat furibundus.[69] Neque enim aliud michi persuadere valeo, quam si equorum armos calcaria urgeant, unus vel eorum alter, vel quod magis mihi timendum est, ambo pariter laetali vulnere confossi pereant omnino. 3. Et quid tum vidua factura sum infoelix? Cui me barbaro iunges? Saltem si qua mihi / de meo Lodovico soboles suscepta fuisset, si quis [f. 17v] mihi ante eius mortem parvulus aula Lodovicus luderet, qui eum tantum ore referret ac moribus, non equidem mihimet nunc sic omnino capta aut deserta viderer.[70] 4. Haec nunc mihi causa potissima est, qua vexor amplius atque sollicitor, ut meis quaerelis tuas aures offendam. Invaserunt me quondam barbaro more, qui ex ultima Britannia[71]

Desiderius in 773-74; but he never went on a crusade. The first trace of an alleged crusade by Charlemagne is to be found in the work of Benedetto di Sant'Andrea del Monte Soratte (10th-11th cent.). See in general G. Paris, *Histoire poétique de Charlemagne* (Paris, 1865; 1905 = repr. 1974). Florio's enthusiastic excursus on the deeds of Charlemagne thus contains a curious mixture of historical facts and legends (*e.g.* the conquest of Jerusalem and Babylon), which was quite common in his days and appears also, for instance, in the *Carlias*, the epic written by his contemporary Ugolino Verino (1438-1516); see the critical edition by Nikolaus Thurn, *Carlias* (München, 1995), and Id., *Kommentar zur Carlias des Ugolino Verino* (München, 2002), pp. 186-187 and *passim*.

67. When Pope Leo III (796-816) was attacked by members of his predecessor's family, he betook himself in 799 to Charlemagne's protection at Paderborn. A few months later Charlemagne went to Rome and conducted a trial, during which Leo III successfully defended himself against the charges of his enemies. On Christmas day 800 he crowned Charlemagne emperor.

68. Cf. Vulg. *Psalm.* 7, 10: 'scrutans renes et corda, Deus', and *Ierem.* 17, 10: 'Ego Dominus scrutans cor et probans renes'.

69. Cf. Sen. *Thy.*, 556-557: 'quem movet crebro furibundus ictu / sanguinem Mavors cupiens recentem.'

70. This entire passage is taken from Verg. *Aen.* 4, 327-330:
Saltem si qua mihi de te suscepta fuisset
ante fugam suboles, si quis mihi parvulus aula
luderet Aeneas, qui te tamen ore referret,
non equidem omnino capta ac deserta viderer.'

71. An allusion to the long war between England and France (1337-1453), the 'Hundred Years War'. For the Ancients Great Britain was at the end of the world, hence 'ultima'; cf., for instance, Catull. 19, 4: 'ultima Britannia', and 11,11-12: 'ultimosque Britannos'; Hor. *carm.* 1, 35, 29-30: 'in ultimos / orbis Britannos.'

sumpserunt originem, mihi semper infaesti Anglici, candidaque mea atque pulcerrima membra obsceno ritu contaminarunt. Nulla mihi mei corporis solida aut firma pars erat / ipsumque caput undique fluctua- [f. 18v] bat.

19.1. Et cum tot angustiis premerer,[72] tot laboribus urgerer, tot anxiarer erumpnis, nunquam tuas aures obtudi, nunquam tuam pacem quaerulis vocibus infaestavi, sed pene sine dote gremio illo meo paupere sponsum meum, Carolum septimum, utcumque modo poteram, confovebam. 2. Cui tandem abs te auxilium presto adfuit, ac divina tua potentia infra breve temporis spatium me totam integraliter recuperavit. Siquidem sua providentia Burgundorum animos sibi conciliavit[73], Anglicos toto regno dispersos ex Gallis, Nor- /manis Aquitanisque finibus deturbavit atque [f. 18v] vi expulsos omnes inglorios ad propria compulit remeare. 3. Quis unquam Romanorum pro suae rei publicae salute conservanda vel ea augenda amplius effecerit? Laudatur quippe Fabius, qui suo consilio et arte <et> cunctatione vires conservavit Romanas[74], sed neque Fabii neque Marcelli[75] laudes, ymo pene Cornelii Scipionis[76] mei sponsi laudibus equiparandas censeo, cuius profecto preconia potius cum magni Caroli laudibus decertare videntur. 4. Namque ille regnum meum ampliavit, quod tamen prius integrum acceperat, hic con- /fractum atque [f. 19r] destructum in pristinam gloriam reduxit. Ille exteras nationes potentia sua Gallorum subiecit imperio; hic non nisi virtute ex alto solus ac nudus barbaros exclusit e regno. Ille Romano ritu psalmodiam voluit cantari in Galliis, hic vero in tantum ecclesias ecclesiasticosque viros decore eximio sublimavit, ut Romana ecclesia Gallico nunc cantu

72. Cf. Vulg. 1. *Par.* 21, 13: 'ex omni parte me angustiae premunt' and *Ruth*, 1, 13; 'angustia magis me premit'.

73. An allusion to the treaty of Arras (1435) between Philip the Good and Charles VII.

74. Quintus Fabius Maximus Verrucosus Cunctator (c. 275-203 BC), who by his cautious strategy avoided a major Roman defeat by Hannibal.

75. Marcus Claudius Marcellus (d. 208 BC) served in the First Punic War and played also an important role in the war against Hannibal. He conquered Syracuse in 212 BC.

76. Publius Cornelius Scipio Africanus Maior (236-183 BC), who defeated Hannibal at the battle of Zama in 202. His fame was immortalized in Petrarch's *Africa* and again in a short prose tract; see Guido Martellotti, 'La *Collatio inter Scipionem Alexandrum Hannibalem et Pyrrum*. Un inedito del Petrarca nella biblioteca della University of Pennsylvania', in *Classical, Mediaeval and Renaissance Studies in Honor of B. L. Ullman*, ed. by Charles Henderson Jr., II (Rome, 1964), pp. 145-168. Another major source was the immensely popular Latin translation of the twelfth *Dialogue of the Dead* of Lucian, dealing with the comparison of the virtues of Alexander the Great, Scipio and Hannibal. It was composed in 1425 by the Italian humanist Giovanni Aurispa (c. 1375-1459) who, however, radically changed the ending, awarding the first place to Scipio instead of to Alexander the Great. See David Cast, 'Aurispa, Petrarch and Lucian: An Aspect of Renaissance Translation', *Renaissance Quarterly*, 27 (1974), 157-173.

gaudeat in divinis. Ille crucem ad exteros portavit, hic intraneos purgavit erroribus.[77]

20.1. Et quid plura? Adeo sponso illo meo letata sum, ut in illo etatem septimam regni finisse, et incipisse octavam / non inmerito dixerim; quem [f. 19v] si fata virum paulo longius servassent, iterum Ierosolima illum[78] quem cruci affixit adoraret.

2. At posteaquam illum vita Lachesis spoliavit, ymo tua miseratio, Iuppiter, eum morte denudavit ac incorruptibili veste voluit decorare, tanti me viri privatione afflictam moestamque omnino tua clementia novo sponso, eius primogenito[79], voluit consolari, qui suo ingressu adeo foelix beatusque fuit, ut numquam me virum meminerim habuisse, qui vel eo magis pacifice, vel universalius integraliusque regnum meum sumpserit ad tempus.

3. Sed heu! Fortuna viris invida fortibus; quae non equa bonis premia dividis![80]/ Ecce namque hi qui paulo ante meo sponso famulari videban- [f. 20r] tur, eiusque semper obtemperare mandatis sacramenta fidelitatis praestitere, nunc illi mihique in arcum sunt pravum conversi, nunc me ludibrio exponere conantur.

4. Hic namque me per bracchia trahit; hic mihi comas evellit; alter me per crura detinens iam pene in terram deicit; hic mecum satagit fornicari; alius verbis, alter muneribus me corrumpere nititur.

5. Et quod peius est, o Iuppiter summe, atque omnino facinore quocumque scelestius, rabidus leo intra meum sinum[81] armata manu sponsum meum ense nudo[82] ausus est appetere / ac si ego, misera Francia, obscenis cani- [f. 20v] bus [83] velut meretrix prostrari deberem.

6. Quis unquam tale vel simile audivit in Galliis, ut sub pretextu pacis ac ut statum corrigant regni[84], Lodovicum virum meum pium atque

77. An allusion to the Pragmatic Sanction, issued at Bourges, 7 July 1438, an assertion of regalian rights over the Church in France.

78. Christ.

79. Louis, the first-born son of Charles VII and later King Louis XI (1423-1483).

80. Sen. *Herc. f.*, 524-525: 'O Fortuna viris invida fortibus / quam non aequa bonis praemia dividis!'

81. The 'rabidus leo' is an allusion to the lion in the coat of arms of the Duke of Burgundy.

82. This common *iunctura* occurs in Verg. *Aen.* 9, 548 and 11, 711 and 12, 305; Stat. *Theb.* 2, 221 and 5, 135.

83. Cf. Verg. *georg.* 1, 470: 'obscenaeque canes importunaeque volucres.'

84. Cf. Commynes, *Mémoires*, p. 56: 'Les requestes et fins des seigneurs estoyent d'entrer dedans Paris pour avoir conversation et amytié avec euls sur le faict de la reformation du royaulme, lequel ilz disoient estre mal conduyt, en donnant plusieurs grans charges au roy.'

clementem crudeliter ignominioseque interficere procurent? An ego talis videor, ut hic Temerarius [85] mecum forte cogitet lenonum more[86] mechari ac pro suo libito michi sponsum auferre legittimum?

7. Non miror audentiam execrandam feri atque inmitis, sed inconstantiam infidelitatemque, ymo proditionem eorum qui virum meum velut agnum ducebant ad mortem, ni tua pietas clementissima aliter disposuisset eve- /nire. [f. 21^{r}]

8. Sed quid alii? Me coram virum meum blasphemant, maledictis detrahunt, vitamque eius vituperant et mores. Nichil regius honor, nichil regia maiestas, nichil Lodovici nomen apud istos valet. Nulla gloriosarum victoriarum, quas adhuc iuvenis et delphinus propria virtute acquisivit, Anglicos ex Normanorum finibus ignominiose expellendo ac Suevos deturbando, apud istos memoria est.[87] Oves accusant pastorem et vilia virgulta Dodoneae[88] quercui insultant.

21.1. Sed esto quod errores mei viri isti emendare atque in melius regnum reformare velint: ad quid ergo omnes pari animo atque consensu arma sump- /serunt? Cur sub hoc velo bona mea predantur? [f. 21^{v}] An armis unquam Romani rem suam publicam reformarunt et non potius legibus? Dimittant ergo arma, coniurationes fugiant, si de pace mea, ut dicunt, disponere intendunt. 2. Sed malo omine videor auguriari [89] non ipsos pacem amare sed bellum, cum iam mihi caput premant et in parte denegent victum. Nam omnia hostili more iam intercipiunt, quae meae Parisiae urbi, vel a superiori parte fluminis, vel ab occiduo, necessaria vel saltem utilia fore videbantur[90], et ut eos omnes uno vocabulo colligam, Catilinae sectam[91] iterum surrexisse for- /mido. [f. 22^{r}]

85. Charles the Bold, duke of Burgundy after the death of his father Philip the Good (†1467).

86. Plaut. *Rud.*, 346: 'si deos decepit et homines, lenonum more fecit.'

87. In 1443 the young prince Louis freed Dieppe besieged by the English; the following year an army of routiers under his command defeated the Swiss at St Jacob near Basel; see Jacques Heers, *Louis XI* (Paris, 1999), pp. 30-35.

88. The oldest Greek oracle was at Dodona in Epirus, where the rustling leaves of the sacred oak produced the oracular responses.

89. 'auguriari' is a rare form for the classical 'augurare/i'.

90. Commynes, who in 1472 deserted the Duke of Burgundy and entered the service of the French King, is of the opposite opinion: 'Car jamais nous n'eusmes faulte de vivres, et dedans Paris à grand peine s'appercevoyent-ilz qu'il y eust homme. Rien ne encherist que le pain, d'un denier seulement sur pain.'; see Commynes, *Mémoires*, p. 58.

91. After having been defeated in the elections of 63 BC and again in those of 62 BC, Catilina organised a conspiracy against the Roman Republic, but he failed.

3. Heu! quid dixi Catilinae factionem, aut Syllae[92] et Marii[93], vel Pompeii[94] aut Caesaris[95] divisiones, cum verius ac sanctius dixissem triformem Gerionem, ymo Lerneum serpentem[96], ydram profecto venenosissimam intra mea viscera iam esse exortam. Siquidem iam meae omnes penitus provinciae pariter sibi volunt libertatem vendicare, omnes suppremam volunt habere iustitiam, omnes volunt parlamentum summum, a quo etiam nolunt ullam appellationem fieri posse.[97]

4. Quaelibet etiam civitas petit universitatem, et dum querunt omnes inscientia proficere in maximam ignoran-/tiam relabuntur, cum hi nunc summi [f. 22v] reputentur, qui in mea iam alma universitate Parisia vix satis digne ultimum locum possidebant. Sic quae quondam omnium studiorum preclaris artibus fulgebam, nunc in me ipsa dispersa vix verum discernere possum a falso. Sed nimia hoc regum indulgentia fecit, qui dum omnium volunt satisfacere votis, vim suam minuunt atque robur.[98]

92. Sulla (born *c.* 138 BC), quaestor under C. Marius in 107, managed to capture Jugurtha and thus bring the Numidian War to an end. He distinguished himself during the Social War (mainly in 90-89BC) and became consul in 88. When the command of his army was taken away from him, he marched on Rome and seized it by surprise a first time in 87. He was outlawed, but in 84 he again openly rebelled against the Roman Republic; he invaded Italy, took Rome and was eventually appointed dictator.

93. Gaius Marius (*c.* 157 BC – 87 BC) won the Numidian war thanks to the diplomatic skills of his quaestor Sulla. When the command in the war against Mithridates was given to Sulla, but afterwards transferred to him, Sulla marched on Rome and Marius had to flee. He joined Lucius Cornelius Cinna, consul in 87, who had been illegally deposed and expelled. Together they captured Rome late in 87, and became consuls in 86 BC.

94. In 59 BC Pompey (106-48 BC) formed a coalition with Caesar and Crassus, which was renewed in 56BC. But Pompey did not remain on good terms with Caesar, and especially after Crassus's death in 53 tension grew between the two men. Eventually Pompey was defeated at Pharsalus, in August 48. He fled to Egypt but was killed as he landed.

95. In 49 BC Julius Caesar (100-44 BC) started a civil war, invading and rapidly conquering Italy from the north. He then crossed to Greece and defeated Pompey at Pharsalus in 48 BC.

96. Geryon was a mythic three-bodied Spanish king, whose oxen were stolen by Hercules. The Hydra of Lerna (a forest and marsh near Argos) was killed by Hercules. Both monsters often appear together, as for instance in Lucr. 5, 26 + 28: 'Lernaeaque pestis /... tripectora tergemini vis Geryonai'; or in Verg. *Aen.* 6, 287 + 289: 'belua Lernae /... et forma tricorporis umbrae.' See n. 5.

97. The first provincial Parlement was that of Toulouse, created 1420. It might be useful to remember that one of the weightiest clauses in the treaty of Péronne (1468) declared that the tribunals of Bruges, Ghent, Ypres and the district of Bruges (Het Brugse Vrije) were no longer within the jurisdiction of the Parliament of Paris.

98. Next to the traditional French universities (Paris, Orléans, Montpellier, etc.) several new ones were established during the fifteenth century. Louis XI himself had a hand in the foundation of several of these, such as Nantes, Valence and Bourges. See Stein, *Charles de France*, p. 43; M. Fournier, *Les statuts et privilèges des Universités françaises depuis leur fondation jusqu'en 1789*, 4 vols (Paris, 1890-1894 = Aalen, 1970).

22.1. Verum ad rem iam tempus est ut redeamus, et cur arma nunc sumpserint non pigeat investigare. Aiunt enim idcirco arma accepisse, quia virum meum timent, quem inconstantiae perfidiaeque nonnulli detractores ca- /lu<m>pniantur. [f. 23r]
2. Satis se poterant ab hac suspitione tutari, si eius clementiam summamque ipsius liberalitatem atque beneficentiam, quam vitiosam prodigalitatem isti appellant, considerarent. Equidem nec humano sanguine ipsum delectari nisi falso incusare possunt, qui etiam proprias iniurias suae coronae illatas dimittendo obliviscitur, et velut novus Caesar[99] etiam eos qui offensas intulerunt, maximis iam honoribus cumulavit.
3. Nonne Iohannem Armaniacum[100], qui nunc me voraci milite premit, omni statu omnique substantia privatum, et merito, mirifice sublimavit, ei totum suum domini-/um exhibendo atque addendo maiora?[101] [f. 23v] Nonne postea quam in recidivationem inciderat, quia fidelitatis sacramentum in mei sponsi dedecus et preiudicium Hesperiae Ultimae regi prestiterat, iterum complures arces et civitatum et opidorum in quibus maxime confidebat, restituit? Et hunc tamen iure ob sua facinora meus Carolus tali privatione dampnaverat, quem nuper meus Lodovicus sua voluit clementia investire.

23.1. Videor namque iterum videre non simul, sed successive Catonem alium aliumque Caesarem[102] mihi tua miseratione esse donatos, quorum primus iustitia ac severitate, alter clementia atque li-/ beralitate, velut duo [f. 24r] lucida sidera effulgeant.
2. Et quis hodie per totum Galliarum regnum dignus, dico, sit, vel pene indignus, qui mei sponsi manus unquam senserit avaras? Nemo profecto! Sed beneficentiae ac liberalitatis virtutes, vitiosam largitatem, bonorum dispersionem, ymo vituperabilem prodigalitatem vocant detractores isti, omniumque humanarum virtutum primam et summam clementiam, qua mortalis homo tibi, Deus alme, simillimus efficitur, infimam detestandam ac execrabilem pusillanimitatem nominare non erubescent. Non deberem ergo commoveri, summi regnator Olimpi[103], si mala faciant pro /

99. Florius refers here to the episodes related by Suet. *Iul.* 73.

100. Concerning Jean V count of Armagnac, see Ch. Samaran, *La maison d'Armagnac au XVe siècle et les dernières luttes de la féodalité dans le Midi de la France* (Paris, 1907), *passim.*

101. After the death of Charles VII on 22 July 1461, Jean V d'Armagnac was rehabilitated by Louis XI on 11 October 1461 and regained all his possessions. See Samaran, *La maison d'Armagnac*, pp. 142-143.

102. The severity of M. Porcius Cato the Elder (234 – 149 BC) was proverbial. For Caesar's mildness and generosity, see Suet. *Iul.* 74-75.

103. A literal quotation from Verg. *Aen.* 7, 558.

bonis, qui virtutes etiam preclaras obscenorum vitiorum vocabulis solent [f. 24v] apellare.

24.1. Venerunt ergo tandem omnes mei regni proceres armato milite pacem componere inter fratres. 0 subdola ac serpentina inventio! Et quis, Pater alme, duorum fratrum pacem conturbavit? Quis Carolum ad Britannos confugere procuravit? Nonne ipsimet eorum latratibus ac detractoriis et adulatoriis vocibus hoc fecerunt? Quid rumoribus caelum implent regis filium ac regis fratrem exulari non licere atque velut Scythani vagas[104] habere do/mos? [f.25r]
2. Quis illum exilio relegavit? Annon ipse solus voluntate propria, sed tamen seductus Britanniam petit, ac securus atque melius apud Britonum ducem quam apud Gallorum regem ac fratrem vitam degere falso sibi confinxit? Quotiens mei sponsi promissa respuit ac preces? Quotiens ad eum requisitus venire contempsit?[105]
3. Nec tamen iuvenem illum forma eximia ac probata virtute decoratum criminari volo, qui adhuc, si fata parcent, vitae superstiti spes altera mihi erit, quique patriis instructus moribus me aliquando mestam solabitur.
4. Sed contra istorum perfidas linguas queror, qui falsis cri-/minationibus [f. 25v] bonorum vitam carpunt, atque adulationibus blandis mores pessimorum laudando efferunt ad astra. Hi profecto sunt, qui pacem meam deturbant, quorum similes etiam totum universum venenoso acconito inficere non desistunt.

25.1. Sed ad quid ego ista, Iuppiter, commemoro, cum tu omnia solus nude videas, omnia solus producas in lucem, apud quem nulla est transmutatio, nulla vicissitudinis obumbratio? Sed ego misera humano more conturbor, quae videns infinitam tuam patientiam circa nostra scelera tantum durare, cogito nonnunquam te in sola tua eternitate be-/atum de no- [f. 26r] stris actibus parum curare persepe.
2. Ceterum a mea mente, quae te semper sincere coluit, absit hic malus error, cum iam a multis temporibus experientia didicerim ac ratione, te etiam minimorum quorumcumque curam gerere, inque suos fines deducere omnino. Nec me ab hoc veritatis tramite persuasiones abducent Ciceronis, non Democriti brocardica argumenta, quod nos recte de tua providentia sentire tuus Unigenitus edocuit.

104. See Hor. *carm.* 3, 24, 9-10: 'Scythae,/ quorum plaustra vagas rite trahunt domos.' Florius uses 'Scythani' instead of 'Scythae'.

105. Louis XI indeed tried to achieve reconciliation with his brother Charles who, however, wrote to the Duke of Burgundy on 16 March 1465 that he felt threatened and had to flee to Brittany; see Stein, *Charles de France*, pp. 56-60.

3. Haec ergo sola parum vigilantius supra me excitetur, nunc supra tuam filiam ac eius salutem cogitet, quae nunc te orat atque pre-/ [f. 26v] catur, ut de duobus fratribus, quos pariter amo ac nimium anxiosa diligo, aliquid procures salutiferum. Namque humanum consilium defecit, humana desiit potentia, ac in tantam iram eorum animi ac furorem exarserunt, ut non nisi proprium sanguinem sitire videantur.

4. Sed cor regis in manu tua est, et quocumque volueris vertes illud. Non ficte in foedera coeant pacis, nec velut Atreus suscepit Thiestem[106], sic alter ab altero recipiatur peto, sed ut vere omnis furor cedat, omnis cesset ira, et omnis animi rancor abscedat, talisque inter eos pax firmetur atque concordia, ut non laetali vulnere / [f. 27r] confossi pereant eternamque meam gloriam proprio sanguine fedent, sed ambo gloriose vivant, ut tales decet, in aevum.

5. Neque enim phas mihi est, cuiquam eorum vitam optare, alteri interitum, cum ambos pio amore diligam atque pari affectu cupiam foelicitari. Amplum siquidem est regnum meum, ac tua miseratione gloriosum, quod non tantum duos germanos, verum omnem Niobeam prolem[107] magnifice valeat enutrire.

6. Tu ergo qui solus es sapiens, modum viamque invenies ac tua potentia efficies, ut ego tandem tot nunc anxia curis ac pressa doloribus, in tua dignatione valeam respirare'. /

26.1. At postquam multis lacrimis ac suspiriis formosa illa mulier verba [f. 27v] complevit, ac omnes caelicolae arrectis auribus[108] elevatisque oculis in summum Iovem suspensi astabant, sic ille tandem vultu, quo caelum tempestatesque serenat[109] ac placido ore[110] hec verba deprompsit:

2. 'Si gens humana, quae sua temeritate ruit per vetitum nephas[111], rapidis semper suis fertur obvia fatis, quid te movere debet, o nata mihi pre caeteris dilecta, si tuae Galliae viridarium urbem Parisiam nunc barbaro more Gallicus furor premit atque devastat?

3. Nonne Titania / [f. 28r] proles[112] me etiam Olimpo regnantem temerario ausu expellere conata est? Nonne Acheronta pervincere voluit Herculeus labor,

106. Atreus and Thyestes were both sons of Pelops. Atreus banished Thyestes, who had committed adultery with his Atreus's wife Aerope. Organizing a feast to celebrate his reconciliation with Thyestes, Atreus killed his brother's sons and served them up to him.

107. Niobe, mythic daughter of Tantalus bore her husband a large family: seven children of either sex according to Ov. *met.* 6, 182-183, six in Homer's Iliad, five or ten in other sources.

108. Verg. *Aen.* 2, 302: 'arrectis auribus.'

109. Verg. *Aen.* 1, 255: 'vultu, quo caelum tempestatesque serenat.'

110. Sil., 6, 457; 6, 536 and 8, 199: 'placido ore'.

111. Hor. *carm.* 1, 3, 25-26: 'audax omnia perpeti / gens humana ruit per vetitum nefas.'

112. The Titans contended with Saturn for the sovereignty of heaven, but his son Jupiter cast them down into Tartarus by his thunderbolts.

et Iapeti genus celestem ignem mala fraude gentibus intulit, atque pennis non homini datis vacuum aera expertus est? Quid quod ipsum caelum stultitia petit humana propago, nec per suum scelus iracunda fulmina me ponere permittit?[113]

4. Verum quoniam hoc non miraris, sed potius times, quando hec te cura remordet[114], paucis adverte docebo, quo nam ordine tua fata tibi profecto inmota maneant[115], quae nec / ipsi celicolae unquam valeant a suo fine [f. 28v] labefactare. Non enim humano more disponitur divinus ordo, ut pro temporum varietate vel eventu mutetur. Nec idcirco, quia particularis causae effectus aliquando suum finem non attingit, divinam et universalem omnium providentiam effugit.

5. Nostram mentem nulla contingentia tangunt, nullus casus apud nos, nulla fortuna locum habet; sed in nostra eternitate beati cuncta suo et infallibili ordine disponimus, quem quia non semper capit mortalis homo, multa sibi casualia accidunt, quae tamen ab eterno mens nostra providit. Nulla preterea minimarum etiam creaturarum nostram gubernationem non / sentit, quae vel per nostram omnipotentiam creata, vel per sapientiam [f. 29r] inesse conservata perdurat.

27.1. Nec credas ergo te a nostra cura excidisse, cuius clementiam in omnibus tuis angustiis tibi adesse novisti, quod si te prius ex ultimis Troiae reliquiis per Scithiam Pannoniamque deduximus[116], si te, cum etiam me

113. The entire passus is taken from Hor. *carm.* 1, 3, 27-40:

Audax Iapeti genus
Ignem fraude mala gentibus intulit.
.....
Expertus vacuum Daedalus aera
Pennis non homini datis:
Perrupit Acheronta Herculeus labor.
Nil mortalibus ardui est:
Caelum ipsum petimus stultitia neque
Per nostrum patimur scelus.
Iracunda Iovem ponere fulmina.

114. Verg. *Aen.* 1, 261: 'quando haec te cura remordet.'

115. Verg. *Aen.* 1, 257-58: 'manent immota tuorum / fata tibi.'

116. The Trojan origins of France rely on two sources of the seventh and eighth century: the Chronicle of Fredegar and the anonymous *Gesta regum Francorum*, both published by Bruno Krusch in the Monumenta Germaniae Historica, Scriptores Rerum Merovingicarum, II. *Fredegarii et aliorum Chronica. Vitae Sanctorum* (Hannover, 1888 = 1956 = 1984). See M. Klippel, *Die Darstellung der frankischen Trojanersage in Geschichtsschreibung und Dichtung vom Mittelalter bis zur Renaissance in Frankreich* (Marburg, 1936); A. Bossuat, 'Les origines troyennes: leur rôle dans la littérature historique du XVe siècle', *Annales de Normandie*, 8 (1958), 187-197; J.P. Bodmer, 'Die französische Historiographie des Spätmittelalters und die Franken', *Archiv für Kulturgeschichte*, 45 (1963), 91-118; G. Uppert, 'The Trojan Franks and their Critics', *Studies in the Renaissance*, 12 (1965), 227-241.

non cognosceres Creatorem, sed cum adulteris, quos deorum nomine colebat gentilitas, quotidie fornicabaris, semper in altum sustulimus, si te saepe a Normanorum insultibus atque barbarorum vastatione, ut iam meministi, liberavimus, quomodo nunc credis nos te in tanto duorum fratrum ac totius regni discrimine deserere debere? / Hoc minime in tuo corde cadat, quam [f. 29v] etiam pre caeteris spetiali privilegio decoravimus.

2. Sed iam pelle timorem, omnisque cura excidat atque sollicitudo. Lodovicus tuus, quem singulari providentia dirigimus, ex Normanorum finibus magno conflato exercitu iterum Parisiam urbem adventabit animosus.[117] Musitabit vulgus et super vario belli eventu fluctuabit. Abscondet sub terra thesaurum mercator avarus, et a furibundo leonis[118] milite suam civitatem funditus deleri timebit.

3. Magnus ubique pavor, sevus ubique terror, sed ira furorque utrumque celabunt. Mars intra sua viscera fremet, et dum a nostra Minerva con-/tinebitur magis atque magis intra semetipsum contabescet. Hucusque pro- [f. 30r] cedere phas erit, quia non ultra divina nostra permissio extendetur.

4. Mirabitur profecto humanus intellectus, atque mortalis homo solo auditu stupebit, cum per nostrum aligerum[119] tantam pacis concordieque serenitatem subito ex alto effulsisse conspiciet. Leo ipse, quem sic timida vocasti, prior superbiam deponet atque celerius ab obsidione recedens in exteras gentes iram suam et odium convertet.[120] Sic alii omnes regni proceres proprios lares petent, et velut duo animi in unum conversi dux Borbonius cum tuo sponso convivia celebrabunt.[121] /

117. Compare Commynes, *Mémoires*, p. 56: 'car il (= Louis XI) vint en très grande compaignie et mist bien dans la ville deux mille hommes d'armes, tous les nobles de Normandie, grant force francs archiers...'; Stein, *Charles de France*, p. 108: '... le roi, venant de Rouen... arrivait à Paris le mercredi 28 <août>... avec 12000 hommes et soixante chariots d'artillerie et de munitions.'

118. Cf. 20.5: 'rabidus leo', alluding to the lion in the coat of arms of the Duke of Burgundy.

119. In classical mythology the winged god Mercury was the messenger of Jove.

120. After the battle of Monthléry, peace treaties were signed at Conflans and at Saint-Maur-les-Fossés on 5 and 29 October 1465, by which Louis XII ceded several cities in Picardy to the Duke of Burgundy and the King's brother Charles received the rich duchy of Normandy in place of that of Berry. Accompanied by Francis II of Brittany, the new Duke of Normandy took possession of his new duchy, while Charles the Bold turned against Liège. The inhabitants of that city had signed a treaty with Louis XI on 17 June 1465 and had revolted against their new bishop, Louis de Bourbon. Abandoned by the French king they had to accept a humiliating peace, which was signed at Sint-Truiden on 22 December. In 1466 followed the destruction of the city of Dinant (25 August). Later on, after the treaty of Péronne in October 1468, Charles the Bold forced the French King to accompany him to Liège and to assist him in the capture (30 October) and the annihilation of the rebellious city. Cf. Stein, *Charles de France*, pp. 123-128 and Commynes, *Mémoires*, pp. 94-98 and 131-168.

121. The Duke of Bourbon sided again with the King in December 1465 and took several cities for him in Normandy; see Stein, *Charles de France*, pp. 150-156.

28.1. Sed paulo post iterum Thesipho[122] Stigiis emissa paludibus in [f. 30v] furorem Gallos accendet, iterumque nudus frater Britanniam advolabit.[123] Neque enim phas erat pro libito eorum pacem servare conditionatam, quam puram, veram ac simplicem demittemus ab alto.

2. Iterum ergo omnes Normanorum urbes atque opida in manus redibunt Lodovici, quibus coronam denudari nec phas permittebat nec iura. Neque tamen perfide sponsus tuus faciet, si eorum luxuriae solo verbo annuens, quod intra sua precordia geret postea producet in lucem.

3. Resumet arma Britannus et vi sua ac robore Normanorum fines tutari conabitur.[124] Sed cum ei auxilium non fuerit / a Burgundo, in se ipso [f. 31r] citius marcescet. At simulata pietate Lincona vulpes suam patriam Carolo donabit, non ut suae subveniat necessitati, sed ut magis tuo sponso incomodet ex illo.[125]

4. Verum Lodovicus magna manu illuc missa Britannos ignominiose a finibus illis expellet, qui tandem coacti iterum non pro sua, sed alterius voluptate pacis conditiones ratificabunt. Tunc Burgundorum legati advenient, et sola humilitate ac reverentia ultra etiam petita obtinebunt.[126]

5. Sed dum se pro concordia fratrum voluerint intromittere, tunc meae dexterae potentiam mortalibus manifestabo. Siquidem cor ferreum a duorum fratrum corporibus auferam / atque carneum dabo ac mite[127], ex quo [f. 31v] fiet ut tui sponsi clementia ultro ac sponte sua Aquitaniae ducatum Carolo condonabit.[128]

122. Tisiphone was one of the Furies.

123. When a small incident seemed to drive a wedge between Charles and Francis II, Duke of Brittany, the King seized the occasion and invaded Normandy in December 1465. But Charles and Francis II were reconciled and Charles fled to Brittany, being at Nantes at the end of February 1466. See Commynes, *Mémoires*, pp. 86-91; Stein, *Charles de France*, pp. 150-181.

124. The Duke of Brittany tried to recapture Normandy for Charles. In October 1467 his army reconquered several cities and even Caen was won back (13/14 October); see Stein, *Charles de France,* pp. 215-219.

125. On 1 October 1467 the Duke of Alençon signed a treaty with the Dukes of Brittany and Normandy, offering to restitute all the cities and castles in Normandy he had in his possession; see Stein, *Charles de France*, p. 207.

126. During the summer of 1468 Louis XI invaded Brittany and forced Francis II to accept the peace of Ancenis (10 September 1468). Charles the Bold marched to the south, halting at Péronne, where the French king arrived on 9 October. The treaty they concluded was humiliating for Louis XI, who was obliged to offer Champagne and Brie to his brother Charles in place of Normandy. See Commynes, *Mémoires*, pp. 122-126 and Stein, *Charles de France*, pp. 254-255.

127. Cf. Vulg. *Ezech.* 11, 19: 'et auferam cor lapideum de carne eorum, et dabo eis cor carneum.'

128. In April 1469 Louis XI succeeded in persuading his brother to accept the duchy of Guyenne instead of that of Champagne, which was reserved to him in the treaty of Péronne. See Commynes, *Mémoires*, pp. 168-171; Stein, *Charles de France*, pp. 255-256.

29.1. Miraberis tu ipsa tantam animorum mutationem, et in uno effectu miserationem nostram laudabis atque iustitiam. Nam quorumdam tunc stratus omnino corruet in terram, multorumque scelera claudo pede poena nullatenus transibit.
2. Nec tu de Lodovici sobole ac successore sollicita sis, qui priusquam mortalitatem exutus sidereas sedes ascendat, gesta mirifica ac toto orbe celebranda efficiet.[129] Namque illi tantam pacis abundantiam tantamque cum exteris nationibus ami-/ citiam atque concordiam donabimus, ut re- [f.32r] novata tempora Salomonis appareant.
3. Et meminimus adhuc preteritorum seculorum quibus ob detractorum invidiam patria domo ac regia aula expulsus linguas barbaras audivit, easque penes multis temporibus velut exul et profugus vitam duxit; quem tamen ut nostram clementiam decebat ad tam opulentam regni gloriam extulimus.[130]
4. Hic profecto si vero corde ac puro eius patrocinia implorabit, quae saepe nostra concessione sibi auxilio fuit, mei Unigeniti matris, ne dubita: sua prece sobolem suscipiet preclaram, cui te optime regendam guber-nandamque / letus ac ilaris dimittet, priusquam longo evo functus cae- [f. 32v] lestem aulam intret gloriosus.
5. Huc usque te nostra verba audisse liceat; quae vero alta nostra mente reposta[131] sunt caetera fatorum tui regni archana cognoscere ne queras. Hoc sat tibi sit, ut scias te spetiali singularique privilegio nostrae maies-tati esse dilectam. Vive foelix atque tuum sponsum ama uniceque fove: quo etiam gaudebis per tempora longiora'.

30.1. Ast ubi summus Iuppiter finem dedit ore loquendi[132], tanta vidi formosam illam mulierem cum suis nimphis exultatione gestire, ut quae prius moesto lacrimosoque / vultu Iove coram accesserit, tunc leto ac ilari summa [f. 33r] cum devotione roseo ac vivido suo ore infinitas gratias redderet Tonanti.
2. Tunc etiam omnis illa caelestis aula mirificis vocibus ex tanto munere Franciae donato tam alte atque gloriose divinas laudes extollebat, ut me pre nimio gaudio tunc visio ac sompnus pariter desererent ac fugerent in auras. Finis.

Φρανκισκωσ Φλωρηοσ Φλορεντινοσ.

129. A son, the future king Charles VIII, was born to Louis XI on 30 June 1470.

130. Louis was banished from the royal court after the discovery of a plot against the French king. He fled first to the Dauphiné (1447-1456), finding a refuge in Burgundian territory during the period 1457-1461, viz. at Genappe in Brabant; see Jacques Heers, *Louis XI* (Paris, 1999), pp. 37-54.

131. Verg. *Aen.* 1, 25: 'manet alta mente repostum.'

132. Verg. *Aen.* 6, 76: 'finem dedit ore loquendi.'

Tania VAN HEMELRYCK

LA MUTACION DE PAIX: L'ÉVOLUTION DES FIGURES EXEMPLAIRES PACIFIQUES DANS LA LITTÉRATURE FRANÇAISE MÉDIÉVALE DU XIVe SIÈCLE AU DÉBUT DU XVIe SIÈCLE

1. INTRODUCTION*

Dès le XIIIe siècle, le goût de l'Antiquité déferle sur la littérature française. Il se manifestera avec emphase dans des œuvres comme l'*Ovide Moralisé*, mais aussi de manière plus ponctuelle, sous les traits de ce qu'il convient d'appeler des figures exemplaires. Elles se rencontrent dans les œuvres de Guillaume de Machaut, Jean Froissart, Eustache Deschamps, Jean Gerson, Christine de Pizan, George Chastelain, ... bref dans l'ensemble du paysage littéraire médiéval.

Ces figures exemplaires, dont le spectre référentiel est infini et demeure tant à la merci de l'histoire que de l'imagination, peuplent massivement les productions en langue vernaculaire dès le début du XIVe siècle.[1]

Ainsi, force est de remarquer que l'émergence de la littérature française pacifique – dont les manifestations tangibles voient le jour au XIVe siècle – n'échappe pas à la veine exemplaire. Au contraire, ces textes se chargent de figures antiques, classiques et chrétiennes, qui participent activement à l'élaboration d'une rhétorique de la paix. Dès lors, les images du passé participent à l'émergence du pouvoir de l'homme de lettres dans l'espace littéraire de la fin du Moyen Âge.

Cette contribution tentera de mettre en exergue la manière dont les figures, mythiques et historiques, de l'Antiquité au sens large furent utilisées par les hommes de lettres médiévaux pour clamer leurs désirs de paix.

Après avoir évoqué furtivement la typologie des figures exemplaires et leur mode de fonctionnement, j'esquisserai une rapide épopée des figures exemplaires qui furent utilisées dans les textes pacifiques à par-

* Tania Van Hemelryck est chercheur qualifié du Fonds National de la Recherche Scientifique – Université catholique de Louvain.

1. Celles-ci sont diverses et variées; elles servent également des textes très différents, cf. T. Van Hemelryck, 'Les figures romanesques dans la littérature des XIVe et XVe siècles. De la réminiscence courtoise à la remotivation satirique', à paraître dans les actes du colloque international pluridisciplinaire *Le romanesque aux XIVe et XVe siècles* (Bordeaux, 5-6-7 juin 2003).

tir des figures de quatre auteurs représentatifs: Eustache Deschamps, Christine de Pizan, George Chastelain et Jean Lemaire de Belges.

Cette dernière étape mettra en exergue l'évolution des figures et des textes pacifiques à la lumière de l'Histoire et de l'histoire littéraire; elle me permettra également d'esquisser les évolutions et contaminations que les œuvres et les personnages pacifiques ont subies dans la portion médiévale de la littérature française pacifique.

2. L'EXEMPLUM ET LA FIGURE EXEMPLAIRE: DÉFINITION RAPIDE

Outre l'*exemplum* traditionnel, défini comme un 'récit bref'[2] et généralement confiné dans des ouvrages didactiques ou de morale religieuse, très souvent en latin, dont la finalité est didactique et persuasive, la littérature française médiévale abrite ce qu'il convient d'appeler des figures exemplaires.

En effet, depuis le XIVe siècle, alors que l'on assiste au déclin de *l'exemplum* traditionnel,[3] la littérature en langue vernaculaire s'est enrichie d'un nouveau procédé littéraire: la figure exemplaire[4] qui se rapproche donc de l'*exemplum* antique[5] où s'entrechoquent la notion de comportement à suivre et l'action ou la parole exemplaire rappelée par un personnage digne de foi. Il s'agit alors d'introduire, non plus des récits, mais de courtes références aux exploits ou vices d'un personnage illustre.

La figure exemplaire devient un procédé poétique mis à l'honneur par une génération de poètes soucieux de cautionner leurs paroles: elle

2. Cl. Brémond, J. Le Goff et J.-Cl. Schmitt, *L'exemplum, Typologie des sources du Moyen Age occidental, fasc. 40, A-VI, C.*9 (Turnhout, Brepols, 1982), pp. 37-38.

3. J.-Th. Welter, *L'exemplum dans la littérature religieuse et didactique du Moyen Âge*, Bibliothèque d'histoire ecclésiastique de France (Paris-Toulouse, Occitania-E.H. Guitard, 1927), pp. 377-378.

4. T. Van Hemelryck, 'Marmoria, Totille et les autres. L'identification des figures dans les textes médiévaux: apport de la base de données Fi-Ex pour les XIVe et XVe siècles', dans Cl. Buridant (éd. sc.), *Le moyen français. Le traitement du texte (édition, apparat critique, glossaire, traitement électronique)*. Actes du IXe colloque international sur le moyen français organisé les 29-31 mai 1997 par le Centre de Linguistique et Philologie Romane et l'Institut National de la Langue Française (Strasbourg, Presses Universitaires de Strasbourg, 2000), pp. 133-148; à ce jour, la base de données Fi-Ex contient 7500 figures répertoriées dans un ensemble de sources littéraires des XIVe, XVe siècles et du début du XVIe siècle.

5. M.-A. Polo de Beaulieu, 'Didactisme ou persuasion? Les recueils d'*exempla* au Moyen Âge', dans *Éducation, apprentissages, initiation au Moyen Âge*. Actes du premier colloque international de Montpellier Université Paul Valéry, novembre 1991, 1993, *Cahiers du C.R.I.S.I.M.A.*, nº 1, t. II, pp. 397-398.

permet d'exprimer un système de valeurs manichéen, inambigu, où le bien fait univoquement face au mal. Dès lors, elle soutient toute l'architecture de la littérature pacifique qui voit le jour au début du XIVe siècle et qui s'ingénie à dénoncer les affres de la guerre, le mal suprême qui s'abat alors sur l'espace européen actuel dans le cours de la guerre de Cent Ans. L'utilisation du procédé participe tant de la rhétorique persuasive de l'écrit pacifique que de la volonté de légitimation des paroles de l'auteur.

3. La figure exemplaire au service de la littérature: quelques exemples

Devant le malaise causé par les affrontements du temps et l'absence royale grandissante, des auteurs, comme Eustache Deschamps ou Christine de Pizan, tentent de fournir des réponses littéraires au désordre politique. Ainsi, les figures exemplaires permettent l'élaboration d'une réalité de mots, fondée sur des valeurs absentes du réel, mais dont la vraisemblance est assurée par l'exemplarité et le pouvoir référentiel dont elles sont investies.

3.1. Eustache Deschamps[6]

Les figures exemplaires occupent une place importante dans les productions poétiques d'Eustache Deschamps. En effet, le recours à ces noms illustres du passé témoigne de deux tendances stylistiques précises, l'une exemplative, l'autre argumentative. L'usage récurrent des autorités dans l'œuvre de Deschamps construit un 'masque d'autorités' autour du regard et de la parole que le poète jette sur la société de son temps. Ainsi, la simple mention de Dieu ou d'Aristote avalise le message poétique, le frappant du sceau de la véracité ou de la révélation. Il est significatif de voir que dans les quelques pièces où Deschamps disserte sur la paix, à chaque fois il s'abrite derrière la toute-puissance divine, garante de ses dires et protectrice de sa personne.

D'autre part, dans sa volonté de construire un miroir du prince aux multiples facettes, l'auteur use de l'image exemplaire des Anciens afin d'asseoir son discours sur des bases didactiques stables et reconnues,

6. Eustache Deschamps, *Œuvres complètes*. Éd. A.-H.-E. de Queux de Saint-Hilaire et G. Raynaud, SATF, 11 vol. (Paris, Didot, 1878-1903).

associant certaines figures, comme les Neuf Preux[7] ou Octovien,[8] à l'état pacifique. Bien que l'utilisation de ces personnages antiques, légendaires ou chrétiens, relève d'une tradition bien ancrée dans la littérature médiévale, couplée au discours sur la paix et insérée dans de courtes productions lyriques, elle témoigne à la fois du caractère profondément conservateur de l'auteur et de son désenchantement face à un réel qui ne semble pas offrir de solution tangible aux problèmes de la guerre. Ainsi, les hommes et leur double exemplaire ne semblent pas aptes à œuvrer en faveur de la paix, peut-être parce qu'ils sont à l'origine de la guerre?

3.2. Christine de Pizan[9]

Dans le cas de Christine de Pizan, l'exemplarité prend les voies de la féminité; en effet, outre son *Livre de Paix*[10] dédié à Louis de Guyenne, l'auteur rédigea des œuvres aux accents pacifiques, dont les femmes étaient parties prenantes: l'*Epistre à la reine*[11] et le *Ditié de Jehanne d'Arc*.[12] Comme si le discours féminin sur des femmes ou à des femmes

7. Dans une pièce, Deschamps appelle explicitement les Neuf Preux et les Neuf Preuses à l'aide en vue de la paix (cf. Eustache Deschamps, *Œuvres complètes. op.cit.* [note 6], t. I, pp. 199-200), tandis que dans une autre, il parle de leur étonnement face au monde d'aujourd'hui, s'ils étaient amenés à revenir parmi nous (cf. Eustache Deschamps, *Œuvres complètes. op.cit.* [note 6], t. III, p. 192).

8. Dans le cas d'Octovien, le rapport à la figure royale est implicite; le roi de France est pressenti comme un nouvel Octovien s'il rétablit la paix (Eustache Deschamps, *Œuvres complètes. op. cit.* [note 6], t. II, p. 5, vv.1-2: 'Quant verray je le temps Octovien, / Que toute paix fut au monde affermée?'; t. VII, p. 251, vv. 1-2: 'Je voy le temps Octovien / Que toute paix fut reformée'; t. VIII, p. 159, v. 34: 'Li temps n'est pas qu'Octoviens / Regnoit! (...)'). *Octavien* est le nom pris par Octave (Auguste) après son adoption par Jules César; l'époque de cet empereur romain vit se développer un état de concorde bénéfique pour la politique, les arts et l'économie, et c'est à cette quiétude pacifique que font allusion les diverses mentions de son nom dans les sources littéraires.
Est-ce par dérision personnelle ou par référence consacrée qu'Octovien de Saint-Gelays utilisa à plusieurs reprises cette figures dans ses compositions pacifiques? cf. 'la paix octovienne' (ms. Paris, B.N., nouv. acq. fr. 1158, f. 23 r, *Complainte de la Justice et de la Paix...*) et 'Octovien apres meinct dur effort' (ms. Paris, B.N., nouv. acq. fr. 1158, f. 51 r, *Ballade*, refrain: 'cil vainct Fortune qui possede concorde').

9. T. Van Hemelryck, 'Christine de Pizan et la paix: la rhétorique et les mots pour le dire', dans *Au Champ des Escriptures. IIIe colloque international sur Christine de Pizan.* Études réunies et publiées par Éric Hicks avec la collaboration de Diego Gonzales et Philippe Simon, Études christiniennes, 6 (Paris, Champion, 2000), pp. 663-689.

10. C.C. Willard (éd. sc.), *The 'Livre de la Paix' of Christine de Pisan: a critical edition with introduction and notes* ('s-Gravenhage, Mouton, 1958).

11. A. J. Kennedy, (éd. sc.), 'Christine de Pizan's *Epistre à la reine* (1405)', dans *Revue des langues romanes*, 92 (1988), pp. 253-264.

12. A. J. Kennedy et K. Varty (éds sc.), *Ditié de Jehanne d'Arc: Christine de Pisan*, Medium Aevum Monographs, n.s., IX (Oxford, Society for the Study of Mediaeval Languages and Literature, 1977).

annihilait l'entropie de la référenciation exemplaire au monde masculin, responsable des malheurs de la guerre.

Avec son *Epistre à la reine*, lettre adressée à Isabeau de Bavière,[13] Christine tente de guider la reine sur la voie pacifique. Percevant le caractère audacieux de sa démarche, elle s'abrite derrière un mur d'*exempla*, exclusivement féminin. Le recours aux figures exemplaires permet à Christine d'illustrer la manière tangible dont la *pourchacerresse de paix* bénéficiera de la renommée perpétuelle par ses actions de paix, qui procureront également le bonheur du peuple.[14]

Dans l'*Epistre à la reine*, l'utilisation de l'artifice rhétorique évoque trois types de figures exemplaires, correspondant à trois chronologies, dans une espèce de mouvement ascendant et circulaire: d'abord antiques, plus spécialement romaines, puis vétéro-testamentaires, contemporaines, religieuses, mais a-temporelle avec l'évocation de la Vierge, pour revenir à l'antiquité, grecque cette fois. Notons que tous les exemples concernent des figures féminines royales, que Christine répartit sur une échelle de vertus dominée par la Vierge Marie, auxquelles s'opposent fugacement deux autres figures, témoins des dérives du pouvoir féminin: Jézabel et Olympias.

Après une ouverture anonyme sur *une tres puissant princesse* romaine,[15] les figures bibliques d'Esther et de Bethsabée apparaissent en reines de vertus. L'époque médiévale, plus spécifiquement la royauté française, est abordée ensuite sous les traits de Blanche de Castille, mère de Louis IX, qui assura d'une main de fer la régence du royaume soulevé par la révolte des grands féodaux. Ensuite, Christine évoque par comparaison implicite la mère de Dieu, à laquelle doivent être comparées toutes

13. Dans le cadre de ce texte, même si Christine use des artifices du clerc, la dimension de son art n'est pas aussi développée que dans d'autres de ses productions. En effet, dans le cas présent, il s'agit d'une production à caractère personnel, où l'auteur entretient un dialogue étroit avec son correspondant épistolaire (à la différence du *Livre de Paix*, qui bien que s'adressant à Louis de Guyenne, englobe l'ensemble de la société, et prend à parti bien des acteurs du conflit, tout en restant sous les feux de la diffusion manuscrite, donc de la vindicte universelle); il ne s'agit nullement d'un texte écrit pour une communauté littéraire et culturelle, sinon pour une individualité ciblée. Dès lors, les armes mises en œuvre dans l'*Epistre* ne sont pas aussi englobantes et se concentrent sur l'unique personnalité visée, en l'occurrence la reine Isabeau de Bavière.

14. Notons que l'*Epistre* manque d'unité dans son organisation; le caractère quasi instantané de la rédaction souffre d'un manque d'unité de ton, ne fût-ce que dans l'organisation du texte. Il convient cependant de préciser qu'il s'agit là de la première production christinienne à caractère politique, l'auteur tâte donc le terrain, privilégiant d'abord la quasi-confidentialité de l'épître avant de se lancer dans des œuvres plus 'ouvertes'.

15. A. J. Kennedy, (éd. sc.), 'Christine de Pizan's *Epistre à la reine* (1405)', dans *Revue des langues romanes*, 92 (1988), pp. 255-256, ll. 62-67.

les reines mues par un sentiment de paix. Loin de se terminer sur cette note superlative, le texte s'abandonne aux malheurs du peuple avant de revenir sur un dernier exemple, mais cette fois du malheur de la reine Olympias, vu comme le résultat de sa mauvaise conduite. Christine conclut avec fracas sur cette note exemplaire défavorable afin de susciter un sursaut moral chez Isabeau de Bavière.

Dans son *Ditié*, la femme sera toujours l'actrice de la paix, mais c'est l'utilisation des figures exemplaires masculines qui accentuera les qualités pacifiques et rédemptrices de Jeanne d'Arc.

En effet, Jeanne devient l'héroïne du miracle pacifique grâce à un savant jeu de parallélismes avec quelques figures exemplaires.[16] Tout d'abord, Christine compare l'action de Jeanne d'Arc à celle de figures masculines vétéro-testamentaires, tels Moïse, Josué et Gédéon, mais aussi à de celles de femmes de l'Ancien Testament, comme Esther, Judith et Déborah.

Jeanne apparaît dès lors dans un réseau comparatif qui la transforme en cours de récit, dans le cours de l'Histoire, en héroïne contemporaine d'un miracle divin supérieur à ceux de l'Écriture: la future paix que Christine souhaite au royaume de France. De fait, Jeanne est égale à Moïse qui sortit *le pueple de Dieu hors d'Egipte*, égalité soulignée par l'adverbe *ainsi* introduisant une comparaison égalitaire; par ailleurs, elle est supérieure à Josué par sa seule condition de féminine sur laquelle Christine insiste. Il en va de même pour Gédéon; le comparant et le comparé semblent se rejoindre dans leur origine modeste – Gédéon était un *simple laboureur* et Jeanne avait été une *simple bergiere* – et dans leur qualité de jouet divin, bien que le miracle de Jeanne dépasse de loin tout ce qui ne fût jamais observé.[17]

L'utilisation des figures exemplaires masculines et féminines, conjointes mais ontologiquement distinctes, permet à Christine de Pizan de dresser le tableau des qualités pacifiques de Jeanne, et donc de sa supériorité quasi universelle. Jeanne d'Arc rejoindra d'ailleurs rapidement le panthéon des héros médiévaux, occupant la place de la dixième preuse, face à son homologue masculin du Guesclin qui prendra celle du dixième preux.[18] Elle entrera dans la légende; on la rencontre d'ailleurs dans la

16. Plus loin, Christine notera que 'Tel force n'ot Hector n'Achilles!' (v. 287).

17. A. J. Kennedy et K. Varty (éds sc.), *Ditié de Jehanne d'Arc: Christine de Pisan*, Medium Aevum Monographs, n.s., IX (Oxford, Society for the Study of Mediaeval Languages and Literature, 1977), vv. 209-216.

18. T. Van Hemelryck, 'Où sont les Neuf Preux? Variations sur un thème médiéval', dans *Studi francesi*, 124 (1998), pp. 1-8.

ballade dite des *Dames du temps jadis* de François Villon ou encore dans le *Séjour d'Honneur* d'Octovien de Saint-Gelays.[19]

L'utilisation du procédé rhétorique glorifie certes le personnage de Jeanne, mais il permet également de cautionner la prise de plume de l'auteur: comme les prophètes de l'Ancien Testament, Christine œuvre pour le renom divin de Jeanne d'Arc. Comme chez Deschamps, les actions des hommes du présent, même épaulées par le renom du passé, ne peuvent garantir le retour de la paix. Dès lors, à l'image de la Vierge Marie, la femme apparaît comme l'émissaire divin porteur du fruit de la concorde.

3.3. George Chastelain[20]

Cependant, de tous les auteurs que l'on pourrait envisager, George Chastelain est celui qui mit le plus judicieusement la figure exemplaire au service du pouvoir de l'écrit. En effet, il sut allier les représentations communes à ses propres innovations thématiques et idéologiques.

Partant de sa *Louenge a la tresglorieuse Vierge*[21] (après 1455?),[22] il associe les figures vétéro-testamentaires de Judith et d'Esther au don de paix, comme le fit déjà Christine de Pizan dans son *Ditié*, lorsqu'elle les associait à la figure de Jeanne d'Arc. Chastelain retournera à l'exemplarité féminine absolue, mère du prince de la paix:

> Forte Judith, humble Ester figurée,
> De qui doulceur et beaulté décorée
> S'enamoura l'offensé roi céleste,
> Mille ans et plus prescrite et proférée
> Premier jamais que fusses engendrée,
> Pour mettre paix et amour restorée
> Seule entre lui et son peuple moleste. (pp. 274-275)

19. Notons cependant cette différence d'utilisation de la figure: chez Villon, Jeanne est introduite dans une strophe construite sur le thème de l'*Ubi sunt*, l'évocation de son nom et de son supplice faisant référence au passé ainsi qu'à d'éventuelles processions de femmes de glace, tandis que dans le *Séjour d'Honneur*, elle hante une fiction narrative, bien que son apparition soit fugace et muette aux côtés de Charles VII [sur la ballade de Villon, voir: P. Verhuyck, 'Villon et les neiges d'antan', dans *Villon. Hier et aujourd'hui. Actes du colloque pour le cinq-centième anniversaire de l'impression du Testament de Villon (…)*, (Paris, Agence Culturelle de Paris, 1993), pp. 177-189.

20 Sur George Chastelain et la paix, voir: E. Doudet, *'Un cristal mucié en un coffre'. Poétique de George Chastelain, 1415-1475*, Bibliothèque du XVe siècle, 67 (Paris, Champion, 2005).

21. *Œuvres de Georges Chastellain.* Publiées par M. le baron Kervyn de Lettenhove, t. VIII: *œuvres diverses*, Académie royale de Belgique (Bruxelles, Victor Devaux, 1866), pp. 269-292.

22. K. Urwin, *Georges Chastelain. La vie, les œuvres* (Paris, P. André, 1937), p. 19: 'Impossible de fixer la date plus exactement. Un manuscrit de la Bibliothèque Nationale nous dit que ce poème fut composé par Chastelain pendant qu'il demeurait à Valenciennes'.

Prolongeant la glorification de la concorde sur le mode encomiastique, il se plaît à louer Philippe le Bon dans son *Epistre au duc de Bourgogne*[23] (août 1456),[24] et plus spécialement à le comparer à *Octavien Auguste,*[25] la figure exemplaire traditionnelle des temps de paix depuis Eustache Deschamps. Tout au long de trois huitains de décasyllabes, l'indiciaire bourguignon dresse un portrait élogieux du grand duc d'Occident à la lumière de son comparant:

> Fortune à luy se rendit toute serve:
> Largue et prodigue en toute sa puissance,
> Et luy submit en paix et en conserve
> Le monde entier sans quelconque réserve,
> Ycy par sens, et là par redoubtance. (p. 150)

Bien entendu sur ce mode élogieux, aucune place n'est faite à la dure réalité de la guerre; seules les vertus chevaleresques priment dans le portrait du duc pacifique:

> Tu as esté un certain duc paisible,
> Bien exploitant sa commission sainte;
> Et au plus près de ton juste possible,
> Tu as esté vers ton peuple entendible
> Pour le mener à salutaire atteinte,
> Encontre toute entreprise et empainte
> De Pharaon parmy la rouge mer:
> Sy t'en doit bien remérir et aimer.
> En ta valeur et vertu singulière,
> Dieu a béni ta terre et les suppos,
> Et y tramis grâce particulière,
> Transquilité, paix, gloire séculière,
> Trop plus qu'ailleurs et de plus long repos. (p. 165)

Sous sa plume, les acteurs politiques vivifieront de leur vivant le panthéon exemplaire,[26] on dépasse donc la reconnaissance posthume qui fut donnée à Jeanne d'Arc ou à Bertrand du Guesclin.

23. *Œuvres de Georges Chastellain.* Publiées par M. le baron Kervyn de Lettenhove, t. VI: *œuvres diverses*, Académie royale de Belgique (Bruxelles, Victor Devaux, 1864), pp. 147-166.

24. K. Urwin, *Georges Chastelain. La vie, les œuvres* (Paris, P. André, 1937), p. 19: 'Les vers 402-403 évoquent l'entrée en Utrecht, le 5 août 1456'.

25. Dans sa *Moralité d'Arras*, Michault Taillevent parle 'Du regne Octovien le bon / Le quarante deuzime annee / Fu celle paix et concordance' (vv. 653-655), selon la représentation répandue à l'époque médiévale. Cf. R. Deschaux, *Un poète bourguignon du XVe siècle: Michault Taillevent (édition et étude)*, P.R.F., 132 (Genève, Droz, 1975), pp. 87-108.

26. Sur l'usage des figures exemplaires chez les indiciaires bourguignons, voir: T. Van Hemelryck, 'Les figures exemplaires au secours du héros bourguignon: exemples de chroniqueurs', dans *Publication du centre européen d'études bourguignonnes (XIVe-XVIe s.). Rencontres d'Edimbourg-Glasgow (28 septembre au 1er octobre 2000)*, n° 41 (2001), pp. 39-51.

La création exemplaire à partir du réel politique fonde ontologiquement l'œuvre littéraire dans l'*Exposition sur verité mal prise,*[27] en effet, pour convaincre Charles VII du bien-fondé d'une action pacifique, dépassant le cadre de la simple adéquation, Chastelain mue le roi en un 'nouveau' personnage, un *second Auguste, nouvel Cesar triumphant sur le monde, autre Charlemaine victorieux* (p. 431). De même, dans *Les hauts faits du duc de Bourgongne* (1467 ou 1468), Philippe le Bon est présenté comme le héros de la paix:

> De paix il usoit en grandes chères, et de guerres en opportunité de causes; … tenoit le salut de France en sa clef et la tranquillité d'Occident en sa main. (p. 217)[28]

La figure exemplaire illustre et donne à voir la pensée politique médiévale: seul le roi juste et bon pourra guider son peuple vers la paix terrestre, préfiguration du bonheur éternel promis par les Écritures.

Par ailleurs, le procédé exemplaire sera subtilement utilisé dans son *Livre de Paix.*[29] En effet, ce texte oppose dans un violent débat des deux allégories: *Sens superficiel* et *Entendement penetrant.* La dernière, double de Chastelain, voit dans la paix signée à Péronne un artifice rhétorique loin de la concorde attendue, tandis que *Sens superficiel* incarne le sens commun face à la paix, soit l'euphorie béate.

Ainsi, ces deux entités allégoriques apparaissent comme les doubles exemplaires de la conscience humaine, mais aussi de l'auteur aux prises avec la réalité pacifique dans l'exercice de sa fonction d'écrivain. Par ailleurs, le texte permet de débattre implicitement du poids des mots et de l'histoire dans la construction d'un raisonnement, puisque les deux entités s'opposent dans leur conception opposée du réel.

Alors que *Sens superficiel* avance des exemples tirés de la vie quotidienne, *Entendement penetrant* expose une brillante démonstration illustrée de cinq récits exemplaires. Dès lors, le récit permet de voir à l'œuvre l'élaboration de la dialectique pacifique confortée par l'utilisation du récit

27. *Œuvres de Georges Chastellain.* Publiées par M. le baron Kervyn de Lettenhove, t. VI: *œuvres diverses*, Académie royale de Belgique (Bruxelles, Victor Devaux, 1864), pp. 243-436.

28. Les mêmes idées sont énoncées en vers dans *La mort du duc Philippe* (*Œuvres de Georges Chastellain.* Publiées par M. le baron Kervyn de Lettenhove, t. VII: *œuvres diverses*, Académie royale de Belgique (Bruxelles, Victor Devaux, 1865), pp. 241-242).

29. Voir George Chastelain, *Le Livre de paix.* Edition critique par Tania Van Hemelryck, à paraître chez Champion dans la Collection 'Classiques Français du Moyen Âge'. Pour l'ancienne édition voir: *Œuvres de Georges Chastellain.* Publiées par M. le baron Kervyn de Lettenhove, t. VII: *œuvres diverses*, Académie royale de Belgique (Bruxelles, Victor Devaux, 1865), pp. 341-422.

exemplaire, qui apparaît comme autant de mises en abyme de la réalité de la paix de Péronne.[30]

Le dédoublement de l'auteur en deux entités, pour ainsi dire exemplarisées et assorties d'une rhétorique propre, dénote la méfiance[31] de Chastelain envers Louis XI et la véracité de ses engagements politiques au lendemain de Péronne. L'ambiguïté référentielle des exemples permet une lecture allusive en ce sens. Il va sans dire que l'utilisation des exemples dépasse les témoignages traditionnels. En effet, d'une part, Chastelain utilise des figures et des situations précises, peu courantes dans les autres récits. D'autre part, il s'agit moins de camper la légitimité des paroles de l'auteur que d'illustrer la précarité de la paix, car l'originalité du *Livre de Paix* réside dans la défiance manifestée par l'auteur bien que l'on vienne de signer la paix.

De fait, alors que les auteurs précédents composaient des écrits d'espoir de paix sur fond dysphorique, c'est-à-dire lors d'une situation historique pacifiquement déficiente, George Chastelain produit un témoignage littéraire consécutivement à une paix sans sombrer dans l'euphorie béate, mais cédant plutôt au scepticisme général, jusque dans l'utilisation des procédés rhétoriques et des ressources de l'écriture.

3.4. Jean Lemaire de Belges

Outre la citation des figures exemplaires, soit pour argumenter le récit en faveur de la paix, soit pour établir une comparaison pacifique avec un personnage, nous assistons parfois à la mise en scène d'une figure exemplaire qui vient se superposer à un personnage réel, perpétuant les prémices d'usages rencontrés chez Christine de Pizan ou encore chez George Chastelain.

Ainsi, dans la *Concorde du genre humain,*[32] la déesse de la paix, Pallas, est explicitement identifiée à Marguerite d'Autriche. Cette déesse se nommait Pallas ou Athéna dans la tradition grecque et Minerve dans la tradition romaine.[33] La base de données Fi-Ex mentionne trente occur-

30. J.-M. Cauchies, *Louis XI et Charles le Hardi. De Péronne à Nancy (1468-1477): le conflit*, Bibliothèque du Moyen Âge, 8 (Bruxelles, De Boeck-Wesmael, 1996).

31. J.-Cl. Delclos, *Le témoignage de Georges Chastellain. Historiographe de Philippe le Bon et de Charles le Téméraire*, P.R.F., 155 (Genève, Droz, 1980).

32. Jean Lemaire de Belges, *La Concorde du genre humain.* Éditée par P. Jodogne, Académie royale de Belgique. Classe des Lettres et des sciences morales et politiques. Collection des anciens auteurs belges. Nouvelle série, 5 (Bruxelles, Palais des Académies, 1964).

33. Dans la *Concorde des deux langages*, elle est décrite de la sorte: 'là où est le temple de Mynerve, laquelle aultrement se nomme Pallas, ou Bellona, deesse de science, d'estude, de vertu, de paix qui est aussi quise par armes, maistresse de tout artiffice et

rences de Pallas – aucune d'Athéna – et dix de Minerve. Les deux noms désignent la même déesse guerrière, qui présidait également aux arts et à la littérature; son ingéniosité aux faits des armes s'étendait également aux faits de la paix: ainsi, elle est reconnue pour avoir introduit l'olivier en Attique.[34] La littérature en langue vulgaire affectionne cette déesse; nous rendons compte ci-après de quelques allusions spécifiquement centrées sur la vertu pacifique de Pallas.

Déjà en 1405 dans son *Vivat rex*, Jean Gerson associait Pallas à la paix:[35]

> C'est elle qui a proprieté de tendre tousjours a paix, car elle est figuree par Pallas, maistresse dez sciencez, qui donna nom a Athenez; par le commun jugement, quant Mars ou Neptunius le vouloit imposer, fut dit que qui produceoit chose plus prouffitable il donroit nom a Athenes. Pallas fit germer ung olivier en signe de paix. Mars un cheval en signe guerre et mort. Paix fut jugiee meilleure. (...).[36]

Dans ses *Folles Entreprises* (1505), Pierre Gringore opposera l'action pacifique de cette déesse à celle des suppôts de *Guerre*:

> Quant Neptunus met sur mer sa nacelle,
> Que Boreas de subit soufflet vente,
> Et que Pluto les autres dieux precelle,
> Guerre monstre sa queue de serpente;
> Se Palas n'est pour l'eure diligente
> De resister à leurs ferocitez.[37]

Notons que déjà dans le *Naufrage de la pucelle*,[38] Jean Molinet comparait implicitement la toute jeune Marie de Bourgogne à la disciple de Pallas; en effet, dans son discours, *Cœur Leal* s'adressant à la princesse, dit:

> Jadis Jepté, Lampeto, Marsepia, Sinope, Arthemise, et autres escollieres d'armes militantes soubz l'estandart de Pallas, deesse armigere, te doibvent

ouvraige, inventeresse d'armures et de tous aultres acoustremens' [Éd. J. Frappier, T.L.F., 9, Paris, Droz, 1947, pp. 45-46].

34. Cf. P. Grimal, *Dictionnaire de la mythologie grecque et romaine* (Paris, P.U.F., 12e éd., 1994).

35. Il conviendrait de s'interroger sur la valeur du recours à Pallas, opposée à Junon, dans l'*Autre balade 14* de Christine de Pizan; cf. T. Van Hemelryck, 'Note sur la *Ballade contre les ennemis de la France*', dans *Le Moyen Français*, 48 (2001), pp. 401-41.

36. Jean Gerson, *Œuvres complètes*. Édition par Mgr P. Glorieux, vol. VII*: *L'œuvre française* (Paris, Desclée de Brouwer, 1968), p. 1145.

37. Pierre Gringore, *Œuvres complètes*. Édition par Ch. d'Héricault et A. de Montaiglon, 2 vol., Bibliothèque elzévirienne (Paris, P. Jannet, 1854), p. 36.

38. Jean Molinet, *Faictz et Dictz*. Éd. N. Dupire, SATF, t. I (1936), pp. 77-99, spécialement pp. 85-86.

> donner vif exemple, solide espoir et amene confortatif pour recouvrer joye pristine, terre perdue et paix entre les hommes. (p. 85, ll. 65-71)

Ainsi, chez Jean Lemaire de Belges, Marguerite est assimilée, par son maintien et son accoutrement armé, à la déesse guerrière Pallas:

> L'autre non maindre, ains aussi belle encore
> portoit harnois qui si bien la decore
> qu'on l'eust jugée une droicte Pallas
> de port royal et magnificque gorre.
> Or sembloit bien son gent corps estre las;
> dont sa compaigne, en deslassant les lacz
> du riche armet, lui esventoit la face
> et s'efforçoit de lui donner solas. (vv. 480-487)[39]

Dans le texte de Lemaire, *Concorde* réutilise la comparaison dans son discours adressé à Maximilien parmi les arguments en faveur de la sacralisation de la noble dame au titre d'Augusta; elle parle encore de son vêtement:

> Car, et combien que elle, par grand alesgresse et zele ardant, ayt incessament endossé ce sainct harnois palladien pour deffendre et garder l'honneur et haultesse de ceste tienne maison et le tenement de ton filz et son nepveu (...). (p. 65, ll. 527-533)

Quant à Minerve, elle apparaît dans la suite du discours de *Concorde* adressé à Maximilien, toujours dans une comparaison explicite avec Marguerite d'Autriche qui, par cette gloire pacifique qu'on lui reconnaîtra en la couronnant de la *palme*, deviendra une seconde Minerve:

> pour la premiere, qu'il te plaira decorer son chief de ceste branche d'olive fructueuse et tousjours verdoyant, significateresse de paix et de concorde, laquelle je lui ay choisie ou jardin de delices, là où est mon repaire avec les bienheureuses ames, affin que par ce signe elle soit pour tout le monde cogneue estre seulle fille naÿfve de toy, Jupiter altitonant, une seconde Minerve prudente et pacificque, engendrée de ton propre chief comme celle qui dés pieça a acquis ce tres exquis surnom de « Paix », substantivement, par singularité d'excellence, en toutes regions. (p. 67, ll. 583-592)

Dans ce texte, l'assimilation exemplaire illustre figurativement l'Histoire. En effet, *la concorde du genre humain* (décembre 1508)[40] fut rédi-

39. Jean Lemaire de Belges, *La Concorde du genre humain*. Éditée par Pierre Jodogne, Académie royale de Belgique. Classe des Lettres et des sciences morales et politiques. Collection des anciens auteurs belges. Nouvelle série, 5 (Bruxelles, Palais des Académies, 1964).

40. P. Jodogne, *Jean Lemaire de Belges...*, p. 312-319; Jean Lemaire de Belges, *La Concorde du genre humain* [cf. note 38]; voir également l'analyse de C.J. Brown, *The Shaping of History and Poetry in Late Medieval France*, pp. 51-55.

gée à la hâte au lendemain des traités de Cambrai. Ce prosimètre célèbre l'intervention active de Marguerite d'Autriche dans la conclusion des accords entre le roi de France et l'Empereur. Les traités signifiaient la fin de la guerre de Gueldre, et concluaient secrètement à une offensive contre Venise[41]. L'œuvre, toute empreinte des influences de Jean Molinet, ne se présente nullement comme une œuvre de réflexion politique, sinon comme un panégyrique à la gloire de la douairière des Pays-Bas. L'association n'est pas la seule que nous trouvions sous la plume de l'indiciaire, puisque les *Illustrations* regorgent d'allusions à cette déesse; la première reprend l'assimilation de Pallas et de Marguerite:

> Par ainsi, tu Princesse pacifique, qui es une autre Pallas, et tressage Minerve, cestadire, Immortelle, etc.[42]

Jean Lemaire de Belges perdure donc la tradition pacifique de la maison de Bourgogne, appliquant ces attributs à Marguerite d'Autriche qui revêt au fil du texte le nom de Pallas et de Minerve. Les figures et leur exemplarité se mêlent pour servir la rhétorique de l'éloge et de la paix.

4. Conclusion

À l'instar d'autres procédés rhétoriques, l'utilisation des figures exemplaires et des autorités permet aux auteurs de légitimer le bien-fondé de leur discours pacifique et de leur prise de parole. Ce procédé poétique est certes intimement lié à la rhétorique encomiastique et à la veine des miroirs du prince, mais ne leur est pas entièrement dévolu, comme nous avons pu le voir.

En fait, les figures exemplaires parfont l'horizon pacifique des ressources littéraires qui se trouvent à la disposition des auteurs. Elles comblent, par leur présence et leur aura exemplaires, le vide du monde.

Grâce à leur dévotion aux mots et aux noms, les auteurs parviennent à transcender par le Verbe le désordre engendré par les faits et gestes de leurs contemporains. Ainsi, l'œuvre littéraire, nouvel alpha et oméga pacifiques, assure la rédemption des hommes.

41. Cette expédition engendra toute une littérature de propagande, dont la *Légende des Vénitiens* de Jean Lemaire ainsi que des œuvres de Pierre Gringore (*L'entreprise de Venise*, *Les folles entreprises*), Symphorien Champier (*Le triumphe du treschrestien roy de France...*) ou encore Claude de Seyssel (*La victoire du roy contre les Veniciens*, etc.); à ce sujet, voir: M. A. Sherman, 'Political Propaganda and Renaissance Culture: French Reactions to the League of Cambrai, 1509-1510', dans *Sixteenth Century Journal*, VIII Supplement (1977), p. 97-128.

42. Jean Lemaire de Belges, *Œuvres*. Édition par J. A. Stecher, 4 vol. (Louvain, Lefever, 1882-1891), t. I, p. 7.

Wim VERBAAL

THE WRITER'S LOVE. LOVE AND THE ACT OF READING: PLATO, AUGUSTINE AND BERNARD OF CLAIRVAUX[1]

When commencing his commentary on the Song of songs and pondering over its abrupt opening verse, its beginning without beginning, Bernard of Clairvaux stresses at first the attractiveness of a text opening on a kiss. 'And it really is a pleasing communication, which takes its beginning from a kiss, and Scripture itself, as if with an attractive face, easily disposes and invites to its reading.'[2] The attractive face of Scripture, offering itself to the reader with a kiss: one cannot deny that Bernard makes use of a striking image when illustrating the intriguing character of the Song of songs. The text of Scripture is not presented in the first place as a referential code, referring to and talking about something outside its own existence. It is itself bodily present, it has a corporality of its own, turning its face toward the reader and offering its lips for a kiss. A kiss on which Bernard will linger for the next eight sermons![3]

The kiss is a sign of peace, is the first definition which Bernard gives,[4] but as his commentary continues, other descriptions are added, some very realistic ('The kiss is taken from a mouth to a mouth and belongs to no one'[5]), others more metaphoric when identifying 'the kiss of the kiss of His mouth' with the Holy Spirit: 'She asks for the kiss, i.e. she invokes the Holy Spirit, by which she receives at the same time the taste of knowledge and the condiment of grace.'[6] And indeed, knowledge is one of the central themes in this part of Bernard's exegesis. Only by the infusing of

1. A first redaction of this article was presented under the title 'Recycling the Word: Silent Reading in the View of Bernard of Clairvaux' at the conference *Manuscripts in Transition*, Brussels 5-9 November 2002.

2. Sermon on the Song of songs {= SC} 1.5, in Jean Leclercq and Henri-Marie Rochais, *Sancti Bernardi Opera* {=*SBO*}, I (Rome, 1957), p. 5.

3. Bernard may have been inspired for this image by two predecessors. John Cassian speaks in his fourteenth *Collatio* of 'the face of the Scriptures' (*Scripturarum facies*), which will innovate according to the progressing innovation of the mind of the reader. Rupert of Deutz refers in his Commentary on the Apocalyps several times to 'the face of Scripture', using both words *facies* and *vultus*.

4. SC 4.2, *SBO* I, p. 19.

5. SC 8.7, *SBO* I, p. 40, speaking about the Incarnated Son as the kiss of God's mouth.

6. SC 8.6, *SBO* I, p. 39.

the Spirit, in which the human soul is kissed by the kiss of God, God reveals himself to man. 'Thus, the Son reveals himself to whomsoever he will, and thus he also reveals the father. No doubt, however, he reveals by means of the kiss, that is by means of the Holy Spirit.'[7] Only 'the anointment learneth' man and the anointment is the experience of the kiss, i.e. of the infusing of the Spirit.[8]

'And the knowledge, which is given in the kiss, is rightly received with love, because the kiss is a sign of love.'[9] Apparently, in the course of reading, the perception of the kiss has undergone an evolution. It was a sign of peace, it has become a sign of love. But as a sign of peace, it referred also to a certain state of mind in the reader: 'Observe in the first place that the name of the Peaceable, who is Salomon, suits the beginning of a book which opens on the sign of peace, i.e. on a kiss. And pay also attention to the fact that by these sort of beginnings only the peaceable minds are invited to understand scripture, who knew already to liberate themselves from the perturbations of the vices and from the confusion of sorrows.'[10] If by its peaceful beginning, the text invites the reader to a peaceful mind, does it not, then, by offering itself for a kiss in a sign of love, invite the reader also to love? But what does love have to do with something as individual and solitary as reading? It might even seem beyond question to look for a connection between love and a medieval monk, especially a monk who is known for his radicalism – not exactly the most obvious messenger of love.

Yet this is exactly what this article hopes to demonstrate. As might become already a bit clearer from the former quotations, Bernard of Clairvaux proves able to transform the solitary activity of reading into an event of the highest tension, indeed of the tension of love. As a writer, Bernard appears to be very sensitive to the distance which separates the author from his reader. Like some of the greatest writers before him, he tries to reduce this distance and to involve his reader in the textual event. In order to succeed, he applies similar literary and rhetorical techniques to those used by some of his predecessors. And for him as for them, his handling of love constitutes the key factor. For this reason, some passages of two other famous writers on love, on the classical Eros or Amor, will first be treated briefly.

7. SC 8.5, *SBO* I, p. 38.
8. Cf. SC 1.11, *SBO* I, p. 7.
9. SC 8.6, *SBO* I, p. 39.
10. SC 1.6, *SBO* I, p. 5.

1. Plato and the distant reader

In any discussion of the authorities on love, the first name to emerge is Plato, author of the *Symposium* and the *Phaedrus*, two dialogues in which Eros occupies a central place. They show many similarities, and as many differences, but it is now generally accepted that in a certain sense the *Phaedrus* continues the theme of Eros as it has already been presented in the *Symposium*.[11]

The *Symposium* contains seven laudations on the god Eros and on his power over man. Though very different from each other, these move towards a sort of culmination in the speech of Socrates, which itself is followed by a final encomium, that of Alcibiades on Socrates himself. Both of these speeches throw light on different aspects of the Eros. Whereas Socrates in his exposition concentrates on the question 'what is Eros?', Alcibiades concretizes this same question by demonstrating what Eros is in Socrates. So, while Socrates' speech really crowns the preceding laudations in being as much a philosophic-theoretical as a poetic oration on the nature of the Eros, Alcibiades rather illustrates the working of Eros, not in an abstract or figurative way, but in the concrete, living personality of Socrates, the man at his side.

The *Phaedrus* is constructed around three speeches, two of which may be characterized as being laudations on some sort of Anteros, the Anti-Eros, the third one singing the Eros itself, after which almost half of the dialogue is occupied by an analysis of the art of rhetoric. So, in spite of the importance of the three speeches, the true emphasis in the work is laid on the last part, the analysis of the art of rhetoric by way of Socrates' well-known dialectic method. In this last part the Eros is no longer subject of the exposition, it rather becomes the analyzing force itself. Thanks to the power of Eros Socrates knows how to fascinate Phaedrus and to make him follow his dialectics and to uncover with him the impotency of nicely constructed oratorical periods as long as the speaker does not himself know what he is speaking about. Inside the dialogue the operation of Eros is no longer merely illustrated. One of the participants, Phaedrus, receives the full force of Eros, being led by Socrates along the paths

11. For recent discussions on the chronology of the traditional 'three' groups, see Julia Annas and Christopher Rowe (ed), *New perspectives on Plato, Modern and Ancient* (Harvard University Press: Cambridge (Mass), 2002), esp. Julia Annas, 'What Are Plato's "Middle" Dialogues in the Middle Of?', p. 1-23 and Charles Kahn, 'On Platonic Chronology', p. 93-127.

of dialectic towards the higher insights into and the supreme view on beauty.[12]

But even then, not much changes for the reader of the dialogue. He remains an outsider, looking at the events described, as if he were looking at a spectacle, some 'pièce de théatre'. According to tradition, Plato originally wrote tragedies and it had been the influence of Socrates which made him abandon these projects. Indeed, the force of the *Symposium* and *Phaedrus* is for a large part due to their high dramatic intensity.[13] As a reader one has the impression of seeing everything happening before one's eyes: as if one were reading a play by Euripides, i.e. as if the force of Eros is performed for him as a spectator, put on a stage and evoked as a living force working upon the actors involved. He himself, however, remains a spectator.[14]

2. Augustine and the uncomfortable reader

For the second author on love who bears on the theme of this article, a move must be made towards the end of Antiquity to hear the voice of a writer at the closing of an epoch. Augustine of Hippo is the most important mediator between Plato in his Neo-Platonic guise and Western Europe. In his *Confessions* he wrote the following famous, beautiful profession of love:

12. This is not the place to discuss in depth the meaning of Eros in these dialogues. For more comprehensive studies we refer to the literature, of which a good recent overview can be found in Blondell.

13. Partly, this originates in the dramatic attitude of Socrates himself. His first speech clearly is meant to be a mocking imitation of Lysias' speech as it has been declaimed by Phaedrus. See on this also the pertinent remarks by R.B.Rutherford in his Comments on Andrea Nightingale, 'Distant Views: "Realistic" and "Fantastic" Mimesis in Plato', in Julia Annas and Christopher Rowe (ed), *New perspectives on Plato, Modern and Ancient* (see n. 11), p. 227-247. The 'Comments' are on p. 249-262, esp. p. 254-255.

14. See now the recent and fascinating study by Ruby Blondell, *The Play of Character in Plato's Dialogues* (Cambridge University Press, 2002). The author argues convincingly that the dramatics of Platonic dialogue are meant to involve the reader as one of the participants in the pedagogical event of the text (esp. p. 37-52). Simultaneously, however, drama's 'fourth wall', consisting of the distance between the spectator and the stage, is never explicitly broken (p. 51). Just as Plato is never involving himself in the textual event, remaining always outside and elusive, the reader too is never obliged to participate in the drama which is performed before his eyes. Before Blondell the suggestive link between reader and spectator already had been made by Jesper Svenbro, 'La grèce archaïque et classique. L'invention de la lecture silencieuse', in Guglielmo Cavallo and Roger Chartier (ed), *Histoire de la lecture dans le monde occidental* (Paris: Seuil, 1997), p. 47-77, esp. p. 66-68 and p. 72-73 (on Phaedrus).

> *Too late I loved Thee, O Thou Beauty both so ancient and so fresh, too late I loved Thee! And behold, Thou wert within, and I without, and there I searched for Thee, and I, unlovely, rushed heedlessly upon those beautiful things Thou hadst made. Thou wert with me, and I was not with Thee. Those things kept me far from Thee, which, unless they were in Thee, were not at all. Thou calledst, and shoutedst, and burstest my deafness. Thou flashedst, shonest, and scatteredst my blindness. Thou breathedst odours, and I drew in breath and pant for Thee. I tasted, and I hunger and thirst. Thou touchedst me, and I burned for Thy peace.*[15]

This short passage suffices to make one realize that the *Confessions* is one of the most alienating books ever penned. Never before had man gone so far in analyzing his own inner movements, in trying to reach the basis of his own experiences and thoughts. And although modern age has become acquainted with psychoanalytic self-descriptions, the confessions of the man Augustine still leave the reader uprooted. They still leave him with a certain uneasiness. They are too smooth, too beautifully constructed, too rhetorical almost to be considered just an honest self-analysis, a sincere attempt at profound self-knowledge. One never escapes the impression that Augustine remains too aware of the presence of the reader.

Sero te amavi: 'Too late I loved Thee'. In the passage quoted Augustine gives in the most concise form a description of the development of his love: the distance between the lover and the beloved, the barriers raised between them, the breaking through and birth of love. *Ecce intus eras et ego foris*: 'Thou wert within and I without'. The distance between the lover and the beloved must not be understood in a linear sense. The separation is based on an inside and an outside, i.e. on two sides or aspects of one and the same reality, which is constituted by the 'me', the 'I', who is not there. For, *ibi te quaerebam*: 'There, outside, I searched for Thee'. Whereas the beloved is stable within, the lover is roaming about on the outskirts of his own being. However, *mecum eras et tecum non eram*: 'Thou wert with me, and I was not with Thee'. The separation appears to be only one-sided: even in his error the lover is not abandoned by the beloved. He simply does not notice the presence of the one for whom he searches, captured as he is by appearances on the rim of his existence.

Vocasti et clamasti et rupisti surditatem meam: 'Thou calledst, and shoutedst, and burstest my deafness'. *Coruscasti, splenduisti et fugasti caecitatem meam*: 'Thou flashedst, shonest, and scatteredst my blind-

15. Augustine, *Confessions* X.38. E.B. Pusey's nineteenth century translation, slightly adapted.

ness'. *Fragrasti et duxi spiritum et anhelo tibi*: 'Thou breathedst odours, and I drew in breath and now I pant for Thee'. *Gustavi et esurio et sitio*: 'I tasted, and now I hunger and thirst'. *Tetigisti me et exarsi in pacem tuam*: 'Thou touchedst me, and I burned for Thy peace'. Love is wakened. The unnoticed presence of the beloved makes itself known, draws the attention towards itself. First there is the voice, calling, then shouting. Next, there is the appearance, flashing, shining. All action originates with the beloved, whereas the lover is passive, besieged by the forces of the beloved. Only after his deafness and blindness have been broken and scattered, can the roles be exchanged. Now the beloved almost limits himself to some sort of non-action: he breathes and becomes tastable. In the lover, on the contrary, all desires are roused: he draws a deep breath and he yearns for the beloved, he tastes and it makes him crave for more. Finally, the beloved touches him and all his love and desire to find peace with the beloved blaze up.

This is no longer a distant and theoretical description of love. It is the voice of experience. It is the confession of a man who has experienced the force of love and who tries to grasp what has happened to him. It could have been the voice of Socrates before going to the Symposium, describing the force of Eros working in him. Or the voice of Phaedrus after the dialogue, describing the force of Socrates' words upon him and the raising of his own desires by it. Yet, at the same time, it cannot be denied that there is something else too: there seems to be less rationality in this passage and more passion, less theory and more experience, less talk and more love.

Indeed, the reader of this passage starts to realize that this is not an exposition on, but rather a profession of, love. As such it is nearer to Alcibiades's 'profession' of Socrates. In the speech in the *Symposium*, however, all emphasis is placed on Socrates, on the source and incorporation of the Eros, as experienced by Alcibiades. In Augustine, all the emphasis is on himself as the inflamed lover, searching for his beloved. In Alcibiades' speech, the Eros is somehow omnipresent, though he is never touched on explicitly. Augustine's confession, on the contrary, is imbued with love: it is the only subject he talks about without being able to touch it, he hardly knows how to express the force of his own experiencing it.

But what has a reader to do with all this? Why is he allowed to hear this intimate profession of love, this self-analysis of a man searching for the truth in his own life? Burcht Pranger of the University of Amsterdam, in a fascinating article, posed this same question on another passage in

Augustine's work. Describing Augustine's behaviour before and after the death of his mother, he remains perplexed by the confidence in the reader shown by the author. While Augustine's own closest friends are not allowed to see his pain and suffering when burying his mother, the reader may follow him into the seclusion of his bedchamber and be the witness of a son's tears. For what reason is the reader allowed what Augustine's closest friends have been denied?[16]

The same pressing question ought to be asked concerning Augustine's profession of love. Why has it been written for someone to read? What does it mean for him who may have read it? *Quid ad nos*? In the same tenth book of his *Confessions* Augustine himself has already given the answer.[17] The fruit of his confessions must be not what he *was*, but what he *is* (*non qualis fuerim, sed qualis sim*), i.e. not his historical past but his actual present; not the past reality of his earthly life as it is described in the first nine books, but the present reality of his life in the book itself, a living voice which will never cease to address the reader.

The reader has become less of an outsider. He is the actual addressee of Augustine's long monologue to God. No longer does he enjoy the distant position of a spectator, though this could be his impression for the autobiographical books. He rather becomes a listener, hearing the voice of a man opening himself in a, what might seem sincere, confession. What he hears does not limit itself to a mere description, to any sort of objective analysis: it is a living voice, an almost immediate expression of experience. The very personal touch of the speaker and of his confession asks some degree of engagement of the reader too. He cannot remain outside. The confidence of the author makes him also a person involved, almost as much as is the author, and even more than Augustine's nearest friends in life. It becomes very hard for the reader to evade his responsibility as a *confidant* of the author. He has to realize that, for Augustine the lover, he is a more trusted person than were even the most familiar friends of the author in life.[18]

16. Marinus Burcht Pranger, 'Tranen in het antieke christendom. Augustinus en de dood', in R.E.V.Stuip and K.Vellekoop (ed), *Emoties in de middeleeuwen* (Verloren: Hilversum, 1998), p.29-47. See also on the passage of love by the same author, 'De zintuigen als verhalend beginsel in Augustinus' *Belijdenissen*', in *Hermeneus,* 74 (2002), p. 132-14.

17. *Confessions* X.6, starting with the phrase: *Hic est fructus confessionum mearum.*

18. For the importance of reading for Augustine, see Marylu Hill, 'Reading without Moving Your Lips: The Role of the Solitary Reader in Liberal Education', in Kim Paffenroth and Kevin L.Hughes (ed), *Augustine and Liberal Education* (Ashgate: London, 2000), p. 179-198, esp.p. 180-182. Also Brian Stock, *Augustine the Reader: Meditation, Self-Knowledge, and the Ethics of Interpretation* (Harvard University Press: Cambridge, 1996).

3. Bernard and the reader beloved

3.1 A writer in love

Seven centuries separate Augustine from Bernard of Clairvaux. It might seem cavalier to ignore these huge time spans. Yet similar annihilations of time occur whenever someone takes up a book to read the words which an author wrote hundreds or even thousands of years ago. Reading breaks down the barriers of time just as modern technology has managed to break down spatial barriers. Nowadays, it is possible to have an immediate conversation with people at the other end of the world and it does not astonish anyone. Modern man, on the other hand, tends to forget that reading admits the voice of someone speaking from another epoch into his own reality, into his actual existence. Twelfth century readers, however, were very aware of this.[19]

Bernard of Clairvaux was a thorough reader of Augustine. Traces of the *Confessions* can be found everywhere in his own works. The most obvious allusion is to be found in his 26th sermon on the Canticle, in the lamentation on his brother Gerard. It opens with the burial of Gerard. In executing the funerary rituals everyone around is astonished to see Bernard without tears. Bernard's lamentation opens where Augustine's story ended. And whereas Augustine only showed his pain to the readers in the seclusion of his sleeping room, Bernard bursts out in tears at the very beginning of his text, as soon as he has finished his description of the funeral. By giving his lamentation the form of a sermon he opposes himself to Augustine's solitary tears: his pain may be seen by everyone, by his supposed audience as well as by readers. The public of his readers is deemed to be equivalent, or even exchangeable with the public of his monastic audience.[20]

19. Only during the Middle Ages, with their cult of the sacrosanct book, does Western European literature seem to have become conscious of the problem of time in writing. Especially twelfth century writers appear to be very sensitive to the possibilities of breaking the limits of time by the act of writing. Many of them seem to be aware of a coexistence of the distance, separating them from their models of Antiquity, and the immediacy and actuality of the voices in the writings of these models. This very specific medieval experience of time in writing (but which in a certain sense appears to be very modern too) finds its origin, of course, in the acquaintance with the Bible, in which the eternal voice of God is heard, being always actual, and which contains all human history from its beginnings to its end. For a discussion on Bernard's approach to time, see my article 'Bernard of Clairvaux's *Sermons for the Liturgical Year*: A Literary Liturgy.' in Nils Holger Petersen, Mette Birkedal Bruun, Jeremy Llewellyn, and Eyolf Østrem (ed), *The Appearances of Medieval Rituals: The Play of Construction and Modification* (Brepols: Turnhout 2003), p. 49-66.

20. See Pranger 1998 p.30-42, as well as my article on sermon 26, 'Preaching the Dead from their Graves. *Bernard of Clairvaux's lament on his brother Gerard*', in *Speculum sermonis* (Brepols: Turnhout, 2004), p. 113-139).

Can allusions be found to Augustine's profession of love too? The preface to Bernard's treatise on consideration, on which he worked during the last years of his life and which he dedicated to his former monk, then Pope Eugenius III, offers one of his most explicit professions of love:

> 'But *Charity never faileth.*[21] It is true that I am discharged from a mother's duties, yet I am not bereft of her affection. Once I bred you in my bowels. You cannot be so easily torn away from my heart. You may *mount up to the heaven*, you may *go down again to the depths:*[22] you will not recede from me, I will follow you wherever you might go. I loved you as you were poor in spirit, I will love you as the father of the poor and of the rich. [...] For this reason I will advise you, not as a master, but as a mother: as someone who loves. Perhaps I might seem rather someone out of his wits, but only to him who does not love, to him who does not feel the force of love.'[23]

Some themes encountered in the former passages indeed return. The person talking here is a lover, someone for whom love is an active working force. An inspiring force too, just as it was experienced by Socrates whose panegyric of love was inspired in him by the love that Phaedrus aroused in him. Even more conspicuous is the affinity with Augustine's profession of love. 'Thou wert with me, and I was not with Thee.' Bernard reverses this: 'Wherever you go, you will not escape me', as if he wants to say: 'I will be with you, even when you do not want to be with me.'

In these words, of course, an allusion can be heard to the verses of the psalm: *Whither shall I go from thy spirit? or whither shall I flee from thy presence? If I ascend up into heaven, thou art there: if I make my bed in hell, behold, thou art there.*[24] Yet, this intertextuality has some strange resonance about it. The psalmist is professing God's omnipresence which he will not escape. In Bernard's text, however, it is he, the writer, who cannot be evaded. He has taken the place of God in the psalm: it is Bernard who will always be there, wherever his addressee might go.

Bernard, the author, has placed himself in the position of the lover, talking to his beloved, just like Socrates in the *Phaedrus*. But by his allusion to the psalm Bernard equates the relation between the lover and the beloved with that between God and the psalmist. The text tells that Bernard, the writer, is with his reader, Eugenius, just as in the psalm God

21. 1 Cor 13:8.
22. Ps 106:26.
23. Bernard of Clairvaux, *De consideratione. Praefatio*. In Jean Leclercq and Henri-Marie Rochais, *Sancti Bernardi Opera*, III (Rome, 1963), p. 393-394.
24. Ps.138:7-8.

is with the psalmist. The psalmist, however, articulates the Word of God himself who is the principal voice in the Bible. The confession of the psalmist, thereby, must be read as divine guidance on the relation of the beloved with God.

To put it briefly: in his words to Eugenius Bernard alludes to the verses of the psalm. In the Bible, however, God is speaking to man at large and the psalmist must be considered as the interpreter of the divine Word, which professes the relationship of man with God. Bernard can be considered, then, as an interpreter of the same sort of relationship, existing between himself as an interpreter and his addressee.

But who is his addressee? Pope Eugenius in the first place, to whom the treatise is dedicated. But Eugenius is present here as a reader, not differing from any actual reader of those same words. So, in an indirect way, in the person of Eugenius, every reader is addressed by the author. This, however, has important consequences for the attitude of the reader towards the text. No longer is he a spectator of some kind of drama evoked in or by the text. Neither can he consider himself as attending, more or less by coincidence, at the passionate monologue of someone talking about himself. No, he must feel himself strongly involved, be it only by the mediation of the real destinary, the reader Pope Eugenius.

3.2 Loving the reader

This opportunity to take refuge behind a historical 'other', behind a person named and individualized to whom one can divert the words and the attention of the author, is not offered in Bernard's sermons. Here, Bernard addresses a nameless audience, which is only addressed by apostrophes such as 'brethren' (*fratres*) and 'you' in both its meanings, plural and singular. A careful study of Bernard's use of the grammatical persons shows that they appear mostly at well-considered places, the plural opening and concluding the sermon, the singular appearing in the body of the text, the plural apostrophe creating only a context of community, while the sermon itself is meant to be taken personally and in an individual sense.[25]

This personal approach to the individual reader by the author never remains abstract, however. The author always appeals to some intermediate biblical personality, held up as a *forma* for reader or author, which

25. See the part of my article which was dedicated to this problem, 'Réalités quotidiennes et fiction littéraire dans les *Sermons sur le Cantique* de Bernard de Clairvaux', in *Cîteaux,* 51 (2000), p. 201-218, esp. p. 205-210. A more comprehensive study is in preparation.

means something more than just an example: the *forma* in the twelfth century very often translating the Platonic concept of the Idea, the spiritual reality of the earthly appearance.[26] Opening his first sermon on the Canticle Bernard applies this to himself: 'To you my brethren, something else has to be said than to the people in the world, and it certainly has to be said in a different way. They are fed with milk and not with meat by him who keeps to the 'form' (*forma*) of the Apostle in teaching (*qui Apostoli formam tenet in docendo*)'.[27] Bernard sees himself as a teacher in the *forma* of the apostle Paul. It is not only that he is taking the apostle as his example which he wants to imitate: he also strives to attain the spiritual reality of Saint Paul in his own teaching. By his teaching Saint Paul has given him, Bernard, the *forma*, the Idea, the spiritual truth, to which his own teaching ought to correspond. Saint Paul, the *magister gentium*, is the Idea for Bernard, the author.

When Bernard, however, strives to attain the *forma* of Saint Paul in his own teaching, then it can be assumed that he expects a similar attitude from his readers. And indeed, as the basic principle for reading his writings, he gives the reader the maxim *Transformamur cum conformamur*: 'We are transformed when we conform ourselves'.[28] In the same way that Bernard wants to transform his teaching by accommodating it to the *forma* (the Idea) of Saint Paul, the reader has to transform himself by conforming to the *forma* which is offered to him in Bernard's text. We must therefore ask which forms Bernard offers the reader.

Of the multitude of independent *formae* which can be found in the different sermons, two stand out, closely connected as they are with the biblical subjects Bernard has exposed most thoroughly, i.e. the scene of the Annunciation (Luke 1:26-38) and the first chapters of the Canticle. It is no accident that both subjects are characterized by high dramatic tension. Transforming oneself by conforming to the *forma* of a biblical personality is indeed founded on the most basic dramatic principles. It means in

26. This appears to be especially true for Bernard. Cf. e.g. the following statement by Bernard: *Forma, autem, sapientia est, conformatio, ut faciat imago in corpore, quod forma facit in orbe. De gratia et libero arbitrio* 33 in Jean Leclercq and Henri-Marie Rochais, *Sancti Bernardi Opera,* III (Rome, 1963), p. 189.

27. Bernard, *Sermon on the Canticle* 1.1 in Jean Leclercq and Henri-Marie Rochais, *Sancti Bernardi Opera,* I (Rome, 1957), p. 3.

28. Bernard, *Sermon on the Canticle* 62.5 in Jean Leclercq and Henri-Marie Rochais, *Sancti Bernardi Opera,* II (Rome, 1958), p. 158. I have treated this theme more extensively in my book *Een middeleeuws drama. Het conflict tussen scholing en vorming bij Abaelardus en Bernardus* (Pelckmans: Kapellen, 2002), esp. p. 244-247.

the first place that the reader is willing to take up the role of the proposed *forma* and to give it life in his own being.[29]

In the commentary on the Annunciation the author himself leads the way. When opening his third homily Bernard realizes that now he will have to give an interpretation of the words the angel speaks to the Virgin. To interpret them means in the first place to speak them, but: 'Alas, how many idle, how many false, how many dirty things I remember having thrown up through this all too filthy mouth of mine, by which I now presume to resume these heavenly words.' Bernard, the author, prays that his mouth be purified so that he might speak the words of the angel in a way that is conform to the angel. Commenting the Bible means in the first place conforming to it.[30]

Yet if Bernard takes up the part of the angel, the reader almost immediately is forced into the *forma* of the Virgin. In the traditional presentations of the Annunciation, Mary is reading when the angel enters. This is the way Bernard also presents her. The Virgin has secluded herself from all human contact. She has locked the doors behind her. No human being can disturb her – only an angel can. Or, actually, only the voice of an angel can, since it is the voice only of the angel that disturbs her in her pious reading. Yet this is precisely what happens when anyone takes up a book and starts reading for himself. A silent reader cuts himself off from the world around. He becomes absorbed in his book. The only voice which can still reach him is the voice in the book, the voice of the writer. Reading the commentary on the Annunciation by Bernard, the silent reader has already assumed in a concrete way the attitude of the reading Virgin. As soon as he realizes that the only voice reaching him is the voice of the author in which the voice of the angel resounds, it becomes clear to him that his silent reading is a rehearsal of the Annunciation scene, that the biblical text has been transformed by the commentary into a sort of script, that the voice of the author is transformed into that of the angel, that he himself has to conform to and to transform into the role of the Virgin and that the final aim of this same commentary is the reincarnation of the divine Word in his own being.

29. See the importance of drama in the Platonic dialogues as demonstrated by Blondell (2002), p. 47-52. The differences must be noted, however. While Plato still leaves some sort of escape to the reader by creating a certain parallel between himself and his public, Bernard, by his direct apostrophe of the reader, leaves no way out.

30. See my close reading of the four homelies on the Annunciation, 'Annoncer le Verbe. Les Homélies sur le *Missus est* de Saint Bernard', in *Collectanea Cisterciensia,* 65 (2003), pp. 111-16 and 193-221.

This may all sound rather theological and perhaps even theoretical. One might with justice ask where Eros and Amor have gone. Of course, the angel of the Annunciation is the messenger of God's love to the Virgin. So Bernard the writer can be considered the messenger of God's love to the reader. Yet even then, this does not immediately implicate the author himself. He remains only a mediator. This will change completely, however, in Bernard's commentary on the Canticle. In this commentary is sung and evoked the true conjunction of the reader with the living Word, hiding in the biblical text and brought to light by the words of the writer. The culmination is reached halfway through the commentary when Bride and Groom sing their nuptial song. When the Groom exclaims: *Behold, thou art fair, my love; behold, thou art fair; thou hast doves' eyes*, he is addressing his Bride in the reader. And when the Bride sings her part: *Behold, thou art fair, my beloved, yea, pleasant*, she confesses in the name of the reader his love for the living Word as it has become alive to him in Bernard's words. Bernard did not remain a simple mediator of divine love to the reader. He became the agent, the originator, indeed, in every sense of the term, the author of the reciprocal love of the reader and the Word.[31]

4. Conclusion: the ideal reader

A long journey has been made from the almost theatrical presentation of Eros as a living force between the actors of a text to the staging of love in the reading process itself, from the reader as spectator to listener and next to an actor himself, from the reader looking upon love at work between people he sees before him to a reader as a *confidant* of someone's most intimate profession of love, and finally to a reader who, somewhat embarrassed, comes to realize that as a silent reader he has become the beloved himself and that now even his own love is awakened. Which reader, however, can go so far? Who would be so innocent as to let himself be seduced by the words of an author? What kind of reader might Bernard have had in mind? He gives the answer in his last sermon on the Canticle, touching upon the modesty, the *verecundia*, of the Bride: 'I should like to take this in my hands somehow and to pluck it like some

31. There is no place here to elaborate Bernard's entire writing strategy as displayed in his eighty-six *Sermons on the Canticle*. It has been done in my Ph.D. thesis, defended in the year 2000. Part of it will be treated in the article on *Sermon* 26 in *Disputatio: Speculum Sermonis* [see note 20]. A study of the entire work will be elaborated later.

beautiful flower from its place and offer it to the youths among us. Not that one should not strive to maintain it into a greater age. It is an ornament for every age. But what shines more clearly and is more beautiful than the grace of modesty in a younger age? What is lovelier than a modest youth?'[32] Here we have come back to our starting point. For Socrates is addressing none other than 'a fair boy, or, more properly speaking, a youth; he was very fair and had a great many lovers'.[33] For Socrates he had a name, Phaedrus, for Bernard he can be anyone, as long as he seeks to be modest and youthful in his reading.

32. Bernard, *Sermon on the Canticle* 86.1 in Jean Leclercq and Henri-Marie Rochais, *Sancti Bernardi Opera,* II (Rome, 1958), p. 317.
33. *Phaedrus* 237b.

Livia VISSER-FUCHS

THE MANUSCRIPT OF THE *ENSEIGNEMENT DE VRAIE NOBLESSE* MADE FOR RICHARD NEVILLE, EARL OF WARWICK, IN 1464

1. INTRODUCTION*

In 1461 both France and England had a new king. Louis XI of France succeeded his father in July; Edward IV, of the house of York, had defeated his predecessor, of the house of Lancaster, in March and was crowned in June. The change of dynasty in England owed much to the greatest magnate in the country, Richard Neville, Earl of Warwick, who because of this and his later political activities is known today as 'the Kingmaker'. During his lifetime the rest of Western Europe was well aware of Warwick's position; indeed, continental princes may have had an almost exaggerated idea of his influence.

The early 1460s saw great diplomatic activity within the triangle of France, England and Burgundy. The ageing Duke Philip the Good, who favoured the house of York, was partly holding on to his allegiance to the French crown, but was above all set on keeping France and England apart and prevent any alliance between them that might turn against himself and his lands. His son Charles, Count of Charolais, was more inclined to favour Lancaster and distance himself from France. Edward IV was busy at home, eradicating remnants of Lancastrian opposition, and wished to be friendly with everyone; he was also on the look-out for a wife. For all three sides economic motives where mixed with political ones and in all matters Warwick played an overwhelmingly important part.[1]

* Since finishing this article I have been in touch with Dr Bernhard Sterchi who kindly showed me an article he had written on the authorship of the *Instruction d'un jeune prince* and the *Enseignement de vraie noblesse*, entitled 'Hugues de Lannoy, auteur de l'*Enseignement de vraye noblesse,* de l'*Instruction d'un jeune prince*, et des *Enseignements paternels*', *Le Moyen Âge*, 110 (2004), 79-117. In this study he argues for the authorship of Hugues on more literary and interpretative grounds than I have done. Though I do not agree with every single point of his argument I very much regret having been unable to refer properly to his impressive contribution and I am grateful for several informative exchanges of ideas.

1. M.-R. Thielemans, *Bourgogne et Angleterre. Relations politiques et économiques entre les Pays-Bas Bourguignons et l'Angleterre, 1435-1467* (Brussels, 1966), 382-424; J. Calmette and G. Perinelle, *Louis XI et l'Angleterre (1461-1483)*, (Paris, 1930), 1-63;

Throughout 1461 to 1465 embassies from England, France *and* Burgundy, crossed and re-crossed the Narrow Seas. Frequently mentioned names on the Burgundian side are those of Jean III, Lord of Lannoy, Jean de Croy, Lord of Chimay, and Antoine de Croy, Count of Porcien. Lannoy and the Croy's, on occasion, represented King Louis as well as Duke Philip, and Jean de Lannoy in particular was very well liked by Edward IV, who tried to take him into his service.[2] English embassies were often headed by John, Lord Wenlock, or George Neville, the earl of Warwick's brother, who was Archbishop of York and Chancellor of England. Richard Whetehill,[3] Captain of Guines Castle near Calais, was an important go-between for all participants. Throughout this period Warwick himself, Captain of Calais since 1455 and well informed about Anglo-French-Burgundian relations, was expected to take part in the negotiations, but his role of defender of the newly risen house of York kept him busy in the North of England, where he reduced one Lancastrian stronghold after another. There were times, however, when both Louis XI and Philip the Good expected the earl almost daily.[4] All this waiting reached its climax in 1464: the arrival of Warwick at St Omer or Hesdin was announced for June, for August,[5] and then again for October, but he never came.[6] In September Edward IV, instead of announcing his marriage to a continental princess – which had been one of the matters Warwick was supposed to deal with – finally confessed to his clandestine marriage to Elizabeth Woodville.[7] She was the widow of a commoner, which caused resentment among the English nobility. The marriage also created friction among continental nobles because Elizabeth, through her mother, was a relative of the Luxembourg family, a niece of Louis, Count of St Pol. He was not only doing a permanent balancing act between France and Burgundy throughout this period, but he was also a great friend of Charles of Charolais, who in his turn was an enemy of the Croy. Anglo-French-Burgundian relations thus became even more complicated, and Warwick even less inclined to leave England.

C.L. Scofield, *The Life and Reign of Edward the Fourth*, 2 vols (London, 1923), 1, bk II; M.A. Hicks, *Warwick the Kingmaker* (Oxford, 1998), 261, seems not to grasp the complexities of the Lannoys' allegiance in those years.

2. Thielemans 1966 [note 1], 394, n. 155.
3. Thielemans 1966 [note 1], 405, n. 217.
4. Febr. 1462: Thielemans 1966 [note 1], 387, n. 119; June 1463, *ibid.*, 306, n. 165.
5. Scofield 1929 [note 1], 1, 345, n. 3.
6. April/May 1464, Thielemans 1966 [note 1], 406, n. 225. Compare the letter of Robert Neville, Warwick's secretary, to Richard Whetehill, 17 Nov. 1464, printed in E. Dupont, ed., *Mémoires de Philippe de Commynes*, 3 vols (Paris, 1840-47), 3, 211-17.
7. C. Ross, *Edward IV* (London, 1974), 91.

While this crisis was coming to a head, an unknown scribe in Bruges had been producing a luxury copy of a text sometimes called the *Imagination*, but more often the *Enseignement de (la) vraie noblesse*. A miniaturist of the same town had been executing a full-page miniature for its opening page and in the margin he had painted the arms and emblem of the earl of Warwick. The book was finished on 4 September 1464.

2. The text

The *Enseignement de vraie noblesse* is one of the many treatises composed in the later Middle Ages on how to live one's life as a knight, nobleman or prince. The most famous of such 'mirrors for princes' is Giles of Rome's *De regimine principum* of 1277-79. Giles was translated by Jean Wauquelin in 1450 at the request of Duke Philip, who already owned three copies of the Latin text.[8] More relevant in the present context than Giles' standard treatise are the many contemporary 'mirrors' written by members of their entourage for Dukes Philip and Charles personally. Their tone is often quite personal, too, which may have something to do with the habit, indeed obligation, of the knights of the Order of the Golden Fleece to criticise each other's conduct, including their sovereign's, during the chapters of the order. Some members of the Lannoy family, which numbered three founding knights of the Order, were tireless writers of practical memoranda and moral advice. In 1430, for example, Hugues de Lannoy, Lord of Santes, wrote a detailed plan of action for Philip the Good on the matter of Anglo-Burgundian cooperation; this had no theoretical content. In 1432/3 he even 'advised' Henry VI, and in 1436, a year after the peace of Arras, he composed another memorandum for the duke, more generally explaining the difficult situation in the duke's lands and the urgent need to make peace with England without loss of honour. A year later again he advised war, because the chances of preserving the peace had become remote. It has been suggested that some of Hugues' advice sowed the seed for the creation of the Great Council at Malines. He certainly advised the duke on financial matters, though not always from altruistic motives.[9]

8. Only one copy of the translation survives, made for Philip in 1452, after Wauquelin's death. Brussels, Bibliothèque Royale (hereafter BR), ms. 9043; see e.g. *Charles le Téméraire, 1433-1477*, catalogue of the exhibition at the Bibliothèque Royale 1977: item 76.

9. On Hugues, Comte B. de Lannoy, *Hugues de Lannoy, le bon seigneur de Santes, 1384-1456* (Brussels, 1957), and e.g. R. Vaughan, *Philip the Good. The Apogee of Burgundy* (London, 1970). The authorship of many of these texts is not beyond doubt.

Hugues' brother Guillebert de Lannoy, Lord of Willerval and another original knight of the Golden Fleece, travelled extensively round Europe and the East, writing reports of an extremely practical nature for diplomatic purposes. He also wrote a letter of fatherly advice to his son, which became well known outside the family circle.[10] A genuine mirror for princes, the *Instruction d'un jeune prince*, is usually also ascribed to him.[11] There is no certainty about the dedicatee of the *Instruction* and it is possible that the text is partly corrupt, but its didactic aim is clear. It claims to be an ancient document, a thirteenth-century treatise on good government written by an aged courtier for a fictional Norwegian prince at the request of his dying father,[12] who did not want his son to make the same mistakes he had made. The work stresses above all the need to fear God, and discusses the four virtues of prudence, justice, restraint and strength of mind, but also honesty and humility, daughter of prudence. A prince should avoid drunkenness, lust, ingratitude and laziness and be generous and high-minded. He should rule with reason and justice; his counsellors should be of high birth, sensible, pious, and not younger than thirty-six years of age. A prince should travel round his lands and see things for himself, thus keeping control of his lieutenants and officers. No wars should be fought unless absolutely necessary, and any youthful excess of energy should not be vented on Christians but on pagans, though even that should only be undertaken after long consideration and with the greatest care. The good running of his own estates is also crucial, and a prince should gather round him perfect knights, whose duties and virtues are illustrated with the story of Hue de Tabarie, a famous crusader. The book should probably be dated 1439-42; the author does not

10. The *Enseignements paternels* survive among others in mss that belonged to Charles the Bold and Margaret of York, and Louis de Gruuthuse.

11. Edited by C.G. van Leeuwen, *Denkbeelden van een Vliesridder. De 'Instruction d'un jeune prince' van Guillebert de Lannoy* (Amsterdam, 1975); Ch. Potvin, *Œuvres de Ghillebert de Lannoy* (Louvain, 1878), 327-432; J. Conell, '*L'Instruction d'ung jeune prince*: a critical edition and analysis', dissertation submitted to the faculty of the School of Arts and Sciences of the Catholic University of America, Washington, DC, 1984. See also C. Lemaire in *La Librairie des ducs de Bourgogne. Manuscrits conservés à la Bibliothèque royale de Belgique*, vol. II, *Textes didactiques*, ed. B. Bousmanne, F. Johan and C. van Hoorebeeck (Brussels, 2003), 222-25, and references given there.

12. Rather amazingly one modern source takes the text to be genuine: *Splendours of Flanders*, catalogue of an exhibition at the Fitzwilliam Museum, 1993, ed. A. Arnould and J.M. Massing (Cambridge, 1993), item 50 (Cambridge, Fitzwilliam Museum, MS 165); the MS bears the arms of Jacques de Luxembourg (*c.* 1420-1487), Lord of Richebourg, without the collar of the Fleece, so it was perhaps produced before 1468.

mince words and it is surprising that both Philip and Charles of Burgundy owned copies.[13]

A cousin of Hugues and Guillebert, Jean, head of the senior branch of the house of Lannoy and knight of the Fleece from 1451, also wrote a literary letter of paternal advice to his young son. Its intentions are very similar to those of the texts discussed above and the book was known outside the family circle, but it was genuinely written for the son, who was so young that the father feared he would not live to instruct him.[14]

The *Enseignement* was written for noble knights in particular.[15] The author explains how, on his way to the shrine of Our Lady of Halle, not actually in a dream, but totally immersed in his prayers, he met Lady Imagination, who is described as the prime mover of all human action. She instructed him at length on how to live a virtuous life and then charged him to go and pass on her precepts to knights and princes, the milieu in which he had been brought up and felt at ease. Imagination stressed that all the evil in the world is caused by the ignorance of princes, lords and knights about what 'nobility' really is, and if they were better instructed *bon et joyeulx temps regneroit* throughout Christianity.

3. The manuscript

The manuscript that bears Warwick's coat of arms is now Geneva, Bibliothèque publique et universitaire, MS fr. 166 **(fig. 1)**.[16] It is a composite manuscript in an eighteenth-century binding. The *Enseignement* is the first item, fol. 1-81, followed by the so-called *Vraie cronique dEscoce*,

13. For the surviving MSS of the *Instruction* see Appendix A, below.

14. B. de Lannoy and G. Dansaert, *Jean de Lannoy le bâtisseur 1410-1493* (Paris and Brussels, 1937).

15. For the contents list of Geneva, BPU, MS fr. 166 see Appendix B, below. For a summary of the text see F. Hachez, 'Un manuscrit de *L'Enseignement de la Vraie Noblesse*, provenant de la bibliothèque de Charles de Croy, Comte de Chimay', *Annales du Cercle archéologique de Mons*, 23 (1892), 91-104. Discussion of the contents in C.C. Willard, 'The concept of true nobility at the Burgundian court', *Studies in the Renaissance*, 14 (1967), 33-48, esp. 41, and M. Keen, 'Some late medieval ideas about nobility', in the same, *Nobles, Knights and Men-at-arms in the Middle Ages* (London and Rio Grande, 1996), 187-207, passim.

16. G. Doutrepont, *La littérature française à la cour des ducs de Bourgogne* (Paris, 1909, repr. Geneva, 1970), 317; H. Aubert, 'Notices sur les manuscrits Petau conservés à la bibliothèque de Genève', *Bibliothèque de l'école des chartes*, 72 (1911), 298-302; B. Gagnebin, 'L'enluminure de Charlemagne à François Ier', *Genava*, ns 24 (1976), 155-56. For the surviving mss of the *Enseignement* see Appendix A, below.

fol. 82-90,[17] a brief text called *Le droit que le roy Charles VIIIme pretend ou royaulme de Naples*, fol. 91, and finally the *Histoire légendaire de sainte Hélène*, fol. 91v-93. The copying of the *Enseignement* was finished on 4 September 1464, according to the manuscript itself, fol. 81, and the writing of the *Vraie cronique* may be of a later date. The two short final texts were added in the 1490s at the earliest and are not really relevant to the present investigation.

Folio 3 has a large miniature and a decorated full margin on all sides. In the lower margin appears the elaborate coat of arms[18] of Richard Neville, Earl of Warwick, surrounded by the Garter.[19] In the right margin is a white bear standing on its hind legs, chained by its collar to a brown tree trunk with very short lopped branches, the trunk obviously representing a 'ragged staff'; tree and bear are standing on a small green 'island'. The bear, and especially the ragged staff were well-known in the Low Countries to be Warwick's emblems. During the English civil war of 1470-71 many chroniclers reported how people changed their allegiance and removed Edward IV's white rose from their clothes to replace it with the ragged staff, *baton nouilleux*, *baculus peregrinantium*.[20]

The rest of the margin is filled with a floral design, acanthus leaves, pinks, strawberries and large blue columbines. The miniature itself shows a landscape: on the left kneels the author, a nobleman wearing what appears to be the collar of the Golden Fleece, his hands joined in prayer; his horse is behind him, his hat on the ground in front of him. On the right is an elegant pale-pink church with a tower on its crossing, tall windows and a blue tiled roof, presumably the shrine of Our Lady of Halle.[21] In the foreground stands a lady, Imagination, in a red gown, covered by a dark purple mantle; her right hand holds up a fold of her mantle, her left hand is raised in a gesture that shows she is speaking to the kneeling

17. The title follows the spelling used by K. Daly, 'The *Vraie cronique dEscoce* and Franco-Scottish diplomacy: an historical work by John Ireland?', *Nottingham Medieval Studies*, 35 (1991), 106-33.

18. Quartered: **1**, parted per pale, 1, Beauchamp, gules, a fess between six crosslets, or, 2, Newburgh Earls of Warwick, chequy or and azure a chevron ermine; **2**, parted per pale. 1, Montagu, argent, three fusils conjoined in fess, gules, 2, Monthemer, or, an eagle displayed, wings depressed, vert, beaked and membered gules; **3**, Neville, Earls of Salisbury, gules, a saltire argent, a label of three points (colour uncertain, should be argent); **4**, quartered, 1 and 4, Clare, or, three chevronels gules, 2 and 3, Spencer, quartered, 1 and 4, argent, 2 and 3, gules, fretty or, over all a bend sable.

19. Warwick became a knight of the Garter in 1460.

20. See e.g. L. Visser-Fuchs, 'Edward IV's "memoir on paper" to Charles, Duke of Burgundy: the so-called "Short Version of the *Arrivall*"', *Nottingham Medieval Studies*, 36 (1992), 167-227, esp. 192, n. 98.

21. Comp. e.g. H. van der Velden, *The Donor's Image* (Turnhout, 2000), 166-78.

man. Trees and rocks are scattered throughout the landscape; there are hills, a broad river and on the horizon appear the pale blue silhouettes of churches and other buildings, probably representing the skyline of Brussels, only ten miles from Halle.

The *Vraie cronique* has a crudely painted coat of arms of Scotland at the beginning, fol. 82, but no other decoration. The semi-cursive, not-quite-professional hand can be dated to any time between December 1463 – the date of the last event recorded in the text – and 1500. On the last page of the text, fol. 90v, is an early sixteenth-century note in a different hand (abbreviations extended and capitals mine): *Ce lyvre me bailla monseigneur dAubigny et fut*[22] *fet par ung grant clerc escosois nomme Irlandia nory*[23] *a Paris lonc tamps.*

The decoration of the first text establishes the earl of Warwick as its first (intended?) owner. The inscription suggests that later the first two texts, or perhaps only the *Vraie cronique,* were owned by Bérault Stuart, 3d Lord of Aubigny (*c.*1452-1508), a Scotsman who spent most of his life in France in the service of Louis XI, Charles VIII and Louis XII. There is a, probably incorrect, tradition that he fought at the head of a Scottish contingent at the battle of Bosworth, where Richard III died to be succeeded by Henry Tudor as Henry VII.[24] Stuart was lieutenant-general of the French army in the Italian wars. Nothing is known about his books except that he himself wrote a treatise on the art of war.[25]

It is remarkable that both texts seem to belong to the same context, that of the diplomatic activities between England, France and Burgundy in 1464, which also included Scotland. The first text, the copy of the *Enseignement*, belongs to this context because of its intended ownership – Warwick, though absent, was the undoubted protagonist whose cooperation was sought by all parties – and its date of completion. The *Vraie cronique dEscoce* has been studied in detail and credibly connected to the proposed negotiations of the spring, summer and finally the autumn of

22. *fut* is inserted above the line.

23. As read by Kathleen Daly and no doubt correct; previous commentators had read *mort*.

24. R.A. Griffiths, R.S. Thomas, *The Making of the Tudor Dynasty* (Gloucester, 1985), 130-31; M. Bennett, *The Battle of Bosworth* (Stroud, 1993), 83, 104, 178 n. 14. Bosworth is not among the many battles discussed in his treatise.

25. The inventory accompanying his testament is very short and has no details, Edinburgh, Scottish Record Office, the testament of Barald Stewart, Lord of Aubigny, GD220/2/1, fol. 114r-v; E. de Comminges, *Traité sur l'art de guerre de Bérault Stuart, seigneur d'Aubigny* (The Hague, 1976), ix-xxxii.

1464.[26] It is also a curious fact that the illuminator of the Warwick *Enseignement*, a collaborator of the famous Willem Vreelant, has recently been called the 'Master of the *Vraie cronique dEscoce*', after his work, in 1464-1467, on Brussels, BR, ms. 9469-70.[27] This latter manuscript contains yet another text connected to the negotiations of 1464, the *Traité contre les prétensions des anglais à la couronne de France*, better known by its opening words as *Pour ce que plusieurs*. These texts in their context of 1464 will be discussed again below.[28]

4. The author

The author of the *Enseignement de vraie noblesse* has been assumed to be Guillebert de Lannoy because of its resemblances to another contemporary 'mirror for princes' the *Instruction d'ung jeune prince*; Guillebert's authorship of the latter is often treated as a fact.[29]

Let us first look at the resemblances between the two texts. The only commentator of the *Enseignement*, Hachez, saw a relation between the two because both authors hide behind an imaginary person to discuss matters that could not be talked about openly.[30] Van Leeuwen, editor of the *Instruction*, correctly argued that the large number of contemporary texts claiming to be written by an imaginary author precludes any conclusions, but he does admit that there seem to be general resemblances in style and in 'philosophy'. Some long sections are actually completely identical: the discussion of the Four Cardinal Virtues and the historical survey of the origins of the 'order' of knighthood; both authors also use

26. Daly 1991 [note 17], 122-25. For the surviving MSS of the *Vraie cronique* see Appendix A, below.

27. B. Bousmanne, *"Item a Guillaume Wyelant aussi enlumineur". Willem Vrelant. Un aspect de l'enluminure dans les Pays-Bas méridionaux sous le mécénat des ducs de Bourgogne, Philippe le Bon et Charles le Téméraire* (Turnhout, 1997), 55-57, and personal information from Dr Bousmanne.

28. On this text: P.S. Lewis, 'War propaganda and historiography in fifteenth-century France and England', *Transactions of the Royal Historical Society*, 15 (1965), 1-21, esp. 12 (n. 2)-14, 17, 20; C. Taylor, 'Sir John Fortescue and the French polemical treatises of the Hundred Years War', *English Historical Review*, 14 (1999), 112-29, esp. 121-29. For the surviving MSS of *Pour ce que plusieurs* see Appendix A, below.

29. See the introductions to the editions in n. 11, above, but also the balanced view of Doutrepont 1909 [note 16], 314-18: 'Le jeu des rapprochements, dans une literature aussi peu originale que celle du xve siècle, est assez dangereux et peut conduire loin. Tant d'analogies s'observent entre les oeuvres d'alors qu'on finirait par attribuer à quatre ou cinq auteurs tous les textes qui nous sont arrives sans signature.'

30. Hachez 1892 [note 15], 104.

the story of Hue de Tabarie, the crusader who instructed Sultan Saladin about the ceremony of creating a Christian knight.[31] None of these resemblances *prove* that the same man wrote both texts, however, for it is well known that prose texts of the period show great similarity,[32] which does not indicate unity of authorship. If the two texts discussed here were composed in the same milieu by men of the same backgrounds the similarity obviously would be even more marked. It is also a fact that many contemporary works were filled in with, or even largely made up out of, existing texts, which can often be found in several separate books by different authors.

The section on the Virtues in the *Instruction* and the *Enseignement* is a set piece that may well exist elsewhere, and so may the 'early history' of chivalry.[33] The instructions and explanations concerning the making of a Christian knight, which the *Instruction* gives in full, is in the *Enseignement* cleverly 'abbreviated' by using the device of a written document which Hugh de Tabarie gives to Saladin:

> Verite est que on treuve en la cronique et conqueste de la Terre Saincte que fist le vaillant Crestien Godeffroy de Buillon, qui entre autres de sa compaignie y ot ung chevalier franchois nonme Hue, qui fu seigneur de Tabarie. Lequel par fortune darmes chey a estre prisonnier au souldan de Surie, nonme Salhadin, lequel le fist venir devant lui et apres pluiseurs paroles et interrogations diverses lui demanda quel chose estoit chevalerie selon lentendement des Crestiens, lequel prinst delay de y respondre. ¶En briefz jours apres lui bailla par escript selon son entendement la maniere que ou temps de lors on tenoit a faire chevalier nouvel en Crestiennete.[34]
>
> [In the chronicle of the conquest of the Holy Land by the valiant Christian Godfrey of Bouillon one finds [the story of] one of the men in his retinue, a French knight called Hugh, who was lord of Tabarie. Through the fortunes of war this man became a prisoner of the sultan of Syria, called Saladin, who had him appear before him and after some conversation and various questions asked him what 'knighthood' was according to Christians. Hugh took his time over answering and a few days later sent a written account of how, according to him, Christians at that time preferred to create new knights.]

The meeting between Hue de Tabarie and Saladin was certainly an existing text.[35] The story, which celebrates knighthood and the symbolic

31. Van Leeuwen 1975 [note 11], xxiii; the identical sections are on 12-14, and 40-49, the story of Saladin on 49-54, at the end of the text.

32. J. Rasmussen, J., *La prose narrative française du XVe siècle* (Copenhague, 1958), *passim*, and Doutrepont quoted in note 29, above.

33. The fact that I have not yet been able to find another copy of these texts is more likely to be due to my ignorance than to their non-existence.

34. Geneva, BPU, MS fr. 166, fol. 32r-v; capitals, u and v modernised.

35. K. Busby, ed., *Raoul de Hodenc: Le Roman des Eles. The Anonymous Ordene de Chevalerie*, Utrecht Publications in General and Comparative Literature, 17 (Utrecht,

meaning of the various ceremonies that accompanied the making of a knight, first occurs briefly in historical sources, and in the thirteenth century was elaborated, altered and written up in verse by a clerical author with the title *Ordene de chevalerie*. Not long after a prose version was made which survives in several manuscripts from the thirteenth to the fifteenth century in various contexts, both historical and literary. The most relevant of these contexts is *l'Histoire de Jean d'Avesnes*, one of those *mises en prose* that were so well liked in Burgundian court circles. One manuscript of *Jean d'Avesnes* occurs in the inventory of Philip the Good,[36] the other bears the arms of Philippe de Croy, Lord of Quiévrain, as well as other indications of Croy ownership.[37] The story is in three parts and relates the life of the semi-historical Jean d'Avesnes, his son, and finally and rather unexpectedly, Saladin. In the third part the meeting of Hue de Tabarie and the sultan was seamlessly included,[38] the text differing little from the version given in the *Instruction d'un jeune prince*. Clearly, many book lovers at the court could have known this version of the story and every author among them could have used it.

The evidence for the authorship of the *Instruction* itself runs as follows. In several presentation miniatures of the text the author wears the collar of the Golden Fleece. He gives his name as *Foliant de Ional*, of which the first part means 'the wanderer' and the third almost certainly is *lanoi* (Lannoy) reversed. The resemblance of the text – in language and construction – to texts known to have been written by one or other of the Lannoy brothers, Hugues and Guillebert, suggests one of them also composed the *Instruction*. Guillebert was a founder member of the order and a great traveller. In one manuscript, one of the Lannoy texts, the so-called *Avis de 1439*,[39] resembles the *Instruction* so closely that it has been assumed to be necessarily by the same author. In the *Avis* Hugues is put forward as a good man to fill an important position, which has been taken to preclude his authorship, leaving Guillebert as the only candidate for the authorship of the *Instruction* itself.

1983), introduction; H. Kjellman, 'Les rédactions en prose de *l'Ordre de Chevalerie*', *Studier i modern sprakvetenskap* (1920), 139-77.

36. Paris, BN, MS fr. 12572; J. Barrois, *Bibliothèque prototypographique ou Librairies des fils du roi Jean, Charles V, Jean de Berri, Philippe le Bon et les siens* (Paris, 1830), no. 1279.

37. Paris, Bibliothèque de l'Arsenal, MS 5208; M. Debae, *La Bibliothèque de Marguérite d'Autriche. Essai de reconstruction d'après l'inventaire de 1523-1524* (Louvain and Paris, 1995), no. [11].

38. L.S. Crist, ed., *Saladin. Suite et fin du deuxième Cycle de la Croisade* (Geneva, 1972), 73-78.

39. Paris, BN, MS fr. 1278, fol. 16 ss.

It is arguable, however, that all the above evidence does not prove that Guillebert rather than Hugues was the author of either text: *both* were knights of the Fleece, *both* travelled extensively.[40] The word *foliant*, on which most of the argument rests,[41] also means 'wandering in the mind', 'being foolish', and may not refer to the author's travels at all; it is quite conceivable that the author called himself 'the fool of Lannoy'![42] It is also debatable whether Hugues would have been incapable of putting himself forward if he was not averse to protesting to the duke about the reduction of his own salary as governor of Holland and Zeeland in March 1438.[43] The name could, moreover, have been inserted in an existing text, without Hugues' knowledge.

There is also more positive evidence for Hugues' authorship, which has not been previously used. In the will of Hugues' wife, Marguérite de Boncourt (or Bécourd), of 14 June 1460,[44] she bequeathed many books to relatives, friends and servants. To Jehan Frémault, son of Lotard, a relative,[45] she leaves *ung livre que fist et composa mon dit feu seigneur*

40. According to his epitaph (see below) Hugues apparently travelled as widely as his brother, and Baudouin de Lannoy 1957 [note 9], 164, without any ulterior motive, calls Hugues' life 'l'existence vagabonde'. The epitaph mentions his visit to *Liflant*, also mentioned at the beginning of the *Instruction.*

41. Potvin 1878 [note 11], p. xxxix.

42. I would also suggest that the names of the some of the principal characters in the book, the three generations of 'Norwegian' rulers, *Ruthegeer*, *Ollerich* and *Rodolph*, were very consciously chosen. The first probably means 'renowned fighter with a spear' and fits John the Fearless very well, the second means 'rich in inherited lands', which is a perfect description of Philip the Good; whether the third, 'famous wolf', fits Charles the Bold is debatable, for he may still have been an unknown quantity at the time the book was written, after 1435 and before 1456 or 1462. If this name does mean to describe Charles it suggests he was already a young man in his teens or twenties and his character was becoming evident when the *Instruction* was composed. Both Hugues and Guillebert could have learned the meaning of such Germanic names while fighting in North-Eastern Europe. See e.g. J. van der Schaar, *Woordenboek van Voornamen. Inventarisatie van de doop- en roepnamen met hun etymologie* (Utrecht and Antwerp, 1964), s.n.

43. R. Vaughan 1970 [note 9], 263-65; De Lannoy 1957 [note 9], 141-42.

44. Printed in De Lannoy 1957 [note 9], 281-95; B. Schnerb, 'Piété et culture d'une noble dame au milieu du XVe siècle: l'exemple de Marguerite de Boncourt, dame de Santes', in *Au cloître et dans le monde. Femmes, hommes et sociétés (IXe-XVe siècle). Mélanges en l'honneur de Paulette L'Hermite-Leclercq*, Cultures et civilisations médiévales, 23, ed. P. Henriet and A.-M. Legras (Paris, 2000), 235-45; Dr Schnerb does not discuss the entry used here as part of the authorship argument, merely saying 'Hugues fut donques l'auteur de deux oeuvres, peut-être didactiques ou littéraires, dont nous ne savons rien'.

45. The Fremaults were as important in Lille in the 15th C. as the Hangouarts – the chronicler Jean de Wavrin married a Hangouart – and the Tenremondes, etc., D. Clauzel, 'Les elites urbaines et le pouvoir municipal: le "cas" de la bonne ville de Lille aux XIVe et XVe siècles', *Revue du Nord*, 78 (1996), 241-67, esp. 250-51; P. d'Feuchere, 'La bourgeoisie lilloise au Moyen Age', *Annales ESC*, 4 (1949), 421-30. Lotard: e.g. M. Sommé, *Isabelle de Portugal, Duchesse de Bourgogne. Une femme au pouvoir au XVe siècle* (Villeneuve d'Ascq, 1998), 363

mary and – even more tellingly – to Hue de Carvin[46] *ung livre couvert de noir, ou sont escrips les deux livres que fist mon dit seigneur mary.* The phrasing of the latter bequest is crucial: it suggests that Hugues de Lannoy wrote two 'books', no more and no less. These are unlikely to be any of the short memoranda and reports he composed for Duke Philip, for those are more numerous and cannot really be called 'books'. So we can legitimately search for two proper, book-length texts written by Hugues. Indeed, there *must* have existed at some point two books written by Hugues,[47] one could be the *Instruction* – which cannot be proved unless we accept the argument about the resemblance of the two texts – the other the *Enseignement*, for which there is more evidence.

In the British Library there are three manuscripts of the *Enseignement*. Chronologically the second one, MS Harley 4397, is a composite book, not illustrated, written on paper in a professional cursive hand; its parchment flyleaves(?) appear to bear the marks of a binding that had clasps and a title frame. The first item in the book is (capitals mine): *le livre de l'Imagination au pelerin de Haulx fait par monsieur de Santes.* This manuscript occurs in the inventory of the library of Charles II, Count of Lalaing, made in 1541.[48] In the same inventory another book occurs, which appears not to have survived and is described as: *Le Pelerinage de Haulx compose par Monseigneur de Sante[s] à l'enseignement des princes escript à la main.*[49]

Equally important and even more interesting is another British Library manuscript, Additional 15469, another paper book, slim, of similar 'A4' size and still in its original binding, which moreover has the remains of two brass clasps on the back board. The clasps are shaped like shields and both bear the same coat of arms: three lions rampant within a engrailed

46. I have not yet found Hue de Carvin elsewhere; his daughter is described as the testatrix's goddaughter and his wife as her cousin.

47. One could, of course, argue that both texts are lost, but that does seem unlikely, given the wealth of written texts from the hands of members of the Lannoy family that does survive.

48. M. Mestayer, 'La bibliothèque de Charles II, comte de Lalaing, en 1541, *Publications du Centre européen d'études bourguignonnes*, 31 (1991), 199-216, esp. 206, lines 20-21:*L'Imagination au pelerin de Haulx fait par monsieur de Sante[s], compile par reverend pere en Dieu Ghillame evesque de Tournay.* This matches the beginning and the end of the contents list – of which the lay-out is identical to those other Lalaing mss e.g. London, BL, MS Harley 4354 – on fol.1 (capitals mine and abbreviations extended): *le livre de l'Imagination au pelerin de Haulx fait par monsieur de Santes*, and *ung Brief et utile traite de conseil compile par reverent pere en Dieu Ghuillaume [Fillastre], Evesque de Tournay*; see Appendix B, below.

49. Mestayer 1991 [note 48], 206, lines 8-9; in both cases the inventory leaves off the –s at the end of *Santes*, but in London, BL, MS Add. 4379 it is certainly there.

border. These are the arms of Hugues who bore argent, three lions rampant vert, armed and crowned or and langued gules, within a engrailed border gules; Guillebert bore the same arms but differenced by a label azure; the label clearly is not on the clasps of the manuscript. Though Guillebert outlived his childless brother by four years and inherited Santes and may have inherited Hugues' arms, it is not known, nor is it likely, that he ever used his elder brother's arms or his title.[50] Usually *le seigneur* – or *le bon seigneur – de Santes* refers to Hugues; Guillebert is the *seigneur de Willerval*; both had borne their titles for a lifetime and people are unlikely to have ever referred to either of them in another way.

In BL, MS Add. 15469 at the end of the text of the *Enseignement*, which has no title, there is one blank page, followed by two flyleaves, fol. 80-81, on which is written in a different, less competent hand, a prose epitaph of Hugues. This epitaph is well known and occurs in several other manuscripts,[51] but is particularly relevant in the context of this manuscript. It was presumably included on purpose, because the owner of the manuscript knew that the text was by Hugues. This copy of the epitaph also appears to be the oldest surviving, apart from the one that was inscribed on a bronze plaque on Hugues' actual tomb in the church of St Peter in Lille.[52]

The manuscript has other remarkable features: its first *and* its last flyleaf, both stuck down, contain otherwise lost sections of the town accounts of Ypres, probably dating from 1410-1420.[53] There are seven miniatures, slightly crude (home-made?) but competent water colours, which are set at the head of each chapter and depict in detail the contents of each. It is especially remarkable that its opening illustration (fol. 3; **fig. 2**), showing the knight kneeling to Lady Imagination, appears to be the only one that attempts to show Imagination's mantle as it should be:

> un mantel … moult estrange, car je la veoie apparoir de toutes les couleurs que onques paintre tant fust soubtil employast en ses paintures. Lesquelles couleurs se diversoient incessaument de couleur a autre, car ce que estoit blanc se moustroit tantost noir, vermeil, azur ou or et ainsy entre meslez de couleur a autre.[54]

50. I am grateful to Dr Jacques Paviot for his help in this matter.

51. Printed in De Lannoy 1957 [note 9], 167-68, and see n. 32 for other editions. The epitaph also occurs in Paris, BN, MS fr. 24020; Lille, Bibliothèque municipale, MS 263; Douai Bibliothèque municipale, MS 968; Brussels, BR, MSS II 3687 and II 1209, but these are all late or very late copies, 16th to 18th C.

52. A.L. Millin, *Antiquités nationals*, 5 vols (Paris, 1790-98), 5, 42-45, pl. LIV [engraving].

53. I am grateful to Dr Rik Opsomer of the Townarchives in Ypres for studying the xeroxes I sent him and for his provisional conclusion about the date of the account entries.

54. Geneva, BPU, MS fr. 166, fol. 3v.

[a mantle that was very strange, for I saw how it appeared to have all the colours that the most subtle painter ever used in his paintings. These colours changed continuously from one to another, for what was white one moment the next moment turned out to be black, red, blue or gold, and so the colours were mixed together.]

The illuminator used dots of different colours to suggest the 'changeability' of the material of the mantle.

The oldest *Enseignement* manuscript of the Bibliothèque Royale Albert I at Brussels, MS 10314 (**fig. 3**), has several puzzling indications about the authorship (or ownership) of the text. The first appears in its only illustration, a drawing with some colour at the beginning of the text. The colours are mainly red and green with some blue; on Lady Imagination's mantle there seems to be a rampant lion in red and an engrailed border, also red. It is just possible that the artist made an error and these were, at least originally, meant to be the arms of Hugues de Lannoy.[55]

5. Bears

Manuscript 10314 at the Brussels Bibliothèque Royale has another remarkable, though not in itself unusual feature: in the margin around the only illustration are four bears, two on either side. They are competently drawn, life-like bears, standing on their hind legs – though not actually standing on anything – holding on to a tree trunk with lopped branches. They are muzzled and chained to the tree; those on the left are facing right, those on the right facing left. In the bottom margin is another, larger but very similar trunk with lopped branches, lying on its side. The bears on the left form a pair, as do those on the right, in that each pair is virtually identical and must have been produced by mechanical copying, tracing on oiled parchment, re-tracing, pricking and pouncing. They are clearly related to the bears used on playing cards and their models. Very similar bears appear on cards showing the 'Beasts of Prey',[56] and were

55. Hachez 1892 [note 5], 96, incorrectly states that Imagination's mantle in Brussels, BR, MS 10314, f. 2, is *bariolé*, multi-coloured (which it should be if the artist had followed the text); comp. F. Lyna, *Les principaux manuscrits à peintures de la Bibliothèque royale de Bruxelles* (Brussels, 1989), 3, pt 1, 369-74, esp. 373, and Debae 1995 [note 37], 405-06. The ms. has, on its first original flyleaf: *du iiij^e^ xviij pepitre le [blank]* in a 15th-century hand.

56. A.H. van Buren and S. Edmunds, 'Playing cards and manuscripts: some widely disseminated fifteenth-century model sheets', *Art Bulletin*, 56 (1974), 12-30, esp. 14, fig. 4; M. Wolff, 'Some manuscript sources for the Playing-Card Master's number cards', *Art Bulletin*, 64 (1982), 587-600.

used, for example, in the early fifteenth-century manuscript of Gaston Phoebus' *Livre de chasse*, Paris, BN, MS fr. 616, fol. 27v.[57]

More interesting than how the bears got into the Brussels manuscript is the question of why they are there. It has been surmised that they were the emblems of the prospective owner of the book, whose coat of arms is supposed to appear on the cloak of Lady Imagination,[58] but no candidate has been put forward. In fact, apart from the earl of Warwick himself, there appears to have been no one who had a bear and ragged staff as his emblem. A well known book owner whose manuscripts show many bears, was Guillaume Jouvenel des Ursins, but his bears are very different and though chained and muzzled, they do not hold ragged staves.[59]

The white bear and ragged staff in the Geneva manuscript were painted in for 'legitimate' and obvious reasons, particularly in combination with Warwick's undoubted coat of arms in the lower margin, but the presence of all those bears in the Brussels manuscript remains mysterious. The first known owner of this Brussels *Enseignement*[60] is Charles de Croy, Count, later Prince, of Chimay (died 1527).[61] His grandfather was the Jean de Croy, Lord, later Count, of Chimay (died 1473), who took part in the negotiations of 1464. Jean was another founding member of the Golden Fleece, and a bibliophile known to have assisted Duke Philip in the acquisition of manuscripts, and a number of texts were produced for him.[62] He was well acquainted with Guillebert and Hugues de Lannoy,

57. Illustrated in e.g. G. Bise, *Medieval Hunting Scenes. ("The Hunting Book" by Gaston Phoebus)*, (Geneva, 1978).

58. Lyna 1989 [note 55], 3, pt 1, 373.

59. E.g. N. Reynaud, 'Les Heures du chancelier Guillaume Jouvenel des Ursins et la peinture parisienne autour de 1440', *Revue de l'art*, 126 (1999), 23-35.

60. There are two other MSS of the text in the Brussels BR, 11047 and 11049; the first appears in the 1467/8 inventory of Philip the Good's library (J. Barrois, *Bibliothèque prototypographique, ou Librairies des fils du roi Jean, Charles V, Jean de Berri, Philippe le Bon et les siens*, Paris 1830, nos 972 and 1802) it has attractive illumination but no miniatures; the second, 11049, has links with Savoy, belonged to Margaret of Austria among others and was made *c.* 1500, Lyna 1989 [note 55], nos 340, 1-2, vol. 3, pt 1, 369-375; vol. 3, pt 2, 472-73, pl. 109.

61. His books: e.g. M. van Houtryve, 'Un manuscrit de l'*Histoire d'Olivier de castile* dans la bibliothèque des Croy', in *Fin du Moyen Age et Renaissance. Mélanges de philologie française offerts à Robert Guiette* (Antwerp, 1961), 115-20.

62. The prose romances *Olivier de Castile* and *Cléomadès* were composed for him, Doutrepont 1909 [note 16], 55-56, 61; M. Debae, 'Une lignée de chevaliers bibliophiles: Jean, Philippe, et Charles de Croy, comtes de Chimay', in *L'ordre de la Toison d'or de Philippe le Bon à Philippe le Beau (1430-1505): ideal ou reflet d'une société?*, ed. P. Cockshaw and C. Van de Bergen-Pantens (Brussels, 1996), 201-05; R. De Smedt, *Les Chevaliers de l'Ordre de la Toison d'or au XVe siècle*, Kieler Werkstücke. Reihe D: Beiträge zur europäische Geschichte des späten Mittelalters 3, gen. ed. W Paravicini, ed. R. de Smedt (Frankfurt am Main, 1994, revised edn 2000), no. 22, and *Nationaal Biografisch Woordenboek* (Brussels, 1964-), 14 (1992), cols. 132-37.

not only as relatives,[63] but also as members of the same court circle and brother knights. They were part of the same 'committee' instituted by Philip the Good in 1445-6 to revise the statutes of the order of the Golden Fleece, which consisted of Anthoine and Jean de Croy, Philippe de Ternant and Guillebert and Hugues de Lannoy.[64] The text they amended and reorganised according to their commission bore certain resemblances to the *Enseignement* and other 'mirrors', but the occasion also threw them together for a period while discussing problems of a moral and literary nature. The *Enseignement* is likely to have been written at around this same time and the fact that Hugues was working on it may well have been known to his colleagues.

The possible ownership of the Brussels BR copy by Jean de Croy may also have certain implications for the ownership of the text by Warwick. If it is true that Jean was sometimes instrumental in providing books for his duke, he must have been even more aware of their value than his book collecting fellow courtiers and it may have been he who decided to give the text to Warwick as a gift at the time of the 1464 diplomatic exchanges. The fact that both texts have bears in their decoration could then be explained in the following tentative way: in the Warwick manuscript the bear was included on purpose, but this book may have set a fashion, inspiring artists of the same or connected workshops to decorate their production in a similar way. Another possible proof of this interpretation is to be found in the margin of the first miniature in yet another manuscript of the *Enseignement,* London, BL, MS Royal 19 C viij, fol. 1.[65] This book was made for King Henry VII of England by his 'librarian', Quentin Poulet,[66] in 1496, 'finished at the manor of Shene on the last day of June' (*parachevee le derrenier jour de Juin au manoir de Shene lan mil CCCC iiij^{xx} et xvj*). Poulet was a native of Lille – the town from which the author of the *Imagination* set out on his pilgrimage – but his preface gives no indication of where he found the text and almost

63. Antoine and Jean de Croy's sister, Jeanne, married Jean II de Lannoy, father of Jean III.

64. De Lannoy 1957 [note 9], 157-58; A.S. Korteweg, 'Le manuscrit KB 76 E 14 de La Haye, le contenu et la décoration des livres des Statuts au xve et xvie siècles', in Cockshaw and Van de Bergen-Pantens 1996 [note 62], 39-40.

65. G.F. Warner and J.P. Gilson, *Catalogue of the Western Manuscripts in the Old Royal and King's Collections*, 4 vols (London, 1921), 3, 336.

66. On Poulet and this MS: J. Backhouse, 'Founders of the royal library', in D. Williams, ed., *England in the Fifteenth Century. Proceedings of the 1986 Harlaxton Symposium* (Woodbridge, 1987), 32-36 and pl. 11 (fol. 3).

suggests that he composed it himself.[67] Though there is no mention of the original author, his exemplar may have influenced the decoration, for in the lower margin of folio 1, below the miniature of a kneeling author presenting a book, among large *trompe l'oeil* pink and white pinks is a tiny, incongruous looking brown bear.

6. 1464

The *Vraie cronique dEscoce* and the *Pour ce que plusieurs*, texts that can both be related, directly or indirectly, by date or by physical link, to Warwick's copy of the *Enseignement*, were both written for a particular purpose. The *Vraie cronique* was composed by a Scotsman resident in France, probably using documents available in the French royal archives. He emphasised Scotland's independence and autonomy and also the alliance between Scotland and France, both issues that were essential to the diplomacy of the 1460s. In these years English claims to Scottish territory and Scottish claims to parts of northern England were part of the background and the Scots and the French needed each other's support against the English. However, the text particularly mentions Scottish indebtedness to France and is more ambiguous about Scottish homage to England than a Scotsman would have been. This background, together with the facts that the last event in the text is the death of Mary of Gueldres in November 1463 and that there seems to be no Scottish exemplar – all surviving copies being French in origin – suggests that the *Vraie cronique* was produced in France, in 1464, as a diplomatic dossier for French use.[68]

Pour ce que plusieurs, as its other title, *Traité contre les pretensions des Anglais à la couronne de France* shows, deals with the English claim to the throne of France. It did so in the way many treatises had done, but it was clearly written after the accession of Edward IV, for the author was no longer able to say that the house of York had a better claim to England than the Lancastrians – as his predecessors in similar texts had done. He was forced to look for different arguments and another emphasis, such as the inability of women to rule or pass on the right of inheritance. The book was also influenced by the then recent work of the Eng-

67. Fol. 1: 'Je ... vous presente ce petit traictie lequel par maniere de passe temps et pour eschevier oyseuse ... ay mis et reduict par lescript de ma simple et rude main.'
68. Daly 1991 [note 17], 110-25.

lish lawyer and politician Sir John Fortescue, which denied any Yorkist right to the English throne.[69]

Both the *Vraie cronique* and *Pour ce que plusieurs* are thus likely to be diplomatic documents made for the use of the French negotiators of 1464 against the English and/or the Scots. Some of these negotiators, technically, were Jean de Lannoy and Jean and Antoine de Croy and it is possible they, too, were equipped with this material, though this is not essential for maintaining a link between these treatises and the *Enseignement.*

The theme of the *Enseignement* is that 'everything is wrong' 'in many countries, but especially in France, England and the neighbouring lands' (*en plusieurs pays et contrees et par especial es parties de France, Angleterre et marches denviron*). This can be remedied by instructing princes, lords and knights in their duties. It was the author's task to pass this message on, which he did by writing it down. Did his relatives, the de Croy's and de Lannoy, take up this task in their turn and considered it useful to have it brought to the attention of their English colleague, the earl of Warwick? Did they think it would be 'good' for him to read these lessons upon the nature of 'true nobility'? If they did, they 'wrapped up' their suggestive present luxuriously in an attractive production by one of the major Bruges workshops of the day. The Franco-Burgundian negotiators were all book owners and book lovers, the gift of a book is something that could well have occurred to them, and they were probably all aware of this impeccable and appropriate family text sitting around to be copied.[70] Books are usually not mentioned separately among (diplomatic) gifts, but that does not mean they were not used as such, particularly when they were considered useful to convince the recipient of the necessity of some particular action or attitude.[71] Of course, the English earl could have found and ordered the book himself – many of his countrymen of equal status did purchase Flemish manuscripts throughout the fif-

69. Taylor 1991 [note 28]: pp. 121-26; the same, 'War, propaganda and diplomacy in fifteenth-century France and England', in C. Allmand, ed., *War, Government and Power in Late Medieval France* (Liverpool, 2000), 70-91.

70. It was only much later that the text became known outside the Burgundian court circle, e.g. when Henry VII's librarian, Quentin Poulet, introduced it into England (see n. 66, above); Poulet was a native of Lille.

71. Like Cardinal Bessarion's copies of his *Orationes* to the emperor, the kings of England and France and the dukes of Burgundy and Savoy to convince them of the need for a crusade, A.F. Sutton and L. Visser-Fuchs, *Richard III's Books* (Stroud, 1997), 33-34, and references given there. Books were also given as New Year gifts, *ibid.*: 40, 69, and were, of course, presented on other occasions by their authors; perhaps being closely related to the author allowed family members to do the same.

teenth century – but if so, why did not the manuscript go to England and end up in an English collection? No other volume from Warwick's library survives, which may mean he either really was not interested in books or that all his marks of ownership were successfully removed. In my opinion, however, Warwick never turned up in St Omer and he never received the gift manuscript. It came into French or Scottish hands, the hands of a man who already possessed a copy of the *Vraie cronique dEscoce* and perhaps other texts, as part of his diplomatic dossier.

Appendix A: the manuscripts of the *Instruction d'un jeune prince*, the *Enseignement de vraie noblesse*, the *Vraie cronique d'Escoce* and *Pour ce que plusieurs.*

A. *Instruction*:

1. Baltimore, Walters Art Gallery, W. 308, parchment, *c.* 1470, owner unknown, ill., contains also *Secret des secretz*, the *Enseignements[du] bon roi Louis ... a sa fille [Isabelle]*, and *La fin du bon roy Saint Louis*. The text in this ms was edited by Conell 1984 [note 11], 1-55.
2. Brussels, Bibliothèque Royale Albert I (hereafter BR), 10976, parchment, 15th-c., Philip the Good?, ill. by the Mr of Guillebert de Lannoy. The text in this ms. was edited by Potvin 1878 [note 11].
3. Cambridge, Fitzwilliam Museum, 165, parchment, 15th-c., Jacques de Luxembourg, ill. by Simon Marmion and Loyset Liedet, contains also René d'Anjou's *Mortifiement de vaine plaisance*.
4. London, British Library (hereafter BL), Cotton Vesp. B i, parchment, 15th-c., Louis de Gruuthuse, ill. by the Mr of the Froissart of Philippe de Comines, contains no other contemporary texts.
5. –, –, Lansdowne 848, paper, late 15th.-c., owner unknown, not ill., contains no other contemporary texts.
6. Munich, Bayerische Staatsbibliothek, Gall. 23, 15th-c., owner unknown, ill. not filled in. The text in this ms. was edited by van Leeuwen 1975 [note 11], 2-54.
7. Paris, Bibliothèque de l'Arsenal, 3521 (314?), paper, 15th-c., owner unknown, not ill., contains also many texts by Alain Chartier.
8. –, –, 5104 (33) parchment, 15th-c., Charles the Bold, ill. by Jean Hennecart, contains also *Enseignements paternels*.
9. Paris, Bibliothèque Nationale de France (hereafter BN), fr. 1216, parchment, 15th-c., Louis de Gruuthuse, ill., contains also *Enseignements paternels*.

10. –, –, fr. 1956, parchment, end 15th c., owner unknown, not ill., contains only minor other contemporary texts.
11. –, –, fr. 1957, paper, 15th-c., owner unknown, not ill., contains also the *Enseignements paternels.*
12. –, –, fr. 5056 (9678), 1469/70, parchment, Jeanne de France, Duchess of Bourbonnais; no illumination; contains also *Pour ce que plusieurs* and Jean Juvénal des Ursins, *Audite celi.*
13. –, –, n.a.fr. 6527, paper, 15th-c., owner unknown, not ill., no other texts.
14. –, Bibliothèque de Sainte-Geneviève, 2218, parchment, 15th c., owner unknown, ill., contains no other texts.
15. –, Collection de la Société des manuscrits des assureurs français, 80-11, parchment, *c.* 1485, François Phebus, Count of Foix, King of Navarre(?), ill. in Flanders and France, contains also Olivier de La Marche *Le chevalier délibéré*. On this ms S.S. Sutch, 'Notice sur l'identification d'un manuscrit "inconnu" du *Chevalier délibéré* d'Olivier de La Marche', *Romania*, 114 (1996), 246-53, and the same,'La production d'un manuscrit du poème intitulé *Le Chevalier délibéré* d'Olivier de La Marche', forthcoming.

B. *Enseignement*:
1. Brussels, BR, 10314, paper, 1460-1470, Croy family, Margaret of Austria, one illustration, contains no other texts, the 'Croy copy'.
2. –, –, 11047, parchment, before 1467, Philip the Good, not ill., contains no other texts, 'Philip the Good's copy'.
3. –, –, 11049, paper, *c.* 1497, Margaret of Austria, 7 miniatures, contains no other texts, the 'Savoy copy'.
4. Chantilly, Musée Condé, 1445, paper, late 15th-c., owner unknown, 7 miniatures, contains no other texts.
5. Geneva, Bibliothèque publique et universitaire (hereafter BPU), fr. 166, parchment, 1464, one miniature, bound in with the *Vraie cronique d'Escoce*, 'Warwick's copy', the ms under discussion.
6. London, BL, Add. 15469, paper, *c.* 1420-1456, Lannoy family, 7 watercolours, followed by epitaph of Hue de Lannoy, Lord of Santes, the 'Lannoy copy'.
7. –, –, Harl. 4397, paper, 15th-c., Lalaing family, not illustrated, followed by *le livre de l'Imagination au pelerin de Haulx fait par monsieur de Santes*, ff. 2-81v; *balade bien substansieuse*, ff. 82-83v; *le Passe temps de Michault [Taillevent]*, ff. 84-95; *le Temps perdu de Pierre Chastelain envoie a Mischault Taillevent*, ff. 95v-104; *Cronique jusques au Roy Charles vij*, ff. 104v-109v; *La Complainte de la mort de Madame*

Ysabel de Bourbon, comtesse de Charolois by Pierre Michault, ff. 109v-114v; *le Testament[?] de Pierre de Nesson*, ff. 114v-120; *Balade de la mort*, ff. 120v-121v; *ung Brief et utile traite de conseil compile par reverent pere en Dieu Ghuillaume [Fillastre], Evesque de Tournay*, ff. 122-167, the 'Lalaing copy'.
8. –, –, Royal 19 C viii, parchment, 1496, Henry VII, 7 miniatures, no other texts, but includes an introduction by Quentin Poulet, Henry VII's librarian, 'Henry VII's copy'.
9. Paris, Bibliothèque de l'Arsenal, 2329, paper, 15th-c., early owner unknown, 7 miniatures, no other texts.
10. –, BN, fr. 1227 (7428), paper, 1496, owner unknown, not ill., no other texts.

C. *Vraie cronique d'Escoce*:
1. Brussels, BR, 9469-70, parchment, 1464-67, Philip the Good, one min. by a collaborator of Willem Vrelant, the so-called 'Master of the *Vraie cronique dEscoce*; contains also *Pour ce que plusieurs*.
2. Geneva, BPU, fr. 166, the ms under discussion, see B 5, above.
3. Paris, BN, fr. 5058 (9680), parchment, late 15th c., Louis de Gruuthuse and Pierre de Ville, 1 miniature, f. 1; *Vraie cronique*, preceded by *Pour ce que plusieurs*, not mentioned by Daly.
4. –, –, n.a.f. 6214 (9679, Barrois 27), parchment, 2nd half 15th c., early owner unknown, no illumination surviving; *Vraie cronique* preceded by *Pour ce que plusieurs*.
5. –, –, n.a.f. 20962, parchment, 1463-77, Jacques d'Armagnac, Duke of Nemours (d. 1477), 1 miniatures, *Vraie cronique* preceded by *Pour ce que plusieurs*.

D. *Pour ce que plusieurs*:
1. Brussels, BR, 9469-70, see C 1, above.
2. –, BR, 12192-4, paper, 1400-30, early owner unknown, not ill., preceded by Pseudo-Turpin and *Traïson Richart II*.
3. Lille, Bibliothèque municipale, 322, paper, 1475-1500, early owner unknown, not ill., contains also texts of the treaties of Brétigny and Troyes, a casus, Jean Juvenal des Ursins, *Audite celi*, Jean Gerson, *Dialogus*, *Opus … de quadam puella*, *Compilatum … de mirabili victoria cuiusdam puelle*, Noël de Fribois, *C'est chose profitable*, and an account of the battle of Nancy.
4. London, BL, Add. 36541, paper, 15th c., early owner unknown, not ill., preceded by the *Traïson Richart II*.

5. Paris, Bibliothèque de l'Arsenal, 3434, parchment, 2nd half 15th c., early owner unknown (arms: *farcé ondé de gueules et d'argent*; Rochechouart, *ex inf.* Hanno Wijsman), not ill., contains no other texts.
6. –, BN, fr. 5056, see A 10, above.
7. –, –, fr. 5058, see C 3, above.
8. –, –, fr. 12788 (Suppl. fr. 607), 15th c., owner?, not ill., contains *Pour ce que plusieurs, Conqueste de Normendie* (by Henry V), Pierre Michault, *Danse aux aveugles,* verse epitaph of Philip the Good ascribed to Jean Molinet, a ballad ascribed to Georges Chastelain plus a response to the latter.
9. –, –, n.a.f. 6214, see C 4, above.
10. –, –, n.a.f. 20962, see C 5, above.
11. –, Bibliothèque Mazarine, 2031 (1183), parchment, 15th c., early owner unknown, no illumination, contains no other texts.
12. Rome, Vatican Library, Reg. 1933, ment. In J. Bignami Odier, 'Les manuscrits de la reine Christine au Vatican' in *Queen Christina of Sweden. Documents and Studies*, Analecta Reginensia, 1 (Stockholm, 1966): 33-43, esp. 35, 43.
13. Turin, Biblioteca reale L II 36, 15th c., no other data available.
14-16. Vienna, Österreichische Nationalbibliothek, 3392 (16th c.), BN fr. 15490 (15/16th c.) and fr. 17969 (17th c.) are too late to be of interest here.

Appendix B: The table of contents of *Enseignement de vraie noblesse* in Geneva, BPU, MS fr. 166.

Capitals and punctuation modernised, abbreviations extended.

Pour maquictier dune promesse que jay faicte a dame de grant renonmee passer temps et eschever oyseuse mere des vices moiennant la grace de Dieu que devotement appelle a mon aide veul exposer une merveilleuse adventure qui nagaires mest advenue. Et pour ce que la cose est longue affin de mieulx entendre lay comprins et departi en sept parties.

La premiere: comment en alant en pelerinaige a Nostre Dame de Halz en la conte de Haynnau Ymagination en personnaige dune dame en moult merveilleus habit sest apparue a moy, et apres pluiseurs parolles finablement me requist que lui vaulsisse faire un message aux princes et chevalerie de Crestiennete.

La seconde en moy declairant la cherge me vouloit donner ma infourme et remoustre quelle chose est vraie noblesse, et comment on la doit entendre et la comprendre en troix parties cy apres declairies.

La tierce comment seignourie temporelle est venue en avant, les causes et moyens pour quoy et qui plus est ce que empereurs, roix et princes sont tenus a faire selon la doctrine de raison et justice, ainsy que cy apres sera plusaplain dit et remoustre.

La quarte de lencommencement et promotion de [p. 2] chevalerie, comment elle est venue en avant des meurs et conditions de chevalier et ce quil est tenus de faire acause de son ordre etc.

La cinquiesme comment ymagination par exemples moustre et ensaigne la providence et sagesse que doivent avoir prinches et chevalerie pour executer et faire deuement ce que reaison et justice leur ont chargie et ordonne comme dessus est dit.

La sixieme la declaration et exposition de la tierce partie de vraie noblesse qui en effect demoustre et ensaigne ce que creature dist et fait en ce monde se par telle attempance et sy bonne maniere que en ce faisant on en puist acquerir grace et bonne renonmee.

La septieme et derreniere partie le bon et joyeulx temps qui regneroit en la chrestiennete se les princes et leur chevalerie avoient en eulx vraie noblesse et se acquitaissent Comme ilz sont tenus de faire sans abuser le haultain et prouffitable guerredon des deux precieuses et glorieuses couronnes que en ce faisant ilz rechepvioient.

Figure 1
Geneva, Bibliothèque publique et universitaire, MS fr. 166, fol. 3.
The opening miniature of the *Enseignement de vraie noblesse,*
by Hugues de Lannoy, Lord of Santes (died 1456)?, in a copy made
for Richard Neville, Earl of Warwick (died 1471), at Bruges?, 1464.
By kind permission of the Bibliothèque publique et universitaire, Geneva.

Figure 2
London, British Library, MS Add. 15469, fol. 3.
The opening miniature of the *Enseignement de vraie noblesse*,
by Hugues de Lannoy, Lord of Santes (died 1456)?,
in a copy perhaps made for the author, in the Lille/Ypres region, 1420-1456.
By kind permission of the British Library, London.

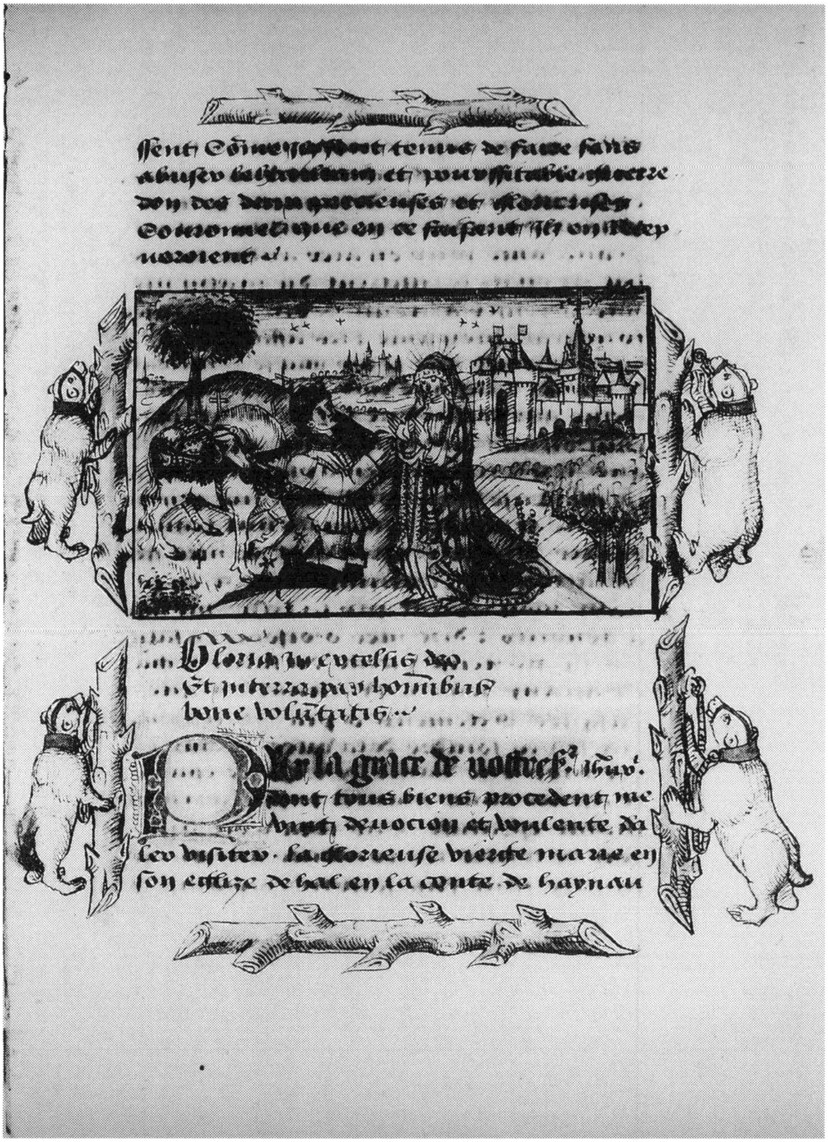

Figure 3
Brussels, Bibliothèque Royale Albert I, MS 10314, fol. 2.
Opening illustration of the *Enseignement de vraie noblesse*,
by Hugues de Lannoy, Lord of Santes (died 1456)?,
in a copy made for a member of the Croy family, 1460-1470.
By permission of the Bibliothèque royale, Brussels.

INDEX LIBRORUM MANU SCRIPTORUM

INDEX LOCORUM ET NOMINUM PERSONARUM